SPIRITUAL EV

Dr. KAMALJIT S. RYATT

ISBN: 978-1-8383868-5-6

SPIRITUAL EVOLUTION
by
Dr KAMALJIT S. RYATT

First Edition: July 2021
PRICE: (India) Rs 1000.00
(UK) £19.95

Published by

i2i
PUBLISHING

i2i Publishing
29 Hope Park Close, Manchester M25 ONL
www.i2ipublishing.co.uk
Email: sales@i2ipublishing.co.uk
Tel: (00)44 (0)161 798 8989
for:
Spiritual Evolution and Awareness (S.E.A.)
Email: sea1304@live.com

DEDICATION

'Sarab dharam mah(i) sresaṭ dharam(u). Har(i) ko Nām(u) jap(i) nirmal karam(u)'.[1]
'ਸਰਬ ਧਰਮ ਮਹਿ ਸ੍ਰੇਸਟ ਧਰਮੁ॥ ਹਰਿ ਕੋ ਨਾਮੁ ਜਪਿ ਨਿਰਮਲ ਕਰਮੁ'॥

'The best of all religions is: always meditate on and remain truly aligned with Nām, the immanent form of the Transcendent Lord, such that your every thought, utterance, and deed is in perfect harmony with It'.

For

Gurmit, my wife
Amrit and Simrit, my daughters
Daniel, my son-in-law
and
Hari and Mani, my grandsons

TABLE OF CONTENTS

TOPIC	PAGE
Front page	1
Copyright/ISBN	2
Dedication	3
For	4
Table of contents	5 - 6
List of abbreviations	7
Key to pronunciation	8 - 10
Foreword	11 - 12
Acknowledgements	13 - 14
Aim	15 - 17
Preface	19 - 27
Mūl Maṅtra	29 - 45
Prologue	47 - 55
Pauṛī 1	57 - 69
Pauṛī 2	71 - 78
Pauṛī 3	79 - 89
Pauṛī 4	91 - 103
Pauṛī 5	105 - 118
Pauṛī 6	119 - 126
Pauṛī 7	127 - 136
Pauṛī 8	137 - 144
Pauṛī 9	145 - 149
Pauṛī 10	151 - 155
Pauṛī 11	157 - 160
Pauṛī 12	161 - 167
Pauṛī 13	169 - 173
Pauṛī 14	175 - 178
Pauṛī 15	179 - 183
Pauṛī 16	185 - 205
Pauṛī 17	207 - 216
Pauṛī 18	217 - 226
Pauṛī 19	227 - 235
Pauṛī 20	237 - 247

Pauṛī 21	249 - 267
Pauṛī 22	269 - 274
Pauṛī 23	275 - 280
Pauṛī 24	281 - 291
Pauṛī 25	293 - 306
Pauṛī 26	307 - 323
Pauṛī 27	325 - 349
Pauṛī 28	351 - 359
Pauṛī 29	361 - 369
Pauṛī 30	371 - 376
Pauṛī 31	377 - 381
Pauṛī 32	383 - 390
Pauṛī 33	391 - 400
Pauṛī 34	401 - 410
Pauṛī 35	411 - 420
Pauṛī 36	421 - 428
Pauṛī 37	429 - 443
Pauṛī 38	445 - 455
Epilogue (Salok)	457 - 465
Glossary of Terms	467 - 534
References	535 - 564
About the Author	565
Spiritual Evolution	567
Reviews	569 - 574

LIST OF ABBREVIATIONS

abbreviation	abbrev
adjective	adj
adverb	adv
arabic	arab
auxiliary verb	aux. v
conjunction	conj
conjunctive verb	conj. v
compound verb	cpd. v
especially	esp.
et cetera	etc
female gender	f
figuratively	fig.
for example	e.g.
gurmukhī	gmkh
interjection	interj
that is to say	i.e.
literally	lit.
male gender	m
Man (in italics)	pronounced 'Mun'
noun	n
particle	p
Persian	pers
phrase	ph
plural	pl
prefix	pref
preposition	prep
pronoun	pron
Sanskrit	skt
singular	s
Srī Gurū Graṅth Sāhib	SGGS
suffix	suff
verb	v
verb transitive	v.t.
verb intransitive	v.i.

KEY TO PRONUNCIATION

Punjābī letter	English equivalent	Sounds like	Example
ਅ	a	u	(as in 'hut')
ਆ	ā	a	(as in 'car')
ਇ	i	i	(as in 'sit')
ਈ	ī	ee	(as in 'sheet')
ਉ	u	u	(as in 'put')
ਊ	ū	oo	(as in 'cool')
ਏ	e	ay	(as in 'say')
ਐ	ai	a	(as in 'sat')
ਓ	o	oa	(as in 'soak')
ਔ	au	o	(as in 'sort')
ਅੰ	ṅ	n	(as in 'sing')
ਆਂ	āṅ	an	(as in 'can't')
ਸ	s	s	(as in 'sing')
ਸ਼	sh	sh	(as in 'she')
ਹ	h	h	(as in 'he')
ਕ	k	k	(as in 'king')
ਖ	kh	kh	(as in 'khaki')
ਗ	g	g	(as in 'leg')
ਘ	gh	gh	(as in 'ghost')
ਚ	ch	ch	(as in 'church')
ਛ	chh	chh	(as in 'Chhattarput')
ਜ	j	j	(as in 'jug')
ਝ	jh	Jh	(as in 'Jhansi')
ਟ	ṭ	t	(as in 'put')
ਠ	ṭh	th	(as in 'thug')

ਡ	ḍ	d	(as in 'doctor')
ਢ	ḍh	dh	(as in 'dhak')
ਣ	ṇ	nn	(as in 'Runn of Kutch')
ਤ	t	t	(as in 'Telugu')
ਥ	th	th	(as in 'thrill')
ਦ	d	th	(as in 'thee')
ਧ	dh	dh	(as in 'dhoti')
ਨ	n	n	(as in 'run')
ਪ	p	p	(as in 'pin')
ਫ	ph	ph	(as in 'phial')
ਬ	b	b	(as in 'bid')
ਭ	bh	bh	(as in 'bhisti')
ਮ	m	m	(as in 'man')
ਯ	y	y	(as in 'yoke')
ਰ	r	r	(as in 'ring')
ਲ	l	l	(as in 'load')
ਵ	v	v	(as in 'vow')
ੜ	ṛ	r	(as in 'Roorkee')

The words 'Chhattarpur', 'Jhansi' and 'Roorkee' are as used in the index given in Philip's Modern School Atlas; similarly, 'Runn of Kutch' is given in the same Atlas in the map of India. The remaining words are found in all English dictionaries.

The letters (i) and (u), used within brackets in this book towards the end of certain words, remain silent and do not affect the pronunciation of the word but correspond to 'sihārī' (ਿ) and 'auṅkaṛ' (ੁ) respectively, and their position relates to the exact spellings of the relevant words as they appear in Srī Gurū Graṅth Sāhib (SGGS). The significance of their usage, however, relates to the rules of grammar. [2-5] Other letters that appear within brackets in the middle of a word impart just a hint of the sound of that letter, e.g., the letter (h), used within brackets, represents (ਅੱਧਾ ੍ਹ) in the foot of the preceding letter and the letter (v), used similarly, represents (ਅੱਧਾ 'ਵ') in the foot of the preceding letter. However, the two identical letters appearing together in succession represent 'accentuation' of that letter and is seen as an (ੱ) ('adhak') over its immediately previous letter. The letter (ṅ) following a letter in a word represents a 'biṅdī' above the immediately previous letter. A word used as 'dehlī dīpak' means that it is being used with two separate words in the same sentence.

FOREWORD

'Jap(u)' is commonly believed to be Gurū Nānak's foremost composition which clearly states his credo and worldview based on his experiential union with the eternal Reality and Its revealed wisdom. Hence, it is rightly given the esteemed rank of the first bānī of the Srī Gurū Granth Sāhib (SGGS), the living Gurū of the Sikhs and the holy text of the Sikh Religion, the fifth largest religion in the world. The Srī Gurū Granth Sāhib includes not only the writings of the six of the ten founding Gurūs but, recognising that no one religion has a monopoly of truth, it also contains writings of Hindu and Muslim saints who share similar spiritual truths.

The teachings of the SGGS underline our common reverence for the one God of us all. They also emphasise the oneness and equality of all members of humanity, regardless of all the artificial man-made barriers of race, colour, gender, class, creed, and geographical borders.

The SGGS is written in the 'Gurmukhī' script used in the Punjab, but the text also includes other languages reflecting the diverse nature of the contributors as well as the regions where the hymns were composed. The writings reach out to a wider world and are expressed in the dialects and styles of the poetry of the region. The verses of the compositions throughout the SGGS Sāhib Jī, except those in 'Jap(u)', are set in musical notation and can be sung to help reflection and contemplation.

Natural evolutionary changes in languages over time, and the establishment of English and Hindi as the dominant languages in Punjab and India, have inevitably led to difficulties in understanding the beauty of texts written during the fifteenth to the seventeenth century. Attempts to translate Sikh scriptures into prose and poetic form have previously had limited success because of the difficulty in trying to adhere to the original poetic format, resulting in transliteration that sometimes fails to convey the underlying deeper and more spiritual message.

There is a relative dearth in the availability of truly scholarly researched material on the Sikh scriptures in the popular languages of the contemporary world. Indeed, this has been one of the main reasons for misinterpretations of the Sikh faith as some sort of an amalgam of Hinduism and Islam - misinformation which has often been advanced by the protagonists of both Hinduism and Islam, and by many Western scholars.

Gurū Nānak's message throughout 'Jap(u)' is one of his experiential knowledge of the eternal Reality, Its awe inspiring creation of universe/s, laws governing every aspect of the evolving creation, human beings' supreme status in the sentient world, the ill-conceived and default state of ego - or 'haumai'- consciousness and our rare and golden opportunity to harmonise perfectly with God - or universal-consciousness. In 'Spiritual Evolution', Dr Ryatt outlines and elucidates clearly the need to move ourselves from an obsession with self to care and concern for others, from being a 'Kūriāṛ(u)' or 'Manmukh' (self-centred being) to becoming a 'Sachiār(u)' or 'Gurmukh' (God-centred being), and to recognise and appreciate our shared responsibility towards His entire creation.

Dr Kamaljit Singh Ryatt is to be congratulated on this well researched and scholarly work which will help those not well versed in the language of the scriptures to gain a fuller understanding of the richness, beauty, and guidance of the Sikh Holy Scriptures. The reader will be rewarded with a greater understanding of the process of spiritual evolution, a lasting change in one's outlook and world view, and the relevance and significance of the Srī Gurū Graṅth Sāhib on this path and to the complex problems of society today.

Lady Singh, Dr Kanwaljit Kaur OBE
President, Global Sikh Council
Deputy Director (Education) Network of Sikh Organisations UK
Education Inspector and Consultant, and Member of Lambeth SACRE

ACKNOWLEDGEMENTS

Amrit and Simrit, my daughters, Daniel, my son-in-law, members of our local Gurbānī Vichār Group in Birmingham, UK, and numerous young Sikhs born within and outside of India are keenly aware of the relative dearth of good quality literature explicating Gurbānī clearly and in contemporary English. This stark gap has been my driving force, and they have all been a source of tremendous encouragement for some years. I am truly indebted to them all.

Dr Meridy Harris of Canterbury has kept faith in me and, once again, put in many hours of hard work in diligently proof-reading the entire manuscript. I owe her an immense debt of gratitude for her generous help. Simrit, my daughter, has also helped in this regard and I am also grateful to her.

Dr Anthony B. John, F.R.C.P., retired Consultant Paediatrician, a good friend over the last forty years and an avid reader of books on a wide range of topics, inspired me to read more widely. My new found 'passion in writing' is probably a serendipitous outcome of this tradition. I am ever so grateful to him.

I have sincerely attempted to elucidate the origin of the words and their numerous literal and tacit meanings, and the hidden concepts behind some of the key words and phrases contained in 'Jap(u)', and have sought help from 'Mahān Kosh' of Bhāī Kāhn Singh Nābhā,[6] 'Srī Gurū Granth Sāhib Darpan' of Prof. Sāhib Singh,[7] Srī Gurū Granth Sāhib (Translation) of Dr Gopal Singh,[8] and Srī Gurū Granth Sāhib (Translation) of Manmohan Singh,[9] and 'Teachings of the Sikh Gurus by Christopher Shackle and Arvind-pal Singh Mandair.[10] Wherever possible, I have supported my view with relevant quotations from the SGGS. However, any misunderstanding and, therefore, any misquotations are entirely due to me, and I humbly apologise for them.

The task of writing this book has kept me away from the key people in my life and my relevant duties for long periods. My wife, Gurmit, daughters Amrit and Simrit, Daniel my son-in-law, and grandsons Hari and Mani have been very understanding and forgiving. I love them all very much and am grateful to them for their support.

i2i Publishing, in particular Lionel Ross, Susan Gleave and Dino Caruana, deserve my special thanks for their generous help and support in achieving the definitive form of the book.

Finally, I accept full responsibility, and unreservedly apologise, for any residual errors of omission or commission that the book may contain despite the generous help and guidance that I have received from Dr Meridy Harris. Indeed, I would be grateful if the readers could bring such errors to my notice so that I may be able to correct them in subsequent editions of this book.

K.S. Ryatt
Spiritual Evolution and Awareness (S.E.A.)
Email: sea1304@outlook.com

AIM

The Sikh faith, of all the major living world faiths, is the youngest, and the most fortunate for having preserved the original manuscript of its scriptures authenticated by the founders of the faith. The holy scripture, Srī Gurū Graṅth Sāhib (SGGS) Ji, revered as the Living Gurū, contains not only the revealed Word as it came to the six of the ten Gurūs but also to other enlightened and saintly people, of high and low caste, born as Hindus and/or Muslims, and from different parts of the Indian sub-continent. Its message transcends all man-made barriers and is truly universal, proclaiming the Fatherhood of God and 'Brotherhood of Man'.[11-2] It also lays emphasis on humanity's deviation from God-consciousness to ego-consciousness[13-4] and the available golden opportunity of this human birth to re-align with God-consciousness.[15] Simultaneously, it also portrays the present state of separation of a lover (the Soul or 'Jīvātmāṅ', metaphorically described as 'the bride' in the scriptures) from the beloved (the Primal Soul or 'Parmātmāṅ', metaphorically described as 'the bridegroom'), and the earnest wish and longing to experience, as well as to be with, that one transcendent and eternal Reality, one's beloved ('Parmātmāṅ' or God) forever.[16-7] This is why the transcendent and eternal Reality has been described herein as the male gender.

Throughout the entire scripture, the revealed Word is beautifully captured and rendered in the various contemporary and popular poetical formats. The rules of these formats have been strictly adhered to, and the compositions of the entire 'Graṅth', except for the first composition, 'Jap(u)', are set in different but appropriate musical 'Rāg' and beat ('tāl'). Their Divine and universal message is meant not only to be internalised but also to be lovingly expressed in our daily life and in the form of singing, which is a powerful and very effective way of influencing oneself and others.[18]

The compositions in the 'Graṅth', commonly referred to as Gurbāṇī - literally meaning words or utterances of the Gurūs - contain the sublime truths about the Creator, the Creation, humanity's status in this Creation, our ideal role and purpose in life, and the path to realise that goal. Furthermore, the study of its universal message of love and peace, and the sublime truths, surely cannot but elevate the reader socially, morally and spiritually. Similar sentiments have also been endorsed by Mohsin Fani,[19]

Max Arthur Macauliffe,[20] H.L. Bradshaw,[21] Dorothy Field,[22] Arnold J. Toynbee,[23] Noel Q. King,[24] Pearl Buck,[25] Janet Lant,[26] Sir Bertrand Russell,[27] and Rabindra Nath Tagore to name a few.

Whilst the 'Gurmukhī' script is used throughout the SGGS the variety of languages used in the hymns clearly points to the diverse backgrounds of the contributors as well as to the regions in which the hymns were composed and to the people at whom the message was initially aimed. The 'Punjābī' language, too, has evolved considerably over the intervening centuries such that the modern 'Punjābī' speaker would now find it difficult to understand fully the message conveyed in these hymns. The vocabulary and the poetic rendering of these compositions thus pose a considerable challenge to their true understanding, not only to Sikhs themselves but also to people of other faiths in the rest of the world.

I have made a unique and serious attempt to enable all those not familiar with the language of the scriptures to understand both the origin of the key words and phrases and their literal meanings and correct pronunciation. Most importantly, I attempt to explain clearly the often, though somewhat latent and perhaps less well understood, hidden concept so that it may purposefully resonate in the contemporary life of the readers.

A word of advice for the two different types of readers, the relative newcomers to 'Sikhī' and those more advanced or academic in nature: the preface is a good start for everyone, as it outlines clearly and briefly Gurū Nānak's worldview. Beginners may find it helpful to focus first on the summary of each verse before going to the conceptual summary at the end of each Pauṛī. However, more advanced readers should examine each word, with its implicit meaning in the context and, where necessary, its full range of meanings in the glossary, e.g., see 'anaṅd', pay attention to rules of grammar and pronunciation, and how the interpretation of each verse (printed in italics) is eventually arrived at.

Finally, although I have attempted to define clearly every new key word or phrase when it first appears in the text, some key words and concepts are also dealt with in some detail in the Glossary. Generally, and where appropriate, I give the root of each word in every line ('tuk' or 'paṅkat(i)' in Gurbāṇī) as well as its various commonly used literal meanings. I then suggest the tacit meaning of the word or phrase in the applied context. Thereafter, the underlying concept in each line or 'tuk' is summarised in italics, and most importantly, the conceptual summary of the entire stanza or 'Pauṛī' is given at the end. I adopted this format in my first book, *Thought*

For the Month[28], which dealt with the 'Bānī' of the fifth Gurū in 'Bārah Mahā' and have carefully retained this format throughout this book to help resolve the challenges alluded to above. I sincerely hope it will make it easier for the reader.

This format has also been adopted in my other writings relating to 'Bānīs', such as Sukhmanī, Rahrās(i), Sohilā, Anaṅd(u), and Āsā dī Vār, soon to be published and made available to a wider readership.

K.S. Ryatt
July 2021

PREFACE

Until a few decades ago, the most basic of all elements, an atom, was believed to comprise a nucleus, itself a composite of a fixed number of protons and neutrons, and a fixed number of electrons, the latter being the only moving and orbiting parts around the nucleus. However, with much progress in science and our greater understanding of nature and its basic constituents, we have now come to know many of the sub-atomic parts, their characteristics, inter-relationship with each other and their continuous orbital movement.

However, the persistent vexing and unanswered questions about the universe are: Who or what is its Prime Mover? What keeps even the most basic of all atoms and sub-atomic parts in orbital motion? What is the source of energy and/or matter involved in the 'big bang'? What is the role of its various integral components, and, finally, what is the purpose of it all?

Some believe that science will unravel this mystery at some point in the future. Although the existing Laws of Physics and Quantum Physics offer some plausible explanations for the puzzling questions posed above, definitive, and evidence-based answers remain somewhat elusive for the time being at least. Others believe that God, who is self-existent and eternal, and perfect and unchanging, is the 'Prime Mover' and the Creator, the 'Cause of all causes', of the laws that govern the universe as well as of everything else in it. Furthermore, they also believe that God, being supernatural and non-physical, is not only beyond the Laws of Physics and Quantum Physics, but also beyond human or any other created being's comprehension.

Gurū Nānak, founder of the Sikh Religion, formed his worldview after he experienced this eternal and transcendent Reality. He sets forth the idea that there was absolutely nothing in the beginning except God, who was then in His transcendent form ('Nirgun sarūp', the form beyond the influence of 'Māyā' and His infinite attributes beyond the grasp of humankind) and in a state of 'trance' ('Aphur Samādhī').[29-30] There was then no air, water, solids, energy or space, the basic rudiments of our empirical world.[31] God, through His Will ('Razā'), then wished to create the universe, a 'world-stage', for its manifold integral components to perform their individual roles. When God so wished, He first came out of that state of 'trance' into an 'active' state ('Sphur Samādhī') and became manifest as 'Nām(u)' (Primal Soul, 'Ātmāṅ' or 'Parmātmāṅ') His immanent form.

This primordial entity then initiated the process of creation and, subsequently, uniformly pervaded its every part.[32-34] Gaseous material came into existence first, and from this came liquids, and the process of further evolution and development of this diverse universe, guided and governed by His Divine Order ('Hukam(u)'), was then set in motion.[35] The empirical world, from the most 'nano' to the most 'macro' form of the cosmos, permeated by 'Nām(u)', thus became His 'Sargun sarūp' (the form which is subject to the influence of 'Māyā' and in which some of His attributes could be within the grasp of humankind). He further states that the immanent 'Nām(u)' is an absolute sine qua non for this process to continue,[36] as existence and/or functional viability of any created basic element, object or being is dependent on 'It' being an integral part of their physical aspect.[37] The all-pervasive 'Nām(u)' just withdraws itself from any basic element, object or being when it becomes superfluous to His creation at any stage. It is then reabsorbed or reintegrated into the 'transcendent Reality' if its presence is no longer required in the creation.[38-40] This ongoing process of change or evolution, from the simplest to the most complex or from an imperfect to the most perfect state, guided and governed by His 'Divine Order', has resulted in the universe as we know it today.

Visualised in this way, life and death can also be considered as the opposite ends of a continuum. For death to be 'something' rather than 'nothing', a soul must exist so that one can think of living and dying as opposites. A living being is alive as long as its soul remains an integral part of its physical structure; without it, it is dead. Gurū Nānak also propounds that the 'soul' ('Ātmāṅ', 'Primal Soul' and 'Nām(u)') is the immanent form of the transcendent God.[41] This is an all-pervasive and integral part of all inanimate objects and living beings, with its most expressive form being operative in humans.[42-44] The basic elements, the most complex compounds, and the functioning sub-units or organs of living beings which lack any degree of autonomy and, therefore, also any free will, simply perform the ultimate functions for which they exist and have evolved.[45] Living beings, on the other hand, have a greater degree of expression of the soul, which imparts to them a variable degree of ability and autonomy to interact with the world outside; the greater the degree of expression of the soul and autonomy or free will, the greater the burden of responsibility for their actions on the individual.[46-48]

For both growth of life and evolution,[49] the creation of a conscious self or ego ('Ha-u' or 'ਹਉ') is a pre-requisite,[50-51] as no animal life could exist without a centre of consciousness with a degree of autonomy in each living being, which would act both as its guardian and guide. This centre of consciousness ('Jīvātmāṅ', Conscious self, '*Man*' or 'Hirdā') comes into being as the 'Ātmāṅ' interacts with, and partially expresses itself within, the body. For this reason, 'Jīvātmāṅ' is also called 'Paṅch-bhoo-ātmāṅ'.[52] This partial expression of 'Ātmāṅ' is primarily by His Will but thereafter the accumulated 'Saṅskārs' of a being also play a significant role in the process which culminates in imparting a unique sense of 'self', free will, ability and the innate nature peculiar to that being. Each independent and functional unit, with this innate ability, can then deploy everything at its disposal for its own survival and for the growth of its kind. Evidently, for 'Jīvātmāṅ' to express itself fully and to interact with its surroundings in any sense, a fully developed and functional nervous system of the body is essential. An extensively damaged and/or very poorly functioning nervous system would create a state of complete disconnection between the body and 'Jīvātmāṅ', a state that can safely be equated with 'brain death'.

However, for 'Ātmāṅ' to remain immaculate and distinct from creation, there had to be a partial and functional surrogate which would afford all parts of the creation a separate identity and a unique innate nature and ability to interact autonomously with its immediate environment. Gurbāṇī' defines this partial and functional surrogate as 'Jīvātmāṅ'.[52] The degree of expression of 'Ātmāṅ', the endowed free will or autonomy and the unique innate nature then governs the ability and scope of the functioning or interaction of any part of the creation. Thus, some constituents of the creation exist to perform only a very limited function. The degree of complexity increases with the greater expression of 'Ātmāṅ', free will or autonomy, and unique innate nature. This is seen in complex molecules, compounds, functioning sub-units or organs of beings, with the greatest expression of 'Ātmāṅ' and free will or autonomy being found in human beings.

In order to create diversity from unity, and for the creation to evolve with time, God first created 'Haumaiṅ', 'Moh' and 'Saṅjog(u) and 'Vijog(u)'.[51, 53-4] Gurū Nānak also suggests that 'Haumaiṅ' or ego-consciousness becomes the driving force for the process of evolution which has put humans at the apex of the evolutionary tree.[47] 'Haumaiṅ' symbolises the growing deployment of the centre of consciousness ('Ha-u' or 'ਹਉ'), purely for the fulfilment of one's self-interest, with total disregard for everything else in this ecosystem. As such, one is characterised as egotistic and one's accompanying consciousness labelled as ego-consciousness. Unfortunately, operating in this default state of ego-consciousness human beings, erroneously consider themselves to be completely different and separate from others and, in collusion with 'Māyā' and 'Avidyā' (misconception), from the Primordial entity itself too, and to have an independent existence, not only from other inanimate and sentient life forms but also from God and His Divine Order.[55-7] It is possible that diverse forms of symbiotic interactions, e.g. mutualistic, commensalistic, parasitic, and others, can be seen in the light of 'Haumaiṅ' in action. If so, good examples of human behaviour under the adverse influence of 'Haumaiṅ' would be the immense damage to the stable global environment currently taking place, not only to land, water and air but also to its vegetation and animal life, with some forms now having become extinct and others threatened to almost extinction, and the inter-state and internecine wars. Nevertheless, Gurū Nānak defines ego-consciousness, coupled with this malady, as the 'Haumaiṅ', and partial and functional expression of 'Ātmāṅ' in such a being as 'Jīvātmāṅ'.[58-60]

However, a human being, though essentially an animal, is superior to others in the animal kingdom because we possess superior ability and a sense of discernment. Not only are we aware of our own thinking process but we can also deliberate over our thinking. Indeed, it is this ability that endows us with a sense of discernment and wisdom, thus enabling us to make the right moral and ethical choices.[46, 48] Gurū Nānak further submits that the second superior attribute in humanity's armament is that, although we operate inherently at the default state of ego-consciousness, we have this golden opportunity and capacity to link with God-consciousness ('Nām-', 'universal-', 'unitary-' or 'higher-' 'consciousness') to realise this goal, the apex position in spiritual evolution ('Sahaj' and 'Anaṅd') and God-realisation (state of 'Jīvan Mukat(i)') in this life, and freedom from 'Āvāgavan', the cycle of transmigration ('Param Mukat(i)' at death.[61-3]

As stated before, it is indeed Gurū Nānak's firm belief that God is the Creator of the universe, and the universe is His creation;[32] though He pervades all His creation uniformly, the creation itself, His 'sargun sarūp', is not God.[64] The creation is limited and bound by Laws of Nature, and continuous change is a feature of this dynamic universe. God, on the contrary, is immutable, infinite, absolutely free,[65] self-existent, and eternal.[66] He is beyond the space-time continuum, and thus cannot be realised with spacio-temporal logic.[67] His Glory is infinite, though He is described as 'father, mother, brother, friend, and protector';[68] 'enlightener, benevolent',[69] 'beneficent and loving';[70] 'helper of the poor and weak, and shelter of the shelterless';[71] 'guide to the erring',[72] 'and generous in rewarding one's efforts';[73-4] 'eyes to the blind, riches to the poor, and fount of all virtues'.[75]

Being inextricably linked with the universe through His immanent form, He is the fount of all attributes, 'values' and 'virtues'.[76-78] It is this aspect of God that clearly alludes to the purpose and direction of His Will and God-consciousness. This not only gives legitimacy and direction to the moral life in the universe but also becomes its gold standard. 'Haumaiṅ' or ego-consciousness and God-consciousness are thus the two opposite ends of a spectrum of consciousness.[79]

One must, therefore, continue to shed one's ego-consciousness and strive to align fully with God-consciousness[80] in order to realise one's spiritual goal of 'Sahaj', 'Anaṅd' and God-realisation in this life. Put differently, 'Jīvātmāṅ' must rid itself of the filth of 'Haumaiṅ', 'Moh' and innate 'Vikārī' tendencies ('Māyā') and become the pure and immaculate expression of 'Ātmāṅ' (nirmal 'Jīvātmāṅ') once again, to align perfectly with 'Nām(u)' ('Ātmāṅ', 'Parmātmāṅ' or the 'Primal Soul'). Alternatively, a 'Manmukh' (someone who submits to ego-consciousness and is misled by one's 'Haumaiṅ') must transform into a 'Gurmukh' (one who submits to the Gurū's Divine Word and Wisdom, ideologically converges with it and aligns with God-consciousness) in order to realise the goal of God-realisation.

However, the tragedy is that a person, afflicted with 'Haumaiṅ'[81] and operating in the default state of ego-consciousness, considers themselves to be independent of the Divine Order ('Hukam(u)').[82-3] With their intellect and cognition subservient to their ego-consciousness, they omit to appreciate the idea of the whole world as one family and ecosystem, and the concept of the universal Fatherhood of God and 'Brotherhood of Man',[84] thus failing miserably to marshal their intellectual and physical talents for the common good of the ecosphere. In this mal-aligned and imperfect state of ego-consciousness, one's 'Jīvātmāṅ' (metaphorically personified as the bride), is in disharmony with, and considered separated from 'Parmātmāṅ'

('Nām(u)', the 'Primal Soul', metaphorically personified as the bridegroom).

One's unconscious-self, or 'Id', to use the Freudian terminology, the storehouse of one's innate nature, basic drives, and repressed desires, constantly drives one towards the physical world and its worldly pleasures in order to achieve inner satisfaction. However, this proves elusive as the insatiable hunger for the worldly comforts and pleasures ('Trishnā') can never be satisfied. Thus, as 'Trishnā' is insatiable in this egotistic state,[85] one struggles to realise lasting inner peace, and suffers forever from the mental unrest and anguish of this never-ending pursuit.[86]

The degree of severity of this predicament may vary in individuals but this remains the default position of human beings, with the resultant persistent inner turbulence or restlessness being due primarily to mal- or non-alignment with God-consciousness. Thus, 'Ātmāṅ' and 'Jīvātmāṅ' being constitutively identical, a lasting inner state of equanimity ('Sahaj') and bliss ('Anaṅd') remains forever one's passionate desire and ultimate goal,[87-8] as expressed in this verse: 'Just as millions of sparks, all with their separate entities, originating from the fire merge in the same fire; millions of dust particles arising from dust merge in the same dust again; and millions of distinct waves, arising from the surface of water of rivers or oceans, merge in the same waters, similarly, the infinite number of animate and inanimate objects, created by and arising out of the supreme Lord seek to merge in the same Lord again.'[89]

This aspect of humanity's state and goal is beautifully captured in the first stanza ('Pauṛī') of 'Jap(u)': 'Kiv sachiārā hoīai kiv kūṛai tuṭai pāl(i)' is the succinct and fundamental question that is raised and 'Hukam(i) rajāī chalṇā Nānak likhiā nāl(i)' is the precise and pithy answer or solution that is offered in the first 'Pauṛī'. 'How do we become godlike and how do we shatter this wall of ignorance that stands between us and the all-pervasive eternal Reality within us? 'We must learn to live by His Will' is the Writ for the whole creation that immediately answers this terse question.

Right at the outset, we must, therefore, appreciate the disparity that exists between our default status as 'Kuṛiārs' and the eternal Reality (a 'Sachiār' or 'Sachiārā'). A 'Kuṛiār' is: (a) one who is misled by 'Haumaiṅ',[90] (b) one whose conscious self ('*Man*', 'Hirdā' or 'Jīvātmāṅ'), afflicted with 'Haumaiṅ' and 'Moh', generates 'Mamtā', 'Trishnā', 'Vikārī predispositions' and 'Vikārs' is forever in a state of struggle and turmoil, and without lasting inner peace and contentment,[91] and (c) one who is, to a greater or lesser extent, engrossed in the transient empirical world to satisfy one's purely selfish and evil innate desires.[91] On the contrary, a 'Sachiār', literally, is God incarnate, godlike or one whose conscious self is attuned perfectly to 'Nām(u)', and in whom 'Nām(u)' manifests its full glory.[92] In fact, Gurū Nānak deploys the term 'Sachiār(u)' in the SGGS for God Himself:

'You are the Creator and my Lord Master, and the fount of all that is eternal' - and this lends further support to the hypothesis developed above.[93]

The root cause of this considerable disparity between us and God is our 'Haumaiṅ', the all-encompassing term for ignorance and/or misconception ('avidyā') of our real self and the empirical world, our ego-consciousness and egotism, and our erroneous belief in our autonomous and independent existence from other inanimate and sentient life forms and from God. Along with 'Moh', humanity's fascination with and irrational and excessive attachment to the empirical world, predisposes and eventually creates an overwhelming and perverse sense of attachment to everything in the material world with total disregard to its transient nature, benefits, and shortcomings, and even the risk of potential harm from the same object. This deeply mistaken sense of ownership or 'belongingness' that stops one from sharing any object of 'Moh' with others is 'Mamtā' or 'Mer'/'Ter', and, similarly, an erroneous sense of self gives rise to a sense of duality ('Dubidā', 'Dvait' and 'Bhram'). The five cardinal instincts or drives ('Kām' (lust), 'Krodh' (wrath), 'Lobh' (greed), 'Moh' (attachment), and 'Ahaṅkār' (egotism), primarily essential for normal survival and growth, now assume their perverse form, transforming one into being ego-centric and egotistic, and making one commit deeds to satisfy those perverse drives, thus increasing the rift between ego-consciousness and God-consciousness, and between us and God.

Clearly, the 'way out'[94-7] is to understand the Divine Order ('Hukam') that governs the entire universe, to submit 'willingly and lovingly' to His Will ('Razā'), and to live in perfect harmony with God-consciousness.[98] But 'Haumaiṅ', 'Moh', one's innate nature and one's limited abilities, preclude one from reaching the final goal through one's own efforts.[99-101] Rather than feeling disheartened and helpless, one must still continue to struggle and work hard sincerely, and humbly seek an alternative solution to this problem. One must, therefore, pray to God and seek His Mercy and Guidance. This comes in the form of guidance and Divine Knowledge from an 'enlightened' person (a 'Sant', 'Sādh', 'Sādhū', 'Bhagat', Gurū, 'Sat(i)gurū' or 'Brahm-gyānī'), one who has realised 'Nām(u)', the immanent form of the transcendent God.[102-3] One then humbly gives way and submits to his Divine Knowledge and Wisdom which, in turn, guides and supports the willing seeker lovingly and altruistically[104] ('Gur prasād(i)'). The seeker then imbibes that Divine Knowledge and Wisdom, and follows the prescribed path with unwavering belief, strict discipline, and steadfast determination ('Jap(u)'). Gradually, one sheds one's 'Haumaiṅ', 'Moh' and 'Vikārī' tendencies (the evil influence of 'Māyā') from one's conscious self ('*Man*', 'Hirdā' or 'Jīvātmāṅ'), learns to live in perfect harmony (a state of 'Sahaj') with 'Nām(u)', and then, with the Grace of God, realises lasting inner bliss ('Anaṅd') and the full glow of the eternal Reality, 'Nām(u)', within one's conscious self, one's goal in this life.[105-6] One's 'Jīvātmāṅ' (without any baggage of 'Haumaiṅ', 'Moh' and 'Saṅskārs') then realises its true self ('nirmal Ātmāṅ') and its unifying source, the Primal Soul, 'Parmātmāṅ' or 'Nām(u)' and merges with the 'Nirgun' or the transcendent Lord (metaphorically depicted as the bridegroom) at death, and finds release from 'Āvāgavan', the cycle of transmigration.

In summary, misled by 'Haumaiṅ', 'Moh' and one's innate nature, one's perverse inner drives become a major hurdle in one's path to alignment with God-consciousness. Thus, misguided and driven to satisfy one's insatiable desire for the material world, its comforts and pleasures ('Trishnā'),[107] one gets entrapped in its web and is sucked deeper and deeper into the whirlpool of the 'world-ocean' ('Bhavjal sāgar') or quagmire of 'Moh' ('Daldal'), and experiences immense suffering in this world.[108] In essence, this is 'Māyā' in action where 'Māyā' is that which makes us susceptible to the captivating spell of the material world and its pleasures and which drives us away from God and God-consciousness (perfect alignment with 'Nām(u)' or 'Nām-consciousness').

Our spiritual wellbeing and ultimate goal thus lie in our understanding of the root problem by regularly subjecting ourselves to introspection ('āpā chīnaṇ' or 'swai paṛchol' in Gurmat - literally defined as 'Gurū dī mat(i)' but encompassing Gurūs' wisdom, teachings, tenets, and directives),[109-112] our willingness to seek cure, and resolutely take the medicine in the form of strict adherence to and practice of the imbibed knowledge of a Gurū's teachings in one's life.[113-5] Perfect alignment with 'Nām(u)' and lasting equanimity ('Sahaj') and inner bliss ('Anaṅd') ensue once 'Haumaiṅ',

‘Moh’ and the ‘Vikārī tendencies’ - the ‘disease’, is cured and the evil influence of ‘Māyā’ removed. One then patiently awaits God’s Grace which instantly leads to the perception of one’s identity, one’s ‘true self’ - the Primal Soul, ‘Parmātmāṅ’ or ‘Nām(u)’ - and the realisation of its full glow - one’s goal in this life.

MŪL MAṄTRA

'Mūl-Maṅtra' - 'Ik O'aṅkār Sat(i)nām(u) Kartā Purakh(u) Nirbhau Nirvair(u) Akāl Mūrat(i) Ajūnī Saibhaṅg Gurprasād(i)' - is the foundational credal statement of Gurū Nānak, the founder of this young and all-embracing faith for all humanity. It encapsulates his unshakeable belief in and spiritual perception of the one Creator of our entire universe/s and forms the basis of his worldview. It precedes 'Jap(u)', the title of the very first composition in 'Srī Gurū Graṅth Sāhib Jī' (SGGS) and serves as an invocation ('Maṅglācharan') of 'Jap(u)', the customary expression of praise and reverence of the contemporary writers. It is incorporated in the very beginning of their major piece of work, for one who is most near and dear, and for whom they have the utmost respect and veneration. It is also Gurū Arjun's 'Maṅglācharan' of the Sikh Holy Scriptures, 'Srī Gurū Graṅth Sāhib Jī'.

The complete or partial forms of 'Mūl-Maṅtra', serving as 'Maṅglācharan' at the top of 'Bānīs' in different 'Rāgs' or 'Bānīs' of different writers, have appeared with variable frequency as follows:

Part/Complete 'Mūl-Maṅtra'	**Number of occurrences**
'Ik O'aṅkār	2
'Ik O'aṅkār Sat(i)nām(u) Gurprasād(i)'	2
'Ik O'aṅkār Sat(i)nām(u) Kartā Purakh(u) Gurprasād(i)'	8
'Ik O'aṅkār Sat(i)nām(u) Kartā Purakh(u) Nirbhau Nirvair(u) Akāl Mūrat(i) Ajūnī Saibhaṅg Gurprasād(i)'	33
'Ik O'aṅkār Sat(i) Gurprasād(i)'	522

'Ik O'aṅkār' (the One eternal, uniformly all-pervasive and immutable Reality) is the very basis of Gurū Nānak's worldview; 'Sat(i)nām(u), Kartā Purakh(u), Nirbhau, Nirvair(u), Akāl Mūrat(i), Ajūnī, and Saibhaṅg', the key attributive aspects of his God, and 'Gurprasād(i)', the embodiment of the only way for humanity to re-align with and realise that God is the real goal in life.

Ik O'aṅkār Sat(i)nām(u) Kartā Purakh(u) Nirbhau
ੴ ਸਤਿ ਨਾਮੁ ਕਰਤਾ ਪੁਰਖੁ ਨਿਰਭਉ

Nirvair(u) Akāl Mūrat(i) Ajūnī Saibhaṅg Gur prasād(i).
ਨਿਰਵੈਰੁ ਅਕਾਲ ਮੂਰਤਿ ਅਜੂਨੀ ਸੈਭੰ ਗੁਰ ਪ੍ਰਸਾਦਿ॥

ik: (a) (adj) one, first of the 1-9 numerals, (b) (adj; synonymous with 'ikallā') alone, by oneself, single-handed or unaided, (c) (adj; synonymous with 'aduttī' or 'lāsānī') unique, unparalleled or without a match, and (d) (n, m) Creator or 'Kartār' (God). In essence, it refers to the One Absolute God ('Wāh(i)gurū' in Gurbānī), unique and unrivalled, 'Niraṅkār' (without any physical form or any perceivable attributes in this form), and transcendent - unfathomable ('agaṅm') and beyond the grasp of human senses and intellect ('agochar'). In addition, He is both 'Nirgun' (without any perceivable attributes in this form and beyond the influence of 'Māyā') and 'Sargun' (immanent in the creation and subject to the influence of 'Māyā' in this form). The following verses from SGGS lend weight to this concept:

My Lord is one and one alone; He is alone and by Himself.[116]

There is none other than just the transcendent Lord; the body and soul are His, and all that happens is in His Will.[117]

Rarely, by imbibing the Gurū's Wisdom, one comprehends that He alone pervades everything; all that exists is nothing but His manifestation.[118]

The one Creator Lord is Merciful, Sustaining and Compassionate, and there is none other. To consider these distinguishing attributes in another person is a misconception and an error. Thus, worship the One alone who is our common Enlightener; we all have the same 'Ātmāṅ' and are all His manifestations.[119]

He is in the 'Maṅdir' as well as in the 'Masjid' and is the focus of Hindu worship and Muslim prayer; all human beings are essentially identical but 'Haumaiṅ' and superficial differences have created the illusion of countless 'others'. The eyes, ears, physical bodies, and their general constitution are identical, and they all represent an amalgam of Earth, fire, water, and air. The God of Muslims and Hindus is the same, and the wisdom in the Purānas and the Qurān is His gift to humanity; all represent His creation as He is their common and shared Creator.[120]

You are the ultimate Master of all, and we can only express Your Glory through the Gurū's Word.[121]

He Himself, who as 'Māyā' has bewitched the world, is both 'nirgun' (beyond the influence of 'Māyā') and sargun' (subject to the influence of 'Māyā') as immanent 'Nām(u)' in the empirical world.[122]

The formless one, beyond the influence of 'Māyā', becomes the empirical world (under the influence of 'Māyā'). God creates diversity from unity but diversity is really His manifestation.[123]

o'aṅkār: (pronounced O'aṅkār) It is a compound word that comprises 'o'aṅ' + 'kār'.

o'aṅ: has roots in the word 'Om' - the symbol of 'dhvanī', the primordial sound ('nād') in the Hindu Vedas. 'Om' pronounced 'o'am', with these three letters depicts the Creator ('a' for 'ākār'), the Sustainer ('o' for 'okār') and the Destroyer ('m' for 'makār'), the three aspects of God represented in Brahma, Vishnu, and Shiva according to Hindu religious texts. Om, the holiest word in the Vedas, is also the symbolic word denoting the Supreme Being - the 'Ocean of Knowledge' and the 'Bliss Absolute' of Rāja Yoga. It is the 'Logos' in Christianity, which becomes the creative force and the immanent Spirit of God; it is 'kun' in Islam, 'O'am' (Vedic rishīs in Hinduism) and 'O'aṅkār' in Jainism. However, for Gurū Nānak, O'aṅkār itself is the Creator ('Kartā'), Sustainer ('Bhartā') and the Destroyer ('Hartā') of everything; He is also transcendent (existing apart from, and not subject to the limitations of His creation), 'agaṅm' (immutable and beyond our reach), and 'agochar' (unfathomable or beyond the grasp of human senses).

The following verses from the SGGS support this concept of the one God being the Cause of all Causes:

The Formless One Himself created the empirical world and this 'world spectacle' ('Saṅsār-' 'khel' or 'līlā') is a witness to His Glory.[124]

The Formless One Himself created this universe; 'Moh(u)' and 'Māiā', too, came to exist by His Divine Order.[125]

You created the empirical world and assigned each part its innate nature and capability, having judged their previous deeds. Having thus created this diverse universe, You keep watch over your own Creation.[126]

He sustains all the non-sentient and sentient life forms and takes care of them every moment and forever.[127]

Countless planets and life forms appear when He deploys His creative power. On the contrary, they all become absorbed in Him, when He deploys His destructive power.[39]

You created this vast universe in diverse ways. Often it was created, assimilated, and then created again. But the One Formless God remained forever uniform and immutable. Countless and diverse forms of beings emanate from Him and become reabsorbed in Him, but none knows His limits. 'He is by Himself and there is none like Him', O' Nānak![128]

He creates and destroys all in a moment but remains distinct and transcendent.[129]

kār: (adj) unchanging, uniform and continuous, especially when used as a 'suffix', e.g., 'na(ṅ)nākār' - unchanging and/or persistent refusal; 'jhanatkār' - uniform and continuous melodious sound; 'jai jaikār' - continuous chanting of 'hail, hail'; 'niratkār' - prolonged and uninterrupted dance; and 'chhuṭkār' - prolonged and continuous escape or liberation. However, as a suffix to 'O'aṅ' it denotes the uniformly all-pervasive as well as the unchanging nature of the One Absolute God. The following verse of the SGGS highlights beautifully this aspect of the Almighty:

'The beauty of the creation, the age of islands, the light of the sun, moon and the stars in the sky, all diminish with time. The age of the Earth, the mountains, and the vegetation; the love for one's wife, son, and brothers; the enchantment of gold, jewels and the diverse empirical world and its pleasures; all diminish with time. Only He, the everlasting Provider of the universe, and the Glory of the 'Sādh jan', are immutable and eternal', O' Nānak![130]

'O'aṅ' and 'O'aṅkār' both appear in the SGGS as well as in 'Vārāṅ' by Bhāī Gurdās as signifying the transcendent and the 'nirgun' aspect of God.

The Formless One pervades all, and everything merges and gets reabsorbed in Him eventually.[131]

The Formless One created Brahma.[132]

The Formless One created the whole universe.[133]

The Formless One created everything, including the days and nights.[134]

The Formless One created the five basic building blocks of the Universe: air, water, Earth, fire (energy), and space.[135]

The symbol ੧ੳ, pronounced as 'Ik Oaṅkār' or both written and pronounced as 'ekaṅkār' ('ਏਕੰਕਾਰ'), is the embodiment of His 'Nirgun' (transcendent and free from the influence of 'Māyā') and 'Sargun' (immanent in the creation and subject to the influence of 'Māyā') aspects of His Unchanging ('kār') Being ('Sarūp' or Form).

He Himself, who as 'Māyā' has bewitched the world, is both 'nirgun' (transcendent and beyond the influence of 'Māyā') and sargun' (subject to the influence of 'Māyā') as immanent 'Nām(u)' in the empirical world.[122]

sat(i)nām(u): a complex word that comprises 'sat(i)' and 'nām(u)'.

sat(i): (synonymous with 'satya' (skt); 'sat(i)', 'sach(u)', sāch(u) and 'sāchā' (gmkh) in Gurbāṇī) (a) (n, m, s; synonymous with 'Pārbrahm' and 'Kartār') the eternal Creator - 'Nām(u)', the immanent form of God, (b) (adj; synonymous with 'sadīvī jyot(i) sarūp') the eternally existent Formless Lord, (c) (n; synonymous with 'ythārath', 'tat(u)' and 'tath(u)') the eternal Truth or Reality, (d) (adj; synonymous with 'sach(u)' or 'asat(i)'-hoṅd vālā') real and not imaginary, (e) (synonymous with 'sarab kalā bharpūr(i)', 'par(i)pūran' and 'sarab-vyāpak') Omnipotent, Omniscient and Omnipresent or all-pervasive, (f) (adj; synonymous with 'shuch(i)', 'pāk', 'nirmal' and 'pavitr') pure or immaculate, and (g) (adj; synonymous with 'pūrā', 'mukaṅmal' and 'ukāī rahit') perfect and flawless. It denotes the one and only eternal Truth, all-pervasive, and the unchanging eternal Reality that is God in SGGS. See sach(u) and sat.

nām(u): (n, m, s) refers to the 'Immanent' form of the transcendent God. Although the transcendent God is 'agaṅm' (immutable and beyond our reach), and 'agochar' (unfathomable or beyond the grasp of human senses), 'Nām(u)', His immanent form, can be perceived. This one word is a surrogate and alone encompasses all the known and unknown attributes of this immanent form of God. 'Nām(u)' also symbolises (a) God's creative power ('Kartār', the Creator, (b) the Divine Order, the sum total of all the Laws of Nature ('Hukam(u)') that sustain and govern the creation, (c) the Divine Word, with which He communicates with His creation ('Sabad', 'Anhad Sabad' or 'Anhad Nād'), and (d) the Divine Will ('Razā'), symbolising how He wishes the entire universe to unfold with time and directs it accordingly, and this is endorsed in the following verses of the SGGS:

The transcendent God first manifested Himself into Nām(u); He then created the world, permeated it and watches over its unfolding and evolving with expectant glee.[33]

By His Order, the wind blows forever, myriads of rivers flow; the sun and moon, whilst moving in their fixed orbits, blaze and shine; the infinite sky vaults above the Earth; countless beings come into this world and go from it.[136]

Sabad (the immanent 'Nām(u)') is my Gurū and surat(i), ('*Man*') attuned to it, is the disciple.[137]

One should contemplate God by word, thought and deed.[138]

O' man! You are supreme in God's creation; now is your opportunity to fulfil or not to fulfil your destiny.[48]

Theologians and others, from all around the globe and of different faiths, especially those who have realised 'Nām(u)' ascribe to Him a variety of names ('Kirtam' or 'Zātī nāms') highlighting His numerous attributes, of which the following are but a few examples: 'Rahīm', 'Karīm', 'Anīl', 'Agaṅm', 'Agochar', 'Anūp', 'Bakhshiṅd', 'Gopāl', 'Gobiṅd', 'Pratipālak', and 'Niraṅkār' amongst many others. However, in the SGGS, 'Sat(i)nām(u)' denotes His primordial nature alone but no attributive character ('Saphātī nām') as highlighted in the following verse:

My tongue can only utter the attributes that I can imagine and relate to, but primordial nature is your eternal attribute.[139]

Thus, although 'Nām(u)' symbolises the totality of God's attributes, it also serves as an interface through which God communicates with His creation, and through which humans can reach and 'perceive' the transcendent Lord. The word 'Sat(i)nām(u)', therefore, symbolises the primordial, absolute, all-pervasive, immanent, and the eternal Reality of the creator of the entire creation. (See 'Nām(u)')

Kartā: (n, m, s; abbrev. for 'Kartār'; 'Sirjanhār' or 'Srishṭā') the doer or the creator of the entire creation.[78]

'He creates and the creation merges or becomes absorbed into Him when He so Wills. He is the sole Creator Integrator. 'The creation of the universe and then its dissolution or doomsday come to be through His Word; His Word again then causes creation and evolution'.[140]

'You are Omnipotent, the Creator and Cause of all Causes, Unfathomable and Infinite', O, Lord![141]

Purakh(u): (n, m, s) (a) literally, a male person, (b) soul as in Bhagvad Gita, (c) (skt) that which diffusely permeates the physical aspect of everything, and implicit here is (d) Primal Soul or 'Nām(u)', the Creator and Sustainer, who is immanent and omnipresent, and yet transcends the creation. In Sūfī and Vaishnavic lore as well as in Gurmat, the essence of the SGGS, the Primal Soul ('Nām(u)') is the only symbolic male, with humanity symbolically being females, and all forever longing to unite with Him. 'There is only one husband in this world and the rest are all His brides. He pervades all 'Hirdās' and is yet detached and unknowable. The perfect gurū reveals Him to us through His Divine Word'.[17] The following verses from the SGGS emphasise this aspect of the Creator's nature:

He permeates the physical world.[142]

He who pervades all worlds is the Creator.[143]

He first manifested Himself from a transcendent to an immanent being ('Nām(u)'); He then created the universe and, pervading its every part, merrily watches over it elaborate and evolve.[33]

Having realised 'Nām(u)' the Guru reveals His presence in all and all to be a part of His being.[144]

Why go and search for Him in the woods? He who pervades everything, and yet remains detached, abides in us all. Search within your 'Hirdā' for Him, who permeates us all uniformly like the fragrance within a flower and one's reflection in the mirror.[145]

Nirbhau: (adj; synonymous with 'be-ḍar' or 'be-khauph') a complex word comprising 'nir' + 'bhau'; it has the following interpretations: (a) 'nir' (without) + 'bhau' ('ḍar' or 'khauph' - fear) i.e., fearless, intrepid or indomitable, and (b) 'nir' (without) + 'bhau' ('bhai' - Order or 'Hukam') i.e., free from any binding order or restraint.

One is normally fearful of a rival or someone more powerful and/or more astute than oneself. However, God is unique and without a rival; in fact, nothing exists, and nor has He created anything that could in any way be a potential threat. There is nothing else but Him, and the whole universe is nothing but His manifestation.[117] The following verses of the SGGS emphasise this aspect of the Creator's nature:

The Lord is great, and most exalted is His position. His Glory is the loftiest of all. If someone were to be as great and exalted, only then would they know that exalted Being.[146]

Everything is bound by His Divine Order, including the flow of the wind, the flow of waters in countless rivers or continuously evolving life in diverse forms. He, the eternal and formless one alone, is not subject to it, O' Nānak.[146]

Only the formless Lord is free and not bound by any spacio-temporal laws; many others like Rām (son of the Hindu King Dasrath) are trivial and insignificant in comparison.[148]

Every constitutive aspect of this universe is subject to His Order; He, the Creator, alone is free of this fear and bondage.[149]

Nirvair(u): (adj, m) a complex word comprising 'nir' (without) + 'vair(u)' (ill will, enmity, animosity, vendetta, or hatred) i.e., all loving, amiable, without rancour, malice, or animosity. This is so because the entire creation is His, and it is nurtured and sustained by His Will ('Razā'). Some of the attributes that encapsulate His innate nature, e.g., 'kripāl', 'da-i-āl', 'rāzak', 'rahīm', 'pratipālak', 'dukh bhañjan' etc. support His loving and caring innate nature. In any case, one normally bears ill will or malice towards one's rivals or peers, but God is not only peerless, but the truth is there is none other than Him in the universe.[117] The following verses of the SGGS emphasise this aspect of the Creator's nature:

You are my father, mother, brother, and kinsman; why would any fear or inner turmoil distress me when You are my refuge everywhere?[68]

He has no rival or peer, nor any enemy.[150]

Akāl mūrat(i): (ad, m) akāl is a complex word comprising 'a' + 'kāl'.

'a', as a prefix to a noun or adjective gives a negative or opposite meaning to the noun or adjective.

'kāl': (a) (adj; synonymous with 'kālā' or 'siāh') black, (b) (synonymous with 'kal(h)', 'aj' or 'parsoṅ') yesterday, today, or tomorrow, (c) (synonymous with 'mrityu' or 'maut') death, and implicit here is (d) (synonymous with 'samāṅ' or 'velā') time.

akāl: (adj) 'a' (without or beyond) + 'kāl' ('samāṅ' or 'velā' - time; 'mrityu' or 'maut' - death) beyond time or not bound by time; eternal.

mūrat(i): (a) (n, m; as 'mūrat(u)' (skt) it is synonymous with 'mahūrat(u)') auspicious or propitious time, and implicit here is (b) (n, f: (skt) synonymous with 'sarūp', 'vajūd', 'hastī', 'hoṅd' or 'astitv') form, shape, or configuration; a being; existence; reality; 'rūp'; embodiment of His Being in whatever form.

akāl mūrat(i): His Being, a definite reality and not a figment of the imagination, and in whatever form, shape, or configuration, that is beyond the limits or restraint of time. This is in contradistinction to everything in creation, whose existence is limited or for a finite time.

The following verses of the SGGS emphasise this aspect of the Creator's nature:

You, who pervades all, are immortal and beyond the scope of time. You are unfathomable, unique, formless and beyond the rules of Karmā.[151]

He is both immortal and eternal.[152]

ajūnī: (adj, m) a complex word comprising 'a' (without) + 'jūnī' (that comes in diverse life forms in this universe) i.e., unborn, beyond, or outside the laws of incarnation or re-incarnation. Individual constituents of the entire creation enter and leave this world, at His Will ('Razā') but He is unborn, and beyond or outside of the laws of incarnation or re-incarnation. The following verses of the SGGS emphasise this aspect of the Creator's nature:

May that tongue burn which alleges that God has a uterine birth.[153]

He, the Creator of the universe, alone is the eternal Reality, the true Lord, and His Glory is eternal. He exists here and now and shall do so forever in the hereafter; He neither incarnates nor dies.[154]

The immaculate Lord ('Nām(u)') does not incarnate and is beyond the suffering associated with birth and death. Such is the Lord and Master of Kabīr who has no mother or father.[155]

saibhaṅg: (adj; synonymous with 'svyambhav' and 'svyambhū' (skt)) a complex word comprising 'svya' (from or by oneself) + 'aṅbhav' or 'aṅbhū' (manifest) i.e., self-created and preserved.[32-3] The following verses of the SGGS emphasise this aspect of His nature:

The immaculate Lord ('Nām(u)') neither suffers from any misfortune, danger or calamity and nor does He incarnate. Kabir's Lord and Master is He who does not have a father or a mother.[155]

He cannot be conceived, nurtured, created or appointed.

He, who exists by Himself, is untainted by 'Māyā' and is thus immaculate.[156]

He, who is by Himself and is forever eternal, is my Lord.[157]

gur: (n, m, s; abbrev. for Gurū) literally, a teacher or a spiritual guide. (u) of 'gur(u)' is missing because of the latent usage of a preposition ('dī' or 'kī') that links it with the next word 'prasād(i)'. In the SGGS, a Gurū is a person who has realised God, and whose every thought ('*Man*'), utterance ('Bachan') and action ('Karam') is in perfect harmony with God and God-consciousness.

It has two parts: 'gu' (darkness or a state devoid of knowledge or wisdom) + 'ru' (light or a state of wisdom/knowledge), and literally means enlightener, that which takes one out of darkness (or a state of ignorance) into light (a state of knowledge or wisdom).

It also has its roots in the word 'gri', meaning (a) to engulf and/or devour, and (b) to inform, instruct or make another understand, i.e., that which destroys ignorance and makes another understand the eternal Reality.

'Anhad Sabad or Nād' ('Nām(u)') is the primordial and perfect Gurū (Enlightener). However, It is only perceived in a state of 'Sahaj' and through the Grace of God. 'Sabad' or 'Anhad Sabad' (the Divine Word) is the Primordial Gurū and It, in turn, inspires or directly communicates through a human being, who is not only aligned perfectly with, but, in a state of 'Sahaj', has also realised or perceived the full glow of 'Nām(u)' within one's conscious self ('*Man*' or 'Hirdā') by the Grace of God. 'Nām(u)' permeates and overwhelms such a person, and manifests in all one's thoughts ('*Man*'), utterances ('Bachan') and deeds ('Karam'). Such a person is a 'spiritual Gurū', and the sermon or words ('bānī', 'bachan', 'bol' or 'updes') that one utters is called Gurbānī which represents the true Glory of God and 'Divine Wisdom' ('brahm giān') for the path to 'Nam-realisation' This is why a Gurū, in Gurmat, is also defined as the 'Sabad

Gurū', i.e., the 'spiritual', or 'Divine Wisdom' packaged or loaded in the Gurū's Words. Logical extrapolation of this concept propounds that Gurbānī, thus, represents 'Sabad' or 'Anhad Sabad' (the Divine Word or 'Nām(u)').

A Gurū (synonymous with a 'Sat(i)gurū', 'Sādh', 'Sādhū', 'Bhagat' or 'Brahm-Gyānī' in Gurbānī) is not God incarnate, even though he has all the virtues, values, and attributes of the Primal Soul ('Nām(u)') which manifest in him; he is thus identified as one with Him. The Gurū is thus 'Nām(u)' - the 'Anhad Sabad' or the Word, disembodied but manifesting through the embodiment of the living Gurū, through which He reveals Himself and His nature. The Gurū's Word or Gurbānī, is, thus, the perfect or true Gurū, the fount or source of Divine Wisdom ('Brahm giān') for one's spiritual evolution and path to 'Nām-realisation'. The following verses of the SGGS lend support to this observation:

'One does not get spiritual wisdom without the Gurū', O Brother! 'Check it out with Lord Brahma, sage Nārad or Vyās who wrote the Vedas'.[158]

A clay pitcher that holds water, cannot itself be made and shaped without water. Similarly, Divine Wisdom holds and stills the *man*(u) but one cannot have Divine Wisdom without the Gurū'.[159]

The Lord pervades all but one realises Him only by imbibing the Divine Wisdom of the Gurū (in essence, the 'Grace of the Gurū').[160]

Only a true Gurū has the wisdom to reveal Him to us; I am, therefore, forever grateful and willing to lay down my life for an audience with him and for alignment with his wisdom.[161]

The following verses from the SGGS underpin the doctrine of Gurū as God ('Nām(u)'), Gurū as a living human being and Gurū as His Divine Word. However, as 'Nām(u)' permeates and expresses its full glow in the conscious self ('*Man*' or 'Hirdā') of a living human being (Gurū), he/she is then identified as one with God and the words then uttered by such a being represent the Primordial Gurū or 'Nām(u)' (the Divine Word, 'Sabad' or 'Anhad Sabad') revealed through him/her. Thus, the true Gurū has always been and shall forever be 'Nām(u)' but the living Gurū's Word (Gurbānī), being Its revelation, is identical with it. Gurbānī is also called 'Aṁmrit Bānī', the spiritually immortalising ('Aṁmrit') utterances ('Bānī') of the Gurūs, who have perceived 'Nām(u)' and whose every thought, utterance and deed is in perfect harmony with 'Nām(u)'. 'Gurbanī' is thus nothing but the Glory of 'Nām(u)' and the path to 'Nām-realisation'. 'Nām(u)', in 'Gurbanī', is often described as 'Nām padārath', 'Nām naunidh(i)', 'Nām-aṅmrit' and 'Nām jal'; just as water, once absorbed, becomes part of one's body, similarly the attributes, values and virtues of 'Nām(u)' once imbibed during contemplation, become part of one's conscious self ('Hirdā or '*Man*').

Gurū as the 'Sabad', 'Anhad Sabad', 'Anhad Nād' or the Divine Word ('Nām(u)')

The eternal Reality, the immaculate Primal Soul that pervades all, and I, are now identical. For I have imbibed His attributes who is the infinite, transcendent and supreme God.[162]

My true Gurū is eternal and neither incarnates nor dies; He is immortal and pervades the entire creation.[163]

'Realising 'Nām(u)' during this lifetime is our real aim; the transcendent and omnipotent, our Lord Master and God, the Primal Gurū, is forever with us', O' Nānak.[164]

I have realised my Gurū, the all-pervasive 'Nām(u)' - the Primal Soul.[165]

My life began with the first breath; it is now the time and the opportunity to imbibe and align with the Gurū's Wisdom. The Word ('Sabad', 'Anhad Sabad'/'Dhun(i)' or 'Nām(u)') is my Gurū and my undivided attention and focus ('Surat(i)') is Its disciple.[137]

He Himself is the Divine Word and the true Enlightener; He utters and thus reveals Himself.[166]

Recognise only Him as my true Gurū, who alone assumed this 'sargun sarūp' from the very beginning and shall continue to do so till the end of time.[167]

The Gurū in the human form - like the ten living Sikh Gurūs

'One does not get spiritual wisdom without the Gurū', O Brother! 'Check it out with Lord Brahma, sage Nārad or Vyās who wrote the Vedas'.[158]

None has realised Him without submitting to a Gurū's Word and Wisdom. God Himself instilled His Divine Wisdom and Knowledge in 'Sat(i)gurū', and by revealing it He proclaims this truth to the world.[168]

One who has perceived the all-pervasive eternal Lord is called a 'Sat(i)gur(u)'.[169]

He alone, ideologically converging with whom one aligns perfectly with 'Nām(u)' and gets lasting inner equanimity ('Sahaj') and bliss ('Anaṅd'), is a true enlightener ('sat(i)gur').[170]

He alone, who is one with Him, who contemplates the One eternal and immaculate Lord, and who overwhelms his five cardinal drives, is the true Gurū.[171]

One who has the full glow of 'Nām(u)' in one's 'Hirdā' is a Sat(i)gur(u).[172]

Words fail to glorify a Gurū truly, for the transcendent Lord has revealed Himself in him and merged with him.[173]

Wondrous is that true enlightener who has realised the eternal Lord; imbibing and aligning with his Divine Wisdom, one attains inner equanimity and bliss and satiates one's 'Trisnā'.[174]

Gurū's word ('Gurbānī') as the Gurū

'Just as I receive the Word of God, so do I expound it', O Lālo![175]

'O' Lord! You are infinite, unfathomable, unique, and incomparable. Your true devotee speaks as You command him to', says Nānak.[176]

The Gurū is his Divine Word and the Word his embodiment; the Word has all the spiritually uplifting virtues.[177]

These words, emanating from the Primal Lord Himself, have demolished all my anxieties.[178]

I know not what to say but say only what is entirely commensurate with Your Divine Order.[179]

'I expound as You enable me to', says Nānak, slave of Your slaves.[180]

'I speak as You empower me to do, for I have no innate ability of my own', O Lord![181]

Recognise the Word of the Gurū as true, for the Lord Himself empowers the Gurū to speak.[182]

Rarely, if one submits to a Gurū, does one then reflect on his Word; it is the word of the truly awakened which enables one to focus on and align with the Primal Soul within one's Hirdā.[183]

The whole world is aware of the true knowledge and wisdom. However, deliverance from one's innate evil drives rests on reflection and implementation, and not just on its observation.[184]

prasād(i): (instrumental case - 'karaṇ kārak') with, by virtue of or through someone's grace. See prasād:

prasād: (a) (n, f; synonymous with 'nadar(i)' or 'mehar dī nazar') literally, gracious glance, (b) (n; synonymous with 'bakhsīs', 'bakhshīsh' or (pers) 'karam(u)') literally, gift, boon, favour or blessing, (c) (n; synonymous with 'nadar(i) karam(u)' or 'mehar-' or 'bakhshish-' 'dī nazar') literally, a gracious glance that results in a positive intercession, and (d) (n, m; synonymous with 'kripā', 'mehar', 'ma-i-ā', 'da-i-ā', 'khushī', 'anugrah') grace, kindness, mercy or favour. However, implicit here is Divine Wisdom and noble or godly attributes, virtues and values wrapped up or contained in the Gurū's Divine Words and his Counsel or Instruction.

gur prasād(i): (instrumental case - 'karaṇ kārak') with, through or by virtue of the Gurū's Grace.

Naturally, this begs the question: What? What is it that one gets with, through or by virtue of the Gurū's Grace? The clue becomes apparent in the first 'Pauṛī' of 'Jap(u)': 'Kiv sachiārā hoīai kiv kūṛai tuṭai pāl(i)' is the key question that is raised and 'Hukam(i) rajāī chalṇā Nānak likhiā nāl(i)' is the pithy answer or solution that is offered. The way and/or means to become a 'sachiārā' is what one achieves with, through or by virtue of the Gurū's Grace. Willing, loving, and unconditional surrender to the Gurū's Will, imbibing his Divine Wisdom and Knowledge and implementing it in one's life is the Gurū's Grace ('Gur prasād') and this is in complete consonance with God's 'nadar(i) karam(u)'.

The key points noted thus far clearly outline that Gurū Nānak's God is the Creator, is simultaneously transcendent and immanent, has a persona with infinite attributes, does not incarnate and is a God of Will and Grace. He is the fount of all wisdom and knowledge, and the evolving empirical world bound by His Divine Order ('Hukam(u') and 'Razā') is forever dependent on His Grace ('nadar(i) karam(u)') for increasingly more and more divine or noble attributes, knowledge and wisdom to progress and evolve in line with His Will. The following verses from the SGGS clearly state humanity's aim and/or goal in this lifetime:

Lost and wandering through myriads of births, you have now got this precious and rare opportunity. Remember and cherish 'Nām(u)' for the day you die is near at hand.[185]

'Why has man, without any devotion to and meditation on 'Nām(u)', come into this world' O, brother? He neither submits to nor cherishes the Gurū's Divine Word and Wisdom in his heart and wastes away this opportunity of a lifetime.[186]

'Our innate nature and evil deeds have led us astray; have Mercy and help us re-align with 'Nām(u)', O' Lord![187]

'Lost and weary of wandering through myriads of births over a long period, you have now been blessed with this human body; this is your time to realise Him, so why don't you meditate on and cherish 'Nām(u)' now?', says Nānak.[188]

Accursed is their life and vain their coming into this world, who neither submit to the true Gurū nor cherish his Divine Message in their 'Hirdā'.[189]

You have been blessed with this human body; this is your time to realise Him.[46]

Humanity is blessed with the apex position amongst the proverbial eighty four lakhs of species; whosoever now misses this opportunity of living by His Will, aligning perfectly with and realising 'Nām(u)' shall suffer the woes of transmigration in 'Āvāgavan'.[47]

O' Man! 'You are here to profit from this lifetime; how vainly are you engaged whilst the twilight of your life is gradually ebbing away.[61]

This was your opportunity to hear and utter His Word and Praise. Instead, engrossed in the material world and forsaking this duty, you are wasting away this golden opportunity.[62]

Humanity has this rare and golden opportunity to link with 'Nām-consciousness' and to realise this goal, the apex position in spiritual evolution - perfect alignment with 'Nām(u)' ('Sahaj') and then, with God's Grace, 'Anand' ('Nām-realisation') in this life, and merger with the Primal Soul or freedom from 'Āvāgavan', the cycle of transmigration, at death.[63]

In several lifetimes you were a worm or a winged insect, an elephant, a fish or a deer, a bird or a serpent, a horse or a bull. You have attained this human birth after a long period, and this is your opportunity to align perfectly with and realise Him.[49]

One who submits to the Gurū's Divine Word, imbibes the noble attributes within one's 'Hirdā' by the Grace of God, attunes perfectly to 'Nām(u)' - the fount of all attributes, - and lives by His Will, realises His Glow within.[190]

What path should one follow and how does one realise one's aim in this life? The following verses from the SGGS illustrate well the way and means to this end:

'How did you realise my Lord?', I go and ask the brides ('Jīvātmāṅs') who have realised God. 'The eternal Lord showered His Grace upon us when we rid ourselves of our sense of duality ('mer ter')', they replied.[191]

'How does one realise the Lord?' Go and ask those who have achieved this. 'Submit to His Will and do away with personal shrewdness and opinionated nature', they reply.[192]

'How should I live my life?', I ask my Gurū. 'He reveals Himself in one's 'Hirdā' when one contemplates and sings His Glory and rids oneself of one's 'Haumaiṅ', replies the Gurū.[193]

One's conscious self becomes pure when one submits to the Guru's Divine Word, reflects upon and ideologically converges with it, examines one's conscious self, and then contemplates 'Nām(u)' and sings His Glory.[194]

Engage in profitable deals ('Nām Simran') lest you come to regret; rid yourself of your evil streak ('Haumaiṅ', 'Moh' and innate evil 'vikārī' tendencies') and imbibe noble attributes within your 'Hirdā' which will be your real assets.[195]

The following verses from the SGGS state clearly how one succeeds in acquiring the Gurū's Grace:

If one should meet and converge ideologically with a true Gurū, rid oneself of 'Haumaiṅ' and align perfectly with and realise 'Nām(u)', then one should surrender to him willingly and lovingly.[196]

The true Gurū helps reveal the Primal Soul within to those who submit to, converge ideologically with, imbibe his Divine Wisdom and Knowledge, and rid themselves of 'Haumaiṅ'.[197]

One who submits to and imbibes the true Gurū's Divine Wisdom in one's Hirdā and aligns one's conscious self with 'Nām(u)' perfectly, realises equanimity ('Sahaj') and lasting inner bliss ('Anaṅd').[198]

Having submitted to and sought the Gurū's Counsel and Wisdom, one needs to abide by it faithfully and resolutely. Thus, one realises 'Nām(u)' when one focuses on 'Nām(u)' and continuously examines one's conscious self.[199]

When one submits to a 'Sat(i)gurū's' Will lovingly and willingly, his unwavering dedication and hard work bears fruit ('Nām-realisation').[200]

One realises Him by surrendering one's all to a Guru willingly and lovingly and through living life by His Will and Order.[201]

Finally, as alluded to above, the Gurū's Divine Word (Gurbānī) represents 'Sabad' or 'Anhad Sabad' (the Divine Word or 'Nām(u)'). Willingly and lovingly surrendering to Gurbānī, and thereby indirectly to His Divine Order and Will, one aligns perfectly with 'Nām(u)' or 'Nām-consciousness', and eventually, through God's Grace, perceives the Primal Soul within, becoming free from 'Haumaiṅ', 'Moh' and innate 'Vikārī' nature ('jīvan mukat(i)') in one's lifetime here and finding release from the cycle of transmigration ('Āvāgavan') at death.

Conceptual summary

The One eternal, transcendent and immutable Reality, Its everlasting, Omnipotent and Omniscient 'Nām(u)' as the Creator, immanent in all Its creation, Sustainer and Destroyer of everything, without fear and enmity, beyond time, Unborn and self-existent, is realised only by the Grace of the Gurū.

PROLOGUE

Jap(u)

॥ਜਪੁ॥

According to popular belief, in AD 1507, God summoned Nānak to His Court, whilst he was bathing in the River 'Beīṅ' in Sultānpur, Punjab, and asked him to promulgate His Glory, 'Hukam(u)' and 'Razā'. Nānak was then blessed with divine inspiration and compiled 'Jap(u)' at God's Court.[202] Another reference to a hand-written account, thought to be mid-sixteenth century in origin and based on the language deployed (currently available in a library, W. Punjab, Pakistan), suggests that, during his last long stint at Kartārpur, Gurū Nānak used Bhāī Lehnā, whom he later appointed as the second Gurū, Gurū Aṅgad, as a scribe for 'Jap(u)'.[203] Bhāī Gurdās also refers to his long stay at Kartārpur and it is quite likely that Gurū Nānak compiled his major works there.[204] It was also towards the end of his life at Kartārpur that Gurū Nānak gave Gurū Aṅgad the 'Pothī' containing all his own 'Bānīs' as well as the 'Bānīs' of various 'Bhagats' that he had personally gathered.

However, the glaring drawbacks, inaccuracies, and lack of authentic evidence that exist in the sources that attempt to answer this question, thus far, clearly lend support to the view that there is no bona fide evidence which corroborates when and where Gurū Nānak, the founder of the Sikh Religion ('Sikhī'), composed Jap(u), the most revered of his compositions ('Bāṇīs').

Whether future research in this area will shed further light, is open to speculation. However, many other questions besides this, demand scrutiny of all the available literature by academics in the field so that a thorough and critical study and examination can turn misrepresentation and fiction into verifiable and evidence-based facts and true knowledge in the future.

Jap(u): (a) (n, m/f, s) Jap(u) is both written and spoken as 'Jap(u) Jī', the suffix 'Jī' denotes reverence for this Bāṇī, and (b) (v, s, second person, imperative mood - 'hukmī bhvikht' - of the verb 'Japṇā') Gurū Nānak's exhortation is to utter, inwardly focus upon and contemplate 'Nām(u)', the one word that embodies and encapsulates the persona and all the known and unknown attributes of the transcendent God, with the eventual aim of imbibing the same attributes in one's conscious self ('*Man*', 'Hirdā' or

'Jīvātmāṅ') and spontaneously express them in one's daily life. The following verse of the SGGS beautifully captures this counsel:

'Remember and contemplate 'Nām(u)', the Omniscient, for this is the sublime fruit of human life'.[205]

The title 'Jap(u)' is followed by the first 'Salok', 'Ād(i) sach(u) Jugād(i) sach(u). Hai bhī sach(u) Nānak Hosī bhī sach(u)', which is also Gurū Nānak's invocation ('Maṅglācharan') for this Bāṇī. The second 'Salok', at the end of this composition, represents a summary or the essence (Epilogue) of 'Jap(u)'. In the thirty-eight 'Pauṛīs' (stanzas) sandwiched between the two 'Saloks', Gurū Nānak develops his worldview and clearly sets forth the way to re-align with 'Nām(u)' and realise our human goal.

'Jap(u)' is Gurū Nānak's attempt to provide an exposition of the 'Mūl-Mantra' and many would boldly go on to state that what follows in SGGS is an exposition of 'Jap(u)'.

'Kiv sachiārā hoīai kiv kūṛai tuṭai pāl(i)' is the succinct and fundamental question that is raised and 'Hukam(i) rajāī chalṇā Nānak likhiā nāl(i)' is the precise and pithy answer or solution that is offered in the first 'Pauṛī'. How do we become godlike and how do we shatter this wall of ignorance that stands between us and the all-pervasive eternal Reality within us? 'We must learn to live by His Will' is the Writ for the whole creation which immediately follows as the answer to this fundamental question.

We must, therefore, appreciate, right at the outset, the disparity that exists between our default status as 'Kuṛiārs' and that of the eternal Reality (a 'Sachiār' or 'Sachiārā'). The path to bridge this gap has been alluded to in the preface and will be developed fully in the ensuing chapters.

Jap: (a) (n, m, pl; (skt) dha - verbal root; synonymous with 'japnā'/'japṇā' or '*man* vich kahiṇā') literally, to utter a word, sentence or a small composition ('Maṅtra') from one of the holy texts repetitively to (i) help in meditation, and (ii) impress and please one's demi-god or god and/or to realise one's ambition successfully, in Hindu tradition, and (b) (v, pl, present tense; synonymous with 'japde han') literally, [they] meditate or contemplate.

The Saṅskrit 'Graṅths' define its three forms as follows: (i) 'Vāchik jap' - the easily audible, meaningful and repetitive utterance of a word or collection of words so that even a person sitting nearby can easily understand its meaning, (ii) 'Upāṅsh jap' - the very softly spoken, meaningful and repetitive utterance of a word or collection of words that even a person sitting nearby cannot hear and understand, and (iii) 'Mānas jap' - the focus on and contemplation of the word or collection of words only in one's conscious self ('*Man*' or 'Hirdā').[206]

Gurmat, however, views it differently. In the initial stages, one needs to have time and quiet space for regular and daily reflection on 'self'. This process of introspection ('āpā chīnaṇ' or 'svai paṛchol') juxtaposes one with 'Nām(u)', the fount of all attributes and sharply brings into focus the need for one's self or inner cleansing. 'Nām Japṇā' is to focus on and devoutly and repeatedly utter the word 'Wāhigurū' (the wonderful enlightener - also known as 'Gur Maṅtrā'), 'Mūl Maṅtrā' (the Credal Statement) or the essence of a part of Gurbānī from the SGGS, loudly enough to be heard in one's immediate proximity, such that the persona and attributes of 'Nām(u)' that it conjures up in one's conscious self, become the focus of one's devotion. With loving and willing surrender to the Gurū's Divine Word and Wisdom, and gradually ideological convergence with it, one begins to cleanse one's conscious self of 'Haumaiṅ', 'Moh' and innate evil 'vikārī' tendencies, to embed noble attributes within it and to begin to express them spontaneously in one's daily life. This would be commensurate with 'Vāchik jap'.

With progress, one engages in 'Nām Japṇā' with increasing fervour and for longer periods but vocalises in such a way that even a person sitting nearby cannot hear. The attributes encapsulated within the Gurū's Divine Word now begin to travel inwardly from one's lips and to resonate in one's vocal cords. With ongoing self-introspection and cleansing, increasing ideological convergence with the Divine Word and the embedding of noble attributes in one's conscious self, gathers pace. This is probably commensurate with 'Upāṅsh jap'.

Gradually, rather than softly uttering, one now merely focuses intensely on the word 'Wāh(i)gurū', 'Mūl Maṅtr' or the essence of any part of Gurbānī from SGGS. The process of self-introspection and cleansing, the permanent embedding of the persona and attributes of 'Nām(u)' in one's conscious self and the expression of these in one's daily life intensifies. This is probably termed 'Nām-' 'Dhiāuṇā', 'Sumarṇā' or 'Arādhanā' and equivalent to 'Mānas jap'.

One inches closer and closer, faithfully adhering to the process and pursuing it with genuine love and unwavering discipline and conviction.

Firm imprinting or embedding of increasingly more and more attributes of 'Nām(u)' gathers momentum, and one eventually reaches perfect alignment or attuning with 'Nām(u)' and achieves a state of lasting inner equipoise ('Sahaj').

At some stage thereafter, and with God's Grace, lasting inner bliss ('Anaṅd') follows, which in itself serves as an overture for the experiential revelation of 'Nām(u)' within one's conscious self ('Jīvātmāṅ', 'Hirdā' or '*Man*'). One perceives the full glow of 'Nām(u)' within one's conscious self, which overwhelms it and expresses itself fully. One's every thought ('*Man*'), utterance ('Bachan') or deed ('Karam') is now inspired and guided by the Divine Word ('Parāvāk', 'Parā-Bāṇī', 'Paṅch Sabad', 'Anhad Sabad' or 'Nām(u)') and one is now a 'Sachiār' or, literally, God incarnate.

In reality, the Divine Word ('Anhad Sabad', 'Anhad Nād or Dhun(i)', 'Parāvāk' or 'Parā-Bāṇī') originates from the primal source ('Nām(u)') and is also described as the 'Unstruck Sound' as it is not produced by the coming together or collision of two objects, is eternal and not heard by ears as opposed to the sound that we hear with our ears and which is transient in nature. 'Parāvāk' or 'Parā Bāṇī' ('Nām(u)') permeates and expresses itself fully in the conscious self ('Jīvātmāṅ', '*Man*' or 'Hirdā') of one who realises 'Nām(u)'.

When word, from such a person enters one's conscious self, it is termed 'Pashyaṅtī Bāṇī'. As it reaches his vocal cords and is softly spoken, it is defined as 'Madhaymā Bāṇī' and when this uttered word becomes clearly audible, it is described as 'Baikharī Bāṇī'.

The word in a Gurū's conscious self or throat/vocal cords is thus identical with 'Parāvāk', 'Parā-Bāṇī', 'Paṅch Sabad', 'Anhad Sabad' or the Divine Word ('Nām(u)'). The process and practice of 'Nām Japnā', as described above, is just a reversal of this process, which takes one from the initial stage of purposeful and focused repetitive uttering of a word or collection of words ('Baikharī Bāṇī') such that it clearly brings forth the persona and/or attributes of 'Nām(u)' in one's conscious self. Gradually and covertly, one progresses through to higher levels, and finally to the stage when the word begins to resonate permanently in one's conscious self. By the Grace of God, one then perceives that 'Unstruck Sound' or 'Dhun(i)' (Divine Word or 'Parā-Bāṇī') and realises the full glow of 'Nam(u)' within one's conscious self ('Jīvātmāṅ', '*Man*' or 'Hirdā'). This is the apogee of spiritual evolution and one's every thought ('Man'), utterance ('Bachan') and deed ('Karam') is then in absolute harmony with 'Nām(u)'. One is now free of 'Haumaiṅ', 'Moh' and evil 'Vikāri tendencies' ('Jīvan Mukat(i)') as one realises one's true self, 'Nām(u)', 'Parmātmān' or universal - or higher-consciousness. One is now a 'Sachiār(u)' or a 'Sachiārā' and lives the rest of one's life by 'Nām-consciousness', finding release ('Param-mukat(i)') from the cycle of transmigration, at death ('Āvāgavan').

Jap(u): (a) (n, f/m, s) literally, meditation or deep contemplation - see 'japṇā'. It is the name of a hymn, a composition of Gurū Nānak, set out in the very beginning of the Sikh Holy Scriptures, the Srī Gurū Granth Sāhib. It forms an obligatory part of an early morning recitation and reflection by a disciple of Gurū Nānak, and (b) (v, s, imperative mood - 'hukmī bhvikht', second person; synonymous with 'tusīṅ japo') literally, you meditate, contemplate, or reflect upon! See japṇā.

japṇā: (v; synonymous with 'Japnā') 'Japṇā', in Gurmat , is to utter a word, phrase or sentence/s ('Baikharī Bāṇī') repetitively such that the persona or the attributes of the object of one's reverence that it conjures up ('Nām(u)') becomes the focus of one's love and devotion. 'Nām Japṇā' is mandatory in Gurmat and its sole purpose is to cleanse, uplift and evolve spiritually, and to transform oneself by imbibing the attributes of 'Nām(u)' in one's conscious self ('*Man*', 'Hirdā' and 'Jīvātmāṅ') and then to be able to express them spontaneously in one's daily life in complete harmony with 'Nām-Consciousness'.

Mere mechanical repetition of a word or God's name, without any concomitant change in one's persona and conscious self, is futile as endorsed by the following verses from the SGGS:

Everyone repeats God's name, but mere repetition does not get one to God. One aligns with and realises 'Nām(u)' by the Grace of the Gurū.[207]

With guile in heart, one practises guile daily but mutters God's name. Surrounded by greed and ignorance of 'Moh', one is just pounding husk and suffers pain.[208]

One mutters God's name but harbours and practises guile; it fails to purify one's conscious self.[209]

However, 'Nām Japṇā', with concomitant cleansing of the filth of 'Haumaiṅ', 'Moh' and innate evil 'vikārī' tendencies, is highlighted in the following verses from the SGGS:

Remember and contemplate upon 'Nām(u)', the omniscient, for this is the sublime fruit of human life.[210]

By focusing on and contemplating 'Nām(u)' alone, I eradicate all my inner turbulence and distress and find lasting inner bliss ('Sahaj' and 'Anaṅd').[211]

Alignment with and realisation of 'Nām(u)' is a prelude to the supreme and lasting inner bliss; this is enshrined in the conscious self of His Bhagats.[212]

Focusing on and contemplating 'Nām(u)' and living by His Will is the most exalted of all duties.[213]

They who submit to, contemplate upon and live by 'Nām(u)' become like It, and eventually perceive Him, the Lord of Wonders, within their 'Hirdā'.[214]

'Forever dwell upon 'Nām(u)', O', my *Man*! He, who ever contemplates the omnipresent and immaculate 'Nām(u)', gets rewarded for honourably discharging his duties both here and in the hereafter.[215]

'Nothing equals realisation of 'Nām(u)'. One achieves 'Jīvan Mukat(i)' and 'Moksh' by surrendering to and imbibing the Gurū's Divine Wisdom and contemplating the persona and attributes of 'Nām(u)', O' Nānak![216]

O' my '*Man*'! 'The noblest amongst all endeavours is to focus and reflect upon the persona and attributes of 'Nām(u)' forever, and then imbibe and reflect the same in your daily life'.[217]

O' you ignorant '*Man*', with no merit or virtue! 'Forever focus and reflect upon the persona and attributes of 'Nām(u)'. Focus on the One who created you, for He shall stand by you till the end of life and in the hereafter', O' Nānak![218]

'One receives honour at His Court by contemplating and living life attuned to 'Nām(u)'. Having achieved 'Jīvan Mukat(i)' and 'Nām-realisation', one's 'Jīvātmāṅ' merges with the Primal Soul in the hereafter', O' Nānak![219]

'Meditate forever upon Him', O' true seeker! This is the most exalted and immaculate of all lifestyles'.[220]

Whom He, having granted His Grace, aligns with 'Nām(u)', achieves 'Sahaj' and thereafter realises 'Jīvan Mukat(i)' and 'Moksh', O' Nānak.[221]

Perfect harmony with and realisation of 'Nām(u)' is one's real wealth and through it one enjoys real beauty in nature. Perfect alignment with 'Nām(u)' offers lasting inner bliss ('Anaṅd').[222]

'Nothing, save the wealth of 'Nām(u)', accompanies one in the hereafter and all else is 'Māyā' and worthless.

Wealth par excellence is to live life in perfect harmony with 'Nām(u)', says Nānak.[223]

'He, whose '*Man*' is imbued with 'Nām(u)' through lovingly hearing His Glory, forever remembers the Lord; the loftiest spiritual status befits him and such is the quality of 'Nām(u)' - the fount of this supreme and lasting inner bliss ('sukhmanī')', says Nānak.[224]

'Bless me with that wisdom and discernment ('bibek') by which I may focus and dwell upon You forever'.[225]

Ād(i) sach(u), Jugād(i) sach(u).
ਆਦਿ ਸਚੁ, ਜੁਗਾਦਿ ਸਚੁ॥
Hai bhī sach(u), Nānak, hosī bhī sach(u).
ਹੈ ਭੀ ਸਚੁ, ਨਾਨਕ, ਹੋਸੀ ਭੀ ਸਚੁ॥

These verses, forming the first 'salok' in Jap(u) and symbolising the prologue, following the title of the composition, represent Gurū Nānak's 'Maṅglā-charan' (Invocation), the customary reverence and devotion dedicated to his 'spiritual guide', God Himself, and are hence incorporated in the very beginning of this major piece of work. A 'Salok' is a composition of couplets or short stanzas, in poetry, dedicated to God's Glory. Thirty-eight 'Pauṛīs' (stanzas) follow, and the composition ends with another 'Salok', an epilogue. Customarily, the writers of the day used it to (a) express their gratitude to their spiritual guide, (b) seek a boon or a blessing from their spiritual guide, or (c) present the very essence of their composition.

Ād(i) sach(u), Jugād(i) sach(u).

ād(i): (a) (n, m, s; synonymous with 'Brahm' and 'Kartār') literally, the Creator or God, and implicit here is (b) (ablative case - 'apādān kārak'; synonymous with 'muḍh toṅ') literally, in the beginning, from the beginning or before the beginning of time. See ād (b and c).

ād: (a) (p; synonymous with 'vagairā' and 'ādik') literally, et cetera, (b) (skt) adj; synonymous with 'ād(i)', 'pahilā' and 'muḍhlā') original, elemental, primary, primeval or primordial, (c) (n, m; synonymous with ‘araṅbh’ and ‘muḍh’) beginning, origin, inception, source or root, and (d) (n, m; synonymous with ‘mūl kāraṇ’) literally, the primary cause.

sach(u): (synonymous with ‘satya’ (skt) and ‘sat(i)’ (gmkh) (a) (n, m, s; synonymous with ‘Pārbrahm’ and ‘Kartār’) the eternal Truth, Reality or Bliss (‘Nām(u)’, the immanent form of God). See sach(u) and sat(i).

jugād(i): (a) (adj; synonymous with ‘yugam’ and ‘dūjā’) literally, second, and implicit here is (b) (ablative case - ‘apādān kārak’; synonymous with ‘jugāṅ de muḍh toṅ’) a complex word comprising: ‘jug’ + ‘ād(i)’, literally meaning ‘ād(i)’ of ‘jugs’, i.e., before the time of the ‘jugs’. See jug(u).

jug(u)**:** (n, m**,** s; synonymous with ‘yug(u)’) The four ‘yugs’ or great epochs and their span, according to Hindu mythology, are as follows: ‘Satyayug’ (1,728,000 years), ‘Tretāyug’ (1,296,000 years), ‘Doāparyug’ (864000 years) and ‘Kalyug’, the current epoch (432,000 years). This would imply that human life has existed for at least 3,888,000 years even if one excludes the current epoch of ‘Kalyug’. Furthermore, it also implies a gradual decline in spirituality, and the practice of spirituality and religion. Socially, ethically, and spiritually, humanity was apparently at its peak during ‘Satyayug’, declined gradually in the ensuing period and is at his lowest in all aspects in this period of ‘Kalyug’. On the contrary, contemporary wisdom tells us that humans have evolved from the Stone, Bronze and the Iron Ages to the Modern Age developing much greater intellect and deductive reasoning as well as greatly refining our understanding of the creation and its likely creator. However, Gurmat and modern science do not support this Vedic view. It merely implies a long period of time during which a pre-eminent or popular worldview prevails, and a unique way of life is practised.

He was there before the beginning of time and has been there since the beginning of the four great epochs.

Hai bhī sach(u), Nānak, hosī bhī sach(u).

hai: (a) (n, m; skt; ‘hyā’; synonymous with ‘ghoṛā’) a horse, (b) (interj; synonymous with ‘dukh bodhak’; pronounced as ‘hā-i’) literally, oh!, (c) (interj; synonymous with ‘shok bodhak’; pronounced as ‘haiṅ’) literally, what!, and implicit here is (d) (aux v, present tense) literally, am, is or are; ‘I am, he is or they are’ and refers to the present time.

bhī: (a) ('bhūt kāl bodhak') indicative of past tense, (b) (conj; synonymous with 'yadī' and 'je') if, in case or provided, (c) (conj; synonymous with 'ate' and 'ar'), (d) (synonymous with 'tad bhī') even then, (e) (synonymous with 'nischya hī') only that (with confidence), and implicit here is (f) (adv; synonymous with 'vī') also or too.

hai bhī sach(u): 'He (God) is here now for sure', 'He exists at present too' or 'His existence in the present time is not imaginary but an absolute reality'.

Nānak: (n, m, s; the founder and the first of the ten Gurūs of the Sikh Faith) (u) of 'Nānak(u)' is missing because of its vocative case - 'saṅbodhan kārak'.

hosī: (v; future tense of the verb 'hoṇā'; synonymous with 'hovegā') shall be or shall exist in the future. See 'hoṇā' (a and c).

'He most certainly exists in the present and shall be here forever in the future too', O' Nānak!

This first 'Salok' is a 'Maṅglā-charan', the customary opening statement of Guru Nanak's absolute faith, reverence, and devotion to his 'Spiritual guide and Master' - God Almighty Himself.

Conceptual summary

God was there before the beginning of time and has been there since the beginning of the four great epochs. He most certainly exists in the present and shall be there forever in the future too.

PAUṚĪ 1
ਪਉੜੀ ੧॥

Sochai, soch(i) n hovaī, je sochī lakh vār.
ਸੋਚੈ, ਸੋਚਿ ਨ ਹੋਵਈ, ਜੇ ਸੋਚੀ ਲਖ ਵਾਰ॥

Chupai, chup n hovaī, je lāi rahā liv-tār.
ਚੁਪੈ, ਚੁਪ ਨ ਹੋਵਈ, ਜੇ ਲਾਇ ਰਹਾ ਲਿਵ ਤਾਰ॥

Bhukhiā, bhukh n utrī, je baṅnā purīā bhār.
ਭੁਖਿਆ, ਭੁਖ ਨ ਉਤਰੀ, ਜੇ ਬੰਨਾ ਪੁਰੀਆ ਭਾਰ॥

Sahas siāṇpā, lakh hoh(i), ta ik n chalai nāl(i).
ਸਹਸ ਸਿਆਣਪਾ, ਲਖ ਹੋਹਿ, ਤ ਇਕ ਨ ਚਲੈ ਨਾਲਿ॥

Kiv sachiārā hoīai, kiv kūṛai tuṭai pāl(i).
ਕਿਵ ਸਚਿਆਰਾ ਹੋਈਐ, ਕਿਵ ਕੂੜੈ ਤੁਟੈ ਪਾਲਿ॥

Hukam(i) rajāī chalṇā, Nānak, likhiā nāl(i). 1
ਹੁਕਮਿ ਰਜਾਈ ਚਲਣਾ, ਨਾਨਕ, ਲਿਖਿਆ ਨਾਲਿ॥ ੧॥

Sochai, soch(i) n hovaī, je sochī lakh vār

sochai: (a) (Instrumental case - 'karaṇ kārak'; synonymous with 'sochaṇ-' 'nāl', 'rāhīṅ', 'duārā' or 'sadkā') with, by, through or by virtue of deliberation or pondering, and implicit here is (b) (Instrumental case - 'karaṇ kārak'; synonymous with 'shochai' (skt) - 'suchtā rakhaṇ-' 'nāl', 'rāhīṅ', 'duārā' or 'sadkā') with, by, through or by virtue of maintaining physical or bodily purity. See sochṇā (d).

sochṇā: (v) (a) (synonymous with 'vichārnā') to deliberate, ponder or critically appraise, (b) (synonymous with 'chiṅtan karnā') to reflect, meditate or contemplate, (c) (synonymous with 'phikar karnā') to worry, feel concerned or be anxious, and implicit here is (d) (synonymous with 'shoch karnā') to cleanse, bathe or physically purify oneself, especially at places of pilgrimage. This connotation is preferred as matters relating to the higher functions of the brain and cognitive ability are especially addressed in the fourth verse of this 'Pauṛī'. The essence of this stanza or 'Pauṛī' is easily understood if one keeps in mind the question posed in the fifth verse ‘kiv sachiārā hoīai, kiv kūṛai tuṭai pāl(i)’ after each verse and the state of one’s conscious self (‘*Man*’).

soch(i): (a) (n, f; synonymous with ‘chiṅtan’ and ‘dhiān’) focus, reflection, meditation or contemplation, and implicit here is (b) (n, f; synonymous with (skt) ‘shoch(i)’, ‘such’, ‘such(i)’ and ‘pavitartā’) morality, uprightness, untaintedness, purity or sanctity. See soch (d).

soch: (n, f) (a) (synonymous with ‘sochṇā’ and ‘vichārnā’) thinking, reflection, contemplation, (b) (synonymous with ‘chiṅtā’ and ‘phikar’) anxiety, apprehension or misgiving, (c) (synonymous with ‘saṅkoch' and ‘suṅgharnā’) shrinking, shrivelling or contracting, and (d) (synonymous with ‘shoch’ (skt), ‘saphāī’ and ‘pavitartā’) ablution, cleanliness or purity. The tacit reference here is to the purity of one’s conscious self.

n: (p; pronounced as ‘nāṅ’) no, not or indicative of a negative implication or connotation.

hovaī: (v, s, f, present tense, third person; synonymous with ‘ho jāṅdī hai’; pronounced as ‘hova-ī) literally, happens, occurs, comes about or befalls. See hovṇā (a).

je: (conj; synonymous with ‘je kar’, ‘yadī’ and ‘agar’) if or in case.

sochī: (a) (instrumental case - ‘karaṇ kārak’; synonymous with ‘sochaṇ-’ ‘nāl’, ‘rāhīṅ’, ‘duārā’ or ‘sadkā’; pronounced as ‘sochīṅ’) with, through or by virtue of pondering or reflecting, and (b) (v, s, first person, imperative mood - ‘saṅbhāv bhvikht kāl’; synonymous with ‘such-’, ‘pavitartā-’ or ‘suchtā-’ ‘banaī rakhī’; pronounced as ‘shochīṅ’) if I were to bathe. See soch (d).

lakh: (adj, pl) many 1×10^5.

vār: (n, m pl) (n, f; synonymous with ‘daphā’, ‘ber’ or ‘vārī’) counter or ‘number of times’. See vār (k).

lakh vār: literally, many times 1×10^5. In essence, countless times.

je sochī lakh vār: if I were to bathe and cleanse myself countless times.

Cleansing or bathing at places of pilgrimage does not result in purity of the conscious self, even though the process is repeated ad infinitum. Or:

One cannot realise Him by thinking or deliberating, even though one may do it hundreds of thousands of times. This is not considered to be the appropriate interpretation of this verse because of reasons alluded to above.

The following verses from the SGGS lend support to this thesis in the first verse of this 'Pauṛī':

No matter how often one bathes at hundreds of places of pilgrimages, it does not wash away the filth of 'Haumaiṅ'.[226]

Mere talk or reading books, without practising or implementing the learned dogmas, does not free us from our evil tendencies. Similarly, by maintaining bodily purity alone, without loving devotion to 'Nām(u)' in one's 'Hirdā', we fail to achieve 'Nām-realisation'.[227]

Even if one cleanses one's body day and night, it fails to cleanse the filth in one's conscious self ('*Man*' or 'Hirdā').[228]

If one could cleanse one's evil tendencies by bathing alone then it would be a doddle for a frog who lives in water day and night. In reality, such a person, like the frog, will enter the cycle of transmigration again and again.[229]

'No one achieves freedom from one's evil tendencies without loving devotion to 'Nām(u)', even if one lives by the banks of the Ganges and drinks pure water'. I just contemplate 'Nām(u)', says Kabīr.[230]

If one's conscious self is soiled and filthy with 'Vikārī' tendencies, the entire body (sensorimotor organs) is then wicked and sinful but bodily cleansing is not its solution. Sadly, the whole of humanity is misled by this misconception and only a rare person understands the truth.[231]

One wanders at places of pilgrimage in spite of harbouring the filth of evil tendencies in one's 'Hirdā'. Ritual bathing for external purity is wasteful when your conscious self is impure.[232]

'You bathe at places of pilgrimage but worship stone idols'. Thus, you remain wicked and sinful ('Vikārī') if your conscious self is not imbued with 'Nām(u)', O' Pandit![233]

Chupai, chup na hovaī, je lāi rahā liv-tār

chupai: (instrumental case - 'karaṇ kārak'; synonymous with 'chup rakhaṇ-' 'nāl', 'rāhīṅ', 'duārā' or 'sadkā'; pronounced as 'chupaiṅ') with, through or by virtue of keeping silence. Yogīs of a certain sect observe and maintain a ritual of prolonged silence, especially with their eyes closed, to still their flirtatious ('chaṅchal') mind ('*Man*') with this exercise.

chup: (a) (interj) shut up, silent, hush or listen, (b) (adj; synonymous with 'khāmosh' and 'maunī') silent or quiet, and implicit here is (c) (n, f;

synonymous with 'khāmoshī' and 'maun') silence, muteness, quietness, or speechlessness.

lāi: (indeclinable past participle or perfect participle - 'pūran pūrab kārdantak'; synonymous with 'lā-', 'lagā-' or 'joṛ-' 'ke') having done, engaged or carried out. See lāuṇā (b).

rahā: (a) (v, s, present tense, first person; synonymous with 'rahindā-' or 'rakhdā-' 'hāṅ'; 'rahindī-' or 'rakhdī-' 'hāṅ'; pronounced as 'rahāṅ') I keep or maintain, and implicit here is (b) (imperative mood - 'saṅbhāv bhvikht kāl - kiās and sharat bodhak'; synonymous with 'je rakhāṅ'; pronounced as 'rahāṅ') if I were to keep and maintain. See rahiṇā (b) and rakhṇā (b).

lāi rahā: (imperative mood - 'saṅbhāv bhvikht kāl - kiās and sharat bodhak'; synonymous with 'lāī rakhāṅ') literally, '[if I] were to maintain'.

liv: (n, f; synononymous with 'birtī-', 'surat(i)-' or 'dhiān-' 'dī ikāgartā') complete focus, concentration, immersion, absorption or engrossment in only one thing, and (b) lasting and unwavering alignment of one's focus, attention or 'surat(i)' on only one thing.

livtār: (n, f; synonymous with 'lagātār virtī'; 'iksār- 'or 'akhaṅḍ-' 'liv') prolonged or constant and intense focus on one thing only.

je lāi rahā livtār: (pronounced as 'lāi rahāṅ livtār') [if I] were to maintain constant and undivided attention or focus on remaining silent or [if I] were to observe and maintain a prolonged and unbroken spell of silence. Mere focus on prolonged, undivided and unbroken periods of silence, undertaken to silence the 'chattering' of the flirtatious mind ('chaṅchal *Man*' or conscious self) and restrain its ceaseless engagement with the material world, in the hope of achieving lasting inner bliss and equanimity ('Sahaj'), is a ritual that has found favour with the 'maundhārī' (those who vow to remain silent) sect of Yogīs and is still diligently practised by them.

Gurū Nānak, however, propounds that it is not just the mere focus on observing and maintaining prolonged and unbroken periods of silence that results in lasting inner equanimity or peace ('Sahaj'), the only route to God-realisation but the focus on 'Nām(u)' - the immanent form of God, and living by His Will. The following verses from the SGGS lend support to this thesis:

How can this silent sādhū, adrift from the right path, awaken from this slumber without the help of a true Gurū?[234]

One may keep silent, use hands as a bowl and wander naked in the forest; one may wander at the river banks of places of pilgrimage and fail to rid oneself of duality; one may crave to live in these holy places and choose to have one's head decapitated by a unique saw ('Karvaṭ'); yet, one would fail to rid oneself of the filth of 'Haumaiṅ' and 'Vikārī' tendencies off one's conscious self, however much one tries.[235]

He, who rids his conscious self of duality, is truly reserved and silent; having thus stilled his '*Man*', he reflects on 'Nām(u)'.[236]

The flirtatious '*Man*', of one sitting idly but vowing to remain silent, binds one to the cycle of transmigration.[237]

He close-crops his hair, keeps a knotted tuft (a 'bodī') and remains silent, feeling proud of this distinctive outward persona. However, his mind wanders in all directions without being imbued with love for Divine Wisdom.[238]

Mere focus on observing and maintaining prolonged and unbroken periods of silence does not silence the chattering mind nor lead to lasting inner peace and God-realisation.

Bhukhiā, bhukh n utrī, je baṅnā purīā bhār

bhukhiā: (a) (instrumental case - 'karaṇ kārak'; synonymous with 'bhukhe rahan-' 'nāl', 'kar ke', 'duārā' or 'sadkā'; pronounced as 'bhukhiāṅ') with, due to, through or by virtue of fasting or starving, and implicit here is (b) (past participle - 'bhūt kirdaṅt'; synonymous with 'Trishnā adhīn rihāṅ') living life subservient to 'Trishnā'; controlled and driven by 'Trisnā'. See trisnā.

trisnā: (n, f; pronounced as 'trishnā') insatiable hunger for the empirical world, its comforts and pleasures in the default state of ego-consciousness or 'Haumaiṅ'.

bhukh: (n, f; synonymous with 'bhūkh') (a) (synonymous with 'khāṇ dī ichhā') hunger or appetite for food, and implicit here is (b) (synonymous with 'ichhā', 'tāṅg' and 'ruchī') incessant craving for the material world, its comforts and pleasures, especially when driven by Trisnā.

utrī: (a) (adj; synonymous with 'utrī dishā') northern direction, (b) (v, s, present tense, third person; synonymous with 'utardī-', 'lahiṅdī-', 'ghaṭdī-' or 'mukdī-' 'hai') literally, subsides, recedes, abates or ceases to exist. See utarṇā (d and g).

n utrī: [the state of craving] does not diminish, subside or abate.

baṅnā: (a) (n, m; synonymous with 'āsrā') help, support, protection or refuge, (b) (n, m; synonymous with 'kaṅḍhā', 'vaṭ', 'vāṛ' and 'hadd') border, boundary, verge or ridge dividing fields, and implicit here is (c) (imperative mood - 'saṅbhāv bhvikht kāl'; synonymous with 'je main-' 'baṅn lavāṅ' or 'sāṅbh lavāṅ') literally, [if I were to] gather and pack it all for myself. See baṅnaṇā.

purīā: (a) (n, f, pl. of 'pūṛī'; pronounced as 'pūṛīāṅ') small quantities of any substance folded and wrapped up in paper, (b) (n, f, pl. of 'purī'; synonymous with 'nagars' or 'shahars'; pronounced as 'purīāṅ') literally, cities, and implicit here is (c) (genitive case - 'saṅbaṅdh kārak'; synonymous with 'nagarāṅ-' or 'shaharāṅ-' 'dā'; pronounced as 'purīāṅ') of shahars or nagars. See purī.

bhār: (n, m; synonymous with 'bojh' or 'vazan') literally, weight, load, luggage or cargo. In essence, reference here is to the enormous amount of weight of all the material objects, useful or valuable for one's survival, comfort and pleasure.

baṅnā purīā bhār: if one were to gather and hoard ('baṅnā') all the desired objects from everywhere in the world ('purīā') and keep them for oneself. Despite this, one's 'trisnā' can never be satisfied and the following verses from the SGGS lend support to this thesis:

A well-read and cultured man is a fool if he indulges in his tastes, greed and 'Haumaiṅ'.[239]

One's tongue never gets tired of slanderous speech, ears of hearing slander and eyes of lascivious gaze, each slavishly seeking its unique sense of pleasure. Gentle rebukes fail to rid them of their desires as a slave to these ardent desires can only be satisfied if he aligns perfectly with and lives by 'Nām-consciousness'.[240]

Rare is the one who has stilled one's craving for the material world. One gathers millions and craves for tens of millions but doesn't dissuade one's '*Man*' from this greed but, instead, struggles to get more and more.[241]

Having earned a thousand, one runs after a hundred thousand; however much one gathers, one is never satiated.[242]

The kings and great landowners could not satisfy their cravings for the material world; engrossed in their material assets and intoxicated by them, they see nothing else. Just as fire cannot be satiated with any amount of wood, how can anyone satisfy one's craving without perfect alignment with 'Nām(u)'.[243]

Beauty, too, does not still one's sense of craving: the more one sees the more one craves. No one, except those with the glow of 'Nām(u)' in their 'Hirdā', has achieved satiety for the material world.[244]

One's craving for more and more of the material world does not diminish, even though one may gather and stockpile all such assets of the world.

Sahas siāṇpā, lakh hoh(i), t ik n chalai nāl(i)

sahas: (adj, pl; synonymous with 'ka-ī hazār') many thousands, i.e., many x 10^3; sahas(u): (adj, s; synonymous with 'ik hazār') one thousand, i.e., 1 x 10^3.

siāṇpā: (n, f, pl; synonymous with 'dānāīāṅ', 'chaturāīāṅ' and 'nipuṅntāvāṅ'; pronounced as 'siāṇpāṅ') wisdom or prudence in many fields; a wide range of knowledge and ability to use wisely; learnt skills. See siāṇap(u).

siāṇap(u): (n, f, s; synonymous with 'sujāntā', 'chaturāī' and 'nipuṅntā') wisdom, intelligence, prudence, astuteness, shrewdness, sagacity or skill.

Undue pride and self-reliance on one's worldly ability, wisdom and skills often turns out to be wanting in the spiritual field. One often falls victim to one, a few, or all of the five perverse innate cardinal drives ('Paṅj Vikārs') and fails to attune to 'Nām-consciousness'. Life lived in 'Haumaiṅ' or ego-consciousness is life wasted; Nānak propounds that a person's goal in this life is to shed this evil influence, submit to 'Nām-consciousness' lovingly and willingly, and live life by His Will.

lakh: (adj, pl; synonymous with 'ka-ī lakh' or many hundred thousands) multiples of 1 x 10^5.

hoh(i): (a) (indeclinable past participle or perfect participle - 'pūran pūrab kārdaṅtak'; synonymous with 'ho ke') by or through being or happening, (b) (v, s, present tense, second person; synonymous with 'huṅdā hai'), and (c) (v, pl, present tense, third person; synonymous with 'huṅde han'), and implicit here is (d) (v, pl, imperative mood - 'saṅbhāv bhvikht kāl - kiās bodhak', third person; synonymous with 'hovaṇ' or 'ho jāṇ';

pronounced as 'hoheṅ') were to be, happen, come about or befall. See hoṇā/hovṇā (a and b).

lakh hoh(i): if thousands of these learnt tricks were to become many hundreds of thousands.

sahas siāṇpā lakh hoh(i): literally, if one's worldly knowledge, wisdom and prudence in many fields and skills were to increase by hundreds of folds. In essence, if one's mental and physical prowess were to develop exponentially.

t: (p and adv; synonymous with 'tad', 'tadoṅ', or 'udoṅ'; pronounced as 'tāṅ') then, thus, because of, and therefore.

ik: (adj) denotes 1 of the 1 - 9 numerals.

chalai: (v, s, present tense, third person; synonymous with 'chaldā-' or 'chaldī-', 'turdā-' or 'turdī-' 'hai') see chalṇā (e).

nāl(i): (adv; synonymous with 'sāth' and 'saṅg') literally, with or in the company of.

nal chalṇā: (v) (a) to accompany another; to be faithful to the end; to last or endure till the end; to stand by and support another.

ik na chalai nāl(i): (a) literally, none ('siāṇpās') comes to the aid of the soul awaiting judgement at God's Court, and (b) none ('siāṇpās') comes to the aid of one's '*Man*' in ridding itself of the filth of 'Haumaiṅ', 'Moh' and innate 'Vikārī' tendencies ('Māyā'). The only way to rid oneself of the adverse influence of 'Māyā' is to submit to the Guru's Divine Word and Wisdom, contemplate 'Nām(u)' and live by God's Will, and this is borne out by the following verses from the SGGS:

It is pointless to give counsel to those who neither hear nor sing the Lord's Praise but pretend to have the sky within their grasp with mere words; it is always better to keep one's distance from one whom God Himself has kept devoid of His devotion.[245]

Only if one ponders over the essence of knowledge, does one become public-spirited and beneficent to all.[246]

'God is not realised by a thousand guiles', O' my *Man*! 'Nanak, His devotee, has realised Him by submitting to and living by the Guru's Will'.[247]

Not a single one of the thousand ritualistic acts or guiles helps one in the end.[248]

What good is it to simply read, ponder over or hear the text of the Vedas or Purānas, when this act alone does not result in inner peace ('Sahaj')?

Why does the ignorant fool not contemplate and align with 'Nām(u)' rather than just reflect upon something else again and again?[249]

'No one has realised God through shrewdness', O' my flirtatious '*Man*'! 'Enchanting 'Māyā', which has created this state of misconception and indecision, has led me astray'.[250]

We read, hear and reflect upon the Divine Word but intuitive love and the realisation of 'Nām(u)' does not transpire due to innate 'Vikārī' tendencies. How would iron (one's conscious self) transmute into gold ('nirmal Jīvātmāṅ') if it does not surrender to 'Nām(u)' (philosopher's stone)?[251]

No matter how accomplished and nimble we are mentally and physically, none of this helps us in neutralising the adverse influence of 'Māyā', here, and during judgement at His Court.

Kiv sachiārā hoīai, kiv kūṛai tuṭai pāl(i)

kiv: (adv; synonymous with 'kaise', 'kiveṅ' or 'kis prakār') how, by what means or in what way.

sachiārā: (a) (adj; synonymous with 'sat(i)vādī', 'dharamātmā' and 'sachā') literally, righteous, saintly, virtuous or truthful, (b) (n, m, s) a complex word comprising 'sach(i)' or 'satya' ('sach', 'tatv giān', godly attributes) + 'ārā' ('vān', 'vālā' or 'vaṅt' - bearer of) bearer of the qualities of 'satya' ('satya dhāran vālā')-one who has attuned to and imbibed the attributes of 'Nām(u)' in one's 'Hirdā' and expresses them in one's daily life, and (c) (n, m, s) a complex word comprising 'sach(i)' ('satya dā' - of godly attributes) + 'ālyā' ('ghar' or 'soma' - source or fount of) literally, the fount of godly attributes ('sach dā-' 'ghar-' or 'somā') i.e., God.

hoīai: (a) (v, s, present tense, third person; synonymous with 'ho sakīdā hai') may become or come to be, and (b) (v, s, imperative mood - 'saṅbhāv bhvikht kāl - prashan bodhak', first person; synonymous with 'hoiā jāve'). See hoṇā/ hovṇā.

kiv sachiārā hoīai: (v, s, imperative mood - 'saṅbhāv bhvikht kāl - prashan bodhak', first person) how do we then attune perfectly to 'Nām-consciousness', and spontaneously and inherently express His persona and attributes in this life?

kūṛai: (genitive case - 'saṅbandh kārak'; synonymous with 'kūṛ dī') of kūṛ. See kūṛ.

kūṛ: (a) (n; synonymous with 'asatya', 'mithiā', 'jhūṭh' and 'kūṛā'; antonym of 'satya' and 'sach') literally, false, baseless or that which is not everlasting, (b) one's misconceived notions of 'Haumaiṅ', 'Dvaitbhāv', and insatiable 'Lobh' for transient worldly things and their short-lived comforts and pleasures, and (c) 'Māyā' which misguides one towards the transitoriness of the material world and its pleasures and leads one away from God, the source of everlasting peace and happiness.

tuṭai: (a) (v, s, present tense, third person; synonymous with 'ṭuṭai' and 'ṭuṭ sakdī hai'), (b) (v, s, imperative mood - 'saṅbhāv bhvikht kāl - prashan bodhak', third person; synonymous with 'ṭuṭe' or 'ṭuṭ jāve') see ṭuṭaṇā.

ṭuṭaṇā: (v) (a) (synonymous with 'tūṭaṇā', 'ṭūṭṇā' or 'alagg ho jāṇā') literally, to break, crack, smash or separate, drop, and implicit here is (b) (synonymous with 'alag hoṇā') literally, to separate, disconnect, become detached or fall apart. In essence, the reference here is to sever links with the wrong path of ego-consciousness and 'Haumaiṅ'.

pāl(i): (a) (adv; synonymous with 'pāl ke' and 'pālan karke') having nurtured, reared, nourished or brought up, (b) (n, f; synonymous with 'paṅkat(i)' and 'katār') a line, row or queue, (c) (n, m; synonymous with 'baṅn') blockage, dam, dyke or embankment, and implicit here is (d) (n, m; synonymous with 'pardā', 'pardāh' and 'kaṅdh') screen, curtain, veil, partition or dividing wall.

kiv kūṛai tuṭai pāl(i): (v, s, third person, imperative mood - 'saṅbhāv bhvikht kāl - prashan bodhak'; synonymous with 'ih kaṅdh kiveṅ-' 'ṭuṭe' or 'ṭuṭ jāve') how do we smash (tuṭai) this wall or barrier (pāl(i)) due to 'Māyā' that exists between us and the all-pervasive God who is within us?

How can we demolish this false barrier of ego-consciousness and re-align perfectly with 'Nām(u)'?

Whilst evolution has firmly put humanity at the apex of the 'tree of evolution', it is now our goal to evolve spiritually, attune and align perfectly with 'Nām-consciousness', and demonstrate our ability to live by the Divine Order ('Hukam(u)') and Will ('Razā').[48] However, by design, 'Haumaiṅ' is the biggest stumbling block to the realisation of this goal; this, colluding with 'Moh', evil 'vikārī' tendencies and together in the form of ignorance, misconception, duality and 'Mamtā' ('Māyā') entrap us in the empirical world and prevent us from realising the assigned goal, our true self ('Parmātmāṅ'). Misled and driven by 'Haumaiṅ' 'Moh', 'Mamtā' and

'Trisnā' to satisfy our inflated and perverse drives of 'Kām', 'Krodh', 'Lobh', 'Moh', and 'Ahaṅkār', we forget our true identity and purpose, and we become engrossed and entrapped in the visible material world and fail to see and realise the all-pervasive 'Primal Soul' - the Prime Mover or the Cause of it all. This is what Gurū Nānak describes as the persona and the life of a 'Kuṛiār(u)'; their misdeeds and sins make them suffer in this life, binding them to the endless cycle of 'births and deaths' ('Āvāgavan'). In the final verse, Gurū Nānak offers the real solution to the most fundamental question that he posed earlier. The only way out is to eat the proverbial humble pie, seek His Grace, attune to and align perfectly with 'Nām(u)', and live by His Will.

Hukam(i) rajāī chalṇā, Nānak, likhiā nāl(i)

hukam(i): (a) (locative case - 'adhikaraṇ kārak'; synonymous with 'hukam vich') in 'hukam(u)', and (b) (instrumental case - 'karaṇ kārak'; 'hukam-' 'nāl', 'rāhīṅ', 'duārā', 'sadkā' or 'anusārī') with, through, by virtue of or according to 'hukam(u)'. See hukam(u).

hukam(u): (n, m) (a) (synonymous with 'rāi', 'phaislā' and 'nirṇā') judgement or decision, and (b) (arab; synonymous with 'phurmān', 'āgiā' and 'ādesh') order, decree, command or Will. The reference here is to the Divine Order and Will that not only creates, sustains, and destroys but also governs the existence and the direction of movement of the entire cosmos.

Whilst complete understanding of His 'Hukam(u)' is also beyond a person's capability, the three different sub-types often come up as subjects of discussion:

(a) 'achet hukam' (automatic or spontaneous in nature) e.g., gravity, daily sunrise or sunset, and all the other natural laws,

(b) 'suchet hukam' (dependent upon our conscious and/or active involvement but judgement is still under His spontaneous/automatic natural laws), e.g.,

'His justice is based only on our deeds and all else is vain prattle. This is the accepted wisdom', I, Nānak, expound.[252]

(c) 'achanchet hukam' (dependent upon our Karmābut beyond our comprehension and scope of time) definitely dependent upon our Karmābut whose consequences are still to be settled. It comes into play quite unexpectedly and at a pre-determined time and place, as is beautifully captured in this verse of the SGGS:

'Man is like a crane, perched quietly and chancing a catch on a riverbank, who gets pounced upon quite unawares and caught by a hawk. Suddenly, all this revelry just vanishes as things, doings of God, which were never in one's conscious self just happen'.[253]

rajāī: (genitive case - 'sanbandh kārak'; synonymous with 'razāī' and 'razā vāle dā'; pronounced as 'razāīṅ') of one whose 'razā' it is. In essence, the reference is to God or 'Nām(u)' - His immanent form. See razā.

hukam(i) rajāī: (a) (locative case - 'adhikaraṇ kārak'; synonymous with 'razā vāle de hukam vich') within God's Divine Order, and (b) (instrumental case - 'karaṇ kārak'; synonymous with 'razā vāle de hukam-' 'nāl', 'rāhīṅ', 'duārā', 'sadkā' or 'anusārī') with, through, by, by virtue of and according to God's Divine Order.

chalṇā: (v; intransitive (a to e); pronounced as 'chalṇāṅ') literally, to walk, proceed, move, leave, go, depart or disappear. Whilst the literal explanations come closer to its meaning, implicit here is: to live one's life. See chalṇā.

hukam(i) rajāī chalṇā: to live one's life by His Divine Order and Will.

Nānak: (n, m, s) (u) of 'Nānak(u)' is missing because of its vocative case - 'sanbodhan kārak'.

likhiā: (v, s, present perfect, third person) literally, [that] has been written. However, the reference here is to the writ or the Divine Order ('Hukam(u)') which has been written since the beginning of creation and of every sentient life form. See likhiā.

nāl(i): (adv; synonymous with 'sāth' and 'saṅg') literally, with or in the company of. However, implicit here is: from the outset; from birth.

Hukam(u) likhiā nāl(i): The Divine Order, written or prescribed for everything, right from its inception.

'Follow His Command as issued right from the outset, and carry out His Will', says Nānak.

Conceptual summary

Of the many ways of realising Truth and Enlightenment, Gurū Nānak here highlights four contemporary and popular ways and means of narrowing the gap between us and Him or ego-consciousness and 'Nām- consciousness'.

He reveals the misguided emphasis on the ritualistic or mechanical aspect of so-called religious acts and their singular failure in bringing about any inner cleansing and/or spiritual awakening of the conscious self. In complete contrast, he then clearly outlines a person's real goal, the biggest hurdle on the way, and the real solution to overcome this predicament. In essence, one has to shed one's ego-consciousness ('Haumaiṅ'), attune to or align perfectly with 'Nām(u)' or 'Nām-consciousness', and live life by His Command ('Hukam') and Will ('Razā'). This is precisely what is required for a 'Kūṛiār' to transform into a 'Sachiār' or 'Sachiārā'. To be godlike ('Sachiār') and 'Jīvan Mukat(i)' in this life is the pre-condition that we must fulfil before we can realise our true selves (the 'Primal Soul'), i.e., one's conscious self ('*Man*', 'Hirdā' or 'Jīvātmāṅ') must align perfectly with 'Nām(u)' (the Primal Soul) and realise its full glow within in this life. Thus, one also achieves 'Moksh' from 'Āvāgavan' in the hereafter.

Endless rounds of deliberation and deductive reasoning do not crystallise all the attributes of the eternal Reality in one's conscious-self ('*Man*', 'Hirdā' or 'Jīvātmāṅ'); it merely boosts one's ego and takes one further away from that ineffable eternal Reality. External acts of bodily cleansing at holy places, no matter how numerous, do not cleanse the filth of 'Haumaiṅ' from one's conscious self. Self-imposed and deliberate acts of observing silence, no matter how prolonged, do not silence the pursuit of the material world in the conscious self. Driven by 'Trisnā' in the default state of 'Haumaiṅ', one could not satisfy one's craving for the material world even if one were to gather and hoard material assets from the entire world as one's goals would just continue to shift like the proverbial shifting sands in this state. Worldly knowledge, wisdom and skills, no matter how vast and perfect, if not deployed to lead a life of high morals and character in this lifetime, do not help one a bit in shedding one's 'Haumaiṅ', 'Moh' and innate 'Vikārī' tendencies here in this life or on the day of judgement at the end of it. Nothing else but one's deeds, in perfect harmony with 'Nām(u)', get recognised on the day of judgement in the hereafter.

How does one then learn to tread the true path and carry out His Will? How does one then smash this veil of ignorance, misconception, 'dubidā' and engrossment in and entrapment by 'Māyā' that is 'kūṛ' and its relentless pursuit that makes us 'kūṛiār', and realise the all-pervasive Primal Soul within? The answer is that one succeeds in realising this assigned goal by following the Divine Order, pre-ordained since one's inception, and by carrying out His Will.

PAURĪ 2
ਪਉੜੀ ੨॥

Hukamī hovan(i) ākār, hukam(u) n kahiā jāī.
ਹੁਕਮੀ ਹੋਵਨਿ ਆਕਾਰ, ਹੁਕਮੁ ਨ ਕਹਿਆ ਜਾਈ॥

Hukmī hovan(i) jīa, hukam(i) milai vaḍiāī.
ਹੁਕਮੀ ਹੋਵਨਿ ਜੀਅ, ਹੁਕਮਿ ਮਿਲੈ ਵਡਿਆਈ॥

Hukmī, utam(u), nīch(u), hukam(i) likh(i), dukh sukhpāīah(i).
ਹੁਕਮੀ, ਉਤਮੁ, ਨੀਚੁ, ਹੁਕਮਿ ਲਿਖਿ, ਦੁਖ ਸੁਖ ਪਾਈਅਹਿ॥

Iknā hukmī bakhsīs, ik(i) hukmī sadā bhavāīah(i).
ਇਕਨਾ ਹੁਕਮੀ ਬਖਸੀਸ, ਇਕਿ ਹੁਕਮੀ ਸਦਾ ਭਵਾਈਅਹਿ॥

Hukmai aṅdar(i) sabh(u) ko, bāhar(i) hukam n koi.
ਹੁਕਮੈ ਅੰਦਰਿ ਸਭੁ ਕੋ ਬਾਹਰਿ ਹੁਕਮ ਨ ਕੋਇ॥

Nānak, hukmai je bujhai, t haumai kahai na koi. 2.
ਨਾਨਕ, ਹੁਕਮੈ ਜੇ ਬੁਝੈ, ਤ ਹਉਮੈ ਕਹੈ ਨ ਕੋਇ॥ ੨॥

Hukamī hovan(i) ākār, hukam(u) na kahiā jāī

hukamī: (synonymous with 'hukmī') (instrumental case -'karaṇ kārak'; synonymous with 'hukam-' 'nāl', 'duārā', 'rāh īṅ' or 'anusār'; pronounced as 'hukamīṅ' or 'hukmīṅ') literally, by lawful means or within the constraints of the law; in essence, according to Divine Order or by His Will.

hovan(i): (v, pl, present tense, third person; synonymous with 'huṅde han') appear with or by His Order. See hovṇā (a).

ākār: (n, m, pl; synonymous with 'sarūp', 'sūrat' and 'rachnā') appearance, figure, dimension, and 3D outline or shape, size and form of the diverse entities in the empirical world. In essence, the diverse empirical world.

hukam(u): (n, m) (a) (synonymous with 'rāi', 'phaislā' and 'nirṇā') judgement or decision, and (b) (arab; synonymous with 'phurmān', 'āgiā' and 'ādesh') order, decree or command. The reference here is to the one primary Divine Order, with all other kinds of laws and orders being subservient to it. The following verses of the SGGS provide a flavour of what 'Hukam(u)' in Gurbānī may comprise:

The perfect Gurū has made clear that the Divine Order is an aspect of 'Nām(u)'.[254]

Do not blame others but blame the deeds we commit; what we sow is what we reap, so why blame others?[255]

By His Order, the wind blows forever, myriads of rivers flow; the sun and moon, whilst orbiting in their fixed orbits, blaze and shine; the infinite sky vaults above the Earth; countless beings come into this world and go from it.[136, 256]

Having created the entire cosmos, He has kept it all under His absolute jurisdiction.[257]

Our deeds ('karmā') bind us to 'Āvāgavan'; our innate nature, the outcome of our repeatedly imagined and/or entertained acts ('Saṅskārs'), makes us dance to its tune.[258]

However one's predestined innate nature drives one, so does one perform the deeds.[259]

Our actions form the basis of our rewards. As we sow, so shall we reap.[260]

Afflicted with the filth of 'Haumaiṅ', astray and wandering aimlessly, humankind is born to die (both spiritually and physically) again and again. We dance to the tune of our endowed innate nature, which only God can revise, and we perform deeds accordingly.[261]

'Jīvātmāṅ' (conscious self, '*Man*' or 'Hirdā') and 'Parmātmāṅ' ('Nām(u)' or Primal Soul) abide together. However, despite this, the two are separated by a strong wall of 'Haumaiṅ'.[262]

'Countless devotees sing His Glory, but none can fathom Him. He has created and fashioned this diverse universe in many ways', O' Nānak![263]

Having planted a tree ('Saṅsār'), God made it produce two kinds of fruits: 'Māyā' ('Bikh') and the spiritually immortalising 'Sabad' ('Aṅmrit'). Being the all-pervasive Creator, He carries out and makes others carry out acts, giving fitting judgement and apportioning just rewards according to His Will.[264]

n: (p; pronounced as 'nāṅ') no, not or indicative of a negative implication or connotation.

kahiā: (a) (n, m; present participle - 'kriyā-phal kirdaṅt'; synonymous with 'kathiā', 'ākhiā' and 'boliā') literally, talk, speech or utterance, (b) (v, past tense; synonymous with 'kathiā' or 'boliā') [I, You or He] said, spoke or uttered, and implicit here is (c) (conj v; synonymous with 'kathiā-', 'ākhiā-' and 'boliā-' 'jāṇā') literally, to be able to state, speak, describe, utter or describe. See kahinā/kahiṇā.

jāī: (v, s, present tense, third person; synonymous with 'jāṅdā-' and 'jā sakdā-' 'hai') see jāṇā (d (v)).

hukam(u) na kahiā jāī: the nature of the Divine Order ('hukam(u)') cannot be described (na kahiā jāī).

All inanimate and animate life forms are created by Divine Order. However, its real nature cannot be defined in any way.

Hukmī hovan(i) jīa, hukam(i) milai vaḍiāī

jīa: (n, pl; synonymous with 'jīv') all sentient beings in the evolutionary tree.

hukam(i): (instrumental case - 'karaṇ kārak'; 'hukam-' 'nāl', 'rāhīṅ', 'duārā', 'sadkā' or 'anusārī') with, through, by virtue of or according to 'hukam(u)'. See hukam(u).

milai: (a) (v, s, present tense, second person; synonymous with 'tūṅ mildā haiṅ' or 'tusīṅ milde ho'), (b) (v, s, imperative mood - 'saṅbhāv bhvikht kāl'; synonymous with 'mil jāve'), and implicit here is (c) (v, s, present tense, third person; synonymous with 'mildā-' or 'mildī-' 'hai') see milṇā (a).

vaḍiāī: (n, f; synonymous with 'vaḍāī', 'mān', 'izzat', 'ābrū', 'mahimā', 'ustat(i)', 't-a-rīf', 'upmā', 'shobhā' and 'pratishṭā') praise, tribute, honour, glory or meritorious award.

vaḍiāī milnī: (conj. v) literally, to be recognized, praised and honoured. This may be both here in this world and/or in the hereafter at His Court. High moral character, ethical living, and altruism as innate nature, are all secondary to good attributes, virtues and values being endowed by God at birth. This is based on His judgment of one's Karmāin an earlier life. His judgement of one's Karmāin the present life determines whether one deserves the status of 'Jīvan Mukat(i)' during one's lifetime and 'Moksh' in the hereafter.

All sentient life forms are both created and honoured according to His Divine Order.

Hukmī, utam(u), nīch(u), hukam(i) likh(i), dukh sukh pāīah(i)

utam(u): (adj; synonymous with 'ūtam', 'at(i) chaṅgā', 'sabh toṅ chaṅgā' and 'sresht̤'; pronounced as 'uttam') literally, perfect, ideal, best, supreme or superlative. In essence, reference here is to one with noble attributes, virtues and values.

nīch(u): (adj); synonymous with 'guṇhīn') low in terms of attributes, virtues and values, i.e., one who is mean, miserly, callous or spiteful or one with innate evil tendencies. See nīch(u).

likh(i): (instrumental case - 'karaṇ kārak'; synonymous with 'likhe anusār') literally, according to or according to the writ or His Divine Order. In essence, everything one is endowed with in one's destiny is judged on the basis of one's previous 'Karmā'. See likh(i).

dukh: (n, m, pl; synonymous with 'dūkh'; antonym of 'sukh') a general term denoting the following: (a) physical and mental ill health, (b) discontent due to lack or absence of the material and/or worldly comforts, and (c) inner turmoil because of being engrossed in the phenomenal world ('māiā') and non-aligned to 'Nām(u)'.

sukh: (n, m, pl; synonymous with 'sūkh') a general term denoting the following: (a) physical and mental well-being, (b) material and worldly comforts, and (c) lasting equanimity and inner bliss ('Sahaj' or 'Anaṅd').

pāīah(i): (v, pl, present tense, third person; synonymous with 'pāīde han') acquire or are apportioned. See pāuṇā (a and d).

One is ascribed high or low status, presence or absence of physical and/or mental good health, of happiness, material comforts and contentment, and of inner turmoil or bliss, here in our destiny, according to His Divine Order.

Iknā hukmī bakhsīs, ik(i) hukmī sadā bhavāīah(i)

iknā: (a) (pron, pl; synonymous with 'kaī') some, and implicit here is (b) (accusative case- 'karam kārak'; synonymous with 'kaīāṅ-' or 'kujh ku-' 'nūṅ') to many, several, some or quite a few.

hukmī: see hukmī (d).

bakhsīs: (synonymous with 'bakhsh' and 'bakhshīsh') (n, f; synonymous with 'kripā', 'mehar' or 'meharbānī') grace, mercy, blessing or boon. The reference here is to His gift of perfect alignment with 'Nām(u)', a gift of

'Jīvan Mukat(i)' in this life and liberation ('Moksh') from the cycle of birth and death ('Āvāgavan'). See bakhsīs.

ik(i): (a) (indefinite pron, pl; synonymous with 'ka-ī') many, several or some, and (b) (dative case - 'sanpardān kārak'; synonymous with 'kaīāṅ-' or 'kujh ku-' 'nūṅ') to some, several or many.

sadā: (adv; synonymous with 'sad', 'nitya' and 'hameshā') forever, always or in perpetuity.

bhavāīah(i): (v, pl, present tense, third person; synonymous with 'ghumāīde-' or 'bhavāīde-' 'han'; 'bhramaṇ karde han'; 'āvāgavan de chakkar vich bhaṭkade han') see bhavāuṇā.

bhavāuṇā: (v; synonymous with 'bhuāuṇā', 'ghumāuṇā' and 'bharmāuṇā') (a) to put one in a quandary; to make one double-minded, unsure and indecisive, (b) to make one go round and round fruitlessly, and (c) to make one wander in the cycle of transmigration ('Āvāgavan').

ik(i) sadā bhavāīaih: some remain in the cycle of life and death forever.

Some are blessed with perfect harmony with 'Nām(u)', 'Jīvan Mukat(i)' and 'Moksh', whilst others deviate and wander fruitlessly in the endless cycle of transmigration forever according to His Divine Order.

Hukmai aṅdar(i) sabh(u) ko, bāhar(i) hukam na koi

hukmai: (a) (accusative case - 'karam kārak';
synonymous with 'hukam nūṅ') to hukam itself, and implicit here is (b) (genitive case - 'saṅbaṅdh kārak';
synonymous with 'hukam de') of 'hukam'.

aṅdar(i): (adv; synonymous with 'vich' and 'bhītar') inside, within or in the midst of.

sabh: (adj; synonymous with 'sabhe', 'sarab', 'sabho' and 'tamām') all, entire, everyone or totality. Reference here is to all elements, different forms of energy and forces, and non-sentient and sentient beings.

ko: (pron; abbrev. for and synonymous with 'koī') someone, anyone, or another; many or several.

bāhar(i): (a) (adj and adv; synonymous with 'alag' and 'vakhrā') detached, removed, isolated or beyond, (b) (adv; synonymous with 'binā' and 'bagair') except, sans or without, and implicit here is (c) (adv; opposite of 'aṅdar(i)') out or outside.

n: (p; pronounced as 'nāṅ') no, not or implying a negative connotation.

koi: (pron and adj; synonymous with 'koī') any, some or certain.
bāhar(i) hukam na koe: nothing (na koe) is outside (bāhar(i)) of this Divine Order.

All are subject to His Divine Order, and none is exempt from it.[147-9]

Nānak, hukmai je bujhai, t haumai kahai n koi

Nānak: (n, m, s) the (u) of 'Nānak(u)' is missing because of its vocative case - 'saṅbodhan kārak'.
hukmai: (a) (genitive case - 'saṅbaṅdh kārak'; synonymous with 'hukam de') of 'hukam', and implicit here is (b) (accusative case - 'karam kārak'; synonymous with 'hukam nūṅ') to hukam itself.
je: (conj; synonymous with 'je kar', 'yadī' and 'agar') if or in case. See je.
bujhai: (v, s, present tense, third person; synonymous with 'jāṇ-', 'bujh-' or 'samajh-' 'laiṅdā hai'), and implicit here is (b) (v, s, third person; imperative mood - 'saṅbhāv bhvikht kāl - sharat bodhak; synonymous with 'je koī-' 'jāṇ-', 'bujh-' or 'samajh-' 'lave') see bujhaṇā (b).
bujhaṇā: (v) (a) to put out or extinguish (fire), [for fire or light] to go out or off, [for thirst] to be quenched, and (b) to comprehend, infer, deduce or solve.
t: (p and adv; synonymous with 'tad', 'tadoṅ', or 'udoṅ'; pronounced as 'taṅ') then, thus, because of or, therefore.
haumai: (n, f; pronounced as 'haumaiṅ') deployment of ego-consciousness and all one's faculties purely for the fulfilment of self-interest, with total disregard for everything else in this eco-system, coupled with an erroneous belief in an independent existence, independent not only of other inanimate and sentient life forms but also of God and His Divine Order, is 'Haumaiṅ'. See 'Haumaiṅ'.
kahai: (a) (v, s, third person, imperative mood - 'saṅbhāv bhvikht kāl'; synonymous with 'biān-' or 'vakhyān-' 'kare bhī') were to express, expound, explicate or elaborate, and implicit here is (b) (v, s, present tense, third person; synonymous with 'ākhdā-' or 'kahiṅdā-' 'hai'; 'varṇan-' or 'vakhyān-' 'kardā hai') literally, state, recount or narrate. See kahiṇā.
Haumai kahai n koi: none gives any credence to the concept of 'Haumaiṅ'. Self-interest or selfishness is no longer the predominant thing

in one's mind, and one then truly believes in and lives by the ideal of the universal Fatherhood of God and the universal Brotherhood of Man.

'If human beings were to grasp this aspect of His Divine Order, then none would rejoice in 'Haumaiṅ', O' Nānak!

Conceptual summary

By His Divine Order (a) the diverse empirical world exists, though its true nature remains ineffable, (b) sentient life exists, honour and/or greatness bestowed, high or low rank conferred, and any happiness or suffering allotted in one's destiny, and (c) some are granted perfect alignment with 'Nām(u)' in this life and 'Moksh' in the hereafter, whilst others are condemned to suffer humiliation in the cycle of transmigration forever. Everything in this universe is governed or bound by His Divine Order, and none is beyond its reach and grasp. One is purged of one's 'Haumaiṅ' only if one truly grasps the basis of this Divine Order.

The key message here is that everything is within the scope and constraint of His Divine Order ('Hukam(u)'). If one really apprehended this then one would rid oneself of this erroneous concept of ego-consciousness and egotism, and more importantly this chronic disease of 'Haumaiṅ'.

As alluded to before, the entire inanimate and animate world, its unfolding or evolution over time is entirely within the scope and constraint of His Divine Order. In reality, this is consequent to the presence of the omnipresent, omnipotent and omniscient Primal Soul, and its degree of expression in all aspects of the creation. In addition, the degree of autonomy (free will) imparted to basic elements, the inanimate and animate forms, determines the ability, potential and scope of their interaction with the world outside. Furthermore, it also endows each independent sentient life with a centre of consciousness - a centre of ego (conscious self, '*Man*' or 'Hirdā') which it deploys with all its physical and mental faculties to interact symbiotically or otherwise with the world outside for its own survival and the growth of its kind.

The deployment of this centre of consciousness and all the faculties at one's disposal for the fulfilment of self-interest alone, with total disregard for everything else in this world, is selfish and egoistic. By design, humans inherently operate in this default state of ego-consciousness and erroneously consider themselves to have an independent existence, independent not only of other inanimate and sentient life forms but also of God and the Divine Order. Ego-consciousness, coupled with this malady of ignorance and misconception of the reality is ‘Haumaiṅ’. Gurū Nānak also considers ‘Haumaiṅ’, along with ‘Moh’ and ‘Sanjog(u) and ‘Vijog(u)’, to be the essential means by which diversity is created from unity[50, 53-4] and ‘Haumaiṅ’ to be the driving force behind the process of evolution, which has put humans at the apex of the evolutionary tree.[43]

However, human beings, though essentially animals, are superior to others in the animal kingdom because we possess a superior sense of discrimination and discernment. Not only are we thus aware of our own thinking processes, but we also have the ability to deliberate over our thinking too. Indeed, this ability endows us with a much greater discriminatory sense and wisdom, which enables us to make the right moral and ethical choices during our daily interactions with others.[47-8] Consequently, even though we operate inherently at the default state of ego-consciousness, we have the potential for usefully exploiting this golden opportunity and deploying the ability to link with ‘God-’, ‘Nam-’, unitary- or higher- consciousness to realise the goal,[61-2] the apex position in spiritual evolution (‘Sahaj’ and ‘Anaṅd’), which eventually leads to true self-realisation/God-realisation, and freedom from this cycle of transmigration (‘Moksh’).[63]

‘Nām(u)’ and ‘Haumaiṅ’ are inherently opposed to each other; the two cannot be at the same place at the same time.[14] The key characteristic of ‘Haumaiṅ’ is that it misleads one to act according to one’s ego.[265] In collusion with ‘Moh’, it engenders a perverse sense of attachment and a sense of partiality and ownership of the material world within one (‘Mamtā’).[266-9] Evil notions, imagined and entertained, adversely affect our innate nature, and evil ‘Vikārī’ tendencies in turn drive us to commit sinful deeds which suck us deeper and deeper into and helplessly entrap us in the clutches of ‘Māyā’, and bind us to the cycle of transmigration (‘Āvāgavan’).[265]

How and where it arises from, and how one rids oneself of its influence are the key questions.

Gurbānī describes ‘Haumaiṅ’ as a chronic disease, the cure for which lies in understanding its true nature.[12]

If one, in His Mercy, submits to a true Gurū and lives by His Divine Order and Will, one can surely rid oneself of this malady’.[265, 270]

PAUṚĪ 3
ਪਉੜੀ ੩॥

Gāvai ko tāṇ(u), hovai kisai tāṇ(u).
ਗਾਵੈ ਕੋ ਤਾਣੁ, ਹੋਵੈ ਕਿਸੈ ਤਾਣੁ॥

Gāvai ko, dāt(i) jāṇai nīsāṇ(u).
ਗਾਵੈ ਕੋ, ਦਾਤਿ ਜਾਣੈ ਨੀਸਾਣੁ॥

Gāvai ko, guṇ, vaḍiāīā chār.
ਗਾਵੈ ਕੋ, ਗੁਣ, ਵਡਿਆਈਆ ਚਾਰ॥

Gāvai ko, vidiā vikham(u) vīchār(u).
ਗਾਵੈ ਕੋ, ਵਿਦਿਆ ਵਿਖਮੁ ਵੀਚਾਰੁ॥

Gāvai ko, sāj(i), kare tan(u) kheh.
ਗਾਵੈ ਕੋ, ਸਾਜਿ, ਕਰੇ ਤਨੁ ਖੇਹ॥

Gāvai ko, jīa lai, phir(i) deh.
ਗਾਵੈ ਕੋ, ਜੀਅ ਲੈ, ਫਿਰਿ ਦੇਹ॥

Gāvai ko, jāpai disai dūr(i).
ਗਾਵੈ ਕੋ, ਜਾਪੈ ਦਿਸੈ ਦੂਰਿ॥

Gāvai ko, vekhai hādrā hadūr(i).
ਗਾਵੈ ਕੋ, ਵੇਖੈ ਹਾਦਰਾ ਹਦੂਰਿ॥

Kathnā, kathī, n āvai toṭ(i).
ਕਥਨਾ, ਕਥੀ, ਨ ਆਵੈ ਤੋਟਿ॥

Kath(i) kath(i) kathī, koṭī koṭ(i) koṭ(i).
ਕਥਿ ਕਥਿ ਕਥੀ, ਕੋਟੀ ਕੋਟਿ ਕੋਟਿ॥

Dedā, de, laide, thak(i) pāh(i).
ਦੇਦਾ, ਦੇ, ਲੈਦੇ, ਥਕਿ ਪਾਹਿ॥

Jugā jugantar, khāhī khāh(i).
ਜੁਗਾ ਜੁਗੰਤਰਿ, ਖਾਹੀ ਖਾਹਿ॥

Hukamī hukam(u), chalāe rāh(u).
ਹੁਕਮੀ ਹੁਕਮੁ, ਚਲਾਏ ਰਾਹੁ॥

Nānak, vigsai veparvāh(u). 3.
ਨਾਨਕ, ਵਿਗਸੈ ਵੇਪਰਵਾਹੁ॥ ੩॥

Gāvai ko tāṇ(u), hovai kisai tāṇ(u)

gāvai: (v, s, present tense, third person; synonymous with 'gāuṅdā hai'; pronounced as 'gāvai') see gāvṇā. However, implicit here is that one illustrates, in awe, that aspect of His Glory which one is fortunate to possess and with which one can identify.

ko: (pron; abbrev for and synonymous with 'koī') someone, anyone or another; many or several.

tāṇ(u): (n, m; synonymous with 'bal', 'shakat(i)' and 'samrathā') ability, capability, authority, strength or power.

gāvai ko tāṇ(u): literally, someone (ko) describes (gāvai) Him, in awe, through His limitless power (tāṇ(u))

hovai: (v, s; third person; present tense; synonymous with 'huṅdā or huṅdī hai' and 'ho jāṅdā hai') literally, happens to have or befalls. See hovṇā.

kisai: (a) (pron; synonymous with 'koī') someone or anyone, (b) (genitive case - 'saṅbaṅdh kārak'; synonymous with 'kisai-' 'dā' or 'dī') of someone or whosoever, and implicit here is (c) (accusative case - 'karam kārak'; synonymous with 'kisai nūṅ') to someone or whomsoever.

hovai kisai tāṇ(u): literally, whosoever (kisai) possesses (hovai) some might or power.

Someone who is blessed with might or power, sings His Glory from the aspect of His Might or Power.

Gāvai ko, dāt(i) jāṇai nīsāṇ(u)

dāt(i): (n, f; synonymous with 'dān', 'khairāt' and 'bakhshīsh') blessing, grace, boon or bestowal. The not so obvious hint of the real nature of this 'dāt(i)' is in the next line, i.e., 'bhagat(i)' - devotional attachment to the attributes, values, and virtues - the persona or the Glory of 'Nām(u)'.

jāṇai: (a) (v, s, present tense, third person; synonymous with 'jāṇdā-' or 'samjadā-' 'hai') see jāṇanā (a and b), and implicit here is (b) (imperative mood - 'saṅbhāv bhvikht kāl - kiās, sharat, ichhā or bevasī bodhak', s, third/first person; synonymous with 'je maiṅ/uh-' 'jāṇ la- ī- e' or 'jānaṇ dā yatan karīe') [if he] becomes acquainted with or gets to understand.

nīsāṇ(u): (n, m, s; synonymous with 'nishān' and 'chin(h)'; pronounced as 'nīshāṇ') a distinguishing mark, sign, brand, logo or trademark; seal or mark of His approval.

dāt(i) jāṇai nīsāṇ(u): whosoever has the intuitive ability to recognise something as His Gift, [describes Him as 'forever the Beneficent and Bountiful'].

Someone, who intuitively recognises the signs of His Gifts or Blessings, sings the Glory of the Beneficent and Bountiful Lord and His Gifts as a mark of His Grace.

Gāvai ko, guṇ, vaḍiāīā chār

guṇ: (n, m, pl; (synonymous with 'visheshaṇ', 'siphat', 'khūbī', 'khāsīat', 'lachhaṇ', 'subhāu/tāsīr') literally, characteristics, properties or attributes of something; however, the tacit reference here is to the Glory of 'Nām(u)'.

vaḍiāīā: (n, f, pl; pronounced as 'vaḍiāīāṅ') see vaḍiāī.

vaḍiāī: (n, f, s; synonymous with 'vaḍāī', 'ustat(i)', 'ƀazurgī', 'uchtā' and 'mahimā') praise, tribute, honour, eulogy, state, venerability or glory.

chār: (adj, pl; synonymous with 'sohaṇīāṅ', 'suṅdar' and 'manohar') beautiful, attractive, appealing, charming or captivating. The word 'char' is being used as 'dehlī dīpak' as it goes with both 'guṇ' and 'vaḍiāīā,' e.g., 'guṇ chār' and 'vaḍiāīā chār'.

chār(u): (adj, s) see above.

chār(i): (adj; digit 4 of the number system) literally, four.

Someone sings His Glory because of His Magnificence and exquisite attributes, virtues and values.

Gāvai ko, vidiā vikham(u) vīchār(u)

vidiā: (a) (n, f; synonymous with 'ilam' and 'giān') learning, education or studies; knowledge or skill, and implicit here is (b) (instrumental case - 'karaṇ kārak'; synonymous with 'vidiā-' 'nāl', 'rāhīṅ', 'sadkā' or 'duārā') with, through or by virtue of knowledge or skill.

vikham(u): (adj; synonymous with 'bikham(u)') (a) unequal or incongruous, (b) (synonymous with 'bhyānak' and 'drāuṇā') dreadful, frightening or ghastly (c) (synonymous with 'dukhdāī') painful, distressing, harrowing or agonising, and implicit here is (d) (synonymous with 'aukhā', 'kaṭhin' and 'mushkil') difficult, hard, arduous, complex or intricate.

vīchār(u): (a) (n, f; synonymous with 'vivek', 'tatv dā nirṇā' or 'aslīyat jāṇan dī kriyā') study, reflection, deliberation, cogitation or speculation about the eternal Reality and (b) (n, m, s; synonymous with 'kudrat de lekhe dī-' 'bīchār' and/or 'bibek') consultation, speculation, consideration or deliberation about the nature, extent, function and the direction of His creation.

Someone with great knowledge and wisdom, ponders over His infinite attributes and the mystery that engulfs the Creation.

Gāvai ko, sāj(i), kare tan(u) kheh

sāj(i): (indeclinable past participle or perfect participle - 'pūran pūrab kārdaṅtak'- 'pūran pūrab kārdaṅtak'; synonymous with 'sāj ke' and 'paidā kar ke') see sājṇā (b).

sājṇā: (a) (vocative case - 'saṅbodhan kārak'; synonymous with 'he sājan') O' Friend! and (b) (v; synonymous with 'sirjaṇā', 'rachṇā' and 'baṇāuṇā') to make, construct, build or create.

kare: (v, s, present tense, third person; synonymous with 'kardā-', 'kar deṅdā-', 'kar sakdā-' or 'kar sakdī-' 'hai') literally, does, undertakes or performs an action. See karnā (g and i (v)).

gāvai ko sāj(i) kare: some describe Him through His amazing and limitless ability to create.

tan(u): (n, m; synonymous with 'srīr'; n, f; synonymous with 'deh') literally, the body, but the reference here is to the sensorimotor organs of the body through which '*man*' expresses itself and interacts with the physical world.

kheh: (n, f, s; synonymous with 'dhūl(i)', 'dhūṛ', 'gard', 'mīṭī' and 'suāh') dust, soil, mud or ashes.

kare tan kheh: literally, destroys the body.

Someone sings His Glory watching Him create a body and then reduce it to dust.

Gāvai ko, jīa lai, phir(i) deh

jīa: (n, f, pl. of 'jīu'; synonymous with 'Rūhāṅ', 'Jīvātmāṅs' and 'Jiṅdāṅ' (pers)) souls.

lai: (indeclinable past participle or perfect participle - 'pūran pūrab kārdaṅtak'; synonymous with 'lai ke') literally, have taken or having taken back. See laiṇā (a and c (ii)).

phir(i): (a) (adv, synonymous with 'phir ke') having wandered about, and implicit here is (b) (adv; synonymous with 'pher', 'dobārā' and 'muṛ ke') again, once again or a second time.

deh: (v, s, present tense, first person; synonymous with 'de deṅdā hai') see deṇā. The letter 'h' of 'deh' is purely to make it rhyme with the last word 'kheh' in the previous verse. The word otherwise is 'de', 'deh(i)' or 'dei'. See 'de', 'deh(i)' and 'deṇā'.

NB: Those who do not believe in 'Āvāgavan' view this paṅkat(i) as 'Gāvai ko, jīa deh, phir(i) lai' which overcomes the issue of introducing 'Āvāgavan'.

Someone sings His Glory knowing that He takes back souls from some and then infuses them into other bodies.

Gāvai ko, jāpai disai dūr(i)

jāpai: (v, s, present tense, third person) (a) (synonymous with 'jāṇīdā-' or 'sojhī āuṅdī-' 'hai') gets to know or understand, and implicit here is (b) (synonymous with jāpdā-', 'bhāsdā-' or 'lagdā-' 'hai'; 'pratīt-', 'mālūm-' or 'mahsus-' 'huṅdā hai') appears, looks, feels, seems or perceives. See jāpṇā.

disai: (a) (imperative mood - 'saṅbhāv bhvikht kāl'; synonymous with 'dis pave', 'nazar ā jāve' or 'darshan ho jāṇ'), and implicit here is (b) (v, s, present tense, third person; synonymous with 'disdā-' or 'nazar āuṇdā-' 'hai'; 'disṇā chāhīdā hai'). See disṇā.

disṇā: (v; synonymous with 'dikhāī deṇā' and 'nazar āuṇā') to appear, be visible, be in sight of, or be able to see.

dūr(i): (adv; adv; synonymous with 'vith-', 'phāsle-' or 'dūrī-' 'te' or 'kar ke') far, far away or remote.

jāpai disai dūr(i): some perceive (jāpai) Him to be far, far away (dūr(i)), or transcendent.

Someone sings His Glory for He appears to be distant or they perceive Him to be remote or transcendent.

Gāvai ko, vekhai hādrā hadūr(i)

vekhai: (v, s, present tense, third person; synonymous with 'vekhdā hai'; pronounced as 'vekhaiṅ') literally, looks, watches, or observes. See vekhṇā (a, c, and f).

hadūr(i): (a) (locative case - 'adhikaraṇ kārak'; synonymous with 'lokāṅ de sā(h)maṇe' or 'khulle maidān vich') out in the open, in front of everyone, and implicit here is (b) (arab; locative case - 'adhikaraṇ kārak'; synonymous with 'sanmukh', 'rūbrū' and 'hadūrī-' or 'hazūrī-' 'vich') literally, in His presence.

hādrā hadūr(i): (adj; synonymous with 'hāzar nāzar' or or 'neṛe toṅ neṛe') manifest, immanent, omnipresent or all-pervasive.

vekhai hādrā hadūr(i): others perceive Him to be omnipresent and very close ('hādrā hadūr(i)') or immanent.

Someone sings His Glory for he finds Him all-pervasive and watching over the entire creation.

Kathnā, kathī, n āvai toṭ(i)

kathnā: (a) (v; synonymous with 'kahiṇā-' and 'biān-' 'karnā'; pronounced as 'kathnāṅ') literally, to say, state, speak, utter, narrate or recount. However, the reference here is to allegorise, and implicit here is (b) (n; infinitive mood - 'bhāvārth kārdaṅtak'; synonymous with 'vyākhiā' and 'biān') commentary, elaboration, exegesis, or discourse.

kathī: (a) (v, present perfect; synonymous with 'kathan-' or 'biān-' 'kītī') literally, have commented, explained or elaborated. However, the implication here is: expounded and extolled His Glory and 'Hukam', and implicit here is (b) (locative case - 'adhikaraṇ kārak'; synonymous with 'kathan-' or 'biān-' 'kītī vich') in that which has been elaborated.

kathnā kathī: (locative case - 'adhikaraṇ kārak'; synonymous with 'kathan-' or 'biān-' 'kīte kathnāṅ vich') literally, in words spoken in praise of Him.

n: (p; pronounced as 'nāṅ') no, not or implying a negative connotation. This is used as 'dehlī dīpak' here:

'kathnā n āvai toṭ(i)' and 'kathī n āvai toṭ(i)'.

āvai: (v, s, present tense, third person; synonymous with 'āuṅdā-' or 'āuṅdī-' 'hai') see āuṇā (a and c (vii)).

toṭ(i): (a) (n, f; synonymous with 'saṅsā' and 'saṅdeh') worldly anxiety, fear or apprehension, suspicion or hesitation, and implicit here is (b) (n, m; synonymous with 'thuṛ', 'ghāṭā' and 'kamī') shortfall, deficit, dearth, lack or loss.

n āvai toṭ(i): (lit.) a shortfall (toṭ(i)) never comes (na āvai); dearth or deficit (toṭ(i)) of this occurs.

There will never be any shortfall in what can be said or what has been said. (The reference here is to His infinite attributes, virtues and values ('guṇ') and to the unknowable nature and extent of His 'Hukam(u)').

Kath(i) kath(i) kathī, koṭī koṭ(i) koṭ(i)

kath(i): (indeclinable past participle or perfect participle - 'pūran pūrab kārdaṅtak'; synonymous with 'kath kath ke') see kathnā.

kath(i) kath(i) kathī: literally, narrated and allegorised countless times.

koṭī: (pl, nominative case - 'kartā kārak'; synonymous with 'kroṛāṅ hī jīvāṅ ne'; pronounced as 'koṭīṅ') literally, tens of millions of human beings.

koṭ(i): (adj; synonymous with 'kroṛ') literally, 1×10^7 or ten million.

koṭ(i) koṭ(i): literally, millions and millions of times.

koṭ(u): (a) (n, m, s; synonymous with 'kil(h)a') a fort; koṭ: (n, m, pl; synonymous with 'kil(h)e') literally, forts.

[Even though] many millions have tried millions of times.

Dedā, de, laide, thak(i) pāh(i)

dedā: (a) (v, s, present tense, third person; synonymous with 'deṅdā hai'; pronounced as 'deṅdā') gives, provides or grants; confers or bestows, and implicit here is (b) (adj, m, s; present participle - 'vartmān kārdaṅtak'; synonymous with 'deṅ vālā', especially 'dātāṅ deṇ vālā' and 'dātār') literally, giver, benefactor or provider but the reference here is to God, and (c) (adj, m, s, 'kartarī-vāchak kirdaṅt'; synonymous with 'deṇ vālā jo deī jā rihā hai') one who forever continues to give.

de: (v, s, present tense, third person; synonymous with 'de(i)', 'ਦੇਇ' or 'deṅdā hai') literally, offers, confers, bestows or grants. However, implicit here is: gives, bestows or grants forever. The reference here is to sustenance (rijak) as well as attributes, virtues and values ('guṇ').

rijak: (n, m; arab; synonymous with 'rozī'; pronounced as 'rizak') literally, daily sustenance.

dedā de: the provider, sustainer, and the ever beneficent Lord (dedā) gives, offers, confers or bestows (de).

laide: (a) (v, pl, present tense, third person; synonymous with 'lai laiṅde han') literally, take, accept, acquire or buy; see laiṇā, and (b) (adj, m, pl; present participle -'vartmān kārdaṅtak'; synonymous with 'laiṇ vāle jīv'; pronounced as 'laiṅde') they who take, obtain or receive. The reference is to gifts of a material nature as opposed to those of a spiritual nature or 'perfect alignment with 'Nām(u)'.

thak(i): (a) (indeclinable past participle or perfect participle - 'pūran pūrab kārdaṅtak'; synonymous with 'thak ke', 'lāchār ho ke' and 'hār ke') having got tired, exhausted, and fatigued; having given in or admitted defeat, and (b) (v; nominative form of 'thakṇā') see thakṇā.

thakṇā: (v; synonymous with 'thak jāṇā', 'ṭhahirnā' and 'ruk jāṇā') to get tired, to become weary, exhausted or fatigued, to feel lost and dejected.

pāh(i): (v, pl, present tense, third person; synonymous with 'paiṅde han' and 'jāṅde han'; pronounced as 'pāh(i)ṅ') see paiṇā (d (v)).

laide thak pāh(i): literally, the beneficiaries or recipients (laide) grow tired (thak pāh(i)) as their basic survival needs are no longer required at the end of life.

The Gracious and Beneficent God forever bestows sustenance and gifts of a material nature, but the recipient mortals grow tired as they reach their end of life.

Jugā jugaṅtar, khāhī khāh(i)

jugā: (a) (n, pl; pronounced as 'jugāṅ') literally, many jugs, and (b) (ablative case - 'apādān kārak') synonymous with 'jugāṅ ton'; pronounced as 'jugāṅ') literally, from ages. See jug.

jug: (n, m; synonymous with 'Yug') age, period, epoch, era or times.

jugaṅtar: (synonymous with 'jugāṅ-' 'vich' or 'aṅdar') literally, between and within the ages.

jugā jugantar: (n, m; synonymous with 'jugāṅ jugāṅtrāṅ-' 'toṅ hī') throughout the ages. However, implicit here is: throughout the four 'yugs'.

khāhī: (a) (adj; synonymous with 'khāhish vālā' or 'trishālū') one who desires or yearns, and implicit here is (b) (adj; synonymous with 'khādik' and 'khāṇ vālā') one who partakes of food and relishes and (c) (adj; synonymous with 'khāṇ vāle'; pronounced as 'khāhīṅ') literally, they who partake of and savour and relish food.

khāh(i): (v, pl, present tense, second person; pronounced as khāheṅ') (a) (fig.) suffer the consequences, and implicit here is (b) literally, they partake of and savour the food, and continue to enjoy other material gifts and attributes allotted in their destiny.

khāhī khāh(i): (lit.) the recipients and consumers of these gifts just continue to consume them as they have done throughout the ages. However, it is worth bearing in mind the never-ending nature of His Bounty; equally, whilst most are just rapt in their enjoyment, they neglect the bestower of these gifts, God ('dātār').

They just seek, subsist and enjoy His Bounty as they have done throughout the ages.

Hukamī hukam(u), chalāe rāh(u)

hukamī: (a) (adj; synonymous with 'hākim' and 'hukam karan vālā'; pronounced as 'hukamī' or 'hukmī') king, sovereign, ruler, governor or commander, and (b) (genitive case - 'saṅbaṅdh kārak'; synonymous with 'hākim-' or 'hukamī-' 'dā') of a ruler or sovereign.

hukam(u): (n, m) (a) (synonymous with 'rāi', 'phaislā' and 'nirṇā') judgement or decision, and (b) (arab; synonymous with 'phurmān', 'āgiā' and 'ādesh') order, decree, or command. The reference here is to the Divine Order.

hukamī hukam(u): God's Divine Order that creates, sustains and directs the creation.

chalāe: (v, s, present tense, third person; synonymous with 'chalāuṅdā-' or 'tordā-' 'hai') literally, moves or sets in motion the unfolding or the evolution of the world. However, implicit here is the affairs, the way and direction of the world or the moral, ethical and spiritual path that leads to 'Nām-realisation'. See chalāuṇā (a and d).

rāh(u): (a) (synonymous with 'mārag', 'rastā' and 'paṅth') literally, the way or path, and implicit here is (b) (n, f; synonymous with 'saṅsār dī kār') literally, unfolding or evolution of the world. However, implicit here is the affairs, the way and direction of the world as well as the moral, ethical and spiritual path that leads to 'Nām-realisation'. See rāh(u).

His Divine Order guides, directs and governs the way of the world.

Nānak, vigsai veparvāh(u)

Nānak: (n, m, s) (u) of 'Nānak(u)' is missing because of its vocative case - 'saṅbodhan kārak'.

vigsai: (a) (v, s, present tense, third person; synonymous with 'pasār-' 'vikās-' or 'phailāu-' 'huṅdā hai'; pronounced as 'vigsaiṅ'), and implicit here is (b) (v, s, present tense, third person; synonymous with 'vigsadā-' or 'khiṛdā-' 'hai'; 'khush-' or 'prasaṅn-' 'huṅdā hai'; pronounced as 'vigsaiṅ') see vigsanā (b).

veparvāh(u): (adj, synonymous with 'beparvāh(u)') a compound word comprising 've' or 'be' (without) + 'parvāh(u)' ('loṛ' or 'muhtājgī'; 'phikar'; 'ḍar'; 'dhiān'; need or dependency; misgivings, concern or apprehension; fear; and focus respectively) i.e., the independent, carefree, intrepid, watchful and engaged God. This is so, as everything is bound by and under the veritable and supreme autonomous governance of His Divine Order ('Hukam(u)').

'He rejoices and blissfully observes it all unfold and flourish', O' Nānak!

Conceptual summary

The mighty and brave amongst us praise Him for His awesome and infinite power. Those blessed with a sense of perception of His Grace glorify Him forever giving away His gifts. Scholars with great depth and breadth of knowledge, grapple with the most intricate and wonderful attributes of His persona, ability and strength. Some praise Him for His ability to create ad infinitum and to reduce His creation to dust at will. Some perceive and praise Him to be distant and transcendent, whilst others perceive and praise Him for being omnipresent and immanent.

Millions have ventured on millions of occasions to fathom Him and to expound the totality of His attributes but have failed miserably. The Beneficent Lord provides generously and unconditionally, as He has done throughout the ages, but the beneficiaries grow tired of His gifts. Blissfully, contentedly, and cheerfully, He watches over the entire creation as it flourishes and evolves within the constraints of His Divine Order.

Not realising the infinite nature of His attributes, human beings, based on their own finite understanding, perception and strength, try to gauge fully the extent of His persona, attributes, virtues and values but come nowhere near and remain in awe of Him.

PAUṚĪ 4
ਪਉੜੀ 4॥

Sāchā sāhib(u), sāch(u) nāi, bhākhiā bhāu apār(u).
ਸਾਚਾ ਸਾਹਿਬੁ, ਸਾਚੁ ਨਾਇ, ਭਾਖਿਆ ਭਾਉ ਅਪਾਰੁ॥

Ākhah(i), maṅgah(i), deh(i) deh(i), dāt(i) kare dātār(u).
ਆਖਹਿ, ਮੰਗਹਿ, ਦੇਹਿ ਦੇਹਿ, ਦਾਤਿ ਕਰੇ ਦਾਤਾਰੁ॥

Pher(i), ki agai rakhīai, jit(u) disai darbār(u).
ਫੇਰਿ, ਕਿ ਅਗੈ ਰਖੀਐ, ਜਿਤੁ ਦਿਸੈ ਦਰਬਾਰੁ॥

Muhau, ki bolaṇ (u) bolīai, jit(u) suṇ(i) dhare piār(u).
ਮੁਹੌ, ਕਿ ਬੋਲਣੁ ਬੋਲੀਐ, ਜਿਤੁ ਸੁਣਿ ਧਰੇ ਪਿਆਰੁ॥

Aṅmrit velā, sach(u) nāu, vaḍiāī vīchār(u).
ਅੰਮ੍ਰਿਤ ਵੇਲਾ, ਸਚੁ ਨਾਉ, ਵਡਿਆਈ ਵਿਚਾਰੁ॥

Karmī āvai kapṛā, nadrī mokh(u) duār(u).
ਕਰਮੀ ਆਵੈ ਕਪੜਾ, ਨਦਰੀ ਮੋਖੁ ਦੁਆਰੁ॥

Nānak, evai jāṇīai, sabh(u) āpe sachiār(u). 4.
ਨਾਨਕ, ਏਵੈ ਜਾਣੀਐ, ਸਭੁ ਆਪੇ ਸਚਿਆਰੁ॥ ੪॥

Sāchā sāhib(u), sāch(u) nāi, bhākhiā bhāu apār(u)

sāchā: (adj, m; 'satya' in Sanskrit and 'sat(i)' in Gurmukhī; synonymous with 'sachā') (a) (synonymous with 'sadīvī jyot(i) sarūp') the eternal Lord or the eternal Reality - 'Nām(u)' as well as the transcendent Lord, (b) (synonymous with 'sarab kalā bharpūr(i)', 'par(i)pūran' and 'sarab-vyāpak') omnipotent, omniscient and all-pervasive and omnipresent, (c) (synonymous with 'satya' and 'hoṅd-' or 'hastī-' 'vālā') real and not imaginary, and (d) (synonymous with 'nirmal', 'pavitr' and 'ukāī rahit') immaculate, perfect and flawless. These are some of the popular and well-known qualities of a God of Infinite Attributes.

sāhib(u): (a) (n, m, s; synonymous with 'kartār') creator (God), and implicit here is (b) (n, m, s; synonymous with 'pat(i)', 'swāmī' and 'mālik') master or lord.

sāch(u): (n and adj, m, s; synonymous with 'satya' and 'sat(i)' or sach(u) of skt and gmkh respectively): (a) (synonymous with 'sadīvī') literally, eternal, and (b) (adj; synonymous with 'pūrā', 'mukaṅmal' and 'ukāī rahit') perfect and flawless. See sāch(u).

nāi: (a) (instrumental case - 'karaṇ kārak'; synonymous with 'Nām(u)-' 'duārā' or 'sadkā') through or by the Grace of 'Nām(u)', (b) (indeclinable past participle or perfect participle - 'pūran pūrab kārdaṅtak'; synonymous with 'n(h)āi ke') through or by bathing, and implicit here is (c) (n, m, s; synonymous with 'nāu') 'Nām(u)' the immanent form of God; 'nāv': (pl of 'nāu'), (d) (n, f; synonymous with 'mahimā' or 'vaḍiāī') literally, praise or glory, and (e) (n, m; synonymous with 'niāi' and 'niyam'; pronounced as 'niāi', 'nyāi' or 'phaislā') order, governance and justice for the evolving world. Viewed this way, it is almost consonant with Divine Order ('Hukam(u)') and as such it is an aspect of 'Nām(u)' as explained before. Here follows an explanation for this reason:

The word 'Nāu' (n, m, s) has been used in place of 'Nām(u)', e.g., 'ūche ūpar(i) ūchā nāu' - Higher than high is His Name. See 'Pauṛī' 24 (pp. 288 - 89).

'Nāu' becomes 'Nāv' in its plural form, e.g., 'Jīa jāt(i) raṅgā ke 'nāv'- the names of diverse kind and colours of creatures. See 'Pauṛī' 16 (pp. 195 - 6).

'Nāu' (nominative or accusative case) becomes 'Nāi' when used as as instrumental case - 'karaṇ kārak', e.g.,

One worships God and gets ferried across this 'bhavjal sāgar' through living life by 'Nām(u)'.[271]

'Nāu', in the form of 'nāi' (pronounced as 'n(h)āi'), has also been used as a verb.

'Tīrath(i) nāvā je tis(u) bhāvā viṇ(u) bhāṇe ki nāi karī' - 'What good does bathing achieve if it does not meet Your approval'? See 'Pauṛī' 6 (pp. 119 – 12).

Another word, 'nāī' (n, f, s; synonymous with mahimā', 'ustat(i)' and 'upmā' - literally, tribute, praise, or glory), closer to 'nāu', has also been used in 'Jap(u)', e.g.,

'Vaḍā Sāhib(u) vaḍī 'nāī' kītā jā kā hovai' - 'Great is the Lord, great is His Name; whatever is visible is His doing'. See 'Pauṛī' 21 (pp. 264-5).

According to the rules of grammar, an adjective which qualifies a noun has the same gender as the noun. Just as the word 'Sāhib' is a noun (nominative case - 'kartā kārak'; m, s) and 'sāchā' is its adjective 'Sāch(u)', similarly, the word 'nāi' should also, therefore, be a noun and of male gender as 'Sāch(u)' is its adjective.

Finally, a similar word 'nāī' is also found in Gurbānī, e.g.,

'But pūj(i) pūj(i) Hindū mūe tūrk mūe sir(u) nāī' - Just as idolatry has caused spiritual death amongst Hindus, ritual bowing of heads to the 'Kābā' has wreaked a similar spiritual demise amongst Muslims.[272]

Here, the word 'nāī' means 'niāī' or 'nivāi', i.e., both meaning bowing or having bowed. Similarly, the word 'nāi' should mean 'niāi', i.e., justice ('phaisalā').

bhākhiā: (a) (v; synonymous with 'sevan kītā' and 'khādhā') literally, ate or partook of, (b) (v, present perfect; synonymous with 'kathan kita', 'ākhiā' and 'uchāriā') uttered, stated or narrated, (c) (v; synonymous with 'ākhdiāṅ'; pronounced as 'bhākhiāṅ') whilst stating or declaring, (d) (n, m; synonymous with 'updesh') lesson, counsel, instruction or precept, and implicit here is (e) (n, f; synonymous with 'bolī' and 'bhāshā') vernacular, language, speech or dialect.

bhāu: (n, m; synonymous with 'prem' and 'piār') love or deep affection.

apār(u): (adj, s; synonymous with 'beaṅt', 'agṇit', 'agādh' and 'athāh') a complex word comprising 'a' (without) + 'pār(u)' (the other end or bank; the opposite end, boundary or limit) i.e., infinite or boundless.

bhākhiā bhāu apār(u): literally, His medium of communication is through infinite love. In essence, He does not just create and stand aside, but is immanent, deeply loves and cares for, and guides, directs and communicates with His creation. A devotee, too, must therefore nurture love for Him and His creation when seeking His Grace.

The governance and justice of the eternal Lord is perfect and infinite love is the medium of His communication.

Ākhah(i), maṅgah(i), deh(i) deh(i), dāt(i) kare dātār(u)

ākhah(i): (v, pl, present tense, third person; synonymous with 'uh ākhde han'; pronounced as 'ākhah(i)ṅ') literally, say, utter or express. See ākhṇā.

maṅgah(i): (v, pl, present tense, third person; synonymous with 'uh maṅgde han'; pronounced as 'maṅgaheṅ') literally, they ask or seek. However, implicit here is: they implore, beseech or supplicate. See maṅgah(i) and maṅgṇā.

Crucially, when we know that everything in this empirical world is of a transitory nature, what is it that we should seek or implore from God? The following verses from the SGGS guide us and come to our aid in this matter:

Supplicating for anything but the realisation of 'Nām(u)' brings me immense grief. Bless me, therefore, with the Blissful 'Nām(u)', O' Lord! So that I may rid myself of this craving for the material world in my '*man*'.[273]

Should an opportunity arise, the supremely wonderful thing to implore from one's Gurū is the ability to sing God's Glory.[274]

For those who have tasted true love for 'Nām(u)', cravings for the material world just cease.[275]

Hear ye all, for I tell the truth, 'Whosoever has true love and devotion for Him realises Him'.[276]

'Your humble devotee implores a gift', O' Lord! 'Have Mercy and make me surrender to and align with 'Nām(u)' lovingly and willingly.[277]

'The entire world acts like a beggar, and the Beneficent Lord gives to all. O', '*man*'! Therefore, remember and contemplate 'Nām(u)', so that your aim of realising Him is achieved', says Nānak.[278]

deh(i): (v, s, imperative mood- 'hukmī bhvikht - benatī bodhak', second person; synonymous with 'tusīṅ-' 'deu' or 'davau') literally, [You] give or grant. In essence, O' Lord! Grant us. However, 'deh(i) deh(i)' implies that we ask for more and more worldly things. See deṇā.

dāt(i): (n, f; synonymous with 'dān karnyog vastū') an object or something worth giving as a free gift. God gives us what we rightfully deserve, all the time. However, being in the grip of 'Māyā', we always ask for more and more of the material world, its comforts and pleasures. The following verse of the SGGS exposes this aspect of our true innate nature:

‘One forsakes the Beneficent Lord, the giver, just as one falls in love with His gifts. The poor, naïve person does not understand that one will succumb to death soon’.[279]

In reality, God is innately and immensely generous, and harbours no ulterior motive, seeking not even a grain in return, as beautifully alluded to in this verse of ‘Jap(u)’: ‘Vaḍā dātā til(u) na tamāi’. See ‘Pauṛī’ 25; pp. 294-5.

The not so obvious hint of the real nature of this ‘dāt(i)’ that we should seek is in the next line, i.e., ‘bhagat(i)’ - devotional attachment to His attributes, values, and virtues - the persona or the Glory of ‘Nām(u)’. This is a ‘dāt(i)’ that He gives only to those who submit to the Guru’s Divine Word and Wisdom willingly, lovingly and unreservedly and live by His Will, and earn His Grace.

kare: (v, s, present tense, third person; synonymous with ‘kardā-’, ‘kar deṅdā-’ or ‘kar sakdā-’ ‘hai’) grants or bestows. See karnā (i, (i and ii)).

dātār(u): (adj, s) a complex word comprising ‘dāt’ (a free gift, donation or grant) + ‘ār’ (synonymous with ‘hār’, ‘vān’ or ‘vālā’), i.e., literally, a giver, donor or bestower of gifts. However, implicit here is the ever beneficent and benevolent benefactor, God.

dāt(i) kare dātār(u): literally, the ever beneficent and benevolent God grants His gifts. In essence, He does not fulfil every single wish of a seeker, but always grants and never withholds what one rightfully deserves.

We, the needy, forever seek His blessings and gifts, and the ever benevolent and benefactor God rightfully and fittingly bestows them upon us.

Pher(i), ki agai rakhīai, jit(u) disai darbār(u)

pher(i): (adv, synonymous with ‘phir’, ‘muṛ ke’ and ‘dobārā’) again, once again or a second time.

ki: (interrogative; synonymous with ‘kiā’ and ‘kī’) what?

agai: (synonymous with ‘āgai’) (a) (n, m; synonymous with ‘āgai’ and ‘parlok vich’) literally, in the hereafter or in one’s future in this life, and implicit here is (b) (adv; synonymous with 'sām(h)ṇe' and 'sanmukh') ahead, in front of or before.

rakhīai: (a) (v, s, imperative mood - 'hukmī bhvikht'; synonymous with 'rakhṇā chāhīdā hai') literally, put or offer, (b) (v, s; imperative mood - 'saṅbhāv bhvikht kāl - prashan bodhak', third person; synonymous with 'rakhīe' or 'rakhiā jāve'). See rakhṇā (c). The reference here is to lay or present something in gratitude as an oblation.

jit(u): (adv; synonymous with 'jis-' 'nāl', 'duārā', 'sadka'or 'toṅ') with, by, through, by virtue of.

disai: (a) (v, s, present tense, third person; synonymous with 'disdā-' or 'nazar āuṇdā-' 'hai'; 'disṇā chāhīdā hai', and implicit here is (b) (imperative mood - 'saṅbhāv bhvikht kāl - ichhā or bevasī bodhak', s, third person; synonymous with 'dis pave', 'nazar ā jāve' or 'darshan ho jāṇ') see disṇā.

disṇā: (v; synonymous with 'dikhāī deṇā' and 'nazar āuṇā') to appear, be visible, be in sight of, or be able to see.

darbār(u): (n, m, s; synonymous with 'bādshāh dī sabhā') a royal court or hall, where an audience is given.

jit(u) disai darbār(u): literally, whereby we may see His Court. In essence, whereby we may perceive His Presence. As He pervades everywhere, this body is also His Court. The following verses lend support to this thesis:

This body is a fort and a temple of God.[280]

The imperceptible and unknowable Lord abides within this body. The unwise egocentrics, ignorant of this reality, search for Him in the world outside.[281]

Everything that exists in this empirical world is His creation. Given this scenario, what does one offer in oblation as a token of one's appreciation and gratitude? The following verses of the SGGS allude to this predicament in the mind of a true devotee:

'I am nothing by myself and everything belongs to You, O' Lord. You are not only transcendent and immanent but also act out this world play between these two extremes'.[282]

What can I offer to you in return, for You, 'Nām(u)', have created all that exists, and I merely extol Your Glory?[283]

‘I own nothing and whatever I have is Yours, O’ Lord. What do I lose if I entrust to You what is Yours?’ says Kabīr.[284]

What can we then offer, whereby we may perceive His Presence within our ‘Hirdā’?

Muhau, ki bolaṇ(u) bolīai, jit(u) suṇ(i) dhare piār(u)

muhau: (ablative case - ‘apādān kārak’; synonymous with ‘mūṅh toṅ’; pronounced as ‘mūhauṅ’) from one’s mouth. See mūṅh.

mūṅh: (n, m) literally, mouth or face.

bolaṇ(u): (n, m; infinitive mood - ‘bhāvārth kārdaṅtak’; synonymous with ‘bol’, ‘bachan’ and ‘akhkhar’) utterances, solemn words and words of honour or pledge.

bolīai: (a) (v, s, imperative mood - ‘hukmī bhvikht’; synonymous with ‘bolīe’ and ‘bolaṇe chāhīde han’), (b) (v, s, imperative mood - ‘saṅbhāv bhvikht kāl - prashan bodhak’, third person; synonymous with ‘bolīe’ or ‘ākhīe’) see bolaṇā.

bolaṇā: (v; synonymous with ‘kahiṇā’) to talk, speak or utter.

muhau ki bolaṇ(u) bolīai: literally, what words can we utter in appreciation and gratitude in our prayer?

‘Nām(u)’ is not just a name in a particular language but a single word representing all the known and unknown attributes and glory of the ineffable transcendent Lord. As a mediator, It also guides a seeker and eventually leads him to the realisation of and merger (perfect alignment or harmony) with God. Though the process may start with contemplation and the simple utterance of a key word, phrase, sentence or a stanza in a routine (‘Nām Japnā’), it eventually overwhelms one’s focus and takes the form of deep contemplation (‘*man* vich surat(i) ate sabad dā mel’) and this is ‘Nām Simran’. Done regularly and without fail, it becomes part of one’s innate nature (‘subhā-u’), and one is consciously and sub-consciously aware of it all the time and one begins to live life by ‘Nām-consciousness’. Gradually, having rid oneself of ‘Haumaiṅ’, ‘Moh’ and innate ‘vikārī’ tendencies, one achieves perfect alignment with ‘Nām(u)’ and eventually, with God’s Grace, one perceives the full glow of ‘Nām(u)’ within one’s ‘Hirdā’ and merges with God.

suṇ(i): (a) (v, s, imperative mood - ‘hukmī bhvikht’, second person; synonymous with ‘dhiān nāl suṇo’ and ‘gaur karo’) literally, listen carefully, and implicit here is (b) (indeclinable past participle or perfect participle - 'pūran pūrab kārdaṅtak'; synonymous with 'suṇ ke') literally, by listening to or having heard. See suṇanā.

dhare: (a) (v, s, present tense, third person; synonymous with 'ṭikāuṅdā-', 'rakhdā-' or 'nīṅh rakhdā-' 'hai') literally, lays or places, lays foundation or secures, and implicit here is (b) (imperative mood - 'saṅbhāv bhvikht kāl', s, third person; synonymous with 'ṭikā-' or 'rakh-' 'deve'; 'rakhe' or 'kare') see dhārṇā.

dharnā: (a) (n, f; synonymous with 'dharan(i) or dharaṇ(i)' and 'prithvī') literally, the Earth, and implicit here is (b) (v; synonymous with 'dharṇā', 'rakhṇā' and 'ṭikāuṇā' to lay, place or support in a stable position or settle securely; to establish.

piār(u): (n, m; synonymous with 'prem', 'prīt' and 'sneh') literally, love or affection. However, implicit here is: a loving bondage with us. The following verses of the SGGS elaborate this further:

Just as in times of discord between a husband and wife, the love of children helps them re-unite, similarly one bonds with the Lord through His Praise and Devotion.[285]

'They, whom a Gurū has enlightened, align and merge with God through His Praise and Devotion and do not need any other guidance', O' Nānak.[286]

What can we then utter from our lips, on hearing which He may bestow His Love?

Aṅmrit velā, sach(u) nāu, vaḍiāī vīchār(u)

aṅmrit: (a) (n, m; synonymous with 'dudh') milk, (b) (n, m; synonymous with 'makhaṇ') butter, (c) (adj, m; synonymous with 'miṭhā' and 'madhur') sweet, tasty, delicious, melodious, and (d) (n, m, adj) literally, an ambrosial nectar, of Greek or Roman mythology. In essence, a compound word comprising 'aṅ' (without) + 'mrit' ('mrityū' (skt) meaning 'death') i.e., that which has an immortalising effect - elixir of life. 'Death' does not refer here to the bodily demise of a being but to one's spiritual downfall - succumbing to one's ego-consciousness ('Haumaiṅ'), 'Moh' and 'Vikārī tendencies' ('Māiā'). Thus, 'aṅmrit' has spiritual death defying power, and the ability to make one eternally spiritually awakened.

velā: (n, m; synonymous with 'samāṅ', 'vaqt', 'din' and 'ghaṛī') literally, time, occasion or opportunity.

aṅmrit velā: (n, m) (a) (synonymous with 'taṛkā' or 'jhalāṅg') the early part of the last quarter of night or the ambrosial hour, when the human mind is rested from the daily chores of the mundane, and implicit here is (b) (synonymous with 'uh samāṅ jadoṅ 'Nām(u)' vich juṛe hoīe') literally, when one is aligned with or in harmony with 'Nām(u)' or 'Nām-consciousness' and one does not succumb to one's ego-consciousness ('Haumaiṅ') and suffer spiritual downfall and death. The following verses of the SGGS lend support to this concept:

Get up early and contemplate 'Nām(u)' and remain focused forever. The daily anxieties won't torment you and your woes shall depart.[287]

He who calls himself a disciple of the true Guru, gets up early and contemplates 'Nām(u)'.[288]

I reflect and meditate upon 'Nām(u)' during the early hours of the morning and seek Your refuge both here and in the hereafter.[289]

'One who fails to get up before the crack of dawn is spiritually dead, though physically alive. You may have forsaken Him but He is still mindful and watches you', says Farīd.[290]

Reflection and contemplation early in the night is useful but even more productive before the crack of dawn. They who are actively engaged in contemplation during this period, are blessed with His Grace.[291]

The seed of 'Nām(u)' sown at just the right time ('aṅmrit velā') flourishes so that the devotee reaps an inexhaustible harvest. By virtue of Its very nature, devotees are blessed with glory, both here and in the hereafter.[292]

sach(u): (adj, m; synonymous with 'sāch(u)') (a) (synonymous with 'sadīvī') literally, eternal. See sach(u).

nāu: (n, s; synonymous with 'Nām(u)') 'Nām(u)', as the one word, is also the embodiment of all His attributes, both known and those unknown to us, as He is the immanent form of the transcendent Lord. See nāu. vaḍiāī: (a) (n, f, s; synonymous with 'vaḍāī', 'ustat(i)', 'tarīph', 'bazurgī', 'uchtā', 'mahimā' and 'pratishṭā') praise, tribute, honour, eulogy, state, venerability or glory, and implicit here is (b) (pl.; genitive case - 'saṅbaṅdh kārak'; synonymous with 'vaḍiāīāṅ dī') literally, of vaḍiāīāṅ.

vīchār(u): (a) (n, f; synonymous with 'vivek', 'tatv dā nirṇā' or 'aslīyat jāṇan dī kriyā') study, reflection, deliberation, cogitation or speculation, and (b) (v, s, imperative mood - 'hukmī bhvikht', second person; synonymous with 'vīchār karo') reflect, ponder or contemplate upon 'Nām(u)', His immanent form, and Its attributes, virtues and values. See vīchār(u).

Reflect and contemplate upon the Glory of the eternal 'Nām(u)' in the ambrosial hour. Or:
The time when one is 'spiritually awakened' by reflecting upon the Glory of the eternal 'Nām(u)', is the spiritual death defying time ('Aṅmrit velā').

Karmī āvai kapṛā, nadrī mokh(u) duār(u)

karmī: (a) (instrumental case - 'karaṇ kārak'; synonymous with 'karam and mehar sadkā'; pronounced as 'karmīṅ'), through His Grace or Mercy, and (b) (instrumental case - 'karaṇ kārak'; synonymous with 'shubh karmāṅ karke'; pronounced as 'karmīṅ') due to or by virtue of one's past noble 'karmā'.

āvai: (v, s, present tense, third person; synonymous with 'āuṅdā hai' and 'mildā hai') [one] gets, acquires or receives. See āvṇā/āuṇā (c).

kapṛā: (synonymous with 'kapaṛā') (a) (n, m) clothes, dress or garment, (b) (n, f; synonymous with 'khilat') a garment or robe of honour bestowed by royalty, and implicit here is (c) (n, f; (fig) synonymous with 'siphat sālāh rūp kapaṛā') alignment with 'Nām(u)' and the gift of living life by His Will, and/or (d) (n; synonymous with 'deh' and 'sarīr') literally, the mortal body, the physical frame of a sentient being.

karmī āvai kapṛā: (a) by virtue of one's past noble 'karmā', one receives the gift of this body, and (b) through His Grace one receives 'siphat-salāh dā kapṛā' ('prem paṭolā'). The following verse from the SGGS alludes to this concept:

'I, Nānak, beseech such a robe ('siphat-salāh dā kapṛā') that enables me to sing Your Glory forever', O' Lord.[293]

An alternative view is: We merit this mortal body as a result of our past good deeds and now, through His Grace, learn to live by His Will. The following verse of the SGGS alludes to this concept:

'We attain this human body after futile wandering over an awfully long period. Why don't we then contemplate Him now for this is the right opportunity to align with and realise 'Nām(u)?', says Nānak.[294]

Whichever explanation of this verse one accepts does not alter the key message of this 'Pauṛī'.

nadrī: (instrumental case - 'karaṇ kārak'; synonymous with 'nadar kar ke' and 'kripā drisṭ(i) sadkā'; pronounced as 'nadrīṅ') through His Grace or Mercy. See nadrī.

mokh(u): (n, m; synonymous with 'moksh' and 'mukat(i)') release, liberation, deliverance, emancipation or freedom from (a) 'Haumaiṅ', 'Moh' and the five cardinal 'Vikārī' tendencies ('Māiā' or 'kūṛ') ['Jīvan Mukat(i)'; 'Māiā-' or 'kūṛ-' 'toṅ khlāsī'], and (b) 'Āvāgavan' - the cycle of birth and death ['Param gat(i)'].

duār(u): (a) (n, f, s) an opening to the interior or exterior, (b) (n, f; synonymous with 'giān-' and 'karam-' 'indrīāṅ') the nine sensorimotor organs with openings to the exterior, and (c) (n, m; synonymous with 'dar', 'darvāzā' and 'dahlīz') literally, entrance, gate, door; threshold or doorsill. However, (fig.) it implies the way, the path or the means, the steps leading to the door.

mokh duār(u): (n, m; synonymous with 'muktī dā dar') (a) literally, threshold or door, and implicit here is (b) the gateway to salvation ('Moksh').

nadrī mokh duār(u): one realises the way to salvation from 'Māiā' ('kūṛ toṅ khlāsī') and 'Āvāgavan' through His Grace.

One receives the gift of a robe ('siphat- salāh dā kapṛā') enabling one to live by and sing His Glory' and realise 'Moksh' through His Grace. Or:

One receives the gift of this human body by virtue of one's past noble deeds but realises 'Moksh' through His Grace.

Nānak, evai jāṇīai, sabh(u) āpe sachiār(u).

Nānak: (n, m, s) the (u) of 'Nānak(u)' is missing because of its vocative case - 'saṅbodhan kārak'.

evai: (a) (adv; synonymous with 'aivai', 'brithā' or 'nisphal'; pronounced as 'aivaiṅ') wasted, futile, worthless or fruitless; for nothing or in vain (b) (adv; synonymous with 'ise trān dā') this is how, like this or similar to, and (c) (adv; synonymous with 'is prakār' or 'iu(ṅ) hī') in this way or by this means.

jāṇīai: (v, s, present tense, third person, 'karam vāch' (passive voice); synonymous with 'uh jāṇiā jāṅdā hai' or 'us nūṅ 'samajh-' or 'anubhav kar-' 'laīdā hai') [he] can be realised, can become evident or be revealed. See jāṇanā (b and d).

sabh(u): (a) (adj; synonymous with 'sabhe', 'sarab' and 'sabho') literally, all, entire, everyone or totality, and implicit here is (b) (adj, m; synonymous with 'har jag(h)ā or thāṅ') literally, in everything and at every place.

āpe: (a) (nominative case - 'kartā kārak', s; synonymous with 'āp-' or 'khud-' 'hī') literally, oneself. The reference here is to He Himself, and (b) (adv, m, s; synonymous with 'āp-' or 'khud-' 'hī' or 'āpah(i)') literally, solely by oneself; God Himself or 'Nām(u)' - the immanent form of God.

sachiār(u): (n, m, s) (a) adj; synonymous with 'sat(i)vādī', 'dharamātmā' and 'sachā') literally, righteous, saintly, virtuous or truthful, (b) (synonymous with 'sachiārā' or 'satyā dhāran vālā') a complex word comprising 'sach(u)' (eternal knowledge and wisdom; persona and attributes of the eternal Reality) + 'ār(u)' or 'ārā' ('vālā', 'vān' or 'vaṅt') one who imbibes and is attuned to the eternal knowledge and wisdom in one's 'Hirdā' and expresses these attributes in one's daily life and implicit here is (c) a complex word comprising 'sach(u)' (eternal knowledge and wisdom; persona and attributes the eternal Reality) + 'ār' or 'ālyā' ('ghar' or 'somā') literally, synonymous with 'sach dā ghar' or the fount of everything eternal, i.e., God Almighty.

'This is how we perceive the eternal Reality that pervades everywhere', O' Nānak!

Conceptual summary

The Lord is eternal as is His Glory, and His Governance and Justice are perfect. He interacts with and cares for His creation, with infinite love as the language and medium of His communication. We, as ordinary mortals, forever seek His Blessings and worldly gifts, and the ever beneficent Provider God rightfully and fittingly bestows them upon us.

What can we then gratefully offer in return whereby we may perceive His Presence within our 'Hirdā'? What can we utter from our lips on hearing which He may bestow His Love upon us?

The answer is: Reflect upon and contemplate the Glory of the eternal 'Nām(u)' in the ambrosial hour. Or:

Become spiritually awakened during this spiritual death defying time ('Aṅmrit velā') by reflecting upon the Glory of the eternal 'Nām(u)'.

One receives the gift of a robe ('siphat-salāh dā kapṛā') which enables one to sing His Glory, live by His Will', and realise freedom from 'kūṛ' or 'māiā' in this life ('Jīvan Mukat(i)') and release ('Param Muakat(i)') from the cycle of transmigration ('Āvāgavan') through His Grace. Or:

One receives the gift of this human body by virtue of one's past noble deeds but achieves salvation from 'kūṛ' or 'māiā' in this life ('Jīvan Mukat(i)') and release ('Moksh' or 'Param Mukat(i)') from the cycle of transmigration ('Āvāgavan') through His Grace.

This is how we perceive the eternal Reality that pervades everywhere.

A true relationship with God, with genuine love and reverence as its basis, cannot be gained merely by offering money, carrying out some sham rituals or carrying out good deeds but it is nurtured by surrendering to and living life by His Will.

PAURĪ 5
ਪਉੜੀ ੫॥

Thāpiā n jāi, kītā n hoi.
ਥਾਪਿਆ ਨ ਜਾਇ, ਕੀਤਾ ਨ ਹੋਇ॥

Āpe āp(i), niraṅjan(u) soi.
ਆਪੇ ਆਪਿ, ਨਿਰੰਜਨੁ ਸੋਇ॥

Jin(i) seviā, tin(i) pāiā mān(u).
ਜਿਨਿ ਸੇਵਿਆ, ਤਿਨਿ ਪਾਇਆ ਮਾਨੁ॥

Nānak, gāvīai guṇī nidhān(u).
ਨਾਨਕ, ਗਾਵੀਐ ਗੁਣੀ ਨਿਧਾਨੁ॥

Gāvīai, suṇīai, *man*(i) rakhīai bhāu.
ਗਾਵੀਐ, ਸੁਣੀਐ, ਮਨਿ ਰਖੀਐ ਭਾਉ॥

Dukh(u) parhar(i), sukh(u) ghar(i) lai jāi.
ਦੁਖੁ ਪਰਹਰਿ, ਸੁਖੁ ਘਰਿ ਲੈ ਜਾਇ॥

Gurmukh(i) nād(n), gurmukh(i) ved(ṅ), gurmukh(i) rahiā samāī.
ਗੁਰਮੁਖਿ ਨਾਦੰ, ਗੁਰਮੁਖਿ ਵੇਦੰ, ਗੁਰਮੁਖਿ ਰਹਿਆ ਸਮਾਈ॥

Gur(u) Īsar(u), gur(u)Gorakh(u), Barmā gur(u), Pārbatī māī.
ਗੁਰੁ ਈਸਰੁ, ਗੁਰੁ ਗੋਰਖੁ, ਬਰਮਾ ਗੁਰੁ, ਪਾਰਬਤੀ ਮਾਈ॥

Je hau jāṇā, ākhā nāhī, kahṇā kathan(u) na jāī.
ਜੇ ਹਉ ਜਾਣਾ ਆਖਾ ਨਾਹੀ ਕਹਣਾ ਕਥਨੁ ਨ ਜਾਈ॥

Gurā, ik deh(i) bujhāī.
ਗੁਰਾ, ਇਕ ਦੇਹਿ ਬੁਝਾਈ॥

Sabhnā jīā kā ik(u) dātā, so mai visar(i) na jāī. 5.
ਸਭਨਾ ਜੀਆ ਕਾ ਇਕੁ ਦਾਤਾ, ਸੋ ਮੈ ਵਿਸਰਿ ਨ ਜਾਈ॥ ੫॥

Thāpiā n jāi, kītā n hoi

thāpiā: (a) (present participle - 'kriyā-phal kirdaṅt'; synonymous with 'rachiā-', 'sirjiā-', 'niṅmiā-', 'sthāpiā-' or 'niyukt kītā-' 'hoiā') appointment, installation or coronation, (b) (past participle - 'bhūt kirdaṅt'; synonymous with 'niyukt kītā aphsar') literally, an appointed officer, (c) (v, s, past or present perfect tense; synonymous with 'thāp dittā sī'; 'thāp dittā hai') did appoint or crown; have appointed, installed or crowned, and implicit here is (d) (conj. v; synonymous with 'sthāpṇā', 'asthāpṇā', 'lāuṇā' and 'niyukt karnā') to appoint respectfully, to designate, install or instate. See thāpṇā (a and c) and see jāṇā (d (ix)).

n: (p; pronounced as 'nāṅ') no, not or implying a negative connotation.

jāi: (conj v and suff.) e.g., 'thāpiā n jāi' (synonymous with 'kise kaṅm-' or 'padvī' 'te niyukt nā hoṇā' - cannot be appointed to a position. See jāi (i (viii) and jāṇā (d (ix)).

thāpiā n jāi; (conj v, s, present tense, third person; synonymous with 'thāpiā-', 'sthāpiā-', 'niṅmiā-', 'lāiā-' and 'niyukt kitā-' 'nahīṅ jā sakdā') literally, cannot be appointed, instated or crowned.

kītā: (a) (present participle - 'kriyā-phal kirdaṅt'; synonymous with 'ih saṅsār us dā-' 'rachiā-', 'sirjiā-' or 'baṇāiā-' 'hoiā hai') [It is His] Creation; see karnā, baṇāuṇā and sirjaṇā, (b) (past participle - 'bhūt kirdaṅt'; synonymous with 'mera kītā hoiā'), literally, my handiwork, and (c) (v, s, past or present perfect; synonymous with 'kītā sī'; 'kītā-' or 'sirjiā-' 'hai') actions taken or deeds done; something has been done or created. See karnā (g) and kītā.

baṇāuṇā: (v) to design, plan, make, build, construct, manufacture, prepare, cook or create.

sirjaṇā: (v; synonymous with 'paidā karnā', 'baṇāuṇā' and 'rachṇā') to make, create, form, construct, prepare or produce.

hoi: (v, s, present tense; synonymous with 'huṅdī-' or 'huṅdā-' 'hai'; 'ho jāṅdī-' or 'ho jāṅdā-' 'hai'; 'ho sakdā hai') literally, occurs, comes to be, or becomes; can occur, happen, or become. See hoi and hoṇā/hovṇā.

kītā n hoi: (synonymous with 'uh-' 'rachiā-', 'baṇāiā-', 'sirjiā-' 'nahi jā sakdā') literally, [He] cannot be conceived, nurtured or created.

In the 'Mūl Maṅtra' Gurū Nānak transparently and succinctly states his coherent and emphatic view about this eternal Reality. God cannot, therefore, be nominated, designated or designed and erected. The following verses from the SGGS and the Dasam Graṅth eloquently express the Gurmat's stance on this subject:

'Whosoever shall call me the Lord will fall into the pit of hell fire'.[295]

The hard work and service of those who call a stone idol their God and bow to its feet, is wasted.[296]

'One piece of stone is loved and venerated whilst another is trodden upon. If one is the image of God so must be the other. However, I only serve the eternal Lord', says Nāmdev.[297]

'Each petal you pluck is full of life but the one for whom you pluck these is lifeless, O gardener. A sculptor, stablising a piece of stone with his feet, carves and fashions an idol out of it and, if the stone were truly a God, then it should devour him for this debasing and defiling act'.[298]

He cannot be conceived, nurtured, created or appointed.

Āpe āp(i), niraṅjan(u) soi

āpe: (a) (nominative case - 'kartā kārak', s; synonymous with 'āp-' or 'khud-' 'hī') literally, oneself. The reference here is to He Himself, and (b) (adv, m, s; synonymous with 'āp-' or 'khud-' 'hī') literally, solely by oneself; God Himself or 'Nām(u)' - the immanent form of God.

āp(i): (a) (pron; synonymous with 'āp-' or 'khud-' 'hī') one oneself or He Himself, and (b) (nominative case - 'kartā kārak', s; synonymous with 'āp-' or 'khud-' 'hī') one oneself or He Himself.

niraṅjan(u): (adj) compound word comprising 'nir' (without or lacking) + 'aṅjan' (literally, collyrium or 'surmā' but figuratively 'Māyā') i.e., perfect, immaculate and untainted by 'Māyā' ('aṅjan rahit' or 'māyā toṅ nirlep').

soi: (pron and adj; synonymous with 'oh' or 'ohī') he, she, it or they. See soi (f).

He exists solely by Himself and is, therefore, immaculate and completely untainted by 'Māyā'.

It will be fruitful now to return to the Mūl Maṅtra' to ponder over it again and to examine the evidence presented there in support of God's persona.

Jin(i) seviā, tin(i) pāiā mān(u)

jin(i): (pron, s; synonymous with 'jis ne' or 'jis(i)') who, whoever or whosoever.

seviā: (v, present perfect; synonymous with 'sevā kītī', 'simriā' and 'upāsanā kītī') see simarnā and sevā karnī.

simarnā: (v; synonymous with 'sumarnā' and 'dhiavaṇā') to focus deeply on and contemplate the persona or attributes of the object of one's devotion, such that they are always at the forefront of one's mind, with the aim of expressing the very same attributes in one's own life.

Prabhū dī sevā karnī: literally, to submit willingly and lovingly to and live one's life in complete harmony with 'Nām(u)' and universal consciousness. The following verses from the SGGS illustrate the concept of service to God ('Prabhū sevā'):

One who submits to, contemplates and imbibes His attributes, virtually becomes His surrogate and acts accordingly.[299]

This *man* assumes the attributes and persona of that which it focuses and ponders on, and acts in the same manner.[300]

Those who rid themselves of 'haumaiṅ' by submitting to the Gurū's Word, contemplate 'Nām(u)' and live by His Will, imbibe and assume the attributes of 'Nām(u)'.[301]

A devotee who submits to the Guru's Word, reflects upon it and converges ideologically with it whilst overlooking public opinion and remarks, and lives life by God's Will, is dear to Him.[302]

Service to God ('Prabhū sevā') is surrendering to and living one's life in complete harmony with 'Nām(u)'; one perceives 'Nām(u)', the fount of eternal bliss ('anaṅd') by submitting to and converging ideologically with the perfect Gurū.[303]

'Sing His Praise', O' my tongue. Bow and submit to His saints forever, converging ideologically with whom I align with 'Nām(u)' and live life attuned to 'Nam-consciousness'.[304]

They who surrender to, and live their life by, 'Nām-consciousness, virtually become His surrogate and act accordingly.[305]

tin(i): (pron, m, s; nominative case - 'kartā kārak'; synonymous with 'tis hī ne') just he or she.

pāiā: (v, s, past or present perfect tense; synonymous with 'hāsal-' or 'prāpat-' 'kītā hai') see pāuṇā (a and d (viii)).

mān(u): (a) (n, m; synonymous with 'abhimān' and 'garūr') vanity, pride, conceit or arrogance, and (b) (n, m; synonymous with 'māṇ(u)', ‘sanmān’, ‘ādar’, ‘satkār’, ‘izzat’, ‘ābrū’ and ‘pratishṭā’) respect, self-respect, accolade, esteem, meritorious status or honour.

One who submits willingly and lovingly to and His Will and lives by it, receives great honour.

Nānak, gāvīai guṇī nidhān(u)

Nānak: (n, m, s) the (u) of ‘Nānak(u)’ is missing because of its vocative case - ‘saṅbodhan kārak’.

gāvīai: (v, pl; imperative mood - ‘saṅbhāv bhvikht kāl -prernā bodhak’, first person; synonymous with ‘gāvīe’ or ‘gāuṇā chāhīdā hai’) literally, we should sing. In essence, we should sing His Praise or Glory. See gāuṇā.

gāuṇā: (v; synonymous with ‘gāvṇā and ‘gāvnā’) literally, to sing, chant or recite. In essence, ‘gāuṇā’ here refers to much more than just singing or chanting and implies that we should imbibe these attributes and express them in our daily lives, as is implicit in the verses alluded to above under Service to God (‘Prabhū sevā’).

guṇī: (a) (adj; synonymous with ‘guṇ vālā’ or ‘guṇvaṅt’) virtuous; gifted, talented or accomplished with qualities or attributes (‘guṇās’), (b) (instrumental case - ‘karaṇ kārak’; synonymous with ‘guṇāṅ-’ ‘nāl’, ‘rāhīṅ’, ‘sadkā’, ‘duārā’ or ‘karke’; pronounced as ‘guṇīṅ’) literally, with, through, by virtue of or due to qualities or attributes, and implicit here is (c) (genitive case - ‘saṅbaṅdh kārak’; synonymous with ‘guṇāṅ dā’) of virtues, qualities or attributes. See guṇ (c).

nidhān(u): (n, m, s; synonymous with ‘kosh’, ‘bhaṅḍār’ and ‘khazānā’) treasure, treasure house, treasure trove or repository.

‘Hence, we too should sing His Glory, who is the treasure trove of all virtues and godly attributes’, O’ Nānak!

Gāvīai, suṇīai, *man*(i) rakhīai bhāu

gāvīai: (v, pl; imperative mood - ‘saṅbhāv bhvikht kāl - ichhā and sharat bodhak’, first person; synonymous with ‘je asīṅ gāvīe’) literally, we should sing. In essence, we should sing His Praise or Glory. See gāuṇā.

suṇīai: (a) (v, pl, first person; imperative mood - 'hukmī bhvikht' - 'updesh-' or 'tākīd-' 'bodhak'; synonymous with 'suṇīe' and 'suṇanā chāhīdā hai') literally, listen attentively! In essence, we should listen attentively to His Praise or Glory in Gurbānī and strive to imbibe those attributes in our 'Hirdā', and (b) (imperative mood - 'saṅbhāv bhvikht kāl - ichhā and sharat bodhak'; synonymous with 'je asīṅ suṇīe') literally, if we were to listen attentively. See suṇanā (Pauṛī 8, pp. 137-8).

man(i): (locative case - 'adhikaraṇ kārak'; synonymous with '*man* vich') in one's conscious self, 'Hirdā' or 'Jivātmāṅ'.

rakhīai: (a) (v, s, present tense, third person; synonymous with 'rakhdā hai') and implicit here is (b) (v, pl, first person; imperative mood - 'hukmī bhvikht' - 'updesh-' or 'tākīd-' 'bodhak'; synonymous with 'rakhīe', 'rakhiā jāve' and 'rakhṇā chāhīdā hai') literally, carefully put or place. See rakhṇā (c and d).

bhāu: (n, m; synonymous with 'prem', 'sneh' and 'piār') love or deep affection. God, being omniscient, clearly sees through our sham rituals. Only our genuine intent and love for Him works, as illustrated by the following verses of the SGGS:

'Having shed their 'Haumai, they plead, O' Lord! Help us submit to and live life in perfect harmony with 'Nām(u)'. They who have savoured real love for Him enjoy lasting inner equanimity and bliss, become content and satisfied forever.[306]

'Hear ye all, for I speak the truth! Whosoever submits to and lives life by His Will willingly and lovingly realises 'Nām(u)' within one's 'Hirdā'.[276]

[Let us therefore] listen attentively to and sing His Praise, and nurture deep faith and love for Him in our 'Hirdā'.

Dukh(u) parhar(i), sukh(u) ghar(i) lai jāi

dukh(u): (n, m, s; antonym of 'sukh(u)') literally, a collective noun for all one's ills and suffering (physical and psychological suffering and distress) that one suffers on being sucked into the web of 'Moh', 'Māyā' and 'Vikārs', and through living life in disharmony with 'Nām(u)' and 'Nām-consciousness'.

parhar(i): (indeclinable past participle or perfect participle - 'pūran pūrab kārdaṅtak'; synonymous with 'parhar ke') see parharnā.

parharnā: (v; a complex word comprising 'par' (another) + 'harnā' (to steal, pilfer, abduct or deprive another of something) i.e., (a) (synonymous with 'par-dhan churāuṇā') to steal, embezzle, burgle or rob another's wealth or assets, (b) (synonymous with 'tyāgaṇā') to give up, sacrifice, forgo, renounce, forsake, rebuff or spurn, and implicit here is (c) (synonymous with 'nivārṇā', 'haṭāuṇā' and 'miṭāuṇā') to remove, dispel, prevent and eradicate.

sukh(u): (n, m, s) literally, a collective term for physical and mental wellbeing and all worldly comforts and happiness. However, implicit here is 'Sahaj', a state of lasting inner equanimity and bliss, which dawns when one abides absolutely by His Will and becomes immune to the evil influence of 'Haumaiṅ', 'Moh' and 'Vikārs' ('Māyā').

ghar(i): (locative case - 'adhikaraṇ kārak'; synonymous with 'ghar vich') literally, in one's home ('ghar') or body ('sarīr' or 'deh'); (fig.) in one's 'Hirdā'. See ghar(u) (h).

lai: (a) (indeclinable past participle or perfect participle - 'pūran pūrab kārdaṅtak'; synonymous with 'lai ke') see laiṇā, and (b) (v, s, present tense, third person; synonymous with 'laiṅdā hai') see laiṇā (b).

jāi: (a) (v, s, present tense, third person; synonymous with 'chale jāṅdā/jāṅdī hai') departs or goes. See jāṇā (b), and (b) (conj v and suff.) as part of the conjunct. verb it helps to complete the meaning of the primary verb), e.g., 'ghar(i) lai jāi' - takes it into one's home or Hirdā'. See jāi (i)

sukh(u) ghar(i) lai jāi: literally, takes 'sukh(u)' into one's 'Hirdā'. However, implicit here is a state of lasting inner equanimity and bliss that takes root and establishes itself in one's 'Hirdā'.

[One who does so (see previous line)] eradicates the pain and suffering secondary to being trapped in the web of 'Māyā', and experiences 'Sahaj' in one's conscious self.

Gurmukh(i) nād(ṅ), gurmukh(i) ved(ṅ), gurmukh(i) rahiā samāī

gurmukh(i): (a) (nominative case - 'kartā kārak'; synonymous with 'gurmukh neṅ'), (b) (ablative case -'apādān kārak'; synonymous with 'gurū de mukh toṅ'), and implicit here is (c) (indeclinable past participle or perfect participle - 'pūran pūrab kārdaṅtak'; synonymous 'gurū val mūṅh karke', ‘gurmukh baṇ ke’, ‘gurū dā pallā phaṛ ke’, ‘gurū dā giān lai ke’ or ‘gurū dī sharan āiāṅ’; pronounced as ‘gurmukhīṅ’) by becoming a ‘gurmukh’ or by surrendering to and imbibing the Gurū’s Word, Wisdom and Teachings (‘Updesh’). See gurmukh(u).

gurmukh(u): (n and adj, m, s; synonymous with ‘jo gurū de sanmukh hai’, ‘gurū dā pallā phaṛan vālā’ or ‘gurū de/dī giān/mat(i) nūṅ dhāran vālā’) literally, one who sits facing the Gurū (‘sanmukh’). However, it implies ‘one who bares one’s soul, submits to the Gurū's Will, strives to align perfectly with ‘Nām(u)’, turns one’s back on ‘Haumaiṅ’, ‘Moh’ and ‘Vikārs’ - evil thoughts, speech, and deeds (‘Māyā’), and, instead, becomes God-orientated, and lives by God’s Will.

nād(ṅ): (n, m; synonymous with ‘anhad nād’, ‘ziṅdagī dī rumak’ or ‘anhad sabad’; pronounced as ‘nādaṅg’) the unstruck and everlasting primordial sound - the communicative aspect of ‘Nām(u)’ - the immanent form of the transcendent God, which is perceived but not heard with ears. See nād.

ved(ṅ): (n, m; synonymous with ‘ruhānī-’ or ‘brahm-’ ‘giān’; pronounced as ‘vedaṅg’) literally, Divine Wisdom according to the written Divine Word.

rahiā: (a) (v, present continuous of ‘rahiṇā’; synonymous with ‘rah rahiā hai’) is staying or continues to stay, (b) (v, present tense; synonymous with ‘rahiṅdā hai’) literally, resides or remains, and (c) (past participle - ‘bhūt kirdaṅt’; synonymous with ‘niraṅtar-’ ‘rukṇā’ or ‘ṭhaharnā’) stopping or staying forever.

samāī: (a) (v, s, present perfect, third person; synonymous with ‘pāī-’ or ‘rakh diṭṭī-’ ‘hai’; ‘ral mil gaī hai’) has been added and dissolved, (b) (v, s, present tense, third person; synonymous with ‘samāiā hai’ or ‘līn huṅdī hai’) becomes engrossed or absorbed and implicit here is (c) (adj; synonymous with ‘viāpak-’ or ‘vyāpak-’ ‘hai’) diffusive or pervasive. See samāī and samāuṇā (b).

gurmukh(i) rahiā samāī: literally, by surrendering to and imbibing the Gurū’s Wisdom and Teachings, one perceives that He pervades all, and one thus develops and nurtures an egalitarian outlook.

One perceives the primordial, unstruck and continual sound, imbibes Divine Knowledge and Wisdom, and perceives His immanence and all-pervasiveness through faithfully following and imbibing the Gurū’s Wisdom and Teachings (‘Updesh’).

Gur(u) Īsar(u), gur(u) Gorakh(u), Barmā gur(u), Pārbatī māī

gur(u): (n, m, s; Nominative case - 'kartā kārak'; abbrev. for Gurū) a complex word comprising 'gu' (darkness or ignorance) + 'ru' (light or knowledge) i.e., one who takes others out of darkness or ignorance and brings them into a state of light or wisdom. See gur(u), pp. 38-41.

Īsar(u): (n, m, s) (a) (skt; synonymous with 'Īshvar') God, and implicit here is (b) (synonymous with 'Shiv' and 'Mahadev') one of the trilogy of Hindu gods, i.e., Brahmā, Vishnu and Shiv.

Gorakh(u): (a) (synonymous with 'prithvī dā rakshak') literally, defender or protector of the Earth. In essence, the Creator God, (b) (synonymous with 'iṅdrīān dā rakshak') literally, protector or saviour of the sensorimotor organs. In essence, 'Parmātmāṅ' ('the Primal Soul'), (c) (synonymous with 'prithvī pālak') literally, Lord Vishnu - sustainer of the world. In essence, God, (d) (synonymous with 'gāīāṅ rakhan vālā') literally, a 'Gavālā' or 'Gopāl', and implicit here is (e) (synonymous with 'Yogīāṅ dā āchāryā') literally, Gorakhnāth - son and disciple of Machhendranāth, who started the 'Kanpaṭā paṅth' of 'Yogīs'.

Barmā: (n, m, s; synonymous with and pronounced as 'Brahmā') Lord Brahmā, one of the trilogy of Hindu gods responsible for creation.

Pārbatī: (n, f; synonymous with 'Umā' or 'Pārvatī') consort of Lord Shiva.

māī: (a) (n, f; synonymous with 'daulat' and 'māiā'; n, m; synonymous with 'dhan') financial assets or wealth, (b) (n, m; synonymous with 'kartār' or 'māyā-pat(i)') the Creator or Lord of 'Māyā', (c) (n, f; synonymous with 'mamtā' and 'merā pan') literally, possessiveness or attachment; partiality or prejudice, (d) (n, f; synonymous with 'avidyā') ignorance, lack of knowledge or wisdom and dubiety about the creator, creation and purpose of life that leads one astray, (e) (n, f; synonymous with 'māyā' or 'shakat(i)') the power and means to the creation of this diverse universe, and implicit here is (f) (n, f; synonymous with 'mātā' and 'māṅ') literally, mother.

The Gurū himself is Shiv, Gorakhnāth, Brahmā and mother Pārbatī for a 'Gurmukh'.

Je hau jāṇā, ākhā nāhī, kahṇā kathan(u) n jāī

je: (conj; synonymous with 'je kar', 'yadī' and 'agar') if or in case.

hau: (a) (n, f; pronounced as 'hauṅ'; abbreviation for 'haumaiṅ') see 'Haumaiṅ', and implicit here is (b) (pron, s; pronounced as hauṅ) literally, I, oneself.

jāṇā: (v, s, imperative mood - 'saṅbhāv bhvikht kāl - kiās bodhak', first person; synonymous with 'maiṅ jāṇ-' or 'samajh-' 'lavāṅ') if I could grasp or perceive.

Je hau jāṇā: (imperative mood - 'saṅbhāv bhvikht kāl - kiās bodhak', first person, s; synonymous with 'je maiṅ jāṇ bhi lavāṅ') literally, if I were to grasp, understand and/or realise ([His Divine Order] (Hukam(u)).

ākhā: (a) (v, s, imperative mood - 'saṅbhāv bhvikht kāl - bevasī bodhak', first person; synonymous with 'ākh-' or 'kah(i)-' 'sakāṅ'; 'varṇan-' or 'biān-' 'karāṅ'; pronounced as 'ākhāṅ') [I] may explain or expound, and implicit here is (b) (v, s, present tense, first person; synonymous with 'ākhdā hāṅ' or 'ākh sakdā hāṅ'; pronounced as 'ākhāṅ'). See ākhṇā.

ākhṇā: (v; synonymous with 'bolaṇā', 'kahiṇā', 'kathan karnā' or 'vakhyān karnā') literally, to say, utter, express, define or expound.

nāhī: (p; synonymous with 'nāṅ' or 'nahīṅ'; pronounced as 'nāhīṅ') no, not or implying a negative connotation. See nāhī.

ākhā nāhī: (synonymous with 'maiṅ ākh nahīṅ sakdā') I cannot explain or expound.

kahṇā: (a) (n; infinitive mood - 'bhāvārth kārdaṅtak'; synonymous with 'ākhṇā', 'ākhaṇ(u)', 'kathan' or 'kathnā') comment, utterance, statement, or observation, and (b) (v; synonymous with 'ākhṇā' or 'kathnā'; 'varṇan-' or 'vakhyān-' 'karnā') literally, to say, utter, recount, narrate or state; to set forth, explain, expound or elucidate.

kathan(u): (n; infinitive mood - 'bhāvārth kārdaṅtak', s; synonymous with 'biān' or 'vakhyān') literally, statement, narration, description or explanation; sermon, advice or dictum.

jāī: (v, s, present tense, third person; synonymous with 'jāṅdā' and 'jā sakdā') literally, I cannot explain and communicate. See jāṇā (d (v)) and jāī (j (x)).

kahṇā kathan(u): (both are nouns and infinitive mood - 'bhāvārth kārdaṅtak') literally, narration, description or explanation. In essence, it refers to God's Glory and His Divine Order.

kahṇā kathan(u) n jāī: God's Glory and His Hukam(u) cannot be explained or expounded.

'If I manage somehow to realise some aspects of His Glory and 'Hukam(u)', I would still be unable to articulate it fully'.

Gurā, ik deh(i) bujhāī

gurā: (vocative case - 'saṅbodhan kārak'; synonymous with 'he gurū jī') O' My Lord! See gur(u).

ik: (adj, s, f; synonymous with 'keval ik') literally, one or only one.

deh(i): (v, s, imperative mood - 'hukmī bhvikht - benat(i) bodhak', first person; synonymous with 'mainūṅ-' 'deu' or 'davo') literally, give or grant. In essence, O' Lord! Grant me. See 'deṇā' (c).

bujhāī: (a) (v, s, present tense, third person; synonymous with 'samjhā deṅdā hai') to make one understand, grasp, realise or perceive, (b) (v; past or present perfect tense; synonymous with 'miṭā-', 'dabā-' or 'ṭhaṅḍī kar-' 'dītti') erased, wiped out or removed, put out or extinguished, and implicit here is (c) (v; imperative mood - 'hukmī bhvikht - benat(i) bodhak'; synonymous with 'bujhā deo', 'sojhī/samjhā deo' or 'samjhāo') make me understand, grasp or realise; grant me this sense or knowledge. See bujhāuṇā (a and b).

ik deh(i) bujhāī: (v, s, imperative mood - 'hukmī bhvikht - benat(i) bodhak', second person; synonymous with 'bujhā deo', 'sojhī deo' or 'samjhāo') literally, reveal this one mystery to me or grant me this sense, knowledge or understanding.

'Grant me the insight of this one precious truth', O' True Enlightener! Or:

'Make me grasp and appreciate just one thing', O' Lord!

Sabhnā jīā kā ik(u) dātā, so mai visar(i) n jāī

sabhnā: (a) (genitive case - 'saṅbaṅdh kārak'; synonymous with 'sābhnāṅ dā'; pronounced as 'sabhnāṅ') of all, (b) (nominative case - 'kartā kārak'; synonymous with 'sābhnāṅ neṅ) literally, everyone, (c) (accusative case - 'karam kārak'; synonymous with 'sābhnāṅ nūṅ') to all, and implicit here is (d) (adj; synonymous with 'sabh') see sabh.

sabh: (adj; synonymous with 'sabhe', 'sarab' and 'sabho') all, entire, everyone or totality.

jīā: (a) (n, f, pl; synonymous with 'rūh', 'jiṅd' and 'jivātmāṅ') souls, (b) (genitive case - 'saṅbaṅdh kārak'; synonymous with 'jīāṅ-' or 'jīvāṅ-' 'dā') of 'jīvs', and implicit here is (c) (n, m, pl; synonymous with 'jīvs'; pronounced as 'jīāṅ' or 'jīvāṅ') all sentient beings.

kā: (prep, m; synonymous with 'dā') of.

ik(u): (a) (adj, s, m; synonymous with 'ikallā') alone, by oneself, single-handed or unaided, (b) (adj, s, m; synonymous with 'lāsāni' or 'adutī') unique, unparalleled or without a match, and (c) (n, m) creator or 'Kartār' (God). In essence, it refers to the One Absolute God, absolutely unique and unrivalled, who is 'Niraṅkār' (without any physical form or any perceivable attributes in this form), and transcendent (unfathomable and beyond the grasp of human senses and intellect).

dātā: (n, m) (a) (synonymous with 'dānī' or 'dānshīl') a generous person, (b) (synonymous with 'dātār') a giver, donor or bestower of gifts ('dāts') without any strings attached, and (c) God - who is the primordial 'sarab thok kā dātā'.

so: (n, m, s; nominative case - 'kartā kārak', synonymous with 'us nūṅ') literally, the same or exactly him. However, the reference is to God Himself, the 'dātār'.

mai: (pron; synonymous with 'ah(ṅ)'; pronounced as 'maiṅ') literally, I.

visar(i): (a) (indeclinable past participle or perfect participle - 'pūran pūrab kārdaṅtak'; synonymous with 'visar-', 'bhul-' or 'bhulā-' 'ke') having omitted, lapsed or unintentionally forgotten, and implicit here is (b) (n, f; synonymous with 'bhul' or 'bhullaṇ dā bhāv') lapse, error, blunder, unintended omission, oversight or slip of memory.

jāī: (conj v and suff.) as part of the conjunct verb it helps to complete the meaning of the primary verb, e.g., (i) 'kathan(u) n jāī' - (synonymous with 'kathan- 'or 'biān-' 'nahī kītā jā sakdā') cannot be described or elaborated, and (ii) 'visar(i) n jāī' - (imperative mood - 'saṅbhāv bhvikht kāl - ichhā and bevasī bodhak'; synonymous with 'maiṅ bhul nāṅ jāvāṅ' or 'maiṅ bhulā nāṅ devāṅ') may I never overlook or forsake [Him]. See jāī.

Being inherently weak and gullible and 'Māyā' being so evil and strong, one is easily and constantly being misguided and tempted to seek more and more material comforts and pleasures. In this pursuit, one gets sucked deeper and deeper into and entrapped in the web of 'Māyā', and forsakes

God, the only Beneficent Provider for us all. The following verses from the SGGS beautifully capture this aspect of human nature:

'Only the one who enjoys the full glow of 'Nām(u)' within one's conscious self lives by Your Will, whilst others just live for self-gratification. Engrossed in the pleasures of the material world, bewitched and intoxicated by the gratification of power and wealth, deluded and defrauded, and dancing unashamedly to their tune, they depart from this world without any honour', O Nānak.[307]

What good are (a) the dainty dishes and beautiful clothes, (b) dry fruit, butter, sweets, refined flour and meat, (c) beautiful costumes, cosy beds and self-indulgence, and (d) armies, royal advisors/assistants and palatial dwellings without living life in harmony with 'Nām(u)', for, in its absence, all these are of merely transitory value?[308]

[That] I may never forget Him, the One who is ever the true Beneficent Provider for us all.

Conceptual summary

He is neither created nor appointed to this exalted position, for the immaculate Lord exists solely by Himself. One who lovingly and willingly submits to and lives by His Will is honoured. Hence, we too, should sing His Glory who is the treasure trove of all virtues and godly attributes. Let us all, therefore, sing and listen attentively to His Praise with genuine love for Him in our conscious selves; [one who does so] eradicates the pain and suffering secondary to being trapped in the web of 'Māyā' and experiences 'Sahaj' in one's conscious self.

Submitting to and carrying out the Gurū's Will, one perceives the eternal, primordial and unstruck sound, attains the Divine Word and Knowledge and realises God's immanence and all-pervasiveness, and thus develops and nurtures an egalitarian outlook. For a Gurmukh, the Gurū himself is Shiva, Gorakhnāth, Brahmā and mother Pārbatī. Even if I were to comprehend some of the mysteries of the eternal Reality and His Divine Order, I would still be unable to articulate it fully.

'Grant me insight of this one precious truth', O' True Enlightener! That I may never be ungrateful and forget Him, the One who is ever the true Beneficent Provider for us all. Or:

'Make me grasp and appreciate just one thing', O' Lord!

That I may never be ungrateful and forget Him, the One who is ever the true Beneficent Provider for us all.

In essence, one who surrenders to 'Nām(u)' and lives willingly and lovingly by His Will finds lasting inner equipoise and bliss, and eventually realises Him. However, one gets this direction and wisdom by converging ideologically with a perfect Gurū. Thus, we should pray to God and seek ideological convergence with a perfect Gurū so that we, too, can realise the true path and wisdom and learn to align with 'Nām(u)' and live by His Will.

PAURĪ 6
ਪਉੜੀ ੬॥

Tīrath(i) nāvā, je tis(u) bhāvā, viṇ(u) bhāṇe, ki nāi karī.
ਤੀਰਥਿ ਨਾਵਾ, ਜੇ ਤਿਸੁ ਭਾਵਾ, ਵਿਣੁ ਭਾਣੇ, ਕਿ ਨਾਇ ਕਰੀ॥

Jetī siraṭh(i) upāī vekhā, viṇ(u) Karmā, ki milai laī.
ਜੇਤੀ ਸਿਰਠਿ ਉਪਾਈ ਵੇਖਾ, ਵਿਣੁ ਕਰਮਾ, ਕਿ ਮਿਲੈ ਲਈ॥

Mat(i) vich(i) rattan, javāhar, māṇik, je, ik gur kī sikh suṇī.
ਮਤਿ ਵਿਚਿ ਰਤਨ, ਜਵਾਹਰ, ਮਾਣਿਕ, ਜੇ, ਇਕ ਗੁਰ ਕੀ ਸਿਖ ਸੁਣੀ॥

Gurā, ik deh(i) bujhāī.
ਗੁਰਾ, ਇਕ ਦੇਹਿ ਬੁਝਾਈ॥

Sabhnā jīā kā ik(u) dātā, so mai visar(i) n jāī. 6.
ਸਭਨਾ ਜੀਆ ਕਾ ਇਕੁ ਦਾਤਾ, ਸੋ ਮੈ ਵਿਸਰਿ ਨ ਜਾਈ॥ ੬॥

Tīrath(i) nāvā, je tis(u) bhāvā, viṇ(u) bhāṇe, ki nāi karī

tīrath(i): (locative case - 'adhikaraṇ kārak', pl; synonymous with 'tīrathāṅ' 'utte' or 'uppar') see tīrath.

tīrath: (n, m, pl; synonymous with 'dharam nāl juṛe hoe pavitr sthān') literally, holy places or places of pilgrimage where believers go to cleanse their sins, to repent, atone and seek forgiveness, favour, Grace, or Mercy from their God. Whilst some just go and visit, others believe in bathing, making offerings of material things and money, and performing acts of charity towards this end.

Tīraths were conveniently situated on the banks of rivers, where it was easier to cross over to the other side. Such places acted as magnets for wandering Hindu 'Bhagats' and 'Sādhūs' who sought a peaceful environment to facilitate reflection and meditation and which also offered easy access to fresh water and sources of food. Ordinary people also held the belief that the spiritual essence of their meditation was absorbed into the surrounding earth and water, and hence the reason for bathing at these places which offered people easy access to 'holy' water for self-cleansing.

Gurmat does not give any credence to such ritualistic acts and, instead, lays emphasis on cleansing the filth ('mal(u)') of 'Haumaiṅ', false pride and evil from one's conscious self by aligning with 'Nām(u)' and 'Nām-consciousness'.

However, 'Tīraths' have now become tourist attractions for the vast majority and no longer serve the purpose of their original intent. Rather than contemplation and reflection and an exercise in inner self-cleansing, many leave conceited with false pride in merely visiting such places, as is illustrated by the following verses of the SGGS:

The filth of 'Haumaiṅ' does not dwindle or fade with bathing at places of pilgrimage. The sham ritualistic deeds, in the garb of religious acts, just feed one's 'Haumaiṅ'.[309]

Those who are innately evil and wicked but have created a façade of honour and prestige in the eyes of public, do not lose their 'Haumaiṅ' and innate vikārī tendencies despite bathing at sixty-eight places of pilgrimage.[310]

One who feels proud at having fasted, been on a pilgrimage, and offered charity, wastes any merit thus earned by nurturing conceit and arrogance and is akin to an elephant who blows dust onto himself after a bath.[311]

I bathe at places of pilgrimage but to surrender to the Guru's Divine Word and Wisdom and align with 'Nām(u)' is the ultimate pilgrimage. Focusing on and contemplating the Guru's Word and imbibing its essence in order to align with 'Nām(u)' is, in reality, a pilgrimage to a 'Tīrath'.[312]

nāvā: (v, s, present tense, first person; synonymous with 'nāhuṅdā hāṅ'; pronounced as 'n(h)avāṅ') literally, I bathe, and implicit here is (b) (imperative mood - 'saṅbhāv bhvikht kāl - sharat bodhak', first person, s; synonymous with 'ishnān karāṅ'; pronounced as 'n(h)āvāṅ') if I were to bathe. In essence, the reference is to external and mechanical rituals which do not bring about inner cleanliness or purity. See n(h)āuṇā.

n(h)āuṇā: (v; synonymous with 'shoch-', 'majan-', 'gusal-' or 'ishnān-' 'karnā') to bathe.

tīrath(i) nāvā: if I were to bathe in holy waters at places of pilgrimage.

je: (conj; synonymous with 'je kar', 'yadī' and 'agar') if or in case.

tis(u): (accusative case - 'karam kārak'; synonymous with 'tis-' or 'us-' 'nūṅ') to him/her. However, implicit here is to God.

bhāvā: (a) (v, s, present tense, first person; synonymous with 'bhāuṅdā-' and 'chaṅgā lagdā-' 'hāṅ'), and (b) (v, s, imperative mood - 'saṅbhāv bhvikht kāl – sharat bodhak', first/third person; synonymous with 'bhā jāvāṅ' or 'chaṅgā lagāṅ') see bhāuṇā.

bhāuṇā: (v, synonymous with 'bhāvṇā' or 'bhāuṇā'; 'chaṅgā-' or 'piārā-' 'lagṇā') literally, to find appealing, desirable, suitable, deserving or worthy.

je tis(u) bhāvā: if it should please Him or meet with His approval. Its ultimate reward is that God may bestow His Grace should one be fortunate enough to please Him. This is the state when all one's thoughts, speech and deeds are in perfect harmony with 'Nām(u)'. An account of the thoughts, utterances and deeds ('Karmā') of such a person will no longer be scrutinised at God's Court as beautifully illustrated in this verse from the SGGS:

He, on whom You bestow Your Grace, does not need to account for his deeds.[313]

viṇ(u): (prep; synonymous with 'bin', 'binā', 'bājh' and 'bagair') literally, without, save, or but for.

bhāṇe: (ablative case - 'apādān kārak'; synonymous with 'bhāṇe toṅ' and 'pasaṅd āuṇ-' or 'chaṅgā lagaṇ-' 'toṅ') literally, from bhāṇā. See bhāṇā.

bhāṇā: (a) (n, m; synonymous with 'Hukam') His Divine Order, (b) (v; synonymous with 'bhāiā' and 'pasaṅd āiā') literally, appealed, liked, desired or approved, and implicit here is (c) (n, f; synonymous with 'ichhā', 'marzī' or 'razā') His Prerogative, Wish or Will.

ki: (interogative; synonymous with 'kiā' and 'kī') what?

nāi: (a) (indeclinable past participle or perfect participle - 'pūran pūrab kārdaṅtak'; synonymous with 'shoch kar-', 'gusal kar-', 'ishnān kar-', and 'n(h)āi-' 'ke'; pronounced as 'n(h)āi) by bathing or having bathed. See n(h)āuṇā.

karī: (a) (n, m; synonymous with 'hāthī') an elephant, (b) (n, f; synonymous with 'bhujā' and 'bāṅ(h)') an arm, (c) (v; past or present perfect tense; synonymous with 'kītī' or 'kītī hai') did or have done; see karnā, and (d) (imperative mood - 'saṅbhāv bhvikht kāl - prashan bodhak', first person; synonymous with 'karāṅ' and 'krāṅgā'; pronounced as 'karīṅ') literally, do or shall do or get and/or will get [something] done. See karnā.

viṇ(u) bhāṇe ki nāi karī: what good would bathing in holy waters serve should it not please Him or meet with His approval? This is precisely the sentiment beautifully captured in this verse of the SGGS:

'Forsake that regime which leads one astray from one's beloved. However, blessed is that love which builds one's credit with the Lord', O' Nānak.[314]

I should bathe at holy places only if it so pleases Him; in other words: what use are such ablutions if they do not meet with His approval?

Jetī siraṭh(i) upāī vekhā, viṇ(u) Karmā, ki milai laī

jetī: (a) (adj, f, s; synonymous with 'jittaṇ vālī') victor or triumphant, and implicit here is (b) (adj, f; synonymous with 'jinnī' and 'jitnī') however much or as much as.

siraṭh(i): (n, f, s; synonymous with 'srishṭ(i)', 'dunīā', 'jagat' and 'saṅsār') the world.

upāī: (v, s, present perfect, third person; synonymous with 'rachī-', 'utpan kītī-' or 'paidā kītī-' 'hai') has been created. See upāī and upjanā.

vekhā: (v, s, present tense, first person; pronounced as 'vekhāṅ') (a) (synonymous with 'khoj kardā hān') I seek, explore, enquire, investigate or search, and implicit here is (b) (v, s; synonymous with 'vekhdā-' or 'dekhdā-' 'hāṅ') literally, [I] see, behold or observe. See vekhṇā (a).

Jetī siraṭh(i) upāī vekhā: as much of the created world as I see.

karmā: (a) (n, f; synonymous with 'kripā-' or 'mehar-' 'toṅ') see karam (f), and (b), (n, m, pl; ablative case - 'apādān kārak'; synonymous with 'shubh karmāṅ toṅ'; pronounced as 'karmāṅ') see karam (a and b). It is, however, noteworthy that one is only deserving of His Grace when one actively seeks and genuinely strives to live in perfect harmony with 'Nām(u)'.

viṇ(u) karmā: literally, without noble deeds and His Grace. A claim to noble deeds alone is not enough, it is His Grace that counts, as represented in the following verse of the SGGS:

The naïve and/or ignorant 'Jīvātmāṅ' implores and wails a lot but does not realise Him in its 'Hirdā'. In reality, no matter how much one may struggle, one does not realise this aim without His Grace.[315]

k(i): is used here as 'dehlī dīpak', e.g. k(i) milai and k(i) laī. 'dehlī dīpak' is a word in grammar which is used with two different words in a sentence.

milai: (a) (v, s, imperative mood - 'saṅbhāv bhvikht kāl'; synonymous with 'mil jāve'), and implicit here is (b) (v, s, present tense, third person; synonymous with 'mildā-' or 'mildī-' 'hai') see milṇā (a).

laī: (a) (n, m, s; synonymous with 'pakh') facet, aspect or partisanship, (b) (prep; synonymous with 'kise vāste') for, for the sake of or in order to, (c) (synonymous with 'laiṇ toṅ' or 'laiṇe se') from getting or obtaining, (d) (v, past tense; synonymous with 'prāpat kītī') got, achieved or obtained, (e) (v, s, third person; imperative mood - 'saṅbhāv bhvikht kāl - kiās or ichhā bodhak'; synonymous with 'lavāṅ' or 'prāpat karāṅ') shall I get, and implicit here is (f) (v, s, present tense, first/third person; synonymous with 'lai sakdā hai') literally, can receive or obtain. See laiṇā (a and b).

ki milai laī: literally, what do I get or achieve? In essence, it means one does not get or achieve anything.

ki laī: literally, what do I get or achieve?

I get or can get nothing without His Grace in this vast creation that I behold. Or:

I get or can get nothing without honest hard work and noble deeds in this vast creation that I behold. Or:

No one, in this vast creation that I behold, can get any spiritual awakening without aligning with 'Nām(u)' and living by 'Nām-consciousness.'

Mat(i) vich(i) rattan, javāhar, māṇik, je, ik gur kī sikh suṇī

mat(i): (n, f; synonymous with 'akal', 'giān', 'samajh' and 'siāṇap') literally, knowledge, intellect or wisdom. It forms the basis and provides 'budh(i)' the ability to reason or discern. It is one of the functions or aspects of '*Man*' in Gurmat. See mat(i).

vich(i): (prep; synonymous with 'bīch', 'bhītar', 'aṅdar' and 'vichkār') within, inside or in the midst.

ratan: (a) (n, m, pl; synonymous with 'kīmatī paththar') precious stones, (b) (synonymous with 'adbhut vastūāṅ') uniquely wonderous things, and implicit here is (c) (n, m, pl; synonymous with 'amolak guṇ') priceless godly attributes, virtues and values.

javāhar: (n, m, pl; arab) pearls or precious stones.

māṇik: (synonymous with 'māṇik') (a) (n, m, s) 'Nām(u)' - the persona and attributes of the transcendent God, (b) (n, m; synonymous with 'lāl raṅg de ratan') literally, priceless rubies, and implicit here is (c) (n, m; synonymous with 'shubh-' or 'ruhānī-' 'guṇ') divine values, virtues and attributes.

ratan javāhar māṇik: (n, m, pl) (a) precious stones, jewels, pearls or rubies, and implicit here is (b) divine attributes, virtues and values. Human beings have mined the Earth for all sorts of minerals, especially diamonds and gold but hardly ever looked deeper into the conscious self where also exists the incomparable and priceless divine attributes, as supported by the following verses from the SGGS:

'Reflect deeply on your *man*', O' friends; only by doing so, can you rid yourself of evil tendencies, and contemplate the Gurū's Divine Words and realise 'Nām(u)' within your conscious self.[316]

'What is in the macrocosm is also in the microcosm. One who is introspective and searches, finds it in one's conscious self. The perfect Gurū reveals the Primal Soul which pervades all, in one's conscious self, pleads Pīpā.[317]

ik: (adj, f, s) one, first of the 1-9 numerals.

gur: (n, m, s; abbrev. for Gurū; synonymous with 'āchārīā') a complex word comprising 'gu' (darkness or ignorance) + 'rū' (light or knowledge) i.e., one who takes others out of darkness or ignorance and brings them into a state of light or wisdom. See gur(u). (u) of 'gur(u)' is missing because of the preposition 'kī' that links it with the noun 'sikh'.

kī: (prep, f; synonymous with 'dī') of or belonging to.

sikh: (a) (n, f; synonymous with 'choṭī' and 'bodī') a tuft of hair left unshorn on top of the head, (b) (n, m, pl; synonymous with 'chele' and 'anuyāī') followers, disciples, novices, pupils or adherents, (c) (n, m, pl) believers in the ten Sikh Gurūs and the Sikh Holy Scriptures Sri Gurū Granth Sāhib Jī, (d) (accusative case - 'karam kārak; synonymous with 'sikhāṅ nūṅ') one's followers or disciples, and implicit here is (e) (n, f, s; synonymous with 'sikhiā' and 'updesh') teaching, instruction or precept.

ik sikh: one instruction, teaching or precept.

suṇī: (a) (v, s, present perfect tense, third person; synonymous with 'suṇī hai') has heard or listened, and implicit here is (b) (imperative mood - 'saṅbhāv bhvikht kāl - sharat bodhak', third person, s; synonymous with 'suṇ la-ī-e' or 'suṇī jāve') [if we were] to listen. See suṇanā.

suṇanā: (v) literally, to hear or listen with one's ears; to pay heed or attention to. However, implicit here is to listen attentively to, understand, reflect upon, and then imbibe or internalise the Divine Message ('gur sikhiā' or 'updesh') or His Glory contained in 'Gurbānī'. It is noteworthy that 'Nām(u)', the immanent form of the transcendent God, in the form of 'Anhad Sabad' or 'Nād', can only be experienced spiritually with the help of a perfect Gurū as emphasised in the following verse from the SGGS:

The priceless jewels that we have within our conscious selves are revealed to us by the Gurū.[318]

The Gurū has revealed the Lord's 'Nām(u)', akin to priceless jewels, hidden in one's 'Hirdā' but the unfortunate egocentric looks instead for lakhs of rupees hidden behind the perishable material assets [that stay here and are not valued in the hereafter] and does not find it there.[319]

The Gurū is akin to an ocean replete with priceless jewels ('noble attributes'), and we, his pupils, are white swans on its banks. Submitting to, focusing upon and contemplating the Gurū's Divine Words, we imbibe these priceless jewels, and our conscious self becomes imbued with love for 'Nām(u)'.[320]

Priceless divine attributes manifest in one's conscious self if one conscientiously listens to, understands, and faithfully accepts and imbibes just one of the Gurū's many teachings.

Gurā, ik deh(i) bujhāī. See 'Pauṛī' 5.
Sabhnā jīā kā ik(u) dātā, so mai visar(i) n jāī. See 'Pauṛī' 5.

Conceptual summary

External and ritualistic bathing at holy places of pilgrimage will only be worthwhile if such acts are pleasing and acceptable to Him, otherwise these would surely be worthless. We get nothing without honest hard work, the performance of noble deeds and God's Grace, and no one, in this vast creation that we behold, achieves any spiritual awakening without aligning with 'Nām(u)' and living by 'Nām-consciousness'. Priceless divine attributes will manifest in one's conscious self if one conscientiously listens to, understands, faithfully accepts, and imbibes just one of the Gurū's many teachings.

Lord! Grant me this insight that 'You are the one true Beneficent Provider for us all' and I may never forget You (or that). Or:

Lord! Make me understand just one thing, which I may never forget, that 'You are the one true Beneficent Provider for us all'.

Sham or ritualistic deeds, in the garb of religious acts, are always found wanting and are never judged to be worthy of His Grace. On the other hand, one who has His Grace submits to the Gurū's Divine Word and Wisdom and strives to align with 'Nām(u)' and live by 'Nām-consciousness'.

PAURĪ 7
ਪਉੜੀ ੭॥

Je, jug chāre ārjā, hor dasūṇī hoi.
ਜੇ, ਜੁਗ ਚਾਰੇ ਆਰਜਾ, ਹੋਰ ਦਸੂਣੀ ਹੋਇ॥

Navā khaṅḍā vich(i) jāṇīai, nāl(i) chalai sabh(u) koi.
ਨਵਾ ਖੰਡਾ ਵਿਚਿ ਜਾਣੀਐ, ਨਾਲਿ ਚਲੈ ਸਭੁ ਕੋਇ॥

Chaṅgā nāo rakhāi kai, jas(u) kīrat(i) jag(i) le-i.
ਚੰਗਾ ਨਾਉ ਰਖਾਇ ਕੈ, ਜਸੁ ਕੀਰਤਿ ਜਗਿ ਲੇਇ॥

Je, tis(u) nadar(i) n āvaī, t, vāt n puchhai ke.
ਜੇ, ਤਿਸੁ ਨਦਰਿ ਨ ਆਵਈ, ਤ, ਵਾਤ ਨ ਪੁਛੈ ਕੇ॥

Kīṭā aṅdar(i) kīṭ(u), kar(i) dosī, dos(u) dhare.
ਕੀਟਾ ਅੰਦਰਿ ਕੀਟੁ, ਕਰਿ ਦੋਸੀ, ਦੋਸੁ ਧਰੇ॥

Nānak, nirguṇ(i) guṇ(u) kare, guṇvaṅtiā guṇ(u) de.
ਨਾਨਕ, ਨਿਰਗੁਣਿ ਗੁਣੁ ਕਰੇ, ਗੁਣਵੰਤਿਆ ਗੁਣੁ ਦੇ॥

Tehā koi n sujhaī, je tis(u) guṇ(u) koi kare. (7)
ਤੇਹਾ ਕੋਇ ਨ ਸੁਝਈ, ਜਿ ਤਿਸੁ ਗੁਣੁ ਕੋਇ ਕਰੇ॥ ੭॥

Je, jug chāre ārjā, hor dasūṇī hoi

je: (conj; synonymous with 'je kar', 'yadī' and 'agar') if or in case.

jug: (n, m, pl; synonymous with 'yug') the four ages, periods, epochs, eras or times according to Hindu mythology. See page 54.

chāre: (adj and adv; synonymous with 'chāroṅ hī') literally, all four.

ārjā: (a) (n, m; synonymous with 'jīvan', 'ziṅdagī' or 'ziṅdgānī') life, lifespan and existence, (b) (n, f, s; synonymous with 'avasthā') state, and implicit here is (c) (n, f; synonymous with 'āyū', 'umar' and 'umr') literally, the age or lifespan.

hor: (adj, f; synonymous with 'aur', 'hor dūjā', 'bākī', 'ziādā'; 'is toṅ-' 'vadh' or 'chhuṭ' and 'adhik') more, additional or different. (u) of 'hor(u)' is missing because it is an adjective of a noun of female gender. See hor(u).

dasūṇī: (adj; synonymous with 'das guṇī') literally, ten times as much.

hoi: (v, s, imperative mood - 'saṅbhāv bhvikht kāl - kiās bodhak', third person; synonymous with 'ho jāve' or 'hove') literally, were to become or were to be. See hoi and hoṇā/hovṇā (a).

je hor dasūṇī hoi: If one could live for ten times the age of four 'jugs'.

If one's lifespan were to be equivalent to that of the four ages or even ten times longer?

Navā khaṅḍā vich(i) jāṇīai, nāl(i) chalai sabh(u) koi

navā: (adj and adv; synonymous with nauvāṅ hī; pronounced as 'navāṅ') literally, all the nine.

khaṅḍā: (n, m, pl; synonymous with 'dīp', 'asthān' and 'desh'; pronounced as 'khaṅḍāṅ') literally, continents, regions or countries. See khaṅḍ(u).

vich(i): (prep; synonymous with 'bīch', 'bhītar', 'aṅdar' and 'vichkār') within, inside or in the midst.

navā khaṅḍā vich(i): (locative case - 'adhikaraṇ kārak', pl; synonymous with 'nauṅ-' 'hissiāṅ or khaṅḍāṅ vich'; 'nauṅ khaṅḍ prithvī vich'; pronounced as 'navāṅ khaṅḍāṅ vich') literally, in the nine parts of the Earth. In essence, throughout this planet Earth.

jāṇīai: (v, s, imperative mood - 'saṅbhāv bhvikht - kiās, sharat or ichhā bodhak'; synonymous with 'jāṇia-' or 'pargaṭ ho-' 'jāe') literally, were to become known, evident, revealed or manifest. See jāṇīai and jāṇanā (a and c).

nāl(i): (adv; synonymous with 'sāth' and 'saṅg') literally, with, along with or in the company of.

chalai: (imperative mood - 'saṅbhāv bhvikht kāl - kiās, sharat bodhak'; synonymous with 'je-' 'chalaṇ' or 'turan') literally, walk, but in essence, to stand by someone. See chalai and chalṇā (a and c).

nāl(i) chalai: (imperative mood - 'saṅbhāv bhvikht kāl - kiās bodhak', pl; synonymous with 'nāl chalan', 'hamāitī hoṇ' or 'pakh karan') literally, were to stand by one, take one's side or be partial to one.

sabh(u): (adj; synonymous with 'sabhe', 'sarab', 'sabho' and 'tamām') all, entire, everyone or totality.

koi: (a) (pron) someone or anyone, (b) (adj; synonymous with 'koī') any, some or certain.

sabh(u) koi: (synonymous with 'har ik manukh') literally, everyone.

If one were to be recognised and acclaimed throughout the world and everyone were to stand by one.

Chaṅgā nāu rakhāi kai, jas(u) kīrat(i) jag(i) le-i

changā: (adj; synonymous with 'uttam', 'sresht', 'shubh' and 'bhalā') literally, ideal, perfect or auspicious.

nāu: (n, f; synonymous with 'nāmaṇā', 'vaḍiāī', 'ustat(i)' and 'mahimā') praise, renown, fame, eulogy, glory or tribute.

chaṅgā nāu: literally, esteemed and honourable status.

rakhāi: (indeclinable past participle or perfect participle - 'pūran pūrab kārdaṅtak'; synonymous with 'rakhā ke' and 'khaṭ ke') having secured or earned.

kai: (a) (prep; synonymous with 'kā', 'ke', 'kī', 'dā', 'de' or 'dī') of, and (b) (prep; synonymous with 'se', 'nāl' or 'toṅ') with or from.

chaṅgā nāu rakhāi kai: literally, having earned or secured an esteemed and honourable status.

jas(u): (n, f; synonymous with 'siphat', 'guṇ' or 'mahimā') praise, merit or glory.

kīrat(i): (n, f; synonymous with 'mahimā', 'ustat(i)', 'vaḍiāī' and 'upmā') praise, tribute, honour or glory.

jag(i): (locative case - 'adhikaraṇ kārak'; synonymous with 'jagat vich') literally, in the world. See jagat.

jagat(u): (n, m, s; synonymous with 'saṅsār' or 'srisṭ(i)') literally, the whole world or universe.

le-i: (a) (v, s, present tense, third person; synonymous with 'laiṅdā hai') would take or grab [for himself], and (b) (imperative mood - 'saṅbhāv bhvikht kāl - kiās bodhak', third person, s; synonymous with 'lai-' or 'prāpat kar-' 'lave') if one were to achieve or acquire. See laiṇā.

jas(u) kīrat(i) jag(i) le(i): [if one were to] achieve or earn praise and glory in the world.

If, having acquired a good name and esteemed status, one were then to net praise, fame, and glory in the world.

Je, tis(u) nadar(i) n āvaī, t, vāt n puchhai ke

tis(u): (genitive case - 'saṅbaṅdh kārak'; synonymous with 'us-' 'de', 'dī', 'ke' or 'kī') literally, his. In essence, the reference here is to God.

nadar(i): (locative case - 'adhikaraṇ kārak'; synonymous with 'kripā drisṭ(i)-' or 'mehar dī nazar-' 'vich') literally, in His Gracious or Merciful gaze. See nadar(i).

n: (p; pronounced as 'nāṅ') no, not or implying a negative connotation.

āvaī: (a) (imperative mood - 'hukmī bhvikht - tāṛnā bodhak'; synonymous with 'ā jāve'), and (b) (v, s, present tense, third person; synonymous with 'āuṅdā-' and 'ā sakdā-' 'hai') see āuṇā/āvṇā.

je tis(u) nadar(i) n āvaī: literally, if one does not come into His notice or if one were judged not to be worthy of His gracious glance.

t: (synonymous with 'tā'; pronounced as 'tāṅ') (p and adv; synonymous with 'tad', 'tadoṅ', or 'udoṅ') then, thus, because of or, therefore.

vāt: (a) (n, m; synonymous with 'vājā') a musical instrument, especially wind instrument, (b) (n, m; synonymous with 'mukh' and 'mūṅh') face or mouth, and implicit here is (c) (n, f; synonymous with 'bāt', 'gal' and 'vārtā') literally, utterance, riddle, narrative or information. It refers to general chitchat or enquiry about one's general health or state of wellbeing ('khabar-sār').

puchhai: (v, s, present tense, third person; synonymous with 'puchhda hai') see puchhaṇā.

puchhaṇā: (v; synonymous with 'prashan karnā', 'swāl karnā' or 'pūchhanā') to ask, question or enquire.

ke: (pron; synonymous with 'koī') someone or anybody.

vāt puchhaṇā: (v; synonymous with 'vāt puchhaṇī', 'galbāt karnā' and 'bātchīt karnā') literally, to narrate, converse or exchange views.

vāt n puchhai ke: literally, no one would stop by to have a general chitchat. In essence, no one would give two hoots about one's fame or status. High moral character, noble deeds, godly attributes, philanthropy and altruism are much more valued here and in the hereafter rather than one's worldly assets alluded to above. In fact, one engrossed purely in one's worldly fame and assets is likely to be arrogant, vain, callous, unsympathetic and certainly not endearing.

None would give two hoots if, despite one's considerable age, good name and esteemed status, one was judged not to be worthy of His favour. Or:

None would pay the slightest notice if, despite one's considerable age, good name and esteemed status, one was judged not to be worthy of His Grace.

Kīṭā aṅdar(i) kīṭ(u), kar(i) dosī, dos(u) dhare

kīṭā: (n, m, pl; pronounced as 'kīṭāṅ') see kīṭ(u) (a).

kīṭ(u): (a) (n, m; synonymous with 'kīṛā' and 'kiram') literally, germ, microbe, worm or insect; a tiny organism that lives in animal or human dung or decaying matter, and (b) (adj; synonymous with 'tuchh', 'adnā', 'nīch' and 'kamīnā') trivial, worthless, insignificant or unimportant; of inferior rank or status. However, implicit here is one who is innately lowly, evil and devoid of or minimally endowed with good attributes, and does evil deeds.

aṅdar(i): (adv; synonymous with 'vich' and 'bhītar) inside, within or in the midst of.

kīṭā aṅdar(i) kīṭ(u): literally, a tiny worm that lives inside another microbe or worm. In essence, lowest of the low, common, trivial or an insignificant person.

kar(i): (indeclinable past participle or perfect participle - 'pūran pūrab kārdaṅtak'; synonymous with 'kar ke') see karnā (g, h and i).

dosī: (adj and n; synonymous with 'aprādhī', 'kukarmī', 'pāpī' and 'kasūrvār'; pronounced as 'doshī') accused, guilty or culprit.

kar(i) dosī: by charging or indicting.

dos(u): (n, m; pronounced as 'dosh(u)') (a) (synonymous with 'avguṇ' or 'aib') vice, demerits, foibles or undesirable traits, (b) (synonymous with 'kaṁzorī') shortcoming, weakness or Achilles' heel, and implicit here is (c) (synonymous with 'klaṅk') blemish, blame, accusation, smear, disgrace or ignominy and (d) (synonymous with 'aprādh', 'gunāh', 'kasūr', 'galatī' and 'pāp') literally, charge, crime, indictment; fault, error or mistake; sin. In essence, the charge or crime of living life engrossed in 'Māiā' and in disharmony with 'Nām(u)'.

dhare: (v, s, present tense, third person; synonymous with 'dhardā-', 'ṭikāuṅdā-', 'rakhdā-' 'hai') see dharnā.

dharnā: (v; synonymous with 'dharṇā', 'rakhṇā', 'tikāuṇā' and 'lāuṇā') literally, to lay, put, place, attach or fix carefully. However, implicit here is to charge or accuse.

dos(u) dhare: literally, accuses, charges or indicts them. The following verse from the SGGS highlights this aspect:

‘One who secures a great name and exalted status, and indulges in the pleasures of one’s *man*, appears, in the eyes of the Lord, just a lowly worm gathering grains for survival.’[321]

God, regarding such a human being as vermin, indicts one of falling foul of ‘Nām(u)’ and of not living by ‘Nām-consciousness’.

Nānak, nirguṇ(i) guṇ(u) kare, guṇvaṅtiā guṇ(u) de

Nānak: (n, m, s) (u) of ‘Nānak(u)’ is missing because of its vocative case - ‘saṅbodhan kārak’.

nirguṇ(i): (a) (accusative case - ‘karam kārak’, s; synonymous with ‘guṇhīn manukh nūṅ’) to one lacking any merit, and implicit here is (b) (locative case - ‘adhikaraṇ kārak’; synonymous with ‘guṇhīn manukh vich’) literally, in one lacking any merit. See nirguṇ.

nirguṇ: (adj, m, pl; synonymous with ‘guṇhīn’) a complex word comprising ‘nir’ (without or lacking) + ‘guṇ’ (attributes, merits or qualities) i.e., lacking or without any worth, merit, goodness or virtue.

guṇ: (n, m, pl) (a) (synonymous with ‘lābh’ and ‘phal’) gain, profit or fruit, (b) (synonymous with ‘vidyā’, ‘hunnar’ and ‘kalā’) knowledge, education or skill, (c) (synonymous with ‘visheshaṇ’, ‘siphat’, ‘khūbī’, ‘khāsīat’, ‘lachhaṇ’, ‘subhāu’ and ‘tāsīr’) literally, the characteristics, properties or attributes of something. However, the tacit reference here is to the attributes of ‘Nām(u)'.

kare: (v, s, present tense, third person; synonymous with 'kardā-’, ‘kar deṅdā-’, ‘kar sakdā-’ ‘hai’) see karnā.

guṇ(u) kare: grants them noble attributes (because judged to be a genuine seeker and earnestly striving towards doing good deeds).

guṇvaṅtiā: (accusative case - ‘karam kārak’; synonymous with ‘guṇvāliāṅ nūṅ’; pronounced as ‘guṇvaṅtiāṅ’) to talented, gifted, meritorious or virtuous people. See guṇvaṅt.

guṇvaṅt: (adj, m, pl; synonymous with ‘gifted, talented, meritorious or virtuous’) a complex word comprising ‘guṇ’ (attributes, characteristics, ‘lachhaṇ’ and ‘visheshaṇ’) + ‘vaṅt’ (‘vān’ and ‘vāle’) i.e., bearers of good attributes or qualities.

de: (v, s, present tense, third person; synonymous with ‘de(i)’, ‘ਦੇਇ’ or ‘deṅdā hai’) literally, offers, confers, bestows or grants. However, implicit here is gives, bestows or grants forever. See deṇā (b and c).

However, the implication here is that He grants noble attributes and virtues to help attune and harmonise perfectly with 'Nām(u)' or 'Nām-consciousness'.

'He grants noble and godly attributes to one who is wretched, abject and ignoble, and to those already gifted and meritorious', O' Nānak!

Tehā koi n sujha-ī, je tis(u) guṇ(u) koi kare

tehā: (adj, m; synononymous with 'taisā' and 'uho jihā') similar to him or similar as that.

koi: (a) (pron) someone or anyone, (b) (adj; synonymous with 'koī') any, some or certain.

sujha-ī: (v, s, present tense, third person; synonymous with 'sujhdā hai') see sujhaṇā (b to d).

sujhaṇā: (v) (a) (synonymous with 'samajh vich āuṇā') to get to know, understand or realise, (b) (synonymous with 'auṛnā' and 'phurnā') to have an idea or to come to mind, (c) (synonymous with 'nazar āuṇā') to come to see, to become visible or to become evident, and (d) (synonymous with 'chete āuṇā') to remember or to recollect.

ji: (a) (adv; synonymous with 'jis toṅ') from whom, which or where, (b) (conj; synonymous with 'je kar') if, in case or provided, (c) (conj; synonymous with 'kioṅ ke' or 'kioṅ jo') because, for or since, and implicit here is (d) (pron; synonymous with 'jo', 'jin(h)' or 'jihṛā') who, which, that, whom or whomsoever.

tis(u): (pron, s; synonymous with 'us' and 'us nūṅ') he, she, that or it. It is noteworthy that the reference here could be to the 'nirguṇ(i)hār' or God - one who is the fount of all attributes, virtues and values, and provider for all.

koi: (a) (pron) someone or anyone, (b) (adj; synonymous with 'koī') any, some or certain.

kare: (a) (v, s, present tense, third person; synonymous with 'kar sakdā-' 'hai' or 'hove') and (b) (imperative mood - 'saṅbhāv bhvikht kāl - kiās, sharat, ichhā bodhak'; synonymous with 'kar-' or 'bakhsh-' 'deve') see karnā (i (i)).

ji tis(u) guṇ(u) koi kare: (a) one who could grant some noble attributes to both the meritorious and those devoid of any merit. Here the word 'who' refers to God, as He is the sole provider of all attributes, and (b) one who could grant Him any attributes. Here the word 'who' refers to any mortal human being, whose ability and stockpile of anything would be limited, and miniscule in comparison to that of God. In reality, this is not plausible as there is only Him in this world, and the latter is just His manifestation.[34, 36 and 391]

It is inconceivable that someone else, save God, could bestow such attributes upon a mere mortal.

Conceptual summary

If one (a) could live for the age of the four 'Yugs', nay, even ten times that, (b) were known and acclaimed in all the nine continents, and entire humanity were to stand by him, (c) had secured a good name, fame and status for oneself, and the whole world were to sing one's praise and glory, none would pay the slightest notice if, despite all this, one failed to come up to the mark and fell from God's Grace. God indicts such a person, regards him as vermin, and accuses him of falling foul of 'Nām(u)' and 'Nām-consciousness'.

God Grants noble attributes, virtues and values to the wretched, abject and ignoble, as well as to those already righteous and meritorious. However, it is unimaginable that someone else, save God, could bestow such attributes upon a mere mortal.

Generally, the greater the craving for long life, the greater the fear of death. 'Yogīs' were known to extend their lifespan through the practice of 'Prāṇāyāmā'- a technique involving deep inhalation through one of the nostrils ('puraka'), a mindful pause for a period after inhalation ('aṅtara kumbhaka'), exhalation through the other nostril ('rechaka') and finally, a mindful pause for a variable period thereafter ('bahya kumbhaka'). With other such attributes harnessed through yogic practice, they were able to command respect from ordinary people and instil fear in their minds. However, lacking total submission to and not living life by 'Nām(u)' or 'Nām-consciousness', they were unable ever to receive God's Grace. An earnest desire to submit totally to 'Nām(u)' and then to live by His Will falls into one's lap only by the Grace of God.

Human birth gives one a golden opportunity to evolve spiritually from being a 'manmukh(u)' to being a 'gurmukh(u)', and then to realise Him, having first aligned perfectly with 'Nām(u)' and 'Nām-consciousness'. Whilst it is obligatory for us to initiate the process and genuinely seek to move in this direction, we must submit to the Gurū's Divine Word and Wisdom, and live life by his Dictum. Thus, we receive God's Grace, align perfectly with 'Nām(u)' and eventually realise 'Sahaj', 'Anaṅd(u)' and 'Nām(u)' - the immanent form of God. The following verses from the SGGS clearly define this path and the precise way to receive His Grace:

As He is supreme and the entire universe is subservient to His jurisdiction, why, then, revere and idolise material riches and miraculous powers?[322]

The gifts are all God's, and nothing influences His Will; some fail to receive even when desirous of His Will and alert to it, whereas He gives spontaneously to others who are just living selflessly by His Will.[323]

Should He grant His Grace, one meets and converges ideologically with the noble and holy, and then reflects upon and sings His Glory in their company.[324]

When the perfect Gurū makes one hear the Divine Word, one rids oneself of the evil effects of 'Māiā', attunes to 'Nām(u)', achieves lasting equanimity ('Sahaj'), and finally, realises 'Nām(u)' by subduing one's 'haumaiṅ'.[325]

One becomes pure by overcoming the influence of 'Māiā'. Having achieved lasting equanimity ('Sahaj') and aligned perfectly with 'Nām(u)', one realises 'Nām(u)' - the immanent aspect of God.[326]

One who submits to and abides by the perfect Gurū's edicts becomes enlightened in his company; one's entire struggle lies in nurturing and harbouring noble virtues and cleansing one's evil 'Vikārī' tendencies.[327]

It is supplication that bears fruit and not one's diktat which does not wash with the Lord.[328]

To chase and idolise material assets and miraculous powers is just a crazy fixation and obsession, and certainly not the way to realise 'Nām(u)' in one's conscious self.[329]

God grants to one to whom He is Merciful, the company and wisdom of the Gurū, helps rid them of their 'Haumaiṅ' and the evil influence of 'Māiā', and achieve lasting equanimity ('Sahaj') and bliss ('Anaṅd').[330]

Death (loss of 'Haumaiṅ', attachment to the material world or infatuation with it), which terrifies the whole world, arouses a sense of inner bliss in my conscious self for, it's with the complete forsaking of 'Moh' and 'Haumaiṅ' (the death of the self), that one realises lasting inner bliss and 'Nām(u)', says Kabīr.[331]

Having strayed and wandered aimlessly over many lifetimes, one receives the Divine Word and Wisdom from a Gurū and imbibes its essence with God's Grace. 'Hear ye! People of the world, there is no one more beneficent than the true Gurū'. The true Gurū helps reveal the Primal Soul within those who submit to and imbibe his Divine Wisdom and Knowledge, and who rid themselves of 'Haumaiṅ'.[332]

'Prāṇāyāmā' may help extend one's life and earn one the respect of humanity far and wide but life devoid of devotion to 'Nām(u)' and harmony with 'Nām-consciousness' does not earn one any credit with God. One receives the gift of noble attributes, virtues and values only from God and one becomes worthy of this only if one genuinely seeks the perfect Gurū's Divine Wisdom, submits to it and follows it faithfully and with dogged determination.

PAUṚĪ 8
ਪਉੜੀ ੮॥

Suṇ(i)ai, sidh, pīr, sur(i), nāth.
ਸੁਣਿਐ, ਸਿਧ ਪੀਰ ਸੁਰਿ ਨਾਥ॥
Suṇ(i)ai, dharat(i), Dhaval, ākās.
ਸੁਣਿਐ, ਧਰਤਿ, ਧਵਲ, ਆਕਾਸ॥
Suṇ(i)ai, dīp, loa, pātāl.
ਸੁਣਿਐ, ਦੀਪ, ਲੋਅ, ਪਾਤਾਲ॥
Suṇ(i)ai, poh(i) n sakai kāl(u).
ਸੁਣਿਐ ਪੋਹਿ ਨ ਸਕੈ ਕਾਲੁ॥
Nānak, bhagtā sadā vigās(u).
ਨਾਨਕ ਭਗਤਾ ਸਦਾ ਵਿਗਾਸੁ॥
Suṇ(i)ai, dūkh, pāp kā nās(u). (8)
ਸੁਣਿਐ, ਦੂਖ, ਪਾਪ ਕਾ ਨਾਸੁ॥ ੮॥

Suṇ(i)ai, sidh, pīr, sur(i), nāth

suṇ(i)ai: (present participle - 'kriyā-phal kirdaṅt' with added reference to case; synonymous with 'suṇiāṅ', 'suṇ ke', 'suṇan nāl' or 'je Nām(u) vich surat(i) joṛī jāe') literally, with or by listening attentively to. However, implicit here is (a) focus of 'surat(i)' on the subject matter heard, (b) understanding of the subject matter, (c) willingly and lovingly imbibing its essence in one's 'Hirdā', and (d) the subject matter to be the persona or attributes of 'Nām(u)' and the way to 'Nām-consciousness'.

Gurbāṇī has the essence of this subject matter. By adhering to this routine with firm commitment, discipline, and order, one learns gradually to focus and contemplate 'Nām(u)' ('Nām-' 'Japnā', 'Simranā', 'Dhiāvanā' or 'Arādhanā'), which, in turn, leads to being perfectly aligned with or attuned to 'Nām(u)', lasting equanimity ('Sahaj'), inner bliss ('Anaṅd') and eventually, 'Nām-realisation'. See suṇanā.

suṇanā: (v) literally, to hear or listen attentively with one's ears; to pay heed or attention to. However, implicit here is to listen attentively to, understand, reflect upon, and then imbibe the Divine Message ('gur-'

'sikhiā' or 'updesh') or His Glory contained in 'Gurbānī'. Crucially, this modality also permits the less fortunate, those unable to read and/or write, to evolve spiritually and to attain their goal of 'Nām-realisation'. It is noteworthy that 'Nām(u)', the immanent form of the transcendent God in the form of 'Anhad Sabad' or 'Nād', can only be experienced spiritually. The following verses from the SGGS help define and develop the scope of 'suṇanā':

'There are many kinds of benefactors and paupers in this world, whose ways are different and who give or beg different objects. 'Nām(u)' is the only worthwhile and acceptable thing to exchange. I am a sacrifice to them who hear and then unreservedly submit to it, and imbibe its essence in their 'Hirdā', says Nānak.[333]

By listening attentively to the Guru's Divine Word (the Gurbānī eulogising the immaculate 'Nām(u)'), one achieves lasting equanimity and inner bliss. But rare is the individual who understands, reflects upon, nurtures and cherishes its essence with conviction, imbibes it in their conscious self, expresses it in their daily life, and eventually realises 'Nām(u)'.[334]

By listening attentively to the Guru's Divine Word (Gurbānī eulogising the immaculate 'Nām(u)'), one achieves lasting inner equanimity ('Sahaj') and bliss ('Anaṅd'). One's '*Man*' is satisfied and delivered from all the sorrows due to being entrenched in the material world. One is not only inspired to reflect upon and contemplate 'Nām(u) but one also earns a good name in the process.[335]

sidh: (n, m, pl) spiritually high ranking Yogīs who have achieved eight unique or mythical psychic, miraculous or supernatural powers. See sidh.

pīr: (a) (n, m, pl; pers; synonymous with 'buḍhe', 'birdh', 'kamzor' and 'bazurg') respectable old and frail men, and implicit here is (b) (n, m, pl; synonymous with 'aulīyā') Muslim religious or spiritual teachers, or holy men. See pīr.

sur(i): (a) (n, m, pl) 'devte' in Hindu mythology, (b) (n, m, s; synonymous with 'uttam purush') the reference is to God, and implicit here is (b) (adj, m, pl; synonymous with 'vaḍḍe') literally, great, senior, elder, and (c) (n, m, pl) human beings with divine attributes ('dayavī guṇ'). See sur and sur(i).

nāth: (n, m) a sect of Hindu ascetics or a member of a sect which follows their yogīrāj Gorakhnāth or Lord Shiva and who has achieved the pinnacle of success on that path.

sur(i) nāth: (n, m; synonymous with 'nātheshwar' and yogīrāj') literally, one who is supreme amongst 'Yogīs'.

By listening attentively to and focusing and reflecting upon the Divine Word and understanding and imbibing its essence in one's 'Hirdā', one achieves the lofty status of the 'Sidhas', 'Pīrs', 'Devtās' and 'Nāths'.

Suṇ(i)ai, dharat(i), dhaval, ākās

dharat(i): (n, f; synonymous with 'prithvī', 'zamīn' and 'bhūmī'; pronounced as 'dhartī') literally, the Earth.

dhaval: (synonymous with 'dhaul(u)') (a) (adj; synonymous with 'chiṭṭā') white, (b) (adj; synonymous with 'ujlā' and 'nirmal') pure and immaculate, and (c) (n, m; synonymous with 'chiṭṭā bail') literally, white ox, which, according to the Hindu Purānas, supports the planet Earth on its horns. In 'Pauṛī' 16, Guru Nanak refutes this argument and states that it is the Divine Order ('Hukam') that supports and stabilises the planets in their specific orbits. However, implicit here is support, buttress or truss propping up the planets.

ākās: (a) (adj; synonymous with 'uchā pad') high rank, position or status, (b) (n, m; synonymous with 'swarg' and 'suarg') heavens or 'devlok', and implicit here is (c) (n, m; synonymous with 'āsmān' and 'aṅbar'; pronounced as 'ākāsh') the sky, the firmament or the heavens above.

By listening attentively to the Divine Word, focusing and reflecting upon it, and understanding and imbibing its essence in one's 'Hirdā', one realises that it is the Divine Order ('Hukam'), and not the horns of a white ox, that stabilises the orbital position of planet Earth and the firmament above.

Suṇ(i)ai, dīp, loa, pātāl

dīp: (a) (n, m, pl; synonymous with 'dīve' and 'chirāg') oil lamps, especially earthen oil lamps, (b) (n, m; synonymous with 'ṭāpū' or 'jazīre') islands, and (c) (n, m; synonymous with 'mahāṅ-dīp') continents.

loa: (n, pl; synonymous with 'lok', 'desh', 'khaṅḍ' and 'bhavan') countries, spheres or planets in a system, e.g., 'Trilok' of Hindu belief and the seven planets below and above Earth in the Islamic tradition. See loa.

pātāl: (a) (n, m, pl) netherworlds, Hades, the underworlds, (b) (n, m) the 'world' below planet Earth according to the Hindu belief of 'Trilok': ('dharat(i)', 'pātāl' below and 'swarg' above, (c) last of the seven worlds beneath the planet Earth according to Islamic mythology. However, the reference here is to planets spatially below planet Earth.

The following verses of the SGGS lend support to the thesis that it is the Divine Order that creates and supports the vast planetary system and diverse life forms wherever they exist:

'Who has created and planted the stars that you see and who supports the star-studded sky above'? Only a fortunate one knows this mystery, O' Paṅḍit. He pervades the entire expanse as well as the sun and moon which blaze to brighten the creation. Only he, who perceives 'Nām(u)' in his 'Hirdā' and whose speech is in harmony with 'Nām(u)', will realise all this', says Kabīr.[336]

By listening attentively to the Divine Word, focusing and reflecting upon it, and understanding and imbibing its essence in one's 'Hirdā', one realises that He pervades all the continents, the countless planets and the underworlds.

Suṇ(i)ai, poh(i) n sakai kāl(u)

poh(i): (pronounced as 'poh') (a) (v, s, present tense, second person; synonymous with 'tusīṅ ḍrā sakde ho'; 'prabhāv-' or 'asar-' 'pā sakde ho'), (b) (v, pl, present tense, first person; synonymous with 'asīṅ ḍrā sakde hāṅ', (c) (v, s, future tense, third person; synonymous with 'uh ḍrā sakaṇge), and implicit here is (d) (v, pl, present tense, third person; synonymous with 'uh ḍrā sakde han'; 'uh prabhāv-' or 'asar-' 'pā sakde han'). The reference here is to the realisation of one's real 'self' ('Jīvātmāṅ') and the notion of a fear of death, which no longer appears menacing or frightening. See pohṇā.

pohṇā: (v) (a) (synonymous with 'ghusṇā' or 'dhakke nāl pravesh karnā') to enter forcibly or to transgress, (b) (synonymous with 'asar-' 'hoṇā' or 'karnā') to influence and/or overwhelm, and (c) (synonymous with 'ḍrāuṇā' and 'dukh deṇā') to oppress and torment.

n: (p; pronounced as 'nāṅ') no, not or implying a negative connotation.

sakai: (modal v, s, present tense, third person; synonymous with 'sākdā hai') literally, may or can perform or carry out an action. See sakṇā.

sakṇā: (modal v, s, present tense, third person) may or can have the ability or strength to carry out an action.

poh(i) na sakaī: does not or cannot overwhelm or forcibly influence.

kāl(u): (n, f; synonymous with 'mrityū' and 'maut') literally, the process and the time of both physical and spiritual demise or death. The fear of death is pre-eminent amongst all other emotions that humans experience. The real 'I' or 'self' is 'Jīvātmāṅ', which is indestructible, and a spiritual demise or death refers to succumbing to one's ego-consciousness ('Haumaiṅ'), 'Moh' and innate 'Vikārī' tendencies ('Māiā'). See kāl(u).

By listening attentively to the Divine Word, focusing and reflecting upon it, and understanding and imbibing its essence in one's 'Hirdā', the fear of both physical and spiritual death does not overwhelm one.

Nānak, bhagtā sadā vigās(u)

Nānak: (n, m, s) (u) of 'Nānak(u)' is missing because of its vocative case - 'saṅbodhan kārak'.

bhagtā: (a) (dative case - 'saṅpardān kārak'; synonymous with 'bhagtāṅ laī') for Bhagats, and implicit here is (b) (genitive case - 'saṅbaṅdh kārak'; synonymous with 'bhagtāṅ de'; pronounced as 'bhagtāṅ') literally, of 'Bhagats'. However, implicit here is in the '*Man*' or 'Hirdās' of 'bhagats'. See bhagat.

However, implicit here is devotees, votaries or they who have realised 'Nām(u)', who live by His Will, and whose every thought ('*Man*'), utterance ('Bachan') and deed ('Karam') is in perfect harmony with 'Nām(u)'. Such a 'bhagat' is synonymous with a 'Saṅt', 'Sādh', Gurū and 'Brahm-gyānī' in Gurmat. The following verses from the SGGS succinctly define and characterise a true 'Bhagat':

Loving and willing surrender to the eternal 'Nām(u)' is the very basis of a true devotee's life; their burning desire is to sing His Glory and live by His Will forever. They humbly follow in the footsteps of the enlightened and enjoy lasting inner bliss forever.[337]

'The lifestyle of His true devotees is unique and extraordinary, and the path they follow is demanding and arduous. Shedding their ardent desire for the material, and shedding greed and egotism, they speak sparingly and only when in need. They follow a rigid, straight and narrow path, finer than a hair or the sharp edge of a sword. They who, with the grace of the Gurū, have shed their ego and egotism make immersion in and merging with 'Nām(u)' their sole desire. The lifestyle of His true devotees has forever been unique and extraordinary', says Nānak.[338]

'Your devotees focus on and contemplate You with love', O, Lord![339]

'He who surrenders to God and lives by His Will, is His true devotee ('bhagat'); he who does not, is fickle and unfaithful', says Nānak.[340]

To regard oneself as naïve even when being wise, to consider oneself weak even when blessed with power, and to share one's possessions with others even when there is little to share, is the mark of a rare person who would be a true devotee of God.[341]

One who accepts both pain and pleasure for what they are and who is forever imbued with love for 'Nām(u)', is a true 'bhagat' of the Lord.[342]

sadā: (adv; synonymous with 'sad', 'nitya' and 'hameshā') forever, always or in perpetuity.

vigās: (a) (n, m; synonymous with 'bikās(u)' or 'vikās') outwardly spread or expansion, development, progress or evolution, (b) (n, f; synonymous with 'chamak' or 'prakash') glow, lustre or enlightenment, and implicit here is (b) (n, f; synonymous with 'anaṅd', 'prasaṅtā', 'khushī' or 'kheṛā') literally, happiness, delight and contentment. In essence, a state of lasting inner equanimity and bliss ('Sahaj') is due to perfect alignment with 'Nām(u)'.

'His 'Bhagats' are forever in a state of inner bliss', O' Nānak! [see next paṅkat(i) for explanation]

Suṇ(i)ai, dūkh, pāp kā nās(u)

dūkh: (n, m, pl; synonymous with 'dukh'; antonym of 'sūkh') collective noun for all one's ills and suffering (physical and/or psychological distress), unhappiness and discontentedness due to lack of material comforts or pleasures, and for inner turmoil resulting from being sucked into the web of

‘Moh’, ‘Māyā’ and ‘Vikārs’, and with living life in disharmony with ‘Nām(u)’ and ‘Nām-consciousness’ (‘life of a Kūṛiār(u)’).

pāp: (n, m, pl; antonym of ‘puṅn’; synonymous with ‘ashubh-’ or ‘māṛe-’ ‘karam’; ‘dushkaram’ and ‘kukaram’) (a) evil thoughts, sins, or misdeeds, exploitatory or detrimental in nature to oneself or other beings, and responsible for one’s own spiritual downfall, and (b) (n, m; synonymous with ‘pāpī birtī or subhāu’) innate evil tendencies.

kā: (prep, m; synonymous with ‘dā’) of.

nās(u): (n, m) (a) (synonymous with ‘bekār-’, ‘viarth-’ or ‘nirārthak-’ ‘jāṇā’) waste, (b) (synonymous with ‘barbād hoṇā’) fall, downfall or ruin, and implicit here is (c) synonymous with ‘nāsh’, ‘vināsh’ and ‘tabāhī’) destruction, eradication or extermination, and (d) (synonymous with ‘marnā’, ‘mukṇā’ and ‘miṭṇā’) death or mortality.

‘By listening attentively to the Divine Word, focusing and reflecting upon it, and understanding and imbibing its essence in one’s ‘Hirdā’, all one’s innate evil tendencies and consequent sufferings just vanish’.

Conceptual summary

By listening attentively to the Divine Word, focusing and reflecting upon it, and understanding and imbibing its essence in one’s ‘Hirdā’, a mere mortal can: (a) acquire the noble attributes normally associated with the ‘Sidhas’, ‘Pīrs’, ‘Devtas’ and supremely ranked ‘Nāth Yogīs’, (b) clearly perceive the mystery surrounding the stable orbital position of planet Earth and the firmament above, (c) truly perceive His all- pervasiveness in the continents, other planets and the netherworlds, and also (d) realise the indestructibility of one’s soul, and so lose the fear of both a spiritual and a physical demise.

His ‘Bhagats’ are forever in a state of inner bliss. For, by listening attentively to the Divine Word, focusing and reflecting upon it, and understanding and imbibing its essence in their ‘Hirdās’, all their innate evil tendencies and their consequent sufferings just vanish.

In essence, by listening attentively to the Divine Word, focusing and reflecting upon it, and understanding and imbibing its essence in one’s ‘Hirdā’, an ordinary person can achieve the lofty heights in spirituality. One not only knows but now perceives His omnipresence and His Divine Order as being the cause of orderliness and stability in the universe. Realising one’s true identity as a spiritual being, one’s fear of death also vanishes.

PAUṚĪ 9
ਪਉੜੀ ੯॥

Suṇ(i)ai, Īsar(u), Barmā, Iṅd(u).
ਸੁਣਿਐ, ਈਸਰੁ, ਬਰਮਾ, ਇੰਦੁ॥
Suṇ(i)ai, mukh(i) sālāhaṇ maṅd(u).
ਸੁਣਿਐ, ਮੁਖਿ ਸਾਲਾਹਣ ਮੰਦੁ॥
Suṇ(i)ai, jog jugat(i), tan(i) bhed.
ਸੁਣਿਐ, ਜੋਗ ਜੁਗਤਿ, ਤਨਿ ਭੇਦ॥
Suṇ(i)ai, sāsat, s(i)m(i)rit(i), ved.
ਸੁਣਿਐ, ਸਾਸਤ, ਸਿਮ੍ਰਿਤਿ, ਵੇਦ॥
Nānak, bhagtā sadā vigās(u).
ਨਾਨਕ, ਭਗਤਾ ਸਦਾ ਵਿਗਾਸੁ॥
Suṇ(i)ai, dūkh, pāp kā nās(u). 9.
ਸੁਣਿਐ, ਦੂਖ, ਪਾਪ ਕਾ ਨਾਸੁ॥ ੯॥

Suṇ(i)ai, Īsar(u), Barmā, Iṅd(u)

suṇ(i)ai: see 'Pauṛī' 8, page 137.

Īsar(u): (n, m, s) (a) (skt; synonymous with 'Īshvar'; pronounced as 'Īshar') God, and implicit here is (b) (synonymous with 'Shiv' and 'Mahadev') one of the trilogy of Hindu Gods - Brahma, Vishnu and Shiv, with Lord Shiv being responsible for death and destruction. Complete detachment from the material world and its comforts, and extreme compassion and mercy rank high amongst the many attributes associated with Lord Shiv.

Barmā: (n, m, s; synonymous with and pronounced as 'Brahmā') Lord Brahmā, one of the trilogy of Hindu Gods, responsible for creation. Wisdom, inquisitiveness, philosophical prowess and deductive reasoning rank high amongst the many attributes associated with Lord Brahmā.

Iṅd(u): (n, m, pl; synonymous with 'Iṅdr', 'Iṅdra', 'Iṅdar' and 'devrāj') (a) literally, Iṅdra or Dev Indra, the mythological king of 'Suarg', 'Swarg' or 'Amrāvatī' - the heavens, where its inhabitants enjoy an eternal and pleasurable life, and (b) God of rain in Hindu mythology.

Numerous good and bad aspects of the characters of various Hindu gods, goddesses, demi-gods and demi-goddesses are described and typified in Hindu religious texts. Whilst Gurmat does not lend any support to their existence or to any supernatural powers ascribed to them, there is reference to some of their commonly known examples of their noble attributes and mythological powers in the SGGS.

By listening attentively to the Divine Word, focusing and reflecting upon it, and understanding and imbibing its essence in one's 'Hirdā', one achieves the noble attributes and the lofty status of Shiv, Brahma and Dev Indra.

Suṇ(i)ai, mukh(i) sālāhaṇ manṅd(u)

mukh(i): (a) (Instrumental Case - 'karaṇ kārak'; synonymous with 'mukh-' 'nāl', 'rāhīṅ', 'duārā' or 'sadkā') with or through one's mukh, and implicit here is (b) (ablative case - 'apādān kārak'; synonymous with 'mukh toṅ') from one's mukh. See mukh(u) (b).

mukh(u): (a) (adj; synonymous with 'mukhīā' or 'pradhān') head, chief or leader, and (b) (n, m, pl; synonymous with 'mūṅh' and 'chehrā') literally, lips or face. In essence, the mouth.

sālāhaṇ: (a) (sālāhan(i); v, pl; synonymous with 'sālāhuṅde han' and 'ustat(i)-' or 'siphat sālāh-' 'karde han') sing His Praise or Glory, and implicit here is (b) (n, f, pl; synonymous with 'ustat(i)', 'tuārīph', 'siphat sālāh' and 'vadiāīāṅ') greatness, praises, merits, glories or eulogies.

maṅd(u): (a) adj; pers; synonymous with 'vān' and vālā' if used as a suffix) e.g., 'akalmaṅd' - wise and 'daulatmaṅd' - wealthy, (b) (adj; synonymous with 'abhāgā' and 'bad-nasīb') unfortunate or ill-fated, and implicit here is (c) (n, m, s; synonymous with 'be-samaj' and 'mūrakh') naive, fool or ignorant, and (d) (n, m, s; synonymous with 'nīch' and 'kamīnā') low, mean or ignoble.

mukh(i) sālāhaṇ maṅd(u): an ill-fated, naïve and ignoble person (maṅd(u)) begins to utter (mukh(i)) His Praise (sālāhaṇ).

By listening attentively to the Divine Word, focusing and reflecting upon it, and understanding and imbibing its essence in one's 'Hirdā', even one who is naïve, ill-fated and ignoble comes to sing His Glory.

Suṇ(i)ai, jog jugat(i), tan(i) bhed

jog: (a) (prep; synonymous with 'nūṅ', 'prat(i)', 'tāṅī', 'laī' and 'vāste') to, up to, or for someone or something, (b) (n, m, pl; synonymous with 'Yogīs') followers of Gorakhnāth or practitioners of the different forms of yoga, (c) (n, m; skt. 'Yog') ways or protocols to focus and still one's very flirtatious mind by Patanjalī, a Hindu Rishī, (d) (adj; synonymous with 'uchit', 'lāik', 'yog', 'yogyatā vālā' or 'samrath') befitting, deserving, proper; capable, competent or powerful enough, (e) (dative case - 'saṅpardān kārak'; synonymous with 'milāp-' 'la-ī' or 'vāste') literally, for meeting, reconciliation or union, and implicit here is (f) (genitive case - 'saṅbaṅdh kārak'; synonymous with 'milāp-' 'dī') of union, reconciliation or meeting.

jugat(i): (n, m; synonymous with 'rahiṇī bahiṇī' and 'jīvan-' 'jāch', 'tarīkā' or 'ḍhaṅg') literally, way of life, art of living, or method, technique or procedure for good living.

jog jugat(i): (synonymous with 'jog-' or 'milāp-' dī jugat(i)) literally, the ways to realise or perceive 'Nām(u)'.

tan(i): (a) (a) (accusative case - 'karam kārak'; synonymous with 'deh-' or 'srīr-' 'nūṅ') to one's body, (b) (instrumental case - 'karaṇ kārak'; synonymous with 'deh-' or 'srīr-' 'nāl', 'rāhīṅ', 'sadkā' or 'duārā') with or through one's body, and implicit here is (c) (genitive case - 'saṅbaṅdh kārak'; synonymous with 'tan-', 'deh-' or 'sarīr-' 'de') literally, of one's body, and (d) (locative case - 'adhikaraṇ kārak'; synonymous with 'tan-', 'deh-' or 'sarīr-' 'vich' or 'aṅdar(i)') in or within one's body or sensorimotor organs. However, implicit here is of or within one's sensorimotor organs that serve the '*Man*'. See tan.

tan(u): (n, m, s; synonymous with 'srīr': n, f, s; synonymous with 'deh') literally, the body but the reference here is to the sensorimotor organs of the body through which '*man*' expresses itself and interacts with the physical world.

bhed: (n, m, pl) (a) (synonymous with 'bhed', 'aṅtar', 'bhiṅntā' and 'pharak') difference, deviation, variance or disparity, and implicit here is (b) (synonymous with 'bhet', 'gupt-bhāv' and 'rāz') literally, secrets, mysteries, intelligence or classified information given in confidence. However, the reference here is to the mystery of one's spontaneous and natural preferences towards the empirical world and vulnerability to the perverse innate 'vikārī' tendencies ('Māyā') of one's '*man*' and sensorimotor organs and the way to overcome this.

By listening attentively to the Divine Word, focusing and reflecting upon it, and understanding and imbibing its essence in one's 'Hirdā', one learns how to temper and/or control the vulnerability of one's sensorimotor organs to 'Māyā', and learns the way to realise 'Nām(u)'.

Suṇ(i)ai, sāsat, sim(i)rit(i), ved

sāst: (a) (n, m; abbreviation for 'sāstr' and 'Shāstra') the following six different sacred books or treatises of the Hindu religion, each with a different philosophical viewpoint and with its different author in brackets: 'Sāṅkh' (Kapal), 'Niāi' (Gautam), 'Vaisheshik' (Kṇād), 'Yog' (Pataṅjalī), 'Mimāṅsā' (Jaiminī) and 'Vedāṅt' (Vyās), and implicit here is (b) (genitive case - 'saṅbaṅdh kārak'; synonymous with 'Shāstrāṅ-' 'dā' or 'dī') literally, of Shāstrās. In essence, the knowledge and wisdom ('giān') of the Shāstrās.

sim(i)rit(i): (n, f) thirty-one religious books containing the code of Hindu law, based on memory of the precepts of their holy Saints or Rishīs, and passed down the generations through oral tradition, and implicit here is (b) (genitive case - 'saṅbaṅdh kārak'; synonymous with 'sim(i)rt(i)īāṅ-' 'dā' or 'dī') literally, of sim(i)rit(i)s. However, implicit here is the knowledge and wisdom ('giān') of the sim(i)rit(i)s.

ved: (n, m, pl; synonymous with 'bed' and 'vedas') the four Hindu Scriptures - 'Rig', 'Yajur', 'Sām' and 'Atharvan', and implicit here is (b) (genitive case - 'saṅbaṅdh kārak'; synonymous with 'vedāṅ-' 'dā' or 'dī') literally, of Veds. However, implicit here is the knowledge and wisdom ('giān') of the Vedas.

By listening attentively to the Divine Word, focusing and reflecting upon it, and understanding and imbibing its essence in one's 'Hirdā', one acquires the Divine Wisdom and Knowledge hidden in the Hindu Shāstrās, s(i)m(i)rit(i)s, and the Vedas.

Nānak, bhagtā sadā vigās(u). See 'Pauṛī' 8
Suṇ(i)ai, dūkh, pāp kā nās(u). See 'Pauṛī' 8

Conceptual summary

By listening attentively to the Divine Word, focusing and reflecting upon it, and understanding and imbibing its essence in one's 'Hirdā', and attuning to 'Nām(u)', a mere mortal can: (a) achieve the noble attributes and the lofty status of Shiv, Brahma and Dev Indra, (b) [an innately naïve and/or evil person] come to sing His Praise, (c) learn how to temper and/or control one's vulnerability to 'Māyā' and learn the way to realise 'Nām(u)', and (d) acquire the divine knowledge and wisdom hidden or expounded in the Hindu Shāstrās, sim(i)rit(i)s, and Vedas.

His 'Bhagats' are forever in a state of inner bliss. For, by listening attentively to the Divine Word, focusing and reflecting upon it, and understanding and imbibing its essence in one's 'Hirdā', all their innate evil tendencies and their consequent sufferings just vanish.

In essence, by gradually listening attentively to the Divine Word, focusing and reflecting upon it, and attuning to 'Nām(u)', a mere mortal can reach the lofty spiritual heights. Perception of one's vulnerabilities to 'Māyā' and their essential preventative safeguards become increasingly transparent, one's innate nature and the characteristics of one's conscious self begin to align closely with 'Nām-consciousness'; and the esoteric Divine Wisdom and Knowledge of religious texts become much more unequivocal and meaningful.

PAUṚĪ 10
ਪਉੜੀ ੧੦॥

Suṇ(i)ai, sat(u), saṅtokh(u), giān(u).
ਸੁਣਿਐ, ਸਤੁ, ਸੰਤੋਖੁ, ਗਿਆਨੁ॥

Suṇ(i)ai, aṭhsaṭh(i) kā isnān(u).
ਸੁਣਿਐ, ਅਠਸਠਿ ਕਾ ਇਸਨਾਨੁ॥

Suṇ(i)ai, paṛ(i) paṛ(i) pāvah(i) mān(u).
ਸੁਣਿਐ, ਪੜਿ ਪੜਿ ਪਾਵਹਿ ਮਾਨੁ॥

Suṇ(i)ai, lāgai sahaj(i) dhiān(u).
ਸੁਣਿਐ, ਲਾਗੈ ਸਹਜਿ ਧਿਆਨੁ॥

Nānak, bhagtā sadā vigās(u).
ਨਾਨਕ, ਭਗਤਾ ਸਦਾ ਵਿਗਾਸੁ॥

Suṇ(i)ai, dūkh, pāp kā nās(u). 10.
ਸੁਣਿਐ, ਦੂਖ, ਪਾਪ ਕਾ ਨਾਸੁ॥ ੧੦॥

Suṇ(i)ai, sat(u), saṅtokh(u), giān(u)

suṇ(i)ai: see 'Pauṛī' 8, page 137.

sat(u): (a) (n, m; synonymous with 'uchā-' and/or 'suchā-' 'ācharn'; 'pat(i)bartā-' or 'istrī-bartā-' 'dharam') high moral character, chastity and faithfulness, and implicit here is (b) (n, m; synonymous with 'hathoṅ chhadaṇ-' and 'dān deṇ-' 'di prakiryā'; 'dān') an act of charity, munificence or largesse.

saṅtokh(u): (a) (n; synonymous with 'prasaṅtā' and 'anaṅd') happiness, pleasure, and spiritual bliss or peace, and implicit here is (b) (n, m, s; synonymous with 'sabar', 'lobh dā tiāg', 'rajj', 'tripat(i)' and 'shāṅtī') literally, contentment or satisfaction, patience, peace or calm, and (c) (synonymous with 'ātmak aḍoltā' or 'Sahaj') lasting inner poise or equanimity.

giān(u): (n, m, s) (a) (synonymous with 'bodh', 'ilam' and 'samajh') knowledge, insight, comprehension, or intelligence, (b) (synonymous with 'vivek' or 'bibek') intuitive insight and knowledge of moral, ethical and spiritual correctness or godliness, and (c) (synonymous with 'tat(u)-', ‘ruhānī-’ or ‘brahm-’ ‘giān(u)’; ‘ruhānī-’ ‘jāgratā’ or ‘sojhī’) spiritual/divine knowledge; an understanding of the Divine Will and true Path; realisation or perception of the eternal Reality.

By listening attentively to the Divine Word, focusing and reflecting upon it, and understanding and imbibing its essence in one’s ‘Hirdā’, and attuning to ‘Nām(u)’, one becomes both charitable and contented, and gains Divine Wisdom and Knowledge.

Suṇ(i)ai, aṭhsaṭh(i) kā isnān(u)

aṭhsaṭh(i): (adj) literally, ‘aṭh’ (8) + ‘saṭh’ (60) i.e., sixty-eight (68). However, implicit here is all the holy places (‘Tīraths’) as this number varies in different Hindu ‘Graṅths’.

kā: (prep, m; synonymous with ‘dā’) of.

isnān(u): (n, m; synonymous with ‘n(h)āuṇā’, ‘majjan(u)’ and (arab) ‘gusal’) ablutions or bathing. However, the reference here is to ritual ablutions at holy places of pilgrimage (‘Tīraths’) to wash away one’s sins. Gurmat does not give any credence to such ritualistic acts and instead lays emphasis on cleansing oneself of the filth of false pride and the evil streak of one’s conscious self by aligning with ‘Nām(u)’ and ‘Nām-consciousness’. The following verses of the SGGS allude to the futility of actions undertaken in the name of one’s faith which fail to cleanse one’s inner evil streak or to bring about any changes within one’s ‘Hirdā’:

The filth of false pride and the evil streak of one’s conscious self is not washed away with ritual ablutions at the approved sixty-eight holy places.[343]

Countless Sādhūs listened attentively to and uttered verses from the Vedās and the Purānās in vain and resigned in defeat; countless others, having adopted various garbs and performed ablutions at numerous holy places, abandoned their pursuit feeling dejected and tired. Just focus your conscious self faithfully on the one Lord who is immaculate and eternal.[344]

Misguided and confused, they engage in ritual ablutions but experience failure and disgrace as it does not wash away the filth of their sins and evil ‘vikārī’ streak.[345]

By listening attentively to the Divine Word, focusing and reflecting upon it, and understanding and imbibing its essence in one's 'Hirdā', and attuning to 'Nām(u)', one gets the equivalence of bathing at sixty-eight holy places.

Suṇ(i)ai, paṛ(i) paṛ(i) pāvah(i) mān(u)

paṛ(i): (indeclinable past participle or perfect participle - 'pūran pūrab kārdaṅtak'; synonymous with 'paṛ ke') see paṛnā.

paṛ(i) paṛ(i): (indeclinable past participle or perfect participle - 'pūran pūrab kārdaṅtak'; synonymous with 'vidyā paṛ paṛ ke') literally, by or having read and studied religious texts or gained worldly education.

paṛnā: (v) literally, to read, recite, study or learn.

pāvah(i): (v, pl, present tense, third person; synonymous with 'uh pāuṅde han'; pronounced as 'pāvaheṅ') they achieve or acquire. See pāvah(i) and pāuṇā (a and b).

mān(u): (a) (v, s, imperative mood - 'hukmī bhvikht', second person; synonymous with 'māno') see maṅnaṇā, (b) (n, m; synonymous with 'abhimān' and 'garūr') vanity, pride, conceit or arrogance, and implicit here is (c) (n, m; synonymous with 'māṇ(u)', 'sanmān', 'ādar', 'satkār', 'izzat', 'ābrū' and 'pratishṭā') respect, self-respect, accolade, esteem, meritorial status or honour.

By listening attentively to the Divine Word, focusing and reflecting upon it, and understanding and imbibing its essence in one's 'Hirdā', and attuning to 'Nām(u)', they achieve accolades equivalent to that of scholars.

Suṇ(i)ai, lāgai sahaj(i) dhiān(u)

lāgai: (a) (v, s, imperative mood - 'hukmī bhvikht', first person; synonymous with 'lag jāve'), and implicit here is (b) (v, s, present tense, third person; synonymous with 'lag jāṅdā hai'; 'lagdā-' or 'lagdī-' 'hai') affects or takes effect. See lagaṇā or lāgaṇā (b, c and e).

lāgaṇā: (v; synonymous with 'lagaṇā') (a) (synonymous with 'mahsūs karnā', 'chhūhṇā', 'lagāuṇā' and 'malnā') to feel, attach, affix, apply, touch or stick, (b) (synonymous with 'shurū karnā') to begin to do something, (c) (synonymous with 'asar hoṇā') to take effect, (d) (synonymous with 'rishtā-' or 'saṅbaṅdh-' 'hoṇā') to be related, and (e) as a prefix or suffix with a verb or noun indicative of the effect of the verb, e.g., 'dhiān(u) lāgaṇā' - to focus on and become totally immersed in an object or concept.

sahaj(i): (a) (adv; synonymous with 's(v)bhāvik' and 'kudratī') instinctively, naturally or intuitively, (b) (adv; synonymous with 'haule haule') gradually, slowly or step by step, (c) (instrumental case - 'karaṇ kārak'; synonymous with 'dhīraj-' and 'shāntī-' 'nāl') patiently and peacefully, and implicit here is (d) (locative case - 'adhikaraṇ kārak'; synonymous with 'shudh sarūp ātmā de aḍol subhāu vich') in a state of lasting inner equanimity. See sahaj (i) and sahaj.

dhiān(u): (n, m, s; synonymous with '*man* vich surat(i) nāl chiṅtan' and 'surat-' or 'birtī-' 'dā ṭikāu') the stilling and focusing of one's wandering mind on the attributes of only one thing in preference to all else, e.g., the eternal 'Nām(u)'.

lāge sahaj(i) dhiān(u): [one] becomes focused and totally immersed (lāge) in a state of deep reflection ('dhiān(u)') and inner equipoise and tranquility ('sahaj(i)').

By listening attentively to the Divine Word, focusing and reflecting upon it, and understanding and imbibing its essence in one's 'Hirdā', and attuning to 'Nām(u)', one becomes deeply reflective and transfixed in a state of lasting inner equipoise.

Nānak, bhagtā sadā vigās(u). See 'Pauṛī' 8
Suṇ(i)ai, dūkh, pāp kā nās(u). See 'Pauṛī' 8

Conceptual summary

By listening attentively to the Divine Word, focusing and reflecting upon it, and understanding and imbibing its essence in one's 'Hirdā', and attuning to 'Nām(u)', a mere mortal can: (a) become both charitable and contented, and gain Divine Wisdom and Knowledge, (b) get the equivalence of bathing at sixty-eight holy places, (c) achieve accolades normally accorded to academics and scholars, and (d) easily become deeply reflective and transfixed in a state of lasting inner equipoise.

His 'Bhagats' are forever in a state of inner bliss. For, by listening attentively to the Divine Word, focusing and reflecting upon it, and understanding and imbibing its essence in one's 'Hirdā', all their innate evil tendencies and their consequent sufferings just vanish.

PAUṚĪ 11
ਪਉੜੀ ੧੧॥

Suṇ(i)ai, sarā guṇā ke gāh.
ਸੁਣਿਐ, ਸਰਾ ਗੁਣਾ ਕੇ ਗਾਹ॥

Suṇ(i)ai, sekh, pīr, pāt(i)sāh.
ਸੁਣਿਐ, ਸੇਖ, ਪੀਰ, ਪਾਤਿਸਾਹ॥

Suṇ(i)ai, aṅdhe pāvah(i) rāh(u).
ਸੁਣਿਐ, ਅੰਧੇ ਪਾਵਹਿ ਰਾਹੁ॥

Suṇ(i)ai, hāth hovai asgāh(u).
ਸੁਣਿਐ, ਹਾਥ ਹੋਵੈ ਅਸਗਾਹੁ॥

Nānak, bhagtā sadā vigās(u).
ਨਾਨਕ, ਭਗਤਾ ਸਦਾ ਵਿਗਾਸੁ॥

Suṇ(i)ai, dūkh, pāp kā nās(u). 11.
ਸੁਣਿਐ, ਦੂਖ, ਪਾਪ ਕਾ ਨਾਸੁ॥ ੧੧॥

Suṇ(i)ai, sarā guṇā ke gāh

suṇ(i)ai: see 'Pauṛī' 8, page 137.

sarā: (a) (n, f; abbrev for 'shrāb') literally, liquor or intoxicating spirit, (b) (n, m; synonymous with 'ghar') home/house, (c) (n, m; synonymous with 'musāphar khānā'; pronounced as 'sarāṅ') literally, an inn or a waiting room, (d) ((arab); synonymous with 'shr-a') straight path, (e) (n, f; synonymous with 'dharam dī maryādā') literally, code of religious practice/tradition, (f) (n, pl; synonymous with 'sarovars', 'jhīlāṅ', 'samuṅdars' or 'sāgars') large tanks, lakes or oceans implicit here is (g) (genitive case - 'saṅbaṅdh kārak', pl; synonymous with 'sarāṅ de'; pronounced as 'sarāṅ') literally, of 'sar' or 'sarovars' or codes of accepted religious practice. See sar (j).

guṇā: (a) (n, m, pl; pronounced as 'guṇāṅ') and implicit here is (b) (genitive case - 'saṅbaṅdh kārak'; synonymous with 'guṇā de') of guṇ. See guṇ(u).

guṇ(u): (synonymous with 'visheshaṇ', 'siphat', 'khūbī', 'khāsīat', 'lachhaṇ', 'subhāu' or 'tāsīr') literally, the characteristics, properties or attributes of something. However, the tacit reference here is to the attributes, values, virtues or Glory of 'Nām(u)'.

ke: (prep, m; synonymous with 'de') of.

gāh: (a) (n, f; skt; synonymous with 'gaṅmbhīrtā' or 'ḍuṅghiāī') seriousness, solemnity or gravity; depth, (b) (n, f; pers; synonymous with 'jag(h)ā' or 'thāṅ') place, location or position, (c) (n, m; synonymous with 'maslan-' or 'kuchlan-' 'dī kriyā' and 'gāhuṇā') the act of trampling, crushing or threshing, (d) (n, m; synonymous with 'grahaṇ-' or 'aṅgīkār-' 'karan dī kriyā') acceptance of an offering; real comprehension or grasp of an issue, and implicit here is (e) (adj; synonymous with 'sūjh-' or 'samjhaṇ-' 'vāle') they who have truly grasped and understood the issue or problem, and (f) (n, m, pl; synonymous with 'gāhak', 'kharīdār' and 'vākaph') customers, buyers or seekers; well acquainted or aware of.

By listening attentively to the Divine Word, focusing and reflecting upon it, and understanding and imbibing its essence in one's 'Hirdā', and attuning to 'Nām(u)', one becomes well-acquainted with and truly knowledgeable about the Ocean of Virtues, 'Nām(u)'. Or:

By listening attentively to the Divine Word, focusing and reflecting upon it, and understanding and imbibing its essence in one's 'Hirdā', and attuning to 'Nām(u)', one truly begins to seek the Fount or Ocean of Virtues, 'Nām(u)'.

Suṇ(i)ai, sekh, pīr, pāt(i)sāh

sekh: (synonymous with and pronounced as 'sheikh') (a) (n, m, s; synonymous with 'shesh nāg') mythological serpent of the Hindu 'Purānas' with one thousand heads, king of serpents and the netherworlds, and one who guards Lord Vishnu with its expanded and hooded neck, (b) (n, m, pl; synonymous with 'jāt(i) toṅ patit hoi brāhmanā dī aulād') progeny of Brahmins who converted to Islam, and implicit here is (c) (n. m, pl) Muslim chiefs or dignitaries, (d) (n, m, pl; synonymous with 'buḍhā' and 'bazurg') respected elderly men, and (e) (n, m, pl; synonymous with 'vidvān') Muslim scholars.

pīr: (a) (n, m, pl; pers; synonymous with 'buḍhā', 'birdh', 'kamzor' and 'bazurg') respectable old and frail men, and implicit here is (b) (n, m, pl; synonymous with 'aulīyā') Muslim religious or spiritual teachers, or holy men.

pāt(i)sāh: (n, m, pl; synonymous with 'pādshāh' and 'bādshāh'and pronounced as 'pātshāh') a complex word comprising 'pāt' + 'sāh'. Literally, Lord Protector and Lord of the imperial throne, i.e., a king. See pāt(i)sāh.

However, implicit here is the status of kings or eternal kings ('sachche pāt(i)sāh') - they who have realised 'Nām(u)' - the source of all attributes, knowledge, wisdom, wealth and power.

By listening attentively to the Divine Word, focusing and reflecting upon it, and understanding and imbibing its essence in one's 'Hirdā', and attuning with 'Nām(u)', one acquires the status and glory of sheikhs, pīrs and kings.

Suṇ(i)ai, aṅdhe pāvah(i) rāh(u)

aṅdhe: (adj, m, pl) (a) synonymous with 'aṅne' and 'netrhīn') literally, blind men, and implicit here is (b) (nominative case - 'kartā kārak'; synonymous with 'agiānī' and 'vichārhīn') literally, stupid, ignorant or lacking worldly and especially, spiritual knowledge, wisdom, and the power of deductive reasoning.

pāvah(i): (v, pl, present tense, third person; synonymous with 'uh pāuṅde han'; pronounced as 'pāvaheṅ') see pāvah(i) and pāuṇā (a and b).

rāh(u): (a) (n, m, s; synonymous with 'tarikā' or 'ḍhaṅg') way, technique or method, and (b) (n, m, s; synonymous with 'mārag', 'rastā' or 'paṅth') literally, the way or path. However, implicit here is the moral, ethical and spiritual path that leads to 'Nām-realisation'. See rāh(u).

By listening attentively to the Divine Word, focusing and reflecting upon it, and understanding and imbibing its essence in one's 'Hirdā', and attuning to 'Nām(u)', even the ignorant find the sublime path to 'Nām-consciousness'.

Suṇ(i)ai, hāth hovai asgāh(u)

hāth: (a) (n, m; synonymous with 'sahārā' and 'āsrā') aid, support, refuge or succour, (b) (n, m, pl; synonymous with 'hath', 'kar', 'dast' and 'hast') hands, (c) (n, m, pl; synonymous with 'chappū') literally, oars, and implicit here is (d) (n, m; synonymous with 'thāh'; 'ḍuṅghiāī-' or 'gahrāī-' 'dā thallā' or 'aṅt') literally, the base, bottom or nadir of depth, and (e) (n, f; synonymous with 'ḍuṅghiāī-' or 'gahrāī-' dī sojhī') an understanding of the depth involved.

hovai: (v, s; present tense, third person; synonymous with 'ho jāṅdā/jāṅdī hai') occurs, becomes or comes to be. See hovai and 'hovṇā'.

hāth hovai: is a phrase that literally denotes that one gets the measure of the depth. However, implicit here is that one really gets to understand the immense complexity of this material world, its comforts, and pleasures, how easily one gets entrapped in it, and how difficult it is to escape from this world-ocean ('Saṅsār Samuṅdar' or 'Bhavsāgar').

asgāh(u): (adj; synonymous with 'agādh' and 'athāh') literally, boundless, unfathomable or bottomless. However, implicit here is the depth or complexity of this world, world-stage or world-ocean ('Saṅsār Samuṅdar' or 'Bhavsāgar').

By listening attentively to the Divine Word, focusing and reflecting upon it, and understanding and imbibing its essence in one's 'Hirdā', and attuning to 'Nām(u)', one fathoms the mystery and complexity of this empirical world and finds the sublime path to 'Nām-consciousness'.

Nānak, bhagtā sadā vigās(u). see 'Pauṛī' 8
Suṇ(i)ai, dūkh, pāp kā nās(u). see 'Pauṛī' 8.

Conceptual summary

By listening attentively to the Divine Word, focusing and reflecting upon it, and understanding and imbibing its essence in one's 'Hirdā', and attuning to 'Nām(u)', a mere mortal: (a) becomes cognisant and a true seeker of the Ocean of Virtues, 'Nām(u)', (b) acquires the status and glory of sheikhs, pīrs and kings, (c) and even the most ignorant find the sublime path to 'Nām-consciousness', and (d) fathoms the mystery and complexity of this empirical world - its inescapable charm, its potential for entrapment in its web, and, more importantly, the way out of it.

His 'Bhagats' are forever in a state of inner bliss. For, by listening attentively to the Divine Word, focusing and reflecting upon it, and understanding and imbibing its essence in one's 'Hirdā', all their innate evil tendencies and their consequent sufferings just vanish.

PAUṚĪ 12
ਪਉੜੀ ੧੨॥

Maṅne kī gat(i), kahī n jāi.
ਮੰਨੇ ਕੀ ਗਤਿ, ਕਹੀ ਨ ਜਾਇ॥

Je ko kahai, pichhai pachhutāi.
ਜੇ ਕੋ ਕਹੈ, ਪਿਛੈ ਪਛੁਤਾਇ॥

Kāgad(i), kalam, n likhaṇhār(u).
ਕਾਗਦਿ, ਕਲਮ, ਨ ਲਿਖਣਹਾਰੁ॥

Maṅne kā, bah(i) karan(i) vīchār(u).
ਮੰਨੇ ਕਾ, ਬਹਿ ਕਰਨਿ ਵੀਚਾਰੁ॥

Aisā, Nām(u) niraṅjan(u) hoi.
ਐਸਾ ਨਾਮੁ ਨਿਰੰਜਨੁ ਹੋਇ॥

Je ko, maṅn(i) jāṇai, *man*(i) koi. 12.
ਜੇ ਕੋ ਮੰਨਿ ਜਾਣੈ ਮਨਿ ਕੋਇ॥ ੧੨॥

Maṅne kī gat(i), kahī n jāi

maṅne: (past participle - 'bhūt kirdaṅt'; synonymous with 'maṅnaṇ-' or 'yakīn kar laiṇ-' 'vālā' and 'patījiā hoiā') literally, one who has submitted to the Gurū's Divine Word and Wisdom lovingly, willingly and unreservedly, deliberated over it and imbibed its essence in one's 'Hirdā' with absolute faith and conviction, striven to attune perfectly to 'Nām(u)' and to live by 'Nām-consciousness'. Gradually, the process becomes spontaneous or automatic ('ajappā jāp') and one achieves perfect harmony with 'Nām(u)' and 'Nām-consciousness'. See maṅnaṇā.

For some, it is not easy to believe what they cannot see or grasp with their senses, but, with faith in their 'messenger of God', others submit to his wisdom, strive to live by God's Will, and hope to find lasting inner equanimity and bliss in this life, and to contribute positively to the wider world. The following verses from the SGGS succinctly and clearly endorse this view:

Yearning to see the eternal Reality doesn't arise easily when objective visualisation is beyond one's scope. On the contrary, the visible empirical world, though short-lived and perishable, is attractive and enticing .[346]

One who forsakes 'Nām(u)', faces a myriad of impediments, and thus dejected, feels condemned to lament like a crow in a deserted house.[347]

Those who have listened attentively to 'Nām(u)'and resolutely believed in It, cease to stray and wander in the material world, and remain focused on 'Nām(u)' within their conscious self ('Hirdā').[348]

I am ever ready to lay down my life for those who, having listened attentively, believe resolutely and have faith in 'Nām(u)'.[349]

The devotion of those who submit to and faithfully follow the Guru's Divine Word willingly, lovingly and unreservedly, bears fruit in God's eyes.[350]

The essence of Divine Knowledge is revealed in the conscious self of whosoever has faithfully aligned with 'Nām(u)' in his 'Hirdā'.[351]

One gets lasting inner bliss and finds release from one's innate evil nature in this lifetime and transmigration at death if one's conscious self submits to and resonates with 'Nām(u)'.[352]

One loses innate wickedness, 'Haumaiṅ' and all one's maladies, and gains spiritual wisdom if one's conscious self submits to and resonates with 'Nām(u)'.[353]

Noble attributes begin to shine in one's conscious self and one attains lasting inner equanimity and bliss if one's conscious self submits to and resonates with 'Nām(u)'.[354]

One's inner focus (surat(i)) on 'Nām(u)' and one's intellect (mat(i)) reaches a higher plane if one's conscious self submits to and resonates with 'Nām(u)'.[355]

kī: (prep, f; synonymous with 'dī') of or belonging to.

maṅne kī: (synonymous with 'maṅn or yakīn kar laiṇ vāle dī' and 'patīje hoi dī') literally, who have accepted with absolute faith and conviction.

gat(i): (n, f; synonymous with 'ruhānī-' 'hālat', 'avasthā', 'dashā' or 'darjā') one's inner or spiritual state, status or rank, with 'Sahaj' or 'Anaṅd' being the highest status or rank of spirituality. See gat(i).

kahī: (a) (n, f, s; synonymous with 'kasī) a spade, (b) (pron; adj; synonymous with 'kisī') any, anyone or someone, (c) (adv; synonymous with 'kahīṅ' or 'kise thāṅ'; pronounced as 'kahīṅ') anywhere or somewhere, and implicit here is (d) (v, s, present tense, third person; synonymous with 'kathan kītī-' or 'ākhī-' 'ja sakdī hai') can be stated, uttered or described. See kahiṇā.

n: (p; pronounced as 'nāṅ') no, not or implying a negative connotation.

jāi: (conj v) e.g., (i) 'n jāi lakhiā' - cannot be ascertained or realised, (ii) 'ghāṭ(i) n jāi' - [His status] does not suffer or shrink, (iii) 'pāiā jāi' ('prāpat kīā jā sakdā hai') - can be achieved or realised, and (iv) 'ākhiā-' or 'kahī-' 'n jāi' - cannot be stated, described or elaborated. See jāi.

When one has deliberated over the Guru's Divine Word and Wisdom and then submitted to it lovingly, willingly and unreservedly, imbibed it with conviction in one's 'Hirdā', and striven to attune perfectly to 'Nām(u)' and live by 'Nām-consciousness', one's inner state or spiritual status cannot be conjured up and put into words.

Je ko kahai, pichhai pachhutāi

je: (conj; synonymous with 'je kar', 'yadī' and 'agar') if or in case.

ko: (pron; abbrev for and synonymous with 'koī') someone, anyone or another; many or several.

kahai: (a) (v, s, present tense, third person; synonymous with 'ākhdā hai-' and 'varṇan-' 'or 'vakhyān-' 'kardā hai') speaks, utters or sings His Glory, and implicit here is (b) (v, s, third person, imperative mood - 'saṅbhāv bhvikht kāl - kiās and sharat bodhak'; synonymous with 'biān-' or 'vakhyān-' 'kare bhī') were to express, utter or elaborate. See kahiṇā.

pichhai: (pronounced as 'pichhchhai') (adv; synonymous with 'pichhoṅ', 'magroṅ', and 'samān bīt jāṇ bād') literally, later, thereafter, afterwards or subsequently. See pichhai.

pachhutāi: (a) (indeclinable past participle or perfect participle - 'pūran pūrab kārdaṅtak'; synonymous with 'pachhutā ke') having regretted, and implicit here is (b) (v, s, present tense, third person; synonymous with 'pachhutāuṅdā hai') see pachhutāuṇā.

pachhutāuṇā: (v, m; synonymous with 'paschātāv-' or 'praschit-' 'karnā') to regret, repent, feel remorse, atone or expiate one's misdeeds or failure to achieve one's objective/s.

If one dares to define it, one would subsequently regret having miserably failed to achieve one's objective.

Kāgad(i), kalam, n likhaṇhār(u)

kāgad(i): (locative case - 'adhikaraṇ kārak'; synonymous with 'kāgaz uppar') literally, on paper. See kāgad.

kāgad: (n, m; synonymous with 'kāgaz') paper or a sheet of paper.

kalam: (n, f; synonymous with 'lekhaṇī') literally, a pen.

likhaṇhār(u): (adj; 'kartarī-vāchak kirdaṅt'; synonymous with 'likh sakan vālā' or 'likhārī') a complex word comprising 'likhaṇ' (to write, inscribe or note down) + 'hār' (synonymous with 'vān', 'vaṅt' or 'vālā'- one who undertakes the activity) i.e., a writer, scribe or calligraphist. However, implicit here is a scholar, philosopher, or a theologian.

The literal interpretation of this verse would be: 'no scholar could capture/conjure up that state and explain it in words with a pen and paper'.

See next verse/pankat(i).

Maṅne kā, bah(i) karan(i) vīchār(u)

kā: (prep, m; synonymous with 'dā') of.

bah(i): (indeclinable past participle or perfect participle - 'pūran pūrab kārdaṅtak'; synonymous with 'baiṭh ke') literally, whilst seated or sitting down. In essence, it refers to having settled down to take a collective decision.

karan(i): (v, pl, present tense, third person; synonymous with 'karde han') literally, undertake or perform an action or a task. See karnā (g).

vīchār(u): (a) (n, m; synonymous with 'anumān' and 'aṅdāzā') estimate, guess or conjecture, and (b) (n, f; synonymous with 'vivek', 'tatv dā nirṇā' or 'aslīyat jāṇan dī kriyā') study, reflection, deliberation, cogitation or speculation. See vīchār(u).

Some resolve to speculate and ponder over their exalted status and attempt to describe the enlightened and blissful state of their 'Man' but none succeeds in defining and capturing that with a pen and paper.

Aisā, Nām(u) niraṅjan(u) hoi

aisā: (adj, m; synonymous with 'ajehā' or 'is prakār dā') like, similar to or resembling this.

Nām(u): (n, m, s) refers to the immanent form of the transcendent God. This one word alone encompasses all the known and unknown attributes of this immanent form of God.

niraṅjan(u): (adj) compound word comprising 'nir' (without or lacking) + 'aṅjan' (collyrium'/'surmā' but fig. 'Vikārs' or 'Māyā'; synonymous with 'aṅjan rahit' or 'māyā toṅ nirlep') i.e., untainted, spotless, flawless or immaculate- in essence, an attribute of God.

hoi: (v, s, present tense; synonymous with 'huṅdī-' or 'hundā-' 'hai'; 'ho jāndī-' or 'ho jāndā-' 'hai'; 'ho sakdā hai') literally, is; occurs, comes to be, or becomes; can occur, happen or become. See hoi.

Such is the Power and Glory of the immaculate 'Nām(u)'...

Je ko, maṅn(i) jāṇai, *man*(i) koi

maṅn(i): (a) (n, m; synonymous with '*man* vich') in one's conscious self, 'Hirdā' or 'Jīvātmāṅ'; the 'tippī' (ṅ) is there solely to increase the 'mātrā', and implicit here is (b) (indeclinable past participle or perfect participle - 'pūran pūrab kārdaṅtak'; synonymous with 'shradhā nāl maṅn ke'; 'shradhā nāl aṅgikār-' or 'manzūr-' 'kar ke') having firmly and unreservedly accepted. See maṅnaṇā.

jāṇai: (v, s, imperative mood - 'saṅbhāv bhvikht kāl - sharat bodhak', third person; synonymous with 'jāṇ lave') see jāṇanā (c and d). However, the reference here is to have absolute faith in and become attuned perfectly to 'Nām(u)'.

maṅn(i) jāṇai: (v, s, imperative mood - 'saṅbhāv bhvikht kāl - sharat bodhak', third person; synonymous with 'pakkā yakīn kar ke jāṇ lave') if one were truly to comprehend the Guru's divine word and message ('Nām-consciousness and 'Nām(u)') and accept it unreservedly and absolutely faithfully, only then could one cleanse one's conscious self of the filth of 'Haumaiṅ', 'Moh' and innate 'Vikārī' tendencies - collectively called 'Māyā', and eventually uplift oneself to realise 'Sahaj' and 'Anaṅd', the apex position in spiritual evolution, according to Gurmat.

man(i): (locative case - 'adhikaraṇ kārak; synonymous with '*man* vich') in one's conscious self, 'Hirdā' or 'Jīvātmāṅ'. See '*man*(u)'.

man(u): (n, m, s) conscious self, 'Hirdā' or 'Jīvātmāṅ'. The commonly used English word 'mind' comes closer to part of the definition of '*Man*' which Gurmat defines as follows: 'O' '*Man*' Thou art the very spark of the

Divine Light; recognise thy essence as such'.[370] '*Man*' (conscious self) is one's centre of consciousness itself, which, in reality, is a partial and functional expression of the Primal Soul ('Parmātmāṅ') within the body. It is also, therefore, described as 'Jīvātmāṅ', and conscious self. '*Man*' and 'Hirdā' are its other commonly used synonyms in Gurbānī.

Gurmat characterises '*Man*' as the ultimate inner sensorimotor organ which orchestrates all our external sensorimotor organs. Its four functional aspects are: '*Man*', the seat of constant and spontaneous generation of ideas ('Saṅkalps') and counter ideas ('Vikalps'), and hence forever fickle and flirtatious ('chaṅchal'), with its three other components: (i) one's innate nature, attention and focus ('Surat(i)', 'Chit' and ('Dhiān'), (ii) knowledge or wisdom of this world ('Mat(i)'), and (iii) one's seat of 'bibek' - the ability to deliberate, discriminate and discern or the power of deductive reasoning ('Budh(i)'). To deliberate and contemplate ('Chiṅtan karnā') and the ability to restrain one's wandering mind and completely transfix on something are also functions ascribed to 'Chit'. See *Man*.

One's 'Jīvātmāṅ' is constitutively of the same lineage as the Primal Soul ('Nām(u)') but not its true functional replica or surrogate. This aspect is beautifully captured in the following verse of the SGGS:

'O' '*Man*'! 'Thou art the very spark of the Divine Light; 'recognise thy essence as such'.[12]

It is one's centre of consciousness, which is a partial and functional expression of the Primal Soul within the body. It is also, therefore, described as one's conscious self, and both '*Man*' and 'Hirdā' are its other commonly used synonyms in Gurbānī. 'Saṅskārs' (indelible imprints of one's repeated thoughts, speech and deeds on the conscious self), secondary to one's 'Haumaiṅ', 'Moh' and innate 'Vikārī' tendencies, accumulated during our present and past lives, somehow accompany us in our next life and cause a hindrance in the process of the complete functional expression of the Primal Soul according to Divine Order ('Hukam(u)'). Hence, for this reason, it is referred to as 'Jīvātmāṅ', '*Man*', 'Hirdā', or 'Aṅtahkaran' when it is present in a body.

One's goal of becoming a 'Sachiār' and the process of spiritual purification or evolution involves fashioning one's '*Man*' and its other functional aspects - 'Surat(i)', '*Mat*(i)' and 'Budh(i)', and ridding oneself of the corrupting baggage of our 'Saṅskārs', thus permitting a perfect expression of the Primal Soul within one's body. In this state, 'Jīvātmāṅ' is 'nirmal' 'Jīvātmāṅ' - a complete functional replica or a surrogate of the Primal Soul, and it (conscious self, '*Man*' or 'Hirdā') realises or perceives the true nature of its 'self' and experiences the full glow of the Primal Soul.

koi: (a) (pron; synonymous with 'koī virlā' or 'ik adhā') rarely or an occasional someone, and (b) (pron; synonymous with 'koī') anyone, someone or certain.

...that if one accepts the Guru's Divine Word ('Nām(u)') and Wisdom faithfully, submits to it willingly, lovingly and unreservedly, and lives by 'Nām-consciousness', one, too, can cleanse the filth of 'Māyā', reach lofty spiritual heights, become spiritually immaculate, and realise the full glow of 'Nām(u)' within one's conscious self ('Man' or 'Hirdā').

Conceptual summary

The enlightened and blissful inner state and the lofty spiritual status of one who submits lovingly, willingly and unreservedly to the Guru's Divine Word and Wisdom, imbibes them with conviction in one's 'Hirdā', strives to attune perfectly to 'Nām(u)' and live by 'Nām-consciousness', just cannot be conjured up and put into words. Should one dare to attempt to do so, one would invariably fail miserably and later come to regret it as the task would turn out to be beyond one's scope and ability. Nonetheless, many wise and erudite men accept the challenge and resolve to capture and transcribe the enlightened state and the exalted status of such a person with pen and paper but fail to do so.

Such is the Power and Glory of the immaculate 'Nām(u) that if one faithfully accepts and submits to the Guru's Divine Word ('Nām(u)') and Wisdom, submits willingly, lovingly and unreservedly to it, and lives by 'Nām-consciousness', one, too, can reach lofty spiritual heights, cleanse the filth of 'Māyā', become spiritually immaculate, and realise the full glow of 'Nām(u)' within one's conscious self ('*Man*' or 'Hirdā').

PAUṚĪ 13
ਪਉੜੀ ੧੩॥

Maṅnai, surat(i) hovai, *man*(i) budh(i).
ਮੰਨੈ, ਸੁਰਤਿ ਹੋਵੈ, ਮਨਿ ਬੁਧਿ॥

Maṅnai, sagal bhavaṇ kī sudh(i).
ਮੰਨੈ, ਸਗਲ ਭਵਣ ਕੀ ਸੁਧਿ॥

Maṅnai, muh(i) choṭā na khāi.
ਮੰਨੈ, ਮੁਹਿ ਚੋਟਾ ਨਾ ਖਾਇ॥

Maṅnai, jam kai sāth(i) na jāi.
ਮੰਨੈ, ਜਮ ਕੈ ਸਾਥਿ ਨ ਜਾਇ॥

Aisā, Nām niraṅjan(u) hoi.
ਐਸਾ ਨਾਮੁ ਨਿਰੰਜਨੁ ਹੋਇ॥

Je ko, maṅn(i) jāṇai, *man*(i) koi. 13.
ਜੇ ਕੋ ਮੰਨਿ ਜਾਣੈ ਮਨਿ ਕੋਇ॥ ੧੩॥

Maṅnai, surat(i) hovai, man(i) budh(i)

maṅnai: (a) (v, s, present tense, third person; synonymous with 'maṅndā-' or 'maṅn laiṅdā-' 'hai') literally, recognises, regards, agrees or accepts, and implicit here is (b) (instrumental case - 'karaṇ kārak; synonymous with 'maṅnaṇ-' 'nāl' or 'sadkā') with, by or by virtue of submitting to the Gurū's Divine Word and Wisdom willingly, lovingly and unreservedly, and harmonising perfectly with 'Nām(u)', and (c) (imperative mood - 'saṅbhāv bhvikht kāl - ichhā, sharat and prernā bodhak'; synonymous with 'je maṅn laīai' or 'je Nām(u) vich-' 'shradhā baṇ-' or 'lagan lag-' 'jāve') literally, if one were to submit to the Gurū's Divine Word and Wisdom willingly, lovingly and unreservedly, and harmonise perfectly with 'Nām(u)'. See maṅnaṇā.

surat(i): (a) (n, f) one of the four parts of the 'Aṅtahkaran', which deals with memory, and (b) (n, f; synonymous with 'dhiān', 'tavajjo', 'birtī', 'suchet pan' and 'vīchār') one of the four parts of '*Man*(u)' in Gurmat that relates to one's focus, attention, alertness, meditation or reflection. See 'aṅtahkaran', '*man*', and 'Pauṛī' 12, pages 165-7.

hovai: (v, s, present tense, third person; synonymous with 'ho jāṅdī/jāṅdā hai') exists, occurs or becomes. See hovai and hovṇā (a).

man(i): in one's conscious self, 'Hirdā' or 'Jivātmāṅ'. See *man* 'Pauṛī' 12, pp. 165-7.

budh(i): (a) (n, f; synonymous with 'akal', 'samajh', 'bibek' or 'bibek shakat(i)') one of the four parts of 'Aṅtahkaran' which deals with deliberation, deductive reasoning and decision making according to the Hindu 'Graṅths', and (b) one of the functions of '*Man*' in Gurmat. It is wisdom, intellect and the rational faculty that gives clarity and sharpness to one's thought and judgement, and the ability to discern right from wrong. See *man* 'Pauṛī' 12, pp. 165-7.

surat(i) hovai man(i) budh(i): one's focus shifts from that of engrossment in the material world and enjoyment of its comforts and pleasures to a more moral, ethical and spiritual way of life as one's innate propensities are challenged by one's sharpened discernment.

By submitting willingly, lovingly and unreservedly to the Gurū's Divine Word and Wisdom and aligning with 'Nām(u)', one's innate nature or focus is underpinned and modulated by the rejuvenated discernment ('bibek budhi(i)') of one's conscious self.

Maṅnai, sagal bhavaṇ kī sudh(i)

sagal: (adj; synonymous with 'sagl', 'sarv', 'sarab', 'sabh', 'sabhe', 'sāre' and 'tmām') literally, all, entire, whole or the totality of something.

bhavaṇ: (a) (n, f; synonymous with 'dishā') direction, (b) (n, m; synonymous with 'ghar') house, mansion or palace, (c) (n, f; synonymous with 'bhramaṇ', 'bhaṭkaṇā', 'chakkar', 'geṛā') a state of vacillation, indecisiveness or dubiety; misconception and/or going astray and wandering about fruitlessly, and implicit here is (d) (n, m; synonymous with 'jagat', 'desh', 'khaṅḍ') world, country or a planet, and (e) (n, m; synonymous with 'maṅḍal') planets orbiting around a big star, e.g., the solar system.

kī: (prep, f; synonymous with 'dī') of or belonging to.

sudh(i): (a) (n, f; synonymous with 'khabar', 'sudh-budh' or 'hosh') awareness, perceptiveness, alertness or presence of mind, (b) (n, f; synonymous with 'samajh', 'sūjh', 'sojhī' or 'jāṇkārī') perception, understanding or comprehension, and (c) (n, f; synonymous with 'vivek shakat(i)') rational ability or discernment; wisdom or prudence; the power of deductive reasoning.

sagal bhavaṇ kī sudh(i): literally, one becomes cognisant of the fact that the whole universe is His creation, and that He is all-pervasive.

By submitting willingly, lovingly and unreservedly to the Gurū's Divine Word and Wisdom and aligning with 'Nām(u)', one becomes cognisant of His omnipresence in the universe and His dominion over it.

Maṅnai, muh(i) choṭā n khāi

muh(i): (locative case - 'adhikaraṇ kārak'; synonymous with 'mūṅh-' 'utte' or 'uppar'; pronounced as 'mūṅh') literally, on their face. See mūh.

mūh: (n, m; pronounced as 'mūṅh') literally, mouth or face.

choṭā: (n, f, pl; synonymous with 'saṭṭāṅ', 'vār' and 'prahār'; pronounced as 'choṭāṅ') blows, strikes or injuries.

n: (p; pronounced as 'nāṅ') no, not or implying a negative connotation.

khāi: (a) (indeclinable past participle or perfect participle - 'pūran pūrab kārdaṅtak'; synonymous with 'khā ke'), and implicit here is (b) (v, s, present tense, third person; synonymous with 'khāṅdā hai') see khāṇā (c (i)).

muh(i) choṭā khāṇā: literally, to be hit or slapped on the face. In essence, it is to suffer or endure punishment, disgrace and humiliation. 'As you sow, so shall you reap' is one of the well-known tenets of Gurmat as well as a generally accepted aphorism. Ignorance, misconception, dubiety and egotism ('Haumaiṅ') and innate 'Vikārī' tendencies ('Māyā') drive one towards the material world and self-fulfillment, and away from godliness or 'Nām-consciousness'. Thus, entrapped by 'Māyā', one commits misdeeds and sins, and suffers the consequences.

By submitting willingly, lovingly and unreservedly to the Gurū's Divine Word and Wisdom and aligning with 'Nām(u)', one avoids the suffering, disgrace and humiliation secondary to one's innate evil nature.

Maṅnai, jam kai sāth(i) n jāi

jam: (n, m, s) literally, 'Yama' (the 'angel of death' in Hindu mythology). It is the commonly held belief that his envoys ('dūts') unceremoniously drag away to hell the souls of individuals steeped in sin or misdeeds. However, the implication here is to 'Haumaiṅ', 'Moh' and 'Vikārs' ('Māyā') whose adverse influence makes one commit sins or misdeeds, thus becoming the cause of one's spiritual downfall or spiritual death. The end result is suffering in every way, both here and in the hereafter, as one remains bound to the cycle of birth and death, which is equivalent to living life in hell. (u) of 'jam(u)' is missing because of the preposition 'kai' and 'sāth(i)' that links it with the verb 'jāi'.

kai: (prep; synonymous with 'kā', 'ke', 'kī', 'dā', 'de' or 'dī') of.

sāth(i): (prep; synonymous with 'saṅg(i)' and 'nāl') with or by your side; in the company of.

jāi: (a) (v, s, present tense, third person; synonymous with 'chale jāṅdā/jāṅdī hai') departs or goes, (b) (conj v) e.g., (i) 'n jāi lakhiā' - cannot be ascertained or realised, (ii) 'ghāṭ(i) n jāi': [His status] does not suffer or shrink, (iii) 'pāiā jāi'- ('prāpat kitā jā sakdā hai') can be achieved or realised, (iv) 'ākhiā n jāi' - cannot be stated, described or elaborated, and (v) 'sāth(i) n jāi' - does not go or accompany someone. See jāi and jāṇā (d).

jam kai sāth(i) jāṇā: literally, to accompany or go with 'Jams'. However, the reference here is to be dragged unceremoniously by the envoys of 'Yama' for sentencing and punishment by 'Dharamrāj' according to the Divine Order. This is a popularly held belief amongst the followers of Hinduism. However, as alluded to above, Gurmat does not support and endorse this view. To be at the mercy of 'Yama' really implies suffering the consequences of one's misdeeds here and, failing judgement at God's Court, having to wander in the many life forms of 'Āvāgavan'- the cycle of birth and death or transmigration.

jam sāth(i) n jāṇā: literally, do not accompany 'Yama' and face the penalty of continued struggle in the cycle of birth and death. In essence, it implies that (a) they do not suffer any ill consequences of their actions but, instead, enjoy their fruits here, (b) they reap the benefits of their good deeds in the next life and (c) they find release from the cycle of 'Āvāgavan'. The following verses from the SGGS shed further light on this concept and endorse it:

The ignorant person, engrossed in the pleasures of the world and failing to submit to the Will of the Creator, gets caught up in the cycle of birth and death and endures a lot of punishment on this long journey.[357]

'Forsaking You, we have come into this world in the form of trees, animals, birds, worms, insects, 'Yogīs', 'Jatīs', 'Tapīs', 'Brahmchārīs', emperors and even beggars. Your real devotees, abiding blissfully by Your Will, live eternally (spiritually) but others, forsaking You, just die. Dejected and tired, we now surrender and seek Your refuge; be Merciful and Bless me with Divine Wisdom', O' Lord.[358]

'Lacking any noble attributes, I have sinned and repeatedly visited this world. Be Merciful and Gracious on this occasion and enable me to live by Your Will and realise You', O' Lord.[359]

'Settle your accounts in this life, hear me O' devotees of the Lord. Pray and seek His Mercy and Blessings so that we don't need to return to this world again', says Kabīr.[360]

By submitting willingly, lovingly and unreservedly to the Gurū's Divine Word and Wisdom and aligning with 'Nām(u)', one does not succumb to 'Haumaiṅ', 'Moh' and 'Vikārī' tendencies' ('Māyā'), nor suffer spiritual downfall or death and its consequences, but finds release from 'Āvāgavan'.

Aisā, Nām niraṅjan(u) hoi. See 'Pauṛī' 12.
Je ko, maṅn(i) jāṇai, *man*(i) koi. See 'Pauṛī' 12.

Conceptual summary

By submitting willingly, lovingly and unreservedly to the Gurū's Divine Word and Wisdom and aligning with 'Nām(u)': (a) one's innate nature, tendency or focus becomes aligned with and underpinned by 'bibek budhi(i)' ('Nām-consciousness'), (b) one becomes cognisant of God's omnipresence in the universe and dominion over it, (c) one avoids suffering, disgrace and humiliation both here and in the hereafter, and (d) one does not succumb to 'Haumaiṅ', 'Moh' and 'Vikārī' tendencies ('Māyā'), nor suffer spiritual downfall or death and its consequences, but enjoys its fruits in this life and may also reap its benefits in the next life or even find release from 'Āvāgavan' - the cycle of birth and death.

Such is the Power and Glory of the immaculate 'Nām(u)' that if one were to accept the Guru's Divine Word ('Nām(u)') and Wisdom faithfully, submit to it willingly, lovingly and unreservedly, and live by 'Nām-consciousness', one, too, could reach lofty spiritual heights, cleanse the filth of 'Māyā', become spiritually immaculate, and realise the full glow of 'Nām(u)' within one's conscious self ('*Man*' or 'Hirdā').

PAURĪ 14
ਪਉੜੀ ੧੪॥

Maṅnai, mārag(i) ṭhāk n pāi.
ਮੰਨੈ, ਮਾਰਗਿ ਠਾਕ ਨ ਪਾਇ॥

Maṅnai, pat(i) siu pargaṭ(u)jāi.
ਮੰਨੈ, ਪਤਿ ਸਿਉ ਪਰਗਟੁ ਜਾਇ॥

Maṅnai, mag(u) na chalai paṅth(u).
ਮੰਨੈ, ਮਗੁ ਨ ਚਲੈ ਪੰਥੁ॥

Maṅnai, dharam setī sanbaṅdh(u).
ਮੰਨੈ, ਧਰਮ ਸੇਤੀ ਸਨਬੰਧੁ॥

Aisā, Nām niraṅjan(u) hoi.
ਐਸਾ ਨਾਮੁ ਨਿਰੰਜਨੁ ਹੋਇ॥

Je ko, maṅn(i) jāṇai, *man*(i) koi. 14.
ਜੇ ਕੋ, ਮੰਨਿ ਜਾਣੈ, ਮਨਿ ਕੋਇ॥ ੧੪॥

Maṅnai, mārag(i) ṭhāk n pāi

maṅnai: see 'Pauṛī' 13, page 169.

mārag(i): (locative case - 'adhikaraṇ kārak'; synonymous with 'mārag-' or 'raste-' 'utte', 'uppar' or 'vich') literally, in or on the way or path. However, implicit here is being en route to perfect alignment with 'Nām(u)' or 'Nām-consciousness'.

mārag: (n, m; synonymous with 'rastā' or 'rāh') literally, the way or path. The reference is to the path of perfect alignment with 'Nām(u)' or 'Nām-consciousness' as opposed to that of 'Haumaiṅ' and ego-consciousness.

ṭhāk: (n, f, pl; synonymous with 'rukāvaṭ' and 'rok') literally, obstacles, stumbling blocks, hurdles or impediments. However, implicit here is the adverse or evil effects of 'Haumaiṅ', 'Moh' and 'Vikārī' tendencies ('Māyā'), impediments on one's path to 'Nām-consciousness'.

n: (p; pronounced as 'nāṅ') no, not or implying a negative connotation.

pāi: (v, s, present tense, third person; synonymous with 'pāuṅdā/pāuṅdī hai' or 'prāpat kardā/kardī hai') finds, achieves or realises. See pāuṇā. The following verses of the SGGS point to the problems one faces on going astray and suggest some preventative measures:

All my drawbacks and sorrows have vanished as the perfect Gurū has firmly aligned me with Nām(u). My innate 'vikārī' tendencies have fled; godliness and lasting equanimity and bliss have pervaded my 'Hirdā'.[361]

One, who forsakes 'Nām(u)', faces a myriad of impediments in life, and thus grieves, feeling condemned to lament like a crow in a deserted house.[347]

By submitting willingly, lovingly and unreservedly to the Gurū's Divine Word and Wisdom and aligning with 'Nām(u)', one does not experience any impediments on the path to perfect harmony with 'Nām-consciousness' and 'Nām-realisation'.

Maṅnai, pat(i) siu pargaṭ(u) jāi

pat(i): n, f; synonymous with 'mān', 'izzat' and 'pratishṭā') honour, good name, self respect or repute. See pat(i).

siu: (a) (prep; synonymous with 'sāth' or 'saṅg') with or in the company of, (b) (adv; synonymous with 'prat(i)', 'se' or 'kol') up to, to whom, and implicit here is (c) (prep; synonymous with 'smet' or 'sahit'; pronounced as 'siuṅ') with, together with, together or along with, in the company of or including.

pargaṭ(u): (adj) (a) (synonymous with 'sāph' or 'nirmal') clean, unsoiled, unsullied or untainted by 'Māyā', and (b) (synonymous with 'pratakh'or 'zāhar') revealed, manifest, evident and apparent.

jāi: (v, s, present tense, third person; synonymous with 'chale jāṅdā/jāṅdī hai') departs or goes. See jāṇā (d).

By submitting willingly, lovingly and unreservedly to the Gurū's Divine Word and Wisdom and aligning with 'Nām(u)', one departs from this world with due credit and honour.

Maṅnai, mag(u) n chalai paṅth(u)

mag(u): (a) (adj; synonymous with 'mag(n)' (skt) -'ḍubbiā hoiā') literally, drowned; entrenched, rapt or engrossed, (b) (n, m; (skt) synonymous with 'mārag', 'rastā' or 'rāh') literally, the way or path, and (c) (locative case - 'adhikaraṇ kārak'; synonymous with 'mārag-' or 'raste-' 'utte') literally, on the way or road. However, the reference here is to the road to 'Nām(u)' or 'Nām-consciousness'.

chalai: (v, s, present tense, third person; synonymous with 'chaldā-' or 'turdā-' 'hai'; pronounced as 'chalaiṅ') see chalṇā (a).

paṅth(u): (a) (n, m; synonymous with 'dharam' or 'mazhab') faith, creed or a religious path to God realisation, (b) (n, m; synonymous with 'mārag' or 'rastā') literally, path, trek or route, and implicit here is (c) (locative case - 'adhikaraṇ kārak'; synonymous with 'mārag utte') literally, on the path or road. In essence, on the byways rather than the established beaten track, main route or highway. The tacit reference here is to mere rituals in the name of religion ('karam kāṇḍs') that do not lend themselves to spiritual enhancement or evolution - a sentiment highlighted in this verse from the the SGGS:

'She ('Jīvātmāṅ') who does not appreciate the love and elation for perfect harmony with 'Nām(u)', gets lost and wanders astray. Forsaking 'Nām(u)', she gets sucked into the depths of the web of 'Māyā' and suffers'.[362]

By submitting willingly, lovingly and unreservedly to the Gurū's Divine Word and Wisdom and aligning with 'Nām(u)', one avoids straying down the byways.

Maṅnai, dharam setī sanbaṅdh(u)

dharam: (n, m, s) (synonymous with 'maryādā') moral, ethical or religious code of conduct, especially that which is completely in line with 'Nām(u)' or 'Nām-consciousness' ('Hukam anusārī')'. It is the Divine Order ('Hukam(u)') which creates, supports, and sustains, governs and guides the entire creation, and directs life towards 'Nām-consciousness'. (u) of 'dharam(u)' is missing because of the preposition 'setī' which joins it to the noun 'sanbaṅdh(u)'.

setī: (a) (prep; synonymous with 'se' and 'toṅ'; pronounced as 'setīṅ') from, and implicit here is (b) (prep; synonymous with 'sāth' or 'nāl'; pronounced as 'setīṅ') by, with or together with.

sanbańdh(u): (n, m; synonymous with 'sańbańdh(u)', 'mel', 'milāp' and 'rishtā nātā') union, relationship, connection, link, alliance or association.

By submitting willingly, lovingly and unreservedly to the Gurū's Divine Word and Wisdom and aligning with 'Nām(u)', one allies oneself directly with the Divine Order and 'Nām-consciousness'.

Aisā, Nām nirańjan(u) hoi. See 'Pauṛī' 12.
Je ko, mańn(i) jāṇai, *man*(i) koi. See 'Pauṛī' 12.

Conceptual summary

By submitting to the Gurū's Divine Word and Wisdom and aligning with 'Nām(u)' willingly, lovingly and unreservedly, one (a) avoids all impediments en route to perfect harmony with 'Nām-consciousness' and 'Nām-realisation', (b) leaves this world with gratitude and honour, (c) avoids straying down uncharted byways and cul-de-sacs that lead nowhere, and (d) connects directly with the Divine Order and 'Nām-consciousness'.

Such is the Power and Glory of the immaculate 'Nām(u)' that if one accepts the Guru's Divine Word ('Nām(u)') and Wisdom faithfully, submits to it willingly, lovingly and unreservedly, and lives by 'Nām-consciousness', one, too, can reach the lofty spiritual heights, cleanse the filth of 'Māyā', become spiritually immaculate, and realise the full glow of 'Nām(u)' within one's conscious self ('*Man*' or 'Hirdā').

PAUṚĪ 15
ਪਉੜੀ ੧੫॥

Maṅnai, pāvah(i) mokh duār(u).
ਮੰਨੈ, ਪਾਵਹਿ ਮੋਖੁ ਦੁਆਰੁ॥

Maṅnai, parvārai sādhār(u).
ਮੰਨੈ, ਪਰਵਾਰੈ ਸਾਧਾਰੁ॥

Maṅnai tarai, tāre gur(u) sikh.
ਮੰਨੈ ਤਰੈ, ਤਾਰੇ ਗੁਰੁ ਸਿਖ॥

Maṅnai, Nānak, bhavah(i) na bhikh.
ਮੰਨੈ, ਨਾਨਕ, ਭਵਹਿ ਨ ਭਿਖ॥

Aisā, Nām niraṅjan(u) hoi.
ਐਸਾ, ਨਾਮੁ ਨਿਰੰਜਨੁ ਹੋਇ॥

Je ko maṅn(i) jāṇai, *man*(i) koi. 15.
ਜੇ ਕੋ ਮੰਨਿ ਜਾਣੈ, ਮਨਿ ਕੋਇ॥ ੧੫॥

Maṅnai, pāvah(i) mokh duār(u)

maṅnai: see 'Pauṛī' 13, page 169.

pāvah(i): (v, pl, present tense, third person; synonymous with 'uh pāuṅde han'; pronounced as 'pāvaheṅ') see pāvah(i) and pāuṇā (a and b).

mokh: (n, m; synonymous with 'moksh' and 'mukat(i)') release, liberation, deliverance, emancipation or freedom from (a) 'Haumaiṅ', 'Moh' and the evil 'Vikārī' tendencies ('Māiā') ['kūṛ toṅ khlāsī' and 'Jīvan Mukat(i)'], and (b) transmigration ('Āvāgavan' - the cycle of birth and death) ['Param gat(i)'].

duār(u): (a) (n, f, s) an opening to the interior or exterior, (b) (n, m; synonymous with 'darbār' or n, f; synonymous with 'kachahrī') hall of audience or a court, (c) (n, f; synonymous with 'giān-' and 'karam-' 'indrīāṅ') the nine sensorimotor organs with openings to the exterior, and implicit here is (c) (n, m; synonymous with 'dar', 'darvāzā' and 'dahlīz') literally, entrance, gate, door; threshold or doorsill. However, (fig.) it implies the way, path or means.

By submitting to the Gurū's Divine Word and Wisdom and aligning with 'Nām(u)' willingly, lovingly and unreservedly, one finds the path to liberation from 'Haumaiṅ', 'Moh' and the evil 'Vikārī' tendencies (the noose and bondage of 'Māyā') and from the cycle of transmigration ('Āvāgavan').

Maṅnai, parvārai sādhār(u)

parvārai: (accusative case - 'karam kārak'; synonymous with 'parvār-' or 'satsaṅgīāṅ-' 'nūṅ') literally, to 'parvār(u)'. In essence, to ideologically convergents or close associates. See parvār(u).

parvār(u): (n, m; synonymous with 'parivār(u)', 'ṭabbar' and 'kuṭaṅb') literally, household, family or extended family. In essence, one's companions, who are ideologically convergent with one.

sādhār(u): (a) (n, m; synonymous with 'gijā', 'gajā' or 'bhojan') good food or sustenance, (b) (n, m; synonymous with 'ādhār', 'āsrā', 'sahārā' or 'ṭek') prop, support or backing, refuge or protection, and implicit here is (c) (adj; synonymous with 'sā' ('sāth', 'nāl' or 'sahit' - with) + 'ādhār' ('āsrā', 'sahārā' or 'ṭek' - support, backing, shelter or protection of alignment with 'Nām(u)') literally, 'ādhār sahit', i.e., aligned with the support, backing or protection of 'Nām(u)'.

parvārai sādhār(u): [one] instils amongst one's extended family members and close associates the real worth of absolute faith in, submission to, and alignment with 'Nām(u)'. The serendipity of this act is clearly stated in this verse of the SGGS:

Contemplate the infinite and unfathomable Lord, reflecting on whom we rid ourselves of all our sins and evil 'Vikārī' tendencies and our non or mal-aligned elders will redeem themselves as well.[363]

By submitting willingly, lovingly and unreservedly to the Gurū's Divine Word and Wisdom and aligning with 'Nām(u)', one consciously directs and firmly links one's family and close companions to this path of 'Nām-consciousness'.

Maṅnai tarai, tāre gur(u) sikh

tarai: (v, s, present tense, third person; synonymous with 'uh tar jāṅdā hai') [he] safely swims across. See tarnā.

tarnā: (v) literally, to swim or swim across to safety, but implicit here is to swim safely across this 'Bhavsāgar'. Put simply, it means to align perfectly with 'Nām(u)' and liberate oneself from the adverse effect of 'Haumaiṅ', 'Moh' and innate evil nature ('Māyā') in this lifetime ('Jīvan Mukat(i)') and find release from 'Āvāgavan' - the cycle of birth and death ('Param Mukat(i)').

bhavsāgar: (synonymous with 'bhaujal', 'bhavjal' or 'saṅsār sāgar') literally, the world-ocean or the world-stage, which Gurmat likens to a very turbulent ocean, where to swim across to safety is well-nigh impossible and spiritual death by drowning in it, is very probable.

tāre: (v, s, present tense, third person; synonymous with 'uh tār deṅdā hai') [he] helps others to swim across. See tārnā.

tārnā: (v) to help another swim across to safety.

gur(u): (n, m, s; abbrev. for Gurū; synonymous with 'āchārīā') a complex word comprising 'gu' (darkness or ignorance) + 'rū' (light or knowledge) i.e., one who takes another out of darkness or ignorance and brings them into a state of light or wisdom. See pp. 38-41.

sikh: (a) (n, f; synonymous with 'choṭī' and 'bodī') a tuft of hair left unshorn on top of head, (b) n, f; synonymous with 'sikhiā' and 'updesh') teachings, instructions or precepts, (c) (n, m, pl) believers in the ten Sikh Gurūs and the Sikh Holy Scripture, the 'Sri Gurū Graṅth Sāhib Jī', (d) (n, m, pl; synonymous with 'shishya', 'chele' and 'anuyāī') followers, disciples, novices, pupils or adherents, and implicit here is (e) (accusative case -'karam kārak; synonymous with 'sikhāṅ nūṅ') to one's followers or disciples. The following verses from the SGGS allude to common impediments in swimming across this 'bhavsāgar':

You will not be able to swim cross this 'bhavsāgar' with the heavy weight of stones ('sins') around your neck and a big bundle of slander ('niṅdā') on your head.[364]

If one's lifeboat is old (twilight of lifetime) and has thousands of holes (innate evil tendencies) then those with lighter loads (fewer 'vikārs') on their heads will swim across whilst others with heavier loads (abundance of 'vikārs'), will drown.[365]

By submitting willingly, lovingly and unreservedly to the Gurū's Divine Word and Wisdom and aligning with 'Nām(u), a Gurū not only swims across himself but also helps his disciples to swim across this 'Bhavsāgar'.

Maṅnai, Nānak, bhavah(i) n bhikh

Nānak: (n, m, s) the (u) of 'Nānak(u)' is missing because of its vocative case - 'saṅbodhan kārak'.

bhavah(i): (a) (ablative case - 'apādān kārak'; synonymous with 'bhav-' or 'bhavsāgar-' 'toṅ') from this world, (b) (v, s, present tense, second person; synonymous with 'tūṅ bhāuṅdā-' or 'bhaṭkadā-' 'haiṅ'), and (c) (v, pl, present tense, third person; synonymous with 'uh bhāuṅde-' or 'bhaṭkade-' 'han'; pronounced as 'bhavaheṅ') see bhavṇā.

bhavṇā: (v) (a) (synonymous with 'dubidhā vich-' 'phirnā', 'laṭkaṇā' or 'rahiṇā') to be in a state of dubiety and indecision, and (b) (synonymous with 'bharmaṇā' or 'bhaṭkaṇā') to go from pillar to post in the fruitless search for something; to stray and wander about aimlessly or fruitlessly in search of something.

n: (p; pronounced as 'nāṅ') no, not or implying a negative connotation. This acts as 'dehlī dīpak' as it goes with both 'bhavah(i)' and 'bhikh', e.g., 'bhavah(i) n' and 'n bhikh'.

bhikh: (n, f; synonymous with 'bhīkh', 'bhikhiā' or 'khair') literally, alms, beggary or act of begging; benefaction, charity or donation. In essence, the reference here is to indebtedness, obligation or dependency upon another when seeking or beseeching knowledge of the true path to 'Nām-realisation'.

By submitting willingly, lovingly and unreservedly to the Gurū's Divine Word and Wisdom and aligning with 'Nām(u)', one avoids obligation to others and dependency upon them, and the need to search high and low for the true path to 'Nām-realisation', O' Nānak!

Aisā, Nām niraṅjan(u) hoi. See 'Pauṛī' 12.
Je ko maṅn(i) jāṇai, *man*(i) koi. 15. See 'Pauṛī' 12.

Conceptual summary

By submitting willingly, lovingly and unreservedly to the Gurū's Divine Word and Wisdom and aligning with 'Nām(u)', one (a) finds the true path to freedom from 'haumaiṅ', 'moh' and 'evil 'vikārī' tendencies' ('kūṛ toṅ khalāsī'-'Jīvan mukat(i)') and the cycle of transmigration ('Āvāgavan'), (b) consciously and deliberately directs and firmly links one's family and companions to the path of 'Nām-consciousness', (c) (a Gurū) not only swims across himself but altruistically also helps his disciples to swim across this 'Bhavsāgar', and (d) avoids dependency upon others and wandering from pillar to post in the fruitless search for the true path to 'Nām-realisation'.

Such is the Power and Glory of the immaculate 'Nām(u)' that if one faithfully accepts the Guru's Divine Word ('Nām(u)') and Wisdom, submits to it willingly, lovingly and unreservedly, and lives by 'Nām-consciousness', one, too, can reach lofty spiritual heights, cleanse the filth of 'Māyā', become spiritually immaculate, and realise the full glow of 'Nām(u)' within one's conscious self ('*Man*' or 'Hirdā').

PAUṚĪ 16
ਪਉੜੀ ੧੬॥

Paṅch parvāṇ, paṅch pardhān(u).
ਪੰਚ ਪਰਵਾਣ, ਪੰਚ ਪਰਧਾਨੁ॥

Paṅche, pāvah(i) dargah(i) mān(u).
ਪੰਚੇ, ਪਾਵਹਿ ਦਰਗਹਿ ਮਾਨੁ॥

Paṅche, sohah(i) dar(i) rājān(u).
ਪੰਚੇ, ਸੋਹਹਿ ਦਰਿ ਰਾਜਾਨੁ॥

Paṅcha kā, gur(u) ek(u) dhiān(u).
ਪੰਚਾ ਕਾ, ਗੁਰੁ ਏਕੁ ਧਿਆਨੁ॥

Je ko kahai, karai vīchār(u).
ਜੇ ਕੋ ਕਹੈ, ਕਰੈ ਵਿਚਾਰੁ॥

Karte kai karṇai, nāhī sumār(u).
ਕਰਤੇ ਕੈ ਕਰਣੈ, ਨਾਹੀ ਸੁਮਾਰੁ॥

Dhaul(u) dharm(u), da-i-ā kā pūt(u).
ਧੌਲੁ ਧਰਮੁ, ਦਇਆ ਕਾ ਪੂਤੁ॥

Saṅtokh(u), thāp(i) rakhiā, jin(i) sūt(i).
ਸੰਤੋਖੁ, ਥਾਪਿ ਰਖਿਆ, ਜਿਨਿ ਸੂਤਿ॥

Je ko bujhai, hovai sachiār(u).
ਜੇ ਕੋ ਬੁਝੈ, ਹੋਵੈ ਸਚਿਆਰੁ॥

Dhavlai upar(i), ketā bhār(u).
ਧਵਲੈ ਉਪਰਿ, ਕੇਤਾ ਭਾਰੁ॥

Dhartī hor(u), parai hor(u) hor(u).
ਧਰਤੀ ਹੋਰੁ, ਪਰੈ ਹੋਰੁ ਹੋਰੁ॥

Tis te bhār(u), talai kavaṇ(u) jor(u).
ਤਿਸ ਤੇ ਭਾਰੁ, ਤਲੈ ਕਵਣੁ ਜੋਰੁ॥

Jīa, jāt(i), raṅgā ke nāv.
ਜੀਅ, ਜਾਤਿ, ਰੰਗਾ ਕੇ ਨਾਵ॥

Sabhnā likhiā, vuṛī kalām.
ਸਭਨਾ ਲਿਖਿਆ, ਵੁੜੀ ਕਲਾਮ॥

Eh(u) lekhā, likh(i) jāṇai koi.
ਏਹੁ ਲੇਖਾ, ਲਿਖਿ ਜਾਣੈ ਕੋਇ॥

Lekhā likhiā, ketā hoi.

ਲੇਖਾ ਲਿਖਿਆ, ਕੇਤਾ ਹੋਇ॥

Ketā tāṇ(u), suāliah(u) rūp(u).
ਕੇਤਾ ਤਾਣੁ, ਸੁਆਲਿਹੁ ਰੂਪੁ॥

Ketī dāt(i), jāṇai kauṇ kūt(u).
ਕੇਤੀ ਦਾਤਿ, ਜਾਣੈ ਕੌਣੁ ਕੂਤੁ॥

Kītā pasāu, eko kavāu.
ਕੀਤਾ ਪਸਾਉ, ਏਕੋ ਕਵਾਉ॥

Tis te hoe, lakh darīāu.
ਤਿਸ ਤੇ ਹੋਏ, ਲਖ ਦਰੀਆਉ॥

Kudrat(i) kavaṇ, kahā vīchār(u).
ਕੁਦਰਤਿ ਕਵਣ, ਕਹਾ ਵੀਚਾਰੁ॥

Vāriā n jāvā, ek vār.
ਵਾਰਿਆ ਨ ਜਾਵਾ, ਏਕ ਵਾਰ॥

Jo, tudh(u) bhāvai, sāī bhalī kār.
ਜੋ, ਤੁਧੁ ਭਾਵੈ, ਸਾਈ ਭਲੀ ਕਾਰ॥

Tū, sadā salāmat(i), Niraṅkār. 16.
ਤੂ, ਸਦਾ ਸਲਾਮਤਿ, ਨਿਰੰਕਾਰ॥ ੧੬॥

Paṅch parvāṇ, paṅch pardhān(u)

paṅch: (a) (adj; synonymous with 'paṅj') five, (b) (n, m, pl; synonymous with 'āgū', 'chaudharī' and 'naṅbardār') one of the five prominent members of the local village management committee ('Paṅchāit'), and implicit here is (c) (n and adj, pl; synonymous with 'Bhagats', 'Sādhū-jan', 'Saṅts' and 'Gurmukhs') they who lovingly submit to the Divine Word and willingly, focus and reflect upon the persona and the attributes of 'Nām(u)' - the immanent form of God, strive to attune perfectly to it, and express the same attributes in their daily lives. Other attributes of 'Paṅch' referred to in the previous Pauṛīs are as follows: (a) they who have absolute faith in the eternal, immaculate, omnipotent, omnipresent and omniscient God described by Gurū Nānak in the 'Mūl Maṅtar', (b) they who live by His Will, (c) they who reflect upon the Glory of 'Nām(u)' in the ambrosial hour, (d) they who never forget the One who provides for and gives to all, (e) they who listen attentively to and reflect upon the Divine Word and sing His Praise, (e) they who have absolute faith in 'Nām(u)' in their 'Hirdā', and strive hard to converge ideologically and harmonise with 'Nām-consciousness'. They are the chosen ones, and the ones who are marked for honour at His Court. See also 'Pauṛī' 34; page 409.

parvāṇ: (a) (adj; synonymous with 'pramāṇit' or 'surkharū'; 'manzūr-', 'kabūl-', 'aṅgīkār-' or 'makbūl-' 'kītā hoiā') approved, authenticated, sanctioned or authorised [by the all-pervasive 'Nām(u)']. See parvāṇ.

pardhān(u): (n and adj, m; synonymous with 'pradhān', 'sreshṭ', 'shromaṇī' and 'mukhīā') head, chairperson or president of an organisation; pre-eminent, foremost, supreme, consummate or unrivalled.

His true 'bhagats' are pre-eminent amongst people in this world and have His seal of approval.

Paṅche pāvah(i), dargah(i) mān(u)

paṅche: (nominative case - 'kartā kārak', pl; synonymous with 'paṅch hī') literally, those or only those paṅch. See paṅch.

pāvah(i): (v, pl, present tense, third person; synonymous with 'uh pāuṅde han'; pronounced as 'pāvaheṅ') see pāuṇā (a).

dargah: (a) (pers; n, f) literally, a 'Darbār' or a 'Court', where the final judgement is passed on deeds carried out in one's lifetime, and implicit here is (b) (locative case - 'adhikaraṇ kārak'; synonymous with 'dargah(i), 'dargāh vich' or 'dargāh upar') literally, in or at God's Court. Since God is all-pervasive and omnipresent, it probably happens here, within our body, before one's 'Jivātmāṅ' leaves the body. There is, therefore, no place elsewhere that is called Heaven where God lives and holds Court, or Hell for that matter, where 'Jivātmāṅs' (re-incarnated in some way) are then punished. However, having once realised 'Nām(u)', life lived here in complete harmony with it is life in heaven. On the contrary, the extreme physical and mental suffering that follows life dissociated from 'Nām(u)' and ensnared by the evil influence of 'Haumaiṅ', 'Moh' and 'Vikārs' ('Māyā'), could be equated with life in hell here.

mān(u): (a) (n, m; synonymous with 'abhimān' and 'garūr') vanity, pride, conceit or arrogance, and (b) (n, m; synonymous with 'māṇ(u)', 'sanmān', 'ādar', 'satkār', 'izzat', 'ābrū' and 'pratishṭā') respect, self-respect, accolade, esteem, meritorious status or honour. In essence, it represents absolute freedom from 'Māyā', 'Jīvan Mukat(i)' and realisation of one's true self ('Parmātmaṅ') in this life and freedom from the cycle of transmigration ('Āvāgavan') in the hereafter.

Only His true 'bhagats' receive honour at His Court.

Paṅche, sohah(i) dar(i) rājān(u)

sohah(i): (a) (v, s, present tense, second person; synonymous with 'tūṅ shobdhdā haiṅ' or 'tusīṅ shobdhde ho'; pronounced as 'sohaiṅ'), (b) (v, pl, future tense, third person; synonymous with 'uh shobhā-' 'pāuṅge' or 'pā laiṅge'; pronounced as 'sohaiṅ', and implicit here is (c) (v, pl, present tense, third person; synonymous with 'uh shobdhe han' or 'uh 'suṅdar lagde han'; pronounced as 'sohaiṅ') see sohṇā lagṇā and sobhṇā.

sohṇā lagṇā: (conj. v, m; 'sohṇī lagṇī' is its feminine counterpart) (a) to look or to appear beautiful or handsome, and (b) to look or to appear graceful, elegant or pleasing.

sobhṇā: (v) to be or to look elegant, graceful, proper, deserving and honourable.

dar(i): (locative case - 'adhikaraṇ kārak'; synonymous with 'dar utte' and 'dar uppar') at the door, threshold or court. See dar (b).

rājān(u): (n, m, s) (a) (synonymous with 'chhatriya' and 'sūrbīr') a warrior, (b) (n, m, s) a ruler, sovereign or king, (c) (n, m, pl; synonymous with 'rāje') many kings, and implicit here is (d) (genitive case - 'saṅbaṅdh kārak'; synonymous with 'rājiāṅ de') of kings.

dar(i) rājān(u): (synonymous with 'rājiāṅ de darbar vich') in the courts or audience halls of kings.

His true 'bhagats' grace the courts of kings.

Paṅcha kā, gur(u) ek(u) dhiān(u)

paṅcha: (genitive case - 'saṅbaṅdh kārak'; synonymous with 'paṅchāṅ dā'; pronounced as 'paṅchāṅ') literally, 'paṅchs'.

kā: (prep, m; synonymous with 'dā') of.

gur(u): (n, m, s; abbrev. for Gurū) a complex word comprising 'gu' (darkness or ignorance) + 'ru' (light or knowledge) i.e., one who takes another out of darkness or ignorance and brings them into a state of light or wisdom.

ek(u): (a) (adj, m; synonymous with 'Kartār') literally, One, but reference is to the one and only God or 'Nām(u)', its persona and attributes as captured in Gurbānī, (b) (adj, m; synonymous with 'adutī') unique, unrivalled or peerless, and implicit here is (c) (adv; synonymous with 'siraph-' or 'keval-' 'ik') only, merely, just or simply one.

gur(u) ek(u): (synonymous with 'keval gurū hī' or 'keval gurū shabad hī') literally, just the Gurū or just the Gurū's Divine Word.

dhiān(u): (n, m, s; synonymous with '*man* vich surat(i) nāl chiṅtan' and 'surat(i)-' or 'birtī-' ' dā ṭikāu') the stilling and focusing of one's wandering mind on the Gurū's Divine Word, i.e., the persona and/or attributes of the eternal 'Nām(u)'.

Their focus is forever just on the Gurū's Divine Word.

Je ko kahai, karai vīchār(u)

je: (conj; synonymous with 'yadī' or 'agar') if or in case.

ko: (pron; synonymous with 'koī') literally, someone, anyone or another. However, the reference here is to a 'Paṅch' or someone on the path to 'Nām-realisation'.

kahai: (a) (v, s, present tense, third person; synonymous with 'kahiṅdā-' 'hai'; 'varṇan-' or 'vakhyān-' 'kardā hai') sets forth, utters, expounds, explicates or sings His Glory, and (b) (v, s, third person, imperative mood - 'saṅbhāv bhvikht kāl - kiās bodhak'; synonymous with 'biān-' or 'vakhyān-' 'ākhe/kare' 'bhī') were to express, expound, explicate or elaborate. See kahiṇā.

karai: (a) (v, s, present tense, third person; synonymous with 'uh kardā hai'), and (b) v, s, third person, imperative mood - 'saṅbhāv bhvikht kāl - kiās bodhak'; synonymous with 'kare bhī') see karnā (g).

vīchār(u): (n, m, s; synonymous with 'kudrat de lekhe dī-' 'bīchār' and/or 'khalāsā/andāzā') speculation, consideration or deliberation about the extent of His Creation. See vīchār(u) (c to f) and vīchārnā.

karai vīchār(u): (conj. v, s, third person, 'saṅbhāv bhvikht kāl - kiās bodhak'; synonymous with 'vīchār-' 'kare' or 'karnā chāhe') if one were to deliberate or should one deliberate.

Traditionally, Hindu seers ('rishīs') would often leave their home to live a simple and very strict and disciplined life and search for inspiration of divine wisdom and revelation in jungles or remote mountains. Some would end up devoting their entire time and effort to deliberating on and recording their observations about the origin, nature and extent of the creation in 'Purānās' and 'Upānishādās' – Hindu religious texts. Gurū Nānak regards the use of their time and effort in this regard, rather than in unreserved surrender to and perfect alignment with 'Nam(u)' and living life by His Will, as a fundamental error and completely futile. Hence the reference to their mistaken belief and notion of a white ox supporting the planet Earth as an example in this 'Pauṛī'.

Should someone dare to speculate about and/or deliberate over and describe the extent of His Creation...

Karte kai karṇai, nāhī sumār(u)

karte: (genitive case - 'saṅbaṅdh kārak'; synonymous with 'karte-' or 'kartār-' 'de') when a masculine and singular noun ending with 'ā' ('kaṅnā') is followed by a preposition the 'ā' changes to 'e' ('lām'), i.e., kartā becomes 'karte'. See kartā.

kartā: (n and adj, m; abbrev. for 'kartār'; synonymous with 'rachanhār', 'rachaitā', 'sirjanhār', 'karan vālā' or 'Pārbrahm') doer, maker, creator, or God.

kai: (prep; synonymous with 'kā', 'ke', 'kī', 'dā', 'de', 'dī', 'se', 'nāl' or 'toṅ') of, from or with.

karṇai: (genitive case - 'saṅbaṅdh kārak'; synonymous with 'karṇe-' or 'krit-' 'dā') of His Creation. See karṇā (c and h).

karte kai karṇai: (synonymous with 'kartār dī srishṭ(i)/ krit dā') literally, of God's Creation.

nāhī: (p; synonymous with 'nāṅ' or 'nahīṅ'; pronounced as 'nāhīṅ') no, not or implying a negative connotation.

sumār(u): (n, f; pers; synonymous with 'giṇtī', 'hisāb' and 'lekhā'; pronounced as 'shumār') reckoning, calculation, computation or estimation.

nāhī sumār(u): literally, beyond reckoning. In essence, infinite. In the past many of different faiths have pondered over when and how the universe was created and supported, and how vast it is. Some have dared to put forward their conclusions which have been found seriously wanting. Some claim that there are just three worlds ('trilok') - 'dharat(i)', 'ākāsh' and 'pātāl', whilst others claim fourteen such worlds - seven above the Earth and six below it. However, as far as Gurū Nānak is concerned, the reality is that there is no one but He who knows the answers to these questions. He is absolutely unique and ineffable and has no rival; in truth, no one else but He alone exists in this universe. It, therefore, behoves us to stop wasting his time and energy on trying to fathom Him and, instead, to submit to the Gurū's Divine Words and Message of living life in 'Nām-consciousness', as captured in the following verses of the SGGS:

'No one knows how vast Your expanse is', O' my Great, Immeasurable and Unfathomable Lord Master.[366]

How can one weigh the immeasurable? Only one who is His rival or peer would know. Therefore, how can we fathom Him as He has no peer or rival?[367]

[One would soon realise that] His Creation is truly immeasurable and infinite.

Dhaul(u) dharm(u), da-i-ā kā pūt(u)

dhaul(u): (a) (adj; synonymous with 'chiṭṭā') white, (b) (adj; synonymous with 'ujlā' and 'nirmal') pure and immaculate, and implicit here is (c) (n, m; synonymous with 'dhaval' and 'chiṭṭā bail') literally, white oxen ('bail'). In reality, sometime in the distant past, some Hindu 'rishīs' deliberated over and wrote about when and how the world came into being, and how vast it is, and recorded their views in the Purānas. They also believed that a mythical white ox supported the planet Earth on one of its horns and that moving the planet Earth from one to the other horn, during periods of recuperation, caused the earthquakes.

dharam(u): (synonymous with 'maryādā') moral, ethical or religious code of conduct, especially that which is in congruence with 'Nām(u)' or 'Nām-consciousness' ('Hukam anusārī'). However, implicit here is the Divine Order ('Hukam(u)'), which creates, supports and sustains, governs and guides the entire creation. The following verse from the SGGS highlights this aspect of the Divine Order ('dharam'):

'He separates the Earth and sky and stretches the canopy of the firmament above. He manifests His 'Nām(u)' and supports the skies above without pillars'.[368]

da-i-ā: (n, f; synonymous with ‘karuṇā’, ‘dayā’, ‘myā’, ‘raham’, ‘kripā’, ‘mehar’, ‘taras’) compassion, mercy, sympathy, benevolence or pity.

kā: (prep, m; synonymous with ‘dā’) of.

pūt(u): (n, m, s) (a) (synonymous with ‘chelā’) literally, a follower or a disciple, and implicit here is (b) (synonymous with ‘putr’ and ‘beṭā’) a son or a male offspring.

His Divine Order, whose existence stems from His compassion, is the mythical bull [that supports and sustains the planet Earth and the other planets].

Saṅtokh(u), thāp(i) rakhiā, jin(i) sūt(i).

saṅtokh(u): (a) (n; synonymous with ‘prasaṅtā’ and ‘anaṅd’) happiness, pleasure, bliss or spiritual peace, (b) (n, m, s; synonymous with ‘sabar’, ‘lobh dā tiāg’, ‘rajj’, ‘tripat(i)’ and ‘shāṅtī’) literally, contentment or satisfaction; patience; peace or calm, and (c) (synonymous with ‘aḍoltā’, ‘Sahaj’ or ‘Anaṅd’) poise, steadiness or tranquillity; lasting inner equipoise and spiritual tranquillity and bliss. However, implicit here is lasting orderliness, stability, equanimity and perfect order.

thāp(i): (indeclinable past participle or perfect participle - ‘pūran pūrab kārdaṅtak’; synonymous with ‘thāp ke’) see thāpṇā.

rakhiā: (v, present perfect; third person) (a) (synonymous with ‘bachāiā’ and ‘rakhyā-’ or ‘hiphāzat’ ‘kītī’) saved, guarded or protected, and implicit here is (b) (synonymous with ‘ṭikāiā’ and ‘ṭikā dittā’) literally, safely placed, kept or installed. See rakhṇā (c and e).

jin(i): (nominative case - ‘kartā kārak’, s; synonymous with ‘jis(i)’ or ‘jis ne’) who, that, which, whoever or whosoever. However, the reference here is to ‘dharam(u)’ - the Divine Order (‘Hukam(u)’).

sūt(i): (locative case - ‘adhikaraṇ kārak’; synonymous with ‘sūtr-’ or ‘sūt-’ ‘vich’) literally, in or by the thread. However, implicit here is in or by the Divine Order. See sūt (b and e).

[And] it is His Divine Order which, by binding everything in the universe under its jurisdiction, controls everything and has established perfect orderliness therein.

Je ko bujhai, hovai sachiār(u)

bujhai: (a) (v, s, present tense, second person; synonymous with 'tūṅ bujh laiṅdā haiṅ' or tusīṅ samajh laiṅde ho'; pronounced as 'bujhaiṅ'), (b) (v, s, present tense, third person; synonymous with 'uh-' 'jāṇ-', 'samajh-' or 'bujh-' 'laiṅdā hai') realises, and implicit here is (c) (v, s, imperative mood - 'saṅbhāv bhvikht kāl - sharat bodhak', third person; synonymous with 'jāṇ-', 'samajh-' or 'bujh-' 'lave') literally, realise [the above concept]. See bujhaṇā (d).

hovai: (v, s, present tense, third person; synonymous with 'huṅdā-' or 'baṇdā-' 'hai'; 'ho jāṅdā hai'). See hovṇā (a and c)

sachiār(u): (n, m, s) (a) a complex word comprising 'sach(u)' (eternal knowledge and wisdom; persona and attributes of the eternal Reality) + 'ār' or 'ālya' ('ghar' or home) literally, synonymous with 'sach dā ghar' or the fount of everything eternal, i.e., God, and implicit here is (b) (synonymous with 'sachiārā' or 'satya dhāran vālā') a complex word comprising 'sach(u)' (eternal knowledge and wisdom; persona and attributes of the eternal Reality) + 'ār(u)' or 'ārā' ('vālā', 'vān' or 'vaṅt'-bearer of) bearer of the qualities of 'satya' ('satya dhāran vālā') - one who has attuned to and imbibed the attributes of 'Nām(u)' in one's 'Hirdā' and expresses them in one's daily life.

One becomes aligned perfectly with 'Nām(u)' - the Divine Order, if one truly comprehends that the Divine Order ('Hukam(u)') is the basis of everything. Or:

Should one claim to have reached the pinnacle of spiritual evolution and to know the nature and modus operandi of the Divine Order? (the reference here is to those with mistaken beliefs as alluded to above).

Dhavlai upar(i), ketā bhār(u)

dhavlai: (genitive case - 'saṅbaṅdh kārak'; synonymous with 'dhaval de') literally, 'on dhaval'. See dhaul (dhaval).

upar(i): (a) (adv; synonymous with 'anusār' and 'mutābik') according to or in accordance with, (b) (adj; synonymous with 'parbal' and 'gālib') strong, forceful, dominant, overpowering and preponderant, and (c) (prep and adv; synonymous with 'utte' and 'uttāṅh'; pronounced as 'uppar') upon, above or on top of [the horns of the 'dhaval'].

ketā: (adj, m; synonymous with 'kitnā' or 'kiṅnā') how much?

bhār(u): (n, m, s; synonymous with 'bojh' or 'vazan') literally, weight, load, luggage or cargo.

However, should one not accept the premise that it is the the Divine Order ('Hukam(u)'), which creates, supports and sustains, governs and guides the entire creation, but still believe that a white ox supports the planet Earth, one would be asked to answer the question here and in the verses that follow.

How heavy is the load borne by this bull?

Dhartī hor(u), parai hor(u) hor(u)

dhartī: (n, f; synonymous with 'prithvī', 'dharat(i)', 'zamīn', 'srishṭ(i)' or 'bhumī') the planet Earth.

hor(u): (adj; synonymous with 'aur' and 'is toṅ vadh or chhuṭ') another, more or in addition. The phrase 'hor(u) hor(u)' alludes to the numerous other planets, not only beneath but also above the planet Earth. However, if one were to accept the premise that a white ox supports the planet Earth on its horns, who or what supports the white ox becomes the next logical question. This is an invalid postulation with no end in sight but the question as to who or what supports the last ox still demands an answer.

parai: (a) (v, s, present tense, third person; synonymous with 'paṛ(h)dā hai'; pronounced as 'paṛaiṅ') literally, reads or recites, (b) (v, s, present tense, third person; synonymous with 'paiṅdā-' or 'paṛtā-' 'hai'; 'pa-iā rahiṅdā hai'; pronounced as 'paṛaiṅ') comes to be, falls or just lies, (c) (v, s, imperative mood - 'saṅbhāv bhvikht kāl - kiās bodhak'; synonymous with 'ḍig-' 'paṛe' or 'pave'; 'nashṭ ho jāve') were to fall or be destroyed or obliterated, (d) (adv; synonymous with 'bād' and 'pichhe') later, subsequently, thereafter; beyond, apart from or out with, (e) (adv; synonymous with 'dūr' and 'pār') far or beyond, (f) (adv; synonymous with 'othe' and 'us pāse') there or in that direction, and implicit here is (g) (adv; synonymous with 'heṭhāṅ', 'nīche' or 'thalle') literally, below planet Earth.

parai hor(u) hor(u): literally, there are many other planets that lie beneath planet Earth.

There are countless planets beneath the planet Earth.

Tis te bhār(u), talai kavaṇ(u) jor(u)

tis: (pron, s; synonymous with 'us') literally, he, she or that. (u) of 'tis(u)' is missing because of the preposition 'te' that links it with the noun 'bhār(u)'. The tacit reference here is to the last bull and how much weight it would be carrying on its horns and what its own support would be.

te: (prep and adv; synonymous with 'utte' and 'uppar') on or above.

tis te bhār(u): how much weight would there be on the last bull?

talai: (prep and adv; synonymous with 'thalle' and 'nīche') under, below or beneath.

kavaṇ(u): (pron; synonymous with 'kavan(u)', 'kauṇ', 'kī' and 'kihṛā') literally, who or what?

jor(u): (n, m; synonymous with 'āsrā' or 'sahārā'; pronounced as 'zor(u)') literally, support or prop. See jor(u).

tis talai kavaṇ(u) jor(u): what is the support beneath that last bull? If planet Earth is borne on the horns of a white ox there must be something else which bears the ox's burden. The next logical question would be: What, in turn, supports the white ox? This state of affairs would continue ad infinitum, failing forever to provide an explanation about the last supporting structure bearing the cumulative burden alluded to above.

[How much load would there be on the last bull], and who or what would then be its own support or prop?

Jīa jāt(i), raṅgā ke nāv

jīa: (n, pl; synonymous with 'jīv' and 'prāṇī') all sentient beings including human beings.

jāt(i): (a) (v, s, present tense, third person; synonymous with 'jāṅdā' or 'jāṅdī') literally, goes, (b) (n, f; synonymous with 'rachnā', 'srishṭ(i)' or 'makhlukāt') creation or universe, (c) (n, f; synonymous with 'got' and 'gotra') sub-caste, and implicit here is (d) (n, f; synonymous with 'kul', 'vaṅsh' and 'shreṇī') kind, class, caste, ethnicity, race or species, and (e) (n, pl; genitive case - 'saṅbaṅdh kārak'; synonymous with 'zātāṅ ate kismāṅ de') of diverse kinds.

raṅgā: (n, m, pl; genitive case - 'saṅbaṅdh kārak'; synonymous with 'raṅgāṅ de'; pronounced as 'raṅgāṅ') of colours or of a range of colours. See raṅg.

ke: (adj; synonymous with 'ka-ī' and 'anek') many or numerous.

nāv: (a) (n, m, s) Nām(u) - the immanent form of God, (b) (n, m, pl; pers; synonymous with 'kishtī', 'naukā' or 'jahāz') ships, and implicit here is (c) (n, m, pl; synonymous with nāṅv) names - for the countless non-sentient elements and sentient beings in the universe, and (d) (n, pl; genitive case - 'saṅbaṅdh kārak'; synonymous with 'nāvāṅ de') of different names.

Diverse kinds and colours of creatures with different names exist in this universe.

Sabhnā likhiā, vuṛī kalām

sabhnā: (a) (nominative case - 'kartā kārak', pl; synonymous with 'sabhnāṅ neṅ') one and all or everyone, and (b) (genitive case - 'saṅbaṅdh kārak', pl; synonymous with 'sabhnāṅ de') of all, everyone, or one and all. See sabh.

sabh: (adj; synonymous with 'sabhe', 'sarab', 'sabho' and 'tamām') all, entire, everyone or totality.

likhiā: (a) (v, pl, present perfect) literally, [they] have all written, and implicit here is (b) (adj, m; past participle -'bhūt kirdaṅt'; synonymous with 'un(h)āṅ dī likhit' or 'un(h)āṅ dā likhiā lekh') literally, His written directive or writ for all, and (c) (n, m; present participle - 'kriyā-phal kirdaṅt'; synonymous with 'likhit', 'lekhā', 'mastak te likhe hoi lekh' or 'tahrīr') literally, a written directive or writ for all that has been worked out and allotted on the basis of their deeds in a previous life/lives which forms the basis of their fate, fortune or destiny in this life.

vuṛī: (adj, f, s; present participle - 'vartmān kārdaṅtak'; synonymous with 'vagdī-', 'vahiṅdī-' or 'chaldī-' 'hoī') literally, flowing or moving in a continuous and uninterrupted fashion, without any need for pause or thought. See vuṛna (b).

kalām: (a) (n, f; synonymous with 'guphtgū bātchīt') a secretive dialogue or conversation, (b) (n, f; synonymous with 'pāk-' or 'nirmal-' 'kathan') sacred utterance, speech or text, and implicit here is (c) (n, f, s; synonymous with 'kalam') literally, pen, and (d) (instrumental case - 'karaṇ kārak'; synonymous with 'kalam-' 'nāl', 'rāhīṅ', 'duārā' or 'sadkā') with, through or by virtue of a pen.

Humans have probed deep into outer space and landed successfully on the surface of the moon and Mars, but no evidence of life, and certainly nothing as complex and comparable to humankind has emerged thus far. The task of determining and defining the extent of this vast and mysterious universe, therefore, rests solely on our shoulders. Whilst science continues to make progress, though its pace has been variable, it still aims to reach its goal of understanding the precise origin, and the extent and normal function, of every constituent of this vast universe, at some point in the future.

On the other hand, Gurū Nānak feels that our limited abilities preclude us from reaching this goal by our own efforts. God, the Creator, has hardwired us so that the mystery and extent of this creation and the extent of His Glory will, forever, remain beyond our scope. Even if all humankind were committed to this task we would not succeed, despite continuing relentlessly without a break ('vuṛī kalām'), as the task is boundless and the unfolding universe continues to evolve while the totality of each of its constituents remains in flux.

The phrase 'sabhnā likhiā' or 'sabhnāṅ dī likhit', therefore, deserves some clarification. In essence, the term relates to the 'likhit'/'lekha'/'mastak de lekh' (see above) not only of all non-sentient and sentient life forms but also of every planet, orbital system, and galaxy of this evolving universe. Indeed, ours is an actively evolving and dynamic world, with the numbers of each species ever in a state of flux, variable and not fixed. Furthermore, the eco-sphere of the planet Earth alone is so vast that humans have yet to succeed in exploring all its aspects, let alone counting the numbers of each species. See Pauṛī 24, pp. 284-7.

Lastly, the task of 'mastak de lekh' for every sentient being rests solely within the domain of God,[369] leaving us just the task of calculating the cumulative total number of each species. Given the above caveat, if humans were to accept this challenge, notwithstanding its enormity, we would not be able to complete it without a pause, a key requirement in the verse.

According to the fifth Nānak, Gurū Arjan Dev, God, the Creator, is the only one who knows the expanse of this universe/s and who has the ability and power to write such an account of every component of this creation as endorsed by the following verse from SGGS:

'With the pen in Your hands, You write our destiny on our foreheads', O' Unfathomable Lord.[369]

Throughout time, created beings have attempted to capture and definitively record the nature and extent of His Creation. (In consonance with Prof. Sahib Singh)[7] *Or:*

He inscribes the fate or destiny of everything and everyone with His uninterrupted stroke of the pen. (Author's preferred interpretation)

Eh(u) lekhā, likh(i) jāṇai koi

eh(u): (a) (adj, m, s; synonymous with 'aisā') like, similar to or resembling this, and (b) (pron, n, s; synonymous with 'yahī' and 'keval eh') this or precisely this.

lekhā: (a) (v, present perfect tense; synonymous with 'likhiā') literally, has been written, and implicit here is (b) (n, m; synonymous with 'likhiā hoiā hisāb') the cumulative number as well as an account of each one's good and bad 'Karmā', and (c) (n, f; synonymous with 'lekh') one's fate or destiny, based on the judgement of one's Karmā ('hisāb' of one's 'saṅskārs') and written on one's forehead, according to popular Hindu belief. See lekh.

likh(i): (a) (indeclinable past participle or perfect participle - 'pūran pūrab kārdaṅtak'; synonymous with 'likh ke') having written, (b) (genitive case - 'saṅbaṅdh kārak'; synonymous with 'likhṇe dī') of noting down or writing something in black and white, and (c) (v; synonymous with 'likhna' or 'likhṇā') literally, the ability to write or note down. See likh(i).

jāṇai: (v, s, present tense, third person; synonymous with 'jāṇdā-' or 'samjadā-' 'hai') knows or understands. See jāṇai and jāṇanā (b and d).

koi: (a) (pron; synonymous with 'koī virlā' or 'ik adhā') rarely or an occasional someone, and (b) (adj; synonymous with 'koī') any, some or certain.

Only a rare individual has the knowledge and ability to record the extent and the basis on which this 'lekhā' of this vast creation is calculated.

If it really were in someone's grasp, it would beg the question captured in the next verse. In reality, no one knows the extent or the basis on which this account ('lekhā jokhā', 'hisāb kitāb' or 'mastak de lekh') of their destiny is worked out.

Lekhā likhiā, ketā hoi

lekhā likhiā: (present participle - 'kriyā-phal kirdaṅt'; synonymous with 'likhiā hoiā lekhā') (a) the written account containing the extent and 'lekhā' of the entire creation ('scribed scroll'), and (b) the written account of every constituent part of this creation and one's entitlement in this life, based on their Karmāin the previous life, which forms the basis of their fate, fortune or destiny.

ketā: (adj, m; synonymous with 'kitnā' or 'kiṅnā') how much? In essence, implicit here is 'limitless or infinite' ('beaṅt') and the word 'ketā' is used here in a merely rhetorical sense.

hoi: (a) (v, present tense; synonymous with 'hundā-' or 'ho jāndā-' 'hai'; 'ho sakdā hai') literally, occurs, comes to be or becomes; can become, and implicit here is (b) (v, s, imperative mood - 'saṅbhāv bhvikht kāl - kiās bodhak', third person; synonymous with 'ho jāve' or 'hove') literally, were to become. See hovṇā (a).

How vast would such a scribed scroll be? Or:
How enormous would this document, containing a record of the extent of the entire creation and 'lekhā' of all its constituent parts, be?

In reality, this is just a rhetorical question as one would never be able to know the answer.

Ketā tāṇ(u), suāliah(u) rūp(u)

ketā: see above.

tāṇ(u): (n, m; synonymous with 'bal', 'shakat(i)', and 'samrathā') ability, capability, authority, strength or power.

suāliah(u): (adj; synonymous with and pronounced as 'suālio') a complex word comprising 'su' ('uttam' and 'suṅdar' - very beautiful) + 'āliah(u)' or 'ālyā' ('ghar' - house) i.e., literally, a beautiful house or a house of great beauty. In essence, a fount of all beauty.

rūp(u): (n, m) (a) (synonymous with 'shakal', 'sūrat', 'sarūp' and 'ākār') literally, form, shape, looks, or appearance, (b) (n, f; synonymous with 'khūbsūrtī', 'sauṅdryā' and 'suṅdartā') literally, good looks, cuteness, beauty or elegance. In essence, the beauty of nature, which, in a way, stands for His beauty, as He pervades all aspects of creation.

How great is His power and how striking is His beauty? Or: Who can speculate about His immeasurable power and striking beauty?

Ketī dāt(i), jāṇai kauṇ kūt(u)

ketī: (adj, f; synonymous with 'kitnī' or 'kiṅnī') how much? In essence, implicit here is limitless or infinite.

dāt(i): (n, f; synonymous with 'khairāt' and 'bakhshīsh') literally, blessing, grace, boon or bestowal; in essence, His bounty.

jāṇai: (a) (v, s, imperative mood - 'saṅbhāv bhvikht kāl - prashan bodhak', third person; synonymous with 'jāṇ lave' or 'samajh sake'), and (b) (v, s, present tense, third person: synonymous with 'uh jāṇdā hai' or 'uh jāṇ sakdā hai') See jāṇanā (a and b).

kauṇ(u): (pron, s; synonymous with 'kaun', 'kavan' or 'kihṛā') who or which? It is used as 'dehlī dipak', e.g., 'kauṇ jāṇai ketī dāt(i)' and 'kauṇ jāṇai kūt(u)'.

kūt(u): (n, m; synonymous with 'aṅdāzā' and 'anumān') estimate, guesstimate or reckoning.

Who can guesstimate or speculate about the extent of His Bounty? In essence, this is just a rhetorical question as His Bounty is infinite, and none can hazard a guess at its extent.

Kītā pasāu, eko kavāu

kītā: (a) (n, f; synonymous with 'krit') creation, and (b) (v, s, past or present perfect; synonymous with 'kītā sī'; 'kītā-' or 'sirjiā-' 'hai') actions taken or deeds done; actions that have been taken or deeds which have been done. See kītā and karnā.

pasāu: (a) (n, m; synonymous with 'prachār' or 'parchār') evangelisation or preaching, and implicit here is (b) (n, m; synonymous with 'visthār', 'phailāu' and 'pasārā') literally, elaboration, expansion, amplification or expatiation. In essence, the reference here is to the vast, evolving expanse or universe - His Creation.

eko: (adj, m; synonymous with 'iko', 'ik hī' and 'keval ik') literally, just or only one.

kavāu: (a) (n, f; synonymous with 'pushāk') attire, uniform, garment, costume or dress, and implicit here is (b) (n, m; synonymous with 'vachan', 'vāk' and 'vākya') a word, and (c) (n, m; synonymous with 'quāu' and 'hukam') command, decree or order.

This vast evolving expanse came into being with just His one word or command.

Tis te hoe, lakh darīāu

tis: see above. The reference here is to His one command.

hoe: (a) (v, s, present tense, third person; synonymous with 'ho jāṅdā hai' or 'ho jāṅde han'), and implicit here is (b) (v, pl, past tense; synonymous with 'ho ga-e', 'hoṅd vich āe', 'baṇ ga-e' and 'upje') literally, came into being. See hoṇā.

lakh: (adj, pl) literally, many 1 x 10^5 but in essence, countless or infinite.

darīāu: (n, m, pl; synonymous with 'darīā' and 'darīyā' (pers)) literally, rivers, and (b) (synonymous with 'samuṅdar' and 'sāgar') seas or oceans.

hoe lakh darīāu: literally, countless rivers gushed forth. In essence, countless or infinite life forms came forth or evolved.

[And] infinite life forms flowed or evolved with that.

Kudrat(i) kavaṇ, kahā vīchār(u)

kudrat(i): (a) (n, f; synonymous with 'māiā') the creative power of God, (b) (n, f; synonymous with 'rachnā' and 'srishṭ(i)') creation or universe, and implicit here is (c) (n, f and adj - (arab) synonymous with 'tākat' and 'shakat(i)') strength, power, energy or ability.

kavaṇ: (pron and adj. f, s; prashan vāchak; synonymous with 'kauṇ' and 'kihṛī') who, what or which? 'u' of 'kavaṇ(u)' is missing because its noun 'kudrat(i)' is of a female form.

kahā: (a) (adv, synonymous with 'kithe', 'kahāṅ', 'kioṅ', 'kaise' or 'kis laī'; pronounced as 'kahāṅ') where, which way, why, how or what for, (b) (pron; synonymous with 'kis') which, (c) (v, s, present tense, first person; synonymous with 'maiṅ kah sakdā hāṅ'; pronounced as 'kahāṅ') literally, describe or explicate [Your creation], and implicit here is (d) (v, s, imperative mood - 'saṅbhāv bhvikht kāl - prashan bodhak', first person; synonymous with 'ākhāṅ', 'maiṅ ākh-' or 'kah-' 'sakāṅ'. See kahinā.

vīchār(u): (n, m, s; synonymous with 'kudrat de lekhe dī-' 'bīchār' and/or 'bibek') speculation, consideration or deliberation about the extent of His Creation. See vīchār(u).

What power and ability have I to interpret and explicate the extent of Your Creation?

Vāriā n jāvā, ek vār

vāriā: (a) past participle - 'bhūt kirdaṅt'; synonymous with 'pichhe rakhiā' or 'lukoiā hoiā') hidden or concealed, and (b) (present participle - 'kriyā-phal kirdaṅt'; synonymous with 'vārnā-', 'balihār-' and 'sadke-' 'jāṇā') to be willing to lay down one's life for another to whom one is devoted and for whom one has an immensely high regard.

n: (p; pronounced as 'nāṅ') no, not or implying a negative connotation.

jāvā: (v, s, present tense, first person; synonymous with 'maiṅ jā sakdā hāṅ'; pronounced as 'jāvāṅ') see jāṇā (d (vi)).

ek: (a) (adj; synonymous with 'ik') literally, one (1 of 1 to 9 numerals), and (b) (adv; synonymous with 'siraph' or 'keval') only, merely, just or simply once. (u) of 'ek(u)' is missing as it is an adjective of 'vār', a noun of female gender.

vār: (n, f, s; synonymous with 'daphā', 'ber' or 'vārī') counter or 'number of times'.

I cannot even once be a sacrifice unto You. Or:
I cannot even once lay down my life for You.

Jo, tudh(u) bhāvai, sāī bhalī kār

jo: (pron; synonymous with 'jihṛā', 'jihṛe', 'jis noṅ', 'jis nūṅ' and 'jin(h)ā nūṅ') who, whom, whosoever or whatever.

tudh(u): (a) (pron, s; synonymous with 'tūṅ', 'tūṅhī', 'tere', 'tainūṅ', 'tujh' and 'tujhe') implicit here is (b) (accusative case - 'karam kārak'; synonymous with 'tainūṅ') to you.

bhāvai: (v, s, present tense, second person; synonymous with 'tainūṅ bhāuṅdā hai') literally, [You] find appealing, desirable, suitable, deserving or worthy. See bhāuṇā.

sāī: (pronominal adj, f, s; synonymous with 'soī', 'soū' and 'ohī') the same or exactly that.

bhalī: (adj, f; synonymous with 'nek', 'shubh', 'chaṅgī', 'sreshṭ' and 'uttam') good, appealing, attractive, ideal or perfect.

kār: (n, f; synonymous with 'karanyog kaṅm') worthwhile or useful work, job or action. See kār.

Only that which appeals to You is a worthwhile deed.
[In essence, it behoves us to live only by Your Will ('razā')].

Tū, sadā salāmat(i), Niraṅkār

tū: (pron; synonymous with and pronounced as 'tūṅ') literally, you; in essence, You (the Almighty).

sadā: (adv; synonymous with 'sad', 'nitya' and 'hameshā') forever, always or in perpetuity.

salāmat(i): (adj) (a) (synonymous with 'kushal' and 'dukh or kalesh rahit') safe and sound, in good health and free of anxiety and apprehension, and implicit here is (b) (synonymous with 'isthit', 'thir', 'sathir' and 'aṭṭal') immutable, immovable, unchangeable, constant and firmly established.

Niraṅkār: (adj, m; synonymous with 'nirākār' or 'ākār rahit') one without a physical shape, i.e., the non-physical, 'spiritual' or the transcendent form of God. The 'u' of 'Niraṅkār(u)' is missing because of its vocative case - 'saṅbodhan kārak'. See Niraṅkār (Glossary).

O' formless Lord! 'You are eternal and forever immutable'.

Conceptual summary

They who have reflected upon and become attuned to the Divine Word, are supreme amongst human beings and have God's seal of approval. They are honoured at God's Court, and their presence graces the courts of kings. They are always focused on and attuned perfectly to the Divine Word, the one and only Gurū. They know in their heart of hearts that not only is God Himself beyond their physical reach and the grasp of their comprehension but also the extent of His Creation. Thus, all efforts to realise the limits of His Creation are in vain and should never even become their aim.

However, should any such person dare to deliberate and speculate about, and explicate the extent and complexity of His creation, they would soon realise the futility of this task as it is truly infinite and beyond anyone's scope and ability. Furthermore, a true devotee or 'bhagat' realises that it is not the horns of the mythological white bull that supports the planet Earth but the Divine Order itself, the offspring of His Mercy. One also realises that it is His Divine Order which, by binding and controlling everything, has established perfect orderliness in the universe like carefully arranged beads in a rosary. Should one genuinely understand, resolutely accept and live life by this Divine Order, one would be worthy of being on the verge of 'Nām-realisation'.

On the other hand, should one waver, falter and refute this, daring to claim that a white ox supports planet Earth, what would be their answer to the question: 'How heavy is the load borne by the horns of that bull'? Furthermore, if a bull supports Earth, then another Earth is required to support it, too; this chain of events would continue ad infinitum and begs the question: How much of a load would there be on the horns of the last bull, the final link in the chain, and who or what would then be its support?

Such a person, who falsely claims to know it all, faces the challenge of other difficult questions which appear later. There is an immense diversity of flora and fauna on Earth and God inscribes their fate or destiny with an uninterrupted stroke of His pen. No one knows how this is done nor understands the basis on which this account of their lot or destiny is written. Should one claim to have the knowhow, would one then know how vast this scribed scroll of a writ would be?

Who can judge His Might, His Beauty or speculate about the extent of His Bounty? He created this vast expanse with just one word or command, and infinite life forms came forth or evolved thereafter.

'What ability and power have I to interpret and explicate the extent of Your creation? I cannot even once be a sacrifice unto You. That which appeals to You is a worthwhile deed. O' formless Lord! 'You are eternal and forever immutable', says Nānak.

In summary, fortunate are they who, like the 'Pañch' alluded to at the beginning of this 'Pauṛī', willingly, lovingly and unreservedly submit to the Guru's Divine Word and Wisdom, nurture the five noble attributes - high moral character ('sat(i)'), contentment (sañtokh(u)'), compassion ('da-i-ā'), living according to His Divine Order ('dharam(u)'), and patience or forbearance ('dhīraj'), and living life by 'Nām-consciousness' and His Will.

In reality, the visible empirical world has its own lure and distracts one from examining one's conscious self, which is so important in one's spiritual progress. However, should one be fortunate enough to begin to tread the Gurū's path, one should not grasp this as an opportunity to engage in the futile search for learning about the mysteries of creation or establishing the expanse of this vast universe as they are both beyond our scope.

PAUṚĪ 17
ਪਉੜੀ ੧੭॥

Asaṅkh jap, asaṅkh bhāu.
ਅਸੰਖ ਜਪ, ਅਸੰਖ ਭਾਉ॥

Asaṅkh pūja, asaṅkh tap tāu.
ਅਸੰਖ ਪੂਜਾ, ਅਸੰਖ ਤਪ ਤਾਉ॥

Asaṅkh, graṅth mukh(i) ved pāṭh.
ਅਸੰਖ ਗਰੰਥ ਮੁਖਿ ਵੇਦ ਪਾਠ॥

Asaṅkh, jog *man*(i) rahah(i) udās.
ਅਸੰਖ, ਜੋਗ ਮਨਿ ਰਹਹਿ ਉਦਾਸ॥

Asaṅkh bhagat, guṇ giān vīchār.
ਅਸੰਖ ਭਗਤ, ਗੁਣ ਗਿਆਨ ਵੀਚਾਰੁ॥

Asaṅkh satī, asaṅkh dātār.
ਅਸੰਖ ਸਤੀ, ਅਸੰਖ ਦਾਤਾਰ॥

Asaṅkh sūr, muh bhakhsār.
ਅਸੰਖ ਸੂਰ, ਮੁਹ ਭਖ ਸਾਰ॥

Asaṅkh mon(i), liv lāi tār.
ਅਸੰਖ ਮੋਨਿ, ਲਿਵ ਲਾਇ ਤਾਰ॥

Kudrat(i) kavaṇ, kahā vīchār.
ਕੁਦਰਤਿ ਕਵਣ, ਕਹਾ ਵਿਚਾਰੁ॥

Vāriā n java, ek vār.
ਵਾਰਿਆ ਨ ਜਾਵਾ, ਏਕ ਵਾਰ॥

Jo, tudh(u) bhāve, sāī bhalī kār.
ਜੋ, ਤੁਧੁ ਭਾਵੈ, ਸਾਈ ਭਲੀ ਕਾਰ॥

Tū, sadā salāmat(i), Niraṅkār. 17.
ਤੂ, ਸਦਾ ਸਲਾਮਤਿ, ਨਿਰੰਕਾਰ॥ ੧੭॥

Asaṅkh jap, asaṅkh bhāu

asaṅkh: (adj, pl; synonymous with 'aṇgiṇat', 'anaṅt', 'beaṅt' and 'beshumār') a complex word comprising 'a' (without or beyond) + 'saṅkh' or 'saṅkhya' ('giṇtī', 'shumār' and 'hisāb' - count, estimation or calculation) i.e., beyond counting, estimation or calculation; innumerable, countless or infinite.

jap: (a) (n, m, pl; skt; synonymous with the act of 'japṇā') literally, the act of repetitive utterance of a word or a collection of words from one of the holy or religious texts, and (b) (v, pl, present tense; synonymous with 'japde han') literally, meditate or contemplate.

bhāu: (n, m; synonymous with 'prem' and 'piār'; 'shradhā'; 'lagan' or 'bhagtī') literally, love or deep affection; faith and reverence; devotion. In essence, it implies cordial, courteous and mutually sympathetic interaction and dealings with non-sentient and sentient life in the creation and/or expression of love or deep affection and reverence for God. See bhāu.

Countless focus and meditate on You and countless express their love for You and the creation in their own ways. Or:

Countless are the ways of focus and meditation, and countless engage in acts of devotion.

Asaṅkh pūja, asaṅkh tap tāu

pūjā: (n, f; synonymous with 'sanmān-', 'sevā-' or 'pūjan- 'or 'archan-' 'dī kriyā') (a) offerings of money or material things in front of a deity or the object of worship or prayers to please and/or to seek some reward in Hindu culture, and (b) (n, f) literally, worship, meditation or prayer. However, in Gurmat, pūjā of 'Prabhū' (God) is prayer or supplication to God to enable one to submit willingly and lovingly to, and to live one's life in complete harmony with, 'Nām(u)' and 'Nām-consciousness'.

Acts and ways of worship, without any concomitant change in one's conscious self and innate nature, prove to be sham and futile as is highlighted in the following verses from the SGGS:

A criminal bows down twice as much as does the hunter of a deer. What good is bowing down one's head when one harbours evil in one's 'Hirdā'?[370]

Being engrossed in, and content with, worshipping the idol of a demi-god, making flower offerings to it, prostrating like a log in front of it, and performing the six kinds of approved acts, only inflated my ego, sucked me deeper and deeper into the web of 'Māyā' but did not help me realise God.[371]

Serve Him, who knows everyone's innermost being and recognises and rewards even an iota of a good deed', O *man*! Surrender yourself and worship Him who is formless, eternal and God of Gods.[372]

I have examined numerous kinds of worship but only that which appeals to You is approved. What can this body, a puppet made of aggregates of the basic elements, accomplish by itself?[373]

tap: (a) (n, f; synonymous with 'tapassiā', 'tap karnā', 'tap sādhnā' or 'tap tāuṇā') strict discipline, austerities, penances or acts of deliberate self-punishment, e.g., tolerance of extreme cold in winter or heat in summer, prolonged fasting, silence or adoption of strange posture, etc., in order to gain full control over one's '*Man*' or conscious self.

tāu: (a) (n, m; synonymous with 'tāp', 'sek' and 'āṅch') literally, fever; heat or warmth; radiated heat, (b) (fig) (n, m, s; synonymous with 'kashṭ', 'dukh' 'ḍar' or 'khatrā') harm, hurt or danger, and implicit here is (c) (n, f; synonymous with 'tapan-', 'tapāuṇ-' and 'tap karan-' 'dī kriyā') undertaking austerities, penances or acts of deliberate self-punishment.

taptāu: (a) (n, m; synonymous with 'tapasyā dā kashṭ') the deliberate imposition of strict self-discipline, austerities or penances to gain control over one's conscious self, and implicit here is (b) (n; synonymous with 'ghāl ghālaṇī'; 'tapāṅ dā-' 'tapṇā' or 'tapāuṇā'; 'kamāī karnī') the process of moving forward with conviction and steadfastness despite having to face hurdles, problems and distress; the act of putting in prolonged, determined and intense effort or painstaking toil.

Countless worship in their own ways, and countless engage in different acts of austerity.

Asaṅkh, graṅth mukh(i) ved pāṭh

graṅth: (a) (v; synonymous with 'guṅdaṇa') to plait, braid or interlace, (b) (n, f, pl; synonymous with 'vaḍīāṅ dhārmak pustakāṅ') literally, large religious or holy books with interlinked or interrelated chapters, and implicit here is (c) (genitive case - 'saṅbaṅdh kārak', pl; synonymous with 'graṅthāṅ de') of graṅths.

mukh(i): (a) (instrumental case - 'karaṇ kārak'; synonymous with 'mukh-' 'nāl', 'rāhīṅ', 'duārā' or 'sadkā') with or through one's mukh, and

(b) (ablative case - 'apādān kārak'; synonymous with 'mukh toṅ') from one's mukh. See mukh.

mukh: (n, m, pl; synonymous with 'mūṅh' and 'chehre') literally, lips or faces; in essence, mouths.

ved: (a) (n, m, pl; synonymous with 'bed') the four Vedas/scriptures of Hindus - 'Rig', 'Sām', 'Yajur' and 'Atharvan' and implicit here is (b) (genitive case - 'saṅbaṅdh kārak', pl; synonymous with 'vedāṅ de') of Vedas.

pāṭh: (a) (n, m, pl; synonymous with 'sabak', 'saṅthā' and 'saṅthiā') literally, assignments, lessons, instructions or precepts, (b) (n, m, pl; synonymous with 'pustak de bhāg' and 'adhayāy') literally, chapters of a book, and implicit here is (c) (n, m; synonymous with 'paṛ(h)āī' and 'paṛ(h)an dī kriyā') the act of daily reading or reciting a sacred text.

graṅth ved pāṭh: (synonymous with 'graṅthāṅ or vedāṅ de pāṭh') reading or recitation from Holy Books or Vedas.

Countless read and recite the various sacred texts and Vedas.

Asaṅkh, jog *man*(i) rahah(i) udās

jog: (a) (prep; synonymous with 'nūṅ', 'prat(i)', 'tāṅi', 'laī' and 'vāste') to, up to, or for someone or something, (b) (adj; synonymous with 'uchit', 'lāik', 'yog', 'yogyatā vālā' or 'samrath') befitting, deserving, proper; capable, competent or powerful enough, (c) (n, m; synonymous with 'milāp') realisation or perception of 'Nām(u)', (d) (genitive case - 'saṅbaṅdh kārak'; synonymous with 'milāp-' 'dī') of union, reconciliation or meeting, (e) (dative case - 'saṅpardān kārak'; synonymous with 'milāp-' 'la-ī' or 'vāste') literally, for meeting, reconciliation or union, and implicit here is (f) (n, m; (skt) 'Yog') ways or protocols to focus and still one's very flirtatious mind by Patānjalī, a Hindu Rishī, and (g) (n, m, pl; synonymous with 'jogīs') followers of Gorakhnāth or practitioners of different forms of yoga.

man(i): (n, m; locative case - 'adhikaraṇ kārak'; synonymous with '*man* vich') see *man*(u).

man(u): (n, m, s) one's conscious self, 'Hirdā' or 'Jivātmāṅ'.

rahah(i): (v, pl, present tense, third person; synonymous with 'uh rahiṅde han'; pronounced as 'raheṅ') literally, live, reside or remain. See rahah(i) and rahiṇā (b).

udās: (a) (adj; synonymous with 'moh rahit') sad, depressed, melancholy or gloomy, and implicit here is (b) (adj; synonymous with 'saṅniāsī', 'virakt', 'vairāgvān' and 'uprām') literally, indifferent, detached or dispassionate. In essence, indifference or detachment is in relation to the empirical world, its pleasures or the lure of 'Māyā'.

Gurmat does not endorse the concept of renouncing one's family and the world in general but rather it emphasises fashioning and subduing one's conscious self at the same time as living the family life and shouldering one's responsibilities:

He lives forever detached in the midst of the household like the lotus flower in water.[374]

One finds the right way to realise God by converging ideologically with the true Gurū and is liberated whilst enjoying the manifold joys of the world.[375]

Countless Yogīs practise indifference and detachment from the material world and its pleasures. Or:

Countless practise indifference and detachment from the material world and its pleasures for the sake of achieving union with God.

Asaṅkh bhagat, guṇ giān vīchār(u)

bhagat: (n, m, pl; synonymous with 'shradhāvān', 'upāsak' or 'bhagtī karan vāle') devotees who worship their deity, preceptor or god with faith and conviction. See bhagat.

guṇ: (genitive case - 'saṅbaṅdh kārak'; synonymous with 'guṇāṅ dī' ['vīchār']) deliberation over the divine attributes. However, the tacit reference here is to the attributes, virtues and values or Glory of 'Nām(u)'.

giān: (n, m, s) (a) (synonymous with 'tat(u)-' 'ruhānī-' or 'brahm-' 'giān(u)'; 'ruhānī-' 'jāgratā' or sojhī') divine or spiritual knowledge; understanding of the Divine Will and true path, and realisation or perception of the eternal Reality, and (b) (genitive case - 'saṅbaṅdh kārak'; synonymous with 'giān dī' ['vīchār']) deliberation over Divine Wisdom and Knowledge.

vīchār(u): (n, f; synonymous with 'vivek', 'tatv dā nirṇā' or 'aslīyat jāṇan dī kriyā') study, reflection, deliberation, cogitation or speculation. See vīchār(u).

guṇ giān vīchār(u): (genitive case - 'saṅbaṅdh kārak'; synonymous with 'guṇāṅ ate giān dī vīchār') literally, deliberation over divine attributes, and divine wisdom and knowledge. 'dī' is the covert preposition ('saṅbaṅdhak') and acts as 'dehlī dīpak', i.e., it links two or more words with another, e.g., 'guṇāṅ dī vīchār' and 'giān dī vīchār'.

Countless devotees reflect upon and deliberate over the Divine Attributes, Wisdom and Knowledge relating to God-realisation.

Asaṅkh satī, asaṅkh dātār

satī: (a) (adj; synonymous with 'satya vaktā') they who never lie and always speak the truth, (b) (adj; synonymous with 'saṅjamī') disciplined, restrained, dispassionate, temperate and placid, (c) (adj; 'saṅtokhī') content, and implicit here is (d) (adj; synonymous with 'dānī' and 'udār-ātmā') generous, benevolent, charitable, righteous and noble. See satī.

dātār: (adj, pl; synonymous with 'dātāṅ deṇ vāle' or 'dānī') (a) a complex word comprising 'dāt' (a free gift, donation or grant) + 'ār' (synonymous with 'hār', 'vān' or 'vālā' - they who carry out the attributes of the noun) i.e., a givers, donors or bestowers of gifts, and (b) a complex word comprising 'dāt' (a free gift, donation or grant) + 'ār' ('ālya' or 'ghar' - source or fount) source or fount of all gifts. See dāt(i).

Countless nobles live a life of righteousness, self-discipline and contentment, and countless give hugely to charity.

Asaṅkh sūr, muh bhakh sār

sūr: (adj, m; synonymous with 'bahādur', 'yodhā' and 'sūrbīr') literally, brave, valiant, courageous or intrepid warriors. In essence, braves who fight 'dharam yudh' ('holy war') with the evil disposition of their innerself and for a noble and righteous cause in the wider world. See sūr.

muh: (a) (n, m, pl; pronounced as 'mūṅh') literally, mouths or faces, and implicit here is (b) (locative case - 'adhikaraṇ kārak', pl; synonymous with 'mūṅhāṅ-' 'utte' or 'uppar') literally, on their faces.

bhakh: (a) (v; synonymous with 'khāṇā') literally, to eat or dine, (b) (n, m; synonymous with 'khāṇyog padārth' as 'bhakh(u)') food fit for eating, and implicit here is (c) (synonymous with 'sahārnā', 'sahiṇā' and 'bradāsht karnā') to bear, suffer or endure and accept the risk of battle wounds and scars.

sār: (n, m; synonymous with 'lohā' and 'phaulād') literally, iron metal. In essence, the reference is to swords or other similar weapons of war made of iron. See sār.

bhakhsār: (nominative case - 'kartā kārak'; synonymous with 'sār-' or 'lohā-' 'khāṇ vāle'; 'shastrāṅ de vār sahiṇ vāle') who face and tolerate strikes or blows of weapons on their faces and/or bodies.

Countless braves, ever ready to defend righteousness, boldly face the steel, risking life and limb, and enduring battle wounds on their faces.

Asaṅkh mon(i), liv lāi tār

mon(i): (a) (n, m; synonymous with 'mun(i)') one who is not restless, agitated or emotionally perturbed in the face of physical or mental suffering, sorrow or grief, (b) (adj, m; synonymous with 'mananshīl' or 'vichārvān') one who is thoughtful, rational or considerate, and (c) (adj, m; synonymous with 'khāmosh', 'chup kītā' and 'maun-dhārī') Hindu 'sādhūs' who have vowed to observe silence and remain absorbed in this act as part of their devotion. These 'sādhūs' associated over-indulgence in dialogue with excessive fickleness of *man*, mental stress and anxiety, loss of focus, and diminution or loss of the ability to discriminate and discern.

liv: (n, f; synononymous with 'birtī- ', 'surat(i)- ' or 'dhiān-' 'dī ikāgartā') complete focus, concentration, immersion, absorption or engrossment in only one thing, and (b) (n, m; synonymous with 'vrit(i) dī ekāgartā' or 'akhaṅḍ dhiān') unwavering and lasting alignment of one's focus, attention or 'surat(i)' with only one thing.

lāi: (a) (v, s, imperative mood - 'hukmī bhvikht', second person; synonymous with 'lā-' or 'lagā-' 'lai' or 'lavo') do, engage or carry out, (b) (indeclinable past participle or perfect participle - 'pūran pūrab kārdaṅtak'; synonymous with 'lā-', 'lagā-' or 'joṛ-' 'ke') having done, engaged or carried out, and implicit here is (c) (v, s, present tense, third person; synonymous with 'lāuṅdā-', 'lāuṅdī-', 'joṛdā-' or 'joṛdī-' 'hai') do, engage or carry out. See lāuṇā (b).

tār: (a) (n, m; synonymous with 'taṅt' and 'ḍorā') literally, a string, (b) (n, f; synonymous with 'ṭhāṭ dī saptak') highest of the three octaves of a musical instrument, (c) (n, f; synonymous with 'britī dī ikāgartā') focus of attention or concentration of mind, and implicit here is (d) (adj; synonymous with 'ik ras', 'akhaṅḍ' and 'lagātār') uninterrupted, continuous, uniform and constant.

livlāi: (synonymous with 'liv lāuṅde-' or 'joṛde-' 'han') literally, engage in intense and prolonged focus on one thing only.

livtār: (n, f; synonymous with 'lagātār virtī'; 'iksār- 'or 'akhaṅḍ-' 'liv') prolonged or constant and intense focus on one thing only.

liv lāi tār: [Countless] lock themselves in a prolonged, unbroken and uniform spell of focus on the object of their attention.

Countless silent 'sādhūs', having vowed to remain mute, maintain prolonged and uninterrupted focus on remaining uncommunicative as part of their devotion.

Kudrat(i) kavaṇ, kahā vīchār. See 'Pauṛī' 16.
Vāriā na java, ek vār. See 'Pauṛī' 16.
Jo, tudh(u) bhāve, sāī bhalī kār. See 'Pauṛī' 16.
Tū, sadā salāmat(i), Niraṅkār. See 'Pauṛī' 16.

Conceptual summary

Countless (a) are the ways of focus and meditation, and countless engage in acts of devotion, (b) engage in different acts of worship, austerity, and self-imposed discipline, (c) read and recite sacred texts and Vedas, (d) Yogīs practise renunciation of the material world in order to reconcile and seek union with God, (e) reflect upon the Divine Attributes, Wisdom and Knowledge relating to God's realisation, (f) nobles live a life of righteousness, self-discipline and contentment, and countless give hugely to charity, (g) braves, resolute and ever ready to defend righteousness, boldly face steel, risking life and limb, and enduring battle wounds on their faces, and (h) uncommunicative Hindu 'sādhūs', having vowed to observe silence, maintain prolonged and uninterrupted focus on this as part of their devotion.

'What ability and power have I to interpret and explain Your Divine Order and the extent of Your creation? I cannot even once be a sacrifice unto You. That which appeals to You is verily a worthwhile deed. O' thou formless Lord! 'You are eternal and forever immutable', says Nānak.

General comment

Pauṛīs 17 to 19 allude to the infinite nature of God and the expanse of His creation. Pauṛī 17 and 18 depict two completely contrasting scenarios: countless striving to live righteously and spiritually vs countless others living as egocentrics, oppressors, exploiters and tyrants. There is just a glimmer of the two opposing ends of such a spectrum in the following two verses from the SGGS:

God, having created the universe (metaphorically, a tree), established both 'Māyā' ('Bikh') and the spiritually immortalising 'sabad' ('Aṅmrit') as the two fruits of this tree. Being the all-pervasive Creator, He carries out, and makes others carry out acts, gives fitting judgement and apportions a just reward (one of these two fruits) according to His and Will.[264]

I am a small-time warrior of God and, like other wrestlers (people of the world), I have gathered here in this wrestlers' pit (the World-Amphitheatre) with God Himself watching us in action. In the humdrum of life, we all act out our unique roles in this world ('amidst the shrieks of bugles and the beating of drums, the wrestlers enter the ring and circle about'). Through meeting the Gurū and acquiring his blessing (ideological convergence with him and alignment with 'Nām(u)'), I subdue all my five fearful opponents ('Paṅj Vikārs') and walk tall with the cloth of honour ('siropāu') on my headgear ('dumālā'). We all come here blessed with a human birth but depart in separate directions having earned different 'Karmā'. The 'gurmukhs' reap the profit of alignment with 'Nām(u)' while the 'manmukhs' depart having lost their original capital/principal.[376]

In Pauṛī 19, there is reference to countless other planets, perhaps supporting simple or even more complex life systems than those found on the planet Earth. The gift to humankind of words and language, aids us, not only in communicating with ourselves and others but also in singing God's Glory. In addition, our ability to be aware of our own thinking and also to deliberate over and scrutinise our thought processes offers us a distinct sense of discernment and wisdom, enabling us to make the right moral choices and ethical decisions.

Notwithstanding our abilities and attributes, the key message in these Pauṛīs is that God's creation alone is so vast and complex that understanding its true nature and extent is beyond the scope of our senses and comprehension. The other staggering reality is that God pervades the entire empirical universe, which is nothing else but His manifestation. To put it simply, it would be simply vain for us to engage in a search to determine the extent of this vast creation and, instead, it behoves us to search for ways and means to align with 'Nām(u)', live by His Will, and realise freedom from 'Haumaiṅ', 'Moh' and innate 'Vikārī' tendencies ('Māyā') ('Jivan Mukat(i)') and to recognise our true selves ('Parmātmāṅ' or Primal Soul) in this lifetime and gain emancipation from 'Āvāgavan', the cycle of transmigration, at death.

PAUṚĪ 18
ਪਉੜੀ ੧੮॥

Asaṅkh mūrakh, aṅdh ghor.
ਅਸੰਖ ਮੂਰਖ, ਅੰਧ ਘੋਰ॥

Asaṅkh chor, harām-khor.
ਅਸੰਖ ਚੋਰ, ਹਰਾਮਖੋਰ॥

Asaṅkh, amar kar(i) jāh(i) jor.
ਅਸੰਖ ਅਮਰ, ਕਰਿ ਜਾਹਿ ਜੋਰ॥

Asaṅkh, galvaḍh hatiā kamāh(i).
ਅਸੰਖ, ਗਲਵਢ ਹਤਿਆ ਕਮਾਹਿ॥

Asaṅkh pāpī, pāp(u) kar(i) jāh(i).
ਅਸੰਖ ਪਾਪੀ, ਪਾਪੁ ਕਰਿ ਜਾਹਿ॥

Asaṅkh kūṛiār, kūṛe phirāh(i).
ਅਸੰਖ ਕੂੜਿਆਰ, ਕੂੜੇ ਫਿਰਾਹਿ॥

Asaṅkh malechh, mal(u) bhakh(i) khāh(i).
ਅਸੰਖ ਮਲੇਛ, ਮਲੁ ਭਖਿ ਖਾਹਿ॥

Asaṅkh niṅdak, sir(i) karah(i) bhār(u).
ਅਸੰਖ ਨਿੰਦਕ, ਸਿਰਿ ਕਰਹਿ ਭਾਰੁ॥

Nānak(u) nīch(u), kahai vīchār(u).
ਨਾਨਕੁ ਨੀਚੁ, ਕਹੈ ਵਿਚਾਰੁ॥

Vāria n javā, ek vār.
ਵਾਰਿਆ ਨ ਜਾਵਾ, ਏਕ ਵਾਰ॥

Jo, tudh(u) bhāvai, sāī bhalī kār.
ਜੋ ਤੁਧੁ ਭਾਵੈ, ਸਾਈ ਭਲੀ ਕਾਰ॥

Tū, sadā salāmat(i), Niraṅkār. 18.
ਤੂ, ਸਦਾ ਸਲਾਮਤਿ, ਨਿਰੰਕਾਰ॥ ੧੮॥

Asaṅkh mūrakh, aṅdh ghor

asaṅkh: (See 'Pauṛī' 17 and pages 207-8).
mūrakh: (a) (adj, m; synonymous with 'nā-tajarbekār') inexperienced,

lacking a particular skill), and (b) (adj, m; synonymous with ‘besamajh’, ‘agiānī’ and ‘budh(i) rahit’) daft, unwise, foolish, stupid or a simpleton.

aṅdh: (a) (adj, m; synonymous with ‘aṅdhā’) literally, blind, (b) (n, m; synonymous with ‘aṅdherā’) pitch darkness, (c) (n, m; synonymous with ‘agiān’, ‘avidiā’ and ‘nādānī’) gross lack of worldly and/or spiritual awareness or knowledge; naivety or ignorance, and implicit here is (d) (adj, m, pl; synonymous with ‘agiānī’ and ‘vichārhīn’) stupid, ignorant or one lacking the power of deductive reasoning.

ghor: (a) (n, m; synonymous with ‘ghoṛā’) a horse, (b) (adj, m; synonymous with ‘da-i-ā hīṇ’ and ‘be-raham’) pitiless, merciless or cruel, (c) (n, f; synonymous with ‘garjan or gajjaṇ dī kriyā’) thunder, (d) (n, f; synonymous with ‘gūṅj’) echo, resonance, reverberation or roar, and implicit here is (e) (adj; synonymous with ‘gāṛā’ and ‘saṅghaṇā’) thick, compact, viscous or dense, and (f) (adj; synonymous with ‘bhayaṅkar’ and ‘ḍrāuṇā’) frightening, dreadful, ghastly, threatening, gruesome.

mūrakh aṅdh ghor: (a phrase; synonymous with ‘mahāṅ mūrakh’; ‘parle darje-’, ‘sikhar-’or ‘choṭī-’ ‘de mūrakh or agiānī’) consummate or ultimate fools.

Countless are naïve or stupid, dreadfully ignorant of any spiritual wisdom and lacking the power of deductive reasoning.

Asaṅkh chor, harāmkhor

chor: (n, m, pl; synonymous with ‘taskars’) burglars, thieves, robbers or pilferers.

harāmkhor: (adj, m, pl) a complex word comprising ‘harām’ + ‘khor’:

harām: (a) (adj; synonymous with ‘murdār khāṇā’) literally, consuming an already dead animal. In essence, usurping the just rights and the rightful finance and property of the meek, weak and powerless by deceit and/or force; morally, ethically or religiously depraved acts, and (b) (adj; synonymous with ‘apvitr’ and ‘dharm anusār varjit’), e.g., consumption of harām food - pork for Muslims and beef for Hindus.

khor: ((pers); suff; synonymous with ‘khāṇ vāle’) they who eat, ingest or consume.

harāmkhor: they who delve in religiously forbidden acts or consume such food, live by perverse or corrupt means and morally, ethically or religiously depraved acts, and who usurp others' assets. The following verse of the SGGS offers the Guru's clear counsel to us on this topic:

'O' brother, foods, forbidden and/or not fit for human consumption which cause bodily pain and instigate evil thoughts in one's *man*, are evil and best avoided'.[377]

Countless behave as thieves who live by perverse and corrupt means and sinful acts, and unlawfully usurp others' assets.

Asaṅkh, amar kar(i) jāh(i) jor

amar: (a) (adj, pl; synonymous with 'maraṇ rahit', 'amiṭ', 'ameṭ', aṭal' or 'achal'; pronounced as 'a-mar') literally, they who do not die; undying, immortal, everlasting or eternal, and implicit here is (b) (n, m; synonymous with 'āmar', 'āmir', 'hākim' or 'hukam karan vāle') rulers, governors or those with authority to command, and (c) (n, m; synonymous with 'āgyā', 'ādesh' and 'hukam') directive, order, command, instruction or permission.

kar(i): (indeclinable past participle; perfect participle - 'pūran pūrab kārdaṅtak'; synomymous with 'kar ke') having done or carried out an act. 'kar(i)' acts as 'dehlī dīpak' as it joins with two separate parts of the sentence, e.g., 'amar kar(i) jāh(i)' and 'kar(i) jāh(i) jor(u)'. See kar(i) and 'karnā' (g).

jāh(i): (v, pl, present tense, third person; synonymous with 'uh jāṅde han' or 'uh jā sakde han'; pronounced as 'jāheṅ') they go or can go. See jāh(i) and jāṇā (d (i and iii).

amar kar(i) jāh(i): depart having imposed their will on others.

jor: (n, m, pl; synonymous with 'dhakkā', 'zulam' and 'vadhīkīāṅ'; pronounced as 'zor') coercion, use of force, oppression, cruelty or persecution. See jor(u).

kar(i) jāh(i) jor(u): depart having deployed unlawful coercion and inflicted cruelty.

Countless impose their will forcefully and mercilessly upon others and depart having deployed unlawful coercion and/or inflicted cruelty and oppression.

Asaṅkh, galvaḍh hatiā kamāh(i)

galvaḍh: (n and adj, pl; synonymous with 'gal vaḍḍaṇ vāle', 'kasāī', 'kātal' and 'khūnī') literally, slayers, killers, assassins or murderers.

hatiā: (n, f; synonymous with 'vadh', 'katal' and 'khūn'; pronounced as 'hattiā') literally, homicide, murder or assassination.

kamāh(i): (a) (v, s, present tense, second person; synonymous with 'tusīṅ kamāuṅde ho'), (b) (v, pl, present tense, first person; synonymous with 'asīṅ kamāuṅde hāṅ'), (c) (v, s, future tense, second person; synonymous with 'tusīṅ kamāuṅge'), and implicit here is (d) (v, pl, present tense, third person; synonymous with 'uh kamāuṅde han'; pronounced as 'kamāheṅ') see kamāuṇā.

kamāuṇā: (v; synonymous with 'kamāvaṇā') (a) (synonymous with 'khaṭṇā', 'kirat kar ke dhan laiṇā' and 'lābh hoṇā') to earn, make money or profit, (b) (synonymous with 'amal vich liāuṇā') to put it into practice, and implicit here is (c) (synonymous with 'phal milnā') to gain the fruits of.

hatiā kamāh(i): literally, [they] commit acts of murder.

People with leanings towards non-vegetarian dietary predispositions view this verse as simply implying exploitation, oppression and tyranny rather than killing. Even if it is the former, the following verses from the SGGS do not support the killing of an animal for one's own proclivities:

'They who ride roughshod over, tyrannise or kill with guile and/or force and then deem it sanctified, will be answerable to the Lord in the hereafter', says Kabīr.[378]

'Use of guile and force is tyranny and the culprits shall be held accountable and duly punished in God's Court', says Kabīr.[379]

What would you call immoral or unholy if you judge killing for sacrificial offering righteous? Who would you then call a butcher when you appoint yourself as a sage, O Pandit?[380]

'You fast to please Allah but you kill other beings for your own pleasure, O Qazi; you just resort to equivocation when you intend to look after your own interests at the cost of others'?[381]

'Call not false the Vedas or the Semitic books, as false is he who fails to sift the truth. Why do you slaughter chickens for food when you say that God is in all'?[382]

Absence of love for the Lord and His Creation turns one into a butcher; this merciless one, then, shows no mercy to others.[383]

One departs to His Court triumphant and with head held high if one causes no suffering to any being.[384]

Countless murderers commit homicide and incur the full wrath of justice.

Asaṅkh pāpī, pāp(u) kar(i) jāh(i)

pāpī: (a) (instrumental case - 'karaṇ kārak'; synonymous with 'pāpāṅ-' 'nāl', 'duārā' or 'rāhīṅ'; pronounced as 'pāpīṅ') with or through pāp, (b) (adj, m, s; synonymous with 'pāp karan vālā' or 'doshī'), and implicit here is (c) (adj, m, pl; synonymous with 'pāp karan vāle' and 'doshī') sinners, miscreants, evildoers, transgressors or reprobates. See pāp(u).

Countless sinners commit evil deeds and depart leaving a trail of committed sins.

Asaṅkh kūṛiār, kūṛe phirāh(i).

kūṛiār: (adj, m) a complex word comprising 'kūṛ(i)' + 'ār'/ārā:

kūṛ: (a) (n; synonymous with 'asatya', 'mithiā', 'jhūṭh' and 'kūṛā'; antonym of 'satya' and 'sach') literally, false, baseless or that which is not everlasting, (b) one's misconceived notions of 'Haumaiṅ', 'Dvaitbhāv', and insatiable 'Lobh' for transient worldly things and their short-lived comforts and pleasures, and (c) 'Māyā' which misleads one towards the transitoriness of the material world and its pleasures and leads one away from God, the source of everlasting peace and happiness.

ār/ārā: (a) (suff; synonymous with 'ālyā' and 'ghar') literally, home or abode but, in essence, source or fount of something, and (b) (suff; synonymous with 'vālā' 'vān' and 'vaṅt') bearer of the attributes of the noun; one who lives out the attributes associated with the noun.

kūṛiār: (a) (adj, m, pl; synonymous with 'jhūṭh bolaṇ vāle' and 'asatyāvādī'; antonym of 'sachiār') literally, liars, untruthful, dishonest and faithless, (b) (n, m, pl; synonymous with 'kūṛ de ghar') source of all perverse evil drives, and (c) (adj, m, pl; synonymous with 'kūṛ vich khachit' or 'kūṛ de vapārī') steeped in and forever dealing with 'kūṛ'. In essence, they who are oblivious of God and His Divine Order and, instead, are rapt in 'Haumaiṅ', duality ('Dvaitbhāv'), and insatiable greed for the fulfilment of their innate evil drives, the transient empirical world and its short-lived comforts and pleasures.

kūṛe: (a) (n, m, pl; synonymous with 'jhūṭhe' and 'asatyāvādī') literally, liars, untruthful, dishonest and faithless, and implicit here is (b) (locative case -'adhikaraṇ kārak'; synonymous with 'kūṛ-' or 'jhūṭh-' 'vich') literally, in falsehood, dishonesty, untruthfulness and perjury. In essence, in falsehood or in the transitoriness of the material world, its comforts and pleasures.

phirāh(i): (a) (v, s, present tense, second person; synonymous with 'tusīṅ phirde ho'), (b) (v, pl, present tense, first person; synonymous with 'asīṅ phirde hāṅ'), (c) (v, s, future tense, second person; synonymous with 'tusīṅ phiroṅge'), and implicit here is (d) (v, pl, present tense, third person; synonymous with 'uh phirde han' or 'rujhe phirde han'; pronounced as 'phirāheṅ') literally, steeped or engrossed in but wandering about aimlessly. See phirnā.

phirnā: (v) (a) (synonymous with 'ṭahlaṇā', 'ghumṇā' or 'vicharnā') literally, to stroll or walk about, (b) (synonymous with 'chaurāsī de geṛ vich rahiṇā') to wander in the cycle of transmigration, (c) (synonymous with 'muṛnā', 'vāpas āuṇā' or 'huṭṇā') to turn back, return or refrain from, and implicit here is (d) (synonymous with 'bharmaṇā' or 'bhaṭkaṇā') to ramble, roam about, go round and round or wander about aimlessly.

Countless are ignorant, misguided and materialistic, and waste their lives steeped in materialism and transitory pleasures [and suffer transmigration].

Asaṅkh malechh, mal(u) bhakh(i) khāh(i)

malechh: (n, m, pl) (a) (synonymous with 'videshī bolī vāle' and 'Āryan-' and/or 'Āryan dharam-' 'virodhī') literally, foreigners, especially those who opposed and oppressed the 'Āryans', their culture and religion, and (b) (synonymous with 'kukarmī', 'anyāy karan vāle' or 'malīn-' or 'khoṭī-' 'mat(i) vāle') literally, degenerate, immoral, unprincipled and depraved; pitiless, cruel, barbaric, tyrannical and oppressors.

mal(u): (a) (n, m; synonymous with 'bhalwān' or 'pahilwān') a wrestler, (b) (v, s, imperative mood -'hukmī bhvikht', second person; synonymous with 'mal lao') claim or occupy; see 'mallaṇā', (c) (n, m; synonymous with 'pāp' or 'gunāh') sin; fault, guilt, crime, (d) (n, f; synonymous with ‘mail(u)’) literally, filth, grime and scum, and implicit here is (e) (adj; synonymous with ‘akhādya’, ‘abhakh’, ‘nā khāṇ yog’, ‘vishṭā’ or ‘gaṅdagī’) literally, excrement or that which is unfit for human consumption. However, ‘Haumaiṅ’ and evil thoughts and deeds, carried out repeatedy and over a long period, that leave a lasting and adversely modifying effect on one’s conscious self and innate nature is ‘mal(u)’ in Gurmat. This is literally what one needs to cleanse oneself in order to realign with ‘Nām(u)’ and ‘Nām-consciousness’.

mallaṇā: (a) (v; synonymous with ‘malṇā’) to wring hands; to rub or massage, and (b) (v; synonymous with ‘kabzā karnā’ or ‘zor nāl āpnā baṇāuṇā’) to claim, possess, occupy and/or own something forcibly.

bhakh(i): (v, pl, present tense, third person; synonymous with ‘hochhiāṅ’ or ‘hābṛiāṅ-’ ‘vāṅg khāṅde han’) eat impatiently and voraciously, and in an undignified manner. See bhakh(i) and bhakshaṇā.

mal(u) bhakh(i): (phrase; n, f; synonymous with ‘apvitr bhojan’ or ‘dharam varjit bhojan’) literally, ‘harām bhojan’; forbidden or proscribed food.

khāh(i): (v, pl, present tense, third person; synonymous with ‘uh khāṅde han’; pronounced as ‘khāheṅ’) literally, they dine, eat, partake of food, consume or ingest; (fig) they suffer the consequences of their deeds. See khāh(i) and khāṇā (b).

bhakh(i) khāh(i): (similar to khāhī khāh(i) in Pauri 3; synonymous with ‘hochhiāṅ- ’or ‘hābṛiāṅ-’ ‘vāṅg khāṅde han’) eat impatiently and voraciously, and in an undignified manner.

mal(u) bhakh(i) khāh(i): literally, consume proscribed food or partake of food not only which is unfit for human consumption but also impatiently, voraciously and in an undignified manner. Equally, this could also imply consuming food bought with money earned through bribery, oppression or immoral and illicit means. The following verse from the SGGS beautifully expresses the nature of such an individual:

Steeped in materialism, one wanders in every direction like a mad dog. The greedy person knows not and partakes of what is acceptable as well as what is forbidden.[385]

Countless foreign tyrants and oppressors voraciously and impatiently consume food unfit for human consumption, and/or live off bribes and income from immoral, illicit or exploitative means.

Asaṅkh niṅdak, sir(i) karah(i) bhār(u)

niṅdak: (n and adj, m, pl; synonymous with 'niṅdā karan vāle') slanderers, blasphemers, backbiters or they who engage in false and malicious slander and disparagement. See niṅdā.

niṅdā: (a) (n, f; synonymous with 'niṅd', 'niṅdiā', 'badnāmī' or 'jhūṭhī tohmat') backbiting, slander, vilification, or malicious insinuations, and (b) (n, f; synonymous with 'augaṇ kaḍaṇ dī kriya') deprecation or denigration of virtues while highlighting or exaggerating one's drawbacks, demerits or flaws.

sir(i): (locative case - 'adhikaraṇ kārak'; synonymous with 'sir-' 'te', 'utte', 'par' or 'uppar') literally, on, upon or above one's head. See sir(i).

karah(i): (a) (v, pl, present tense, third person; synonymous with 'uh karde-' or 'kardīāṅ' 'han' or 'kar sakde han'; pronounced as 'karheṅ') do, perform or carry out. See karah(i) and karnā (g).

bhār(u): (a) (n, m s; synonymous with 'bojh' or 'vazan') literally, weight, load, luggage or cargo, implicit here is (b) (synonymous with 'ahsān', 'pharz' and 'jumevārī') (fig.) onus, obligation or burden of responsibility. In essence, the reference here is to the guilt, crime and punishment of slander.

sir(i) karah(i) bhār(u): literally, bear the burden on their heads. However, the reference here is to the ramifications of their action.

By their very nature, an egocentric person normally resorts to belittling another's virtues and exaggerating their handicaps to boost their own ego. However, this tendency isn't particularly fruitful as it deflects one from reflecting on one's own weaknesses. The following verses from the SGGS expose this aspect of a slanderer:

It is wrong to slander another, a practice in which the unwise and egocentric indulge; their faces are blackened and they are thrown into the depths of Hell (they are maligned and shunned, and their lives become miserable and unbearable).[386]

The slanderers, overlooking their own sorrowful state, wash the accumulated dirt of another and, thus, reap what they sow. Neither do they get any inner peace here and now nor any reward at God's Court, eventually suffering in the cycle of transmigration.[387]

Countless slanderers bear the burden of the repercussions of their slander.

Nānak(u) nīch(u), kahai vīchār(u)

Nānak(u): (n, m, s) the founder and the first of the ten Sikh Gurūs.

nīch(u): (adj; synonymous with 'nimāṇā', 'nitāṇā', 'nāchīz' and 'guṇhīn') low in terms of noble attributes, virtues and values, i.e., one who is mean, miserly, callous or spiteful or one with innate evil tendencies. See nīch(u).

Nānak(u) nīch(u): (synonymous with 'nīch(u) Nānak(u)' or 'Nānak(u)-' 'vechārā' or 'garīb') literally, humble and lowly Nānak(u).

kahai: (v, s, third person, present tense; synonymous with 'ākhdā-' or 'kahiṅdā-' 'hai'; 'varṇan-' or 'vakhyān-' 'kardā hai') literally, says or states. See kahai and kah(i)ṇā.

vīchār(u): (n, m, s; synonymous with 'kudrat de lekhe dī-' 'bīchār' and/or 'bibek') speculation, consideration or deliberation of the extent of His creation. See vīchār(u).

Nānak(u) nīch(u): literally, 'nīch(u) Nānak(u)' or 'guṇhīn Nānak(u)' and this is virtually similar to the phrase 'kudrat kavaṇ' in 'Pauṛī' 16, 17 and 19.

kahai vīchār(u): (a) (synonymous with 'tuchh vichār pesh kardā hāṅ') literally, I, humble and lowly Nānak, offer my insignificant view or opinion, and implicit here is (b) (synonymous with 'kuchh bhī kah sakāṅ') what ability do I have that I could make even a small contribution towards the extent and expanse of Your Creation?

'I, Nānak, lowly and humble, and lacking any noble attributes or virtues, offer my humble but considered view. Or:

What noble attributes or virtues do I, lowly Nānak, possess that I could even dare to debate the expanse of Your Creation?

Vāria n javā, ek vār. See 'Pauṛī' 16.
Jo, tudh(u) bhāvai, sāī bhalī kār. See 'Pauṛī' 16.
Tū, sadā salāmat(i), Niraṅkār. See 'Pauṛī' 16.

Conceptual summary

Countless are (a) dreadfully ignorant of any wisdom and devoid of the power of deductive reasoning, (b) thieves who live unlawfully off their perverse and corrupt means and usurp what belongs to others, (c) tyrants who forcefully and mercilessly impose their will upon others, and depart from this world having inflicted cruelty and oppression on others, (d) murderers who commit homicide and stand to incur the wrath of justice, (e) sinners who commit evil deeds and depart from this world leaving a trail of sins behind, (f) ignorant and materialistic, who waste their lives steeped in materialism and its transitory pleasures, and suffer transmigration, (g) foreign tyrants and oppressors who partake of food not fit for human consumption and live off bribes or income from immoral, illicit or exploitative means, and (h) slanderers who bear the burden of the aftermath of their slander.

'What noble attributes or virtues do I, lowly Nānak, possess that I could even dare debate the extent and expanse of Your Creation? I cannot even once be a sacrifice unto You. That which appeals to You is verily a worthwhile deed. O' thou formless Lord! 'You are eternal and forever immutable', says Nānak.

PAURĪ 19
ਪਉੜੀ ੧੯॥

Asaṅkh nāv, asaṅkh thāv.
ਅਸੰਖ ਨਾਵ, ਅਸੰਖ ਥਾਵ॥

Agaṅm, agaṅm, asaṅkh loa.
ਅਗੰਮ, ਅਗੰਮ, ਅਸੰਖ ਲੋਅ॥

Asaṅkh kahah(i), sir(i) bhār(u) hoi.
ਅਸੰਖ ਕਹਹਿ, ਸਿਰਿ ਭਾਰੁ ਹੋਇ॥

Akhrī nām(u), akharī sālāh.
ਅਖਰੀ ਨਾਮੁ, ਅਖਰੀ ਸਾਲਾਹ॥

Akhrī, giān(u), gīt guṇ gāh.
ਅਖਰੀ, ਗਿਆਨੁ, ਗੀਤ, ਗੁਣ ਗਾਹ॥

Akhrī, likhaṇ(u), bolaṇ(u) bāṇ(i).
ਅਖਰੀ, ਲਿਖਣੁ, ਬੋਲਣੁ ਬਾਣਿ॥

Akhrā, sir(i) saṅjog(u) vakhāṇ(i).
ਅਖਰਾ, ਸਿਰਿ ਸੰਜੋਗੁ ਵਖਾਣਿ॥

Jin(i) eh(i) likhe, tis(u) sir(i) nāh(i).
ਜਿਨਿ ਏਹਿ ਲਿਖੇ, ਤਿਸੁ ਸਿਰਿ ਨਾਹਿ॥

Jiv phurmāe, tiv tiv pāh(i).
ਜਿਵ ਫੁਰਮਾਏ, ਤਿਵ ਤਿਵ ਪਾਹਿ॥

Jetā kītā, tetā nāu.
ਜੇਤਾ ਕੀਤਾ, ਤੇਤਾ ਨਾਉ॥

Viṇ(u) nāvai, nāhī ko thāu.
ਵਿਣੁ ਨਾਵੈ, ਨਾਹੀ ਕੋ ਥਾਉ॥

Kudrat(i) kavaṇ, kahā vīchār.
ਕੁਦਰਤਿ ਕਵਣ, ਕਹਾ ਵੀਚਾਰੁ॥

Vāriā na java, ek vār.
ਵਾਰਿਆ ਨ ਜਾਵਾ, ਏਕ ਵਾਰ॥

Jo, tudh(u) bhāve, sāī bhalī kār.
ਜੋ ਤੁਧੁ ਭਾਵੈ, ਸਾਈ ਭਲੀ ਕਾਰ॥

Tū, sadā salāmat(i), Niraṅkār. 19.
ਤੂ, ਸਦਾ ਸਲਾਮਤਿ, ਨਿਰੰਕਾਰ॥ ੧੯॥

Asaṅkh nāv, asaṅkh thāv

asaṅkh: (See 'Pauṛī' 17 and pages 207-8).

nāv: (n, m, pl; synonymous with and pronounced as 'nāṅv') names for the countless elements, non-sentient and sentient beings in the universe. See nāv.

thāv: (n, f, pl; synonymous with 'thāuṅ' and 'ṭhāṅvāṅ'; pronounced as 'thāṅv') literally, places or locations which elements, non-sentient and sentient beings inhabit.

Countless are the names of the created elements, non-sentient and sentient beings, and countless the places where they are found. Or:

Countless are Your Names and Titles, and countless the places which You pervade and where You exist.[8-10]

Agaṅm, agaṅm, asaṅkh loa

agaṅm: (adj, m; synonymous with 'agam'; pronounced as 'agaṅm') (synonymous with 'apahuṅch') inaccessible, unreachable, unapproachable, unfathomable or beyond human reach. See agaṅm.

loa: (n, pl; synonymous with 'lok', 'khaṅḍ', and 'bhavan') islands, countries or continents; domains, spheres or planets in a system, e.g., 'trilok' of Hindu belief, and the fourteen planets (seven planets below and seven above planet Earth), in the Islamic tradition. See loa.

Countless domains, spheres or planets are beyond human reach.

Asaṅkh kahah(i), sir(i) bhār(u) hoi

kahah(i): (a) (v, s, present tense, second person; synonymous with 'tūṅ ākhdā haiṅ' or 'tusīṅ ākhde ho'), (b) (v, pl, present tense, first person; synonymous with 'asīn ākhde hāṅ'), and implicit here is (c) (v, pl, present tense, third person; synonymous with 'uh kahiṅde- 'or 'ākhde-' 'han'; pronounced as 'kahaheṅ') see kahiṇā.

asaṅkh kahah(i): literally, [they who even dare to speculate and] postulate the extent of His creation as countless ('asaṅkh'). In essence, they who use the word 'asaṅkh' to assign limits to His creation are committing an error, for both He and His creation are limitless, and the word 'asaṅkh', too, fails to do the issue full justice. The word ineffable ('akath') perhaps comes closer and signifies Gurū Nānak's true meaning.

sir(i): (locative case - 'adhikaraṇ kārak'; synonymous with 'sir-' 'te', 'utte', 'par' or 'uppar') literally, on one's head. See sir(i).

bhār(u): (a) (n, m; synonymous with 'bojh' and 'vazan') literally, weight, load, luggage or cargo, (b) (n, s; (fig.) synonymous with 'ahsān', 'pharz' and 'jumevārī') onus, obligation or burden of responsibility. In essence, the reference here is to the guilt, blame and punishment of this error.

hoi: (v, s, present tense; synonymous with 'huṅdī- 'or 'huṅdā-' 'hai'; 'ho jāṅdī- 'or 'ho jāṅdā-' 'hai'; 'ho sakdā hai') literally, occurs, comes to be or becomes; can occur, happen or become. See hoi and hoṇā (a and c (iii)).

They who use the word 'asaṅkh' to define the limits to His creation, bear the blame and liability of this error upon themselves. Or:

They who use the term 'asaṅkh' to express limits to His creation, bear the consequences of committing this error.

Akhrī nām(u), akharī salāh

akhrī: (instrumental case - 'karaṇ kārak'; synonymous with 'akhrāṅ-', 'varaṇ-' or 'lipī-' 'duārā' or 'rāhīṅ'; pronounced as 'akhrīṅ') with or through the use of words.

nām(u): (n, m, s) immanent aspect of God. However, tacit reference here is to the names we ascribe to God and 'Nām Japṇā' - His Glory or the attributive aspect of 'Nām(u)' which one imbibes in one's conscious self or 'Hirdā' as one aligns and harmonises with 'Nām(u)'.

sālāh: (n, f; synonymous with 'ustat(i)', 'mahimā', 'shalāghā', 'vaḍiāī' and 'siphat salāh') His Glory or Praise.

[However, whilst words, like 'asaṅkh', fail to capture the limits of His creation] it is only through words that we explicate the intangible 'Nām(u)' and sing His Glory.

Akhrī, giān(u), gīt, guṇ gāh

giān(u): (n, m, s; synonymous with 'tat(u)-' 'ruhānī-' or 'brahm-' 'giān(u)'; 'ruhānī-' 'jāgratā' or 'sojhī') divine or spiritual knowledge; intuitive insight and knowledge of godliness; an understanding of His

Divine Will and the true path to the realisation or perception of the eternal Reality. See giān.

gīt: (n, m, pl) (a) (synonymous with 'gāuṇ vāle pad') songs, (b) (synonymous with 'bhajan' or 'pūjā de gīt') hymns or songs of Praise (God's Glory), but the implication here is to Gurbāṇī, God's Praise as contained in the SGGS, or any other sacred text for that matter, and (c) (genitive case - 'saṅbaṅdh kārak'; synonymous with 'gītāṅ de') of gīts.

guṇ: (a) (n, m, pl; synonymous with 'visheshaṇ', 'siphat', 'khūbī', 'khāsīat', 'lachhaṇ' and 'subhāu' or 'tāsīr') literally, characteristics, properties or attributes of something, and the tacit reference here is to the attributive aspects or Glory of 'Nām(u)', and (b) (genitive case - 'saṅbaṅdh kārak'; synonymous with 'guṇāṅ de') of guṇ.

gāh: (n, m; synonymous with 'gāhak', 'kharīdār' and 'vākaph') literally, real customers, buyers or seekers; well-acquainted and well-aware of the value of the product. See gāh.

gīt guṇ gāh: literally, seekers of noble attributes of the hymns and songs of praise.

Through words we acquire divine or spiritual knowledge, and with words we grasp and imbibe His attributes and sing songs of His Praise.

Akhrī, likhaṇ(u), bolaṇ(u) bāṇ(i)

likhaṇ(u): (infinitive mood - 'bhāvārth kārdaṅtak'; synonymous with 'likhṇā', 'likhat', 'lekh', 'lip(i)', 'tahrīr' and 'likhaṇ dī kriyā') the act or art of capturing words in written form.

bolaṇ(u): (n, m; infinitive mood - 'bhāvārth kārdaṅtak'; synonymous with 'vachan' and 'kathan') literally, speech, utterance or pledge; solemnly given word.

bāṇ(i): (a) (n, f; synonymous with 'bolī'; pronounced as 'bāṇī') language, dialect or mode of communication, and (b) (genitive case - 'saṅbaṅdh kārak'; synonymous with 'bāṇī-' or 'bolī-' 'dā') of language or spoken words. See bāṇ(i) and bāṇī.

likhaṇ(u) bolaṇ(u) bāṇ(i): (synonymous with 'bāṇī'/ 'bolī-' 'dā likhṇā ate bolṇā') literally, the writing or utterance of language or words of wisdom.

Through words we speak and communicate the essence of our oral or written expression. Or:

A language can only be spoken or written with words.

Akhrā, sir(i) saṅjog(u) vakhāṇ(i)

akhrā: (instrumental case - 'karaṇ kārak'; synonymous with 'akhrāṅ-', 'varaṇ- 'or 'lipī-' 'nāl', 'duārā' or 'rāhīṅ'; pronounced as 'akhrāṅ') with or through the use of words.

sir(i): see above. The outcome of God's judgement of one's Karmā ('karam phal' or 'bhāg'; fate or destiny) is inscribed on one's forehead ('mastak de lekh') right from birth, according to popular belief. It signifies the sum total of one's attributes, innate nature, circumstances and opportunities for the realisation or otherwise of one's potential in life.

saṅjog(u): (a) (n, m; synonymous with 'saṅbaṅdh' or 'itphāk') connection or concordance, (b) (n, m, s; synonymous with 'upāya' or 'yatan') means, remedy or measure, and implicit here is (c) (n, m, s; synonymous with 'milāp'; antonym of 'vijog') a subsidiary of the Divine Order ('Hukam') that brings together circumstances, events or two things or beings previously separated and (d) (n, m; synonymous with 'bhāg' or 'karam phal', and n, f; synonymous with 'kismat') consequence of one's action, one's lot; fate or destiny.

vijog(u): (n, m, s; antonym of 'saṅjog(u)') (a) a subsidiary of the Divine Order ('Hukam') which brings about circumstances or events that lead to separation of two things or beings previously together, for example, the 'vemukh person' and 'Nām(u)', and (b) (n, m; synonymous with 'vichhoṛā' or 'judāī') separation or parting from a dear one.

vakhāṇ(i): (a) (indeclinable past participle or perfect participle - 'pūran pūrab kārdaṅtak'; synonymous with 'vakhiān-' or 'biān-' 'kar ke') by narrating or describing; having described or expounded, (b) (n, m; synonymous with 'vakhiān-' or 'biān-' 'kartā') one who explains, describes, reveals or expounds, and implicit here is (c) (v; synonymous with 'vakhiān- 'or 'biān-' 'kītā jāṅdā hai'; pronounced as 'vakhāṇī'). See vakhānaṇā.

vakhānaṇā: (v; synonymous with 'vakhāṇanā', 'vakhyānaṇā', and 'vakhiān-' or 'biān-' 'karnā') to describe, elaborate, elucidate, expound or expatiate.

An account of our destiny, allegedly inscribed on our forehead right from birth, can be explained only with words.

Jin(i) eh(i) likhe, tis(u) sir(i) nāh(i)

jin(i): (pron, s; nominative case - 'kartā kārak'; synonymous with 'jis(i)' and 'jis ne') who, whoever or whosoever. However, the tacit reference here is to God.

eh(i): (pron; pl of 'eh') literally, only these or just these. The reference here is to an account of one's destiny ('saṅjogāṅ-' or 'mastak-' 'de lekh').

likhe: (a) (v, s, present tense, third person; synonymous with 'likhdā hai') literally, writes or inscribes, and implicit here is (b) (v, s, present perfect, third person; synonymous with 'likhe han') literally, have written. The tacit reference here is to accounts or details of one's fate or destiny ('lekh') which God writes or has apparently inscribed, on one's forehead, i.e., 'saṅjogāṅ-' or 'mastak-' 'de lekh'.

tis(u): (genitive case - 'saṅbaṅdh kārak'; synonymous with 'us-' 'de' or 'ke') literally, his. However, the tacit reference here is to God.

sir(i): see sir(i) (d).

nāh(i): (a) (n, m; synonymous with 'nāth', 'swāmī' or 'mālik'; 'pat(i)') Lord; husband, and (b) (indeclinable past participle or perfect participle - 'pūran pūrab kārdaṅtak'; synonymous with 'n(h)ā ke' or 'isnān kar ke') having bathed, and implicit here is (c) (p; pronounced as 'nāh(i)ṅ') no, not or implying a negative connotation.

tis(u) sir(i) nāh(i): literally, no such words are inscribed on His forehead as He is completely immune to and beyond this space-time logic or rules of governance.

However, God Himself, who writes everyone's destiny, has no such account written on His forehead.

The following verses from the SGGS also point towards this sentiment:

'This visible, infinite, empirical world, His manifestation ('sargun sarūp' of 'Nām(u)'), is the creation of His Divine Order but the transcendent and ineffable Lord Himself is beyond its scope'.[388]

Jiv phurmāe, tiv tiv pāh(i)

jiv: (adv; synonymous with 'jioṅ, 'jis prakār', 'jaise' and 'jiveṅ') howsoever, as, in the manner of, as though, for instance.

phurmāe: (v, s, present tense, third person; synonymous with 'phurmāuṅdā-' or 'hukam kardā-' 'hai'; pronounced as 'phurmāe') literally, wills, orders or commands.

tiv: (adv; synonymous with 'tiveṅ', 'taise' or 'us trāṅ') similarly or in the same manner.

pāh(i): (v, pl, present tense, third person; synonymous with 'pāuṅde-' or 'prāpat karde-' 'han'; pronounced as 'pāheṅ') see pāuṇā (a and d). The reference here is to 'saṅjogāṅ- 'or 'mastak-' 'de lekh'.

What He Ordains, so the mortals receive.

Jetā kītā, tetā nāu

jetā: (adj, m) (a) (synonymous with 'jetū', 'vij-a-ī' and 'jittan vālā') winner, victor, victorious or triumphant, and (b) (synonymous with 'jiṅnā' and 'jitnā') however much or as much as.

kītā: (n, f; synonymous with 'krit') creation. See kītā.

tetā: (adv; synonymous with 'utnā') that much or equivalent to.

nāu: (n, s; synonymous with 'Nām(u)') 'Nām(u)', as the one word is also the embodiment of all His attributes, both known and unknown to man, and His being and immanent form. 'Nām(u)' - the Primal Soul - is also the sole creator which pervades every aspect of its creation. Nothing exists without the presence of 'Nām(u)' within. Yet, despite this, He is transcendent and not identical to the creation.

As vast as is Your creation, it just reflects Your Glory. Or:
The entire creation is nothing but Your 'virtual' manifestation.

Viṇ(u) nāvai, nāhī ko thāu

viṇ(u): (prep; synonymous with 'bin', 'binā', 'bājh' and 'vagair') literally, without, save, or but for.

nāvai: (ablative case - 'apādān kārak'; synonymous with 'Nāv-' or 'Nām-' 'toṅ') literally, from 'Nām(u)'.

viṇ(u) nāvai: (synonymous with 'Nāv-' or 'Nām-' 'toṅ binā') literally, without 'Nām(u)'.

nāhī: (a) (v, s, present tense; synonymous with 'n(h)āuṅdā-' or 'isnān kardā-' 'hai'; pronounced as 'nāhīṅ') bathes, (b) (adj, m; synonymous with ‘varjaṇ vālā’ or ‘prat(i)baṅdhak’) administrator, enforcer, or one who forbids, and (c) (p; synonymous with ‘nāṅ’ or ‘nahīṅ’; pronounced as ‘nāhīṅ’) no, not or implying a negative connotation.

ko: (pron; abbrev for and synonymous with ‘koī’) someone, anyone or another.

thāu: (n, f; synonymous with ‘thāṅ’, ‘asthān’, ‘jag(h)ā’, ‘tikāṇā’, ‘ḍerā’ and ‘dishā’; (pl) thāv; pronounced as ‘thāuṅ’) place, resting place, dwelling, location, space, region or direction. His pervasiveness in the universe is beautifully captured in the following verses from the SGGS:

This vast empirical world that you see is nothing but His manifestation; in reality, it is all that you see.[389]

The unfathomable Lord is not only within everything but is also without. He pervades every ‘Hirdā’ and being.[390]

There is no place without ‘Nām(u)’ - the all-pervasive Primal Soul.

Kudrat(i) kavaṇ, kahā vīchār. See ‘Pauṛī’ 16.
Vāriā na java, ek vār. See ‘Pauṛī’ 16.
Jo, tudh(u) bhāve, sāī bhalī kār. See ‘Pauṛī’ 16.
Tū, sadā salāmat(i), Niraṅkār. See ‘Pauṛī’ 16.

Conceptual summary

Countless are the names of the created sentient beings, and countless the places where they exist. Countless are Your Names and Titles, and countless the places where You manifest. Countless domains, spheres or planets are beyond human reach. They who use the word ‘asaṅkh’ to ascribe limits to His creation, bear the consequences of committing this error. However, whilst words, like ‘asaṅkh’ fail to capture the limits of His creation, it is only through words that we expound the ineffable ‘Nām(u)’ and sing His Glory. Through words we acquire Divine Knowledge, and with words we grasp His attributes and sing songs of His Praise. Through words we communicate in speech and writing. Indeed, an account of our destiny, allegedly inscribed on our forehead right from birth, can only be explained with words. Whilst God inscribes the accounts of mortals’ destinies, He Himself has no such account written on His forehead. The reality is that what He ordains, is what mortals receive. The entire creation is nothing but His mere virtual manifestation, and, indeed, there is no place without 'Nām(u)', the all-pervasive Primal Soul, His immanent form.

'What ability and power have I to interpret and explicate Your Divine Order and the extent of Your creation? I cannot even once be a sacrifice unto You. That which appeals to You is verily a worthwhile deed. O' thy formless Lord! 'You are eternal and forever immutable', says Nānak.

In summary, Gurū Nānak alludes to the beginning of this vast and diverse empirical world and humbly guides us away from our vain attempts to find its limits and even from using the word 'asaṅkh'. He envisages the whole world as His manifestation and further suggests that whilst God has granted us words and language to sing His Glory, this gift should not be abused in an attempt to define the extent of His Glory or His creation.

PAUṚĪ 20
ਪਉੜੀ ੨੦॥

Bharīai hath(u), pair(u), tan(u), deh.
ਭਰੀਐ ਹਥੁ, ਪੈਰੁ, ਤਨੁ, ਦੇਹ॥

Pāṇī dhotai, utras(u) kheh.
ਪਾਣੀ ਧੋਤੈ, ਉਤਰਸੁ ਖੇਹ॥

Mūt palītī, kapaṛ(u) hoi.
ਮੂਤ ਪਲੀਤੀ, ਕਪੜੁ ਹੋਇ॥

De sābūṇ(u), la-ī-ai oh(u) dhoi.
ਦੇ ਸਾਬੂਣੁ, ਲਈਐ ਓਹੁ ਧੋਇ॥

Bharīai mat(i), pāpā kai saṅg(i).
ਭਰੀਐ ਮਤਿ, ਪਾਪਾ ਕੈ ਸੰਗਿ॥

Oh(u) dhopai, nāvai kai raṅg(i).
ਓਹੁ ਧੋਪੈ, ਨਾਵੈ ਕੈ ਰੰਗਿ॥

Puṅnī, pāpī, ākhaṇ(u) nāh(i).
ਪੁੰਨੀ, ਪਾਪੀ, ਆਖਣੁ ਨਾਹਿ॥

Kar(i) kar(i) karṇā, likh(i) lai jāh(u).
ਕਰਿ ਕਰਿ ਕਰਣਾ, ਲਿਖਿ ਲੈ ਜਾਹੁ॥

Āpe bīj(i), āpe hī khāh(u).
ਆਪੇ ਬੀਜਿ, ਆਪੇ ਹੀ ਖਾਹੁ॥

Nānak, hukmī āvah(u) jāh(u) (20)
ਨਾਨਕ, ਹੁਕਮੀ ਆਵਹੁ ਜਾਹੁ॥ ੨੦॥

Bharīai hath(u), pair(u), tan(u), deh

bharīai: (a) (v, s, present tense, third person; synonymous with 'bhar- 'or 'gaṅdā ho-' 'jāṅdā hai') becomes dirty, smeared or defiled, (b) (v, pl, imperative mood - 'hukmī bhvikht', first person; synonymous with 'sānūṅ bhar laiṇā chāhīdā hai') we should fill to the brim, and implicit here is (c) (v, s, 'saṅbhāv bhvikht kāl - kiās bodhak'; first person; synonymous with 'je bhar- ', 'libbaṛ- 'or 'gaṅdā ho-' 'jāve') [if something] should become laden, heavily coated or smeared with [dust, scum or filth]. See bharnā (b and c (vii)).

hath(u): (n, m, s; synonymous with 'kar(u)', 'dast(u)' and 'hast(u)') one hand; hath: (n, m, pl) both hands.

pair(u): (n, m, s; synonymous with 'pad(u)', 'charan(u)' or 'pāṅv(u)') one foot; pair: (n, m, pl) both feet.

tan(u): (n, m, s; synonymous with 'srīr'; n, f, s; synonymous with 'deh') literally, the body or the physical frame through which '*man*' expresses itself and interacts with the physical world.

deh: (a) (n, m; (pers) synonymous with 'piṇḍ' and 'grām') village, and implicit here is (b) (n, f, s; synonymous with 'tan(u)', 'jisam', and 'sarīr') being a noun of female gender, its singular form lacks the (u) at the end.

Should one's hand, foot or body become soiled or heavily covered with dust...

Pāṇī dhotai, utras(u) kheh

pāṇī: (a) (n, m; synonymous with 'jal') water, and implicit here is (b) (instrumental case - 'karaṇ kārak'; synonymous with 'jal-' 'nāl', 'rāhīṅ', 'sadkā' or 'duārā') with or through water.

dhotai: (a) (present participle - 'kriyā-phal kirdaṅt'; synonymous with 'dhotiāṅ', and (b) (instrumental case - 'karaṇ kārak'; synonymous with 'dhovan- 'or 'dhoṇ-' 'nāl') by cleansing or washing.

utras(u): (v, s, present tense, second person; synonymous with 'mail-', 'dard-' or 'pīṛ-' 'uttar jāṅdī hai') literally, disappears, ceases to exist or vanishes. See utarnā (c, d and g).

kheh: (n, f, s; synonymous with 'dhūl(i)', 'dhūṛ', 'gard', 'miṭṭī' and 'suāh') dust, soil, mud or ashes.

It can be cleansed with water.

Mūt palītī, kapaṛ(u) hoi

mūt: (n, m; synonymous with 'mūtar' and 'peshāb') urine.

palītī: (a) (n, f; synonymous with 'palīdtā', 'palītpan' and 'apvitrata') pollution, filth or defilement, and (b) (adj; synonymous with 'palīdtā vālā', 'palīt' and 'nāpāk') unclean, polluted, impure or defiled.

palīt: (adj; synonymous with 'palīd' (pers), 'apvitr' and 'nāpāk') unclean, polluted, impure or defiled.

kapaṛ(u): (a) (adj, m, s; synonymous with 'līrāṅ dī godṛī pah(i)raṇ vālā') beggar or vagabond, (b) (n, m, s) synonymous with 'khillat') a robe of honour, (c) (n, m, s) synonymous with 'deh' or 'sarir') body or physical frame, and implicit here is (d) (n, m, s) synonymous with 'vastr') cloth, fabric, garment or dress.

hoi: (v, s, imperative mood - 'saṅbhāv bhvikht kāl - kiās bodhak', third person; synonymous with 'ho jāve' or 'hove') literally, were to become or were to be. See hoi and hovṇā (a and c).

Should one's garment become soiled and defiled with bodily excrement...

De sābūṇ(u), la-ī-ai oh(u) dhoi

de: (indeclinable past participle or perfect participle - 'pūran pūrab kārdaṅtak'; synonymous with 'lā ke') literally, by applying and rubbing.

sābūṇ(u): (n, m; arab; synonymous with 'sābun' or 'sāban') soap.

la-ī-ai: (a) (v, pl, imperative mood, first person; synonymous with 'japīe' or 'simrīe') meditate, reflect or contemplate, (b) (v, s, present tense, third person; synonymous with 'laiṅdā hai') buys, gets, receives or acquires, (c) (v, s, imperative mood - 'hukmī bhvikht', first person, pl; synonymous with 'laiṇā chāhidā hai') literally, we should do or should be able to do, and implicit here is (d) (conj. v, s, present tense, third person; synonymous with 'la-ī-dā hai'), e.g., 'dho la-ī-dā hai' - is washed or gets washed.

oh(u): (pron and adj, s; synonymous with 'uh' and 'vah') literally, he or that. In essence, the reference here is to an unclean or defiled cloth, garment or dress.

dhoi: (a) (v, s, imperative mood - 'saṅbhāv bhvikht kāl - prernā bodhak', second person; synonymous with 'dhovo') wash or cleanse, (b) (indeclinable past participle or perfect participle - 'pūran pūrab kārdaṅtak'; synonymous with 'dho ke') by washing or cleansing, and implicit here is (c) (v; s, present tense, third person; synonymous with 'dhoṅdā hai' or 'dhotā jā sakdā hai') washes or cleanses; can be washed or cleansed. See dhoṇā.

dhoṇā: (v; synonymous with 'dhovṇā', 'dhāvan karnā' and 'pāṇi'/'sāban nāl-' 'sāph or ujlā karnā') to wash or launder something with soap and/or water.

It can be washed with soap and water.

Bharīai mat(i), pāpā kai saṅg(i)

mat(i): (n, f; synonymous with 'akal', 'giān', 'samajh' and 'siāṇap') knowledge, intellect, wisdom, and ability to reason or discern. This is one of the aspects or functions of '*man*' in Gurmat. See mat(i).

pāpā: (instrumental case - 'karaṇ kārak'; synonymous with 'pāpāṅ-' 'nāl', 'kāran' or 'duārā'; pronounced as 'pāpāṅ') with pāp. See pāp(u).

kai: (prep; synonymous with 'kā', 'ke', 'kī', 'dā', 'de' or 'dī') of. See kai.

saṅg(i): (a) (n; synonymous with 'sāthī') companion, (b) (n; synonymous with 'saṅbaṅdhī') relative or kinsman, (c) in the company or society of, or in association with (saṅg), and implicit here is (d) (prep; synonymous with 'sāth', 'sāth se', 'nāloṅ' or 'nāl') with, along with, along-side or together with.

The following verses from the SGGS allude to the sentiments expressed in this verse:

Thus, trapped in this 'vikārī' way of life (mired in enmity, lust, disproportionate anger and attachment, falsehood, evil, guile, and unchecked greed), he has lived many lives and made little progress. 'O' Lord! Grant Your Grace and save him', supplicates Nānak![391]

This '*man*' is polluted in every way with the filth of 'haumai' and 'vikārs' of many lives and, like the oilman's duster, it cannot now be cleansed even though it may be washed hundreds of times. However, one's mindset changes when one surrenders to and imbibes the Guru's Wisdom and Knowledge and loses one's 'haumaiṅ'; one, then, no longer succumbs to 'Māyā' nor remaind bound to 'Āvāgavan'.[392]

All the deeds one does under the influence of 'haumaiṅ' create chains for one's neck, and the undue sense of ownership in one's mind ('mamtā') creates leg irons for one's ankles.[393]

All one's innate 'vikārī' tendencies make one commit sins which in turn become chains for one's neck; in contrast, divine attributes, virtues and values are one’s real kith and kin and friends, for they help negate and/or eliminate them. Moreover, as the innate ‘vikārī’ tendencies and burden of one’s sins accompany one in the hereafter and attract no reward, one should rid oneself of these by any means.[394]

Should one’s intellect or deductive reasoning be defiled with innate evil tendencies…

Oh(u) dhopai, nāvai kai raṅg(i)

oh(u): see above. In essence, the reference here is to the corrupted, unclean or defiled knowledge, wisdom (‘mat(i)’) or discerning ability of ‘*man*’.

dhopai: (a) (v, pl, imperative mood - ‘hukmī bhvikht’, first person; synonymous with ‘sānūṅ dho laiṇā chāhīdā hai’) should wash or cleanse, and (b) (v, s, present tense, third person; synonymous with ‘dhotā jāṅdā hai’ or ‘dhotā jā sakdā hai’) is or can be washed or cleansed. See dhoṇā.

nāvai: (genitive case - ‘saṅbaṅdh kārak’; synonymous with ‘Nāv-’ or ‘Nām-’ ‘de nāl’) with ‘Nām(u)’.

raṅg(i): (instrumental case - ‘karaṇ kārak’; synonymous with ‘raṅg-’ or ‘prem-’ ‘nāl’, ‘duārā’ or ‘rāhīṅ’) see raṅg(u) (a and j).

nāvai kai raṅg(i): literally, with or by the dye or love of ‘Nām(u)’. However, implicit here is ‘submitting to, imbibing the attributes of and aligning with ‘Nām(u)’ willingly and lovingly’. The following verses of the SGGS lend further weight to this thesis:

When one submits to the Guru’s Divine Word and Wisdom and imbibes it, one realises that by contemplating and singing His Glory, one aligns perfectly with and realises Him - the fount of all attributes, virtues and values.[395]

Those who submit to the Gurū’s Divine Word and Wisdom and imbibe it, rid themselves of their ‘haumaiṅ’ and live by God’s Will, become like Him.[396]

That can be cleansed by lovingly imbibing the attributes of ‘Nām(u)’.

Puṅnī, pāpī, ākhaṇ(u) nāh(i)

puṅnī: (a) (v; synonymous with 'pūrī hoī'; pronounced as 'puṅnī') fulfilled, (b) (adv; instrumental case - 'karaṇ kārak'; synonymous with 'puṅnaṅ kar ke'; pronounced as 'puṅnīṅ') through or by virtue of 'puṅn', and implicit here is (c) (adj, m; synonymous with 'puṅnya-vān' or 'puṅn karan vālā'; pronounced as 'puṅnī') one who performs noble deeds.

puṅn: (n, m;) (a) (synonymous with 'sukaram'; 'bhale-', 'uttam-', 'sukrit-', 'shubh-', 'sreshṭ-', 'pavitr-' or 'nek-' 'karam') acts of virtue, merit, charity, or altruism, and (b) acts deemed good and auspicious, and of positive value in one's spiritual progress, in Hindu belief.

pāpī: (a) (instrumental case - 'karaṇ kārak'; synonymous with 'pāpāṅ-' 'nāl', 'duārā' or 'rāhīṅ'; pronounced as 'pāpīṅ') with or through 'pāp', and implicit here is (b) (adj, m, s; synonymous with 'pāp karan vālā' or 'doshī') and (c) (adj, m, pl; synonymous with 'pāp karan vāle' and 'doshī') sinners, miscreants, evildoers, transgressors or reprobates. See pāp(u).

ākhaṇ(u): (a) (v: (ākhaṇ and ākhaṇ(i)); synonymous with 'kahiṇā' and 'kathan karnā') see ākhṇā, and (b) (n, m, s; infinitive mood - 'bhāvārth kārdaṅtak'; synonymous with 'bolaṇ', 'kathan', 'biānaṇ' and 'vakhiānaṇ') literally, speech, utterance, statement or elaboration. In essence, not just mere words.

nāh(i): (a) (n, m; synonymous with 'nāth', 'swāmī' or 'mālik'; 'pat(i)') Lord; husband, (b) (indeclinable past participle or perfect participle - 'pūran pūrab kārdaṅtak'; synonymous with 'n(h)ā ke' or 'isnān kar ke') having bathed, and implicit here is (c) (p; pronounced as 'nāh(i)ṅ') no, not or implying a negative connotation.

ākhaṇ(u) nāh(i): literally, are not mere statements or sayings. However, the tacit reference here is to their consequences - the just reward and befitting punishment for good and bad deeds respectively.

Saints or sinners are not mere statements or labels.

Kar(i) kar(i) karṇā, likh(i) lai jāh(u)

kar(i): (indeclinable past participle; perfect participle - 'pūran pūrab kārdaṅtak'; synomymous with 'kar ke') having done or carried out an act. See karṇā (f and g).

likh(i): (indeclinable past participle or perfect participle - 'pūran pūrab kārdaṅtak'; synonymous with 'likh ke') literally, by writing or noting; having written. See likhṇā.

likhṇā: (v; synonymous with 'likhat vich liāuṇā') literally, to note or write down. However, the tacit reference here is to a record of good and bad thoughts and deeds ('Karmā'). It is believed that thoughts and deeds, repeated over and over again, assume the form of a habit which leaves an indelible mark or a permanent imprint ('Saṅskār') on one's conscious self ('Jīvātmāṅ'). The record or account of these 'Saṅskārs', based on one's 'Karmā', forms the basis of one's judgement at God's Court, and one's fate or destiny (whatever one is endowed with at birth, both the qualitative and quantitative aspects of one's virtues and/or vices; one's physical, psychological and spiritual potential; coming together ('Saṅjog') or parting/loss ('Vijog') of objects, people or wealth) is then written on one's forehead ('mastak de lekh' or 'mathai jo likhiās(u)'). 'Mastak de lekh' and 'Saṅskārs' contribute towards and influence one's future innate nature, drives and desires, and thus one's actions later in this life and in the next.

lai: (indeclinable past participle or perfect participle - 'pūran pūrab kārdaṅtak'; synonymous with 'lai ke') see laiṇā (a and b).

jāh(u): (a) (imperative mood - 'hukmī bhvikht'; synonymous with 'jāo', 'jāvo' or 'janmo'; pronounced as 'jā(h)o') go, depart or be born, (b) (v, pl, present tense, second person; synonymous with 'tusīṅ lai jāṅde ho'; pronounced as 'jāo') take with you or accompany you, and implicit here is (c) (v, pl, future tense, second person; synonymous with 'tusīṅ lai jāoge' or 'jāvoge'; pronounced as 'jāo') see jāṇā (a and d (i) and (viii)).

likh(i) lai jāh(u): literally, 'Saṅskārs', inscribed on your conscious self ('Jīvātmāṅ'), accompany your 'Jīvātmāṅ' to God's Court.

The following verses forewarn us that our good and bad deeds are recorded and will be subject to God's scrutiny and justice:

'Be ever so mindful of sins you may commit inadvertently', O' my careless '*Man*'; therefore, seek the refuge of the most Merciful Lord who grants noble and godly attributes to the abject and ignoble, and dispels all their fears'.[397]

We reap the fruits of our past deeds and cannot lay the blame on others. Forsaking alignment with and allegiance to 'Nām(u)', we fall into the clutches of 'Haumaiṅ', 'Moh' and our innate evil nature ('Māyā'), and all kinds of suffering and ills overwhelm us. Having deserted 'Nām(u)' and, therefore, succumbed to 'Māyā', we commit sins and misdeeds, and forfeit any notion of reconciliation for many lifetimes.[398]

Our deeds ('karmā') bind us to 'Āvāgavan'; the imprints they leave on our conscious self ('Saṅskārs') become our innate evil nature ('subhāu' or 'kirat(i)') which, in turn, makes us dance to its tunes. [258]

'Saṅskārs', the indelible marks or permanent imprints of often repeated thoughts and actions, get inscribed on our conscious self and accompany our 'Jīvātmāṅ' in the hereafter.

Āpe bīj(i), āpe hī khāh(u)

āpe: (pron, m, s; nominative case - 'kartā kārak'; synonymous with 'āp- 'or 'khud-' 'hī') literally, solely oneself.

bīj(i): (indeclinable past participle or perfect participle - 'pūran pūrab kārdaṅtak'; synonymous with 'bīj ke') having sown the seeds or lived a particular lifestyle. See bījaṇā (a and b).

bījaṇā: (v) (a) (synonymous with 'boṇā' or 'bīj bījṇā') literally, to sow seeds, (b) (fig.) to conduct oneself according to one's innate nature and beliefs, and (c) (fig.) to labour, toil or work hard.

hī: (a) (prep; synonymous with 'dā', 'nūṅ', 'toṅ', 'neṅ'; 'trāṅ', 'prakār' and 'vich') of; to; from; kind, sort, category or manner; within, inside, among or between respectively, (b) (p or adv; synonymous with 'nischai' or 'yakīnan') surely, certainly or without fail, (c) (adv or emphatic particle; synonymous with 'keval' and 'siraph') only, indeed, exactly or verily, (d) (adj; synonymous with 'acharj') strange, quaint, astonishing or wondrous, (e) (n, f, s; synonymous with with 'ur' or 'chhātī') chest, (f) (aux v) hai, (g) sār, (h) (adv; synonymous with 'vī' or 'bhī') also, (i) (interj; synonymous with 'haiṅ') what?, and implicit here is (j) (n, m, s; synonymous with 'svai/svayam', '*man*' or 'hirdā') one's conscious self or oneself.

khāh(u): (a) (v, pl, imperative mood - 'hukmī bhvikht', second person; synonymous with 'tusīṅ-' 'khāo' or 'khāvo') you eat, ingest or consume, (b) (v, pl, present tense, second person; synonymous with 'tusīṅ khāṅde ho') you eat or consume, and implicit here is (c) (v, pl, future tense, second person; synonymous with 'tusīṅ khāvoge'; pronounced as 'khā(h)o') you will eat or consume; you will bear the consequenes of. See khāṇā (b and c (i)).

āpe bīj(i) āpe hī khāh(u): (a) you will enjoy the fruits of your labour, and (b) you will suffer the consequences of your actions. The following verses from the SGGS express this sentiment clearly and eloquently:

We must settle our accounts for the deeds we commit.[399]
One is rewarded for one's own good and bad deeds.[400]
We bear the fruit according to the deeds we commit.[401]
Blame not others but, instead, blame the deeds we ourselves commit; for what we sow now is what we reap later, so why blame others?[255]

What we sow now is what we reap later.

Nānak, hukmī āvah(u) jāh(u)

Nānak: (n, m, s; vocative case - 'saṅbodhan kārak') O Nānak! The (u) of 'Nānak(u)' is missing because of its vocative case - 'saṅbodhan kārak'.

hukmī: (instrumental case - 'karaṇ kārak'; synonymous with 'hukam-' 'nāl', 'duārā', 'rāhīṅ' or 'anusār'; pronounced as 'hukamīṅ' or 'hukmīṅ') literally, legally, by lawful means or within the constraints of the law. In essence, according to Divine Order or by His Will. See hukmī.

āvah(u): (a) (v, pl, imperative mood - 'hukmī bhvikht', second person; synonymous with 'tusīṅ āu' or 'tusīṅ janam lavo'), (b) (v, pl, future tense, second person; synonymous with 'tusīṅ āvoge' or 'tusīṅ janam lavoge'), and implicit here is (c) (v, pl, present tense, second person; synonymous with 'tusīṅ āuṅde ho' or 'tusīṅ janam laiṅde ho'; pronounced as 'āva(h)o') you come or are born. See āuṇā (b).

jāh(u): see jāh(u) (c).

āvah(u) jāh(u): (ph) literally, a phrase meaning you repeatedly come and go. However, in essence, it refers to 'Āvāgavan' - the cycle of birth and death or transmigration.

'We come into and depart from this world by His Will', O' Nānak!

Conceptual summary

If one's hand, foot or body gets soiled or heavily smeared with dust, one removes it by cleansing it with water; if one's garment becomes contaminated or defiled with bodily excrement, it is washed clean with soap and water. However, if one's conscious self ('Jīvātmāṅ') becomes corrupted or defiled with evil tendencies, it is cleansed by lovingly submitting to and imbibing the attributes of 'Nām(u)'. Virtues and sins or saints and sinners are not mere statements or labels; if repeated often enough, good and bad deeds leave their imprints on our conscious self and accompany us to our day of judgement. God's Will prevails, and we reap what we sow. 'Thus, our coming into and departure from this world (liberation or transmigration for the soul) is determined by His Will', O' Nānak!

The following verses from 'Jap(u)' highlight God's modus operandi – the Divine Order ('Hukam(u)') that autonomously and spontaneously governs all aspects of this evolving world:

'How can we demolish this false barrier of ego-consciousness and re-align perfectly with 'Nām(u)? Follow His Command as prescribed right at the outset, and carry out His Will', says Nānak. Pauṛī 1, pages 66-68.

'One is accredited high or low status, physical and/or mental good health, happiness, material comforts and contentment, and inner turmoil or bliss in one's destiny according to His Divine Order'. Pauṛī 2, page 74.

'We come into and depart from this world according to His Divine Order', O' Nānak. Pauṛī 20, pages 245.

Thus, the Divine Order ('Hukam(u)' and its subsidiary set of rules and laws) governs all aspects of this empirical world. Accordingly, as we sow, so shall we reap.

One's repetitive thoughts or deeds become habits which, in turn, leave an imprint ('Saṅskārs') on one's conscious self. They form the basis of one's judgement in the hereafter and one's position as well as fate/destiny ('Mastak de lekh') in the hierarchical system of Āvāgavan determined by His 'Hukam(u)'.

We could choose to become engrossed in the empirical world, and remain bound to transmigration or live by His Will, and find release from the clutches of 'Haumai', 'Moh' and evil 'Vikārī proclivities' ('Jīvan Mukat(i)') and, realising our true self, find freedom from this system of transmigration ('Param Mukat(i)').

'Haumai', 'Moh' and evil 'Vikārī' proclivities ('Māyā') always lure and drive one towards the empirical world and 'Vikārs', and thus, one's conscious self becomes corrupted and defiled (ego-consciousness). Rapt in the empirical world and detached from ‘Nām-consciousness’, one experiences inner turmoil and physical and psychological problems, and loses inner calmness and contentedness. ‘Nām Japnā’ is the way to cleanse this filth of ego-consciousness and realise lasting inner equipoise and bliss but its purpose is not to enable one to ascertain the extent of this creation and its creator.

PAUṚĪ 21
ਪਉੜੀ ੨੧॥

Tīrath(u), tap(u), da-i-ā, dat(u) dān(u).
ਤੀਰਥੁ, ਤਪੁ, ਦਇਆ, ਦਤੁ ਦਾਨੁ॥

Je ko pāvai, til kā mān(u).
ਜੇ ਕੋ ਪਾਵੈ, ਤਿਲ ਕਾ ਮਾਨੁ॥

Suṇiā, maṅniā, *man*(i) kītā bhāu.
ਸੁਣਿਆ, ਮੰਨਿਆ, ਮਨਿ ਕੀਤਾ ਭਾਉ॥

Aṅtargat(i) tīrath(i), mal(i) nāu.
ਅੰਤਰਗਤਿ ਤੀਰਥਿ, ਮਲਿ ਨਾਉ॥

Sabh(i) guṇ tere, mai nāhī koi.
ਸਭਿ ਗੁਣ ਤੇਰੇ, ਮੈ ਨਾਹੀ ਕੋਇ॥

Viṇ(u) guṇ kīte, bhagat(i) n hoi.
ਵਿਣੁ ਗੁਣ ਕੀਤੇ, ਭਗਤਿ ਨ ਹੋਇ॥

Suāst(i) āth(i), bāṇī barmāu.
ਸੁਅਸਤਿ ਆਥਿ, ਬਾਣੀ ਬਰਮਾਉ॥

Sat(i), suhāṇ(u), sadā *man*(i) chāu.
ਸਤਿ ਸੁਹਾਣੁ ਸਦਾ ਮਨਿ ਚਾਉ॥

Kavaṇ(u) s(u) velā, vakhat(u) kavaṇ(u), kavaṇ thit(i), kavaṇ vār(u).
ਕਵਣੁ ਸੁ ਵੇਲਾ, ਵਖਤੁ ਕਵਣੁ, ਕਵਣ ਥਿਤਿ, ਕਵਣੁ ਵਾਰੁ॥

Kavaṇ(i) s(u) rutī, māh(u) kavaṇ(u), jit(u) hoā ākār(u).
ਕਵਣਿ ਸਿ ਰੁਤੀ, ਮਾਹੁ ਕਵਣੁ, ਜਿਤੁ ਹੋਆ ਆਕਾਰੁ॥

Vel n pāīā paṅḍatī, j(i) hovai lekh(u) purāṇ(u).
ਵੇਲ ਨ ਪਾਈਆ ਪੰਡਤੀ, ਜਿ ਹੋਵੈ ਲੇਖੁ ਪੁਰਾਣੁ॥

Vakhat(u) n pāio kādīā, j(i) likhan(i) lekh(u) qurāṇ(u).
ਵਖਤੁ ਨ ਪਾਇਓ ਕਾਦੀਆ, ਜਿ ਲਿਖਨਿ ਲੇਖੁ ਕੁਰਾਣੁ॥

Thit(i), vār(u), nā jogī jāṇai, rut(i) māh(u) nā koī.
ਥਿਤਿ, ਵਾਰੁ, ਨਾ ਜੋਗੀ ਜਾਣੈ, ਰੁਤਿ ਮਾਹੁ ਨਾ ਕੋਈ॥

Jā kartā sirṭhī kau saje, āpe jāṇai soī.
ਜਾ ਕਰਤਾ ਸਿਰਠੀ ਕਉ ਸਾਜੇ, ਆਪੇ ਜਾਣੈ ਸੋਈ॥

Kiv kar(i) ākha, kiv sālāhī, kio varnī, kiv jāṇā.
ਕਿਵ ਕਰਿ ਆਖਾ, ਕਿਵ ਸਾਲਾਹੀ, ਕਿਉ ਵਰਨੀ, ਕਿਵ ਜਾਣਾ॥

Nānak, ākhaṇ(i) sabh(u) ko ākhai, ik du ik(u) siāṇā.
ਨਾਨਕ, ਆਖਣਿ ਸਭੁ ਕੋ ਆਖੈ, ਇਕ ਦੂ ਇਕੁ ਸਿਆਣਾ॥

Vaḍā Sāhib(u), vaḍī nāi, kītā jā kā hovai.
ਵਡਾ ਸਾਹਿਬੁ, ਵਡੀ ਨਾਈ, ਕੀਤਾ ਜਾ ਕਾ ਹੋਵੈ॥

Nānak, je ko āpau jāṇai, agai ga-i-ā nā sohai (21)
ਨਾਨਕ, ਜੇ ਕੋ ਆਪੌ ਜਾਣੈ, ਅਗੈ ਗਇਆ ਨ ਸੋਹੈ॥ ੨੧॥

Tīrath(u), tap(u), da-i-ā, dat(u) dān(u)

tīrath(u): (n, m, s; synonymous with 'dharam nāl juṛe hoe pavitr sthān') literally, a place of pilgrimage where believers of different faiths go to cleanse themselves of their sins, to atone, to seek favour, grace, mercy, or forgiveness. Whilst it is essential for some just to go and visit, others believe in bathing, making offerings of material things and money, and performing acts of charity towards this end. Gurmat does not give any credence to such ritualistic acts. Instead, it lays emphasis on cleansing the filth ('mal(u)') of 'Haumaiṅ', false pride and the evil streak from one's conscious self by aligning with 'Nām(u)' and 'Nām-consciousness'. See 'Pauṛī' 6; pp. 119-22.

tap(u): (a) (n, f; synonymous with 'tapassiā', 'tap karnā', 'tap sādhnā' or 'tap tāuṇā') strict discipline, austerities, penances or acts of deliberate self-punishment, e.g., tolerance of extreme cold in winter or heat in summer, prolonged fasting, silence or adoption of strange posture, etc., all to gain full control over one's '*Man*' or conscious self.

da-i-ā: (n, f; synonymous with 'karuṇā', 'myā', 'raham', 'kripā', 'mehar', 'taras') pity, compassion, sympathy, mercy or benevolence.

dat(u): (a) (n, m; synonymous with 'tiāgaṇ dā bhāv') an act of renunciation, and implicit here is (b) (n, m; synonymous with 'dittā hoiā dān') that which has been given away freely.

dān(u): (a) (p and suff; synonymous with 'vān', 'vaṅt' or 'vālā') e.g., 'kalamdān' - an inkstand for pen and ink, 'juzdān' - bookshelf, a satchel or a bag for books, and 'ātishdān', 'aṅgīṭhī' or fireplace, (b) (n; synonymous with 'dān vich dittī vastū') something given as a gift, and (c) (n, m; synonymous with 'khairāt') alms, donation, charity or a free gift to the needy, from a donor who neither intends nor desires to have something in return.

Generally approved acts, in the name of a faith system, may prove motivating and may lead to irrational customary practice but fail to leave a lasting commitment amongst followers to be morally and ethically responsible, to accept the thesis of the Fatherhood of God and the Brotherhood of Man, and to regard the planet Earth as a common and shared eco-system for all life, be it non-sentient or sentient. Hence, Gurmat emphasises submission to, strict focus on, and imbibement of the real essence of the Divine Word (Gurū's 'Updesh') in one's 'Hirdā' with loving conviction and does not attach a lot of weight to acts just carried out ritualistically. The following verses from the SGGS merit closer scrutiny as they relate to and highlight different attitudes of human behaviour in this regard:

By deliberating, one submits to the Gurū's Divine Wisdom, aligns with 'Nām(u)' and reaps its just rewards, and learns how to give to charity wisely. This is the true path and the rest is the mere twaddle of a deceitful man, says Nānak.[402]

The outwardly considerate and caring sense a feeling of contentedness with thoughts of charitable acts in their '*man*' but hidden behind this lies their expectation of much gratitude and indebtedness of the humanity, in return.[403]

Only one who earns through honest hard work and shares it with the needy knows the righteous path.[404]

See next paṅkat(i).

Je ko pāvai, til kā mān(u)

je: (conj; synonymous with 'je kar', 'yadī' and 'agar') if or in case.

ko: (pron; abbrev for and synonymous with 'koī') someone, anyone or another; many or several.

pāvai: (a) (v, s, present tense, second person; synonymous with 'tusīṅ pāuṅde ho'), (b) (imperative mood - 'saṅbhāv bhvikht kāl - kiās, sharat, or ichhā bodhak'; synonymous with 'je prāpat ho jāve'; 'je prāpat kar la-īe'), and implicit here is (c) (v, s, present tense, third person; synonymous with 'uh pāuṅdā-', 'pā sakdā-' or 'prāpat kar sakdā-' 'hai'; pronounced as 'pāvaiṅ') see pāuṇā (a).

til: (a) (n, m, s) sesame seed, and (b) (adj) miniscule like a sesame seed. (u) of 'til(u)' is missing because of the preposition 'kā' that links it with the noun 'mān(u)'.

kā: (prep, m; synonymous with 'dā') of.

mān(u): (a) (n, m; synonymous with 'abhimān' or 'garūr') vanity, pride, conceit, or arrogance, and (b) (n, m; synonymous with 'māṇ(u)', 'sanmān', 'ādar', 'satkār', 'izzat', 'ābrū' and 'pratishṭā') respect, self-respect, accolade, esteem, meritorious status or honour.

If someone were to earn recognition and honour in return for acts of pilgrimage, austerity, compassion, and charity, it would be worth only a tiny grain.

Suṇiā, maṅniā, *man*(i) kītā bhāu

suṇiā: (a) (v, s, present perfect; third person; synonymous with 'suṇ liā hai' or 'anubhav kar liā hai') see suṇanā, and implicit here is (b) (present participle - 'kriyā-phal kirdaṅt'; synonymous with 'jis ne 'Nām(u)-' 'sun liā hai' or 'vich surat(i) joṛī hai') whosoever has focused on 'Nām(u)'. See suṇanā, Pauṛī' 8, pp. 137-8.

maṅniā: (a) (v, s, present perfect, third person; synonymous with 'maṅn liā hai') see maṅnaṇā, and (b) (present participle - 'kriyā-phal kirdaṅt'; synonymous with 'jis ne 'Nām(u)' nūṅ suṇ ke maṅn liā hai') one who has listened attentively to the Divine Word, submitted to it, and has imbibed its message in one's conscious self with conviction. See maṅnaṇā.

man(i): (locative case - 'adhikaraṇ kārak'; synonymous with '*man* vich') in one's conscious self ('Jivātmāṅ', '*Man*' or 'Hirdā').

kītā: (v, present perfect; synonymous with 'jis ne bhī kītā hai') literally, [whosoever] has acted or done the deeds. See kītā.

bhāu: (a) (n, m; synonymous with 'shradhā' and 'vishvāsh') faith, trust, confidence, or devotion, and (b) (n, m; synonymous with 'prem' and 'piār') love or deep affection. See bhāu.

One who has focused on the Gurūs 'updesh' (Divine Word), submitted to and imbibed it in one's 'Hirdā' with loving conviction...

Aṅtargat(i) tīrath(i), mal(i) nāu

aṅtargat(i): (a) (n, f; synonymous with 'aṅtarmukhī vrit(i) or birtī') a complex word comprising 'aṅtar' (within) + 'gat(i)' (spiritual state or level) i.e., one's focus on one's conscious self ('*Man*' or 'Hirdā'), and (b) (adv; synonymous with ('aṅdar prāpat hoiā') literally, already available in one's 'Hirdā'.

tīrath(i): (synonymous with 'tīrath utte or upar') literally, in, at or over a holy place.

aṅtargat(i) tīrath(i): literally, at or in one's conscious self ('*Man*' or 'Hirdā') where one's 'Jīvātmāṅ' resides. However, implicit here is where one contemplates, focuses on, and submits to the Gurū's Divine Word unreservedly, and genuinely strives to imbibe His Message and align with 'Nām(u)' with loving conviction.

mal(i): (adv; synonymous with 'mal mal ke') by rubbing or scrubbing vigorously. See malnā (d).

malnā: (a) (v; synonymous with 'hath malnā') to wring one's hands, (b) (v; synonymous with 'lāuṇā') to apply, (c) (v; synonymous with 'maslaṇā') to trample and to rub and crush forcefully, and (d) (v; synonymous with 'ragharṇā') to rub, scrub or massage vigorously.

nāu: (a) (v, s, present tense, first person; synonymous with 'n(h)āuṅdā hai'; pronounced as 'n(h)āu') literally, I undertake ablutions or bathe, and (b) (v, past tense or present perfect tense; synonymous with 'n(h)āiā' or 'n(h)āiā hai').

mal(i) nāu: (a) (v, s, present tense, first person; synonymous with 'mal mal ke 'n(h)āuṅdā hai') literally, I vigorously scrub to cleanse the filth off, and (b) (v, past tense or present perfect tense; synonymous with 'mal mal ke n(h)āiā hai') literally, vigorously scrubs to clean the filth off. The reference here is to the sustained, determined, and rigorous introspection and contemplation upon 'Nām(u)', which metaphorically acts as a detergent to remove the filth of 'Haumaiṅ', 'Moh' and innate evil 'Vikārī' tendencies from one's conscious self.

...has really scrubbed and bathed, at the holy place within [and cleansed the 'filth' from one's conscious self].

Sabh(i) guṇ tere, mai nāhī koi

sabh(i): (adj; synonymous with 'sabhe', 'sabho', 'sarab' and 'tamām') all.

guṇ: (n, m, pl; synonymous with 'visheshaṇ', 'siphat', 'khūbī', 'khāsīat', 'lachhaṇ', 'subhāu/tāsīr') literally, characteristics, properties, or attributes of something; however, the tacit reference here is to attributes, values, virtues associated with 'Nām(u)'.

tere: (pron, pl) literally, yours but implicit here is 'Prabhu's'.

mai: (pron; synonymous with 'merā', 'mere' or 'mainūṅ' or 'mujhe') mine or to me.

nāhī: (p; pronounced as 'nāhīṅ') no, not or implying a negative connotation.

koi: (a) (pron) someone or anyone, (b) (adj; synonymous with 'koī') any, some or certain.

mai nāhī koi: literally, I have no ability. In essence, whatever little virtue I have is due to You, and not of my making.

You are the fount of all noble attributes and virtues; whatever little I have, is due to You.

Viṇ(u) guṇ kīte, bhagat(i) n hoi

viṇ(u): (prep; synonymous with 'bin', 'binā', 'bājh' and 'bagair') without, save, or but for.

kīte: (a) (adv; synonymous with 'kar ke' and 'paidā kītiāṅ') by generating, (b) (v, pl, past tense; synonymous with 'paidā- 'or 'utpaṅn-' 'kīte') produced or generated, and (c) (imperative mood - 'saṅbhāv bhvikht kāl - sharat or shradhā bodhak'; synonymous with 'je tūṅ-''kareṅ' or 'paidā kar deveṅ') if You were to generate. See karnā (i (iii)).

viṇ(u) guṇ kite: (synonymous with 'guṇ paidā kītiāṅ bina' or 'je tūṅ mere aṅdar guṇ nāṅ paidā kareṅ') (a) without developing or harbouring noble attributes, and (b) without You manifesting and nurturing these noble attributes in my 'Hirdā'. It should be clear from the previous verses and 'Pauṛīs' that one first needs to seek genuinely and actively and then follow the Gurū's path to alignment with and realisation of 'Nām(u)' with absolute faith and determination before one becomes worthy of His Grace. Since He is the fount of all attributes, virtues and values, His Grace manifests as the harbouring, nurturing, and expression of these noble attributes within oneself.

bhagat(i): (n, f; synonymous with 'sevā', 'shradhā' and 'upāsanā'; pronounced as 'bhagatī') literally, faith, trust, reverence, meditation, love, devotion or worship. In essence, it is unwavering faith in, love for, focus and meditation on or devotional attachment to the persona (attributes, virtues and values) or the Glory of 'Nām(u)' (or any object of one's devotion), such that one imbibes the same attributes within one's Hirdā, and innately or spontaneously reflects them in one's daily life.

n: (p; pronounced as 'nāṅ') no, not or implying a negative connotation.

hoi: (v, s, present tense; synonymous with 'huṅdī- 'or 'ho sakdī-' 'hai') see hoi and hoṇā/hovṇā (a).

And one cannot innately and spontaneously reflect the noble attributes and express one's devotion in one's daily life without Your instilling and nurturing them in one's 'Hirdā' first. Or:

Expression of my devotion or worship of You is not possible without my harbouring and nurturing noble virtues and values in my 'Hirdā' first.[8 - 10]

Suāst(i) āth(i), bāṇī barmāu

suāst(i): (a) (p; synonymous with 'aṅgīkār bodhak') words denoting approval, e.g., 'hāṅ' or 'ṭhīk', (b) (n, f; synonymous with 'ashīrvād' and 'āsīs') a blessing or benediction of good health, happiness and contentment, and implicit here is (c) (synonymous with 'O'aṅkār dī dhun(i)', 'jai hove terī' and 'tainūṅ namaskār hai') 'Anhad Nād', I salute You, I bow to You or 'Wāhegurū terā hī āsrā', (d) (p; 'kushal bodhak') e.g., 'maṅgal ho!' or 'kushal ho!' i.e., prosper, be in good health and may God save you, and (e) (n; synonymous with synonymous with 'kalyāṇ-', 'chhutkārā-' or 'bachāo-' 'bodhak') literally, liberate, escape or find freedom.

āth (i): (a) (n, f; synonymous with 'iṅdrīyāṅ de vishiāṅ vich) engrossed in the perverse drives related to the various sensory organs, (b) (adv; synonymous with 'thakkiā hoiā' and 'niḍhāl') extremely tired, fatigued or exhausted, (c) (adv; synonymous with 'ast' or 'lop hoiā') having set, disappeared or become invisible, (d) (adv; synonymous with 'ithe' or 'aithe') here, (e) (adj; synonymous with 'ichhā vālā' or 'khāhishmaṅd') literally, desirous or aspiring, and implicit here is (d) (n, f; synonymous with 'arth', 'dhan', 'daulat' and evil 'Vikārī' tendencies ('māiā')) wealth, material assets, and material comforts and pleasures, and (e) (ablative case - 'apādān kārak'; synonymous with 'māiā toṅ') literally, from 'māiā.

suāst(i) āth(i): (a) O' Lord! I salute You, for You have created material comforts and pleasure ('Māyā'),[7-10] and (b) literally, freedom from the clutches of 'Māyā'.

bāṇī: (n, f; synonymous with Gurbāṇī or Gurū's 'bachan', 'bol' or words) spiritually uplifting and divinely inspired words of knowledge and wisdom or utterances of one who has realised 'Nām(u)', and whose every thought, utterance and deed is in harmony with 'Nām(u)'. See bāṇī.

barmāu: (a) (adj; synonymous with 'Brahmā dī'; pronounced as 'brahmāu') of Brahmā, (b) (synonymous with 'Brahmā', 'Brahmā dī rachnā' and 'Brahmā dī Ved-bāṇī') Brahmā himself; Brahmā's Ved-bāṇī.

bāṇī barmāu: (synonymous with 'Brahmā dī' bāṇī') literally, Brahmā's bāṇī. However, implicit here is the Divine Word uttered by someone who is in perfect harmony with 'Nām(u)' ('Anhad Nad, Dhun(i) or Sabad), viz., Gurū's 'bachan', 'bol' or words (Gurbāṇī).

'O' Lord! I salute You. From You issued forth the 'Anhad Nād' ('Nām(u)'), material assets, comforts and pleasures (Māyā), Divine Word, Brahmā, and the Creation'.[7-10] *Or:*

Find freedom ('suāst(i)') from the clutches of 'Māyā' (āth(i)) by submitting to and imbibing the Gurū's Divine Word.

Sat(i), suhāṇ(u), sadā *man*(i) chāu

sat(i): The Sanskrit word 'satya' is written as 'sat(i)' in Gurbānī and used in the following context: (a) (adj; synonymous with 'sadīvī') eternally existent, (b) (adj; synonymous with 'ythārath', 'tat(u)' and 'tath(u)') eternal truth, (c) (adj; synonymous with 'pāk', 'pavitr', 'nirmal' and 'pūrā') immaculate, perfect and flawless, (d) (adj; synonymous with 'sreshṭ' and 'utam') the ultimate in everything, and (e) (n, m, s; synonymous with 'Kartār' and 'Kartā Purakh') the Creator, the one and only eternal Truth, all-pervasive, and the unchanging eternal Reality. See sat(i).

suhāṇ(u): (a) (adj; synonymous with 'shobhnīk' or 'suṅdar') beautiful, elegant, or charming, and (b) (adj; synonymous with 'pavitr' or 'sub-hān' (arab)) the immaculate Primal Soul (God).

sadā: (adv; synonymous with 'sad', 'nitya' and 'hameshā') forever, always or in perpetuity.

man(i): (locative case - 'adhikaraṇ kārak'; synonymous with '*man* vich') in one's conscious self ('Jivātmāṅ', '*Man*' or 'Hirdā').

chāu: (n, m; synonymous with 'umaṅg', 'utshāh' and 'kheṛā') aspiration, yearning; eagerness, zeal, inspiration, or motivation; intense delight or happiness.

You are the eternal Reality, Immaculate, and forever the fount of eternal Bliss.[7-10] *Or:*

One then becomes spiritually eternal ('Jīvan Mukt'), immaculate and forever optimistic, in ascendency and in bliss.

Kavaṇ(u) s(u) velā, vakhat(u) kavaṇ(u), kavaṇ thit(i), kavaṇ(u) vār(u)

kavaṇ(u): (pron and adj, m; synonymous with. 'kavan(u)', 'kauṇ', 'kihṛā' or 'kī') who, which or what?

s(u): (pron and adj; synonymous with 'so', 'uh' and 'ohī') that, he, or she.

velā: (n, m, s; synonymous with 'samaṅ', 'din' and 'ghaṛī') literally, time, occasion, or opportunity. However, implicit here is the period of the day, i.e., morning, afternoon or evening etc.

vakhat(u): (n, m; synonymous with 'vakat', 'velā' and 'samaṅ') literally, time, period or age. However, implicit here is the precise time of the day or night.

kavaṇ: (pron and adj, f) see above. (u) of 'kavaṇ' is missing because of its link with 'thit(i)', a noun of female gender. See thit(i) (b).

thit(i): (n, f; synonymous with 'tith(i)' and 'mit(i)') a day or date according to the movement of the moon around its axis. See thit(i).

vār(u): (n, m, s; synonymous with 'din') days of the week based on the movement of Earth around the sun. See vār(u).

What was that period, precise time, lunar day, or the day of the week?

Kavaṇ(i) s(i) rutī, māh(u) kavaṇ(u), jit(u) hoā ākār(u)

kavaṇ(i): (pron and adj, f; synonymous with 'kauṇ' or 'kihṛī') who or what?

s(i): (pron and adj; synonymous with 'uh', 'vah' or 'so') he, she, that, the same or they.

rutī: (n, f, pl of 'rut', 'rut(i)' and 'rit(i)'; synonymous with 'rut' and 'mausam') seasons; rit(u): (n, m, s; (skt) 'mausam') season.

māh(u): (n, m, s; synonymous with 'mahīnā') literally, month of the year.

jit(u): (adv, pron and adj; synonymous with 'jadoṅ', 'jis vele' and 'jab ke') when.

hoā: (a) (v, s, present perfect; synonymous with 'hūā' or 'hoiā hai') has been, has happened or has occurred, (b) (v, s, present tense; synonymous with 'bhaiā' or 'ho jāṅdā hai') (i) comes to be or becomes (ii) turns, and (iii) changes, and implicit here is (c) (v, past tense; synonymous with 'hoiā', 'hoṅd vich āiā' or 'baṇ ga-i-ā') came into existence or was created. See hoṇā (b).

ākār(u): (n, m; synonymous with 'akār(u)', 'sarūp', 'sūrat') literally, physical shape, form, appearance, or an outline. In essence, the diverse empirical world.

The common belief about creation held by different faiths is that the empirical world came into being at the behest of just one word - 'logos' (Christianity), 'kuṅn' (Islam), 'O'am' (Hinduism), 'O'aṅkār (Jainism) and 'kavāo'(Sikh) as the following verses from the SGGS state:

'kītā pasāu, eko kavāu'. See Pauṛī 16, p. 200.

Through His Word came the creation and then the disintegration of planets. Thereafter, creation and then evolution followed, again at the behest of His Word.[405]

There was nothing else when He manifested Himself. He consults no one and just deliberates by Himself, and what He Wills, happens. There was then neither sky nor the underworld nor the three Hindu worlds; the Formless One was by Himself and nothing was yet created. What He Wills comes about, for there is nothing else but Him.[406]

What was the season and the month when the whole world came into being?

Vel n pāīā panḍatī, j(i) hovai lekh(u) purāṇ(u)

vel: (n, f, s; synonymous with 'velā', 'samāṅ', 'din' or 'ghaṛī') see velā.

pāīā: (a) (n, m; synonymous with 'pā' or 'pāu') a quarter of a basic unit of weight ('ser'), (b) (v, s, f, present perfect tense, second person;

synonymous with 'hāsal or prāpat kītī hai'; 'khaṭṭī hai'; 'pahnī hai'; 'milāī' or pā dittī hai'; 'anubhav kītī hai') has achieved, gained, worn, added, poured or put, realised or perceived respectively, (c) (v, s, present tense, first person; synonymous with 'maiṅ pāuṅdī-', 'hāsal' or 'prāpat kardī-' 'hāṅ') I achieve, (d) (present participle - 'kriyā-phal kirdaṅt'; synonymous with 'jo kichh(u) pāīā') that or whatever is my achievement, and implicit here is (e) (v, past tense; synonymous with 'hāsal- 'or 'prāpat-' 'kītī hai') see pāuṇā (a and c).

paṅḍatī: (a) (accusative case - 'karam kārak', m, pl; synonymous with 'paṅḍatāṅ nūṅ'; pronounced as 'paṅḍatīṅ') literally, to 'Paṅḍits', and implicit here is (b) (nominative case - 'kartā kārak', m, pl; synonymous with 'paṅḍatāṅ neṅ'; pronounced as 'paṅḍatīṅ'). See Paṅḍit.

paṅḍit: (n, m, s) (a) (synonymous with 'jo tihāṅ gunā dī paṅḍ utāre' and 'jo āpnā *Man* parbodhah') one who sheds the influence of 'Māyā' or one who sheds spiritual ignorance and aligns perfectly with 'Nām(u)', and implicit here is (b) (adj; synonymous with 'vidyā vich nipuṅn purakh', 'gyānī' and 'vidvān') a learned man, a man of letters, literary person, knowledgeable, highly educated or a scholar.

j(i): (conj; synonymous with 'je kar', 'yadī' and 'agar') if, in case or provided.

hovai: (v, s, imperative mood - 'saṅbhāv bhvikht kāl - kiās/ichhā bodhak', third person; synonymous with 'ho jāve' or 'je huṅdā') were to exist, occur or become. See hovṇā.

j(i) hovai: literally, (a) if it happens, and implicit here is (b) if it had happened. In essence, it really means 'if the paṅḍits had known the precise time of the origin of this world'.

lekh(u): (a) (n, f; synonymous with 'lekh', 'likhat' or 'nibaṅdh') fate, fortune, or destiny, and implicit here is (b) (n, m; synonymous with 'ālochanātmak graṅth') a composition, critique or treatise.

purāṇ(u): (n, m, pl; synonymous with 'purānas') 18 ancient Hindu texts written by Rishi Vyas and others.

lekh(u) purāṇ(u); (synonymous with 'jagat de araṅbh bāre purāṇ vāṅg(u) lekh') literally, a composition or treatise, like a purāṇ(u), on the topic of the origin of the world.

Had the 'Paṅḍits' really known the origin of the world, it would have been recorded in a unique treatise like the 'Purānas'.

Vakhat(u) n pāio kādīā, j(i) likhan(i) lekh(u) Qurāṇ(u)

vakhat(u): (n, m; synonymous with 'vakat', 'velā' or 'samāṅ') literally, time, period, age, or era.

pāio: (v, past tense; synonymous with 'un(h)āṅ prāpat- 'or 'hāsal-' 'kītā'; 'labhbhā') they achieved, gained, or realised.

kādīā: (n, m, pl; nominative case - 'kartā kārak';

synonymous with 'kādīāṅ ne'; pronounced as 'kādīāṅ') literally, 'Qādīs'. See qādī.

qādī: (n, m, s; arab; synonymous with 'qāzī') literally, an interpreter of Islamic law ('Sharīā'); a Muslim magistrate or judge. The Arabic letters 'zuād' and 'ze' are pronounced with the Punjabi letter 'ਦ' (d).

likhan(i): (v, pl, m, present tense, third person; synonymous with 'likh deṅde') see likhṇā.

likhṇā: (v; synonymous with 'likhat vich liāuṇā') literally, to write; to note down or record.

Qurāṇ(u): (n, m; synonymous with 'korān') holy scriptures of the Mohammedans. The suffix 'majīd' or 'sharīph' is used as a mark of respect, e.g., 'Qurān(u)-' 'majīd' or 'sharīph'. The words or verses ('Āyats') came directly to prophet Muhammad, occasionally in his dreams or via Archangel Gabriel over a period of twenty three years but prophet Muhammad himself did not know how to read or write.

Each of the verses was taught by Archangel Gabriel and formally declared by prophet Muhammad. It is believed that the meaning of some 'āyats' in Qurān(u) is only known to God Himself. 'Āyat', an abbreviation for 'Āyatullah', is a feminine name of Islamic origin which refers to the verses of the Quran and a sign from God. It also has the latent meaning of a 'miracle' or 'proof' that describes the verses in the Quran.

Twelve close companions of Caliph Abu Bakr collected verses, scribed on paper, cloth, leather, and other material by forty two scribes as well as from those who had memorised them, and compiled them into their holy book, the Quran as we know it today. One of the oldest copies of the Quran, currently kept in The British Library, appears to date between year 700 and 799 A.D. However, it contains only two-thirds of the text that appears in today's copy.

Had the Qāzīs known the precise time of the origin of the world, it would have been documented as one of the verses in the Qurān.

Thit(i), vār(u), nā jogī jāṇai, rut(i), māh(u) nā koī

nā: (p, pronounced as 'nāṅ' though written as just 'n') no, not or indicative of a negative implication or connotation.

jogī: (a) (n, m; synonymous with 'saperā') a snake charmer, (b) (adj; synonymous with 'jinnā' or 'jitnā'; 'jinnī' or 'jitnī') as much as, (c) (adj; synonymous with 'lāik' or 'yogyatā vālā') capable, deserving or worthy, and implicit here is (d) (n, m, s; synonymous with Yogī) a follower of Gorakhnāth or a practitioner of different forms of yoga, who claims to have mastered full control over their '*Man*' and the five cardinal drives and/or achieved 'Nirvānā'.

jāṇai: (v, s, present tense, third person; synonymous with 'jāṇdā-' or 'samjadā-' 'hai') see jāṇanā (a and b).

rut(i): (n, f, s; synonymous with 'rit(u)' in skt) a season.

koī: (pron and adj; synonymous with 'koī ik') literally, anyone, someone or rare one.

No Yogī knows the lunar day, the day of the week, the season, or the month [when the world came into being].

Jā kartā sirṭhī kau sāje, āpe jāṇai soī

jā: (pron and adj; synonymous with 'jis' or 'jihṛā') who, whom, which or that.

kartā: (n, m; abbrev. for 'kartār'; synonymous with 'rachanhār' and 'rachaitā') doer, maker, creator, or God.

sirṭhī: (synonymous with 'sirṭh', 'sirṭh(i)' and 'srishṭī') (a) (n, f; synonymous with 'rachnā' or 'krit') Creation, and (b) (n, m; synonymous with 'jagat' or 'saṅsār') the world or the universe.

kau: (prep; synonymous with 'tāṅī', 'ko', 'nūṅ', 'neṅ', 'toṅ' or 'dā/kā') to, for, from, up to, in return and of.

sāje: (v, s, present tense, third person; synonymous with 'sājdā hai') see sājṇā.

sājṇā: (a) (vocative case - 'saṅbodhan kārak'; synonymous with 'he sājan') O' Friend! and implicit here is (b) (v; synonymous with 'sirjaṇā',

‘rachṇā’ or ‘baṇāuṇā’) to make, construct, build or create.
āpe: (pron, m, s; synonymous with ‘āp-’ or ‘khud-’ ‘hī’) God Himself or ‘Nām(u)’, the immanent form of God.
jāṇai: (v, s, present tense, third person; synonymous with ‘jāṇdā hai’) see jāṇanā (b).
soī: (pron and adj; synonymous with ‘ohī’) literally, the very same person or being.

Only the Creator Himself, who creates and fashions the world, knows the precise time of creation.

Kiv kar(i) ākhā, kiv sālāhī, kio varnī, kiv jāṇā

kiv: (adv; synonymous with ‘kaise’ or ‘kiveṅ’) how, by what means or in what way.
kar(i): (a) (locative case - ‘adhikaraṇ kārak’; synonymous with ‘hath- ’‘vich’ or ‘uppar’) literally, in or on one’s hands, (b) (indeclinable past participle; perfect participle - ‘pūran pūrab kārdaṅtak’; synomymous with ‘kar ke’) having done or carried out an act, and (c) (v, s, imperative mood, second person; synonymous with ‘kar’ and ‘karo’. See ‘karnā’.
kiv kar(i): (adv; synonymous with ‘kis trāṅ’) how, by what means or in what way.
ākhā: (a) (v, s, present tense, first person; synonymous with ‘ākhāṅ’, ‘kahāṅ’ or ‘biān karāṅ’; ‘maiṅ ākhdā-’ ‘or ‘ākh sakdā-’ ‘hāṅ’), and (b) (v, s, imperative mood - ‘saṅbhāv bhvikht kāl - bevasī and prashan bodhak’; synonymous with ‘ākh-’ or ‘kah(i)-’ ‘sakāṅ’; ‘varṇan-’ or ‘biān-’ ‘karāṅ’; pronounced as ‘ākhāṅ’), first person; synonymous with ‘ākhāṅ’) see ākhṇā.
ākhṇā: (v) to say, utter, express; to ask, plead, beseech or earnestly implore.
kiv kar(i) ākhā: (v, s, imperative mood - ‘saṅbhāv bhvikht kāl - bevasī and prashan bodhak), first person; synonymous with ‘maiṅ-’ ‘kis trāṅ- ’or ‘kiveṅ-’ ‘ākhāṅ’ or ‘varṇan- ’or ‘biān-’ ‘karāṅ’? How do I state?
sālāhī: (a) (v; synonymous with ‘sālāh deṇ vālā’ and ‘maṅtrī’) adviser, (b) (adj, m; synonymous with ‘ustat(i) karan vāle’) who praise or eulogise others, (c) (n, m, s; synonymous with ‘Kartār’) God, (d) (adj, m; synonymous with ‘shalāghnīyā’ or ‘sālāhuṇ-yog’) literally, praiseworthy. In essence, the reference is to God, whose Glory is infinite, (e) (v, present tense, first person; synonymous with ‘ustat(i) kardāṅ- ’or ‘ustat(i) kar

sakdā-' 'hāṅ'; pronounced as 'sālāhīṅ'), and implicit here is (f) (v, s, imperative mood - 'saṅbhāv bhvikht kāl - bevasī and prashan bodhak'; first person; synonymous with 'sālāhāṅ' or 'siphat karāṅ'; pronounced as 'sālāhīṅ') see salāhuṇā.

salāhuṇā: (v; synonymous with 'shalāghā-', 'mahimā- 'or 'siphat salāh-' 'karnī; 'gun gauṇe') to praise, extol, or eulogise, but implied here is to align perfectly with 'Nām(u)' and sing His Glory. The following verse states in all humility that God's Praise is truly ineffable:

'Your Glory is truly eternal', O' my true Lord. You are the infinite and transcendent Lord and Your power is just beyond words.[407]

kio: (adv; synonymous with 'kaise', 'kis prakār' or 'kis vāste') how, why, or what for.

varnī: (a) (v, s, present tense, first person; synonymous with 'varṇan-' or 'biān-' 'kardāṅ hāṅ'; 'biān kar sakdā hāṅ'; pronounced as 'varnīṅ'), and implicit here is (b) (v, s, imperative mood - 'saṅbhāv bhvikht kāl - bevasī and prashan bodhak', first person; synonymous with 'maiṅ varṇan karāṅ'; pronounced as 'varnīṅ') see varṇan karnā.

varṇan karnā: (v; synonymous with 'kathan- 'or 'biān-' 'karnā') to state, describe, narrate, or expound.

jāṇā: (v, s, imperative mood - 'saṅbhāv bhvikht kāl - ichhā bodhak', first person; synonymous with 'maiṅ jāṇ-' or 'samajh-' 'lavāṅ') [how] I could know, grasp, or perceive. See jāṇanā and jāṇā.

How can I express and sing Your Glory, describe Your attributes, and realise or perceive You?

Nānak, ākhaṇ(i) sabh(u) ko ākhai, ik dū ik(u) siāṇā

Nānak: (n, m, s) the (u) of 'Nānak(u)' is missing because of the vocative case - 'saṅbodhan kārak'.

ākhaṇ(i): (accusative case - 'karam kārak'; synonymous with 'ākhaṇ-' or 'kahaṇ-' 'nūṅ') to stating or declaring. See ākhaṇā or ākhṇā. See ākhaṇ(i).

sabh(u): (adj; synonymous with 'sabhe', 'sarab', 'sabho' and 'tamām') all, entire, everyone or totality.

ko: (a) (pron; abbrev for and synonymous with 'koī') someone, anyone, or another; many or several. See ko.

ākhai: (a) (v, s, present tense, second tense; synonymous with 'tūṅ ākhdā haiṅ' or 'tusīṅ ākhde ho'), (b) (imperative mood - 'saṅbhāv bhvikht kāl - kiās, sharat, ichhā or bevasī bodhak', s, third/first person; synonymous with 'je maiṅ- ' 'ākhāṅ' or 'kahāṅ'), and implicit here is (c) (v, s, present tense, third person; synonymous with 'ākhdā hai') see ākhṇā.

ik: (pron; synonymous with 'koī ik') someone or anyone. (u) of 'ik(u)' is missing because of the preposition 'dū' that links it with 'ik(u)'.

dū: (a) (adj; (skt) synonymous with 'bechain') restless, anxious, nervous or worried, (b) (adj; synonymous with 'do', 'dūjā' or 'dūsrā') two, second or another, and implicit here is (c) (suff and prep; synonymous with 'se', 'toṅ' or 'koloṅ'), and (d) (locative case - 'adhikaraṇ kārak'; synonymous with 'ik dūsre toṅ') one from another.

ik(u): (adj, m, s; synonymous with 'ik', 'ikallā', 'lāsāni' or 'adutī') one, first of the 1-9 numerals, alone, by oneself, unaided or unique, and (b) (pron; synonymous with 'koī ik') someone or anyone.

siāṇā: (adj, m; synonymous with 'siānā', 'sujān', 'budhīmān', 'chatur', 'chālāk' and 'dīragh drashṭā') wise, intelligent, prudent, circumspect, or cunning.

'However, everyone else pretends to know and claims to be wiser than the other', O' Nānak!

Vaḍā Sāhib(u), vaḍī nāī, kītā jā kā hovai

vaḍā: (adj, m) (a) (synonymous with 'at(i)' and 'bahut') very much, plenty, plentiful or abundant, (b) (synonymous with 'visthar vala') big, huge, large or tall, (c) (synonymous with 'laṅbā') literally, tall, (d) (synonymous with 'birdh' or 'virdh') senior or elder, and implicit here is (e) (synonymous with 'mukhīā', 'shiromani' and 'sreshṭ') principal, premier or superior.

Sāhib(u): (n, m; synonymous with 'pat(i)', 'swāmī' and 'mālik') Master or Lord.

vaḍī: (adj, f) see vaḍā.

nāī: (a) (n, m) a barber, (b) (adv; synonymous with 'nivā ke' and 'jhukā ke') by bowing or having stooped, (c) (instrumental case - 'karaṇ kārak'; synonymous with 'Nām-' 'karke', 'nāl' and 'duārā') due to, with or through 'Nām(u)', (d) (locative case - 'adhikaraṇ kārak'; synonymous with 'Nām vich') in 'Nām(u)', and implicit here is (e) (n, f; synonymous with 'vaḍiāī', 'mahimā' or 'shobhā') praise, fame or glory.

kītā: (a) (present participle - 'kriyā-phal kirdaṅt'; synonymous with 'krit(u)'; 'rachiā-', 'kariā-' or 'baṇāiā-' 'hoiā hai') creation; something created, done or made; see karnā, baṇāuṇā and sirjaṇā, and implicit here is (b) (past participle - 'bhūt kirdaṅt', m; synonymous with 'kītā-' or 'kariā-' 'hoiā kaṅm'; 'sirjiā saṅsār') literally, completed actions or deeds; created and developed world. See kītā.

jā: (pron and adj; synonymous with 'jis') who, whom, which or that. See above.

kā: (prep, m; synonymous with 'dā') of.

jā kā: (synonymous with 'jis dā') whose.

hovai: (a) (v, s, present tense, third person; synonymous with 'huṅdā hai'). See above.

He is the Lord Master, Great is His Glory, and all that happens in this world is His doing.

Nānak, je ko āpau jāṇai, agai ga-i-ā nā sohai

je: (conj; synonymous with 'je kar', 'yadī' and 'agar') if or in case.

ko: (pron; synonymous with 'koī') someone, anyone, or another.

āpau: (ablative case - 'apādān kārak'; synonymous with 'āpah(u)', 'apne se' and 'āp toṅ'; pronounced as 'āpauṅ') by oneself or by one's own ability and capacity.

jāṇai: (a) (v, s, present tense, third person) see jāṇanā, and (b) (imperative mood - 'saṅbhāv bhvikht kāl - kiās bodhak'; synonymous with 'jānaṇ dā yatan kare' or 'jānaṇā chāhe') see jāṇanā (a, b, or d).

agai: (a) (adv; synonymous with 'sām(h)ṇe' and 'sanmukh') ahead or in front of; before, (b) (locative case - 'adhikaraṇ kārak'; synonymous with 'is pichhoṅ', 'bhvikh vich' or 'aglī ziṅdagī vich') literally, sometime in the future or in the next life, (c) (adv; synonymous with 'pahiloṅ hī') beforehand or in advance, and implicit here is (d) (locative case - 'adhikaraṇ kārak'; synonymous with 'āgai', 'parlok vich' or 'Prabhū dī hazūrī vich'; pronounced as 'aggai') literally, after one's demise in the hereafter, i.e., at God's Court. However, as God is omnipresent, His Court, too, is not elsewhere or in some mythological place called heaven.

ga-i-ā: (a) (conj v and suff) synonymous with 'bīt ga-i-ā'; 'chal basiā' or 'muk-', 'miṭ-' or 'tur-' 'ga-i-ā') literally, has gone or elapsed; has passed, deceased or died, (b) (v, m, s, present tense, first person; synonymous with 'maiṅ jāṅdāṅ hāṅ') [I] go, leave or depart, and implicit here is (c) (indeclinable past participle or perfect participle - 'pūran pūrab kārdaṅtak'; synonymous with 'ho ke' and 'jā ke'; pronounced as 'ga-i-āṅ') having become; having got or gone there.

sohai: (v, s, present tense, third person; synonymous with 'ādar pāuṅdā-', 'shobdā- 'or 'suṅdar lagdā-' 'hai'; pronounced as 'sohaiṅ') literally, gets honoured; appears graceful, respectable, or honourable.

'One is not honoured at His Court in the hereafter, should one claim to know the extent of His Glory and the mystery behind His creation by one's own intellect and ability', O' Nānak!

Conceptual summary

If one is fortunate enough to undertake acts of pilgrimage, austerity, compassion, and charity, one earns recognition and honour at God's Court worth only a tiny grain. On the other hand, focusing on and imbibing the Gurū's Divine Word and message with conviction in one's Hirdā is commensurate with bathing and scrubbing of the filth of 'Haumaiṅ', 'Moh' and innate 'Vikārī' tendencies in one's own holy place ('Hirdā').

You are the fount of all attributes, virtues, and values; whatever little I have, is due to You. Equally, one can neither express one's devotion nor reflect the noble attributes innately and spontaneously in one's daily life without first harbouring and nurturing them in one's Hirdā.

'O' Lord! I salute You. From You issued forth the 'Anhad Nād' ('Nām(u)'), material assets, comforts, and pleasure ('Māyā'), the Divine Word, and Brahmā. You are the immaculate, eternal Reality and the fount of eternal Bliss'. Or:

One finds freedom from the clutches of 'Māyā' by submitting to and imbibing the Gurū's Divine Word and Wisdom, and then becomes spiritually eternal ('Jīvan Mukt'), immaculate and forever optimistic, in ascendency and in bliss.

What was that period, precise time, lunar day or the day of the week, the season, or the month when the world came into being? Had the 'Paṅḍits',

‘Qāzīs’ or ‘Yogīs’ known the answer, it would have been recorded in a unique treatise like the Purānas or in some verses of the Qurān. In reality, no one really knows, as it is only the creator, who creates and sustains the world, who knows the precise time of when and how the creation came into being.

‘How can I express and sing Your immeasurable Glory, explain, or illustrate Your attributes, and apprehend or perceive You? Yet, surprisingly, everyone else pretends not only to know but also claims to be wiser than the other?’, O’ Nānak! ‘You are the Lord Master, great is Your Glory, and all that happens in this world is Your doing. One who claims to have the answer to this mystery of creation, and to know the extent of Your Glory by his own ability, is not considered worthy of honour at Your Court in the hereafter’, O’ Nānak!

One’s conscious self (‘Jīvātmāṅ’, ‘*Man*’ and ‘Hirdā’) becomes pure and sacrosanct when one lovingly submits to, focuses on and contemplates ‘Nām(u)’ and lives by His Will. However, this is, without any shadow of a doubt, subject to submitting to and imbibing the Gurū’s Divine Word and Message in one’s ‘Hirdā’ willingly, lovingly and unreservedly. This in turn, happens by the Grace of God. Focusing on and contemplating ‘Nām(u)’ and living by His Will, does not mean cognisance of and access to all aspects of His Glory, which is infinite and beyond our capability. There is a lot that truly remains a mystery, and that is precisely what continues to generate a sense of wonder about the Creator and His Creation.

PAUṚĪ 22
ਪਉੜੀ ੨੨॥

Pātalā pātāl, lakh, āgasā āgās.
ਪਾਤਾਲਾ ਪਾਤਾਲ, ਲਖ, ਆਗਾਸਾ ਆਗਾਸ॥

Oṛak oṛak bhāl(i) thake, ved kahan(i) ik vāt.
ਓੜਕ ਓੜਕ ਭਾਲਿ ਥਕੇ, ਵੇਦ ਕਹਨਿ ਇਕ ਵਾਤ॥

Sahas aṭhārāh, kahan(i) katebā, as(u)lū ik(u) dhāt(u).
ਸਹਸ ਅਠਾਰਹ, ਕਹਨਿ ਕਤੇਬਾ, ਅਸੁਲੂ ਇਕੁ ਧਾਤੁ॥

Lekhā hoi, t likhīai, lekhai hoi vinās(u).
ਲੇਖਾ ਹੋਇ, ਤ ਲਿਖੀਐ, ਲੇਖੈ ਹੋਇ ਵਿਣਾਸੁ॥

Nānak, vaḍā ākhīai, āpe jāṇai āp(u). (22)
ਂਨਕ, ਵਡਾ ਆਖੀਐ, ਆਪੇ ਜਾਣੈ ਆਪੁ॥ ੨੨॥

Pātalā pātāl, lakh, āgasā āgās

pātalā: (a) (n, m, pl; synonymous with 'pātalāṅ de'; pronounced as 'pātālāṅ') literally, of 'pātāls', and implicit here is (b) (locative case - 'adhikaraṇ kārak'; synonymous with 'pātalāṅ de heṭh'; pronounced as 'pātalāṅ') below or beneath the 'pātāls'. See pātāl.

pātāl: (a) (n, m, pl) the worlds below the planet Earth according to the Hindu belief of 'Trilok' ('dharat(i)', 'pātāl' below and 'swarg' above), (b) last of the seven worlds beneath the planet Earth according to Hindu and other mythology, and implicit here is (c) (n, m) netherworld, Hades, the underworld or the habitable worlds beneath the planet Earth according to Hindu mythology. However, Gurū Nānak does not give any credence to the view that there are 'Pātāls' for lesser human beings and some lower life forms, and heaven ('Swarg') for Devīs, Devtās and other beings of high moral character or of faith in their earlier life as humans on this Earth. Thus, 'pātāl' just refers to planets lying below the planet Earth in the spatial sense as it comes across clearly in this verse of the SGGS:

The sun and the moon are like two lamps and the fourteen planets of the universe are like the shopping malls of this world-city. All living beings act out as traders and shoppers.[408]

lakh: (adj, pl) literally, many 1 x 10^5. However, implicit here is countless. The word 'lakh' acts as 'dehlī dīpak' as it joins with 'pātalā pātāl lakh' on one side and 'lakh āgasā āgās' on the other.

pātalā pātāl lakh: literally, there are many lakhs of 'worlds' beneath the planet Earth.

āgasā: (a) (n, m, pl; synonymous with 'āgasāṅ de'; pronounced as 'āgasāṅ') of āgas, and implicit here is (b) (locative case - 'adhikaraṇ kārak'; synonymous with 'āgasāṅ uppar'; pronounced as 'āgasāṅ') above or beyond the skies or heavens. See āgās.

āgās: (a) (n, f) Haumaiṅ, (b) (n, m) the all-pervasive God or 'Nām(u)', and implicit here is (c) (n, m; synonymous with 'gagan', 'khagol', 'āsmān', 'aṅbar', 'ākāsh') the sky, the firmament, or the heavens above. In essence, it refers to the space or atmosphere arching over and above the planets. Thus, if there are countless planets, there must be countless firmaments.

lakh āgasā āgās: literally, there are many lakhs of planets above the planet Earth with their own skies or firmaments.

There are countless planets beneath the planet Earth, and countless skies and firmaments above it according to the Vedas.

Oṛak oṛak bhāl(i) thake, ved kahan(i) ik vāt

oṛak: (n, m; synonymous with 'had', 'had-baṅna', 'aṅt' and 'avdh(i)') the end, extreme or the outermost limit.

bhāl(i): (indeclinable past participle or perfect participle - 'pūran pūrab kārdaṅtak'; synonymous with 'bhāl- 'or 'khoj-' 'ke') see bhālaṇā or khojaṇā.

bhālaṇā: (v; synonymous with 'ḍhūṅḍhaṇā' and 'khojaṇā') to seek, search, investigate, explore, or discover.

khojaṇā: (v) to search, inquire, investigate, or discover.

thake: (a) (v, s, present tense, third person; synonymous with 'thak- 'or 'hār-' 'jāṅdā hai') becomes weary and tired, and gives up, and implicit here is (b) (v, pl, past tense or present perfect tense, third person; synonymous with 'uh thak- 'or 'hār-' 'gae') they became weary and tired and gave up; they have become weary and tired and have given up. See thakṇā.

thakṇā: (v; synonymous with 'thak jāṇā', 'ṭhahirnā' and 'ruk jāṇā') to get tired; to become weary, exhausted, or fatigued and to rest; to feel lost and dejected.

ved: (n, m, pl; synonymous with 'bed') the four 'Vedas' of Hindus - Rig, Sām, Yajur and Atharvan.

kahan(i): (v, pl, present tense, third person; synonymous with 'kahinde' or 'ākhde-' 'han') see kahiṇā.

ik: (adj, f) one, first of the 1-9 numerals. The (u) of 'ik(u)' is missing as it is an adjective qualifying a female noun 'vāt'.

vāt: (a) (n, m; synonymous with 'vājā') a musical instrument, especially a wind instrument, (b) (n, m; synonymous with 'mukh' and 'mūṅh') face or mouth, and (c) (n, f; synonymous with 'bāt', 'gal' and 'vārtā') utterance, riddle, narrative, or information. It refers to some general information or inquiry about one's general health or state of wellbeing ('khabar-sār').

ik vāt: (synonymous with 'ik hi vāt') the ultimate or the definitive and unanimous statement or pronouncement.

'Exhausted and dejected in their pursuit to find the limits of creation, countless sages have reluctantly given up their search', state the Vedas categorically, succinctly and unanimously.

Sahas aṭhārāh, kahan(i) katebā, asulū ik(u) dhāt(u)

sahas: (adj, pl; synonymous with 'hazār') many thousands (1 x 10^3).

aṭhārāh: (adj) eighteen.

sahas aṭhārāh: literally, eighteen thousands (18 x 10^3). However, implicit here are: (a) God has created eighteen thousand kinds of inanimate and sentient life forms according to the Islamic book 'Basāyar', (b) that there are a total of eighteen thousand 'ālams' ('vidvān' -scholars or truly enlightened individuals created by God) according to the four Semitic books, and (c) there are eighteen thousand worlds ('ālams') altogether in this creation.

katebā: (n, f, pl; synonymous with 'katābāṅ'; pronounced as 'katebāṅ') see kateb.

kateb:(n, f; synonymous with 'kitāb' and 'pustak') literally, a book, a textbook or publication but reference here is to the four Semitic books: the Zabūr (Book of David), the Torah (Book of Moses), the Bible (Injīl-Book of Isa), and the Quran.

as(u)lū: (adv; synonymous with 'muḍhoṅ', 'asal vich' and 'aslīyat vichāran toṅ'; pronounced as 'aslū') from the beginning or outset, from the very roots, in reality, or in essence. (u) that appears after 's' in 'as(u)lū' denotes that 's' is the letter 'suād' in the Arabic language.

ik(u): (adj, m) see above.

dhāt(u): (a) (n, f; synonymous with 'khaṇij padārth') element, mineral or metal, (b) (n, m; synonymous with 'paṅj tat' - the five basic ingredients of the body) air, water, Earth, fire and space, (c) (n, m; synonymous with 'iṅdrīs') the five sensorimotor organs (eyes, ears, nose, mouth/tongue and skin), (d) the perverse influences to which the sensorimotor organs are subservient ('rūp', 'shabad', 'sugaṅdh', 'ras' and 'sparsh' respectively), (e) (n, f) 'māyā', (f) (n, f; synonymous with 'avidyā') ignorance, (g) (n, f) 'jīvātmāṅ', (h) (n, m; synonymous with 'guṇ') attributes, virtues or values, (i) (n, f; synonymous with 'ruchī' and 'subhāu') innate tendencies, predispositions or proclivities, (j) (n, f; synonymous with 'dauṛ bhaj' and 'bhaṭkaṇā') to become engrossed and lost in the material world, and implicit here is (k) (n, m, s; synonymous with 'kartār') the creator God.

The four Semitic books state that the creator, God, is in essence, the fount of the eighteen thousand truly enlightened people, different species, and worlds.

Lekhā hoi, t likhīai, lekhai hoi vinās(u)

lekhā: (a) (v, past or present perfect tense; synonymous with 'likhiā') literally, wrote or that has been written, (b) (n, m, s; synonymous with 'lekh') one's fate or destiny that is based on the judgement of one's Karmā ('hisāb' of one's 'saṅskārs'), and written on one's forehead according to popular Hindu belief, and implicit here is (c) (n, m; synonymous with 'likhiā hoiā hisāb') an account of every one's good and bad 'Karmā'.

hoi: (v, imperative mood - 'saṅbhāv bhvikht kāl - kiās or sharat bodhak', third person; synonymous with 'ho jāve' or 'ho sake') literally, were to become or were to be. See hoi.

lekhā hoi: (synonymous with 'hisāb kitāb ho sake') if the limits could be recorded or if it were possible to record the limits.

t: (synonymous with 'tā'; pronounced as 'tāṅ') (p and adv; synonymous with 'tad', 'tadoṅ', or 'udoṅ') then, thus, because of, and therefore.

likhīai: (a) (v, s, imperative mood - 'hukmī bhvikht', first person; synonymous with 'likhṇā chāhīdā hai') should be depicted or portrayed as, and (b) (v, s, present tense, third person; synonymous with 'likhiā jāṅdā hai'; 'likhiā- 'or 'aṅkit kitā-' 'jā sakdā hai'; 'likh sakīdā hai') is characterised as, can be depicted as or recorded. See likhṇā.

likhṇā: (v; synonymous with 'likhat vich liāuṇā') literally, to note or write down.

lekhā hoi tā likhīai: literally, if only it were possible to determine the extent of this creation, its limits could then be recorded.

lekhai: (a) (locative case - 'adhikaraṇ kārak'; synonymous with 'lekhe de hisāb kitāb vich') in one's fate or destiny, (b) (instrumental case - 'karaṇ kārak'; synonymous with 'lekhe de hisāb kitab-' 'nāl', 'anusār' or 'sadkā') with, according to or by virtue of one's destiny, and implicit here is (c) (genitive case - 'saṅbaṅdh kārak'; synonymous with 'lekhe dā hisāb kitāb') an account of one's lekh or lekhā.

hoi: (v, s, present tense; synonymous with 'huṅdī- 'or 'huṅdā-' 'hai'; 'ho jāṅdī- 'or 'ho jāṅdā-' 'hai'; 'ho sakdā hai') literally, occurs, comes to be or becomes; can occur, happen or become.

viṇās(u): (n; m, s; synonymous with 'vinās(u)' or 'nās'; pronounced as 'vināsh') decay or death, destruction, extermination, or ruin.

lekhai hoi vinās(u): literally, the counting system fails as the accounts themselves are infinite and never ending, thus becoming beyond the reach of the people of the times. The following verses of the SGGS clearly encapsulate this sentiment:

'You are an ocean of virtues and Your extent unfathomable, and no one knows the dimensions of Your vast expanse', O' my great Master.[409]

Even saintly men with divine attributes failed and reluctantly abandoned this chase after their numerous serious attempts, for the extent of His wonderful creation is immeasurable. How can a son witness the birth of his father? He has strung together the entire creation in His Divine Order.[410]

If only this account could be determined, it would be recorded. However, the accounting system fails as the constitutive parts are infinite.

Nānak, vaḍā ākhīai, āpe jāṇai āp(u)

Nānak: (n, m, s) O' Nānak! The (u) of 'Nānak(u)' is missing because of its vocative case - 'saṅbodhan kārak'.

vaḍā: (adj, m) (a) (synonymous with 'at(i)' and 'bahut') plenty, plentiful or abundant, (b) (synonymous with 'visthār vālā') big, huge, large, or tall,

(c) (synonymous with 'birdh or virdh') senior or elder, and implicit here is (d) (synonymous with 'mukhīā', 'shiromanī' and 'sreshṭ') principal, premier or foremost.

ākhīai: (a) (v, s, present tense, third person; synonymous with 'ākhiā jāṅdā hai' or 'ākhī jāṅdī hai'), and implicit here is (b) (v, pl, imperative mood - 'hukmī bhvikht', first person; synonymous with 'ākhīdā hai' or 'ākhṇā chahīdā hai') see ākhṇā.

ākhṇā: (v; synonymous with 'bolaṇā', 'kahiṇā', 'kathan karnā' or 'vakhyān karnā') to say, utter, express, define or expound.

āpe: (pron, m, s; synonymous with 'āp hī' and 'āpah(i)') literally, solely by oneself; in essence, God Himself or Nām(u) - the immanent form of God.

jāṇai: (v, s, present tense, third person: synonymous with 'uh jāṇdā hai') see jāṇanā (b and d).

āp(u): (a) (n, m; synonymous with 'āpābhāv', 'haumaiṅ', 'ahaṅkār', 'khudī', 'apṇat' or 'mamtā') vanity, conceit, ego, or possessiveness, and implicit here is (b) (n, m, s; synonymous with 'khud') oneself.

āpe jāṇai āp(u): He alone knows His Glory and the bounds of His Creation.

'We should call Him Great, for He alone knows His Glory and the bounds of His Creation', says Nānak.

Conceptual summary

The number 'lakhs' becomes meaningless when one considers its uselessness in defining the extent of this universe and its constitutive parts. It is truly infinite and beyond the scope of our numbering system.

The definitive and unanimous statement of all the Vedas is that there are numerous worlds below and firmaments above this planet, Earth, and no one could ever fathom the true extent of this vast universe. In contrast, the four Semitic books state that there are eighteen thousand enlightened sages, different species and different worlds that issue forth from just the one Creator God.

In reality, an account of the true extent of the creation and its constitutive parts could only be recorded if this were possible. However, the accounting system fails as the constitutive parts are infinite. We should simply call Him Great, for He alone knows His Glory and the bounds of His Creation.

PAUṚĪ 23
ਪਉੜੀ ੨੩॥

Sālāhī sālāh(i), etī surat(i) n pāīā.
ਸਾਲਾਹੀ ਸਾਲਾਹਿ, ਏਤੀ ਸੁਰਤਿ ਨ ਪਾਈਆ॥

Nadīā atai vāh, pavah(i) samuṅd(i), n jāṇīah(i).
ਨਦੀਆ ਅਤੈ ਵਾਹ, ਪਵਹਿ ਸਮੁੰਦਿ, ਨ ਜਾਣੀਅਹਿ॥

Samuṅd sāh sultan, girhā setī māl(u) dhan(u).
ਸਮੁੰਦ ਸਾਹ ਸੁਲਤਾਨ, ਗਿਰਹਾ ਸੇਤੀ ਮਾਲੁ ਧਨੁ॥

Kīṛī tul(i) n hovnī, je tis(u) manah(u) n vīsrah(i). (23)
ਕੀੜੀ ਤੁਲਿ ਨ ਹੋਵਨੀ, ਜੇ ਤਿਸੁ ਮਨਹੁ ਨ ਵੀਸਰਹਿ॥ ੨੩॥

Sālāhī sālāh(i), etī surat(i) n pāīā

sālāhī: (a) (v, s, present tense, first person; synonymous with 'ustat(i) kardāṅ- 'or 'ustat(i) kar sakdā-' 'hāṅ'; pronounced as 'sālāhīṅ'), (b) (v, s, imperative mood - 'saṅbhāv bhvikht kāl - bevasī and prashan bodhak', first person; synonymous with 'sālāhāṅ' or 'siphat karāṅ'), (c) (v; synonymous with 'sālāh deṇ vālā' and 'maṅtrī') adviser, (d) (adj, m; synonymous with 'ustat(i) karan vāle') who praise or eulogise others, and implicit here is (e) (n, m, s; synonymous with 'Kartār') God, and (f) (adj, m; synonymous with 'shalāghnīyā' or 'sālāhuṇ-yog') literally, praiseworthy. In essence, the reference here is to God, whose Glory is infinite. See salāhuṇā.

sālāh(i): (a) (v, pl, present tense, third person; synonymous with 'sālāhuṅde han'), and implicit here is (b) (indeclinable past participle or perfect participle - 'pūran pūrab kārdaṅtak'; synonymous with 'siphat-sālāh- 'or 'shalāghā-' 'kar ke') by singing His praise or Glory. See sālāhuṇā.

salāhuṇā: (v; synonymous with 'shalāghā-', 'mahimā- 'or 'siphat-salāh-' 'karnī'; 'gun gauṇe') to praise, extol, or eulogise, but implicit here is to align perfectly with 'Nām(u)' and sing His Glory.

etī: (adj; synonymous with 'itnī' and 'ainī') this much or so much.

surat(i): (n, f; synonymous with 'samajh' and 'sojhī') spiritual knowledge or wisdom. See surat(i).

n: (p; pronounced as 'nāṅ') no, not or implying a negative connotation.

pāīā: (a) (v, past tense; synonymous with 'hāsal- 'or 'prāpat-' 'kītī'), and (b) (v, s, f, present perfect tense, second person; synonymous with 'hāsal or prāpat kītī hai'; 'khaṭṭī hai'; 'pahnī hai'; 'milāī' or 'pā dittī hai'; 'anubhav kītī hai') has achieved; gained; worn; added, poured or put; realised or perceived respectively. See pāuṇā (a).

etī surat(i) n pāīā: (synonymous with 'itnī sojhī nahīṅ aī') literally, [no one] really understood this. In essence, implicit here is that no one really gained any understanding of the extent of His true Glory as this verse of the SGGS clearly states:

'His 'Bhagats' have realised lasting inner peace and equanimity through immersing themselves in reflection upon His attributes and persona. However, no one has ever realised the full extent of the One who pervades all', O' Nānak![411]

None, having extolled and sung His Praise, realised His full Glory. Or: Countless sing the praise of the Venerable Lord but none realise His full Glory.

Nadīā atai vāh, pavah(i) samuṅd(i), n jāṇīah(i)

nadīā: (n, f, pl; pronounced as 'nadīāṅ') brooks, streams small rivers or rivulets.

atai: (conj; synonymous with 'au', 'ate' and 'te') and or as well as.

vāh: (a) (adj; synonymous with 'adhbhut' or 'acharj') strange, unique, wonderful, or surprisingly beautiful, (b) (adj; synonymous with 'khūb' and 'hachhchhā') good or nice, (c) (n, f and interj; synonymous with 'vāh vāh', 'shābāsh' or 'āphrīn') bravo, well done or wonderful, (d) (n, m; synonymous with 'hal vāhuṇ dī kriyā') the act of ploughing, and implicit here is (e) (n, f, pl; synonymous with 'pravāh' or 'nāle') small flowing streams.

vāhuṇā: (v; synonymous with 'bāhṇā') (a) (synonymous with 'hal nāl khet vāhuṇā') to plough, and (b) (synonymous with 'bal nāl shastar chalāuṇā' or 'prahār karnā') to wield a sword, shoot an arrow, throw a spear, or discharge a gun.

pavah(i): (v, pl, present tense, third person; synonymous with 'uh paiṅde-' or 'pai jāṅde-' 'han') see paiṇā.

samuṅd(i): (locative case - 'adhikaraṇ kārak'; synonymous with 'samuṅd vich') see samuṅd.

samuṅd: (n, m, pl; synonymous with 'samuṅdr') seas or oceans.

jāṇīah(i): (v, s, present tense, third person, passive voice; synonymous with 'jāṇīde' or 'jāṇe jāṅde') literally, are known or recognised. See jāṇanā (a).

n jāṇīah(i): (synonymous with 'nahīṅ-' 'jāṇīde' or 'jāṇe jāṅde') literally, are not known or recognised. However, implicit here is that [small rivers and rivulets] lose their identity [as they flow into oceans] and are no longer seen as distinct. This verse of the SGGS beautifully captures Gurū Nānak's central thesis and message for humanity.

Just as rivulets and rivers lose their distinct identity when they merge with the oceans, one, too, rids oneself of 'Haumaiṅ' and the notion of separate existence when one lives in harmony with Nām(u)' and by His Will.
Or:

Just as small rivers and rivulets that flow into and merge with oceans, lose their own distinctiveness, similarly, living in perfect harmony with 'Nām(u)' and by His Will, His 'bhagats' remain oblivious of the extent of His attributes.

Samuṅd sāh sultan, girhā setī māl(u) dhan(u)

samuṅd: (genitive case - 'saṅbaṅdh kārak', pl; synonymous with 'samuṅdrāṅ de') of oceans.

sāh: (n, m, s) (a) (synonymous with 'dam', 'suās' and 'svās') a breath, (b) (abbrev. for and synonymous with 'shāhukār'; pronounced as 'shāh') a merchant, a banker, a moneylender, or a businessman, (c) (synonymous with 'swāmī' and 'pat(i)'; pronounced as 'shāh') Lord, Master, husband, and implicit here is (d) (pers; synonymous with 'shāh' and 'bādshāh'; pronounced as 'shāh') a king or an emperor.

sultān: (n, m; synonymous with 'bādshāh') a ruler, king, or emperor.

samuṅd sāh sultan: (a) extremely wealthy seafaring traders and emperors who controlled large oceans, and (b) literally, kings or emperors - rulers of vast oceans.

girhā: (a) (n, f; (pers) synonymous with 'girh', 'gaṭhrī' or 'gaṭh') a large bale, bundle or package tied in a piece of cloth, (b) (n, m; synonymous with ‘ghar’) home, and implicit here is (c) (n, m; synonymous with ‘gir(i)’ (skt), ‘parbat’ or ‘pahāṛ’) a mountain.

setī: (a) (prep; synonymous with ‘se’ and ‘toṅ’; pronounced as ‘setīṅ’) from, and implicit here is (b) (prep; synonymous with ‘sāth’ or ‘nāl’) by, with or together with.

māl(u): (n, m; arab; synonymous with ‘dhan’, ‘saṅpadā’ and ‘daulat’) one’s wealth, valuable goods, or assets.

dhan(u): (a) (interj; synonymous with ‘vāh’ and ‘khūb’) bravo, well done or wonderful, (b) (adj; synonymous with ‘dhanya’ and ‘punyavān’) pious, saintly or virtuous, (c) (adj; synonymous with ‘sālāhuṇ-yog’) praiseworthy, (d) (n, f; synonymous with ‘sarīr/deh’, ‘juān istrī’ and ‘jīvātmāṅ’) physical body, a mature woman and soul, and implicit here is (e) (n, m; synonymous with ‘daulat’ or ‘saṅpat(i)’) literally, wealth, riches, assets, high post or rank.

girhā setī māl(u) dhan(u): literally, with assets heaped as high as mountains. The reference here is to their vast assets and riches, which cannot be traded for noble attributes and lasting inner bliss, and which often lead them astray and deeper and deeper into the web or ‘māyā’.

Kings and emperors with dominions as vast as oceans and mountains of material assets and wealth.

Kīṛī tul(i) n hovnī, je tis(u) manah(u) n vīsrah(i)

kīṛī: (a) (n, f; synonymous with ‘kīṭī’ or ‘chīṭī’) literally, an ant, (b) (adj, m; synonymous with ‘tuchh’ or ‘adnā’) of low quality, rank, or status; trivial, unimportant or inconsequential. However, implicit here is an ordinary or insignificant person of little or no means.

tul(i): (a) (n, m; synonymous with ‘chittarkār dā bursh’) a small soft brush for painting, (b) (n; synonymous with ‘tulnā’, ‘tol’ and ‘vazan’) comparison, equivalence, or weight, and implicit here is (c) (adj; synonymous with ‘samān’ and ‘brābar’) equal, equivalent, comparable, resembling or matching. The (i) in ‘tul(i)’ is there as it is an adjective qualifying a noun of female gender.

hovnī: (v, pl, present tense, third person; synonymous with ‘huṅde han’; pronounced as ‘hovnīṅ’) see hovṇā (a).

je: (a) (conj; synonymous with ‘je kar’, ‘yadī’ and ‘agar’) if or in case.

tis(u): (a) (pron, m, s; synonymous with 'us') literally, he, she or that person, and implicit here is (b) (genitive case - 'sanbandh kārak'; synonymous with 'us-' 'de', 'dī', 'ke' or 'kī') literally, his or its.

manah(u): (ablative case - 'apādān kārak'; synonymous with '*man* se' or '*man* ton'; pronounced as 'manah(u)ṅ') from one's '*man*' ('Jīvātmāṅ', Conscious self or 'Hirdā').

vīsrah(i): (v, s, imperative mood - 'sanbhāv bhvikht kāl - sharat bodhak', second person; synonymous with 'je tūṅ visar- 'or 'bhul-' 'jāveṅ'). See vīsrah(i), visarnā and visārnā.

Je tis(u) manah(u) n vīsrah(i): (a) (synonymous with 'jihṛā us-nuṅ manah(u)n nahīṅ bhulāuṅdā') one who does not let Him slip from his conscious self, and (b) (synonymous with 'je us kīṛī de *man* vichoṅ tūṅ nāṅ visar jā-iṅ') literally, if that 'kīṛī' was not to let You slip from its conscious self ('*man*'). In essence, to let 'Nām(u)' slip from your '*man*' is akin to befriending or aligning deliberately and willingly with another, i.e., to ally with and serve 'Haumaiṅ' willingly, in preference to aligning with 'Nām-consciousness'.

Thus, misguided and misled by 'Haumaiṅ', lured by 'Moh' of the material world, its comforts and pleasures, and driven by 'Trishnā', one becomes engrossed and ensnared in the web of 'Māyā', loses one's inner peace, and suffers forever from the inner turmoil and anguish that accompanies this never-ending pursuit. Thus, the comparison here is between one lacking any material assets but with lasting inner equipoise and bliss due to 'Nām(u)' in one's 'Hirdā' and the other with an abundance of worldly riches and comforts but with no noble attributes, inner peace, contentment or happiness. The following verses from the SGGS support the central thesis of this Pauṛī:

In whosoever's 'Hirdā' God makes an inkling of 'Nām(u)' to establish and flourish, his fame or greatness becomes inestimable or boundless.[412]

'Whom He blesses with willing, loving and unconditional surrender to, love for and perfect alignment with 'Nām(u)' is the King of Kings or the most reverend of all', O' Nānak! See Pauṛī 25, pp. 304-6.

Do not equal one of little or no means and repute but who never forgets God in one's conscious self ('Jīvātmāṅ', 'Man' or 'Hirdā').

Conceptual summary

None, having extolled and sung His Praise, realise His full Glory though they may become totally absorbed in Him, just as the small rivers and rivulets that flow into and merge with the oceans lose their distinctiveness but remain unaware of their expanse.

Kings and emperors, with dominions as vast as oceans and assets heaped as high as mountains do not equal one of little or no means and influence but who never forgets God in his conscious self ('Jīvātmāṅ', '*Man*' or 'Hirdā').

Submitting to 'Nām(u)' and living by His Will may lead to the realisation and full glow of 'Nām(u)' in one's 'Hirdā' but it does not mean that one can determine and define His Glory. Realising and revelling in the full glow of 'Nām(u)' in one's 'Hirdā' remains the sole aim and purpose in life but the struggle to define His Glory ends in vain.

PAUṚĪ 24
ਪਉੜੀ ੨੪॥

Aṅt(u) n siphtī, kahaṇ(i) n aṅt(u).
ਅੰਤੁ ਨ ਸਿਫਤੀ, ਕਹਣਿ ਨ ਅੰਤੁ॥

Aṅt(u) n karṇai, deṇ(i) n aṅt(u).
ਅੰਤੁ ਨ ਕਰਣੈ, ਦੇਣਿ ਨ ਅੰਤੁ॥

Aṅt(u) n vekhaṇ(i), suṇaṇ(i) n aṅt(u).
ਅੰਤੁ ਨ ਵੇਖਣਿ, ਸੁਣਣਿ ਨ ਅੰਤੁ॥

Aṅt(u) n jāpai, kiā *man*(i) maṅt(u).
ਅੰਤੁ ਨ ਜਾਪੈ, ਕਿਆ ਮਨਿ ਮੰਤੁ॥

Aṅt(u) n jāpai, kītā ākār(u).
ਅੰਤੁ ਨ ਜਾਪੈ, ਕੀਤਾ ਆਕਾਰੁ॥

Aṅt(u) n jāpai, pārāvār(u).
ਅੰਤੁ ਨ ਜਾਪੈ, ਪਾਰਾਵਾਰੁ॥

Aṅt kāraṇ(i), kete bil-lāh(i).
ਅੰਤ ਕਾਰਣਿ, ਕੇਤੇ ਬਿਲਲਾਹਿ॥

Tā ke aṅt, n pāe jāh(i).
ਤਾ ਕੇ ਅੰਤ, ਨ ਪਾਏ ਜਾਹਿ॥

Eh(u) aṅt(u), n jāṇai koi.
ਏਹੁ ਅੰਤੁ, ਨ ਜਾਣੈ ਕੋਇ॥

Bahutā kahīai, bahutā hoi.
ਬਹੁਤਾ ਕਹੀਐ, ਬਹੁਤਾ ਹੋਇ॥

Vaḍā sāhib(u), ūchā thāu.
ਵਡਾ ਸਾਹਿਬੁ, ਊਚਾ ਥਾਉ॥

Ūche ūpar(i), ūchā nāu.
ਊਚੇ ਉਪਰਿ, ਊਚਾ ਨਾਉ॥

Evaḍ(u) ūchā, hovai koi.
ਏਵਡੁ ਊਚਾ, ਹੋਵੈ ਕੋਇ॥

Tis(u) ūche kau, jāṇai soi.
ਤਿਸੁ ਊਚੇ ਕਉ, ਜਾਣੈ ਸੋਇ॥

Jevaḍ(u) āp(i), jāṇai āp(i) āp(i).
ਜੇਵਡੁ ਆਪਿ, ਜਾਣੈ ਆਪਿ ਆਪਿ॥

Nānak, nadrī karmī dāt(i). (24)
ਨਾਨਕ, ਨਦਰੀ ਕਰਮੀ ਦਾਤਿ॥ ੨੪॥

Aṅt(u) n siphtī, kahaṇ(i) n aṅt(u)

aṅt(u): (n, m; synonymous with 'oṛak', 'sīmā' and 'hadd') end, boundary, finale, or extremity.

n: (p; pronounced as 'nāṅ') no, not or implying a negative connotation.

siphtī: (a) (instrumental case - 'karaṇ kārak'; synonymous with 'siphtāṅ-' 'nāl', 'rāhīṅ' or 'duārā'; pronounced as 'siphtīṅ'), and implicit here is (b) (synonymous with 'siphtāṅ dā'; pronounced as 'siphtīṅ') literally, of His Praise or Glory. See siphat.

siphat: (a) (adj; synonymous with 'siphat sālāh', 'vaḍiāī', 'mahimā', 'ustat(i)', 'upmā', 'jas' and 'guṇ') greatness, praise, merit, glory, grandeur, or eulogy.

kahaṇ(i): (kahaṇ: infinitive mood - 'bhāvārth kārdaṅtak') (a) (accusative case - 'karam kārak'; synonymous with 'kahaṇ nūṅ') to stating, (b) (locative case - 'adhikaraṇ kārak'; synonymous with 'kahaṇ vich') in saying or explicating, and implicit here is (c) (instrumental case - 'karaṇ kārak'; synonymous with 'kahaṇ-''nāl', 'rāhīṅ'/'duārā' or 'sadkā') with, through or by virtue of narrating or expounding. See kahaṇ (d) and kahiṇā.

God is not only omnipotent, omnipresent, and omniscient, but His Glory is infinite, too, as the following verses from the SGGS emphasise:

'If I were to make ink of all the oceans, pens of all the woods and paper from the entire Earth, I would still not be able to write Your Glory', says Kabīr.[413]

How can the Immeasurable be measured? Only a rival, if there were one, would know. As He has no rival, how can one, therefore, evaluate Him?[414]

The extent or measure of His attributes is truly overwhelming and indefinable. Only a rival, if there were one, would know.[415]

Your intuitive knowledge of others' innermost thoughts ('dānā') and Your foresight or farsightedness ('binā') is as vast as an ocean; how can I, a mere small fish, know Your magnitude.[416]

The Vedas know not His magnificence; many, like Brahma, did not know the mystery of His mind; the incarnated demi-gods do not know the extent of His expanse. The transcendent Lord, God of Gods, is infinite and only He knows His Majesty whilst others merely expound it by hearsay.[417]

You know the woes of my conscious self without my uttering even a word, and can make me contemplate 'Nām(u)'.[418]

Who else can one go to and implore when the omniscient God Himself knows the state of my 'Hirdā'?[419]

His Glory is not only infinite but also ineffable too.

Aṅt(u) n karṇai, deṇ(i) n aṅt(u)

karṇai: (genitive case - 'saṅbaṅdh kārak'; synonymous with 'karṇā- 'and 'krit-' 'dā') of His creation. See karṇa (c and h).

deṇ(i): (a) (infinitive mood - 'bhāvārth kārdaṅtak'; locative case - 'adhikaraṇ kārak'; synonymous with 'dātāṅ deṇ vich') literally, in giving, offering or donating, and (b) (infinitive mood - 'bhāvārth kārdaṅtak'; instrumental case - 'karaṇ kārak'; synonymous with 'dātāṅ deṇ-''nāl', 'rāhīṅ', 'sadkā' or 'duārā') due to, with, through or by virtue of giving. The reference here is to confer, grant or bestow something worldly and/or even His Grace to attune and harmonise perfectly with 'Nām(u)' or 'Nām-consciousness'. See deṇā (b and c).

deṇ(i) n aṅt(u): (synonymous with 'us dīāṅ dātāṅ dā bhī aṅt nahīṅ') limitless is His bounty.

Infinite is His Creation, and infinite His bounty and treasure of gifts.

Aṅt(u) na vekhaṇ(i), suṇaṇ(i) n aṅt(u)

vekhaṇ(i): (infinitive mood - 'bhāvārth kārdaṅtak') (a) (instrumental case - 'karaṇ kārak'; synonymous with 'vekhaṇ-''nāl', 'rāhīṅ' or 'duārā') due to, with or through looking or observing, and (b) (locative case - 'adhikaraṇ kārak'; synonymous with 'vekhaṇ vich') literally, in looking or observing. See vekhṇā.

suṇaṇ(i): (infinitive mood - 'bhāvārth kārdaṅtak') (a) (locative case - 'adhikaraṇ kārak'; synonymous with 'suṇaṇ vich') literally, in listening, and (b) (instrumental case - 'karaṇ kārak'; synonymous with 'suṇaṇ nāl') with listening. See suṇaṇā, pp. 137-8.

There is mention of just two of the sensory organs here, but the implicit reference is to all the sensory organs which can only work within the confines of their limits. Whilst the universe is bound by time and space, and limited, the Creator is completely free and unlimited. It is hardly surprising that God is not only beyond our reach but also beyond the grasp of our human senses.

His Glory is unfathomable, both by the power of observation and of hearing.

Aṅt(u) n jāpai, kiā *man*(i) maṅt(u)

jāpai: (a) (v, s, present tense, third person; synonymous with 'jāṇīdā-' or 'sojhī āuṅdī-' 'hai') gets to know or understand, and (b) (v, s, present tense, third person; synonymous with 'jāpdā-', 'bhāsdā-'or 'lagdā-' 'hai'; 'pratīt-', 'mālūm-'or 'mahsus-' 'huṅdā hai') appears, looks, feels, seems or perceives. See jāpai and jāpṇā.

kiā: (a) (pron; synonymous with 'kyā' or 'ki') what, and (b) (p; synonymous with 'prashan bodhak') used in the interrogative sense. See kiā.

man(i): (locative case - 'adhikaraṇ kārak'; synonymous with '*man* vich') in one's conscious self, 'Hirdā' and 'Jīvātmāṅ'. See *man*.

maṅt(u): (n, m; abbreviation for 'maṅtr') (n, m) (a) (synonymous with 'kānāphūsī', 'ghusar musar' and 'lukvī galbāt') whisper in one's ear, (b) (synonymous with 'ved and/or mūl pāṭh') recitation of a part of any Veda, (c) recitation of a holy verse to please or charm a 'Devī' (a demi-Goddess) or 'Devtā' (a demi-God) for success in one's ambition, (d) (n, m; synonymous with 'jo maṅnan karīe') that which one reflects on or ponders over and imbibes faithfully, (e) (synonymous with 'Gurū updes') instruction or precepts of a Gurū, and (f) (n; synonymous with 'salāh' and 'mashvarā') counsel, advice or opinion, and implicit here is (g) (n; synonymous with '*Man* aṅdar(i) guphatgū') one's innermost, personal and secretive thoughts, views or feelings. Gurū Nānak's 'Ik O'aṅkār', as portrayed in the 'Mūl Maṅtra', is unique; He is by Himself and the creation is nothing but His manifestation. This verse of the SGGS highlights another key characteristic of His God:

'He neither consults another nor seeks another's counsel; whatever He does, He does it by Himself'.[420]

Limitless are the mysteries of His mind. Or:
No one, at any given moment, knows or perceives the mysteries of His mind.

Aṅt(u) n jāpai, kītā ākār(u)

kītā: (a) (n, f; synonymous with 'krit') creation, (b) (past participle or 'bhūt kirdaṅt', m; synonymous with 'us dā kariā-', 'sirjiā-' or 'baṇāiā-' 'saṅsār') this universe created and developed by Him. See kītā.

ākār(u): (n, m; synonymous with 'akār', 'sarūp', 'sūrat' and 'rachnā') shape, size, form, figure, dimensions, appearance. In essence, the diverse empirical world.

Bounds of His creation are beyond our comprehension. Or:
Limitless are the bounds of His creation.

Aṅt(u) n jāpai, pārāvār(u)

pārāvār(u): (n, m) complex word comprising 'pār' ('parlā'- the opposite or far side - 'kinārā', 'taṭ', 'hadd' or 'sīmā') bank or limit + 'āvār' ('urlā' - the near side- 'kinārā', 'taṭ', 'hadd' or 'sīmā') bank or limit, i.e., the extent, vastness, the opposite extremes or farthest limits.

The limits of this vast creation are inconceivable and immeasurable. Or:
The limits of the two opposite extremes of this creation are unfathomable.

Aṅt kāraṇ(i), kete bil-lāh(i)

aṅt: see aṅt(u) (a). (u) of ('aṅt(u)') is missing because of the preposition 'kāraṇ(i)' that follows and links it with the rest of the sentence.

kāraṇ(i): (prep; synonymous with 'kāraṇ-' 'vāste' or 'laī') literally, for what purpose or the aim of it all. See kāraṇ.

kāraṇ: (a) (adv; synonymous with 'vāste', 'laī', 'het(u)' and 'nimit') what for or for what purpose, and (b) (n) the cause, motive, purpose or means of an action, e.g., 'upādān kāraṇ' - material cause: 'mīṭī' for a pitcher or 'sūt' for cloth; 'nimit kāraṇ' - efficient cause: a weaver or spinning wheel for cloth; 'formal cause' - that which imparts physical and functional characteristics, and the 'final cause'- the purpose or the object of creation.

kete: (adj, m, pl; synonymous with 'kaī' and 'kitne') numerous, many, several or quite a few.

bil-lāh(i): (a) (v, s, present tense, second person; synonymous with 'tūṅ bil-lāuṅdā haiṅ' or 'tusīṅ bil-lāuṅde ho') you cry over [something], (b) (v, s, imperative mood - 'saṅbhāv bhvikht kāl - kiās, sharat, ichhā bodhak', second person; synonymous with 'je tusīṅ bil-lāho') if you lament over [something], (c) (v, pl, present tense, first person; synonymous with 'asīṅ bil-lāhuṅde hāṅ') we cry over [something], (d) (v, pl, future tense, third person; synonymous with 'uh bil-lāhuṇge') they will cry over [something], and implicit here is (e) (v, pl, present tense, third person; synonymous with 'uh bil-lāuṅde han'; pronounced as 'bil-lāheṅ') they cry or lament over [something]. See bil-lāhuṇā.

bil-lāhuṇā: (v; synonymous with 'vilkaṇā', 'roṇā', 'vilāp- 'or 'virlāp-' 'karnā', 'arṛāhuṇā' or 'duhāī pāuṇī') to wail, lament, whine, whimper, cry, cry loudly and at a high pitch.

Countless beings struggle and lament in their vain pursuit of finding the limits of His Glory and of the creation...

Tā ke aṅt, n pāe jāh(i)

tā: (synonymous with 't'; pronounced as 'tāṅ') (pron; synonymous with 'tis' or 'us') literally, his or her. See tā.

ke: (prep, m; synonymous with 'de') of or for.

aṅt: (n, m, pl; synonymous with 'hadd baṅne') see aṅt (c). (u) of ('aṅt(u)') is missing because it is in the plural form.

pāe: (a) (adv; synonymous with 'pairīṅ' or 'charanāṅ nāl'; pronounced as 'pāeṅ') to or with feet, (b) (v, pl, past tense; synonymous with 'prāpat kīte'), (c) (v, s, present tense, third person; synonymous with 'ḍāleṅ or ḍāldā-', 'pāuṅdā- 'or 'pā sakdā-' 'hai') adds, pours, or puts on, and (d) (conj v) e.g. 'pāe jāh(i)'- 'pāe- 'or 'labhe ja-' 'sakde han'- can be got or found. See pāuṇā.

jāh(i): (a) (v, pl, present tense, third person; synonymous with 'jāṅde han', 'jā sakde'; 'dūr ho- 'or 'miṭ- ''jāṅde- ' 'han'; pronounced as 'jāhen') they go or can go, and (b) (conj v and suff), e.g. 'pāe jāh(i)'-'pāe- 'or 'labhe ja-’ ‘sakde han’- can be got or found; ‘n kathne jāh(i)’- cannot be described. See jāṇā (d).

...but they cannot fathom the extent of His Glory or depict the limits of His Creation.

Eh(u) aṅt(u), n jāṇai koi

eh(u): (pron and adj, m, s; synonymous with ‘yahī’ and ‘keval eh’) this or precisely this.

jāṇai: (v, s, present tense, third person: synonymous with ‘uh jāṇdā hai’ or ‘jāṇ sakdā hai’) see jāṇanā (b and d).

koi: (pron and adj; synonymous with ‘koī’) any, some or certain. The following verses of the SGGS beautifully capture His ineffable Glory and the limitlessness of His Creation:

Everyone says He is great, just on the basis of hearsay. However, how great He is can only be defined by seeing Him.[421]

He has no peer or rival, and none bears any ill will towards Him.[150]

Your intuitive knowledge of others’ innermost thoughts (‘dānā’) and Your foresight or farsightedness (‘bīnā’) is as vast as an ocean; how can I, a mere small fish, know Your magnitude.[416]

None can fathom Him and/or His Glory and know the limits of His Creation. Or:

Both He and His Glory and the limits of His Creation elude us all.

Bahutā kahīai, bahutā hoi

bahutā: (adj; synonymous with ‘bahut’, ‘adhik’, ‘vadhere’ and ‘ziādā’) plenty, plentiful, abundant, or much.

kahīai: (a) (v, s, present tense, third person; synonymous with ‘ākhdā-’or ‘biān kardā-’ ‘hai’) elucidates or expounds, (b) (v, pl, imperative mood - ‘hukmī bhvikht’, second person; synonymous with ‘ākhṇā chāhidā hai’ or ‘biān karnā chāhidā hai’) should elucidate or expound, and implicit here is (c) (imperative mood - ‘saṅbhāv bhvikht kāl - kiās or sharat bodhak’, s, third/first person; synonymous with ‘je bhāveṅ uh/asīṅ us nūṅ vaḍḍā kahīe’) literally, if we epitomise His Greatness [and wonder about the vastness of the creation]. See kahiṇā.

hoi: (v, s, present tense; synonymous with 'huṅdī- 'or 'huṅdā-' 'hai'; 'ho jāṅdī- 'or 'ho jāṅdā-' 'hai'; 'ho sakdā hai') literally, occurs, comes to be, or becomes; can occur, happen or become. See hoi.

The more we discover and define, the more there is to know of Him and His Creation.

Vaḍā sāhib(u), ūchā thāu

vaḍā: (adj, m; synonymous with 'mukhīā', 'shiromani' and 'sreshṭ') principal, premier or the most superior.

sāhib(u): (n, m; synonymous with 'swāmī', 'mālik' and 'pat(i)') Master or Lord (sāhib).

ūchā: (adj, m) (a) (synonymous with 'uchā' and 'tībar'; 'āvāz or dhun(i) vich uchā') loud, (b) (synonymous with 'sur vich uchā') to be at a higher point than the desired musical note, (c) (synonymous with 'ūchāī vich uchā') tallest amongst the tall or highest amongst the high, and (d) (synonymous with 'sthān or padvī vich uchā') high or higher in rank or status.

thāu: (a) (n, f) post, position, station or office, (b) (suff) signifying region or land, e.g., Rājasthān, and implicit here is (c) (synonymous with 'thāṅ', 'asthān', 'jagah(i)', 'tikāṇā' and 'ḍerā'; pronounced as 'thāuṅ') (a) (n, f) place, location, space or dwelling.

ūchā thāu: literally, His place of dwelling is high. However, implicit here is 'He is agaṅm and agochar'.

The Lord is Great, and exalted is His position.

Ūche ūpar(i), ūchā nāu

ūche: (adj, m; synonymous with 'ūchtā vāle') (a) very tall or high, (b) very worthwhile or valuable; of high rank or lofty status, and (c) (synonymous with 'ūche toṅ') literally, from the highest or the loftiest.

ūpar(i): (a) (adv; synonymous with 'anusār' and 'mutābik') literally, according to or in accordance with, (b) (adj; synonymous with 'parbal' and 'gālab') strong, forceful, dominant, overpowering, and preponderant, and implicit here is (c) (prep and adv; synonymous with 'utte' and 'utāṅh') upon, above or on top of.

ūchā: see above.

ūche ūpar(i) ūchā: (synonymous with 'bahut ūchā', 'at(i) ūchā' and 'sabh toṅ ūchā') literally, taller than the tall; higher than the high. However, implicit here is the highest ranking or the topmost position.

nāu: (n, f; synonymous with 'nāmaṇā', 'vaḍiāī', 'ustat(i)' and 'mahimā') praise, eulogy, glory, or tribute. See nāu.

Higher than high or loftiest is His Glory.

Evaḍ(u) ūchā, hovai koi

evaḍ(u): (adj and adv; synonymous with 'itnā-'or 'ainā-' 'vaḍḍā') so much or this much.

hovai: (v, s, imperative mood - 'saṅbhāv bhvikht kāl - kiās and sharat bodhak', third person; synonymous with 'hove' or 'ho jāve') see hovṇā (a).

If someone were to be so exalted.

Tis(u) ūche kau, jāṇai soi

tis(u): (pron and adj; synonymous with 'us') literally, he, she or that person. The reference here is to God.

kau: (prep; synonymous with 'tāṅī', 'ko', 'nūṅ', 'neṅ', 'toṅ', 'dā/kā') literally, of, to, for, from and up to.

soi: (pron and adj; synonymous with 'oh' or 'ohī') he, she, it or they; the same. See soi.

Only then he would know that exalted Being.

Jevaḍ(u) āp(i), jāṇai āp(i) āp(i)

jevaḍ(u): (adj; synonymous with 'jitnā vaḍḍā') as much as, as great as or as big as. In reality, God has no equal or rival.

āp(i): (pron; synonymous with 'āp- 'or 'khud-' 'hī') one oneself or He Himself.

Only He knows however great and/or exalted He is.

Nānak, nadrī karmī dāt(i)

Nānak: (n, m, s) the (u) of 'Nānak(u)' is missing because of its vocative case - 'sanbodhan kārak'.

nadrī: (a) (adj; synonymous with 'nadar karan vālā') one with the ability of a compassionate glance, i.e., God, and (b) (genitive case - 'sanbandh kārak'; synonymous with 'nadar karan vale dī') literally, God's.

karmī: (synonymous with 'karam- 'or 'mehar-' 'sadkā'), through His Grace or Mercy.

dāt(i): (n, f; synonymous with 'dān', 'khairāt' and 'bakhshīsh') blessing, grace, boon, or bestowal. The reference here is to the knowledge or perception of His indefinable Glory or attributes and the vastness of His Creation. See dāt(i).

'The Compassionate Lord bestows every blessing and the gift of 'Nām(u)' through His Grace', O' Nānak!

Conceptual summary

Infinite is His Glory, the devotees that sing it, and endless the ways to express it. Infinite is His Creation and Bounty. His Glory is unfathomable and beyond our powers of observation and hearing. Limitless and unfathomable are the mysteries of His mind.

Limitless are the bounds of His Creation and the expanse between. Countless struggle and lament in their vain pursuit of finding the limits of His Glory and Creation but fail miserably.

In reality, none can fathom Him or the vastness of this creation. The more we discover and define, the more mystery and perplexity surrounds Him and His Creation.

The Lord is great, and exalted is His position; higher than high or loftiest is His Glory. He is unique and only His equal or rival would know His true Glory and status.

'The Compassionate Lord bestows all blessings, even the gift of 'Nām(u)', through His Grace', O' Nānak!

In summary, God is the fount of all attributes, virtues, and values, and both His Glory and His Creation are infinite. In reality, there is no other but Him in this universe, let alone the possibility of there being an equal or a rival. Thus, the struggle to define and depict Him and His Creation are completely in vain.

PAUṚĪ 25
ਪਉੜੀ ੨੫॥

Bahutā karam(u), likhiā nā jāi.
ਬਹੁਤਾ ਕਰਮੁ, ਲਿਖਿਆ ਨਾ ਜਾਇ॥

Vaḍā dātā, til(u) na tamāi.
ਵਡਾ ਦਾਤਾ, ਤਿਲੁ ਨ ਤਮਾਇ॥

Kete maṅgah(i), jodh apār.
ਕੇਤੇ ਮੰਗਹਿ, ਜੋਧ ਅਪਾਰ॥

Ketiā, gaṇat nahī vīchār(u).
ਕੇਤਿਆ, ਗਣਤ ਨਹੀ ਵੀਚਾਰੁ॥

Kete, khap(i) tuṭah(i) vekār.
ਕੇਤੇ, ਖਪਿ ਤੁਟਹਿ ਵੇਕਾਰ॥

Kete, lai lai, mukar(u) pāh(i).
ਕੇਤੇ, ਲੈ ਲੈ, ਮੁਕਰੁ ਪਾਹਿ॥

Kete mūrakh, khāhī khāh(i).
ਕੇਤੇ ਮੂਰਖ, ਖਾਹੀ ਖਾਹਿ॥

Ketiā, dūkh bhūkh sad mār.
ਕੇਤਿਆ, ਦੂਖ ਭੂਖ ਸਦ ਮਾਰ॥

Eh(i) bhī dāt(i), terī, dātār.
ਏਹਿ ਭਿ ਦਾਤਿ, ਤੇਰੀ, ਦਾਤਾਰ॥

Baṅd(i) khalāsī, bhāṇai hoi.
ਬੰਦਿ ਖਲਾਸੀ, ਭਾਣੈ ਹੋਇ॥

Hor(u), ākh(i) na sakai koi.
ਹੋਰੁ, ਆਖਿ ਨ ਸਕੈ ਕੋਇ॥

Je ko khāik(u), ākhaṇ(i) pāi.
ਜੇ ਕੋ ਖਾਇਕੁ, ਆਖਣਿ ਪਾਇ॥

Oh(u) jāṇai, jetīā muh(i) khāi.
ਓਹੁ ਜਾਣੈ, ਜੇਤੀਆ ਮੁਹਿ ਖਾਇ॥

Āpe jāṇai, āpe dei.
ਆਪੇ ਜਾਣੈ, ਆਪੇ ਦੇਇ॥

Ākhah(i), si bhi, ke-ī ke(i).
ਆਖਹਿ, ਸਿ ਭਿ, ਕੇਈ ਕੇਇ॥

Jis no bakhse, siphat(i) sālāh.
ਜਿਸ ਨੋ ਬਖਸੇ, ਸਿਫਤਿ ਸਾਲਾਹ॥

Nānak, pāt(i)sāhī pāt(i)sāh(u). (25)
ਨਾਨਕ, ਪਾਤਿਸਾਹੀ ਪਾਤਿਸਾਹੁ॥ ੨੫॥

Bahutā karam(u), likhiā nā jāi

bahutā: (adj, m; synonymous with 'bahut', 'adhik', 'ziādā' and 'vadhere') literally, plentiful, abundant, excessive, profuse or in large quantity. However, implicit here is limitless or endless.

karam(u): (n, f; pers; synonymous with 'kripā', 'meharbānī' and 'bakhshīsh') kindness, favour, grace, mercy, or compassion. It is, however, noteworthy that one is deserving of His Grace only when one genuinely strives to live by His Will and in perfect harmony with 'Nām(u)'.

likhiā: (conj v) e.g., (i) 'likhiā n jāi' - literally, that cannot be written, noted or recorded and (ii) 'ih likhiā ga-i-ā hai'- this has been written or recorded.

n: (p; pronounced as 'nāṅ') no, not or implying a negative connotation. See likhiā.

jāi: (conj v and suff.) as part of the conjunct verb it helps to complete the meaning of the primary verb, e.g., (i) 'n jāi lakhiā' - cannot be ascertained or realised, (ii) 'likhiā n jāi' - that cannot be written or recorded. See jāi.

His Grace and Bounty are both abundant, and too generous and vast to be recorded.

Vaḍā dātā, til(u) na tamāi

vaḍā: (adj, m) (a) (synonymous with 'bahut' and 'at(i)') very much, great, inordinate, immense, or tremendous, and (b) (synonymous with 'shiroman(i)' and 'mukhīā') principal, premier, ultimate, supreme, or foremost.

dātā: (n, m) (a) (synonymous with 'dānī', 'dānshīl' or 'dāt deṇ vālā') a generous person, (b) (synonymous with 'dātār') a giver, donor or bestower of gifts (dāts) without any strings attached, and implicit here is (c) God - who is the primordial 'sarab thok kā dātā', the Great Giver or the Great Benefactor.

til(u): (a) (n, m, s) sesame or mustard seed, and (b) (adj) miniscule like a sesame seed, figuratively used to denote an insignificant amount.

tamāi: (a) (n, f; synonymous with 'tamā' (skt), 'rātr(i)' or or 'rāt'' darkness and night, (b) (n, f; synonymous with 'hiras', 'ruchī', 'ichhchhā' and 'tām' (skt)) desire, craving, and inclination, and implicit here is (c) (n, m; synonymous with 'tam-ā' (arab), 'lālach' and 'trishnā') greed, avarice, and covetousness. God is innately loving and compassionate and infinitely generous. He always gives and grants His Grace and seeks nothing in return.

He is innately and immensely generous, and harbours no ulterior motive and seeks not even a grain in return.

Kete maṅgah(i), jodh apār

Kete: (adj; synonymous with 'kaī' and 'kitne') numerous, many, several or quite a few.

Maṅgah(i): (v, pl, present tense, third person; synonymous with 'uh maṅgde han'; pronounced as 'maṅgaheṅ') literally, [they] ask or seek. However, implicit here is [they] implore, beseech, or supplicate. See maṅgah(i) and maṅgṇā. The reality is that He gives to all and not just to His 'Bhagats'. There is really no need for any alarm as the basic needs for survival are provided to all and, in addition, whatever else a being is judged to be deserving of, based on its 'Karma', is also granted in its 'mastak de lekh' as illustrated in this verse of the SGGS:

'Why waver and lose faith when the Creator is committed to sustain and protect you', O man! He who created you and will surely afford you succour'.[422]

jodh: (n, m, pl; synonymous with 'jodhe', 'yodhe' and 'bahādur') literally, knights, warriors, and braves, especially those who fight injustice, tyranny, oppression, a holy war or engage in battle with their innate evil tendencies.

Apār: (adj, s; synonymous with 'beaṅt', 'agṇit', 'agādh' and 'athāh') compound word comprising 'a' (without) + 'pār' (the other end or bank, the opposite end, bourndary or limit), meaning infinite or boundless.

Countless hugely brave and just knights beg for physical and inner strength from You.

Ketiā, gaṇat nahī vīchār(u)

ketiā: (adj, m; genitive case - 'saṅbaṅdh kārak'; synonymous with 'kaīāṅ- 'or 'kitniāṅ-' 'dī'; pronounced as 'ketiāṅ') literally, many or of many. See ketiā.

gaṇat: (a) (v; synonymous with 'gaṇanā') to count, (b) (n, f; synonymous with 'giṇtī': n, m; 'hisāb' and 'shumār') count, reckoning, calculation or census. See gaṇanā.

gaṇanā: (v) to count, note, enumerate, or estimate.

nahī: (p; pronounced as 'nahīṅ') no, not, expressing a negative meaning. cannot count, countless.

vīchār(u): (a) (n, f; synonymous with 'vivek', 'tatv dā nirṇā' or 'aslīyat jāṇan dī kriyā') study, reflection, deliberation, or cogitation, (b) (synonymous with 'kudrat de lekhe dī-' 'bīchār' and/or 'bibek') consultation, speculation, consideration or deliberation, and (c) (n, m; synonymous with 'anumān' and 'aṅdāzā') estimate, guess, speculation or conjecture. See vīchār(u).

Countless others, beyond conjecture and speculation, beg for fulfilment of their needs.

Kete, khap(i) tuṭah(i) vekār

khap(i): (indeclinable past participle or perfect participle - 'pūran pūrab kārdaṅtak'; synonymous with 'khap khap ke') see khapṇā (c and e).

khapṇā: (v) (a) (synonymous with 'preshān hoṇā', 'khijhṇā', 'taṛpaṇā' and 'chiṅtā karnī') to fret, worry, agonise or brood, (b) (synonymous with 'baṅne jaṇā') to be tied, chained, bound, (c) (synonymous with 'nāsh hoṇā') to be destroyed, obliterated or eradicated, (d) (synonymous with 'kharch hoṇā') to be spent or consumed, and implicit here is (e) (synonymous with ‘jazab hoṇā’ and ‘khachṇā’) to permeate, assimilate and lose self-identity; to become engrossed or absorbed.

tuṭah(i): (a) (v, s, present tense, second person; synonymous with ‘tusīṅ rah-’, ‘muk- ’or ‘khatam ho-’ ‘jāṅde ho’), (b) (v, pl, present tense, first person; synonymous with ‘asīṅ rah-’, ‘muk-’or ‘khatam ho-’ ‘jāṅde hāṅ’), (c) (v, pl, future tense, third person; synonymous with ‘uh khatam ho jāṅge’), and implicit here is (d) (v, pl, present tense, third person; synonymous with ‘uh rah- ’or ‘muk-’ ‘jāṅde han’; ‘uh ṭuṭde- ’or ‘alag ho jāṅde-’ ‘han’). See tuṭaṇā.

tuṭṇā: (v) (a) (synonymous with ‘tūṭaṇā’, ‘ṭūṭṇā’ or ‘alagg ho jāṇā’) literally, to break, crack, smash or separate; drop, and implicit here is (b) (synonymous with ‘alag hoṇā’) literally, to separate, disconnect, become detached or fall apart. In essence, the reference here is to severing links with the true path of ‘Nām-consciousness’ and ‘Nām(u)’.

vekār: (a) (n, m, pl; synonymous with ‘bekār’) work or deeds with no useful outcome, (b) (n, m, pl; synonymous with ‘pāp’) evil thoughts, sins, or misdeeds, exploitative or detrimental in nature to other beings, and responsible for one’s own spiritual downfall, and implicit here is (c) (n, m, pl; synonymous with ‘vikārs’) evil, immoral, sinful or perverse thoughts, speech or deeds resulting from an innate evil nature and warped persona with the five basic tendencies - ‘kām’, ‘krodh’, ‘lobh’, ‘moh’ and ‘haṅkār’- having now become perverted, and (d) (locative case - ‘adhikaraṇ kārak’; synonymous with ‘bikārāṅ-’ or ‘vikārāṅ-’ ‘vich’) literally, in ‘vekār’.

Countless beings, engrossed in the material world and in evil deeds because of their innate evil nature, inadvertently self-destruct and breakaway from the true path of ‘Nām-consciousness’.

Kete, lai lai, mukar(u) pāh(i)

lai: (indeclinable past participle or perfect participle - ‘pūran pūrab kārdaṅtak’; synonymous with ‘lai ke’) literally, having got, obtained or acquired. See laiṇā (a and b). The reference here is to the sustained provision of basic needs for everyone’s survival.

mukar(u): (a) (n, m; skt; synonymous with ‘darpaṇ’ and ‘shīshā’) mirror or looking glass, and implicit here is (b) (n, m; synonymous with ‘munkir- ’or ‘inkār-’ ‘dī bhāvnā or kriyā’) denial, retraction, or disclaimer.

pāh(i): (v, pl, present tense, third person; synonymous with 'paiṅde- 'or 'jāṅde-' 'han'; pronounced as 'pāheṅ') literally, lie, achieve, go, get ready and eager to act or engage. See pāh(i) and paiṇā (d (vi)).

mukar(u) pāh(i): (conjunct v; synonymous with 'mukar(u) jāh(i)', i.e., 'mukar(u) jāṅde han') literally, deny, renege, disclaim or go back upon. Bhāī Gurdās, the scribe of the SGGS and maternal uncle of Gurū Arjun Dev, the fifth Gurū, bestows upon the ungrateful ones ('akirtghan') 'the leper complex' and depicts them as a category of people 'to be shunned like the plague'.

Except for an ungrateful person, supreme amongst evil persons, none of the following is truly a burden on the Earth: tall mountains that almost touch the sky, countless huge forts visible from many miles away, the oceans into which many rivers merge, all the fruit-laden trees of the world and the countless sentient life forms wandering the Earth.[423]

A scavenger woman ('Chūhaṛī'), having appeased her lust, was seen carrying a foul-smelling bowl (a human skull) containing dog meat, cooked in wine, and covered with a bloodstained cloth. When asked to clarify, she explained that she had covered the meat she had cooked to hide it from the sight of an ungrateful person in order to avoid it being defiled.[424]

Countless ungrateful beings deny ever receiving these gifts in spite of their continual procurement of the basic needs for survival.

Kete mūrakh, khāhī khāh(i)

mūrakh: (a) (adj, m; synonymous with 'nā-tajarbekār') inexperienced, lacking a particular skill), and (b) (adj, m; synonymous with 'besamajh', 'agiānī' and 'budh(i) rahit') daft, unwise, foolish, stupid, simpleton or short-sighted.

khāhī: (a) (adj; synonymous with 'khāhish vālā' or 'trishālū') one who desires or yearns, and implicit here is (b) (adj, s; synonymous with 'khādik' and 'khāṇ vālā') one who partakes of food and relishes it and implicit here is (c) (adj, pl; synonymous with 'khāṇ vāle'; pronounced as 'khāhīṅ') literally, they who partake of and savour and relish food.

khāh(i): (a) (v, s, present tense, second person; synonymous with 'tūṅ khāṅdā haiṅ' or 'tusīṅ khāṅde ho'; pronounced as 'khāheṅ') you partake of food; (fig) you suffer the consequences of your actions, (b) (v, pl, present tense, first person; synonymouse with 'asīṅ khāvāṅge') we will partake of food, (c) (v, s, imperative mood - 'saṅbhāv bhvikht kāl - kiās, sharat, ichhā bodhak', first/second person; synonymous with 'je asīṅ/tusīṅ khāvīe'), (d) (v, pl, future tense; synonymous with 'uh khāṇge'), and implicit here is (e) (v, pl, present tense, third person; synonymous with 'uh khāṅde han'; pronounced as 'khāheṅ') literally, they dine, eat, partake of food, consume or ingest or (fig) they suffer the consequences of their deeds. See khāṇā (b and c).

Countless fools voraciously and ungratefully consume and enjoy Your Gifts.

Ketiā, dūkh bhūkh sad mār

ketiā: (adj, m; accusative case - 'karam kārak'; synonymous with 'kaīāṅ-' or 'kitniāṅ-' 'nūṅ'; pronounced as 'ketiāṅ') to many.

dūkh: (n, m, pl; synonymous with 'dukh'; antonym of 'sūkh') collective noun for all one's ills and suffering from physical and/or psychological distress; unhappiness and discontentedness due to real or apparent lack of material comforts or pleasures, and inner turmoil because of being engrossed in the web of 'Moh', 'Māyā' and 'Vikārs', and with living the life of a 'Kūṛaiār(u)' in disharmony with 'Nām(u)' and 'Nām-consciousness'.

bhūkh: (n, f; synonymous with 'bhukh') (a) (synonymous with 'khāṇ dī ichhā') hunger or appetite for food, and (b) (synonymous with 'ichhā', 'tāṅg' and 'ruchī') incessant craving for the material world, its comforts, and pleasures, especially when driven by 'Trisnā'.

sad:(adv; synonymous with 'sadā', 'sadīvī' and 'hameshā') ever, forever, always, or perpetually.

mār: (a) (n, m; pers; synonymous with 'sarp') a serpent, (b) (n, f; synonymous with 'vāsnā' in Budhism) lewdness or sensual desire, (c) (n, f; synonymous with 'mrityū' and 'maut') death, (d) (n; synonymous with 'bimārī' and 'rog') illness, and implicit here is (e) (n, f; synonymous with 'prahār', 'aghāt', 'choṭ', 'saṭ' and 'ṭhokar') literally, blows, knocks or assault. In essence, affliction with distress, pain, illness, and hunger.

Countless beings suffer forever with pain, distress, and hunger.

Eh(i) bhī dāt(i), terī, dātār

eh(i): (pron; pl of 'eh') only these or just these.

bhī: (a) (synonymous with 'tad bhī') even then, and implicit here is (b) (adv; synonymous with 'vī') literally, also or too. See bhī.

dāt(i): (n, f; synonymous with 'dān', 'khairāt' and 'bakhshīsh') blessings, grace, boon, or bestowal.

terī: (pron, f) yours.

dātār: (n, adj, s; synonymous with 'dātā, 'dāt deṇ vāle', 'dānī' or 'dānshīl') a complex word comprising 'dāt' (a free gift, donation or grant) + 'ār' ('ālya' or 'ghar' -source or fount) they who bestow gifts and whose treasures are boundless. However, implicit here is the ever beneficent and benevolent God ('sarab thok kā dātā'). (u) of 'dātār(u)' is missing because of its vocative case - 'saṅbodhan kārak'.

'Anguish and pain, secondary to sinful deeds, become the cure, and engrossment in worldly comforts and pleasure, the malady. However, one is saved from all this when one is blessed with lasting inner equanimity and bliss. You, the Creator, are the real doer of everything and I can do nothing; it does not behove me to claim to know or understand the underlying mystery'.[425]

'These too are Your Blessings or Gifts', O' You, the Beneficient Lord!

Baṅd(i) khalāsī, bhāṇai hoi

baṅd(i): (a) (locative case - 'adhikaraṇ kārak'; synonymous with 'vaṅd(i)-' (skt), 'baṅdhan-', 'kaid-' and 'jel-' 'vich') literally, in bondage, confinement or captivity, and implicit here is (b) (ablative case - 'apādān kārak'; synonymous with 'vaṅd(i)-' (skt), 'baṅdhan-', 'kaid-' and 'jel-' 'toṅ') literally, from bondage or confinement. However, implicit here is bondage or entrapment in the lure of the empirical world and its pleasures ('Moh of Māyā') and the cycle of transmigration ('Āvāgavan'). See baṅdh(u).

baṅdh(u): (a) (n, m, s; synonymous with 'saṅbaṅdh') relationship, connection or association, (b) (n, m, s; synonymous with 'baṅn') dam, dyke, blockage or obstruction, (c) (n, f, s; synonymous with 'rukāvaṭ' or 'vighan') barrier, stumbling block or impediment, (d) (n, f, s; synonymous with 'ṭhal', ‘ṭhahrāo’ or ‘rok’) stoppage, curb or check, and implicit here is (e) (n, m, s; synonymous with ‘baṅdhan’) bondage, restraint or limitation.

khalāsī: (a) (n, f, s; arab; synonymous with ‘nirbaṅdh’, ‘chhuṭkārā’ or ‘āzādī’) literally, liberation, deliverance or freedom but implicit here is (b) (n, f; synonymous with ‘rihāī’, ‘muktī’ or ‘mukat(i)’) exoneration from the evil influence of ‘Haumaiṅ’, ‘Moh’ and ‘Vikārs’ (‘Māyā’) in this lifetime (‘Jīvan-Mukat(i)’), and release from ‘Āvāgavan’, the cycle of transmigration, in the hereafter (‘Moksh’ or ‘Param gat(i)’).

bhāṇai: (a) (instrumental case - ‘karaṇ kārak’ ‘nāl’, ‘rāhīṅ’, ‘duārā’ or ‘sadkā’; synonymous with ‘bhāṇe anusār turiāṅ’) according to His Will, and (b) (locative case - ‘adhikaraṇ kārak’; synonymous with ‘bhāṇe vich turiāṅ’) living by His Will. See bhāṇā.

bhāṇā: (a) (v; synonymous with ‘chaṅgā lagā’, ‘pasaṅd āiā’, ‘bhāiā’ and ‘bhā ga-i-ā’) literally, appealed, liked, desired or approved, and implicit here is (b) (n, m; synonymous with ‘Hukam’) His Divine Order, and (c) (n, f; synonymous with ‘ichhchhā’ and ‘marzī’) His Prerogative, Wish or Will.

hoi: (v, s, present tense; synonymous with ‘huṅdī- ’or ‘huṅdā-’ ‘hai’; ‘ho jāṅdī- ’or ‘ho jāṅdā-’ ‘hai'; ‘ho sakdā hai’) literally, occurs, comes to be, or becomes; can occur, happen or become. See hovṇā (a and c).

Release from ‘Haumaiṅ’, ‘Moh’ and innate ‘Vikārī’ tendencies (‘Māyā’) in the here and now, and from ‘Āvāgavan’, the cycle of transmigration, in the hereafter, is by Your Decree only.

Hor(u), ākh(i) na sakai koi

hor(u): (a) (pron; synonymous with ‘anya’, ‘dūjā’, ‘dūsrā’ and ‘vakhrā’) another, different and someone or something else, and (b) (adj; synonymous with ‘aur’ and ‘is toṅ-’ ‘vadh’ or ‘chhuṭ’) another, more or in addition.

ākh(i): (indeclinable past participle or perfect participle - ‘pūran pūrab kārdaṅtak’; synonymous with ‘ākh- ’or ‘bol-’ ‘ke’) by saying, uttering, or illustrating. See ākhṇā.

n: (p; pronounced as ‘nāṅ’) no, not or implying a negative connotation.

sakai: (modal v, s, present tense, third person; synonymous with ‘sakdā hai’ and ‘samrath ho sakdā hai’) see sakṇā.

sakṇā: (modal v, s, present tense, third person) may or can.

koi: (a) (pron; synonymous with ‘koī ik’ and ‘virlā’) rare one or occasional someone, (b) (pron and (adj; synonymous with ‘koī’) any, certain or someone.

ākh(i) n sakai koi: (synonymous with ‘bol ke nahīṅ das sakdā’) no one can explain by word of mouth.

None can vouch for an alternative route.

Je ko khāik(u), ākhaṇ(i) pāi

je: (conj; synonymous with ‘je kar’, ‘yadī’ and ‘agar’) if or in case.

ko: (pron; abbrev. for ‘koi’; synonymous with ‘koī’ and ‘koi’) someone, anyone, or another.

khāik(u): (a) (n, m; synonymous with ‘tiḍḍā’ or ‘pataṅgā’ (pers)) winged insect, (b) (n and adj, m; synonymous with ‘khādik’ or ‘peṭū’) gluttonous, piggish or a guzzler, and implicit here is (c) (n, m; synonymous with ‘kathakkaṛ’, ‘vaqta’, ‘gappī’, ‘gapauṛū’ or ‘jhakh māran vālā’) blabbermouth, gossipmonger, rumourmonger, or prattler. In essence, naïve or foolish.

ākhaṇ(i): (genitive case - ‘saṅbaṅdh kārak’; synonymous with ‘ākhaṇ-’or ‘kahiṇ-’ ‘dī/dā’) see ākhaṇ(i) and ākhṇā.

pāi: (n, m; synonymous with ‘ihsās’, ‘shakat(i)’, ‘bal’, ‘pāiāṅ’ and ‘hauṅsalā’; pronounced as ‘pā(i)ṅ’) a feeling or realisation; courage and moral strength. See pāi.

Should a naïve blabbermouth dare suggest this?

Oh(u) jāṇai, jetīā muh(i) khāi

oh(u): (pron and adj, m, s) he, she, it or that.

jāṇai: (v, s, present tense, third person; synonymous with ‘jāṇdā- ’or ‘samjadā-’ ‘hai’) see jāṇanā (a, b, and c).

jetīā: (adj, f, pl; synonymous with ‘jiṅnīāṅ’ or ‘jitniāṅ’; pronounced as ‘jetiāṅ’) however much or as much as, or however many.

muh(i): (locative case - ‘adhikaraṇ kārak’; synonymous with ‘mūṅh-’ ‘utte’ or ‘uppar’; pronounced as ‘mūṅh’) literally, on one’s face. See mūṅh.

mūṅh: (n, m) literally, mouth or face.

khāi: (a) (indeclinable past participle or perfect participle - 'pūran pūrab kārdaṅtak'; synonymous with 'khā ke'), and implicit here is (b) (v, s, present tense, third person; synonymous with 'khāṅdā hai') see khāṇā (c (i)).

He knows how many slaps or blows he has to withstand on his face and the shame he has to endure.

Āpe jāṇai, āpe dei

āpe: (a) (pron; nominative case - 'kartā kārak', s; synonymous with 'āp' or 'khud-' 'hī') literally, solely oneself. The reference here is to 'He (God) Himself'.

jāṇai: see above. The reference here is to the deserving needs of all beings, a sentiment beautifully captured by this verse from the SGGS:

You know the woes of my conscious self without my uttering even a word, and can make me contemplate 'Nām(u)'.[418]

dei:(v, s, present tense, third person; synonymous with 'deṅdā hai') see deṇā (a, b, and c). However, the reference here is to noble attributes, virtues, and values and to help attune to and harmonise perfectly with 'Nām(u)' or 'Nām-consciousness'.

God alone knows our just needs and provides accordingly.

Ākhah(i), si bhi, keī kei

ākhah(i): (v, pl, present tense, third person; synonymous with 'ākhde han'; pronounced as 'ākhaheṅ') see ākhṇā.

si: (pron and adj, f, s; synonymous with 'uh', 'vah' or 'ih') literally, she, that, or it. In essence, the reference here is to the notion that He Himself knows what to grant and to whom.

bh(i): (p and adv; synonymous with 'bhī' and 'vī') also or too. See bh(i).

ke-ī ke(i): (a) (pron and adj, m; synonymous with 'koī') anyone or someone, and implicit here is (b) (adj, m; synonymous with 'virle') some rare people.

Though only the exceptional few and grateful acknowledge this.

Jis no bakhse, siphat(i) sālāh

jis: (pron, s, third person; synonymous with 'jin(i)') he, she, it, or that; who, whom or whomsoever. (u) of 'jis(u)' is missing because of the preposition 'no' that follows and links it with the rest of the sentence.

no: (p; pronounced as 'noṅ' and synonymous with 'nūṅ') with or to.

bakhse: (v, s, present tense, third person; synonymous with 'bakhshadā hai') see bakhshaṇā.

bakhshaṇā: (v; synonymous with 'bakshaṇā'; pronounced as 'bakhshaṇā') (a) (synonymous with 'muāph karnā') to be merciful or gracious; to exempt, pardon or forgive, and implicit here is (b) (synonymous with 'inām deṇā' to bestow a grant, gift, or honour, and (c) (synonymous with 'kripā- 'or 'mehr-' 'karnī') to bless with compassion.

siphat(i) sālāh: (n, f; synonymous with 'mahimā', 'upmā', 'vaḍiāī', 'ustat(i)', 'jas', 't-a-rīf') literally, His Praise and Glory. In essence, His devotion ('Bhagat(i)') i.e., a willing, loving and unconditional surrender to, love for, and endeavor to align perfectly with 'Nām(u)'. One cannot achieve the noble attribute of His 'siphat sālāh' by one's own effort; its gift lies solely in His domain as the following verses of the SGGS explain:

Rarely is one blessed with His devotion and praise; whosoever is so blessed is then not asked to account for his actions.[426]

The Benificent Lord bestows the gift of 'Nām(u)' to whosoever He finds deserving as this privilege is solely His. They, who are imbued with His love, enjoy lasting inner bliss here and are honoured in the hereafter.[427]

'Whom He Blesses with willing, loving, and unconditional surrender to, love for and perfect alignment with 'Nām(u)'...

Nānak, pāt(i)sāhī pāt(i)sāh(u)

Nānak: (n, m, s) (u) of 'Nānak(u)' is missing because of the vocative case - 'saṅbodhan kārak'.

pāt(i)sāhī: (a) (n, f; synonymous with 'pātshāhī') kingship, dominion, or empire, (b) (adj; synonymous with 'shāhī' or 'rājkī') royal, regal or imperial, (c) (n, f; synonymous with 'gurtā' or 'sachī bādshāhat') eternal rule, dominion or empire (in Spirituality), and implicit here is (d) (genitive case - 'saṅbaṅdh kārak', pl; synonymous with 'pāt(i)sāhāṅ dā'; pronounced as 'pātshāhīṅ') of 'pātshāhāṅ'. See pāt(i)sāh.

pāt(i)sāh(u): (n, m, s; synonymous with 'pādshah' and 'bādshah' and pronounced as 'pātshāh') a complex word comprising 'pāt' or 'pāt(i)' + 'sāh(u)'. Literally, Lord Protector and Lord Master of the imperial throne, i.e., a King. See pāt(i)sāh(u).

sachā pāt(i)sāh: one who has realised 'Nām(u)', the fount of all attributes, virtues and values within one's 'Hirdā'.

... *'He is the King of Kings or the Most Reverend of all', O' Nānak!*

Conceptual summary

God's Grace and Bounty are abundant and beyond all reckoning. He is innately and enormously generous, harbours no selfish ulterior motive, and seeks not even a grain in return.

'Countless hugely brave and just knights beg for physical and inner strength from You, and countless others, beyond my conjecture and speculation, beg for their needs too. Countless beings (a) deeply entrenched in the empirical world and its pleasures and in evil deeds because of their innate evil nature, inadvertently self-destruct on this slippery slope, and turn away from the true path of 'Nām-consciousness', (b) keep receiving the gifts but deny You, the Benefactor, and countless fools voraciously and ungratefully consume and enjoy Your Gifts, and (c) suffer forever in pain, distress and hunger; but 'these too are Your Blessings or Gifts', for they prompt them to learn to live by Your Will, O' the Ever Munificent Lord!

Release from 'Māyā' and 'Āvāgavan', the cycle of transmigration, is by Your Decree only, and none can vouch for an alternative route. However, should a naïve loudmouth dare suggest one, he would know the shame he would endure and the punishment he would incur thereafter.

God alone knows our just needs and provides accordingly, though only the exceptional few acknowledge this. 'He whom God Blesses with willing, loving, and unconditional surrender to, love for and perfect alignment with 'Nām(u)', is the King of Kings', O' Nānak!

In summary, His Glory is surely infinite, but His Grace and Compassion, too, know no bounds. You spontaneously and forever fulfil the basic needs of all and yet all the high and mighty of the world still beg for more at your door.

In return, we indulge in, and become entrenched in material gifts and pleasures, and forsake You, the Benefactor. Greed for more and more ('Trisnā') thrusts us deeper and deeper into the web of 'Māyā', from which it is difficult to escape, and hence suffer the consequences. Inner turmoil from loss of inner peace, physical and mental suffering and general discontentment, eventually exhort us to change our course from ego-consciousness to 'Nām-consciousness', in order to seek the most precious gift of willing and loving surrender to the Gurū's Divine Word and Wisdom, and to promise resolutely to live by Your Will.

PAUṚĪ 26
ਪਉੜੀ ੨੬॥

Amul guṇ, amul vāpār.
ਅਮੁਲ ਗੁਣ, ਅਮੁਲ ਵਾਪਾਰ॥

Amul vāpārīe, amul bhaṅḍār.
ਅਮੁਲ ਵਾਪਾਰੀਏ, ਅਮੁਲ ਭੰਡਾਰ॥

Amul āvah(i), amul lai jāh(i).
ਅਮੁਲ ਆਵਹਿ, ਅਮੁਲ ਲੈ ਜਾਹਿ॥

Amul bhāi, amulā samāh(i).
ਅਮੁਲ ਭਾਇ, ਅਮੁਲਾ ਸਮਾਹਿ॥

Amul(u) dharam(u), amul(u) dībāṇ(u).
ਅਮੁਲੁ ਧਰਮੁ, ਅਮੁਲੁ ਦੀਬਾਣੁ॥

Amul(u) tul(u), amul(u) parvāṇ(u).
ਅਮੁਲੁ ਤੁਲੁ, ਅਮੁਲੁ ਪਰਵਾਣੁ॥

Amul(u) bakhsīs, amul(u) nīsāṇ(u).
ਅਮੁਲੁ ਬਖਸੀਸ, ਅਮੁਲੁ ਨੀਸਾਣੁ॥

Amul(u) karam(u), amul(u) phurmāṇ(u).
ਅਮੁਲੁ ਕਰਮੁ, ਅਮੁਲੁ ਫੁਰਮਾਣੁ॥

Amulo amul(u), ākhiā n jāi.
ਅਮੁਲੋ ਅਮੁਲੁ, ਆਖਿਆ ਨ ਜਾਇ॥

Akh(i) ākh(i), rahe liv lāi.
ਆਖਿ ਆਖਿ, ਰਹੇ ਲਿਵ ਲਾਇ॥

Akhah(i), ved pāṭh purāṇ.
ਆਖਹਿ, ਵੇਦ ਪਾਠ ਪੁਰਾਣ॥

Akhah(i), paṛe, karah(i) vakhiāṇ.
ਆਖਹਿ, ਪੜੇ, ਕਰਹਿ ਵਖਿਆਣ॥

Akhah(i) Barme, akhah(i) Iṅd.
ਆਖਹਿ ਬਰਮੇ, ਆਖਹਿ ਇੰਦ॥

Akhah(i) gopī, tai Goviṅd.
ਆਖਹਿ ਗੋਪੀ, ਤੈ ਗੋਵਿੰਦ॥

Akhah(i) Īsar, ākhah(i) Sidh.
ਆਖਹਿ ਈਸਰ, ਆਖਹਿ ਸਿਧ॥

Akhah(i), kete kīte Budh.
ਆਖਹਿ, ਕੇਤੇ ਕੀਤੇ ਬੁਧ॥

Akhah(i) dānav, ākhah(i) dev.
ਆਖਹਿ ਦਾਨਵ, ਆਖਹਿ ਦੇਵ॥

Akhah(i), sur(i) nar, mun(i) jan, sev.
ਆਖਹਿ, ਸੁਰਿ ਨਰ, ਮੁਨਿ ਜਨ, ਸੇਵ॥

Kete ākhah(i), ākhaṇ(i) pāh(i).
ਕੇਤੇ ਆਖਹਿ, ਆਖਣਿ ਪਾਹਿ॥

Kete, kah(i) kah(i), uṭh(i) uṭh(i) jāh(i).
ਕੇਤੇ, ਕਹਿ ਕਹਿ, ਉਠਿ ਉਠਿ ਜਾਹਿ॥

Ete kite, hor(i) kareh(i).
ਏਤੇ ਕੀਤੇ, ਹੋਰਿ ਕਰੇਹਿ॥

Tā, ākh(i) na sakah(i), keī ke-i.
ਤਾ, ਆਖਿ ਨ ਸਕਹਿ, ਕੇਈ ਕੇਇ॥

Jevaḍ(u) bhāvai, tevaḍ(u) hoi.
ਜੇਵਡੁ ਭਾਵੈ, ਤੇਵਡੁ ਹੋਇ॥

Nānak, jāṇai sāchā soi.
ਨਾਨਕ, ਜਾਣੈ ਸਾਚਾ ਸੋਇ॥

Je ko ākhai, bol(u) vigāṛ(u).
ਜੇ ਕੋ ਆਖੈ, ਬੋਲੁਵਿਗਾੜੁ॥

Tā likhīai, sir(i) gāvārā gāvār(u). 26.
ਤਾ ਲਿਖੀਐ, ਸਿਰਿ ਗਾਵਾਰਾ ਗਾਵਾਰੁ॥ ੨੬॥

Amul guṇ, amul vāpār

amul: (adj, m; synonymous with 'anmol', 'amol', 'amulik', 'amulīk' and 'amolak') a complex word comprising 'a' (without) + 'mul' (price or value) i.e., literally, priceless, precious, invaluable, irreplaceable or treasured; that which cannot be bought with any amount of money or by an exchange of other goods.

guṇ: (n, m, pl) (a) (synonymous with 'visheshaṇ', 'siphat', 'khūbī', 'khāsīat', 'lachhaṇ', 'subhāu' or 'tāsīr') literally, characteristics, properties, or attributes of something. However, the tacit reference here is to God's attributes, virtues and values or the Glory of 'Nām(u)'.

vāpār: (n, m; synonymous with 'vaṇaj', 'vapār(u)', 'viopār' or 'biopār') buying and selling; trade or business dealings.

Noble or godly attributes and spiritual wisdom, the tutelage of a Gurū, devotional love for God, the Grace of God, and realisation of 'Nām(u)' are all priceless and beyond the discipline of procurement with exchange for money or other valuable goods. Furthermore, one cannot achieve these by one's own effort and their gift is solely the prerogative of God; hence, these are also called 'dātāṅ'. This is entirely consistent with the sentiments expressed in the following verses from the SGGS:

The Benificent Lord bestows the gift of 'Nām(u)' on whosoever He finds deserving as this privlege is solely His. They, who are imbued with His love, enjoy lasting inner bliss here and are honoured in the hereafter.[427]

Your Glory is inestimable, priceless and ineffable. They who engage in this act, align perfectly with and become totally immersed in You.[428]

Your 'Nām(u)' cannot be bought for any amount of money or in exchange for goods as Its attributes are priceless.[429]

He is inscrutable and thus immeasurable. Many have striven in vain for He is beyond evaluation.[430]

Priceless are Your attributes and priceless is their trade.

Amul vāpārīe, amul bhaṅḍār

vāpārīe: (n, m, pl; synonymous with 'vaṇaj karan vāle' or 'vyāpārī') literally, dealers, traders, or businessmen, especially those engaged in buying and selling some commodities. However, the emphasis here is on the dealers and and the goods they deal in, the trade of Divine attributes, values, and virtues as advocated in the following verses of the SGGS:

Trade by what is right according to 'Nām-consciousness', O' trader, for its reward will stand you in good stead at His Court'.[431]

There is nothing that I can claim to be mine and all that I have is Yours. I entrust unto You what is Yours and do not lose out in any way', says Kabir.[284]

By submitting to and imbibing the Guru's Divine Word and Wisdom, one realises that one aligns perfectly with and realises Him - the fount of all attributes, virtues and values - by contemplating and singing His Glory.[395]

Your bhagats who are beyond the scope of 'Āvāgavan', come into this world for altruistic causes. They bless others with spiritual life and devotion to God, and thus align them with 'Nām(u)'.[432]

Let's imbibe and share these noble and Divine attributes together, for their stockpile does not diminish and is forever replete.[433]

Deal in just what you have come into this world to do and you align perfectly with 'Nām(u)' only by submitting to the Divine Knowledge and Wisdom of a Gurū.[434]

Submit and commit to aligning yourself with 'Nām(u)' and inspire others to do so as well.[435]

bhaṅḍār: (a) (n, m, pl; synonymous with 'bhaṅḍsāl', 'mālgudām', 'zakhīre' and 'khazāne') literally, stocks, treasures, repositories or storehouses of tradeworthy goods, (b) (n, m, pl; synonymous with 'rasoī-'or 'laṅgar- ''de samān dā khazānā') a place for stockpiling of food items or a pantry; stockpiles of all the essential ingredients for survival, safe upkeep and physical, mental, and especially, spiritual well-being.

Precious are the traders who engage in this trade, and precious Your treasure.

Amul āvah(i), amul lai jāh(i)

āvah(i): (e) (v, pl, present tense, third person; synonymous with 'uh āuṅde han'; pronounced as āvaheṅ') see āvṇā or āuṇā (b). However, implicit here is those who come into the world to engage in this trade. See āvah(i) and āuṇā (b).

lai: (indeclinable past participle or perfect participle - 'pūran pūrab kārdaṅtak'; synonymous with 'lai ke') see laiṇā (b).

jāh(i): (a) (v, pl, present tense, third person; synonymous with 'jāṅde han', 'jā sakde'; 'dūr ho-' or 'miṭ-' 'jāṅde han'; pronounced as 'jāhen') they go or can go, and (b) (conj v and suff), e.g., (i) 'pāe jāh(i)'-'pāe- 'or 'labhe ja-' 'sakde han' - can be got or found; (ii) 'n kathne jāh(i)' - cannot be described; (iii) 'lai jāh(i)' - they get, acquire or earn and depart. See jāṇā (a and d (i)).

Priceless are they who come into this world to engage in this trade and depart having earned these treasured attributes.

Amul bhāi, amulā samāh(i)

bhāi: (a) (n, f; synonymous with 'prem') literally, love, intense fondness, amity or preference, and implicit here is (b) (locative case - 'adhikaraṇ kārak'; synonymous with 'prem vich') in love or to have deep affection and reverence for. In essence, those who are in love with or express deep devotion and reverence for Him. See bhāi.

amulā: see amul.

samāh(i): (a) (v, s, present tense, second person; synonymous with 'tusīṅ samā-' or 'līn-' 'ho jāṅde ho'; pronounced as 'samāheṅ', (b) (v, s, future tense, first person; synonymos with 'asīṅ samā jāvāṅge'), (c) (imperative mood - 'saṅbhāv bhvikht kāl - kiās, sharat or ichhā bodhak'; synonymous with 'je tusīṅ samā jāo'), (d) (v, pl, future tense, third person; synonymous with 'uh samā-' or 'līn-' 'ho jāṇge'; pronounced as 'samāheṅ'), and implicit here is (e) (v, pl, present tense, third person; synonymous with 'uh samā-' or 'līn-' 'ho jāṅde han'; pronounced as 'samāheṅ') literally, they who totally immerse themselves in Him, align perfectly with Him, and become one with Him. See samāuṇā (c).

Precious are those who are truly in love with and forever immersed in reflecting on 'Nām(u)' and living by His Will.

Amul(u) dharam(u), amul(u) dībāṇ(u)

dharam(u): (n, m; synonymous with 'maryādā') moral, ethical or religious code of conduct, especially that which is in line with 'Nām(u)' or 'Nām-consciousness'. However, implicit here is the Divine Order ('Hukam(u)'), which creates, supports, and sustains, governs and guides the entire creation and the way of life in complete congruence with 'Nām(u)' or 'Nām-consciousness' ('Hukam anusārī')'. See dharam(u).

dībāṇ(u): (n, f; synonymous with 'kachahirī') a royal Court or a Court of Justice. There is no favour or bias at His Court and His Justice is just and priceless as it is based solely on evidence of one's Karmā and cannot be bought with anything. See dībāṇ(u).

Priceless is the Divine Order and treasured Your Court.

Amul(u) tul(u), amul(u) parvāṇ(u)

tul(u): (n, f; synonymous with ‘tulā’, ‘takṛī’ and ‘tarāzū’) literally, the scale or balance; figuratively, a symbol of His perfect justice.

parvāṇ(u): n, m; synonymous with ‘vaṭṭā’) literally, weight or weights used in a scale. See parvāṇ(u). However, implicit here is the Divine Order, the sole basis for His justice, as referred to in the following verse of the SGGS:

The immaculate, unknowable and infinite Lord weighs up or judges the world without any scales.[436]

Priceless are the scales and incomparable the weights for the carriage of Your perfect justice.

Amul(u) bakhsīs, amul(u) nīsāṇ(u)

bakhsīs: (synonymous with ‘bakhsh’ and ‘bakhshīsh’) (n, f; synonymous with ‘rahmat’, ‘kripā’, ‘da-i-ā’ or ‘meharbānī’) grace, mercy, or blessing.

nīsāṇ(u): (n, m, s; synonymous with ‘nishān’ and ‘chin(h)’; pronounced as ‘nīshāṇ’) mark, sign, brand, logo, or trademark; seal or mark of His approval. The fact that His Grace or Blessing is truly precious is stated clearly in the following verses of the SGGS:

He whom You bless, sings Your Praise.[437]

Rarely is one blessed with His devotion and praise; whosoever is so blessed with this treasure is then not asked to account for his actions.[426]

No one has gained these psychic or intuitive powers without Your Grace. Only, he, to whom You grant Your Grace, secures them and experiences no obstacles in the process simultaneously.[438]

Precious is Your Blessing, and invaluable the mark of Your approval.

Amul(u) karam(u), amul(u) phurmāṇ(u)

karam(u): (n, f; pers; synonymous with ‘rahmat’, ‘kripā’, ‘meharbānī’ and ‘bakhshīsh’) grace, mercy, blessing, compassion, or favour. It is, however, noteworthy that one is only worthy of His Grace when one genuinely seeks and strives to live in perfect harmony with ‘Nām(u)’.

phurmāṇ(u): (a) (n, m; pers; synonymous with 'āgyā-patr' or 'hukam-nāmā') written command or edict, and (b) (n, m; pers; synonymous with 'phurmān', 'āgyā', 'hukam(u)') order, command, directive, mandate, or judgement.

Precious is Your Mercy and Grace, and treasured Your Verdict and Edict.

Amulo amul(u), ākhiā n jāi

amulo amul(u): (synonymous with 'amolak hi amolak', 'amul toṅ amul' or 'aṅdāziāṅ toṅ pare') priceless and invaluable beyond words.

ākhiā: (a) (adj; past participle - 'bhūt kirdaṅt') e.g., 'merā ākhiā bachan' - a word or statement that I voiced, (b) (n, m; present participle - 'kriyā-phal kirdaṅt'; synonymous with 'ākhaṇ', 'kahiṇ', 'bachan', 'kathan' or 'bol') e.g., 'ih 'bol' merā ākhiā hoiā hai' - I uttered this word or statement, and implicit here is (c) (conj v) e.g. 'ākhiā n jāi') literally, that cannot be uttered or spoken, and (ii) 'ih ākhiā ga-i-ā hai' - this has been voiced or articulated. See ākhṇā. However, implicit here is to guesstimate or speculate about the limits or extent of God's attributes or Glory.

n: (p; pronounced as 'nāṅ') no, not or implying a negative connotation.

jāi: (v, s, present tense, third person; synonymous with 'jāṅdā' or 'jā sakdā hai') literally, cannot be stated or described. See jāi and jāṇā.

ākhiā n jāi: literally, cannot be stated or described. However, implicit here is that it cannot be guessed, estimated or fathomed.

You and Your Glory are simply ineffable.

Akh(i) ākh(i), rahe liv lāi

ākh(i): (indeclinable past participle or perfect participle - 'pūran pūrab kārdaṅtak'; synonymous with 'ākh ke') literally, by uttering, but implicit here is by speculating or guesstimating. See ākhṇā.

rahe: (a) (v, s, present tense, second person; synonymous with 'tuṅ rahiṅdā haiṅ' or 'tusīṅ rahiṅde ho'), (b) (v, s, present tense, third person; synonymous with 'uh rahiṅdā hai'), and implicit here is (c) (v, pl, present continuous tense, third person; synonymous with 'uh thak' or 'rah jāṅde han') literally, [they] give up having become weary and exhausted. See rahiṇā (e).

liv: (n, f; synononymous with 'birtī-', 'surat(i)-' or 'dhiān-' 'dī ikāgartā') complete and unwavering focus, concentration, immersion, absorption or engrossment in only one thing, and (b) (n, f; synonymous with 'vrit(i) dī ekāgartā' or 'akhaṅḍ dhiān') unwavering and lasting alignment of one's focus, attention or 'surat(i)' on only with one thing.

lāi: (a) (v, s, present tense, third person; synonymous with 'lāuṅdā-', 'lāuṅdī-', 'joṛdā-' or 'joṛdī-' 'hai') do, engage or carry out, (b) (v, s, imperative mood - 'hukmī bhvikht', second person; synonymous with 'lā-' or 'lagā-' 'lai' or 'lavo') do, engage or carry out, and implicit here is (c) (indeclinable past participle or perfect participle - 'pūran pūrab kārdaṅtak'; synonymous with 'lā-', 'lagā' or 'joṛ-' 'ke') having done, engaged or carried out. See lāuṇā (b and c).

liv lāi: (synonymous with 'liv lā ke') by focusing or having focused.

They who focus on and speculate about the extent of His Glory, just fail and give up feeling weary and dejected. Or:

Having speculated about Him and His Glory and failed, they just submit to Him and align with Him lovingly.

Akhah(i), ved pāṭh purāṇ

ākhah(i): (a) (v, pl, present tense, third person; synonymous with 'ākhde han'; pronounced as 'ākhaheṅ') literally, speak, voice or utter, but implicit here is: [that they] guesstimate or speculate about the full extent of His Glory. See ākhṇā.

ved: (n, m, pl; synonymous with 'bed') the four vedas or scriptures of Hindus- 'Rig', 'Sām', 'Yajur' and 'Atharvan'.

pāṭh: (a) (n, m; synonymous with 'sabak', 'saṅthā' and 'saṅthiā') literally, assignment, lesson, instruction, or precept, (b) (n, m; synonymous with 'pustak dā bhāg' and 'adhayāy') literally, chapter of a book, and implicit here is (c) (n, m; synonymous with 'paṛ(h)āī' and 'paṛ(h)an dī kriyā') the study or the act of daily reading or reciting a sacred text.

purāṇ: (n, m, pl; synonymous with 'purānas') 18 ancient Hindu texts written by Rishi Vyās and others.

ved pāṭh purāṇ: (synonymous with 'vedāṅ-' and/or 'purāṇāṅ-' 'dā adhyan' or 'vedāṅ-' and/or 'purāṇāṅ-' 'dī saṅthiyā') literally, study of the ‘vedāṅ’ and/or the ‘purāṇās’ or readings and/or reciting of the‘vedās’ and/or ‘purāṇās’.

See next ‘Paṅkat(i)’ (Verse).

Akhah(i), paṛe, karah(i) vakhiāṇ

paṛe: (a) (v, s, present tense, second person; synonymous with ‘tusīṅ paṛde ho’), (b) (v, s, present tense, third person; synonymous with ‘uh paṛda hai’), (c) (v, pl, present tense, third person; synonymous with ‘uh paṛde han’; pronounced as ‘paṛ(h)eṅ’), and implicit here is (d) (present participle - ‘kriyā-phal kirdaṅt’; pl; synonymous with ‘vidvān’; pronounced as ‘paṛ(h)e’) learned, scholars or men of letters. See paṛ(h)nā.

paṛ(h)nā: (a) (v; synonymous with ‘pāṭh karnā’) to read, recite, study, or learn, and (b) v; synonymous with ‘paṛhāī karnī’) to study.

paṛnā: (v; synonymous with ‘parnā’, ‘paiṇā’ or ‘paṛṇā’) (a) (synonymous with ‘paiṇā’ or ‘letṇā’) to lie down, (b) (synonymous with ‘digṇā’ or ‘girnā’) to fall or lie down, (c) (synonymous with ‘pāṭh karnā’) to read, learn or study, and (d) (conj. v) e.g., ‘samajh paṛnā’ - to acquire knowledge or to understand; ‘saran paṛnā’ - to submit humbly and seek another’s protection.

karah(i): (v, pl, present tense, third person; synonymous with ‘uh karde-’or ‘kardīāṅ-’ ‘han’ or ‘kar sakde han’; pronounced as ‘karheṅ’) literally, to do, undertake, perform, or carry out an action or a task. See karnā (g and i).

vakhiāṇ: (n, m; synonymous with ‘bakhiān’, ‘vikhiāṇ’, ‘kathan’, ‘byān’ or ‘nirūpaṇ’) debate, discourse, lecture, illustration, or elaboration.

See next ‘Paṅkat(i)’ (Verse).

Akhah(i) Barme, akhah(i) Iṅd

Barme: (n, m, pl; synonymous with ‘ka-ī Brahmā varge’; pronounced as ‘Brahmeṅ’) literally, many like Brahmā.

Iṅd: (n, m, pl; abbrev. for Iṅdar devtā; synonymous with ‘ka-ī Iṅdar varge’) literally, many like Iṅdar devtā.

See next Paṅkat(i) (Verse).

Akhah(i) gopī, tai goviṅd

gopī: (n, f, pl) (a) (synonymous with 'giān ate karam indrīāṅ') sensorimotor organs, and implicit here is (b) (synonymous with 'gavālans' and 'ahīrans') milkmaids or dairymaids.

tai: (conj; synonymous with 'aur' and 'ate') literally, and. See tai.

goviṅd: (n, m, pl; synonymous with 'Gobiṅd(u)'; 'ga-ūāṅ chāran vālā' or 'gavālā') one who takes others' cows for grazing in the fields; one of the many names for Lord Krishna.

See next Paṅkat(i) (Verse).

Akhah(i) Īsar, ākhah(i) Sidh

Īsar: (n, m, pl) (a) (skt; synonymous with 'Īshvar') God, and implicit here is (b) (synonymous with 'Shiv' and 'Mahādev' varge - many like 'Shiv'.

Sidh: (n, m, pl) Yogīs who have (a) achieved the eight mythical psychic powers, 'bibek' - the power of deductive reasoning and ability to judge right from wrong, and 'Nirvānā' through yogic practices, and (b) subdued their '*Man*', the five cardinal drives and their innate evil nature.

See next Paṅkat(i) (Verse).

Akhah(i), kete kīte Budh

kete: (adj; synonymous with 'kaī' and 'kitne') numerous, many or several.

kīte: (a) (v, pl, present pefect tense, third person; synonymous with 'kar- 'or 'baṇā-' 'lae han') literally, have made, shaped, modulated or set right, (b) (v, past tense; synonymous with 'paidā-'or 'utpaṅn-' 'kīte-', 'baṇāe-'or 'sirje') made or created, implicit here is (c) (past participle - 'bhūt kirdaṅt', m, pl; synonymous with 'kīte-'or 'baṇāe-' 'hoe').

Budh: (a) (n, m, pl; synonymous with 'kaī Mahātmā Budh), and (b) (n, m, pl; synonymous with 'kaī' Mahātmā Budh varge') many like Gautama Budhā.

kete kīte Budh: (synonymous with 'Prabhū de ka-ī Budh varge paidā kīte') literally, many like Gautama Budh that God has created.

See next Pańkat(i) (Verse).

Akhah(i) dānav, ākhah(i) dev

dānav: (n, m) (a) children of 'dān(u)' (mother) and 'kashyap' (father) in Hindu mythology, and (b) (synonymous with 'daiṅt', 'rākhash' and 'rākhshash'; antonym of 'dev' and 'devtā') demons, ignoble or vile persons lacking virtues.

dev: (n, m, pl; abbrev. for 'devtā' and 'devte') (synonymous with 'devtās' and 'sur') eternal beings with Divine powers who live in heaven of Hindu mythology.

See next Pańkat(i) (Verse).

Akhah(i), sur(i) nar, mun(i) jan, sev

sur(i): (a) (adj, m, pl; synonymous with 'vaḍḍe') literally, great, senior, elder, and implicit here is (b) (genitive case - 'saṅbaṅdh kārak'; synonymous with 'devtiāṅ de') of 'devtās', and (c) (n, m, pl; synonymous with '('dayavī guṇaṅ vāle manukh') human beings with Divine attributes. See sur, dev and sur(i).

sur: (n, m) (a) a musical note, and implicit here is (b) (synonymous with 'devtā') see dev.

nar: (a) (n, m, s) a word for 'Brahmā', 'Vishnu', 'Shiv'; Arjun (one of five Pāṅdavas of Mahābhārtā); Kartār or Pārbrahm, (b) (adj, m; synonymos with 'uddamī' or 'purshārthī'; 'daler' or 'himmatī') industrious and enterprising; daring, courageous or brave, and implicit here is (c) (n, m; synonymous with 'purush', 'mard' and 'manukh') literally, men.

sur(i) nar: literally, men with Divine attributes.

mun(i): (a) (n and adj, m; synonymous with 'vichār karan vālā' or 'maṅnanshīl') considerate, rational, thoughtful, philosopher or sage, (b) (n, m; synonymous with 'jis dā *man* dukh vich vyākul n hovai', 'a rikhī' or 'rishī', a 'Sādh' and a 'Saṅt') one who remains calm even in states of adversity, and implicit here is (c) (n, m; synonymous with 'maunī', 'chup kītā' and 'maun dhāran vālā manukh') one who vows not to or deliberately avoids speaking, an ascetic.

jan: (n, pl) (a) (synonymous with 'sevak' and 'dās') servants or slaves, (b) (synonymous with 'smūh' or 'smudāi') multitudes, crowds, or groups,

(c) (synonymous with 'istrīāṅ', 'nārīāṅ', 'jorūs', 'vahuṭīāṅ' or 'bhāryāṅ'; (pers) 'zan') wives, (d) 'bhagats', 'sādhūs', 'jigiāsūs', devotees or seekers of absolute Truth and eternal Reality, and implicit here is (e) (synonymous with 'purakh' or 'prānī') beings or persons.

mun(i) jan: (synonymous with 'mun(i) lok') literally, ascetics with a degree of self-control in speaking.

sev: (n, m; synonymous with 'sevaks', 'sevādārs', 'dās' and 'khidmatgārs') literally, attendants, servants, waiters, or devout followers.

The scripts of the Vedās and Purāṇās, many erudite scholars of these texts, others like Brahma, Indra, Krishna and dairymaids, Shiva, Sidh Yogīs, Budhā, demons and 'devtās', men with noble attributes, ascetics with self-control and devout followers whom You have created, seek to define and illustrate Your Glory.

Kete ākhah(i), ākhaṇ(i) pāh(i)

ākhaṇ(i): (infinitive mood - 'bhāvārth kārdaṅtak') (genitive case - 'saṅbaṅdh kārak'; synonymous with 'ākhaṇ dā') of ākhaṇ.

pāh(i): (v, pl, present tense, third person; synonymous with 'pāuṅde han', 'jāṅde han'; 'tatpar huṅde han' and 'tatpar lagde han') achieve, go, get ready and eager to act or engage, and (e) (conj v) e.g., 'pāh(i) jāi'.

ākhaṇ(i) pāh(i): literally, appear eager and ever ready to do so.

Numerous others are similarly engaged, and many dare, and appear ever ready, to do so.

Kete, kah(i) kah(i), uṭh(i) uṭh(i), jāh(i)

kah(i) kah(i): (adv; conjunctive participle; synonymous with 'ākh ākh ke') literally, having expressed or expounded Your Glory. See ākhṇā.

uṭh(i): (indeclinable past participle or perfect participle - 'pūran pūrab kārdaṅtak'; synonymous with 'uṭh ke') see uṭhṇā.

ūṭhṇā: (v; synonymous with 'uṭhaṇā' or 'ūṭhṇā') (a) (synonymous with 'jāgṇā') to wake up, (b) (synonymous with 'khaṛe hoṇā') to stand up or rise from a sitting position, (c) (synonymous with 'sāvdhān hoṇā') to become alert, attentive, circumspect, and vigilant, and implicit here is (d) (synonymous with 'upjanā' and 'utpan hoṇā') to sprout, be born, and grow.

jāh(i): (v, pl, present tense, third person; synonymous with 'uh jāṅde han' or 'jā sakde han'; pronounced as 'jāheṅ') they go or can go. See jāṇā (d (i)).

uṭh jāṇā: (conj v; synonymous with 'chale-', 'tur-', 'mar-'or 'miṭ-' 'jāṇā' or 'maut ho jāṇī') literally, to depart, cease to exist, or die.

uṭh(i) jāh(i): (conj v; synonymous with 'paidā ho ke tur jāṅde han') literally, having been born, depart from this world.

Many depart from this world having sought to define Your Greatness.

Ete kīte, hor(i) kareh(i)

ete: (adj and adv; synonymous with 'itne', 'aine' and 'is kadar') literally, so many.

kīte: (a) (v, pl, past tense; synonymous with 'kīe', 'kare', 'sirje' or 'baṇāe') literally, created, and (b) (v, pl, present perfect; synonymous with 'sirje- 'or 'baṇāe-' 'ga-e han').

hor(i): (a) (pron; synonymous with 'anya') literally, another some other, and implicit here is (b) (adj and adv, pl; synonymous with 'aur') many more, further or additional.

kareh(i): (a) (v, pl, present tense, third person; pronounced as 'karehṅ'), and implicit here is (b) (v, s, imperative mood - 'saṅbhāv bhvikht kāl - kiās or sharat bodhak', second person; synonymous with 'kar deveṅ'; pronounced as 'karehṅ') if You were to create many more.

If You were to create many more than You have already created.

Tā, ākh(i) n sakah(i), keī ke-i

tā: (p and adv; synonymous with 'tad-', 'tadoṅ-', or 'udoṅ-' 'bhī') because of, thus, then, even then.

ākh(i): (indeclinable past participle or perfect participle - 'pūran pūrab kārdaṅtak'; synonymous with 'ākh ke') see ākhṇā.

sakah(i): (v, pl, m, present tense, third person; synonymous with 'uh-' 'yog- 'or 'samrath-' 'ho sakde han'; pronounced as 'sakaheṅ') [they] would be able to do so.

ākh(i) n sakah(i): literally, [they] would not be able to define accurately [His Greatness].

ke-ī ke-(i): (a) (pron; synonymous with 'koī'; pronounced as 'ke-ī ke') anyone or someone, and (b) (adv; synonymous with 'virle') some rare people.

n keī ke-i: literally, no one or none.

None could define Your Greatness or Glory even then.

Jevaḍ(u) bhāvai, tevaḍ(u) hoi

jevaḍ(u): (adj; synonymous with 'jitnā vaḍḍā') as much as, as great as or as big as.

bhāvai: (v, s, present tense, third person; synonymous with 'bhāuṅdā-', 'piārā lagdā- 'and 'chaṅgā lagdā-' 'hai'; pronounced as 'bhāvaiṅ') fancies, finds appealing, deserving, or worthy. See bhāuṇā.

jevaḍ(u) bhāvai: literally, however big or great He wishes to be.

tevaḍ(u): (adj; synonymous with 'utnā vaḍḍā') literally, that much or as much as that.

hoi: (v, s, present tense, synonymous with 'huṅdā hai' and 'ho jāṅdā hai') literally, becomes or comes to be.

You become and make the creation however great or vast You wish it to be.

Nānak, jāṇai sāchā soi

Nānak: (n, m, s) the (u) of 'Nānak(u)' is missing because of its vocative case - 'saṅbodhan kārak'.

jāṇai: (v, s, present tense, third person; synonymous with 'jāṇdā hai') see jāṇanā (a and b).

sāchā: (adj, m; 'satya' in (skt) and 'sat(i)' in (gmkh); synonymous with 'sachā') (a) (synonymous with 'sadīvī jyot(i) sarūp') the eternal Lord or the eternal Reality - 'Nām(u)' as well as the transcendent Lord, (b) (synonymous with 'sarab kalā bharpūr(i)', 'par(i)pūran' and 'sarab vyāpak') omnipotent, omniscient, and all-pervasive and omnipresent, (c) (synonymous with 'satya' and 'hoṅd-'or 'hastī-' 'vālā') real and not imaginary, and (d) (synonymous with 'nirmal', 'pavitr' and 'ukāī rahit') immaculate, perfect and flawless. These are some of the popular and well-known attributes of the God of infinite attributes.

soi: (pron and adj; synonymous with 'oh' or 'ohī') he, she, it or they; the same.

'Only You, the eternal Lord, know the extent of Your Glory and the expanse of Your Creation', O' Nānak!

Je ko ākhai, bol(u) vigāṛ(u)

je: (conj; synonymous with 'yadī' or 'agar') if or in case.

ko: (pron; synonymous with 'koī') someone, anyone, or another.

ākhai: (a) (v, s, present tense, third person; synonymous with 'ākhdā hai' and 'vakhyān kardā hai'), and (b) (imperative mood - 'saṅbhāv bhvikht kāl - kiās bodhak', s, third person) see ākhṇā.

bol(u): (n, m, s; synonymous with 'vākyā', 'kathan' and 'bachan') speech, utterances, or solemn words.

vigāṛ(u): (a) (n, m; synonymous with 'vikār') an action without any useful outcome; an evil thought, utterance or deed, and (b) (n, f; synonymous with 'virodh-', 'nāchākī-', 'vigrah-' and 'laṛāī-' 'karnā) a deliberate act of opposition, argument, dispute or fracas.

bol(u)-vigāṛ(u): (adj, m, s; synonymous with 'bakbādī') one who is quick off the mark or flies off the handle, and deliberately uses bad language, argues, or disputes and creates an uneasy, frosty and hostile atmosphere; tactless, outspoken, foul-mouthed or scurrilous.

je ko bol vigāṛ(u) akhai: literally, if an unwise and outspoken person makes a statement. However, implicit here is if an unwise and outspoken person enters into debate and makes a wild, ill-judged statement, relating to knowledge about the extent of His Glory and His Creation.

However, if an impetuous loudmouth dares to speculate about His greatness and/or the extent of creation and claims to define it.

Tā likhīai, sir(i) gāvārā gāvār(u)

tā: (p and adv; synonymous with 'tad', 'tadoṅ', or 'udoṅ') then, thus, because of.

likhīai: (a) (v, s, imperative mood - 'hukmī bhvikht',

third person; synonymous with 'likhṇā chāhīdā hai') should be depicted or portrayed as, and (b) (v, s, present tense, third person; synonymous with 'likhiā jāṅdā hai' and 'aṅkit kitā jā sakdā hai') is depicted or characterised as. See likhṇā.

likhṇā: (v) literally, to write. In essence, to describe, portray, characterise, or depict.

sir(i): (locative case - 'adhikaraṇ kārak'; synonymous with 'sir-' 'te', 'utte', 'par' or 'uppar') literally, on, upon or above one's head.

sir(i) gāvārā: (n, pl; synonymous with 'gāvārāṅ de sir te') see gāvār(u).

gāvār(u): (a) (suff; (pers)) imparts the meaning of 'anukūl' (favourable or conforming to) or 'pasaṅd' (preferring or preference), e.g., khush-gāvār(u) - one with a jolly and cheerful predisposition, and implicit here is (b) (adj, m; synonymous with 'peṅḍū', 'dehātī', 'mūrakh' or 'asabhya') uncultured, rustic, naive, crass, stupid, or unwise.

sir(i) gāvārā gāvār(u): (synonymous with 'gāvārāṅ de sir te gāvār', 'mūrakhāṅ sir mūrakh' or 'mahāṅ mūrakh') extremely uncultured, dense and ignorant.

He then gets branded as the most ignorant amongst the foolish.

Conceptual summary

Priceless are (a) Your attributes, and their trade, (b) the traders who engage in this trade and Your treasures, (c) they who come into this world to engage in this trade and depart having earned the invaluable noble attributes, and (d) Your true devotees who have deep affection for and are immersed in reflection upon 'Nām(u)' and who live by Your Will.

Precious is (a) the Divine Order and treasured Your Court, (b) Your Balance and incomparable the weights for carriage of Your Perfect Justice, (c) Your Blessing and invaluable the Seal of Your approval, and (d) Your Mercy and Grace, and incomparable Your Verdict and Edict.

You and Your Glory are simply ineffable, as none has the ability or capacity to evaluate Your attributes. They who focus on and speculate tirelessly about the extent of Your Glory, just fail and abandon this chase feeling weary and dejected. Alternatively, having speculated about Him and His Glory and failed, they just submit to and align with Him lovingly.

The scripts of the Vedās and Purāṇās, many erudite scholars of these texts with their discourses, many like Brahma, Indra, Krishna and his dairymaids, Shivā and the Sidh Yogīs, Budhā, demons and 'devtās', men with noble attributes, ascetics with self-control, and devout followers that You have created seek to define and delineate Your Glory and Majesty.

Numerous others are similarly engaged whilst others rush eagerly and dare to enter this rat race with gusto. Many leave this world having attempted but failed to define Your Glory. If You were to create still many more, no one could define Your Glory and Greatness even then. You become and make Your creation as great or vast as You wish and only You, the eternal Lord, know Your Glory and the expanse of Your creation. However, if an impetuous loudmouth dares to speculate about and attempt to define Your Greatness and Majesty, he shall be characterised as the most ignorant amongst fools.

In conclusion, numerous erudite scholars and spiritual masters have come and gone, and shall continue to bless this Earth in future, but none has and none shall be able to define and depict Your Glory and the vastness of Your creation. No one else, save You, knows Your infinite Glory and repository of Your treasure. You are simply ineffable and one who foolishly dares to attempt to speculate can only be described as flippant, shallow, myopic and of limited discernment.

PAUṚĪ 27
ਪਉੜੀ ੨੭॥

So dar(u) kehā, so ghar(u) kehā, jit(u) bah(i) sarab samāle.
ਸੋ ਦਰੁ ਕੇਹਾ, ਸੋ ਘਰੁ ਕੇਹਾ, ਜਿਤੁ ਬਹਿ ਸਰਬ ਸਮਾਲੇ॥

Vāje nād, anek asaṅkhā, kete vāvaṇhāre.
ਵਾਜੇ ਨਾਦ, ਅਨੇਕ ਅਸੰਖਾ, ਕੇਤੇ ਵਾਵਣਹਾਰੇ॥

Kete rāg parī siu kahīan(i), kete gāvaṇhāre.
ਕੇਤੇ ਰਾਗ ਪਰੀ ਸਿਉ ਕਹੀਅਨਿ, ਕੇਤੇ ਗਾਵਣਹਾਰੇ॥

Gāvah(i) tuhno, pauṇ(u), pāṇī, baisaṅtar(u), gāvai rājā dharam(u) duāre.
ਗਾਵਹਿ ਤੁਹਨੋ ਪਉਣੁ, ਪਾਣੀ, ਬੈਸੰਤਰੁ, ਗਾਵੈ ਰਾਜਾ ਧਰਮੁ ਦੁਆਰੇ॥

Gāvah(i) chit(u) gupat(u) likh(i) jāṇah(i), likh(i) likh(i) dharam(u) vichāre.
ਗਾਵਹਿ ਚਿਤੁ ਗੁਪਤੁ ਲਿਖਿ ਜਾਣਹਿ, ਲਿਖਿ ਲਿਖਿ ਧਰਮੁ ਵੀਚਾਰੇ॥

Gāvah(i) īsar(u), barmā, devī, sohan(i) sadā savāre.
ਗਾਵਹਿ ਈਸਰੁ, ਬਰਮਾ, ਦੇਵੀ, ਸੋਹਨਿ ਸਦਾ ਸਵਾਰੇ॥

Gāvah(i) ind iṅdāsan(i) baiṭhe, devtiā dar(i) nāle.
ਗਾਵਹਿ ਇੰਦ ਇਦਾਸਣਿ ਬੈਠੇ, ਦੇਵਤਿਆ ਦਰਿ ਨਾਲੇ॥

Gāvah(i) sidh samādhī aṅdar(i), gāvan(i) sādh vichāre.
ਗਾਵਹਿ ਸਿਧ ਸਮਾਧੀ ਅੰਦਰਿ, ਗਾਵਨਿ ਸਾਧ ਵਿਚਾਰੇ॥

Gāvan(i) jatī satī saṅtokhī, gāvah(i) vīr karāre.
ਗਾਵਨਿ ਜਤੀ ਸਤੀ ਸੰਤੋਖੀ, ਗਾਵਹਿ ਵੀਰ ਕਰਾਰੇ॥

Gāvan(i) paṅḍit paṛan(i) rakhīsar, jug(u) jug(u) vedā nāle.
ਗਾਵਨਿ ਪੰਡਿਤ ਪੜਨਿ ਰਖੀਸਰ, ਜੁਗੁ ਜੁਗੁ ਵੇਦਾ ਨਾਲੇ॥

Gāvah(i) mohaṇīā *man*(u) mohan(i), surgā machh pa-i-āle.
ਗਾਵਹਿ ਮੋਹਣੀਆ ਮਨੁ ਮੋਹਨਿ, ਸੁਰਗਾ ਮਛ ਪਇਆਲੇ॥

Gāvan(i) ratan upāe tere, aṭh-saṭh(i) tīrath nāle.
ਗਾਵਨਿ ਰਤਨ ਉਪਾਏ ਤੇਰੇ, ਅਠਸਠਿ ਤੀਰਥ ਨਾਲੇ॥

Gāvah(i) jodh mahā-bal sūrā, gāvah(i) khāṇī chāre.
ਗਾਵਹਿ ਜੋਧ ਮਹਾਬਲ ਸੂਰਾ, ਗਾਵਹਿ ਖਾਣੀ ਚਾਰੇ॥

Gāvah(i) khaṅḍ maṅḍal varbhaṅḍā, kar(i) kar(i) rakhe dhāre.
ਗਾਵਹਿ ਖੰਡ ਮੰਡਲ ਵਰਭੰਡਾ, ਕਰਿ ਕਰਿ ਰਖੇ ਧਾਰੇ॥

Seī tudh(u) no gāvah(i), jo tudh(u) bhāvan(i), rate tere bhagat rasāle.

ਸੇਈ ਤੁਧੁਨੋ ਗਾਵਹਿ, ਜੋ ਤੁਧੁ ਭਾਵਨਿ, ਰਤੇ ਤੇਰੇ ਭਗਤ ਰਸਾਲੇ॥

Hor(i) kete gāvan(i), se mai chit(i) n āvan(i), Nānak(u) kiā vīchāre.
ਹੋਰ ਕੇਤੇ ਗਾਵਨਿ, ਸੇ ਮੈ ਚਿਤਿ ਨ ਆਵਨਿ, ਨਾਨਕੁ ਕਿਆ ਵੀਚਾਰੇ॥

Soī soī sadā sach(u), sāhib(u) sāchā, sāchī nāī.
ਸੋਈ ਸੋਈ ਸਦਾ ਸਚੁ, ਸਾਹਿਬੁ ਸਾਚਾ, ਸਾਚੀ ਨਾਈ॥

Hai bhī, hosī, jāi n jāsī, rachnā jin(i) rachāī.
ਹੈ ਭੀ, ਹੋਸੀ, ਜਾਇ ਨ ਜਾਸੀ, ਰਚਨਾ ਜਿਨਿ ਰਚਾਈ॥

Raṅgī raṅgī bhātī kar(i) kar(i), jinsī māiā jin(i) upāī.
ਰੰਗੀ ਰੰਗੀ ਭਾਤੀ ਕਰਿ ਕਰਿ, ਜਿਨਸੀ ਮਾਇਆ ਜਿਨਿ ਉਪਾਈ॥

Kar(i) kar(i) vekhai kītā āpṇa, jiv tis dī vaḍiāī.
ਕਰਿ ਕਰਿ ਵੇਖੈ ਕੀਤਾ ਆਪਣਾ, ਜਿਵ ਤਿਸ ਦੀ ਵਡਿਆਈ॥

Jo tis(u) bhāvai, soī karsī, hukam(u) n karṇā jāī.
ਜੋ ਤਿਸੁ ਭਾਵੈ, ਸੋਈ ਕਰਸੀ, ਹੁਕਮੁ ਨ ਕਰਣਾ ਜਾਈ॥

So pāt(i)sāh(u), sāhā pāt(i)sāhib(u), Nānak, rahaṇ(u) rajāī. 27.
ਸੋ ਪਾਤਿਸਾਹੁ, ਸਾਹਾ ਪਾਤਿਸਾਹਿਬੁ, ਨਾਨਕ, ਰਹਣੁ ਰਜਾਈ॥ ੨੭॥

'Where is that place or through which door do I enter to find You? Dejected and wandering about in vain, I now long for someone to come and show me the way'.[439]

'The Creator Lord pervades absolutely the waters, the Earth and the firmament. He extends into and manifests in countless ways in the universe', O' Nānak.[440]

'The Lord first creates nature, then pervades it'.[441]

As we look around, we see ourselves deeply entrenched in achieving our worldly aims, enjoying the fruits of our labour and successes, and continuing with our struggle to enhance our quality of life. Inquisitiveness about the nature of one's true self, our true purpose in life, and the prime mover as the basis of all existence, comes about only when one is either discontented with the empirical world or has had one's fill of it. This 'Pauṛī' poses and deals with such questions that arise in our conscious self from time to time and deals with them.

So dar(u) kehā, so ghar(u) kehā, jit(u) bah(i) sarab samāle

so: (pron and adj; synonymous with 'oh', 'uh' or 'ohī') literally, that. See so.

dar(u): (n, m, s;) (a) (abbrev. for 'darbār') a court, and (b) (pers; 'dwār', 'duār', 'dahlīz', 'chaukhaṭ' and 'darvāzā') literally, the bottom part of the threshold of a door, or door, the movable barrier to the entrance of a room, a building, or the outermost part of a house.

kehā: (adv and adj, m; synonymous with 'kihā', 'kaisā', 'kis trāṅ dā' and 'kis prakār dā') literally, what sort, what kind, or like what? However, implicit here is the question of how big, how beautiful, how wonderful or how awe-inspiring.

ghar(u): (a) (n, m, s; synonymous with 'sarīr' and 'deh') one's body, (b) (n, m; synonymous with 'shāstr') a holy book that contains the credo of a belief system or 'dharma', (c) (n, m; synonymous with conscious self, '*Man*' and 'Hirdā') an abstract but innermost part of one's body where it eventually perceives 'Nām(u)' or 'Parmātmāṅ', and implicit here is (d) (n, m, s; synonymous with 'grih' and 'nivās') literally, home. The reference here is to God's home. However, it is worth noting here that God is all-pervasive and immanent throughout creation. Thus, the entire visible empirical world is His home. See ghar(u).

jit(u): (adv; synonymous with 'jithe' and 'yahāṅ') where.

bah(i): (indeclinable past participle or perfect participle - 'pūran pūrab kārdaṅtak'; synonymous with 'baiṭh ke') literally, whilst seated or sitting down. In essence, it refers to having settled down to deliberate and take a decision. See baiṭhṇā (a and b).

baiṭhṇā: (v; synonymous with 'bahiṇā') (a) to sit down or take a seat, (b) to settle down, (c) to sink, and (d) to cave in or withdraw. However, it generally implies to sit beside one and demonstrate like-mindedness, unanimity and harmony of thought and opinion.

sarab: (adj; synonymous with 'sabh', 'sabhe' and 'tamām') literally, all. However, implicit here is His entire creation.

samāle: (v, s, present tense, third person; synonymous with 'uh sam(h)āladā- 'or 'saṅbhāladā-' 'hai'; pronounced as 'sam(h)āleṅ') literally, to look after, to take care of, or to support or sustain. See samālanā (a, b and c).

samālanā: (v, synonymous with 'samālaṇā' or 'saṅbhālaṇā'; pronounced as 'sam(h)ālanā)' (a) (synonymous with 'dekh bhāl karnī') to sustain, nourish and protect, (b) (synonymous with 'sahārā deṇā') to support, prop or help, (c) (synonymous with 'sāṅbhaṇā') to take care of or to look after, and (d) (synonymous with 'yād karnā' or 'simarnā') to keep in mind, remember, reflect, or contemplate.

How great and beautiful is that door or entrance of that mansion where You sit and take care of all Your creation?

Vāje nād, anek asaṅkhā, kete vāvaṇhāre

vāje: (a) (n, m; synonymous with 'sāz') musical instruments, and implicit here is (b) (v, pl, present tense, third person; synonymous with 'vajde han') literally, are played. See vajṇā.

vajṇā: (v) (a) (synonymous with 'prasidh hoṇā') to become famous or to be acclaimed, (b) to ring, chime, bang, collide or strike against, and implicit here is (c) (synonymous with 'vādan hoṇā') to sound a musical note.

nād: (n, f) (a) (synonymous with 'saṅkh') conch, (b) (synonymous with 'sabad', 'dhun(i)', 'anhad nād', 'parā-vāk' or 'parā- bāṇī') the unstruck, everlasting primordial sound or 'dhun(i)' - the Divine Word - with which God communicates with His creation; one who perceives 'anhad nād' realises 'Nām(u)' - the Immanent form of God, (c) (synonymous with 'saṅgīt') melodious and enchanting music, and implicit here is (d) (synonymous with 'avāz' - sounds of different pitch, amplitude and timbre from different objects, instruments and diverse life forms. See nād.

anek: (adj; synonymous with 'anik', 'bahut' and 'nānā') countless or numerous.

asaṅkhā: (synonymous with 'asaṅkhāṅ hī'; pronounced as 'asaṅkhāṅ') literally, countless. See asaṅkh.

asaṅkh: (adj; synonymous with 'aṇgiṇat', anaṅt', 'beshumār') a complex word comprising 'a' (without or beyond) + 'saṅkh' or 'saṅkhya' ('giṇtī', 'shumār' or 'hisāb' - counting, estimation or calculation) i.e., beyond counting, estimation or calculation; innumerable, countless or infinite.

kete: (adj, m, pl; synonymous with 'kaī' or 'kitne') numerous, many, several or quite a few.

vāvanhāre: (n, m, pl and adj; 'kartarī-vāchak kirdaṅt'; synonymous with 'vajāuṇ vāle') literally, players of those instruments. The reference is to the sound or noise of activity from all the participants in the creation. See vajāuṇā.

vajāuṇā: (v) (a) (synonymous with 'prasidh-' or 'mash-hūr-' 'karnā') to make famous; to propagate or spread one's renown, and implicit here is (b) (synonymous with 'vādan karnā' and 'koī sāj vajāuṇā') literally, to play an instrument, e.g., to ring the bells, to beat the drums or to play any other instrument.

Countless sounds ring out there, and countless are their sources and players.

Kete rāg parī siu kahīan(i), kete gāvaṇhāre

rāg: (n, m, pl) vocal or instrumental musical metres or melodies.

parī: (a) (v, s, past or present perfect tense; synonymous with 'pa-ī' and 'paṛī') lay or has laid, (b) (v, s, past or present perfect tense; synonymous with 'ḍigī' or 'ḍigī hoī') fell or collapsed; has fallen or collapsed, (c) (n, s; synonymous with 'parāṅ-'or 'paṅkhāṅ-' 'vālā priṅdā') a bird, (d) (n, f, s; synonymous with 'apsarā' or 'hūr') a female dancer in 'Indrapurī' or 'swarg', (e) (n, f, s; synonymous with 'suṅdar istrī') a beautiful woman, and implicit here is (f) (n, f, s; synonymous with 'rāgnī') a subset of a major 'rāg(u)'.

siu: (prep; synonymous with 'sāth', 'nāl', 'saṅg', 'smet', 'sahit', 'se' or 'kol'; pronounced as 'sioṅ') with, together with, including, to/from whom.

rāg parī siu: literally, rāgs along with their subsets and variations.

kahīan(i): (v, pl, present tense, third person; synonymous with 'ākhde-', 'kahiṅde- 'or 'gāuṅde-' 'han') see kahiṇā.

kahiṇā: (a) (infinitive mood - 'bhāvārth kārdaṅtak'; synonymous with 'ākhṇā', 'ākhaṇ(u)', 'kathan' or 'kathnā') comment, utterance, or observation, and (b) (v; synonymous with 'ākhṇā' or 'kathnā'; 'varṇan-' or 'vakhyān-' 'karnā') literally, to say, utter, recount, narrate or state; to set forth, explain, expound or elucidate. However, implicit here is 'siphat sālāh karnī' or to sing His Glory.

gāvaṇhāre: (n and m, pl; 'kartarī-vāchak kirdaṅt'; synonymous with 'gāvaṇ vāle') literally, singers. They who produce the countless different sounds alluded to above. See gāuṇā or gāvṇā.

Countless sing Your Praise in different rāgs and their subtle subsets. (literal). Or:

Countless express outwardly their innate nature, physical assets and abilities (as a result of their endowed attributes, virtues and values), and engage in different activities, some with subtle variations.

Gāvah(i) tuhno, pauṇ(u), pāṇī, baisaṅtar(u), gāvai rājā dharam(u) duāre.

gāvah(i): (v, pl, present tense, third person; synonymous with 'uh gāuṅde han'; pronounced as 'gāvaheṅ') literally, it means 'they sing'. See gāvah(i) and gāvṇā (b and c).

However, the implicit meaning of the word 'gāvṇā' is completely different. As alluded to earlier, all the constitutive parts of this creation have a variable degree of expression of that higher- or universal- consciousness and are allotted their unique innate nature, attributes, abilities, and free will by God. These form the basis of the range and level of tasks they can perform and the interactions they can be involved in. Indeed, within each category of task or interaction, there is a vast range, each being achieved and performed according to the endowed attributes of that constitutive part or being. Where there is no free will, that part of the creation can only perform what it has been designed and created to do. On the other hand, where there is a much greater allotment of free will as well as an expression of that higher consciousness, the greater is the range of tasks and interactions and the greater the burden of moral, ethical, and spiritual responsibility for one's deeds and interactions. Therefore, each constitutive part of this universe singing His Praise, therefore, just represents an expression of their endowed attributes and consciousness in the form of deeds carried out. However, to live by His Will, within these constraints, is what He expects from us and from others with a degree of free will.

tuhno: (pron; synonymous with 'tujhe' and 'tainūṅ') literally, to you or to thee. However, implicit here is 'O Lord!

pa-uṇ(u): (a) (n, m; synonymous with 'prān') (i) ('swās' or 'dam') breath, (ii) (jīvan) life or lifetime, (iii) ('*man*' or 'chit') conscious self, and (iv) ('bal' or 'shaktī') strength, power or vigour, and (b) (n, f; synonymous with 'havā', 'vāyū' and 'pavaṇ') air or wind; gases or a mixture of all gases. The raging winds, blowing from an area of high pressure towards one of low pressure, have a distinct sound, and their force, speed and direction are all within the bounds of His Divine Order.

pānī: (n, m) (a) (instrumental case - 'karaṇ kārak'; synonymous with 'pāṇī-' 'nāl', 'rāhīṅ', 'sadkā' or 'duārā') e.g., 'pāṇī dhotai utras(u) kheh', and implicit here is (b) (synonymous with 'jal') water, and (c) liquids. Pitter-patter, slapping or rumbling torrents and waves all have their unique sounds, with water always flowing from a higher to a lower altitude.

baisaṅtar(u): (n, f) (a) (synonymous with 'agan(i)') literally, fire, and (b) (fig.) energy. Crackling, rustling, popping, whooshing, and hissing are some of the words associated with sounds of a fire burning.

gāvah(i) tuhno pauṇ(u) pāṇī baisaṅtar(u): literally, the air, water and fire sing Your praise. In essence, they act exactly according to their innate nature, ability and free will and subject to Your Divine Order.

gāvai: (v, s, present tense, third person: synonymous with 'uh gāuṅdā hai') see gāvṇā.

rājā dharam(u): (n, m, s; synonymous with 'dharam rāj') the Lord of moral justice - a mythological character in Hindu mythology who is appointed to carry out God's justice. He keeps an account of everyone's good and bad deeds, written under the supervision of 'Chitr' and 'Gupt', in a huge register which is kept in a place called 'Agrsaṅdhānī'. See dharam rāj. In contrast, the Lord of Gurū Nānak is omnipotent, omnipresent, and omniscient. If He can create the universe in the flicker of an eyelid, then He can deliver perfect justice for one and all without any help.

'sachā āp(i) sachā darbār(u)'- the eternal Lord is omnipresent, and His Court, too, is truly just. See Pauṛī 34.

duāre: (a) (n, m, pl; synonymous with 'giān-' and 'karam-' 'indrīāṅ') sensorimotor organs, (b) (n, m, pl; synonymous with 'dar', 'dahlīzāṅ' or 'darvāze') thresholds of a door, or doors, movable barriers to the entrance of a room or hall, and implicit here is (c) (locative case - 'adhikaraṇ kārak'; synonymous with 'duār-'or 'dar-' 'te') literally, at your door. See dar and duār.

gāvai rājā dharam(u) duāre: literally, 'Dharamrāj' sings Your Praise at Your door. In essence, the judgement of one's Karmā and the final verdict is entirely by Your Divine Order ('Hukam(u)').

O' Lord! Wind, water, and fire sing Your praise; and Dharam rāj sings Your praise at Your doorstep.

Gāvah(i) chit(u) gupat(u) likh(i) jāṇah(i), likh(i) likh(i) dharam(u) vichāre

chit(u): (a) (n, m) one of the four parts of 'Antahkaraṇ' which forms the basis of memory. 'Antahkaraṇ' (skt), in turn, refers to a non-physical organ, deep within one's body that performs the ultimate sensory function, and which orchestrates one's definitive motor responses and functions. Gurbānī probably refers to it as 'surat(i)' or 'dhiān' (focus), one of the attributes of '*Man*' (conscious self, 'Jīvātmāṅ' or 'Hirdā'), and (b) (n, m; synonymous with 'chitrgupt' and 'kāith chetū') a purānic character who was extremely good at keeping accounts, and was later appointed as a clerk, in the office of 'Dharamrāj', to keep an account secretly ('gupt') of the good and bad deeds of all beings.

chit(u) gupat(u): the two angels of 'dharam rāj', 'Chitr' and 'Gupt', who record all our good and bad deeds according to Hindu belief; 'chit(u)' records the deeds done consciously and 'gupt(u)' records the deeds done subconsciously.

Similarly, the Quran also points to 'Kirāman' and 'Kātibīn', the two angels who sit on one's right and left shoulder and secretly keep an account of one's good and bad deeds.

However, Gurmat believes that one's good and bad deeds leave their impressions in one's unconscious self ('Achet *Man*'), a functional part of one's conscious self, thus creating a permanent record within it.

likh(i): (a) (indeclinable past participle or perfect participle - 'pūran pūrab kārdaṅtak'; synonymous with 'likh ke') literally, having written, and implicit here is (b) (v; synonymous with 'likhṇā') to write, scribe or note. See likhṇā.

jāṇah(i): (v, pl, present tense, third person; synonymous with 'uh jāṇde han'; pronounced as 'jānaheṅ') see jāṇah(i) and jāṇana (a and b).

likh(i) jāṇah(i): (synonymous with 'likhṇā jāṇde han') literally, they know how and what to write.

likh(i) likh(i): (a) (instrumental case - 'karaṇ kārak'; synonymous with 'likhe anusār') literally, according to the writ of His Divine Order, (b) (indeclinable past participle or perfect participle - 'pūran pūrab kārdaṅtak'; synonymous with 'likh likh ke') by writing or noting down, and implicit here is (c) (accusative case - 'karam kārak'; synonymous with 'likhe hoe nūṅ') that which has been so recorded or an account thus written or recorded.

dharam(u): (a) (n, m, s; synonymous with 'maryādā') moral, ethical or religious code of conduct. In essence, the Divine Order ('Hukam(u)'), which creates, supports, and sustains, governs and guides the entire creation and way of life in complete congruence with 'Nām(u)' or 'Nām-consciousness' ('Hukam anusārī'), and (b) (n, m, s; synonymous with 'Dharamrāj') see dharamrāj.

vichāre: (v, s, present tense, third person; synonymous with 'bīchāre' and 'vīchārdā hai') see vīchārnā.

likh(i) likh(i) dharam(u) vichāre: (synonymous with 'likhe hoe nūṅ dharamrāj vīchārdā hai') literally, dharam rāj weighs up the evidence thus recorded.

As stated earlier, Gurmat does not lend any support to this view. Such views or belief systems cast doubt on and belittle God's power and ability. On the contrary, the God of Gurū Nānak is the all-pervasive eternal Reality, who is omnipotent, omnipresent, and omniscient, and the fount of all attributes, virtues and values. The entire creation and its constitutive parts are nothing but His manifestation. In other words, there is no one else besides Him, in reality. However, the actions of all beings with a degree of autonomy or free will are subject to His scrutiny as the following verse from the SGGS explains clearly:

All the good and the bad are judged at His Court; with a lifestyle engrossed in the empirical world and opposed to 'Nam-consciousness', the disloyal wail and feel remorse at having wasted this opportunity, as they are cast out.[442]

Chitr and Gupt are well-versed in keeping records of our good and bad deeds; and Dharamrāj adjudicates based on this gathered evidence.

Gāvah(i) Īsar(u), Barmā, devī, sohan(i) sadā savāre

Īsar(u): (n, m, pl) (a) (skt; synonymous with 'Īshvar') God, and implicit here is (b) (synonymous with 'Shiv', 'Mahesh' and 'Mahādev') Lord Shivā, one of the trilogy of Hindu Gods, responsible for death and destruction.

Barmā: (n, m, s; synonymous with and pronounced as 'Brahmā') Lord Brahmā, one of the trilogy of Hindu Gods, responsible for creation.

devī: (n, f, s) (a) (synonymous with 'sadāchārī istrī' and 'pat(i)vartā istrī') a faithful and obedient wife of high moral character, (b) (synonymous with 'dev patnī') consort of a devtā, and (c) demi-goddess in Hindu mythology.

Whilst Brahmā, Vishnū and Shiv and many other 'devis' and 'devtas' have special roles and positions in Hindu mythology, they hold no such prominent position in Sikh belief and practice. However, many people, like them, live out their lives, as they do, according to their innate nature, attributes and abilities and are inherently desirous of aligning perfectly with 'Nām(u)' and eventually realising its full glow in their Hirdās.

sohan(i): (v, pl, present tense, third person; synonymous with 'sohṇe-' and 'shobhnīk-' 'lagde han') appear elegant, graceful and praiseworthy.

sadā: (adv; synonymous with 'sad', 'nitya' and 'hameshā') forever, always or in perpetuity

savāre: (adj; synonymous with 'sajāi-', 'shiṅgāre-', 'rās kite-' or 'savāre-' 'hoe') adorned, bedecked, and embellished.

Shiv, Brahmā and the demi-goddesses, adorned with noble attributes and appearing forever elegant, sing Your praise.

Gāvah(i) Ind iṅdāsan(i) baiṭhe, devtiā dar(i) nāle

Ind(u): (n, m, s; abbrev. for 'Indr') king of 'devs' or 'devtās', and God of rain in Hindu mythology.

Ind: (n, m, pl) numerous like dev Indra.

iṅdāsan(i): (locative case - 'adhikaraṇ kārak'; synonymous with 'Indar de-' 'āsan or takhat-' 'upar') upon the throne of dev Indra.

baiṭhe: (adj; synonymous with 'baiṭhe hoi') seated or having taken their seats.

Ind iṅdāsan(i) baiṭhe: (synonymous with 'ka-ī Indra devtā varge āpṇe āsaṇā uppar baiṭhe hoe') many like Indra Dev, sat on their thrones.

devtiā: (genitive case - 'saṅbaṅdh kārak'; synonymous with 'devtiāṅ de'; pronounced as 'devtiāṅ') with other demi-gods. See dev (f).

dar(i): (locative case - 'adhikaraṇ kārak'; synonymous with 'dar- 'utte' or 'uppar') literally, at one's door. However, the reference here is: at Your door. In essence, implicit here is: by focusing on and contemplating You, as You, God Almighty, are everywhere. See dar.

nāle: (adv; synonymous with 'sāth', 'saṅg' and 'smet' or 'nāl hī') literally, in the company of, with or along with.

devtiā nāle: (synonymous with 'devtiāṅ smet' or 'devtiāṅ de smet') literally, alongside other devtās.

Many others like dev Indra, along with other demi-gods, seated on their thrones, sing Your praise at Your doorstep.

Gāvah(i) sidh samādhī aṅdar(i), gāvan(i) Sādh vichāre

sidh: (n, m, pl) Yogīs who (a) have achieved eight psychic or miraculous powers, harnessed through practice of their yogic techniques, (b) have achieved 'sidhī' - spiritual wisdom and knowledge, and subdued their '*Man*', the five cardinal drives and innate evil tendencies, and (c) are considered to be above human beings but below 'devtās', according to old Saṅskrit texts.

samādhī: (n, f; synonymous with 'liv-līnatā') a state of intense and prolonged focus on and contemplation of an object of one's reflection whilst sitting in a particular posture ('āsanā').

aṅdar(i): (adv; synonymous with 'vich' and 'bhītar) inside, within, or amidst.

gāvan(i): (v, pl, present tense, third person; synonymous with 'uh gāuṅde han') see gāvṇā.

sādh: (a) (n, m, pl; synonymous with 'Saṅt', Gurū, 'Sat(i)gurū', 'Brahmgyānī' or 'Bhagat') they who have realised 'Nām(u)', and whose every thought, utterance and deed is in harmony with it, and implicit here is (b) they who are on a spiritual quest to attain perfect alignment with 'Nām(u)' and enlightenment.

vīchāre: (indeclinable past participle or perfect participle - 'pūran pūrab kārdaṅtak'; synonymous with 'vichār kar ke') by focusing on and contemplating noble and godly attributes. See vīchārnā.

Sidhas, sitting on their 'āsanās' and engrossed in deep meditation, and Sādhs, through focus and contemplation, sing Your praise.

Gāvan(i) jatī satī saṅtokhī, gāvah(i) vīr karāre

gāvan(i): see above.

jatī: (n, m, pl & adj) (a) (synonymous with 'brahmchārī') virtuous or holy persons who have subdued their conscious self, and implicit here is (b) celibates, they who have absolute control over their sensual urges, and abstain from sexual relationships.

satī: (adj, pl; synonymous with 'dānī' and 'udār-ātmās') generous, benevolent, charitable, righteous, and noble.

saṅtokhī: (adj; synonymous with 'sabar vāle' and 'lobh de tyāgī') contented, satisfied and always at peace with one's inner self.

vīr: (n, m, pl) (a) (synonymous with 'bhāī' and 'bharā') brothers, and implicit here is (b) (synonymous with 'yodhās' and 'bahādurs') braves, knights, valiants or warriors.

karāre: (a) (adj, m; synonymous with 'tez' and 'tikhe') spicy, (b) adj, m; synonymous with 'khastā' and 'bhurbharā') crisp, and implicit here is (c) (adj, m; synonymous with 'dhīraj ate tākat vāle') endowed with patience, serenity, commitment, resolve, fortitude, and forbearance.

Numerous abstinent, contented, and charitable beings, and the fiercest of braves, sing Your praise.

Gāvan(i) paṅḍit paṛan(i) rakhīsar, jug(u) jug(u) vedā nāle

paṅdit: (n, m, s) (a) (synonymous with 'jo tihāṅ gunā dī paṅḍ utāre' and 'jo āpnā *Man* parbodhah') one who sheds the influence of 'Māyā' or one who sheds spiritual ignorance and aligns perfectly with 'Nām(u)', and implicit here is (b) (adj; synonymous with 'vidya vich nipuṅn purakh', 'gyānī' and 'vidvān') a learned man, man of letters, literary person, knowledgeable, highly educated or a scholar.

paṛan(i): (v, pl, present tense, third person; synonymous with 'paṛ(h)de han') see paṛnā (c).

paṛnā: (v; synonymous with 'parnā', 'paiṇā' or 'paṛṇā') (a) (synonymous with 'paiṇā' or 'leṭṇā') to lie down, (b) (synonymous with 'digṇā' or 'girnā') to fall or lie down, (c) (synonymous with 'pāṭh karnā') to read, learn or study, and (d) (conj v) e.g., 'samajh paṛnā' - to acquire knowledge or understanding; 'saran paṛnā' - humbly to submit and seek another's protection.

rakhīsar: (n, m, pl; synonymous with 'rakhīsur', 'rikhīsur' and 'mahā-rishīs') a complex word comprising 'rakhī' or 'rikhī ('saint' or 'sage') +

'sar' or 'sur' ('sresht' or 'Īshvar') i.e., supreme amongst seers, saints and sages.

jug(u): (n, m, s; synonymous with 'yug') age, period, epoch, or era. The four 'yugs' or great epochs, according to Hindu mythology, are as follows: 'Satyayug', 'Tretāyug', 'Doāparyug' and 'Kalyug', the current epoch.

jug(u) jug(u): literally, throughout the four ages. In essence, forever.

vedā: (a) (n, m, pl; synonymous with 'bed'; pronounced as 'vedāṅ') the four 'Vedas' or holy scriptures of Hindus - 'Rig', 'Sām', 'Yajur' and 'Atharvan', and implicit here is (b) (instrumental case - 'karaṇ kārak'; synonymous with 'vedāṅ-' 'nāl', 'rāhīṅ', 'duārā' or 'sadkā').

vedā nāle: (synonymous with 'vedāṅ smet') along with the Vedas too.

Paṅḍits and great seers, who read and recite the Vedas, forever sing Your praise.

Gāvah(i) mohaṇīā *man*(u) mohan(i), surgā machh pa-i-āle

mohaṇīā: (n, f, pl; synonymous with 'suṅdar istrīāṅ' and 'apsrāṅ'; pronounced as 'mohaṇīāṅ') beautiful and charming women.

man(u): (a) (n, m, s) one's conscious self, 'Hirdā' or 'Jīvātmāṅ', and (accusative case - 'karam kārak'; synonymous with '*man* nūṅ') to *man*.

mohan(i): (v, pl, present tense, third person; synonymous with 'moh laiṅdīāṅ han') see mohṇā.

mohṇā: (v) (a) (synonymous with 'mohan- 'or 'mohit-' 'karna') literally, to attract, charm, enchant, bewitch, or captivate, and (b) (synonymous with 'bhulāuṇā' or 'dhokhe vich phsāuṇā') to mislead, deceive and defraud.

However, implicit here is: to charm and subjugate another.

man(u) mohan(i): (synonymous with '*man*(u) nūṅ moh laiṇ vāliāṅ'): [they] who are capable of charming and overwhelming another's conscious self ('Jīvātmāṅ' or 'Hirdā').

mohaṇīā *man*(u) mohan(i): enchantingly beautiful women who charm and overwhelm another's conscious self. Beauty is just another example of one of His gifts. The power of beauty to attract and captivate another's conscious self is an example of this attribute of God in action.

surgā: (locative case - 'adhikaraṇ kārak'; synonymous with 'surg-' or 'swarg-' 'vich') literally, in surag.

surag: (n, m; synonymous with 'swarg', 'devlok' and 'bahisht') literally, heaven or paradise. There is no concept of heaven, outside of this Earth and life, in Gurmat. Being self-reliant for one's basic and general needs, having enough access to and comforts of the material world, being in sound physical and mental health, and enjoying lasting equipoise and inner bliss is probably counted as being in 'heaven' here on Earth.

machh: (locative case - 'adhikaraṇ kārak'; synonymous with 'māt-lok vich') see machh.

machh: (n, m; synonymous with 'māt-lok' and 'dharat(i)') our Earth.

pa-i-āle: (locative case - 'adhikaraṇ kārak'; synonymous with 'pa-i-āl vich' and 'pātāl vich') literally, in pa-i-āl. See pa-i-āl.

pa-i-āl: (n, synonymous with 'pātāl' (skt.)) believed to be the planet below Earth, according to the old Hindu concept of 'Tri-lok' - heaven ('swarg'/'suarg'), Earth, and 'pātāl', (b) the last of the seven planets below or beneath the planet Earth according to Islamic belief, and (c) (n, m) literally, the netherworld, the underland, Hades or Hell. Gurmat, however, discounts this notion altogether as there are countless planets on all sides of the planet Earth.

surgā machh pa-i-āle: in or of the celestial, terrestrial and the netherworld.

Enchantingly beautiful women of the celestial, terrestrial and the netherworlds sing Your praise.

Gāvan(i) ratan upāe tere, aṭh-saṭh(i) tīrath nāle

ratan: (a) (n, m, pl; synonymous with 'ratan rūp' and 'guṇvān manukh') 'saṅts', 'sādhs', 'bhagats', 'gurūs,' and 'brahmgyānīs', and (b) (n, m, pl; synonymous with 'ratan rūp' and 'amolak guṇ') priceless godly attributes, virtues, and values. See ratan.

upāe: (a) (past participle - 'bhūt kirdaṅt'; synonymous with 'upāe ratan'), (b) (v, pl, present tense, third person; synonymous with 'paidā karde han'), and implicit here is (c) (v, pl, present perfect, third person; synonymous with 'upjāe' and 'utpan- 'or 'paidā-' 'kīte han') see upāuṇā.

upāuṇā: (v; synonymous with 'upjaṇā'; 'utpādan-' or 'utpan-' 'karnā') to grow, generate, produce, or create.

tere: (pron and adj, pl, m) literally, thine, your or yours. However, implicit here is God's ('Prabhū's').

ratan upāe tere: 'uttam padārath', 'ratan rūp guṇvān manukh' and 'ratan rūp amolak guṇ' that You created. All these priceless commodities are often seen together at places of pilgrimage: free food ('laṅgar') made of 'uttam padārath', saintly and enlightened people freely and altruistically sharing the Divine Word and Message and of course piety, love, humility, free and voluntary service ('sewā'), compassion, contentment and other such 'amolak guṇs' in action.

aṭh-saṭh(i): (adj) literally, 'aṭh' (8) + 'saṭh' (60) i.e., sixty-eight (68).

tīrath: (n, m, pl) literally, places of pilgrimage where believers of different faiths go to cleanse themselves of their sins. Whilst it is essential for some just to go and visit, others believe in bathing, making offerings of material things and money, and performing acts of charity towards this end.

aṭh-saṭh(i) tīrath nāle: literally, along with the sixty-eight holy places of pilgrimage.

Your created noble food items and godly attributes and their bearers, along with the sixty-eight places of pilgrimage, sing Your praise.

Gāvah(i) jodh mahābal sūrā, gāvah(i) khāṇī chāre

jodh: (n, m, pl; synonymous with 'yodhe') literally, braves, knights, or warriors, especially those who fight injustice, tyranny, oppression, a holy war or who engage in battle with their own innate evil tendencies.

mahābal: (adj, m; synonymous with 'balvān', 'balvaṅt', 'mahābalī' and 'at(i) tākatvar') a complex word comprising 'mahā' (great) + 'bal' (might or power) i.e., very strong and powerful; mighty and brave.

sūrā: (adj, m; synonymous with 'bahādur', 'yodhā', 'sūrbīr' and 'sūrme') literally, brave, valiant, courageous, or intrepid. In essence, the braves who engage in an internal mental battle or who engage in a battle deemed appropriate with the principles of 'dharam'.

khāṇī: (genitive case - 'saṅbaṅdh kārak'; synonymous with 'khāṇāṅ de') of sources of life. See khāṇ.

khāṇ: (n, f, pl) (a) mines - source of minerals, and (b) source or origin of sentient beings. Traditionally, four such sources are recognised: (a) 'aṅḍaj' - through an egg, (b) 'jeraj' - through a placenta, (c) 'setaj' - through sweat, moisture or sporification, and (d) 'utbhuj' - through Earth. However, Gurmat alludes to numerous ways of production.

chāre: (adv; synonymous with 'chāroṅ hī') literally, all four of them.

chār(i): (adj; digit 4 of the number system) literally, four.

khāṇī chāre: (a) (synonymous with 'chauhāṅ hī khāṇāṅ de jīv jaṅtū') literally, sentient life from all four sources of life, and (b) (ablative case - 'apādān kārak'; synonymous with 'chauhāṅ khāṇāṅ toṅ paidā hoe jīv/jaṅt') all life forms born of these routes.

Warriors, mighty and brave, spiritual crusaders, and the life forms from these four sources of life, sing Your praise.

Gāvah(i) khaṅḍ maṅḍal varbhaṅḍā, kar(i) kar(i) rakhe dhāre

khaṅḍ: (n, m, pl) planets (khaṅḍ) in the universe (brahmaṅḍ). See khaṅḍ.

maṅḍal: (n, m, pl; synonymous with 'golākār gherā' and 'dāyrah') many circular orbits; many planetary systems, with planets orbiting around a sun or star. See maṅḍal.

varbhaṅḍā: (n, m, pl; synonymous with 'brahmāṅḍs' or 'varbhaṅḍs') literally, many universes; sum total of all galaxies and universes.

kar(i) kar(i): (indeclinable past participle or perfect participle - 'pūran pūrab kārdaṅtak'; synonymous with 'kar kar ke', 'paidā kar ke' and 'sirj ke') literally, having created. See karnā (g).

rakhe: (a) (v, s, present tense, third person; synonymous with 'uh rakhdā hai'), (b) (imperative mood - 'saṅbhāv bhvikht kāl', s, second/third person; synonymous with 'je tūṅ/uh rakh-' or 'bachā-' 'lave'), (c) (v, past tense; synonymous with 'us ne rakhkhe' or 'us ne rakh ditte'), (d) (past participle - 'bhūt kirdaṅt'; synonymous with 'rakhe khaṅḍ maṅḍal') literally, Your created and securely placed planets in orbits, and implicit here is (e) (v, pl, present perfect, third person; synonymous with 'rakhe-' or 'ṭikāe-' 'hoe') created and securely settled in place. See rakhṇā (c).

dhāre: (a) (v, s, present tense, third person; synonymous with 'uh dhardā-', 'ṭikāuṅdā-', 'rakhdā-'or 'nīṅh rakhdā-' 'hai'), (b) (v, past tense; synonymous with 'us ne dhare' or 'us ne dhar ditte'), (c) (imperative mood - 'saṅbhāv bhvikht kāl', s, second/third person; synonymous with 'je tūṅ/uh ṭikā-' or 'rakh-' 'deve') see dhārṇā, (d) (past participle - 'bhūt kirdaṅt'; synonymous with 'dhāre-'or 'ṭikāe-' 'hoe khaṅḍ maṅḍal') safely and securely places planets and orbits, and (e) (v, pl, present perfect, third person; synonymous with 'dhāre-'or 'ṭikāe-' 'hoe han') safely and securely settled in place. See dhārnā (b).

dhārnā: (synonymous with dhārṇā) (a) (v; synonymous with 'dhāran karnā') to put on, assume or adopt, (b) (v; synonymous with 'pakaṛnā', 'phaṛnā' or 'rakhṇā') to grab hold; to put or place safely, (c) (n; synonymous with 'samajh' and 'driṛ nischā') understanding and firm belief, view, or notion, and (d) (n, f; synonymous with 'dharam dī rahit') religious code of conduct.

The planets, orbits, constellations, and the universe, created and securely put in place by You, sing Your praise.

Seī tudh(u) no gāvah(i), jo tudh(u) bhāvan(i), rate tere bhagat rasāle

seī: (pron and adj; synonymous with 'ohī' or 'vahī') the same or exactly they.

tudh(u): (pron; synonymous with 'tere', 'tainū', 'tujh' and 'tujhe') you or yours.

no: (prep; synonymous with 'nūṅ'; pronounced as 'noṅ') to.

jo: (pron and adj; synonymous with 'jihṛe' or 'jin(h)ā nūṅ') who, whom or whosoever.

bhāvan(i): (v, pl, present tense, third person; synonymous with 'bhāuṅde han' and 'piāre lagde han') see bhāvṇā.

bhāvṇā: (v, synonymous with 'bhāuṇā' and 'piārā- 'or 'chaṅgā-' 'lagṇā') literally, to find appealing or desirable. In essence, suitable, deserving, or worthy.

rate: (a) (past participle - 'bhūt kirdaṅt'; synonymous with 'ratte-' or 'prem vich raṅge-' 'bhagat'; pronounced as 'ratte'), (b) (adj, m, pl; vocative form of 'ratā'; synonymous with 'raṅge-''hoe') literally, steeped or imbued in the red colour or dye of love. However, implicit here is that they are exhibiting the attributes associated with perfect harmony with 'Nām(u)'.

bhagat: (n, m, pl; synonymous with 'upāsaks', 'saṅts', 'sādhs', 'gurūs' and 'brahm-gyānīs') literally, devotees, votaries or they who have perceived the celestial 'Nād' ('Nām(u)'), live by His Will, and whose every thought, utterance and deed is in perfect harmony with 'Nām(u)'. See bhagat.

rasāle: (adj, m, pl; synonymous with 'ras vāle', 'ras ālya', 'ras de ghar', 'rasik' and 'rasīe') a complex word comprising 'ras' ('prem/love' or 'amrit') + 'āle'/ālya' ('ghar/grih' or 'jagā/place'), i.e., steeped in or oozing with love for 'Nām(u)'.

In essence, they who are steeped in the hue of 'Nām(u)' please You, and sing Your praise.

Hor(i) kete gāvan(i), se mai chit(i) n āvan(i), Nānak(u) kiā vīchāre

hor(i): (a) (pron; synonymous with 'anya') literally, another or some other, and implicit here is (b) (adj and adv; pl; synonymous with 'aur', 'avar', 'hor dūje' and 'bākī') more, further, additional.

gāvan(i): (v, pl, present tense, third person; synonymous with 'gāuṅde han') see gāvan.

se: (a) (adj; synonymous with 'jaise' or 'jehe') same as, and implicit here is (b) (pron and adj, pl; synonymous with 'uh', 'veh' or 'uhī') they or the same.

mai: (pron; synonymous with 'merā', 'mere', 'mainūṅ' and 'mujhe') mine or to me. See mai.

chit(i): (locative case - 'adhikaraṇ kārak'; synonymous with 'chit vich') literally, in one's cognition or consciousness. See chit.

chit: (n, m) (a) one of the four parts of 'Aṅtahkaraṇ' which forms the basis of memory, and (b) (n, f; synonymous with 'surat(i)' or 'dhiān' of '*Man*') cognition, attention, awareness or consciousness. See 'Aṅtahkaraṇ' and '*Man*'. See 'Pauṛī' 12, pp. 165-7.

n: (p; pronounced as 'nāṅ') no, not or implying a negative connotation.

āvan(i): (v, pl, present tense, third person; synonymous with 'uh āuṅde han') that I cannot remember. See āuṇā (a).

Nānak(u): (n, m, s) the first of the ten founders of the Sikh faith.

kiā: (a) (pron; synonymous with 'kyā' or 'ki') what, and (b) (p; synonymous with 'prashan bodhak') used in the interrogative sense. See kiā.

vichāre: (a) (v, s, present tense, third person; synonymous with 'bīchāre' and 'vīchār kar sakdā hai'), and (b) (v, s, imperative mood - 'saṅbhāv bhvikht kāl - prashan and bevasī bodhak', first person; synonymous with 'maiṅ kī vichār- ''karāṅ' or 'kar sakdā hāṅ') ponder, reflect or deduce. See vīchārnā.

Many others who I cannot even conceive, sing Your praise; how can, I, lowly Nānak, conceptualise that? Or:

'Many others, who I, lowly Nānak, cannot even envisage, sing Your praise'.

Soī soī sadā sach(u), sāhib(u) sāchā, sāchī nāī

soī: (pron and adj; synonymous with 'ohī') the same or exactly that. See soī.

sadā: (adj; synonymous with 'sad', 'nitya' and 'hameshā') forever, always or in perpetuity.

sach(u): (adj, m; synonymous with 'sach(u)') (a) (synonymous with 'sadīvī') eternal, (b) (synonymous with 'pūrā', 'mukaṅmal', 'sarab kalā bharpūr(i)', 'par(i)pūran' and 'sarab-vyāpak') omnipotent, omniscient, and all-pervasive and omnipresent, (c) (synonymous with 'satya' and 'hoṅd or hastī vālā') real and not imaginary, and (d) (synonymous with 'nirmal', 'pavitr' and 'ukāī rahit') perfect, flawless and immaculate. In essence, it implies the perfect, immaculate and the eternal Reality - 'Nām(u)'.

sāhib(u): (n, m; synonymous with 'pat(i)', 'swāmī' or 'mālik') Master or Lord.

sāchā: ((skt) 'satya' and (gmkh) 'sat(i)') (a) (adj; synonymous with synonymous with 'satya' and 'hoṅd or hastī vālā') real and not imaginary, (b) (adj; synonymous with 'nirmal', 'pavitr' and 'ukāī rahit') eternally true, perfect or flawless, and implicit here is (c) (n, m, s; synonymous with 'sadīvī jyot(i)' - the Primal Soul) the eternal Reality or 'Nām(u)'. See sach(u), sāchā and sat(i).

sāchī: (adj, f) (a) (synonymous with 'nirmal' and 'pavitr') perfect, flawless, or immaculate, and (b) (synonymous with 'sadīvī' and 'aṭal') eternal.

nāī: (a) (n, m) a barber, (b) (adv; synonymous with 'niāī', 'nivā ke' and 'jhukā ke') by bowing or having stooped, (c) instrumental case - 'karaṇ kārak'; synonymous with 'Nām(u)'- 'karke', 'nāl' and 'duārā') due to, with or through 'Nām(u)', (d) (locative case - 'adhikaraṇ kārak'; synonymous with 'Nām(u) vich') in 'Nām(u)', and implicit here is (e) (n, f; synonymous with 'vaḍiāī', 'shobhā' and 'nāmaṇā') praise, fame or glory.

He and He alone is the eternal Reality, the true Lord, and His Glory is eternal too.

Hai bhī, hosī, jāi n jāsī, rachnā jin(i) rachāī

hai: (aux v, s, present tense) literally, am, is or are. See hai.

bhī: (adv, synonymous with 'vī') also or too. See bhī.

hosī: (v; future tense of 'hoṇā', synonymous with 'hovegā') shall be or shall exist in the future.

jāi: (v, s, present tense, third person; synonymous with 'jaṅmdā- 'or 'paidā huṅdā-' 'hai') literally, takes birth or is born. See jāi.

n: (p; pronounced as 'naṅ') no, not or implying a negative connotation. 'n' acts as 'dehlī dīpak' here as it joins with 'jāi' and 'jāsī' as 'jāi n' and 'n jāsī'.

jāi n: (a) literally, does not go, and implicit here is (b) does not take birth or is not born.

jāsī: (v, future tense; synonymous with 'jāvegā'; pronounced as 'jāsīṅ') literally, shall go. However, implicit here is: shall die.

n jāsī: literally, shall not go. However, implicit here: shall not die.

rachnā: (a) (n, f; synonymous with 'kalākār dī peshkash' and 'kavī dā kāvyā') composition, production or construction of any master artist, (b) (n, f; synonymous with 'baṇāun dī kriyā') an act of creation, (c) (v; synonymous with 'banāuṇā') to make, create, form, construct, prepare or produce, (d) (synonymous with 'abhed hoṇā') to pervade, permeate and saturate, (e) (synonymous with 'magan- 'or 'līn-' 'hoṇā') to become deeply attached, absorbed or engrossed, and implicit here is (f) (n, f; synonymous with 'srishṭ(i)') the universe.

jin(i): (nominative case - 'kartā kārak'; genitive case - 'saṅbaṅdh kārak', s; synonymous with 'jis(i)' and 'jis ne') who, that, which, whoever or whosoever.

rachāī: (v, s, present perfect, third person; synonymous with 'rachī-', 'utpan kītī- 'or 'paidā kītī-' 'hai') literally, has created. See rachnā.

He who has created this universe, exists here and now, and shall forever henceforth, and never incarnates or dies.

Raṅgī raṅgī bhātī kar(i) kar(i), jinsī māiā jin(i) upāī

raṅgī: (genitive case - 'saṅbaṅdh kārak'; synonymous with 'raṅgāṅ dī'; pronounced as 'raṅgīṅ') of many colours. See raṅg (i).

raṅgī raṅgī: of a variety of different colours.

bhātī: (genitive case - 'saṅbaṅdh kārak'; synonymous with 'bhāṅtāṅ dī'; pronounced as 'bhāṅtī') of different kinds. See bhāṅt.

bhāṅt: (a) (synonymous with 'salīkā', 'tarīkā' and 'ḍhaṅg') manner or method, and implicit here is (b) (n, f; synonymous with 'bhāṅt(i)', 'prakār' and 'kism') kind, sort, variety, or form.

jinsī: (genitive case - 'saṅbaṅdh kārak'; synonymous with 'kaī jinsāṅ dī; pronounced as 'jinsīṅ') of many different kinds of sentient life. See jins.

jins: (a) (n, f; synonymous with 'vastu') literally, product or commodity, (b) (n, f; synonymous with 'anāj') grains or agricultural produce, (c) (n, f; synonymous with 'sāmagrī') materials, ingredients and tools or appliances collectively, and implicit here is (d) (n, f; synonymous with 'jātī', 'kism' or 'bhāṅt') literally, kind, sort, species, or genus.

māiā: (n, f; synonymous with 'māyā') (a) (synonymous with 'mātā') mother, (b) (synonymous with 'kapaṭ', 'chhal' or 'dhokhā') trickery, guile, sham or illusion, (c) (synonymous with 'avidyā', 'bhram' or 'bhulekhā') misconception and ignorance, which cause dubiety ('dubidā'), and implicit here is (d) that which lures one to the physical world and its transitory pleasures in preference to living life in complete harmony with 'Nām(u)' or 'Nām-consciousness'. See māyā or māiā.

upāī: (a) (v, past tense; synonymous with 'paidā kītī'), and (b) (v, s, present perfect, third person; synonymous with 'rachī-', 'utpan kītī- 'or 'paidā kītī-' 'hai') has been created.

He who created the diverse hues and kinds of sentient life has also fashioned their 'Māiā'.

Kar(i) kar(i) vekhai kītā āpṇa, jiv tis dī vaḍiāī

vekhai: (v, s, present tense, third person; synonymous with 'vekhdā hai'; pronounced as 'vekhaiṅ') literally, to guard, care, support and sustain. See vekhṇā (g).

kītā: (a) (past participle or 'bhūt kirdaṅt', m; synonymous with 'āpṇa kariā-', 'sirjiā-' or 'baṇāiā-' 'saṅsār') this universe created, built, or developed by Him and (b) (n, f; synonymous with 'krit') creation. See kītā (a, c and e).

āpṇa: (adj, m; synonymous with 'nij dā', 'swai dā' and 'khud dā') personal, appertaining to or belonging to self.

jiv: (adv; synonymous with 'jioṅ', 'jis prakār', 'jaise' and 'jiveṅ') as, in the manner of, as though, for instance.

tis: (pron, s; synonymous with ‘us’) literally, his. In essence, His. The (u) of ‘tis(u)’ is missing because of the preposition ‘dī’ that links it with the noun ‘vaḍiāī’.

dī: (a) (v, past tense or present perfect; synonymous with ‘dittī’) offered or gave, and implicit here is (b) (prep; synonymous with ‘saṅbaṅdh bodhak’) of or belonging to.

vadiāī: (a) (n, f; synonymous with ‘mahimā’, ‘ustat(i)’, ‘bazurgī’, ‘t-a-rīf’, ‘vaḍāī’, ‘upmā’, ‘shobhā’, ‘mān’, ‘siphat-sālāh’, ‘ābrū’ and ‘razā’) literally, praise, tribute, honour, or glory, and (b) (n, f; synonymous with ‘razā’ and ‘marzī’) His Will.

Having created, He sustains and watches over His creation according to His Will.

Jo tis(u) bhāvai, soī karsī, hukam(u) n karṇā jāī

jo: (pron; synonymous with ‘jihṛā’ and ‘jis trāṅ’) that, what, who, whoever, whosoever or whatever.

bhāvai: (v, s, present tense, third person; synonymous with ‘bhāuṅdā-’, ‘piārā lagdā- ’or ‘chaṅgā lagdā-’ ‘hai’; pronounced as ‘bhāvaiṅ’) literally, fancies; finds appealing, deserving, or worthy. See bhāvai and bhāuṇā/bhāvṇā.

soī: (pron and adj; synonymous with ‘ohī’ or ‘vahī’) literally, ‘the very same’ person, or being; the same or exactly that. See soī.

karsī: (v, s, future tense, third person; synonymous with ‘karegā’; pronounced as ‘karsīṅ’) literally, shall do, undertake, or carry out. See karnā (g).

hukam(u): (n, m) (a) (synonymous with ‘rāi’, ‘phaislā’ and ‘nirṇā’) judgement or decision, and implicit here is (b) (arab; synonymous with ‘phurmān’, ‘āgiā’ and ‘ādesh’) order, decree, or command. The reference here is to the Divine Order.

jāī: (v, s, present tense, third person; synonymous with ‘jāṅdā-’ and ‘jā sakdā-’ ‘hai’) see jāī and jāṇā (d).

n karṇā jāī: (synonymous with ‘nahīṅ kītā jā sakdā’) literally, cannot be done.

hukam(u) n karṇā jāī: literally, one cannot raise objection to and challenge His command. It has already been stated that His Divine Will and

Order are the final arbiters in what happens in this world. One's prayer is one's only saving grace as is supported in the following verse of the SGGS:

'It is not command but one's prayer that works with the Lord Master', O' Nānak.[443]

He does whatever He desires, and none can challenge His command.

So pāt(i)sāh(u), sāhā pāt(i)sāhib(u), Nānak, rahaṇ(u) rajāī

so: (pron and adj; synonymous with 'oh' and 'ohī') the same or exactly this or that.

pāt(i)sāh(u): (n, m; synonymous with 'pādshāh' and 'bādshāh'; pronounced as 'pātshāh') a complex word comprising 'pāt' + 'sāh'. Literally, Lord Master of the throne, i.e., a King. See pāt(i)sāh.

pāt(i)sāhib(u): (n, m) a complex word comprising 'pāt(i)' (see above) + 'sāhib(u)' ('swāmī' or 'mālik' - Lord Master) literally, Lord Protector or king.

sāhā pāt(i)sāhib(u): literally, King of Kings.

Nānak: (n, m, s) the (u) of 'Nānak(u)' is missing because of its vocative case - 'saṅbodhan kārak'.

rahaṇ(u): (n, m; infinitive mood - 'bhāvārth kārdaṅtak'; synonymous with 'rahiṇā', 'vasṇā' and 'nivās karnā') literally, living, residing, or inhabiting. However, implicit here is: behoves to remain or to live.

rajāī: (locative case - 'adhikaraṇ kārak'; synonymous with 'razā-', 'hukam- 'or 'bhāṇe-' 'vich') by His Will. See razā (c).

'He is the King of Kings, and it behoves us to accept and live by His Will', O' Nānak!

Conceptual summary

As alluded to earlier, 'Nām(u)', the Primal Soul and the immanent form of God, pervades all, and its presence is an absolute sine qua non for the existence and/or functional viability of any of the most basic created elements or the most complex sentient beings.

The Primal Soul, whilst interacting with and able to express itself fully within the developing body, gives rise to a perfect centre of consciousness ('nirmal Jīvātmāṅ', '*Man*', 'Chit' or 'Hirdā'), which enables the body to interact perfectly with the world outside. This is commensurate with 'Nām(u)' being manifest in that body or, put another way, the entity being synonymous with God-incarnate.

However, from the very beginning, a human being is also endowed with a unique mixture of 'Haumaiṅ', 'Moh', innate nature and degrees of innate evil tendencies ('Māyā') which impede the full expression of the Primal Soul and, in turn, gives rise to a sub-optimal centre of consciousness (conscious self, 'Jīvātmāṅ', '*Man*' or 'Hirdā') with a degree of autonomy or free will. This unique mixture of 'Māyā' evolves with the passage of time and over many lifetimes as one sheds, or gathers 'Saṅskārs' during one's interaction with the physical world.

In turn, 'Māyā' creates a spectrum of consciousness that ranges between ego-consciousness and 'Nām-', higher- or universal- consciousness. The word 'gāvah(i)' really alludes to reflecting or demonstrating the degree of alignment or harmony with 'Nām(u)' rather than just 'singing' or 'singing His Glory'. Thus, the natural behaviour of everything is enacted according to the endowed key elements alluded to above, which is all controlled or governed by His Divine Order.

Equally, every constituent part of this universe has a target or purpose imposed by the Creator, and He expects that we all strive to achieve that. This is precisely what pleases Him and what is described as living by His Will. This is exactly how we become worthy of His favoured glance, His Grace ('Nadar(i)' or ('Nadar(i) karam'). The verse 'Seī tudh(u) no gāvah(i) jo tudh(u) bhāvan(i) rate tere bhagat rasāle' accurately refers to and supports this concept and hence the reason why those who live in perfect harmony with 'Nām(u)' are really engaged in singing His Glory.

Finally, 'Nām(u)' - the immanent form of the transcendent God, is the only eternal Reality which pervades, creates, sustains, and guides everything in the universe. Whilst the entire creation is limited and bound by His laws of nature, He is beyond the space-time continuum, and thus cannot be realised with spacio-temporal logic. Hence the reason why there is no one who can fathom why, how and from where He operates and governs this vast creation. When our design and abilities are such that the Creator will forever be unfathomable, then it behoves us to surrender and accept to live by His Will. This is the only way that we can minimise the gap between us and Him or shatter the wall of ignorance that remains as a barrier between us and Him, who really resides in us as well as in everything else in the universe.

How great and beautiful is that door and how wondrous that mansion where You sit and take care of all Your creation! Countless sounds are heard and countless are the sources and players of those instruments in this world; these sounds, in different 'rāgās' and their offshoots, which we hear (representative of their outward expression of their innate nature; attributes, virtues and values and abilities; and engagement in different activities with their subtle variations), symbolise the singing of Your Glory.

The following sing Your praise: wind, water and fire; 'Dharam rāj' at Your doorstep; 'Chitr' and 'Gupt', experts in keeping records of our good and bad deeds, and Dharamrāj, who adjudicates on the basis of this evidence; Shiv, Brahmā and the demi-goddesses, adorned with noble attributes and appearing forever elegant; many others like dev Indra, along with other demi-gods, seated on their thrones; 'Sidhas', engrossed in deep meditation, and 'Sādhs' in reflection and contemplation; numerous celibates, saints, serene and contented, and the fiercest of braves; 'Paṅdits', great seers and scholars along with the Vedas; enchantingly beautiful women of the celestial, terrestrial and the netherworlds; Your created noble attributes and their bearers over the sixty-eight places of pilgrimage; the warriors, mighty and brave, spiritual crusaders, and the four sources of life; the planets, constellations and the universe, created and securely put in place by You.

In reality, they who please You and are steeped in the hue of 'Nām(u)', sing Your praise. 'Many others, that I cannot even imagine and recall, sing Your praise'; what ability do, I, Nānak, even have to ponder or speculate?

He and He alone is the eternal Reality, the true Lord, and His Glory is eternal too. He who has created this universe, never incarnates nor dies, exists here and now, and shall remain so forever. He, who has created the diverse hues and kinds of sentient life and fashioned their 'Māiā', having created, sustains and watches over His creation according to His Will. He does whatever He desires, and none can challenge His command. 'He is the King of Kings, and it behoves us to accept this and live by His Will', O' Nānak!

PAUṚĪ 28
ਪਉੜੀ ੨੮॥

Muṅdā saṅtokh(u), saram(u) pat(u) jholī, dhiān kī karah(i) bibhūt(i).
ਮੁੰਦਾ ਸੰਤੋਖੁ, ਸਰਮੁ ਪਤੁ ਝੋਲੀ, ਧਿਆਨ ਕੀ ਕਰਹਿ ਬਿਭੂਤਿ॥

Khiṅthā kāl(u), kuārī kāiā jugat(i), ḍaṅḍā partīt(i).
ਖਿੰਥਾ ਕਾਲੁ, ਕੁਆਰੀ ਕਾਇਆ ਜੁਗਤਿ, ਡੰਡਾ ਪਰਤੀਤਿ॥

Āī paṅthī sagal jamātī, *man*(i) jītai jag(u) jīt(u).
ਆਈ ਪੰਥੀ, ਸਗਲ ਜਮਾਤੀ, ਮਨਿ ਜੀਤੈ ਜਗੁ ਜੀਤੁ॥

Ādes(u), tisai ādes(u).
ਆਦੇਸੁ, ਤਿਸੈ ਆਦੇਸੁ॥

Ād(i), anīl, anād(i), anāhat(i), jug(u) jug(u) eko ves(u). (28)
ਆਦਿ, ਅਨੀਲੁ, ਅਨਾਦਿ, ਅਨਾਹਤਿ, ਜੁਗੁ ਜੁਗੁ ਏਕੋ ਵੇਸੁ॥ ੨੮॥

Rishī Patāṅjalī established Yoga to realise one's 'true self' and Gorakh Nāth became its other key proponent sometime thereafter. Yogīs worship Lord Shiva. During the time of Gurū Nānak, their beliefs, practice and lifestyle had gained considerable prominence and engendered both fear and reverence in the general populace. This arose from their supposed ability on one hand to offer boons to satisfy the needs and hopes of the masses and, on the other hand, from the fear of being damned and cursed should there be any cause for their displeasure or annoyance.

Yogīs often moved around in small groups and would establish a temporary base ('Maṭh') on the outskirts of small villages in the mountains or forests. A senior and revered member, a 'Nāth(u)', would be appointed as a leader, and younger members or new recruits, would be sent to the nearby villages to gather food for their general sustenance. Yogīs had their twelve separate groups ('Paṅths'), each wearing some unique bodily marks and ornaments, with the 'Āī Panthīs' regarding themselves as the foremost, and looking down upon members of the other groups.

They believed that one could perceive one's true self, the eternal Reality ('Ātmāṅ') by focusing and stilling one's mind ('Manās') for long periods. Renunciation of the world and its comforts ('Tyāg'), the practice of austerities ('Tapasyā') and paltry helpings of food ('Alap ahār') were key to achieving their aim. Control of their breath ('Prāṇāyām'), the adoption of eighty-four body postures ('Āsanās') and prolonged periods of focus ('Samādhī') helped them to achieve perfect focus of their mind and apparently, also led them to enjoy much longer lifespans. This practice apparently helps release increasing amounts of some spiritual energy which helps open a mythical gateway in the brain ('Dasam duār'), creating a state of absolute mental stillness ('Aphur Samādhī') and enabling 'Jīvātmāṅ' ('Manās') to perceive its true self, the eternal Reality ('Parmātmāṅ'). Whilst en route to this stage, they also enjoyed the acquisition of certain mystical and miraculous powers ('Ridh(i)' and 'Sidh(i)'), which they exploited to create both fear and reverence amongst the naive and gullible masses.

Gurmat, however, does not lend any credence to the following: (a) the wearing of external or bodily marks or ornaments and the practice of rituals ('Karam kāṅḍ') without the concomitant reduction of evil characteristics or a gain of noble attributes in one's innate nature, and (b) the view that one can achieve full control and stillness of one's mind ('Aphur Samādhī') with one's own effort and without complete focus on 'Nām(u)' and the Grace of 'Nām(u)' (Primal Soul or 'Parmātmāṅ'). The following verses from the SGGS lend weight to this thesis:

Having practised the eighty-four āsanās of Sidhās I feel dejected and tired; despite the long life I have achieved, I suffered spiritual death on many occasions and failed to realise the Primal Soul.[444]

The filth of 'Haumaiṅ' and one's innate evil nature does not diminish or vanish even if one learns to adopt the 'asanās' of the Sidhās and control of one's five senses.[445]

Eating good food and wearing fine clothes are in vain, and damned are the miraculous supernatural powers, without living life by 'Nām-consciousness'. Indeed, if God were to bless one with 'Nām(u)' and such abilities were its direct consequence, then they would be truly miraculous powers. Perfect alignment with and realisation of 'Nām(u)' within one's 'Hirdā' through submitting to and imbibing the Gurū's Word and Wisdom, is the real miracle.[446]

Even if I were to become an accomplished Yogī (a 'Sidhā'), with the incumbent miraculous supernatural powers manifesting at my command and even if people were to revere me, in awe of my power to manifest or become invisible in a moment, I pray that I would not become conceited and forget to remain in perfect harmony with You.[447]

Willing surrender to the Gurū's Divine Word and Message is the right way to 'Nām-consciousness' and to realisation of 'Nām(u)'. Thus, one gets liberated from the evil 'Vikārī' tendencies whilst enjoying the manifold joys of the world.[448]

Be entrepreneurial and live and enjoy a wholesome life with your honest earnings; by focusing on and contemplating 'Nām(u)', one rids oneself of all one's anxieties, aligns with and realises 'Nām(u)'.[449]

Muṅdā saṅtokh(u) saram(u) pat(u) jholī dhiān kī karah(i) bibhūt(i)

muṅdā: (a) (adj; present participle - 'vartmān kārdaṅtak'; synonymous with 'baṅd kītīāṅ' or 'baṅd hoīāṅ') literally, closed or shut; see muṅdaṇā, (b) (n, f; synonymous with 'mohar' or 'chhāp') stamp or seal; imprint or impression, and (c) (n, m, pl; synonymous with 'muṅdrāṅ'; pronounced as 'muṅdāṅ') literally, earrings in the form of ringlets or large earrings. Earrings were, and are, often worn by yogīs, especially by the 'kanphaṭā' sect of yogīs or 'gorakhpaṅthīs' and represent one of their few outward symbols. Members of this sect also believe that piercing or slitting of the earlobes interferes with, or interrupts, the flow towards and into one's '*Man*' (conscious self or 'Hirdā'), of 'vikari' (evil) thoughts which lead one astray. Reference to a few other outward symbols of their dress code, symbolic of unique aspects of their way of life, appears later. Gurū Nānak, however, lays emphasis on focusing on and contemplating the Divine Word and Wisdom and imbibing the noble attributes in one's conscious self and he does not lend any support to the prominence being given to sham outward symbols of religious practice.

'Indulgence in dancing and merrymaking is the way of the world and merely an instinct of the conscious self. However, only they, who have fear and regard for the Divine Order, are truly desirous of loving and serving You', O' Nānak.[450]

santokh(u): (a) (n; synonymous with 'prasaṅtā', 'khushī' or 'nischiṅt avasthā') happiness, pleasure, and a state of freedom from anxiety, and (b) (n, m, s; synonymous with 'sabar', 'lobh dā tiāg', 'rajj', 'tripat(i)' and 'shāntī') literally, contentment or satisfaction; patience; peace or calm but reference here is to lasting inner equipoise ('Sahaj').

saram(u): (n, f) (a) (pers; synonymous with 'sharam', 'hyā' or 'lajjā') honour; humiliation, shame, and implicit here is (b) (skt; synonymous with 'shram', 'mihnat', 'uddam', 'ghālaṇā' or 'purshārath') endeavour, toil, or labour. As part of their order, Yogīs renounce the world and its comforts and pleasures and become non-contributory members of society. Gurmat disapproves of this lifestyle and strongly endorses an alternative which is highlighted in the following verses from the SGGS:

Be entrepreneurial and live and enjoy a wholesome life with your honest earnings; focusing on and contemplating 'Nām(u)', one rids oneself of all one's anxieties, aligns with and realises 'Nām(u).[449]

He who earns through honest hard work and shares it with the needy, alone knows the righteous path.[451]

pat(u): (a) (n, m, s; skt; in the form of 'pat(i)') 'khasam', 'bhartā', 'swāmī' and 'mālik') husband and master, (b) (n, f; in the form of 'pat(i)') 'pratishṭā', 'mān', 'izzat', 'ābrū' and 'vaḍiāī') self-respect, honour, dignity and respectability, (c) (n, m, s; synonymous with 'patr(u)'; n, m, pl; 'patr') leaves of trees, and implicit here is (d) (n, m, s; skt; in the form of 'pātr'; synonymous with 'bhāṅḍā', 'piālā' and 'khappar') a bowl, pot, vessel or begging bowl.

jholī: (n, f, s) (a) (n, m; synonymous with 'kachh or pyjāme dā āsaṇ') gusset, and implicit here is (b) a pouch or the spread out part of a shirt or dress, in front of the abdomen and pelvis, and (c) (synonymous with 'guthlī', 'chhoṭī thailī' and 'chhoṭā jholā') a small bag or satchel made of cloth.

dhiān: (n, m, s; synonymous with '*man* vich surat(i) nāl chiṅtan' and 'surat(i)- 'or 'birtī-' 'ṭikāuṇī') stilling and focusing of one's wandering mind on the persona and/or attributes of only one thing in preference to all else, i.e., the eternal 'Nām(u)'. The (u) of 'dhiān(u)' is missing because of the preposition 'kī' which links it with the noun 'bibhūt(i)'.

kī: (prep, f; synonymous with 'dī') of or belonging to.

karah(i): (v, s, imperative mood - 'saṅbhāv bhvikht kāl - sharat bodhak', second person; synonymous with 'je tūṅ karaheṅ') literally, if you do. See karnā (g).

bibhūt(i): (n, f) (a) (synonymous with 'dhan', 'daulat' and 'saṅpadā') wealth, riches, property, or assets, and implicit here is (b) synonymous with 'vibhūt(i)', 'bhasam', 'rākh' and 'suāh') literally, ash or cinders. A covering of ash on the body, a prominent feature amongst some meandering 'Yogīs', not only signifies renunciation of the material world but also apparently, it also toughens up the skin as a barrier, offers protection from extremes of heat and cold, protects them from body and/or hair lice, serves as a very useful insect repellant, and, more importantly, serves to prevent the influence of 'Vikārs' on one's '*Man*'.

Let contentment and modesty be your earrings, honest hard work your pouch and begging bowl, and the focus and contemplation of 'Nām(u)' the ashes that you smear on your body.

Khiṅthā kāl(u) kuārī kāiā jugat(i) ḍaṅḍā partīt(i)

khiṅthā: (a) (n, f, s; synonymous with 'deh' and 'sarīr') body, and (b) (n, f, s; synonymous with 'kaṅthā', 'godṛī' and 'rajāī') a patched blanket or a light quilt; rags sewn or knitted together to make a shawl.

kāl(u): (n, m) (synonymous with 'maut' or 'mrityū') death. Fear of death and the 'day of judgement' brings into sharp focus one's immoral thoughts and unethical deeds and keeps alive in one's mind the thought of the omnipotent and omnipresent God. See kāl(u).

kuārī: (a) (adj; synonymous with 'māiā- 'or 'vikārāṅ-' 'toṅ abhij') chaste; untouched, untainted, or uncorrupted with inner evil drives, and (b) (n, f, s; synonymous with 'un-viāhī- 'or 'bedāg-' 'kanyā') an unmarried woman, a spinster or a virgin.

kāiā: (n, f, s; synonymous with 'deh' and 'sarīr'; pronounced as 'kāiāṅ') literally, body.

jugat(i): (n, m; synonymous with 'rahiṇī bahiṇī' and 'jīvan-' 'jāch', 'tarīkā' or 'ḍhaṅg') method, technique, procedure or way of life.

ḍaṅḍā: (a) (n, f; synonymous with 'daṅḍ' or 'sazā') punishment or penalty, and implicit here is (b) (n, m, s; synonymous with 'daṅḍ' and 'soṭā') literally, a staff, wooden bar, or a stave. A 'ḍaṅḍā' is a tool often deployed as a means of support during walking or climbing, or as defence, and to gauge or measure the depth of water during their travels.

partīt(i): (n, f; synonymous with 'pratīt(i)', 'nischyā', 'shradhā', 'sidak', 'bharosā' or 'vishvāsh') faith, trust, belief, confidence, or reverence. Yogīs have their faith in, and are devoted to, Lord Shiva. For Gurū Nānak, it stands for absolute faith or belief in His eternal status, reverence for all His attributes, virtues and values, and belief in Him as the cause of all causes and the source of everything as emphasised in the following verses from the SGGS:

The essence of Divine Knowledge is revealed in the conscious self of whoever firmly believes in His eternal and spiritual existence in their Hirdā.[351]

Whosoever has absolute faith in the Gurū in their conscious self, meditates upon and aligns with 'Nām(u).[452]

Make the fear of death the patched blanket you wear, purity of thought, deed, and chastity your way of life, and absolute faith in God, your staff.

Āī paṅthī sagal jamātī *man*(i) jītai jag(u) jīt(u)

āī paṅthī: (a) (n, m; synonymous with 'rāh jāṇ vālā' or 'rāhī') traveller or wayfarer, and implicit here is (b) (instrumental case - 'karaṇ kārak'; synonymous with 'āī paṅth nāl') literally, with or belonging to the 'āī paṅth'. In essence, 'āī paṅthīs' regard themselves as noble, upper class, or supreme in spirituality amongst the twelve sects of Yogīs. See āī paṅth.

āī paṅth: one of the 12 sects (paṅth) of Yogīs, and one that is regarded by them as the highest ranking. Traditionally, 'Āī paṅthīs' look down upon and keep themselves aloof from others of different sects. This is considered an evil trait in Gurmat and the following verse of the SGGS lends weight to this thesis:

'They who reckon themselves to be great but regard others as trite or insignificant and nurture this attitude in their persona, create hell for themselves here', says Kabīr.[453]

sagal: (adj, synonymous with 'sagl', 'sarv', 'sarab', 'sabh', 'sabhe', 'sāre' and 'tmām') all, entire or whole.

jamātī: (adj, m) (a) synonymous with 'jamāt nāl saṅbaṅdh rakhan vālā') committed to and expressing allegiance to a particular class, and (b) (synonymous with 'ham-jamātī' and 'brābar dā') literally, populist, democrat or egalitarian.

sagal jamātī: literally, they who believe in and practise populism, equality or egalitarianism.

āī paṅthī sagal jamātī: literally, one, who treats all as equal and as friends, is really an 'āī paṅthī'.

man(i): (accusative case - 'karam kārak'; synonymous with '*man* nūṅ') one's mind. See *man*(u).

jītai: (a) (v, s, second person; synonymous with 'tūṅ jit jāṅdā haiṅ' or 'tusīṅ jit jāṅde ho'), (b) (v, s, present tense, third person; synonymous with 'uh jit jāṅdā hai'; pronounced as 'jītaiṅ'), and implicit here is (c) (instrumental case - 'karaṇ kārak'; synonymous with 'jittiāṅ-' or 'jittan-' 'nāl', 'rāhīṅ', 'duārā' or 'sadkā'; pronounced as 'jītaiṅ') and (d) (v, s, imperative mood - 'saṅbhāv bhvikht kāl, third person; synonymous with 'je jitt lave'; pronounced as 'jītaiṅ') see jittaṇā.

jittaṇā: (v; synonymous with 'jitt pāuṇī', 'fateh karnī' and 'saphal hoṇā') to win, triumph or conquer; to succeed.

man(i) jītai: (synonymous with '*man* nūṅ jitiāṅ'; '*man* nūṅ 'jittan-' 'nāl', 'rāhīṅ', 'duārā' or 'sadkā') by conquering one's conscious self; with, by/through and by virtue of conquering one's conscious self.

jag(u): (n, m, s; abbrev for 'jagat'; synonymous with 'saṅsār') literally, the world. However, implicit here is 'Haumaiṅ', innate 'vikārī' tendencies and 'Moh' of the material world ('Māyā').

jīt(u): (a) (adj; especially if used as a suffix, e.g., 'Indrajīt(u)') one who gains victory, triumph or success over one's sensorimotor organs; Meghnāth, Son of Rāvan, who gained victory over Indra Dev, and implicit here is (b) (n, f; synonymous with 'jīt' and 'phate' or 'phatah(i)') victory, triumph or success.

jag(u) jīt(u): (synonymous with 'jagat-' 'utte' or 'upper-' 'jit(u)') literally, victory over the world. However, implicit here is victory over 'Māyā' which leads one astray and away from godliness and God.

Make egalitarianism your mark of high rank and conquering man your conquest over the world and 'Māyā'.

Ādes(u) tisai ādes(u)

ādes(u): (n, f, s; pronounced as 'ādesh(u)') (synonymous with 'namaskār' or 'praṇām') a humble bow and submission, deferential homage, salutation, obeisance, or hail. 'Yogīs' recite the 'ādes maṅtra' as a prayer to Lord Shiva prior to their partaking of food. However, Gurū Nānak exhorts them to pray to an immaculate being, the eternal Reality, who is the God of all gods. See ādes(u) (d).

tisai: (pron and accusative case - 'karam kārak'; synonymous with 'us-' 'nūṅ' or 'ko') to Him.

I bow humbly and submit only unto Him. Or:
Hail! Hail only unto Him.

Ād(i) anīl anād(i) anāhat(i) jug(u) jug(u) eko ves(u)

ād(i): (adj; synonymous with 'muḍh toṅ'; ād (b and c)) literally, in the beginning or before the beginning of time, primary, original, primeval, or primordial. In essence, the reference here is to God, the Creator, who was there before the beginning of time. See ād (b, c, and d).

anīl: (adj; synonymous with 'klaṅk- 'or 'Māyā' 'raṅg-' 'rahit'; 'shudh sarūp' or 'pavitr') literally, un-adulterated, not contaminated or defiled by the black dye or colour of 'Māyā'.

anād(i): (adj) a complex word comprising 'an' ('binā', 'rahit' or 'without') + 'ād(i)' ('āraṅbh', 'muḍh', 'origin' or 'beginning') i.e., that which has no beginning.

anāhat(i): (adj) a complex word comprising 'an' ('without') + 'āhat' ('death' or 'destruction') i.e., literally, everlasting or eternal.

jug(u): (n, m; synonymous with 'yug') literally, age, period, epoch, era, or times.

jug(u) jug(u): (a) (locative case - 'adhikaraṇ kārak'; synonymous with 'har ik yug vich') literally, in every 'yug', age, period, or epoch, and (b) (adv; synonymous with 'sadā') forever or throughout the four ages.

eko: (adj, m; synonymous with 'iko', 'ik hī' and 'keval ik') literally, just or only one but implicit here is that 'which does not alter'.

ves(u): (n; synonymous with 'bhekh', 'shakal' and 'rūp') form, figure, appearance, caricature, or silhouette. See ves(u).

eko ves(u): [one who] never changes and is eternally uniform.

[Who is] primeval, immaculate, without beginning, immortal, and immutable throughout the ages.

Conceptual summary

Make contentment and modesty your earrings, honest hard work your pouch and begging bowl, spiritual awakening, focus and contemplation upon 'Nām(u)', the ashes smeared on your body, your symbol of renunciation. Make the fear of death the patched blanket you wear, chastity and purity of thought and deed your way of life, and resolute faith in God, your staff. Make egalitarianism, the symbol of high rank, and conquest of the mind, your victory over 'Māyā' and the world.

Humbly bow and submit only unto Him, who is primordial, immaculate, without a beginning, immortal, and immutable throughout the ages.

Yogīs of the day put undue emphasis on their different techniques of 'āsanās', meditation ('samādhī'), outward appearance, and way of life. However, these were not helping them rid their 'Haumai', 'Moh', innate evil drives and bad 'Saṅskārs'. 'Jog(u)' or 'Yog(u)' is really coming together and perfect alignment ('milāp') with, and eventually realisation or perception of 'Nām(u)' - the Primal Soul, the immanent form of the transcendent God. Gurū Nānak portrays himself as a different kind of Yogī. He lays emphasis on acts that help rid one's conscious self of the evil baggage of innate 'vikārī' tendencies as these create a gap between us and our creator. They maintain this sense of disunity as well as supporting a parallel path between ego-consciousness and 'Nām-consciousness', thus becoming an impediment for their convergence.

Gradually, as we commit to submitting to the Gurū's Divine Word and Message willingly and lovingly, and strive to live by God's Will, we begin to learn and accept Him as the only eternal Reality. We thus become more contented, in the worldly sense, and commit to work hard and to earn an honest day's living ('Kirat karnī'), to share our assets with the needy ('Vaṅḍ chhakṇā'), to love, revere and serve Him and His creation ('Nām Japṇā') and to adopt them as our motto and way of life whilst we remember that the judgement of our deeds ('karmā') at the end of life is our means to liberation from the cycle of birth and death ('Āvāgavan').

All this restrains us from evil deeds and drives us towards alignment with 'Nām-consciousness' ('Nām Japnā'). Consequently, we avoid becoming engrossed in the empirical world which takes us away from 'Nām-consciousness' or becoming a recluse and completely renouncing the world and its pleasures, and thus becoming an inactive and non-contributory member of society.

PAUṚĪ 29
ਪਉੜੀ ੨੯॥

Bhugat(i) giān, da-i-ā bhaṅdāraṇ(i), ghaṭ(i) ghaṭ(i) vājah(i) nād.
ਭੁਗਤਿ ਗਿਆਨੁ, ਦਇਆ ਭੰਡਾਰਣਿ, ਘਟਿ ਘਟਿ ਵਾਜਹਿ ਨਾਦ॥

Āp(i) nāth(u), nāthī sabh jā kī, ridh(i) sidh(i) avrā sād.
ਆਪਿ ਨਾਥੁ, ਨਾਥੀ ਸਭ ਜਾ ਕੀ, ਰਿਧਿ ਸਿਧਿ ਅਵਰਾ ਸਾਦ॥

Saṅjog(u) vijog(u) due kār chalāvah(i), lekhe āvah(i) bhāg.
ਸੰਜੋਗੁ ਵਿਜੋਗੁ ਦੁਇ ਕਾਰ ਚਲਾਵਹਿ, ਲੇਖੇ ਆਵਹਿ ਭਾਗ॥

Ādes(u), tisai ādes(u).
ਆਦੇਸੁ, ਤਿਸੈ ਆਦੇਸੁ॥

Ād(i), anīl, anād(i), anāhat(i), jug(u) jug(u) eko ves(u). 29.
ਆਦਿ, ਅਨੀਲੁ, ਅਨਾਦਿ, ਅਨਾਹਤਿ, ਜੁਗੁ ਜੁਗੁ ਏਕੋ ਵੇਸੁ॥ ੨੯॥

A Yogī, the group's lead ('bhaṅdārī') in distributing free food ('chūrmā' or 'rast') amongst its clan, would signal the mealtime by blowing a horn (a 'siṅghī') - a tradition which still continues to this day. The 'Nāth', the group leader, and seated high in the midst of a circle, is served first and the rest are served afterwards. 'Ādes maṅtra', an invocation to Lord Shiva, is recited prior to their partaking of food and a thanksgiving prayer is offered to Lord Shiva and Gorakh Nāth at the end of the meal when they all leave the circle to wash their own utensils.

Whilst balanced food is essential for the wellbeing of the body, Gurū Nānak emphasises that spiritual knowledge ('brahm giān') is similarly indispensable for the welfare of one's conscious self ('Jīvātmāṅ', '*Man*' or 'Hirdā'). According to His Will and His Mercy, God offers this to a willing seeker through the Divine Word and Wisdom of a Gurū. The seeker's actions, his accumulated karma thus far, form the basis of this opportune moment ('saṅjog(u)') while His Divine Order ('Hukam(u)' with its subsidiaries 'Saṅjog(u)' and 'Vijog(u)') determine what is apportioned to each being. This is how God governs and directs the affairs of the world. The only way to realise His Grace is to submit to His Divine Word and Wisdom and strive to live by His Will. On the other hand, all efforts to seek psychic or supernatural powers is counterproductive and just vain.

Bhugat(i) giān da-i-ā bhaṅdāraṇ(i) ghaṭ(i) ghaṭ(i) vājah(i) nād

bhugat(i): (a) (n, m; synonymous with 'bhog' and 'bhogṇā') joy and enjoyment of the material world - good food, material comforts and pleasures, and sensual pleasures, and implicit here is (b) (n, f; synonymous with 'bhojan' and 'chūrmā'; just as 'mukat(i)' is pronounced as 'muktī', 'bhugat(i)' should be correctly pronounced as 'bhugtī') literally, a meal made from crushed bread, butter, 'dāl' and sugar, the simple, nutritious and balanced food of Yogīs, which they partake of themselves and share with others. See 'chūrmā'.

chūrmā: (n, m) (a) tiny shredded pieces of a 'chapāttī' or 'roṭī' - a thin pancake of unleavened dough or bread cooked on a griddle - and mixed with butter, some sugar, and 'dāl', and (b) small round pancakes of unleavened dough mixed with lots of butter, cooked on a griddle, and then shredded into small pieces.

giān(u): (n, m, s) (synonymous with 'tat(u)-' 'ruhānī-' or 'brahm-' 'giān(u)'; 'ruhānī-' 'jāgratā' or 'sojhī') divine or spiritual knowledge about the one eternal Reality, its all-pervasive, sustaining and creative power; intuitive insight and knowledge of godliness; an understanding of the Divine Will and the true path to realisation or perception of the eternal Reality. See giān(u). The following verses from the SGGS relate to and expound the significance of 'brahm giān(u)':

'Nām(u)' creates everything and 'Nām(u)' is the fount of all knowledge, attributes, virtues, and values.[454]

'Jin(i) seviā, tin(i) pāiā mān(u). Nānak, gāvīai guṇī nidhān(u)'. However, He grants these only to a willing and deserving seeker and through the medium of a perfect Gurū. See Pauṛī 5.

The Divine Wisdom of His Will and true path to His realisation is the real sustenance for the truly enlightened.[455]

The eternal 'Nām(u)', which has subdued all my worldly cravings, is my rock.[456]

I found lasting inner equanimity by aligning perfectly with 'Nām(u)' and I now live purely by 'Nām-consciousness'.[457]

da-i-ā: (n, f; synonymous with 'karuṇā', 'myā', 'raham', 'kripā', 'mehar', 'taras') pity, compassion, sympathy, mercy, or benevolence.

bhaṅdāraṇ(i): (n, f, s; synonymous with 'bhaṅdār rakhaṇ vālī') literally, the safekeeper of materials or provisions for a common kitchen ('laṅgar'), a cook, and one who prepares and serves the food.

bhaṅdārī: (n, m, s; synonymous with 'bhaṅdār rakhaṇ vālā', 'rasoīā' and 'lāṅgrī') a male steward. See bhaṅdār.

bhaṅḍār: (a) (n, m, pl; synonymous with 'bhaṅḍsāl', 'mālgudām', 'zakhīre' and 'khazāne') literally, stocks, treasures, repositories or storehouses of tradeworthy goods, (b) (n, m, pl; synonymous with 'guṇī nidhān' or 'guṇāṅ da khazānā') literally, 'nau nidh(i) Nām(u)', and (c) (n, m, pl; synonymous with 'rasoī-' or 'laṅgar-' 'de samān dā khazānā') literally, a place for the stockpiling of food items or a pantry; stockpiles of all the essential ingredients for survival, safe upkeep and general well-being.

da-i-ā bhaṅdāraṇ(i): literally, make compassion the server. However, the reference here is to (a) renounce your cold-heartedness, indifference and callousness, and practise compassion, (b) actively engage in an honest day's hard work and then share your earnings with the needy, and (c) share the Divine Word and Wisdom freely and altruistically with others as God, in His Mercy, offers this to all willing seekers.

ghaṭ(i): (indeclinable past participle or perfect participle - 'pūran pūrab kārdaṅtak'; synonymous with 'hirde-'or 'sarir-' 'vich') in one's body; in one's '*Man*' or 'Hirdā'.

ghaṭ(i) ghaṭ(i): in everybody; in every '*Man*' or 'Hirdā'. See ghaṭ.

ghaṭ: (a) (adj; synonymous with 'ghaṭṭ', 'kam' or 'ghaṭṭṇā') short, deficient, inadequate or less, (b) (n, m, s; synonymous with 'baddlāṅ dī ghaṭā') heavy and dark clouds, (c) (n, m, s; synonymous with 'ghaṛā' and 'kalsā') pitcher or an earthen waterpot, (d) (n, f, s; synonymous with 'ghāṭī' and 'darā') a valley or downward slope of a hill, (e) (n, f, s; synonymous with 'udar(i)' or 'Peṭ' of a woman) literally, the uterus or loosely referred to as the abdomen of a woman, and implicit here is (f) (synonymous with 'deh' and 'sarīr') physical body of a person, and (g) (synonymous with 'aṅtahkaraṇ', 'dil', '*man*' or 'hirdā ghar') apparently where one's soul resides, and where one perceives the Primal Soul.

vājah(i): (v, pl, present tense, third person; synonymous with 'vajde han') see vajṇā (a).

vajṇā: (v) (a) (synonymous with 'vādan hoṇā') to sound a musical note, (b) to ring, chime, bang, collide or strike against, and (c) (synonymous with 'prasidh hoṇā') to become famous or to be acclaimed.

nād: (n, f) (synonymous with 'sabad', 'dhun(i)', 'anhad nād', 'parā-vāk' or 'parā-bānī') is the unstruck, everlasting primordial sound or 'dhun(i)' - the Divine Word with which God communicates with His creation; one who perceives 'anhad nād' realises 'Nām(u)'- the Immanent form of God. Yogīs wear a conch around the neck and its sound alerts and summons all for a meal. Similarly, this unstruck primordial 'dhun(i)' ('anhad nād') serves as one's inner voice or calling that echoes spontaneously and occasionally from deep within and becomes one's guiding beacon.

ghaṭ(i) ghaṭ(i) vājah(i) nād: literally, the unstruck, everlasting primordial 'dhun(i)' that echoes and works its magic in every 'Hirdā' and body. It is an exhortation to the Yogīs to look deep within and pay heed to their conscious self, to aim to 'perceive' this 'dhun(i)' in their own and everyone else's 'Hirdā', and to recognise not only His all-pervasiveness but also the commonality amongst all fellow beings.

Make divine knowledge your banquet for sharing, and compassion your desire to dispense, and recognise the unstruck and everlasting sound that resonates in every 'Hirdā' as the sound of your conch.

Āp(i) nāth(u) nāthī sabh jā kī ridh(i) sidh(i) avrā sād

āp(i): (pron; synonymous with 'āp or khud hī') one oneself or He (God) Himself.

nāth(u): (a) (n, m) (synonymous with 'bhartā' and 'pat(i)') literally, husband, and (b) (synonymous with 'swāmī' and 'mālik') literally, master, protector and God. See nāth(u).

nāthī: (a) (n, f; synonymous with 'nāth dī padvī') rank or status of a 'Nāth', (b) (adj; synonymous with 'nāth vālā') one who is a lord or master, and (c) (synonymous with 'nathī-', 'baṅnī-', 'kābū kītī-' 'hoī') curbed, checked, controlled, bridled, or restrained. See nathaṇā.

nathaṇā: (v) (a) (synonymous with 'nak viṅnaṇā') to pierce a nose to enable one to wear a stud or a ring, (b) (synonymous with 'nakel pāuṇī' and 'kābū karnā') to check, restrain, curb or bridle; to apprehend, seize or bring under control. In reality, the Divine Order controls all aspects of this evolving empirical world and its reference to humanity is clearly defined in this verse from the SGGS:

'God has the controlling yoke (nose ring) - His Will in His Hand and our innate nature (based on our past Karmā and His Divine Order) leads us now. The reality is that we just dance to its tune now', O' Nānak.[458]

sabh: (adj; synonymous with 'sabhe', 'sarab' or 'sabho') literally, all, entire, everyone or totality; in essence, the reference here is to the entire universe.

jā: (pron; synonymous with 'jis') who, whom, which or that. See jā.

kī: (prep, f; synonymous with 'dī') of or belonging to. See kī.

nāthī sabh jā kī: literally, under whose sway is the entire universe.

ridh(i): (a) (n, f; synonymous with 'dhaṅn', 'daulat' or 'saṅpadā') material or worldly assets, affluence, or prosperity; promotion in rank or status, (b) (n, f; synonymous with 'vaḍiāī' or 'pratāp') success, influence, renown or power secondary to worldly assets, rank or status in worldly affairs, and (c) (n, f; synonymous with 'dhaṅn-', 'daulat-' or 'saṅpadā-' 'paidā karan vālīāṅ shakatīāṅ') miraculous powers to realise 'dhaṅn', 'daulat' or 'saṅpadā'.

sidh(i): (n, f) (a) (synonymous with 'kāraj-' 'saphaltā-' or 'kāmyābī') realisation of success in one's ambition, (b) (synonymous with 'vikārāṅ toṅ muktī') 'Moksh' from one's evil tendencies or the five cardinal sins, and implicit here is (c) the prominent eight of the eighteen miraculous or supernatural powers: (i) 'aṇimā' - the ability to become as small as one wants, (ii) 'laghimā' -the ability to become as light as one wants, (iii) 'prāpatī' - the ability to have any material thing one wants, (iv) 'prākāmayā' - the ability to have your own way (dictatorial power), (v) 'mahimā' - the ability to become as big as one wants, (vi) 'īshitv' - the ability to assume sovereignty, supremacy or sway, (vii) 'vashitv' - the ability to get another under your influence or control, and (viii) 'kāmāvāsāitā' - the ability to have absolute control over your sensuality.

avrā: (pron, pl; synonymous with 'dūjā' and 'koī hor') literally, another, different or some other. The reference here is to that which takes one away from godliness and 'Nām-consciousness'.

sād: (a) (n, f; synonymous with 'shād' (pers), 'khushī' and 'prasaṅtā') satisfaction in fulfillment of one's expectation, and gain of others' approval, (b) (n, m; synonymous with 'sidhāṅt') doctrine, tenet, credo or precept, and implicit here is (c) (n, m; synonymous with 'svād, 'ras', 'chaskā' and 'ādat') taste, relish or pleasure; passionate desire, habit or addiction. In essence, the tacit reference here is to distractions that lead one astray or the sway that leads one away from God.

The Yogīs of the day had deviated from the real goal of their lives (union with and/or realisation of God) and the correct path for achieving this goal. They believed in (i) withdrawing from the world, which they thought was a serious distraction from, and hindrance to, their spiritual progress, (ii) selfish and egocentric outlook - concern for their own welfare only, (iii) reliance on simple food for survival or alms from the common man, (iv) ritualistic acts which did nothing to cleanse their inner evil tendencies, (v) undue prominence to the achievement of 'ridh(i)s' and 'sidh(i)s', their abuse for personal gain and terrorising the common masses, and many other beliefs and practices which today seem anachronistic and counterproductive to their aim. The following verse from the SGGS emphasises this notion:

Craving for worldly assets and miraculous powers is nothing but infatuation with the material world and proves futile in aligning one's conscious self with 'Nām(u)'.[329]

Make God your Lord Master, under whose sway is the entire universe, and give up the pursuit of worldly renown and influence or miraculous powers which are nothing but false and futile.

Saṅjog(u) vijog(u) dui kār chalāvah(i) lekhai āvah(i) bhāg

saṅjog(u): (synonymous with 'saṅyog(u)') (n, m) (a) (synonymous with 'saṅbaṅdh' and 'itphāk') connection or concordance, (b) (n, m, s; synonymous with 'upāya' or 'yatan') means, remedy or measure, and implicit here is (c) (synonymous with 'bhāg', 'kismat' and 'karam phal') fate, destiny, consequence of or reward for one's actions, and (d) (n, m, s; synonymous with 'milāp'; antonym of 'vijog') a subsidiary of the Divine Order ('Hukam') which brings back together two things or beings previously separated.

vijog(u): (n, m) (a) (synonymous with 'vichhoṛā' and 'judāī') separation or parting from a dear one, loss of noble virtues or values or separation from a desired object, and implicit here is (b) a subsidiary of the Divine Order ('Hukam') which brings about the separation of two things previously together, e.g., the 'Manmukh' and 'Nām(u)'.

One's accumulated Karmā forms the basis of both 'saṅjog(u)' and 'vijog(u)' and together they are not only related to one's destiny but also to sudden and unexpected events in one's life. It is believed that the relevant details of the process that brings about these desired actions are recorded ('likhiā') in one's destiny ('Mastak de lekh') right from one's birth ('dhur(i)'). The following verses from the SGGS explicate 'Hukam(u)' as the basis of the creation:

God first created 'Haumaiṅ' and, by its virtue, the diverse flora and fauna thereafter.[50]

How was the world constructed and how does all one's suffering vanish? The world came into being in 'Haumaiṅ', and forsaking 'Nām(u)' one experiences all one's suffering.[51]

God first created a sense of desire and attachment, and thereafter followed the creation of the universe.[53]

All sentient beings are like little pawns in Your Divine Game; some, having been together, separate ('vijog(u)') whilst others come together ('saṅjog(u)') by Your Will.[459]

Having first created 'Saṅjog(u)' and 'Vijog(u)', God established the very basis of this universe. He then created the universe according to His Will and so will 'Jīvātmāṅ' merge with the Primal Soul.[460]

dui: (a) (adj; synonymous with 'do') literally, two, and (b) (adj, pl; synonymous with 'duhū', 'dohāṅ', 'doveṅ' and 'donoṅ') both, i.e., saṅjog(u) and vijog(u).

kār: (synonymous with 'srisṭ(i) rachnā') literally, the act of creation and its evolution over time. In essence, the reference here is to the way of the world, how it moves, flows or unfolds and evolves both in the Darwinian and spiritual sense. See kār.

chalāvah(i): (a) (v, s, present tense, second person; synonymous with 'tusīṅ chalāuṅde ho' or 'tūṅ chalāuṅdā haiṅ'), (b) (v, s, imperative mood - 'saṅbhāv bhvikht kāl - sharat bodhak', second person; synonymous with 'je tūṅ chalāvaheṅ'), (c) (v, pl, future tense, third person; synonymous with 'uh chalāuṇge'), and (d) (v, pl, present tense, third person; synonymous with 'uh chalāuṅde han'; pronounced as 'chalāvaheṅ') see chalāuṇā (a and d).

chalāuṇā: (v) (a) to set in motion, to cause to move or to start or drive something, (b) to discharge or fire (a firearm), (c) to shoot an arrow, and (d) to manage, govern, conduct, or direct.

lekhai: (a) (adv; 'lekhā kardiāṅ') of accounts or whilst accounting, (b) (genitive case - 'saṅbaṅdh kārak'; synonymous with 'lekhe dā') of one's destiny, (c) (locative case - 'adhikaraṇ kārak'; synonymous with 'lekhe vich') in one's destiny, and implicit here is (d) (instrumental case - 'karaṇ kārak'; synonymous with 'lekhe-' or 'karmāṅ de hisāb-' 'anusār') with or according to the judgement of one's previous Karmā and, therefore, in one's destiny. The prevalent folklore dictates that details of one's fate or destiny (the sum total of one's attributes, virtues, values, innate nature, circumstances and opportunities for realisation or otherwise of one's potential in life with 'Saṅjog(u)' and 'vijog(u)', determined on the basis of one's 'karmā'), is written on one's forehead ('mastak'). This is often described as 'mastak de lekh' or 'mastak de bhāg'. See lekhā. The following verse from the SGGS captures and illustrates well the concept of 'Saṅjog(u)':

One meets one's mother, father, wife, son, relatives, loving friends, and brothers through the erstwhile 'Saṅskārs' etched in one's previous life, but none come to one's help on the day of judgement.[461]

āvah(i): (v, pl, present tense, third person) literally, come, arrive or appear. See āuṇā (a).

bhāg: (n, m, pl) (a) (synonymous with 'khaṅḍs' and 'ṭukṛe') literally, fractions, segments, or portions, (b) (synonymous with 'khitte' and 'desh') countries or parts of a country, and implicit here is (c) (synonymous with 'hisse') literally, shares or contributions, and implicit here is (d) (synonymous with 'bhāgya' or 'kismat') our lot, share, fortune, fate or destiny. However, the implication is to whatever God endows us with at birth [both the qualitative and quantitative aspect of one's attributes, virtues, and values, one's physical, psychological and spiritual potential, the coming together ('Saṅjog') or parting/loss ('Vijog') of objects, people or wealth] on the basis of one's previous Karmā and 'Saṅskārs'.

'Saṅjog' and 'vijog', the two subsidiary laws of the Divine Order ('Hukam(u)'), together control how the world unfolds, and our Karmā determines our fates.

Ādes(u) tisai ādes(u). See 'Pauṛī' 28.

Ād(i) anīl anād(i) anāhat(i) jug(u) jug(u) eko ves(u). See 'Pauṛī' 28.

Conceptual summary

Make Divine Knowledge your banquet, and compassion your stewardess to dispense freely, and recognise the unstruck and everlasting sound that resonates in every 'Hirdā' as the sound of your conch. Make God, under whose sway is the entire universe, your Lord Master, give up the vain search for worldly celebrity status, influence and miraculous powers, all of which are nothing but false and futile. Remember that 'saṅjog' and 'vijog', the two subsidiary laws of the Divine Order, together control how the world evolves and our Karmā determines our fates.

Finally, remember to bow and submit humbly only unto Him, who is primordial, immaculate, without a beginning, immortal, and immutable throughout the ages.

The focus on, contemplation of, and devotion to the Gurū's Divine Word and Message makes us aware and appreciate the Divine Order that governs the entire universe, His omnipresence, the principle of the universal Fatherhood of God and Brotherhood of Man, and the need for moving away from one's obsession with self to care and concern for others as responsible saints and soldiers of God. We also learn how God, deploying 'Haumai', 'Moh' and 'Sanjog' and 'Vijog', created this diverse world, how we come into it and depart from it, how our destiny brings us together or separates us from what we have come to love, and how not to make worldly renown our false aim but, instead, that living by His Will is the path to follow in order to achieve perfect harmony with 'Nām-consciousness' and eventually to realise 'Nām(u)'.

PAUṚĪ 30
ਪਉੜੀ ੩੦॥

Ekā māī, jugat(i) viāī, tin(i) chele parvān(u).
ਏਕਾ ਮਾਈ, ਜੁਗਤਿ ਵਿਆਈ, ਤਿਨਿ ਚੇਲੇ ਪਰਵਾਣੁ॥

Ik(u) saṅsārī, ik(u) bhaṅdārī, ik(u) lāe dībāṇ(u).
ਇਕੁ ਸੰਸਾਰੀ, ਇਕੁ ਭੰਡਾਰੀ, ਇਕੁ ਲਾਏ ਦੀਬਾਣੁ॥

Jiv tis(u) bhāvai, tivai chalāvai, jiv hovai phurmāṇ(u).
ਜਿਵ ਤਿਸੁ ਭਾਵੈ, ਤਿਵੈ ਚਲਾਵੈ, ਜਿਵ ਹੋਵੈ ਫੁਰਮਾਣੁ॥

Oh(u) vekhai, onā nadar(i) n āvai, bahutā eh(u) viḍāṇ(u).
ਓਹੁ ਵੇਖੈ, ਓਨਾ ਨਦਰਿ ਨ ਆਵੈ, ਬਹੁਤਾ ਏਹੁ ਵਿਡਾਣੁ॥

Ādes(u), tisai ādes(u).
ਆਦੇਸੁ, ਤਿਸੈ ਆਦੇਸੁ॥

Ād(i), anīl, anād(i), anāhat(i), jug(u) jug(u) eko ves(u). (30)
ਆਦਿ, ਅਨੀਲੁ, ਅਨਾਦਿ, ਅਨਾਹਤਿ, ਜੁਗੁ ਜੁਗੁ ਏਕੋ ਵੇਸੁ॥ ੩੦॥

In Pauṛī 21, page 257-61, Gurū Nānak stated clearly that no one, save God Himself, knows precisely how and when this vast universe came into being. However, according to the prevailing pre-Vedic and Vedic Hindū belief, the Primal Mother ('Jagat janan(i)', 'Prakrit(i)' or 'Māyā'), alone and somehow mysteriously, conceived and bore three obedient sons. 'Brahmā' was entrusted with the role of the Creator, 'Vishnū' the role of the Sustainer, and 'Shiv' or 'Mahādev' the role of Adjudicator and Destroyer. Together the three deities or Gods, supported by their aides, guide and govern the emergence of the universe and its unfolding, or evolution. However, Gurū Nānak refutes this ideology and categorically states that God Himself works, drives, directs, and governs the world according to His Will, as stated so emphatically in this Pauṛī.

Ekā māī jugat(i) viāī tin(i) chele parvān(u)

ekā: (a) (n; synonymous with 'saṅkhya bodhak aṅg 1') one, (b) (n, m; synonymous with 'adutī ik' or 'kartār') literally, creator God, and implicit here is (c) (adj, f or m; synonymous with 'keval iko', 'ikallī' or 'ikallā' and 'iko ik') literally, the only one, alone or by herself.

māī: (a) (n, f; synonymous with 'daulat' and 'māiā'; n, m; synonymous with 'dhan') financial assets or wealth, (b) (n, m; synonymous with 'kartār' or 'māyā-pat(i)') the creator or lord of 'Māyā', (c) (n, f; synonymous with 'mamtā' and 'merā pan') literally, possessiveness or attachment; partiality or prejudice, (d) (n, f; synonymous with 'avidyā') ignorance, lack of knowledge or wisdom and dubiety about the creator, the creation and the purpose of life that leads one astray, and implicit here is (e) (n, f; synonymous with 'māyā') the power and the means to the creation of this diverse universe, and (f) (n, f; synonymous with 'mātā' and 'māṅ') literally, mother. 'Jagat janan(i)' is also known as 'Durgā', 'Aditī', and 'Jagadambhā', and some equate her with the primordial energy which manifests in various forms: the creative force, 'Māyā', Mother Nature, and 'Prakritī', for example. The term 'Māyā' is used here as the force and means of creating this diverse world, separating the creation from its creator.

jugat(i): (n, m; synonymous with 'rahiṇī bahiṇī' and 'jīvan-' 'jāch', 'tarīkā' or 'ḍhaṅg') method, technique, or procedure.

viāī: (a) (past participle - 'bhūt kirdaṅt'; synonymous with 'prasūt hoī') literally, pregnant and expectant, and (b) (v, s, past tense; synonymous with 'prasūt hoī') literally, was impregnated or became pregnant. See viāuṇā.

viāuṇā: (v; synonymous with 'biāuṇā') (a) (synonymous with 'bāhar āuṇā', 'ugṇā' and 'paidā hoṇā') to grow, to sprout or to be delivered, and (b) (synonymous with 'prasūt hoṇā' and 'bachchā deṇā') to be impregnated and then deliver.

tin(i): (adj; synonymous with 'trai' and 'tīn') literally, number three. See tin(i).

chele: (n, m, pl; synonymous with 'cheṭak', 'chāṭṛe', 'chere' and 'shishya') literally, pupils, disciples, followers, or apprentices. However, implicit here is the three obedient sons ('Brahmā', 'Vishnu' and 'Shivā') according to Hindu mythology.

parvān(u): (adj; synonymous with 'pramāṇit' or 'surkharū'; 'saphal-', 'manzūr-', 'kabūl-', 'aṅgīkār-' or 'makbūl-' 'kītā hoiā') approved, authenticated, sanctioned, or authorised. See parvān(u).

The Primal Mother, 'Māyā', alone and mysteriously, conceived and manifestly had three disciples.

Ik(u) saṅsārī ik(u) bhaṅdārī ik(u) lāe dībāṇ(u)

ik(u): (a) (adj) one, first of the 1-9 numerals.

saṅsārī: (a) (n, f; synonymous with 'saṅsār dī rīt' and 'dunīā dī chāl') literally, the way of the world, (b) (n, m; synonymous with 'grihasthī') a householder, (c) (adj; 'saṅsārik' and 'duniāvī') worldly, mundane, temporal and physical, and implicit here is (d) (n, m; synonymous with 'saṅsār rachan vālā') literally, the creator of the universe. The tacit reference here is to 'Brahmā', one of the trilogy of Hindu deities who is regarded as the creator.

bhaṅdārī: (a) (n, m; synonymous with 'bhaṅḍār rakhaṇ- 'or 'gudām saṅbhālaṇ-' 'vālā') warehouse owner or storekeeper, and (b) (n, m; synonymous with 'rasoī dā samān rakhaṇ vālā', 'rasoīā' and 'lāṅgrī') cook and safekeeper of materials or provisions for the common kitchen ('laṅgar') literally, a steward. However, the tacit reference here is to 'Vishnū', one of the trilogy of Hindu deities, who is regarded as the austainer. See bhaṅḍār.

bhaṅḍār: (a) (n, m, pl; synonymous with 'bhaṅḍsāl', 'mālgudām', 'zakhīre' and 'khazāne') literally, stocks, treasures, repositories or storehouses of tradeworthy goods, (b) (n, m, pl; synonymous with 'rasoī-'or 'laṅgar-''de samān dā khazānā') a place for the stockpiling of food items or a pantry; stockpiles of all the essential ingredients for survival, safe upkeep and general wellbeing.

lāe: (v, s, present tense, third person; synonymous with 'lāuṅdā hai') see lāuṇā (c (i)).

dībāṇ(u): (n, f; synonymous with 'kachahirī') a royal court or a court of justice, where the Karmā of every being is judged. In essence, the tacit reference here is to 'Shiv' or 'Mahādev', who presides over this court and is responsible for the justice and destruction of all aspects of the creation.

One then assumes the role of the creator ('Brahmā'), another the role of the sustainer ('Vishnū'), and the third the role of an adjudicator and destroyer ('Shiv' or 'Mahādev').

Jiv tis(u) bhāvai tivai chalāvai jiv hovai phurmāṇ(u)

jiv: (adv; synonymous with 'jioṅ', 'jis prakār', 'jaise' and 'jiveṅ') howsoever, as, in the manner of, as though, for instance.

tis(u): (pron, s; accusative case - 'karam kārak'; synonymous with 'tis nūṅ') to him. However, the tacit reference here is to God. See tis(u).

bhāvai: (v, s, present tense, third person; synonymous with 'uh bhāuṅdā hai') literally, sees fit; finds appealing, desirable or deserving. See bhāvai and bhāuṇā.

tivai: (adv; synonymous with 'tiv', 'taise' and 'us prakār'; pronounced as 'tivaiṅ') similarly, that is how or in the same manner.

chalāvai: (a) (v, s, present tense, second person; synonymous with 'tūṅ chalāuṅdā haiṅ' or 'tusīṅ chalāuṅde ho'), (b) (imperative mood - 'saṅbhāv bhvikht kāl - kiās, sharat, ichhā bodhak', s, third/first person; synonymous with 'je chalāveṅ'), and implicit here is (c) (v, s, present tense, third person; synonymous with 'uh chalāuṅdā hai') literally, works, moves, drives, directs, governs, or controls. See chalāuṇā.

jiv tis(u) bhāvai tivai chalāvai: [In reality] God works, drives, directs and governs the world as He sees fit. In contrast, this is the reality as Gurū Nānak sees it.

hovai: (v, s, present tense, third person; synonymous with 'ho jāṅdī/jāṅdā hai'; 'huṅdā-' or 'huṅdī-' 'hai') exists, occurs, or becomes. See hovṇā (a and c).

phurmāṇ(u): (a) (n, m; pers; synonymous with 'āgyā-patr' or 'hukam-nāmā') written command or edict, and implicit here is (b) (n, m; pers; synonymous with 'phurmān', 'āgyā', 'hukam(u)') order, command, directive, mandate, or judgement. The following verses from the SGGS highlight the operative powers of His Divine Order ('Hukam(u)'):

Coming into and departing from this empirical world is a game or a spectacle that You have created, making 'Māiā', which facilitates this flux in the empirical world, obey Your Will.[462]

One who by listening attentively to the Guru's Word and Wisdom and God's Glory aligns one's conscious self perfectly with Nām(u), firmly believes that the formless One not only created this world-spectacle but its unfolding, infatuation with the material world ('Moh') and 'Māyā', too, came into being by His Divine Order.[463]

In reality, He works, drives, directs and governs the world as He Wills.

Oh(u) vekhai onā nadar(i) n āvai bahutā eh(u) viḍāṇ(u)

oh(u): (pron and adj, s) literally, he, she, or that. However, implicit here is God Himself.

vekhai: (v, s, present tense, third person; synonymous with 'dekh bhāl-' or 'saṅbhāl-' 'kardā hai'; pronounced as 'vekhaiṅ') literally, cares, maintains, guards, and protects. See vekhai and vekhṇā (g).

onā: (a) (adj; synonymous with 'utnā') that much or as much as, (b) (pron, pl; nominative case - 'kartā kārak', pl; synonymous with 'un(h)āṅ neṅ'; pronounced as 'on(h)āṅ') they or them, (c) (pron, pl; genitive case - 'saṅbaṅdh kārak', pl; synonymous with 'un(h)āṅ de'; pronounced as 'on(h)āṅ') theirs, and implicit here is (d) (pron, pl; accusative case - 'karam kārak', pl; synonymous with 'un(h)āṅ nūṅ'; pronounced as 'on(h)āṅ') to them. However, the tacit reference here is to the generally accepted three deities alluded to above, and to humanity whose figment of imagination these deities are.

nadar(i): (a) (n, f; arab; synonymous with 'drisṭ(i)', 'nigāh' and 'nazar') sight, vision, field of vision, watch or notice, and (b) (locative case - 'adhikaraṇ kārak'; synonymous with 'drisṭ(i)-', 'nigāh-' and 'nazar-' 'vich') literally, in one's sight or notice. See nadar(i).

n: (p; pronounced as 'nāṅ') no, not or implying a negative connotation.

āvai: (a) (imperative mood - 'saṅbhāv bhvikht kāl - kiās, sharat, ichhā bodhak', s, third/first person; synonymous with 'ā jāve'), and implicit here is (b) (v, s, present tense, third person; synonymous with 'āuṅdā-' or 'āuṅdī-' 'hai') literally, comes or arrives. See āvṇā (c).

bahutā: (adj; synonymous with 'bahut', 'adhik', 'vadhere' and 'ziādā') plenty, plentiful, abundant, or much.

eh(u): (pron and adj, m, s; synonymous with 'yahī' and 'keval eh') this or precisely this.

viḍāṇ(u): (a) (synonymous with 'viḍaṅbban', 'āḍaṅmbbar' and 'dikhāvā') literally, sham, ostentation, or pretentious display, (b) (synonymous with 'niṅdā karni') slander, vilification, disparagement or defamation, (c) (synonymous with 'makhaul' and 'ṭhaṭhā') mockery, ridicule or derision, (d) (adj, m; synonymous with 'begānā' and 'oprā') unrelated or stranger, and implicit here is (e) (synonymous with 'hairat', 'hairānī' and 'hairāngī') astonishment, amazement, surprise, shock or perplexity.

And the most astonishing reality is: He watches over the creation and takes care of it though He remains invisible to the three deities and their disciples or votaries.

Ādes(u) tisai ādes(u). See 'Pauṛī' 28.
Ād(i) anīl anād(i) anāhat(i) jug(u) jug(u) eko ves(u). See 'Pauṛī' 28.

Conceptual summary

The prevalent belief in Hindu mythology is that the Primal Mother, 'Māyā', alone and mysteriously, conceived and bore three obedient sons. One ('Brahmā') was entrusted the role of the creator, another ('Vishnū') the role of the sustainer, and the third ('Shiv' or 'Mahādev') the role of an adjudicator and destroyer. However, Gurū Nānak refutes this ideology and categorically states that God Himself works, drives, directs, and governs the world as He Wills. Moreover, the most staggering reality is that He watches over and takes care of all, though He remains unseen to the three deities and their adherents and advocates.

It therefore behoves us to bow and submit humbly only unto Him, who is primordial, immaculate, without a beginning, immortal, and immutable throughout the ages.

The focus on and contemplation of and devotion to the Gurū's Divine Word and Message makes one strive hard to align with 'Nām-consciousness' and keep alive the burning desire to achieve lasting equanimity ('Sahaj'), inner bliss ('Anaṅd') and, to realise 'Nām(u)' eventually. As one devotedly treads this path, one confidently begins to discount others' firmly held beliefs of separate rival entities entrusted with the roles of a creator, a sustainer and an adjudicator. Instead, he hearkens to the imbibed wisdom of the Gurū that it is 'Nām(u)', the immanent form of the transcendent God, which creates ('Kartār'), sustains ('Pālanhār'), guides and directs ('Anhad Sabad'), and governs and adjudicates ('Hukam' and 'Razā'). Furthermore, though 'Nām(u)' is the immanent and invisible form of the transcendent God, one can perceive It by submitting to and imbibing the Guru's Divine Word and Message, living life devotedly and accordingly, achieving 'Sahaj' and 'Anaṅd', and eventually, with the Grace of God, realising the full glow of 'Nām(u)' within one's 'Hirdā'.

PAUṚĪ 31
ਪਉੜੀ ੩੧॥

Āsaṇ(u) loi loi bhaṅḍār.
ਆਸਣੁ ਲੋਇ ਲੋਇ ਭੰਡਾਰ॥

Jo kichh(u) pāiā, su ekā vār.
ਜੋ ਕਿਛੁ ਪਾਇਆ, ਸੁ ਏਕਾ ਵਾਰ॥

Kar(i) kar(i) vekhai sirjaṇhār(u).
ਕਰਿ ਕਰਿ ਵੇਖੈ ਸਿਰਜਣਹਾਰੁ॥

Nānak, sache kī sāchī kār.
ਨਾਨਕ, ਸਚੇ ਕੀ ਸਾਚੀ ਕਾਰ॥

Ādes(u), tisai ādes(u).
ਆਦੇਸੁ, ਤਿਸੈ ਆਦੇਸੁ॥

Ād(i), anīl, anād(i), anāhat(i), jug(u) jug(u) eko ves(u). (31)
ਆਦਿ, ਅਨੀਲੁ, ਅਨਾਦਿ, ਅਨਾਹਤਿ, ਜੁਗੁ ਜੁਗੁ ਏਕੋ ਵੇਸੁ॥ ੩੧॥

Āsaṇ(u) loi loi bhaṅḍār

āsaṇ(u): (a) (n, m) an additional strip of cloth sewn into the crotch part of the garment to strengthen or enlarge that part, (b) (n, m; synonymous with 'baiṭṭhaṇ laī-' 'vastū', 'gaddī' or 'gaddā') a thick cotton mat or a padded sheet to sit on, (c) (n, m) one of the eighty-four Yogic postures, and implicit here is (d) (n, m; synonymous with 'tikāṇā') a base, resting place or abode.

loi: (a) (n, m; synonymous with 'log', 'jan' and 'lukāī') disciples, followers, devotees, or humanity, (b) (n, m; synonymous with 'prakāsh' and 'chānaṇ') glow, radiance or enlightenment, and implicit here is (c) (n, m; synonymous with 'lok', 'desh' and 'bhavan') literally, planets, worlds, continents or countries, and (d) (locative case - 'adhikaraṇ kārak'; synonymous with 'lok-' or 'bhavan-' 'vich') literally, in a continent, planet or galaxy. However, the reference here is not to the three ('tri-lok') or the seven worlds of Hindu and Islamic mythology but to the infinite number of planets in the whole universe.

loi loi: (locative case - 'adhikaraṇ kārak'; synonymous with 'har ik lok' or 'bhavan-' 'vich') literally, in every planet or world of this universe.

bhaṅḍār: (a) (n, m, pl; synonymous with 'bhaṅḍsāl', 'mālgudām', 'zakhīre' and 'khazāne') literally, stocks, treasures, repositories, or storehouses of tradeworthy goods, (b) (n, m, pl; synonymous with 'rasoī-'or 'laṅgar-' 'de samān dā khazānā') a place for the stockpiling of food items or a pantry; stockpiles of all the essential ingredients for survival, safe upkeep and general wellbeing.

āsaṇ(u) loi loi: literally, His dwelling is in every planet of every world or universe. In 'Āsā dī Vār', Gurū Nānak emphatically states:

'The self-existent God manifested Himself into 'Nām(u)'; He then created the world, permeated it and revealed Himself in His Creation.[33]

āsaṇ(u) bhaṅdār: the safe and secure placement of stockpiles of all the essential ingredients for survival, safe upkeep, and sustained orderliness. This was indeed an essential pre-condition for any evolving process and was certainly not overlooked by God, as the following verses from the SGGS state:

'Why fret and fuss when God Himself is committed to sustaining all His creation?' O' my *Man*. Was sustenance not provided for all creatures prior to their creation amidst rocks?'[464]

'You first assured the provision of sustenance and then created the life form dependent upon it. There is no one as mighty and great as You are, O' Lord, and no one comes close to being Your rival'.[465]

He established His presence and created stockpiles of everything essential for everyone and everywhere in every planet in the universe.

Jo kichh(u) pāiā su ekā vār

jo: (pron and adj; synonymous with 'jihṛā' or 'jis nūṅ') that, what, who, whoever, whosoever or whatever.

kichh(u): (a) (pron; synonymous with 'koī ik') something or someone, (b) (adj, m, s; synonymous with 'kiṅchit', 'thoṛā' or 'tanik') small in quantity, meagre, or inadequate, and implicit here is (c) (adj, m, s; synonymous with 'kuchh(u)' and 'kujh(u)') something or anything.

pāiā: (v, s, present perfect tense, first/third person; synonymous with 'hāsal or prāpat kītā'; 'khaṭṭiā'; 'pahniā'; 'milāiā' or 'pā dittā hai'; 'anubhav kītā hai'- has achieved; gained; worn; added, poured, or put; realised or perceived respectively) see pāuṇā (d (i)).

su: (pron and adj; synonymous with 'so', 'uh' or 'ohī') that, he, or she.

ekā: (a) (n; synonymous with 'saṅkhya bodhak - aṅg 1') one, (b) (n, m; synonymous with 'adutī ik' or 'kartār') literally, creator God, and implicit here is (c) (adj, f or m; synonymous with 'keval iko', 'ikallī' or 'ikallā' and 'iko ik') literally, the only one or the one and only.

vār: (n, f; synonymous with 'daphā', 'ber' or 'vārī') counter or number of times.

eko vār: literally, just once or once and for all. However, implicit here is that His repositories or stockpiles are inexhaustible ('akhuṭ(u)'), a view supported by the following verse from the SGGS:

Notwithstanding the amount we consume, His treasures are inexhaustible.[466]

Whatever is there was put there just once and for all.

Kar(i) kar(i) vekhai sirjaṇhār(u)

kar(i) kar(i): (indeclinable past participle or perfect participle - 'pūran pūrab kārdaṅtak'; synonymous with 'kar kar ke') having created. See karnā (b and g).

vekhai: (v, s, present tense, third person; synonymous with 'vekhdā hai' and 'dekh bhāl' or 'saṅbhāl kardā hai'; pronounced as 'vekhaiṅ') literally, cares, supports and sustains. See vekhṇā (g).

In essence, the reference here is to His Divine Order which extends to creation, its preservation and safeguard, adjudication, and guidance and direction.

sirjaṇhār(u): (n and adj, m, s; 'kartarī-vāchak kirdaṅt'; synonymous with 'kartā', 'kartār' and 'rachanhār') -

(a) a complex word comprising 'sirjaṇā' (v; synonymous with 'paidā karnā', 'baṇāuṇā' and 'rachnā' - to create, construct or produce) + 'hār' (synonymous with 'vaṅt', 'vān' and 'vālā'- one who carries out the relevant function of the verb) i.e., the Creator, and

(b) a complex word comprising 'sirjaṇā' (n; synonymous with 'sirjanā' or 'rachnā' - creation) + 'hār' (synonymous with 'vaṅt', 'vān' and 'vālā' -

one who possesses the attributes hidden in or related to the noun and carries out that action.

He creates and, having created, nurtures and cares for His Creation.

Nānak sache kī sāchī kār

Nānak: (n, m, s) the (u) of 'Nānak(u)' is missing because of its vocative case - 'saṅbodhan kārak'.

sache: (n, m, s; synonymous with 'sadīvī Prabhū') the Eternal Lord. When a noun that ends with 'ā' ('ʇ' or 'kaṅnnā') is followed by a preposition, its 'kaṅnnā' is replaced with a '͡' ('lām') represented here with 'e', e.g., 'sachā + kī' becomes 'sache kī'.

kī: (prep, f; synonymous with 'dī') of or belonging to. sāchī: (adj, f) (a) (synonymous with 'nirmal' and 'pavitr') pure or immaculate, and implicit here is (b) (synonymous with 'sadīvī' and 'aṭal') eternal, (c) (synonymous with 'uttam', 'ukāī rahit' or 'saṅpan') perfect, and (d) (synonymous with 'hukam baṅdh') conforming to or in harmony with 'Nām(u)'.

kār: (a) (n, m; synonymous with 'kaṅm') work, job, or an action, and (b) (n, m; synonymous with 'karanyog kaṅm') worthwhile or useful work, job, or action.

The following verses from the SGGS endorse the latent sentiments in this verse:

His Grace, whose creation is perfect in every way, forever bears fruit. He who is eternal and is the fount of everything, creates everything that is perfect.[467]

He, whose creation is perfect, is eternal, immaculate, omnipotent, and omniscient.[468]

'The deeds of the eternal One are flawless and perfect', O' Nānak!

Ādes(u) tisai ādes(u). See 'Pauṛī' 28.
Ād(i) anīl anād(i) anāhat(i) jug(u) jug(u) eko ves(u). See 'Pauṛī' 28.

Conceptual summary

He pervades everything and ensures that the essential and relevant existential support and systems exist on every planet.

Whatever was deemed essential was put there once and for all. He creates, and having created, nurtures and cares for His creation. According to Gurū Nānak, the deeds of the eternal One are forever flawless and perfect.

Gurū Nānak, therefore, humbly bows in deference and submits only unto Him, who existed before the beginning of time, is immaculate, has no beginning, is eternal, and has remained unchanged since the beginning of time.

In conclusion, His creation and its constitutive parts are infinite. His Divine Order sustains, supports and safeguards the survival and wellbeing of all created beings without any fear or favour and ensures inexhaustible means to this end, too.

PAUṚĪ 32
ਪਉੜੀ ੩੨॥

Ik dū jībhau lakh hoh(i), lakh hovah(i) lakh vīs.
ਇਕ ਦੂ ਜੀਭੌ ਲਖ ਹੋਹਿ, ਲਖ ਹੋਵਹਿ ਲਖ ਵੀਸ॥

Lakh(u) lakh(u) geṛā ākhīah(i), ek(u) nām jagdīs.
ਲਖੁ ਲਖੁ ਗੇੜਾ ਆਖੀਅਹਿ, ਏਕੁ ਨਾਮੁ ਜਗਦੀਸ॥

Et(u) rāh(i) pat(i) pavaṛīā, chaṛīai hoi ikīs.
ਏਤੁ ਰਾਹਿ ਪਤਿ ਪਵੜੀਆ, ਚੜੀਐ ਹੋਇ ਇਕੀਸ॥

Suṇ(i) galā ākās kī, kīṭā āī rīs.
ਸੁਣਿ ਗਲਾ ਆਕਾਸ ਕੀ, ਕੀਟਾ ਆਈ ਰੀਸ॥

Nānak nadrī pāīai, kūṛī kūṛai ṭhīs. (32)
ਨਾਨਕ ਨਦਰੀ ਪਾਈਐ, ਕੂੜੀ ਕੂੜੈ ਠੀਸ॥ ੩੨॥

Ik dū jībhau lakh hoh(i) lakh hovah(i) lakh vīs

ik: (adj) one, first of the 1-9 numerals.

dū: (a) (adj; synonymous with 'do', 'dūjā' or 'dūsrā') literally, two, second or another, (b) (adj; skt; synonymous with 'be-chain') restless, anxious, nervous, or worried, and implicit here is (c) (suff and prep; synonymous with 'se', 'toṅ' or 'koloṅ') literally, from.

ik dū: (locative case - 'adhikaraṇ kārak'; synonymous with 'ik dūsre toṅ' or 'ik toṅ'), literally, from one or one from another.

jībhau: (ablative case - 'apādān kārak'; synonymous with 'jībh toṅ'; pronounced as 'jībhauṅ') literally, from one's tongue or of one's tongue. see jībh.

jībh: (n, f; synonymous with 'rasnā', 'jihbā' or 'zubān') literally, tongue.

lakh: (adj, pl) many 1 x 10^5.

hoh(i): (a) (v, s, present tense, second person; synonymous with 'huṅdā hai'; pronounced as 'hoiṅ') see hoṇā, and implicit here is (b) (v, pl, imperative mood - 'saṅbhāv bhvikht kāl, third person; synonymous with 'hovaṇ', 'hoṇ' or 'ho jāṇ') happen, come about or befall; were to happen or occur. See hovṇā/hoṇā (a).

hovah(i): (a) (v, pl, present tense, third person; synonymous with 'uh huṅde han', 'uh ho jāṅde han' or 'uh ho jāṅdīaṅ han'; pronounced as ‘hovaheṅ’), and implicit here is (b) (imperative mood - ‘saṅbhāv bhvikht kāl - kiās, sharat and ichhā bodhak’; synonymous with ‘ho jāṇ’; pronounced as ‘hovaheṅ’) see hovṇā/hoṇā (a).

vīs: (adj; synonymous with ‘vīh’) literally, twenty.

lakh vīs: (adj; synonymous with ‘vīh lakh’) literally, 20 x 10^5.

If one tongue were to become one hundred thousand tongues, and if this number were then to increase by another twentyfold.

Lakh(u) lakh(u) geṛā ākhīah(i) ek(u) nām jagdīs

geṛā: (a) (n, m, s; synonymous with ‘chaurāsi dā chakkar’) the mythological figure of 84 x 10^5 forms of life forms that complete the cycle of birth and death (‘Āvāgavan’), and implicit here is (b) (n, m; synonymous with ‘pherā’, ‘ghumāu’ and ‘golākār chakar’) a circuit, a round trip, and (c) (synonymous with ‘daphā’ and ‘vār’) [a given number of] times, turns or chances.

ākhīah(i): (a) (v, s, present tense, second person; synonymous with ‘tuṅ ākhdā haiṅ’ or ‘tusīṅ ākhde ho’), (b) (v, pl, future tense, third person; synonymous with ‘uh ākhaṇge’), (c) (v, pl, present tense, third person; synonymous with ‘uh ākhde han’), and implicit here is (d) (v, pl, imperative mood - ‘saṅbhāv bhvikht kāl - kiās and sharat bodhak’, third person; synonymous with ‘akhe jāṇ’ or ‘ākhiā jāve’) see ākhṇā or kahiṇā.

lakh lakh geṛā ākhīah(i): literally, [if one] were then to say it a hundred thousand times.

ek(u): (adv; synonymous with ‘siraph-’ or ‘keval-’ ‘ik’) only, merely, just, or simply.

nām: (n, m, s) literally, a name. In essence, that which relates to and characterises an object, a place, or a being.

jagdīs: (n, m; synonymous with ‘jagdīsh’ and ‘jagat dā īsh’; pronounced as ‘jagdīsh’) compound word comprising ‘jag’ or ‘jagat’ (world) + ‘īsh’ (abbreviation for ‘īshvar’, God) i.e., Lord of the World.

ek(u) nām jagdīs: literally, just the one name of the Lord. The tacit reference here is to: (a) merely mechanical repetition, without any concomitant change towards or re-alignment with ‘Nām-consciousness’, and (b) one’s preconceived conceitedness and arrogance in being judged worthy of that ultimate reward of God-realisation. However, it is humility, willing and unreserved surrender to the Divine Word and Wisdom, and commitment to living by His Will that gets noticed and makes one worthy of His Grace, the cornerstone of every successful act.

If each one of them were then merely to utter the one name of the Lord hundreds of thousands of times [one would still not be able to realise God].

Et(u) rāh(i) pat(i) pavaṛīā chaṛīai hoi ikīs

et(u): (a) (adj and adv, m; synonymous with 'itnā' and 'ainā') literally, so much or this much, and implicit here is (b) (pron; synonymous with 'is') literally, this.

rāh(i): (locative case - 'adhikaraṇ kārak'; synonymous with 'raste vich' and 'raste uppar') see rāh(u).

rāh(u): (n, m; synonymous with 'mārag', 'rastā' and 'paṅth') literally, the way or path. However, implicit here is the moral, ethical and spiritual path that leads to 'Nām-realisation'.

et(u) rāh(i): literally, on this path, i.e., the path to perfect alignment with God or 'Nām-consciousness'.

pat(i): (a) (n, m; synonymous with 'bhartā', 'patī' and 'khāvaṅd') husband, and (b) n, m; synonymous with 'swāmī' and 'mālik') Lord or Master. See pat(i).

pavaṛīā: (n, f, pl; synonymous with 'pauṛīāṅ'; pronounced as 'pavaṛīāṅ') steps of a ladder. See pauṛī.

pauṛī: (a) (n, f) a stanza ('chhaṅd') of a particular style of poetic writing, especially associated with depicting and narrating the noble attributes of warriors, valour and chivalry, (b) (n, f; synonymous with 'padvī' and 'maṅzil') a rank or status in a hierarchical structure; the ultimate goal, and implicit here is (c) (n, f, s; synonymous with 'ārohaṇ' and 'sīṛī') a ladder.

et(u) rāh(i) pat(i) pavaṛīā: literally, the steps to perfect alignment with 'Nām-consciousness'.

chaṛīai: (a) (v, s, present tense, second person; synonymous with 'tūṅ chaṛdā haiṅ' or 'tusīṅ chaṛde ho'), (b) (imperative mood - 'saṅbhāv bhvikht kāl - kiās, sharat, ichhā or bevasī bodhak', s, third/first person; synonymous with 'chaṛ jā-ī-e' or 'chaṛ jāṇā chāhīdā hai'), and implicit here is (c) (v, s, present tense, third person; synonymous with 'chaṛiā jāṅdā hai' and chaṛiā jā sakdā hai') see chaṛnā (a).

chaṛnā: (v) (a) (synonymous with 'uppar val jāṇā') to go up, rise, climb, or ascend, (b) (synonymous with 'savār hoṇā') to board, ride or mount, (c) (synonymous with 'chaṛāī kar jāṇā' and 'parlok-gaman karnā') to decease or die, and (d) (synonymous with 'vairī uppar chaṛāī karnā', 'dhāvā bolṇā' and 'hallā karnā') to attack, ascend upon or invade.

hoi: (indeclinable past participle or perfect participle - 'pūran pūrab kārdaṅtak'; synonymous with 'ho ke') having become or having been. See hoṇā (a).

ikīs: (a) (adj; pronounced as 'ikkīs') literally, twenty one, (b) (n, f; synonymous with 'ikīh' and 'parmātmāṅ') the Primal Soul, [the sages have ascribed the whole universe or 'Māyāvī Saṅsār' as 'vīh', 'bīs' or 'bīs bisve', and the stage beyond as 'ikīh', 'turīā pad' or the Primal Soul, and (c) (n, m; synonymous with 'ik-īsh' and 'ik-īshvar') a complex word comprising 'ik' (One) + 'īs' (abbrev for 'īsh' or 'īshvar' - God) i.e., the One God.

chaṛīai hoi ikīs: literally, one climbs or ascends by gradually aligning perfectly with 'Nām(u)' or becoming Godlike. The reference here is to losing or shedding, gradually, the baggage of one's 'Haumaiṅ', 'Moh' and innate evil 'Vikārī' tendencies leading steadily to perfect harmony with 'Nām-consciousness' which then permits the full glow or manifestation of the Primal Soul within one's Hirdā. One's conscious self ('*Man*' or 'Jīvātmāṅ') then becomes the true image of 'Parmātmāṅ' (the Primal Soul). This contrasts with the ritualistic or mechanical methodology alluded to above. Both these aspects are emphasised in the following verses from the SGGS:

We are good at talking but exhibit disgraceful conduct. Physically we appear whiter than white but are deceitful and depraved from within.[469]

The filth of 'Haumaiṅ' and innate 'Vikārī' tendencies in one's conscious self are cleansed by one's focus on and contemplation of 'Nām(u)'.[470]

The filth in one's innate nature comes off with singing His Praise and abiding by His Will. Thus, one's inflated ego and erroneous belief of an independent existence, the all-consuming poison, vanishes.[94]

By submitting to the Guru's Divine Wisdom, one contemplates the Lord, aligns perfectly with 'Nām(u)' and lives by it, body and soul, says Nānak.[471]

'Why do you, Nāmdev, bewitched by māiā, continue to print sheets and not contemplate 'Nām(u)'? asks Trilochan. O' Trilochan, work with your hands and feet and utter His Glory with your tongue but remain focused on 'Nām(u)'', says Nāmdev.[472]

Just as one buys paper, cuts out a kite and flies it across the skies while chatting with friends but remains focused on the string that controls it, similarly, my '*Man*', having aligned perfectly with 'Nām(u)', is now focussed on it like that of a goldsmith chatting with customers whilst remaining sharply focused on gently fashioning his creation.[5]

One advances towards one's goal of 'Nām-realisation' by gradually shedding one's 'Haumaiṅ' and becoming increasingly aligned to 'Nām(u)' and Godlike.

Suṇ(i) galā ākās kī kīṭāāī rīs

suṇ(i): (indeclinable past participle or perfect participle - 'pūran pūrab kārdaṅtak'; synonymous with 'suṇ ke') literally, by listening to, upon hearing or having heard. See suṇanā.

suṇanā: (v) literally, to hear or listen attentively with one's ears; to pay heed or attention to.

galā: (n, f, pl; pronounced as 'gallāṅ') literally, chit chat, stories or message. However, implicit here is that others talk about the lasting inner equipoise ('Sahaj'), bliss ('Anaṅd'), the stage of 'Nām-realisation' and deliverance from 'Āvāgavan' but overlook the pre-condition of submission to the Gurū's Divine Word and Message and the uphill struggle that one has to engage in to achieve this goal. See gal.

gal: (a) (n, m; synonymous with 'kaṅṭh') literally, the throat or a part of the neck, and implicit here is (b) (n, f, s; synonymous with 'galbāt' and 'guphat-gū') chitchat, dialogue, or general conversation.

ākās: (a) (adj; synonymous with 'uchā pad') high rank, position, or status, (b) (n, m; synonymous with 'swarg' and 'suarg') heavens or 'dev-lok', and implicit here is (c) (n, m; synonymous with 'āsmān' and 'aṅbar'; pronounced as 'ākāsh') literally, the sky, the firmament or the heavens. However, the reference here is to lasting inner peace ('Sahaj') and bliss ('Anaṅd'), the peaceful and contented life in a mythological heaven ('swarg').

kī: (prep, f; synonymous with 'dī') of or belonging to.

suṇ(i) galā ākās kī: literally, on hearing of (a) the praise of the heavenly abodes, and (b) the praise or glory of those who have reached these lofty heights. In essence, on hearing the glory of those who have aligned perfectly with 'Nām(u)'.

kīṭā: (accusative case - 'karam kārak'; synonymous with 'kīṭāṅ nūṅ'; pronounced as 'kīṭāṅ') literally, to small, and lowly crawling creatures.

However, implicit here is: to those who are lowly or engrossed and entrapped in 'Māyā' and who resort to the seemingly easier but ritualistic and imperfect ways of achieving the goal of lasting equanimity ('Sahaj') and inner bliss ('Anaṅd'). See kīṭ (b).

kīṭ: (a) (n, m, s; synonymous with 'kīṛā' and 'kiram') a worm, a microbe, an ant, or a pest, and (b) (adj; synonymous with 'tuchh', 'adnā', 'nīch' and 'kamīnā') literally, lowly, worthless, insignificant, mean or of low caste. In essence, the reference here is to the ignorant, rapt by the material world and trapped in it, and engaged in sham acts of worship and evil deeds.

āī: (a) (v, f, s, present tense, third person; synonymous with 'āuṅdī- 'or 'janam laindī-' 'hai'; 'ā jāṅdī hai'), and (b) (v, f, s, present perfect tense; synonymous with 'ā gaī hai') see auṇā (a).

rīs: (n, f) (a) (synonymous with 'brābarī' and 'tulnā') equivalence or parity, and (b) (synonymous with 'nakal', 'anusāran', 'anukaran' and 'rashak' (pers)) literally, emulation, imitation, or copy. The tacit reference here is to copying and blindly following others in mere mechanical chanting but without the concomitant shedding of one's 'Haumaiṅ' or any progress towards alignment with 'Nām-consciousness'. The sham and dishonest are forever wishful of striking lucky but never keen to put in the hard graft, as emphasised in the following verse from the SGGS:

Hordes follow the way of the 'Paṅḍits' but only Kabīr engages in this uphill struggle en route to 'Nām-realisation'.[474]

On hearing of the exaltations of His true 'bhagats', even the ignorant, rapt, and trapped in the material world, are aroused to imitate.

Nānak nadrī pāīai kūṛī kūṛai ṭhīs

Nānak: (n, m, s) the (u) of 'Nānak(u)' is missing because of its vocative case - 'saṅbodhan kārak'.

nadrī: (instrumental case - 'karaṇ kārak'; synonymous with 'mehar dī nadar nāl' and 'kripā drisṭ(i) sadkā'; pronounced as 'nadrīṅ') through His Grace or Mercy. Loving, willing and completely unreserved surrender to His Will and perfect alignment with 'Nam-consciousness' is the way to His Grace or Mercy and not the outwardly, self-imposed, strict religious worship and austerities.

pāīai: (a) (v, pl; present tense, imperative mood - 'hukmī bhvikht', first person; synonymous with 'pāiā jā sakīdā 'hai'; 'prāpat karnā chāhīdā hai'), and implicit here is (b) (v, s, present tense, third person; synonymous with 'pā laīdā hai' and 'prāpat kar laīdā hai') see pāuṇā (a).

kūṛī: (a) (adj, f; synonymous with 'kūṛ vālā', 'jhūṭhā', 'chhalīā' and 'pākhaṅḍī') a cheat, a charmer, untruthful or dishonest, and implicit here is (b) (adj; synonymous with 'jhūṭhī') baseless, fake, sham and disingenuous.

kūṛai: (genitive case - 'saṅbaṅdh kārak'; synonymous with 'kūṛe manukh dī') of a 'kūṛ' or 'kūṛā manukh'.

kūṛā: (adj, m; synonymous with 'jhūṭhā') fake, phoney, sham, liar or dishonest.

ṭhīs: (a) (n, f; synonymous with 'chiṅtā' or 'phikar') anxiety, concern, apprehension, or misgiving, (b) (n, f; synonymous with 'choṭ', 'saṭ' and 'sadmā') hurt, injury, strike, a blow or a whack; trauma, shock or a mental blow, and implicit here is (c) (n, f; synonymous with 'shekhī', 'ḍīng', 'phaṛ' and 'gapp') rumour, gossip, bunkum, poppycock or a vain boast.

kūṛī ṭhīs: (n, f, s; synonymous with 'jhūṭhī gapp') literally, a false rumour.

[However, they need to realise that] 'His Grace alone is the route to His realisation; the rest is just the vain boast of a liar', O' Nānak!

Conceptual summary

If one tongue were to become one hundred thousand tongues, and if (a) if this were then to increase by another twentyfold, and (b) if each one of them were then merely to utter the one name of the Lord hundreds of thousands of times, one would still not be able to achieve 'Sahaj', 'Anaṅd' or realisation of God within one's 'Hirdā'. In reality, one advances towards perfect alignment with 'Nām(u)' by gradually shedding one's 'Haumaiṅ' and increasingly becoming Godlike.

However, not unsurprisingly and in complete contrast, on hearing the exaltations of His true 'bhagats', even the naïve and ignorant, rapt by the material world and trapped in it, are aroused merely to imitate.

'His Grace alone is the route to His realisation; the rest is just the vain boast of a liar', O' Nānak!

The stark reality is that, misguided and driven to satisfy one's insatiable desire for the material world, its comforts and pleasures, one gets entrapped and sucked deeper and deeper into the web of 'Moh' and 'Māyā', and experiences immense inner turbulence and suffering. In contrast, when one hears about the lasting inner state of equipoise or bliss of His true devotees, aligned perfectly to 'Nām-consciousness' and living by His Will, one is naturally attracted towards that goal but, without the initial willing and unreserved surrender to the Gurū's Will, and dedication and commitment thereafter, one falls for the rituals, the easy way out, rather than the more arduous but true path to 'Nām-consciousness'.

Willing and loving surrender to the Gurū's Divine Word and Message, and a genuine inner struggle to live by God's Will, is the only way to find His Grace. Only thus, does one achieve lasting inner equipoise and bliss, and perceive the full glow of 'Nām(u)' within one's 'Hirdā'.

PAURĪ 33
ਪਉੜੀ ੩੩॥

Ākhaṇ(i) jor(u), chupai nah jor(u).
ਆਖਣਿ ਜੋਰੁ, ਚੁਪੈ ਨਹ ਜੋਰੁ॥

Jor(u) n maṅgaṇ(i), deṇ(i) n jor(u).
ਜੋਰੁ ਨ ਮੰਗਣਿ, ਦੇਣਿ ਨ ਜੋਰੁ॥

Jor(u) n jīvaṇ(i), maraṇ(i) n jor(u).
ਜੋਰੁ ਨ ਜੀਵਣਿ, ਮਰਣਿ ਨਹ ਜੋਰੁ॥

Jor(u) n rāj(i), māl(i), *man*(i) sor(u).
ਜੋਰੁ ਨ ਰਾਜਿ, ਮਾਲਿ, ਮਨਿ ਸੋਰੁ॥

Jor(u) n surtī, giān(i) vīchar(i).
ਜੋਰੁ ਨ ਸੁਰਤੀ, ਗਿਆਨਿ ਵੀਚਾਰਿ॥

Jor(u) n jugatī, chhuṭai saṅsār.
ਜੋਰੁ ਨ ਜੁਗਤੀ, ਛੁਟੈ ਸੰਸਾਰੁ॥

Jis(u) hath(i) jor(u), kar(i) vekhai soi.
ਜਿਸੁ ਹਥਿ ਜੋਰੁ, ਕਰਿ ਵੇਖੈ ਸੋਇ॥

Nānak, utam(u), nīch n koi. (33)
ਨਾਨਕ, ਉਤਮੁ, ਨੀਚੁ ਨ ਕੋਇ॥ ੩੩॥

The Primal Soul ('Parmātmāṅ' or 'Nām(u)', the immanent form of God), pervades all and is an integral part of all inanimate elements and living beings. The degree of expression and autonomy, or free will, which it imparts increases with the increasing complexity of non-sentient and sentient life; its most expressive form, with the greatest degree of free will, is operative in humans.

'Parmātmāṅ' gives rise to a centre of consciousness as it interacts and expresses itself in the body. This centre of consciousness is the unique 'self' or 'I' which, using the body as a mere tool, enables the 'self' to interact with the world outside. Such a centre of consciousness, with a degree of autonomy or free will, is an absolute pre-requisite for the survival of each living being and for their adaptation to a changing environment, and, as such, it serves both as their guardian and guide.

Whilst God Himself apportions uniquely different 'Haumaiṅ', 'Moh', innate nature and free will to inanimate and sentient life and creates diversity right at the outset, any subsequent change in their characteristics is directly and purely due to their unique interactions with the surrounding material world and their impressions of it.

At present, we consider the deployment of this centre of consciousness purely for the fulfilment of our own self-interest and with total disregard for everything else in this eco-system as egotistic and one's consciousness as ego-consciousness. However, Gurmat regards this as the deviant and default operative state when one considers oneself to have an independent existence, independent not only of other inanimate and sentient life forms but also of God and His Divine Order. Such a state of ego-consciousness, coupled with this malady, is 'Haumaiṅ' in Gurmat, and the expression of 'Parmātmāṅ' in such a being is 'Jīvātmāṅ' (conscious self, '*Man*' or 'Hirdā').

Gurū Nānak propounds that the vast diversity that exists in human beings, in its physical form as well as its intellectual prowess and moral and spiritual ability, is due to the inherent differences in the endowed 'Haumaiṅ', 'Moh', innate 'Vikārī' tendencies [altogether our innate nature] because of our erstwhile 'Sanskārs'. Indeed, it is these 'Sanskārs' which become an obstacle in the complete manifestation of the Primal Soul.

The conscious self ('*Man*', 'Hirdā' or 'Jīvātmāṅ') is thus a partial and distorted manifestation of the Primal Soul. This leads to the erroneous perception that one's self harbours a unique persona and innate nature with inimitable innate drives and tendencies. Our fate or destiny, from the present moment onwards, is thus determined on the basis of our past 'Karmā'; this forms the basis of our innate nature, drives and tendencies, our ability, capacity, and potential, and the coming together or parting of objects, beings and events ('saṅjogs' and 'vijogs') which play a role in the realisation or otherwise of our potential ('mastak de lekh').

Our innate nature, drives and tendencies, spontaneously and automatically, and sometimes against our better judgement, indulge us in thoughts, speech and actions that we subsequently come to regret, as highlighted in the various verses of this 'Pauṛī'. Furthermore, undue, and unjust pride in personal ability and strength encourages egoism, generates egotism, destroys inner equanimity and peace, and becomes an impediment to general deliberation and learning. In addition, an egotist is likely to succumb to greed and the fulfilment of their own desires. The following verses of the SGGS explicate how intricately intertwined the relationship is between the Divine Order, our fate or destiny, our 'Sanskārs' and our innate nature:

The Lord binds humans to the bondage of our deeds; innate nature, secondary to our repeated thoughts and deeds ('sanskars'), drives us accordingly.[258]

He can not only do all Himself but can make the created beings do His bidding too. In the end, what He Wills happens.[475]

Say! 'What can one do by oneself'? In reality, what God Wills is what gets done. If it were in our control, we would grab it all for ourselves. In fact, we does exactly what God Wills.[476]

What can a wooden puppet do? Only the puppeteer who directs it from behind, knows. The puppeteer just brings it out, dressed suitably for the role he wants it to play.[477]

Ākhaṇ(i) jor(u) chupai nah jor(u)

ākhaṇ(i): (locative case - 'adhikaraṇ kārak'; synonymous with 'kahan-'or 'ākhaṇ-' 'vich'; 'bhāvārth kārdaṅtak') for the sake of stating or declaring; in stating or declaring. See ākhaṇ(i).

jor(u): (n, m; synonymous with 'vas'; pronounced as 'zor') authority, control or controlling power. See jor(u).

chupai: (pronounced as 'chupaiṅ') (locative case - 'adhikaraṇ kārak'; synonymous with 'chup rakhaṇ vich') in maintaining silence or remaining speechless. A certain sect of Yogīs observes and maintains a ritual of prolonged silence, especially with their eyes closed, to still their flirtatious ('chaṅchal') minds ('*Man*') with this exercise. See chupai, chup and chup rahiṇā.

nah: (p; pers; synonymous with 'nah(i)' (skt)) no, not or expressing a negative meaning. 'nah' operates here as 'dehlī dīpak' as it joins two parts of the sentence.

ākhaṇ(i) jor(u) nah: literally, I have no control or controlling power over what I say.

chupai nah jor(u): literally, I have no control or controlling power over when to remain silent.

'Bol(u) vigāṛ(u)' is a good example of this characteristic: see 'Pauṛī' 26, p. 321.

It is not within our controlling power to speak or remain silent.

Jor(u) n maṅgaṇ(i) deṇ(i) n jor(u)

n: (p; pronounced as 'nāṅ') no, not or implying a negative connotation.

maṅgaṇ(i): (infinitive mood - 'bhāvārth kārdaṅtak'; locative case - 'adhikaraṇ kārak'; synonymous with 'maṅgaṇ vich') literally, in asking, seeking or begging. See maṅgṇā. In reality, the act of asking, seeking, or begging for help exposes one's inadequacies and hurts one's ego; egocentricity will, therefore, deter someone from this act.

maṅgnā: (v; synonymous with 'maṅgṇā' and 'yāchnā karnī') literally, to ask, demand, borrow, request, seek or beg. However, implicit here is to plead, implore, beseech, or supplicate.

deṇ(i): (infinitive mood - 'bhāvārth kārdaṅtak'; locative case - 'adhikaraṇ kārak'; synonymous with 'deṇ vich') literally, in giving, offering, or donating. See deṇā (a and b). One who is prone to duality, 'Moh', 'Mamta', excessive greed and lacks contentment ('santokh') will find it difficult to donate or share. In contrast, the concepts of Unity in Diversity, the Fatherhood of God and Brotherhood of Man, shine through in this verse of the SGGS:

You are everywhere as You permeate all Your creation and are thus cognisant of all that is in the innermost parts of all beings. The bountiful and benevolent, and the destitute and beggars are the wondrous contrasts of Your creation. I see no other than You as the Benefactor and as the Receiver.[4]

It is not within our controlling power to ask for help or give help to the needy.

Jor(u) n jīvaṇ(i) maraṇ(i) n jor(u)

jīvaṇ(i): (infinitive mood - 'bhāvārth kārdaṅtak'; locative case - 'adhikaraṇ kārak'; synonymous with 'jīvaṇ vich') literally, in subsisting, surviving, or remaining alive. See jīvaṇā.

jīvaṇā: (v) (a) literally, to subsist, survive or live, and (b) to live morally, ethically, and spiritually; to live life in perfect harmony with 'Nām(u)-'or 'Unitary-' 'consciousness.'

maraṇ(i): (infinitive mood - 'bhāvārth kārdaṅtak'; locative case - 'adhikaraṇ kārak'; synonymous with 'maraṇ vich') literally, in dying spiritually and/or physically. See marnā.

marnā: (v; synonymous with 'marṇā') (a) (synonymous with 'dehāṅt; 'sarīrak maut- 'or 'mrityū-' 'ho jāṇī') to pass away, expire, decease or die physically, (b) (synonymous with 'jīvat marnā') to shed or lose completely the influence of 'Haumaiṅ', 'Moh' and 'Māyā', and (c) (synonymous with 'ātmak maut ho jāṇī') to suffer 'spiritual downfall or death' - literally, succumbing to the evil influence of Haumaiṅ', 'Moh' and 'Māyā' during one's lifetime. The following verses of the SGGS explicitly state how everything is governed by His Divine Order and falls within its scope:

His Divine Order governs one's birth and death; one is born or dies according to His Will'.[479]

One is born in this world, with death pre-recorded in one's destiny.[480]

We are born with a finite number of days and breaths, which neither increase nor decrease even by an iota. One who is lured by attachment to this empirical world and seeks long life, is a fool', O' Nānak.[481]

One has no control over the time and place of one's birth or death.

Jor(u) n rāj(i) māl(i) *man*(i) sor(u)

rāj(i): (locative case - 'adhikaraṇ kārak'; synonymous with 'rāj vich'. However, implicit here is 'rāj prāpat karan vich') literally, in acceding to the throne. However, the reference here is to in getting control, sway or power of government. See rāj.

rāj: (n, m) reign, dominion, sway, rule, or stately power.

māl(i): (locative case - 'adhikaraṇ kārak'; synonymous with 'māl-', 'milak-'or 'dhan-''vich'. However, implicit here is 'māl prāpat karan vich') literally, in amassing wealth, riches or assets. See māl.

māl: (n, m; arab; synonymous with 'dhan', 'daulat' and 'saṅpadā') wealth, riches, or assets (property and other possessions).

man(i): (locative case - 'adhikaraṇ kārak'; synonymous with '*man* vich') in one's '*man*'. See '*Man*'.

man: (n, m, s) one's conscious self, 'Hirdā' or 'Jīvātmāṅ'.

sor(u): (n, m, s; synonymous with 'shor', 'raulā', 'ḍaṅḍ' and 'phūṅ-phāṅ'; pronounced as 'shor' (skt)) literally, pride, self-conceit, haughtiness, vanity, or arrogance.

It is not within our control to gain stately power, riches, or excessive self-pride.

Jor(u) n surtī giān(i) vīchār(i)

surtī: (locative case - 'adhikaraṇ kārak'; synonymous with 'surat vich'; pronounced as 'surtīṅ) in focusing. In essence, it is 'ātmak jāg vich', i.e., in spiritual awakening or alertness. See surat(i).

giān(i): (locative case; synonymous with 'giān vich'. However, implicit here is 'giān prāpat karan vich') in acquiring spiritual knowledge and wisdom. See giān(u) (b and c).

vīchār(i): (locative case - 'adhikaraṇ kārak'; synonymous with 'vīchār karan vich') in deliberating or deducing. See vīchār(u) (e and f) and vīchārnā.

It is not within our control to be spiritually awakened and remain immersed in deliberation and Divine Wisdom.

Jor(u) n jugtī chhuṭai sansār(u)

jugtī: (locative case - 'adhikaraṇ kārak'; synonymous with 'jugat-' or 'rahit-' 'vich'; pronounced as 'jugtīṅ') in abiding by a particular order, code of conduct or 'Maryādā'. See jugat(i) (f). The reference here is to ritualistic acts which do not assist in shedding 'Haumaiṅ' and aligning perfectly with 'Nām(u)'.

chhuṭai: (a) (imperative mood - 'saṅbhāv bhvikht kāl - kiās, sharat, ichhā or bevasī bodhak', third/first person; synonymous with 'je chhuṭ jāīai'), and implicit here is (b) (v, s, present tense, third person; synonymous with 'muktī ho jāṅdī hai' or 'chhuṭkārā ho jāṅdā hai') see chhūṭṇā.

chhuṭṇā: (v, synonymous with 'chhūṭṇā') to break loose, extricate or escape. However, implicit here is to find release, liberation, or emancipation from 'Haumaiṅ', 'Moh' and innate 'vikārī' tendencies in this life and 'Āvāgavan' (cycle of birth and death) at death.

sansār(u): (a) (n, m; synonymous with 'jagat', 'jahān' and 'dunīā') literally, the ever-changing empirical world, (b) (n, f; synonymous with 'sansār de log' and 'lukāī' or 'lokāī') the whole of humanity, and implicit here is (c) (n, f; synonymous with 'Māyā') literally, anything that leads one astray and away from 'Nam-consciousness', and (d) (n, m; synonymous with 'Āvāgavan') the cycle of transmigration.

chhuṭai sansār(u): literally, one extricates oneself from the clutches of 'Haumaiṅ', 'Moh' and innate 'vikārī' tendencies in this life and 'Āvāgavan' (cycle of birth and death) at death. Our inadequacies, 'vikārī' tendencies and 'Haumaiṅ', the chronic disease, become the obstacles and render this beyond our scope. The following verses from the SGGS clearly outline the way out:

No one achieves all the noble virtues, austerities, noble deeds, and miraculous powers of Sidhas without You.[482]

Release from 'Māyā' and 'Āvāgavan', the cycle of transmigration, is only by Your Decree. See Pauri 25, pp. 300-1.

It is not within our control to find release from the clutch of 'Māyā' and 'Āvāgavan', the cycle of transmigration.

Jis(u) hath(i) jor(u) kar(i) vekhai soi

jis(u): (a) (pron, s) who, whom, whosoever, whomsoever or that, and implicit here is (b) (genitive case - 'saṅbaṅdh kārak'; synonymous with 'jis de/dā') literally, whose.

hath(i): (locative case - 'adhikaraṇ kārak'; synonymous with 'hath vich') literally, in one's hands. However, implicit here is: within one's control or power. See hath.

hath: (n, m, pl; synonymous with 'hāth', 'kar', 'dast' and 'pāṇ(i)') literally, hands.

Jis(u) hath(i): literally, in whose hands. However, implicit here is that it is in God's hands.

kar(i): (indeclinable past participle or perfect participle - 'pūran pūrab kārdaṅtak'; synomymous with 'kar ke') having done or having carried out an act. See karnā (g).

vekhai: (v, s, present tense, third person; synonymous with 'dekh bhāl-' or 'saṅbhāl-' 'kardā hai'; pronounced as 'vekhaiṅ') literally, cares, maintains, guards, and protects.) see vekhṇā (g).

soi: (pron and adj; synonymous with 'oh' or 'ohī') literally, he or she. In essence, the same who holds or wields power, i.e., God. See soi.

He who has the ultimate authority and power, creates and watches over the creation in action.

Nānak utam(u) nīch n koi

Nānak: (n, m, s) the (u) of 'Nānak(u)' is missing because of its vocative case - 'saṅbodhan kārak'.

utam(u): (adj; synonymous with 'ūttam', 'at(i) chaṅgā', 'sabh toṅ chaṅgā' and 'sreshṭ'; pronounced as 'uttam') par excellence, superlative, perfect, ideal, or best.

nīch: (a) (n; synonymous with 'gulām' and 'dās') a slave or a humble servant, (b) (adj; synonymous with 'karam kar ke nīvāṅ' or 'kāmā'; 'jāt(i) kar ke nīvāṅ') low in terms of a feudal or social class system, or a 'Shūdra' of the Hindu caste system, (c) (adj; synonymous with 'nimāṇā', 'nitāṇā', 'nāchīz' and 'guṇhīn') low in terms of livelihood, ability, nobility and virtues, i.e., one who undertakes a lowly, menial job; one who is mean, miserly, callous or spiteful, or has innate evil tendencies, and implicit here is (d) lowly, lacking virtues or good attributes.

utam(u) nīch n koi: literally, none is either high or low, noble or ignoble, and Lord Master or serf [by one's choice or efforts]. This would only be true if this were within our scope. The reality is that our destiny rests within the constraints of His judgement of our Karmā or 'Saṅskārs' and it is His judgement that confers what is apportioned to us as our 'bhāg' or 'mastak de lekh' at birth.

It is the deeds one does, and not one's worldly honour, fame, or status, which earns one high or low rank in God's eyes. The ability, capacity, or potential to do anything is entirely due to His Gift. However, one must become worthy of His Grace to achieve this and ever greater heights in the worldly and/or spiritual sense. The key to His Grace is our rightful entitlement or deserving', for otherwise, the fount or the source of everything is within us as well, from the most nano to the most macro constituent of this creation. These sentiments are clearly expressed in the following verses of the SGGS:

'He holds and wields the power and enacts and dispenses noble attributes to whom He wills', says Nānak.[483-4]

You are the fount of all attributes, virtues, and values; whatever little I have, is due to You. See Pauṛī 21, pp. 254-5.

Everything is the Lord's manifestation, and nothing exists without Him.[485]

It is the Lord's spark ('Jīvātmāṅ') that speaks within all of us. Who else is it, save the Lord Himself, that speaks? [486]

'The Lord pervades the entire creation, and the creation is within Him. Who can then be labelled bad when nothing exists without His presence within?', asks Farīd.[487]

koi: (adj; synonymous with 'koī') any, some or certain.
n koi: literally, no one. See koi.

'No one is perfect or flawed by oneself', O' Nānak! Or
'No one is high or low by oneself or by social design', O' Nānak!

Conceptual summary

It is not within our control or power to speak or remain silent, to ask for help or to give help to the needy, to determine the time or place of our birth or death, to gain stately power, riches or egotism, to be spiritually awakened and remain immersed in deliberation and divine wisdom, or to find release from the grip of 'Māyā' in this life and from 'Āvāgavan', the cycle of transmigration, at death.

He, who wields the ultimate authority and power, creates, and watches over the creation in action. 'No one is perfect or flawed by one's own choice, O' Nānak!

Our conscious self, innate nature and being in this world is not of our choice or our birthright. Instead, God, according to His Will, grants us the package of attributes, virtues and values in the form of 'Haumain', 'Moh', innate 'Vikārī' tendencies and free will which translates into our physical being along with our abilities, virtues, good or bad proclivities, potential and fate or destiny in this world.

If we truly submit to the Gurū's Divine Word and Message, learn to focus on and to contemplate 'Nām(u)', shed the evil influence of 'Haumaiṅ', 'Moh' and evil 'Vikārī' tendencies, and begin to align perfectly with 'Nām-consciousness', we become worthy of His gracious glance ('nadar(i) karam'). In essence, it is the good deeds that one does, and His Grace, that makes one high or low in His eyes and not the high or low rank at birth.

PAUṚĪ 34
ਪਉੜੀ ੩੪॥

Rātī, rutī, thitī, vār.
ਰਾਤੀ, ਰੁਤੀ, ਥਿਤੀ, ਵਾਰ॥

Pavaṇ, pāṇī, agnī, pātāl.
ਪਵਣ, ਪਾਣੀ, ਅਗਨੀ, ਪਾਤਾਲ॥

Tis(u) vich(i) dhartī, thāp(i) rakhī dharamsāl.
ਤਿਸੁ ਵਿਚਿ ਧਰਤੀ, ਥਾਪਿ ਰਖੀ ਧਰਮ ਸਾਲ॥

Tis(u) vich(i), jīa jugat(i) ke raṅg.
ਤਿਸੁ ਵਿਚਿ, ਜੀਅ ਜੁਗਤਿ ਕੇ ਰੰਗ॥

Tin ke nām, anek anaṅt.
ਤਿਨ ਕੇ ਨਾਮ, ਅਨੇਕ ਅਨੰਤ॥

Karmī karmī, hoi vīchār.
ਕਰਮੀ ਕਰਮੀ, ਹੋਇ ਵੀਚਾਰੁ॥

Sachā āp(i), sachā darbār(u).
ਸਚਾ ਆਪਿ, ਸਚਾ ਦਰਬਾਰੁ॥

Tithai sohan(i), paṅch parvāṇ(u).
ਤਿਥੈ ਸੋਹਨਿ, ਪੰਚ ਪਰਵਾਣੁ॥

Nadrī karam(i), pavai nīsāṇ(u).
ਨਦਰੀ ਕਰਮਿ, ਪਵੈ ਨੀਸਾਣੁ॥

Kach pakāī, othai pāi.
ਕਚ ਪਕਾਈ, ਓਥੈ ਪਾਇ॥

Nānak, ga-i-ā jāpai jāi. (34)
ਨਾਨਕ, ਗਇਆ ਜਾਪੈ ਜਾਇ॥ ੩੪॥

'Dharam khaṅḍ' is the first of the five rungs of the ladder of spiritual evolution. 'Dharam' is (a) that which outlines and clearly defines the attributes of a Divine Order, (b) 'maryādā' that brings out clearly the way to freedom from 'Haumaiṅ', 'Moh', innate 'vikārī' tendencies and/or 'Āvāgavan' ('Moksh'), (c) the innate nature, duty or justice of Nature, (d) the Divine Word and Wisdom worth imbibing and aligning to, and (e) a system or Divine Order ('Hukam(u)') which governs the entire empirical world. In 'Pauṛī' 16, Gurū Nānak alludes to the Divine Order ('Dharam' or 'Hukam(u)') as being an offshoot of God's eternally compassionate nature which has established and maintained orderliness, stability and tranquillity ('saṅtokh(u)') by making everything abide by it unreservedly. Nothing is outside the scope of this Divine Order ('Dharam') and nothing escapes its justice.

This 'Pauṛī' outlines the following salient aspects of this stage: (a) the establishment of Earth, amidst the vastness of the empirical world, for humankind to demonstrate its willingness to abide by His Will, (b) judgement of our 'karams' (thoughts, speech and deeds) and the verdict based on their degree of alignment or otherwise with 'Nām-consciousness', (c) perfect alignment with 'Nām-consciousness' being His preferred state, and (d) His seal of approval ('Nisāṇ(u)') for those judged to be perfect. The following verses of the SGGS emphasise these aspects:

You have come to listen to and utter the Divine Word. Forsaking 'Nām(u)', you have entrenched yourself in the pleasures of the empirical world and are wasting this precious life.[488]

You have been blessed with this beautiful human body and this is your chance to harmonise with and realise 'Nām(u)'.[15]

O man, you have come to earn spiritual credit. What vain pursuits are you engaged in when finite available time is just slipping by?[489]

'Having created this diverse life form, God established 'dharam' to scrutinise and judge their deeds, O' Nānak. Whilst the righteous are judged pure, and honoured, the deviants and sinners are separated and incriminated at His Court'.[490]

One reaps what one sows and earns the fruits of one's actions.[491]

They who truly love Him with their hearts, are His true devotees; they whose actions differ from what's in their minds, are recognised as sham.[492]

Truth is supreme amongst virtues but higher still is truthful living.[493]

Our accumulated 'karmas' (thoughts, speech and actions) of this life are scrutinised and judged at His Court; good and bad 'karmas' are thus separated, and their balance forms the basis of His Verdict ('bhāg' or 'mastak de lekh').[494]

He governs by His Will and His pen writes His judgement based on our deeds.[495]

Rātī, rutī, thitī, vār

rātī: (a) (adj, f; synonymous with 'mast or magan') deeply absorbed or engrossed, (b) (adj; synonymous with 'rattī bhar' and 'tanik') a tiny or miniscule amount, (c) (adj, f; synonymous with 'prem vich raṅgī or 'lāl bhaī) steeped in or imbued with the symbolic deep red colour or dye of love - to be in perfect harmony with 'Nām(u)', (d) (synonymous with rāt nūṅ' or 'rāt de sameṅ; pronounced as 'rātīṅ') at night, and implicit here is (e) (n, f, pl; synonymous with 'rātāṅ'; pronounced as 'rātīṅ') literally, nights.

rutī: (n, f, pl of 'rut', 'rut(i)' and 'rit(i)'; synonymous with 'rut' and 'mausam'; pronounced as 'rutīṅ') the different seasons. See rut.

rut: (n, f, s; synonymous with 'mausam', 'rut(i)' and 'rit(i)' (skt)) a season.

thitī: (n, m, pl of and synonymous with 'tith(i)' and 'mit(i)'; pronounced as 'thitīṅ') literally, days ('thitāṅ') based on the lunar movement around the Earth. See thit(i) (b).

vār: (n, m pl; synonymous with 'din') days of the week based on the movement of Earth around the sun. The whole verse alludes to the establishment of the fourth dimension, the beginning of time. See vār.

Amidst nights, seasons, lunar dates, and days...

Pavaṇ, pāṇī, agnī, pātāl

pavaṇ: (n, f; synonymous with 'havā', 'vāyū', 'pavaṇ' and 'suās') air (mixture of different gases) or wind.

pāṇī: (n, m) (a) (synonymous with 'jal') literally, water, and (b) liquids.

agnī: (n, f; synonymous with 'agan(i)') literally, fire. In essence, energy - the very first of the five primordial aspects of creation - others being air (gases), water (liquids), Earth (dharat(i) - solids), and ākāsh (ether or space). Vedic scholars allude to three kinds: (i) 'dāvā agan(i)' - that which destroys forests or that which enables one to digest one's food, (ii) 'divya agan(i)' -energy in the form of lightening in the sky, and (iii) 'Jaṭhar agan(i)' - that which drives and maintains bodily functions and temperature. Gurmat alludes to its four sub-types in the body: (a) 'Trishnā/Lobh dī agan(i)', (b) 'Krodh dī agan(i)', (c) 'Kaṭhortā dī agan(i)' - the fire of mercilessness or indifference, and (d) 'Jaṭhar agan(i)' - the fire in the mother's body.

pātāl: (a) (n, m, pl) the worlds below planet Earth according to the Hindu belief of 'Trilok' ('dharat(i)', 'pātāl' below and 'swarg' above), (b) last of the seven worlds beneath planet Earth according to both Hindu and Islamic mythology, and implicit here is (c) (n, m) netherworlds, Hades, the underworld or the habitable worlds beneath planet Earth according to Hindu mythology. This dictates further claims that 'Pātāl' is for lesser human beings and some lower forms of life whilst 'Swarg' ('Heaven') is for 'Devīs', 'Devtās' and other beings of high moral character or of faith in their earlier life as humans on this Earth. Gurmat, however, does not give any credence to this ideology and, instead, infers that the term depicts the spatial orientation of a planet in relation to another above it.

The verse alludes to the five basic elements, the building blocks, essential for this diverse creation: air, water, fire/energy, Earth (mother of all elements and life) and ether/space. This concept is entirely consistent with the following verses of the SGGS:

He Himself causes the world to appear and evolve from the five basic elements into which He infuses His essence ('Ātmaṅ').[496]

You have created this vast empirical world from the five basic elements; let someone create a sixth element if one dares.[497]

...amidst gases, liquids, energies, and lower worlds...

Tis(u) vich(i) dhartī, thāp(i) rakhī dharamsāl

tis(u): (pron and adj; synonymous with 'us') literally, he, she, or that.

vich(i): (prep; synonymous with 'bīch', 'bhītar', 'aṅdar' and 'vichkār') within, inside or in the midst.

dhartī: (n, f; synonymous with 'prithvī', 'dharat(i)', 'zamīn' or 'bhumī') the planet Earth.

thāp(i): (indeclinable past participle or perfect participle - 'pūran pūrab kārdaṅtak'; synonymous with 'thāp ke') having lovingly and securely installed and stationed. See thāpṇā.

rakhī: (v, present perfect; third person; synonymous with 'rākhī') (a) (synonymous with 'bachāī' and 'rakhyā- 'or 'hiphāzat-' 'kītī') guarded, saved, or protected, and (b) (synonymous with 'ṭikāī' and 'ṭikā dittī') literally, placed or installed. See rakhṇā (c).

dharamsāl: (n, f) (a) (synonymous with 'musāpharāṅ laī muphat nivās') free rest house for travellers, (b) (synonymous with 'dharam asthān') a place of worship for Sikhs where the needy get food and a place to rest, and implicit here is (b) a complex word comprising 'dharam' + 'sāl'('sālā' or 'shālā' - a house/place; synonymous with 'dharam kamāuṇ dī thāṅ') a place where one learns and then strives to live by the Will of God. See dharam.

The following verse of the SGGS beautifully captures our purpose in life in this world:

Vegetation flowers in order to bear fruit and, at fruition, flowers just vanish. Similarly, our daily struggle revolves around survival and through it we seek eternal knowledge for lasting bliss. Once enlightened, the need for purely worldly gain just disappears.[498]

The Earth is safely and securely established to serve as a place for learning to live by the Will of God.

Tis(u) vich(i), jīa jugat(i) ke raṅg

jīa: (n, pl; synonymous with 'jīv') all sentient beings.

jugat(i): (n, m; synonymous with 'rahiṇī bahiṇī' and 'jīvan-' 'jāch', 'tarīkā' or 'ḍhaṅg') literally, way of life, art of living or method, technique, or procedure. See jugat(i).

jīa jugat(i): (synonymous with 'jīvāṅ dī-' 'jugatī' or 'rahiṇī bahiṇī-' 'dā ḍhaṅg') literally, the way of life of beings.

ke: (a) (adj; synonymous with 'ka-ī' and 'anek') many or numerous. See ke.

raṅg: (n, m, pl) (a) (synonymous with 'kisam' and 'prakār') category, manner, or mode, and (b) (synonymous with 'varaṇ') different hues or colours. See raṅg (h and j).

An infinite variety of sentient life of diverse forms and colours inhabits it.

Tin ke nām, anek anaṅt

tin: (a) (n, m, s; synonymous with 'triṇ', 'ghāh' or 'phūs') dried-up grass or straw, (b) (genitive case - 'saṅbaṅdh kārak', pl; synonymous with ‘tinā-’, ‘tin(h)-’ and ‘tin(h)ā-’ ‘de’) their, and implicit here is (c) (pron and adj, pl; synonymous with ‘tinā-’, tin(h)-’ and ‘tin(h)ā-’) they or theirs.

nām: (n, pl) literally, names. In essence, a word or words that relate to or describe a place, an object, a sentient being or a person.

anek: (adj; synonymous with ‘anik’, ‘bahut’ and ‘nānā’) countless or numerous.

anaṅt: (adj) compound word comprising ‘an’ (without) + ‘aṅt’ (ending, limit or boundary), i.e., endless, infinite or eternal - an attribute of God.

Numerous are their names and infinite their number.

Karmī karmī, hoi vīchār(u)

karmī: (instrumental case - ‘karaṇ kārak’; synonymous with 'karmāṅ-’ ‘karke' or ‘anusār’; pronounced as ‘karmīṅ’) due to or by virtue of one’s past karmā. See karmī.

hoi: (v, s, present tense; synonymous with ‘huṅdī-’ or ‘huṅdā-’ ‘hai’; ‘ho jāṅdī-’ or ‘ho jāṅdā-’ ‘hai’; ‘ho sakdā hai’) literally, occurs, comes to be, or becomes; can occur, happen or become. See hovṇā/hoṇā (a).

vīchār(u): (n, m; synonymous with ‘nirṇā’ and ‘phaislā’) conclusion, judgement, or decision. See vīchār(u).

They are judged by the deeds they commit.

Sachā āp(i), sachā darbār(u)

sachā: (synonymous with (skt) ‘satya’ and (gmkh) ‘sat(i)’) (a) (adj; synonymous with ‘nirmal’, ‘pavitr’ and ‘ukāī rahit’) eternally true, perfect or flawless, and implicit here is (b) (n, m, s; synonymous with ‘sadīvī jyot(i)’ - the Primal Soul) the eternal Reality - ‘Nām(u)’, the immanent form of God.

āp(i): (pron; synonymous with ‘āp-’ or ‘khud-’ ‘hī’) one oneself or He Himself.

sachā: see sach(u) (e).

darbār: (n, m, s; synonymous with ‘bādshāh dī sabhā’) a royal court or hall, where an audience is given; a royal court where a judgement is pronounced. Gurmat does not give any credence to the view that God lives somewhere in the ‘heavens’, and hence there is no specific place assigned for this purpose. However, Gurū Nānak emphatically states that He is everywhere in the creation, as endorsed by this verse from Āsā dī Vār in the SGGS:

The self-existent God first manifested as 'Nam(u)'; He then created the world and permeated it, and now joyfully watches it unfold and evolve.[33]

God Himself is the eternal Reality, and His Court is impartial, flawless, and just.

Tithai sohan(i), paṅch parvāṇ(u)

tithai: (adv; synonymous with 'othe' and 'vahāṅ') there.

sohan(i): (v, pl, present tense, third person; synonymous with 'sohṇe-' or 'shobhnīk-' 'lagde han'; 'sobhde han') appear elegant, graceful, honourable, and praiseworthy.

paṅch: (n and adj; synonymous with 'Bhagats', 'Sādhū-jan', 'Saṅts' and 'Gurmukhs') they who submit to, focus, and reflect upon the persona and the attributes of 'Nām(u)', the immanent form of God, lovingly and willingly and strive to attune with it and express the same attributes in their daily lives. See paṅch in 'Pauṛī' 16; pp. 186-89.

parvāṇ(u): (a) (adj; synonymous with 'pramāṇit' or 'surkharū'; 'manzūr-', 'kabūl-', 'aṅgīkār-' or 'makbūl-' 'kītā hoiā') approved, authenticated, sanctioned, or authorised [by the all-pervasive 'Nām(u)'] and (b) (adj, m; synonymous with 'pramān duārā sidh', 'pratakhkh' or 'zāhir') evident, tangible and explicit. See parvāṇ(u).

Approved true devotees appear manifestly graceful and glorious there.

Nadrī karam(i), pavai nīsāṇ(u)

nadrī: (a) (adj; synonymous with 'nadar karan vālā' or 'kartār'; pronounced as 'nadrī') one with the ability of a compassionate glance, i.e., God, and (b) (genitive case - 'saṅbaṅdh kārak'; synonymos with 'nadar karan vāle di') literally, of one with a compassionate glance. In essence, the reference is to God. See nadrī.

karam(i): (a) (instrumental case - 'karaṇ kārak'; synonymous with (skt) 'karmāṅ-' 'duārā' or 'sadkā') through good deeds in harmony with 'Nām(u)', and implicit here is (b) (instrumental case - 'karaṇ kārak';

synonymous with (arab) 'karam-' or 'bakhshish-' 'duārā' or 'sadkā') through or with His Grace or Mercy. It is, however, noteworthy here that one is only deserving of His Grace when one strives to live in harmony with 'Nām(u)'.

pavai: (v, s, present tense, third person; synonymous with 'paiṅdā-' or 'pai jāṅdā-' 'hai') see paiṇā (d (iv)).

nīsāṇ(u): (n, m, s; synonymous with 'nishān' and 'chin(h)'; pronounced as 'nīshāṇ') mark, sign, brand, logo, or trademark; seal or mark of His approval. See nīsāṇ(u).

The mark of His approval is by the Grace of the Merciful Lord.

Kach pakāī, othai pāi

kach: (n, f; synonymous with 'kachcha pan' and 'kachiāī') literally, half-baked, or undeveloped state; raw, immature, unripe, half-baked or undeveloped state.

pakāī: (a) (v, present perfect; synonymous with 'riṅn(h)ī') literally, cooked, and implicit here is (b) (n, f; synonymous with 'pakiāī', 'pakkā pan' and 'driṛtā') ripe and mature state, firmness, and steadfastness. In essence, the reference here is to the degree of perfect alignment with 'Nām(u)' ('pakkā'), or otherwise ('kachchā').

othai: (adv; synonymous with 'us asthān te' and 'vahāṅ') literally, there. In essence, at God's Court. However, He is immanent in all aspects of His creation; His Court is, therefore, not somewhere else.

pāi: (v, s, present tense, third person; synonymous with 'pāuṅdā hai' or 'prāpat kardā hai') finds, achieves, or realises. See pāuṇā (c).

How raw or ripened, or good or bad one is, is revealed there.

Nānak, ga-i-ā jāpai jāi

Nānak: (n, m, s) the (u) of 'Nānak(u)' is missing because of its vocative case - 'saṅbodhan kārak'.

ga-i-ā: (a) (synonymous with 'bīt ga-i-ā'; 'chal basiā' or 'muk-', 'miṭ-' or 'tur-' 'ga-i-ā') literally, has gone or elapsed; has passed, deceased or died, (b) (v, m, s, present tense, first person; synonymous with 'maiṅ jāṅdā hāṅ') [I] go, leave or depart, and implicit here is (c) (indeclinable past participle or perfect participle - 'pūran pūrab kārdaṅtak'; synonymous with 'jā ke' and 'ho ke'; pronounced as 'ga-i-āṅ') having become; having got or gone there, i.e., at God's Court.

jāpai: (a) (v, s, present tense, third person; synonymous with 'jāṇīdā-' or 'sojhī āuṅdī-' 'hai') gets to know or understand, and (b) (v, s, present tense; synonymous with 'jāpdā-', 'bhāsdā-' or 'lagdā-' 'hai'; 'pratīt-', 'mālūm-' or 'mahsus-' 'huṅdā hai') seems or appears; feels, realises or appreciates. See jāpai (b, d, and e) and jāpṇā (a and b).

jāi: (conj v and suff.; synonymous with 'jāṅdā-' or 'jā sakdā-' 'hai') e.g., (i) (v, s, imperative mood - 'saṅbhāv bhvikht kāl - kiās or ichhā bodhak', second person; synonymous with 'jāve' or 'miṭe'; 'jāvāṅ' or 'jāṅvāṅ') vanish or disappear; wish I could know or understand, and implicit here is (ii) 'jāpai jāi' - get to know or is understood. See jāi.

jāpai jāi: (a) (imperative mood - 'saṅbhāv bhvikht kāl - kiās or ichhā bodhak', first person; synonymous with 'jāṅiā jāve'), and implicit here is (b) (v, s, present tense, third person; synonymous with 'jāṅiā jāṅdā hai') literally, get to know or understand.

'But His judgement is realised only on arrival there', O' Nānak!

Conceptual summary

The Earth, along with nights, seasons, lunar dates and days, air, water, fire, is positioned and assigned as a place for learning and earning righteousness and for learning to live by the Will of God. An endless array of sentient life of varied forms, colours and names, infinite in number, exist therein. They are judged by the deeds they commit; the judgement of His Court, like the eternal Reality, is absolutely impartial, flawless and just.

'Only the approved devotees appear glorious and elegant there as the Merciful Lord, by His Grace, singles them out with His mark of approval. How raw or ripened, or good or bad they are, is revealed there but this judgement is realised only on arrival there', O' Nānak!

By His Grace, one realises: (a) one's reason and purpose in life on this Earth, (b) that one, like all others, will be judged by the deeds one commits, and the degree of success or failure will be revealed on the day of judgement, (c) that what counts is not one's worldly fame or status but His mark of approval and robe of honour, (d) one's wrongly held concept of ego-consciousness and egotism and the need to move towards the principle of universal Fatherhood of God and Brotherhood of Man, and (e) that this is just the first rung of the ladder of spiritual evolution (‘Dharam Khaṅḍ’).

PAUṚĪ 35
ਪਉੜੀ ੩੫॥

Dharam khaṅḍ kā, eho dharam(u).
ਧਰਮ ਖੰਡ ਕਾ, ਏਹੋ ਧਰਮੁ॥

Giān khaṅḍ kā, ākhah(u) karam(u).
ਗਿਆਨ ਖੰਡ ਕਾ, ਆਖਹੁ ਕਰਮੁ॥

Kete pavaṇ pāṇī vaisaṅtar, kete kān mahes.
ਕੇਤੇ ਪਵਣ ਪਾਣੀ ਵੈਸੰਤਰ, ਕੇਤੇ ਕਾਨ ਮਹੇਸ॥

Kete barme ghāṛat(i) ghaṛīah(i), rūp raṅg ke ves.
ਕੇਤੇ ਬਰਮੇ ਘਾੜਤਿ ਘੜੀਅਹਿ, ਰੂਪ ਰੰਗ ਕੇ ਵੇਸ॥

Ketīā karam bhūmī, mer kete, kete dhū updes.
ਕੇਤੀਆ ਕਰਮ ਭੂਮੀ, ਮੇਰ ਕੇਤੇ, ਕੇਤੇ ਧੂ ਉਪਦੇਸ॥

Kete iṅd chaṅd, sūr kete, kete maṅḍal des.
ਕੇਤੇ ਇੰਦ ਚੰਦ, ਸੂਰ ਕੇਤੇ, ਕੇਤੇ ਮੰਡਲ ਦੇਸ॥

Kete sidh budh, nāth kete, kete devī ves.
ਕੇਤੇ ਸਿਧ ਬੁਧ, ਨਾਥ ਕੇਤੇ, ਕੇਤੇ ਦੇਵੀ ਵੇਸ॥

Kete dev dānav, mun(i) kete, kete ratan samuṅd.
ਕੇਤੇ ਦੇਵ ਦਾਨਵ, ਮੁਨਿ ਕੇਤੇ, ਕੇਤੇ ਰਤਨ ਸਮੁੰਦ॥

Ketiā khāṇī, ketiā bāṇī, kete pāt nariṅd.
ਕੇਤੀਆ ਖਾਣੀ, ਕੇਤੀਆ ਬਾਣੀ, ਕੇਤੇ ਪਾਤ ਨਰਿੰਦ॥

Ketiā surtī, sevak kete, Nānak, aṅt(u) n aṅt(u). (35)
ਕੇਤੀਆ ਸੁਰਤੀ, ਸੇਵਕ ਕੇਤੇ, ਨਾਨਕ, ਅੰਤੁ ਨ ਅੰਤੁ॥ ੩੫॥

Having realised one's limitations and drawbacks at the outset and the scale of the task ahead, one eagerly reaches out for further guidance from the Divine Words and Wisdom of a Gurū. Surrendering to the Gurū's Divine Words and Wisdom willingly, lovingly and unreservedly, one vows to imbibe them in one's 'Hirdā' and implement them in one's daily life. Undoubtedly, it transpires to be an uphill struggle as it is not easy to shake and ward off the opposing and misleading influence of 'Māyā'. But the process begins with deliberating and understanding the Divine Word, contemplation of 'Nām(u)' and introspection ('swai paṛchol' or 'āpā chīnaṇ').

Dharam khaṅḍ kā, eho dharam(u)

dharam: (n, m, s; synonymous with 'maryādā') moral, ethical or religious code of conduct, especially that which is in congruence with 'Nām(u)' or 'Nām-consciousness'. The (u) of 'dharam(u)' and 'khaṅḍ(u)' is missing because of the preposition 'kā' that joins it with another noun 'dharam(u)', at the end of the sentence.

khaṅḍ: (n, m; synonymous with 'avasthā') state, stage, condition, domain, or realm. See khaṅḍ(u).

kā: (prep, m; synonymous with 'dā') of. See kā.

eho: (a) (pron and adj; synonymous with 'yahi' and 'iho') this or as alluded to, and (b) (adj; synonymous with 'keval ih') only this, just this or merely this.

dharam(u): see dharam (b and c).

eho dharam: literally, this is precisely one's aim and duty in this first stage of spiritual awakening and evolution.

Such is the way of life of the realm of righteousness.

Giān khaṅḍ kā, ākhah(u) karam(u)

Newly gained wisdom now transforms one's worldly knowledge ('mat(i)') and discernment ('budh(i)') into intuitive knowledge ('uchī mat(i)' and 'anbhavī giān') and wisdom ('bibek budh(i)'). Gradually, one's subjugation to 'Haumaiṅ', 'Moh' and innate 'vikārī' tendencies lessens and one's flirtatious '*man*' begins to calm down and become increasingly attracted to and aligned with 'Nām-consciousness'. One's narrow focus on and concern for oneself loosens its grip, one examines and reassesses one's undue self-conceit in the wider context of the world, and one begins to empathise, care and have concern for others and align with the ideals of universal Fatherhood of God and Brotherhood of Man. Suddenly, a 'eureka moment' dawns and the pursuit of one's purpose in life comes to an end as everything falls into clear perspective, as is beautifully captured in the following verse of the SGGS:

Look, O' friends! 'The storm of new ideas and insight ('eureka moment') has struck'. It has blown away the thatched roof of misconception and dubiety propped up by 'māiā'.[499]

During this stage, one learns about the infiniteness of the creation and the insignificance of oneself in comparison. One's misconception of 'Haumaiṅ' comes into sharp focus and a passion for climbing up one rung of the ladder of spiritual evolution is aroused within one's 'Hirdā'. The following verses of the SGGS clearly show how one now intuitively begins to experience the eternal Reality and Divine Order:

'Awestruck, I am a sacrifice unto You, for You pervade the entire empirical world and Your Glory is infinite.[500]

'The formless and eternal Reality, immune to the influence of 'Māyā', manifests itself not only as the evolving empirical world, forever vulnerable to 'Māyā' but also, in a state of constant trance Himself. He creates all, and as 'Jīvātmāṅ' in all Its creation, He remembers and meditates on Himself too', says Nānak.[29]

He who dedicates his life to serve others in this world, gets recognised and honoured at His Court.[501]

giān: (n, m, s) (a) (synonymous with 'vivek' or 'bibek') intuitive insight and knowledge of moral, ethical, and spiritual correctness or godliness, and (b) (synonymous with 'tat(u)-' 'ruhānī-' or 'brahm-' 'giān(u)'; 'ruhānī-' 'jāgratā' or 'sojhī') divine or spiritual knowledge; intuitive insight and knowledge of godliness; an understanding of the Divine Will and the true path to the realisation or perception of the eternal Reality. See giān(u).

ākhah(u): (a) (v, pl, present tense, second person; synonymous with 'tusīṅ ākhde ho') you say, state or explain, (b) (imperative mood - 'hukmī bhvikht'; second person; synonymous with 'dasso', 'varṇan karo' or 'samajh lavo') [you] explain or rationlise, and implicit here is (c) (v, s, present tense, first person; synonymous with 'ākhdāṅ-' or 'dasdāṅ-' 'hāṅ'; pronounced as 'ākhau(h)ṅ') I describe, explain, or expound.

karam(u): (n, m; synonymous with 'kartav' or 'pharz') duty.

I now describe one's duty or way of life in this realm of knowledge and wisdom.

Kete pavaṇ pāṇī vaisaṅtar, kete kān mahes

kete: (adj; synonymous with 'kaī' and 'kitne') numerous, many, several or quite a few. In essence, the adjective refers to the large numbers and diverse types of inanimate and sentient life forms that God has created in Nature.

pavan: (n, f; synonymous with 'havā', 'vāyū', 'pavaṇ' and 'suās') literally, air or wind. In essence, different types of gaseous material.

pāṇī: (n, m, pl) (a) (synonymous with 'jal') literally, water. In essence, different types of liquids.

vaisaṅtar: (n, f, pl; synonymous with 'baisaṅtar') literally, fire. In essence, different sources of heat or energy.

kān: (a) (n, m, pl; synonymous with 'kaṅn') ears, (b) (n, m; synonymous with 'tīr', 'bāṇ' and 'vāṇ') arrows, (c) (n, f; pers; synonymous with 'khaṇ(i)') mines, and implicit here is (d) (n, m, pl; synonymous with 'kān(h)') literally, many like Lord Krishna.

mahes: (n, m, pl; synonymous with 'Mahesh', 'Maheshwar', 'Mahādev', 'Shiv', 'Rudr', 'jagatnāth' and 'mahī dā īsh'; pronounced as 'mahesh') literally, many like Lord Shiv, Lord of the Earth, one of the trinity of Gods in the Hindu religion.

There are many types of gases, liquids, and energies, and many like Krishna and Shiv in this world.

Kete barme ghāṛat(i) ghaṛīah(i), rūp raṅg ke ves

barme: (genitive case - 'saṅbaṅdh kārak'; synonymous with 'Brahmā varge dīāṅ'; pronounced as 'brahmeṅ') literally, many like Lord Brahmā. In essence, the reference here is to the sources of different types of creation.

ghāṛat(i): (locative case - 'adhikaraṇ kārak'; synonymous with 'ghāṛat vich') literally, in the shape or form of. See ghāṛat.

ghāṛat: (n, f; synonymous with 'ghaṛat', 'banāvaṭ' and 'rachnā') literally, the physical form, shape, design, or final structure.

barme ghāṛat(i): (synonymous with 'Brahmā dī ghāṛat vich' or 'Brahmā varge') in the character of Brahmā.

ghaṛīah(i): (a) (imperative mood - 'saṅbhāv bhvikht kāl - prernā bodhak', second person; synonymous with 'ghaṛo'), and implicit here is (b) (v, pl, present tense, third person; synonymous with 'ghaṛe jāṅde han'; pronounced as 'ghaṛīaih') literally, are carved, sculpted, or fashioned. See ghaṛnā.

barme ghāṛat(i) ghaṛīah(i): fashioned in the likeness of Brahma.

rūp: (n, m) (a) (n, f; synonymous with 'khūbsūrtī', 'sauṅdryā' and 'suṅdartā') literally, good looks, cuteness, beauty, or elegance, and implicit here is (b) (synonymous with 'shakal', 'sūrat', 'sarūp' and 'ākār') literally, form, shape, looks, or appearance.

raṅg: (n, m, pl) (a) (synonymous with 'kisam' and 'prakār') category, manner, or mode, and (b) (synonymous with 'varaṇ') different hues or colours. See raṅg (h and j)

ke: (adj; synonymous with 'ka-ī' and 'anek') many. See ke.

ves: (n; synonymous with 'bhekh', 'shakal' and 'rūp') form, figure, appearance, caricature, or silhouette. See ves.

Many of the ilk of Brahmā are fashioned in diverse forms, colours, and guises.

Ketīā karam bhūmī, mer kete, kete dhū updes

ketīā: (adj, f; synonymous with 'kitnīā' and 'kiṅnīā'; pronounced as 'ketīāṅ') literally, many or how many?

karam: (n, m; synonymous with 'kartav' or 'pharz') literally, duty. See 'karam(u)' (d).

bhūmī: (n, f) (a) (synonymous with 'jagāṅ', 'thāṅ' and 'prithvīāṅ') literally, places, lands, and planets, like the planet Earth. In essence, different places for different beings to perform their rightful duties.

karam bhūmī: (n, f, pl; synonymous with 'karam and dharam kamāuṇ laī thāvāṅ or dhartīāṅ') literally, fields of action; places like the planet Earth for the diverse life forms to live out their lives.

mer: (a) (n, f; synonymous with 'merāpan', 'mamtā', 'khudī' and 'apṇat') strong feeling of mine and thine, partiality, of ownership and possessiveness, (b) (adj; synonymous with 'pradhān' and 'shiromaṇī') literally, head, principal, chairman or supreme, (c) (n, m; synonymous with 'mālā dā shiromaṇī maṇkā') literally, the top bead in a rosary, and implicit here is (d) (n, m, pl; synonymous with 'pahāṛ' and 'gir(i)') large mountains, like the mythological Sumer mountain.

dhū: (n, m, s; synonymous with 'dhrav') a 'bhagat' in Hindu mythology, who shines like the polestar in the galaxy amongst other 'bhagats' in the world.

updes: (n, m; synonymous with 'sikhyā', 'gurdīkhyā' and 'sidhāṅt'; pronounced as 'updesh') lesson, sermon, counsel, doctrine, precept and religious or moral instruction or teachings.

There are innumerable places for the diverse life forms to live out their lives, numerous huge mountains, and many supreme 'bhagats' like 'Dhrū' and their teachings.

Kete Iṅd Chaṅd, Sūr kete, kete maṅḍal des

Iṅd: (n, m, pl; synonymous with 'Indra, 'Indar' and 'devraj') (a) God of rain in Hindu mythology, and (b) literally, Lord Indra or Dev Indra, the mythological king of 'Suarg', 'Swarg' or 'Amrāvatī' - the heavens, where the inhabitants enjoy eternal life.

chaṅd: (a) (adj; pers; synonymous with 'kuchh', 'tanik' and 'thoṛā') a little, some, scanty, meagre, or inadequate, (b) (n, f, pl) souls ('Jīvātmāṅs'), and implicit here is (c) (n, m, pl; synonymous with 'Chāṅd' and 'Chaṅdarmā') literally, moons.

sūr: (n, m, pl; synonymous with 'sūraj') literally, suns. See sūr.

maṅḍal: (n, m; synonymous with 'golākār gherā' and 'dāyrah') a planetary system, with planets orbiting around a sun or a star. See maṅḍal.

brahmaṅḍ: (n, m, pl) (a) (synonymous with 'rachna') the sum total of all the planetary systems; the whole collection of galaxies; the entire universe or the entire cosmos, and (b) (synonymous with 'dunīā', 'srish(i)' and 'saṅsār') the whole world.

des: (a) (n, m; synonymous with 'malkīat') literally, ownership or property, (b) (n, m, pl; synonymous with 'deh de aṅg') parts of the body, and implicit here is (c) (n, m, pl; synonymous with 'mulk', 'vatan' and 'khitte') country or region.

There are many like dev Indra, moon, sun, countries, and planetary systems.

Kete Sidh Budh, Nāth kete, kete devī ves

sidh: (n, m, pl) yogīs who have achieved: (a) eight unique or mythical psychic, miraculous or supernatural powers, and (b) sidh(i). See sidh.

sidh(i): (a) (n; synonymous with 'karāmāt', 'alokik shakat(i)') miraculous or supernatural power, (b) (n, f; synonymous with 'kāmyābī' or 'saphaltā') success, (c) (n, f; synonymous with 'nijāt' or 'mukat(i)') freedom or emancipation, (d) (n; synonymous with 'saṅpadā') one's assets, and (e) eighteen miraculous or supernatural powers, of which eight are pre-eminent.

Budh: (a) (n, m, s) literally, planet Mercury, whose name is used for one of the days of the week 'Budhvār' (Wednesday), (b) (adj, m; synonymous with 'jāgiā hoiā') literally, spiritually enlightened, and implicit here is (c) (n, m, s) literally, Mahātamā Gautam Budh - believed to be the ninth incarnation of Lord Vishnū according to Hindu mythology.

nāth: (n, m) a sect of Hindu ascetics or any of their members who follow their 'Yogīrāj' Gorakhnāth or Lord Shiva and who have achieved the pinnacle of success on that path.

devi: (n, f, s) (a) (synonymous with 'sadāchārī istrī' and 'pat(i)vartā istrī') a faithful and obedient wife of high moral character, (b) (synonymous with 'dev patnī') consort of a devtā.

ves: see above. See ves (g and h).

There are many 'Sidhas', 'Budhas', 'Nāth Yogīs', and many others in the guise of incarnations of goddesses.

Kete dev dānav, mun(i) kete, kete ratan samuṅd

dev: (n, m, pl; abbrev. for 'devtā' and 'devte') (synonymous with 'sur') eternal beings with Divine powers, who live in heaven in Hindu mythology. See dev.

dānav: (n, m) (a) children or progeny of 'dan(u)' (mother) and 'kashyap' (father) in Hindu mythology, and (b) (antonym of 'dev'; synonymous with 'daiṅt', 'rākhash' or 'rākhshash') a demon, an ignoble or vile person lacking all virtues.

mun(i): (a) (n and adj, m; synonymous with 'vichār karan vālā' or 'maṅnanshīl') considerate, rational, thoughtful, philosopher or sage, (b) (n, m; synonymous with 'jis dā *man* dukh vich vyākul n hovai', 'a rikhī or rishī', a 'Sādh' and a 'Saṅt') one who keeps calm even in states of adversity, and implicit here is (c) (n, m; synonymous with 'maunī', 'chup kītā' and 'maun dhāran vālā manukh') one who vows not to speak or deliberately avoids speaking; an ascetic, a sect of yogīs who vow to remain silent for long periods to avoid inner unrest or turmoil, and who strive to control their fickle and flirtatious '*Man*'.

ratan: (a) (n, m, pl; synonymous with 'ratan rūp' and 'guṇvān manukh') 'saṅts', 'sādhs', 'bhagats', 'gurūs', and 'brahmgyānīs', and (b) (n, m, pl; synonymous with 'ratan rūp', 'amolak guṇ') priceless godly attributes, virtues, and values. See ratan.

samuṅd: (n, m, pl; synonymous with 'samuṅdr') literally, seas or oceans.

ratan samuṅd: (a) (synonymous with 'ratnāṅ de samuṅdr') vast oceans of precious stones, jewels, or noble attributes, virtues, and values, and implicit here is (b) (synonymous with 'guṇvān manukh') literally, men replete with noble attributes as vast as the oceans.

There are numerous demi-gods, demons, 'rishīs', and holy men with oceans of noble attributes.

Ketiā khāṇī, ketiā bāṇī, kete pāt nariṅd

khāṇī: (a) (n, f, pl) literally, mines or abundant sources of basic raw minerals or resources, and (b) the four main sources of life: 'anḍaj' (through eggs), 'jeraj' (through placenta), 'setaj' (through sweat) and 'utbhuj' (through the Earth). See khāṇ(i).

khāṇ(i): (n, f, s; synonymous with 'khāṇ' and 'kān') literally, a mine.

bāṇī: (n, f, pl; synonymous with 'bāṇ(i)', 'bāṇīāṅ' and 'bolīāṅ') languages, dialects, or modes of communication. See bāṇī and bāṇ(i) (f).

pāt: (a) (n, m; synonymous with 'pattā') leaf, (b) (n, m; synonymous with 'par', 'khaṅbh' or 'paṅkh') wing, (c) (v, s; abbrev. for 'pāvat'; synonymous with 'pāuṅdā hai') gets, achieves, or receives; literally, wears but (fig.) endures, (d) (v, s; synonymous with 'ḍigdā hai') literally, falls or sinks to a lowly position, (e) (n, m; synonymous with 'takhat' and 'siṅghāsan') a throne or royal seat, and implicit here is (f) (n, m; synonymous with 'trātā', 'rakshak' and 'rakhiak') protector, saviour, guardian or 'pāt(i)shah'.

nariṅd: (n, m) a complex word comprising 'nar' ('people') + 'iṅd/iṅdr' (a king); synonymous with 'manukhāṅ dā rājā', i.e., a king over people; a man at the helm of a nation, a king.

pāt nariṅd - literally, emperors and kings.

There are numerous sources of life, languages (modes of communications), and kings of kings.

Ketiā surtī, sevak kete, Nānak, aṅt(u) n aṅt(u)

surtī: (a) (n, f; pl of surat(i); synonymous with 'surtāṅ', 'samaj', 'sojhī', 'giān' and 'mat(i)') spiritual knowledge or wisdom, states of inner/spiritual awakening or alertness, and (b) (n, f; pl of surat(i); synonymous with 'surtāṅ', 'samādh(i)', 'liv' or 'dhiān') literally, many or different types of focus or attention. See surat(i) (b).

ketiā surtī: (a) (n, f, pl; synonymous with 'ka-ī prakār dī sojhī, samajh or mat(i)') different kinds of knowledge, understanding or wisdom, and implicit here is (b) (n, f, pl; synonymous with 'ka-ī prakār dī liv') literally, different ways or means of focusing.

sevak: (n, m, pl) (a) (synonymous with 'sevā karan vāle', 'dās' and 'khidmatgār') servant or attendant, and (b) (synonymous with 'chelā', 'murīd', 'anuyāī', 'shardhālū' and 'upāshak') disciples, followers, or devotees.

Nānak: (n, m, s) the (u) of 'Nānak(u)' is missing because of its vocative case - 'saṅbodhan kārak'.

aṅt(u): (n, m; synonymous with 'oṛak', 'sīmā' and 'had') literally, the end, boundary, finale, or extremity.

n aṅt: literally, there is no end to this end, i.e., the reference is to infinity

'Countless are the devotees and the ways they focus singularly on their object of devotion; His creation is truly infinite', says Nānak.

Conceptual summary

The five 'khaṅḍs' allude to the distinct levels or stages in one's spiritual evolution or enlightenment. Having realised one's purpose in life and the reality of the scrutiny and judgement of one's deeds, one now truly seeks to understand the vastness of the creation and one's insignificant position and role within it.

Until now, with ego-consciousness being the default operative control centre, one was egocentric as regards oneself and one's nuclear family, and was also deeply engrossed in the material world, its comforts, and pleasures. Recognising one's inability to satisfy one's 'trisnā' and the transitoriness of worldly comforts and pleasures, one now seeks more lasting ways of achieving inner stability and bliss.

One is now eager to broaden one's horizon and truly understand oneself and one's position, role and purpose in the wider world, beyond the narrow range of self, family, religion, race and country. This path and the journey to realise one's real self and to shed one's 'Haumaiṅ', 'Moh' and evil innate 'Vikārī' tendencies now suddenly becomes much more rewarding and gratifying.

'Such is one's duty and way of life in the realm of righteousness', and I, Nānak, 'now describe one's duty, conduct and way of life in the realm of knowledge and wisdom'.

There are many: (a) types of gases, liquids and energies, and many like Krishna and Shiv, (b) of the ilk of Brahmā, who are fashioned in diverse forms, colours and guises, (c) places for the diverse life forms to live out their lives, numerous huge mountains, and supreme 'bhagats', like Dhrū, and their teachings, (d) like dev Indra, moon, sun, countries and planetary systems, (e) Sidhas, Budhās, Nāth yogīs, and others in the guise of the incarnation of goddesses, (f) demi-gods, demons, rishīs, and holy men with oceans of noble attributes, (g) sources of life, modes of communications, emperors and kings, and (h) kinds and ways of focus which many devotees practise. However, the reality is that His creation is limitless.

'Countless are the devotees and the ways they focus singularly on their object of devotion; His creation is truly infinite', says Nanak.

PAUṚĪ 36
ਪਉੜੀ ੩੬॥

Giān khaṅḍ mah(i), giān(u) parchaṅḍ(u).
ਗਿਆਨ ਖੰਡ ਮਹਿ, ਗਿਆਨੁ ਪਰਚੰਡੁ॥

Tithai, nād binod koḍ anaṅd(u).
ਤਿਥੈ, ਨਾਦ ਬਿਨੋਦ ਕੋਡ ਅਨੰਦੁ॥

Saram khaṅd kī, bāṇī rūp(u).
ਸਰਮ ਖੰਡ ਕੀ, ਬਾਣੀ ਰੂਪੁ॥

Tithai, ghāṛat(i) ghaṛīai, bahut(u) anūp(u).
ਤਿਥੈ, ਘਾੜਤਿ ਘੜੀਐ, ਬਹੁਤੁ ਅਨੂਪੁ॥

Tā kīa gala, kathīā nā jāh(i).
ਤਾ ਕੀਆ ਗਲਾ, ਕਥੀਆ ਨਾ ਜਾਹਿ॥

Je ko kahai, pichhai pachhutāi.
ਜੇ ਕੋ ਕਹੈ, ਪਿਛੈ ਪਛੁਤਾਇ॥

Tithai ghaṛīai, surat(i) mat(i) *man*(i) budh(i).
ਤਿਥੈ ਘੜੀਐ, ਸੁਰਤਿ ਮਤਿ ਮਨਿ ਬੁਧਿ॥

Tithai ghaṛīai, surā sidhā kī sudh(i). (36)
ਤਿਥੈ ਘੜੀਐ, ਸੁਰਾ ਸਿਧਾ ਕੀ ਸੁਧਿ॥ ੩੬॥

Giān khaṅḍ mah(i) giān(u) parchaṅḍ(u)

giān: (a) (n, m, s; synonymous with 'vivek' or 'bibek') intuitive insight and knowledge of moral, ethical, and spiritual correctness or godliness, and (b) (synonymous with 'tat(u)-' 'ruhānī-' or 'brahm-' 'giān(u)'; 'ruhānī-' 'jāgratā' or 'sojhī') divine or spiritual knowledge; intuitive insight and knowledge of godliness; an understanding of the Divine Will and the true path to realisation or perception of the eternal Reality. See giān and 'Pauṛī' 35.

khaṅḍ: (n, m; synonymous with 'avasthā') state, stage, condition, domain, or realm. See khaṅḍ (j) and 'Pauṛī' 35, page 412-3.

mah(i): (prep; synonymous with 'māh(i)', 'aṅdar' or 'vichkār') inside, within, or in the midst of.

parchaṅḍ: (a) (adj; synonymous with 'vaḍḍā krodhī') extremely angry, wrathful, or irate, (b) (n, f; synonymous with 'agan(i)') literally, fire; heat or energy, (c) (adj; synonymous with 'bahut tikhkhā' or 'tez') literally, very sharp or strong, (d) (adj; synonymous with 'pratāpī' and 'tejasvī') great, renowned, powerful or majestic, and implicit here is (e) (adj; synonymous with 'parbal', 'balvān', 'zorāvar', 'tez' and 'tībar') literally, strong, powerful, mighty, burning desire.

Spiritual awakening or enlightenment reigns supreme in this realm of knowledge and wisdom.

Tithai nād binod koḍ anaṅd(u)

tithai: (adv; synonymous with 'othe' and 'vahāṅ') there.

nād: (a) (n, f; synonymous with 'anhad nād') literally, the unstruck everlasting primordial sound or 'dhun(i)', neither arising from the collision of two objects nor heard by the ears but perceived with one's 'surat(i)' aligned perfectly with and focused on 'Nām(u)', and implicit here is (b) (n, f; synonymous with 'saṅgītak dhun(i)') literally, melodious vocal or the enchanting musical sounds of 'rāgās'. See nād. Option 'b' is preferred as one's '*Man*' (conscious self or 'Hirdā') is neither yet fashioned, nor in a steady state of equanimity ('Sahaj') to perceive the 'anhad nād'.

binod: (synonymous with 'vinod') (a) (n, f; synonymous with 'chāu' and 'umaṅg') desire, yearning, ambition, or aspiration, and implicit here is (b) (n, m, pl; synonymous with 'kautakī-' 'choj', 'khel' or 'tamāshe') literally, wondrous acts, ploys or spectacles.

koḍ: (a) (n, m; synonymous with 'biṅg or viṅg', 'ramzāṅ') literally, a metaphor; a sarcastic or satirical twist to meaning, (b) (n, m, pl; synonymous with 'kautakī-' 'choj', 'khel' or 'tamāshe') literally, wondrous acts, ploys or spectacles, and implicit here is (c) (adj; synonymous with 'kroṛ' and 'koṭ(i)') 1×10^7. This is the preferred option as option 'b' has already been referred to in the word 'binod'.

anaṅd(u): (n, f; synonymous with 'anad', 'suād', 'khushī' and 'prasaṅtā') happiness, delight, jubilation, rejoicing and contentment. See anaṅd(u).

There one experiences joy equal to that of myriads of musical melodies and wondrous acts, pageants, magical trickery and spectacles.[7] *Or:*

There, one perceives the eternal unstruck sound ('anhad nād') and enjoys lasting and wondrous inner equipoise and bliss, and ecstasy beyond the joy of crores of worldly events.[9]

[The first interpretation is preferred by the author but other views, which appear somewhat ambivalent, also exist in the literature][8,10, 20]

Saram khaṅd kī bāṇī rūp(u)

As the surge of spiritual knowledge gathers momentum, one looks ahead and commits to whittling down the adverse influence of 'Haumaiṅ', 'Moh', innate 'Vikārī' tendencies ('Māyā') on one's 'surat(i)', 'mat(i)', '*man*(i)' and 'budh(i)', i.e, all aspects of one's conscious self. Pursuing this path with dogged determination and resoluteness, one successfully fashions and aligns one's 'surat(i)', 'mat(i)', '*man*(i)' and 'budh(i)' perfectly with 'Nām-consciousness'. Having rid oneself of the evil influence of 'Māyā', to live by His Will now instinctively becomes one's burning desire and ultimately embedded in one's innate nature ('kudratī subhā-u').

He who unreservedly accedes to living by His Will, deserves to be known as 'Jīvan mukat(i)'. Happiness and joy are to him, as is grief and sorrow; neither of the two states shakes his inner equipoise. He enjoys, forever, the state of inner bliss ('Anaṅd(u)'), where one never detaches from perfect alignment with 'Nām(u)'.

saram: (n, f) (a) (pers; synonymous with 'sharam', 'hyā' or 'lajjā') honour; humiliation and shame, and implicit here is (b) (skt; synonymous with 'shram', 'ghālanā' or 'pursһārath') endeavour, toil, or labour.

saram khaṅd: literally, the realm of labour and commitment. The forging of one's conscious self continues and, with steadfastness and hard work, perfect alignment with 'Nām-consciousness' is eventually achieved. The state of one's conscious self, at this stage, in perfect alignment and harmony with 'Nām(u)', is just beyond words.

kī: (prep, f; synonymous with 'dī') of or belonging to. See kī.

bāṇī: (n, f; synonymous with 'rachnā', 'baṇtar' and 'banāvaṭ') creation, composition, production, any work of art, craft, or literature; structure, build or design. See bāṇī.

rūp(u): (n, m) (a) (synonymous with 'shakal', 'sūrat', 'sarūp' and 'ākār') literally, form, shape, looks, or appearance, and implicit here is (b) (n, f;

synonymous with 'khūbsūrtī', 'sauṅdryā' and 'suṅdartā') literally, good looks, cuteness, beauty, or elegance.

The state and design of one's conscious self, in this realm of spiritual effort, is both beautiful and indefinable.

Tithai ghāṛat(i) ghaṛīai bahut(u) anūp(u)

ghāṛat(i): (locative case - 'adhikaraṇ kārak'; synonymous with 'ghāṛat-', 'ghaṛat-' or 'banāvaṭ-' 'vich') literally, in the shape, form or design of. See ghāṛat.

ghaṛīai: (a) (v, pl, first person, imperative mood - 'hukmī bhvikht'; synonymous with 'ghaṛ laiṇe chāhīde han'), and implicit here is (b) (v, s, present tense, third person; synonymous with 'ghaṛīdā-' or 'ghaṛīdī-' 'hai'; 'ghaṛī jandi hai') see ghaṛnā. The object to be sculpted or fashioned is one's conscious self - 'surat(i)', 'mat(i)', '*man*' and 'budh(i)'.

bahut(u): (adj; synonymous with 'bahutā', 'adhik', 'vadhere' and 'ziādā') plentiful, abundant or in large quantity.

anūp(u): (adj; synonymous with 'be-misāl') complex word comprising 'an' (without or beyond) + 'ūp' ('upmā'-praise or eulogy), i.e., beyond praise, extraordinary, unique, unrivalled or unparalleled.

One forges one's conscious self ('Jīvātmāṅ', 'Man' or 'Hirdā') into a supremely beautiful state there.

Tā kīa galā kathīā nā jāh(i)

tā: (synonymous with 't'; pronounced as 'tāṅ') (pron; synonymous with 'tis' or 'us') his or her. In essence, that state or realm of spiritual enlightenment. See tā.

kīa: (a) (v, s, past tense; synonymous with 'kītā') literally, did or carried out etc., (b) (past participle - 'bhūt kirdaṅt', synonymous with 'kītā', 'kariā' or 'kīā') done, carried out, undertaken, or created, and implicit here is (c) (pron, p, pl; synonymous with 'kīāṅ' and 'dīāṅ'; pronounced as 'kīāṅ') of or belonging to that state of spiritual enlightenment.

galā: (n, f, pl; synonymous with 'bātāṅ'; pronounced as 'gallāṅ') literally, talks, conversations or utterances. In essence, qualities, characteristics or essence.

kathīā: (v; synonymous with 'kathan-' or 'biān-' 'kītīāṅ'; pronounced as 'kathīāṅ') literally, stated or described. See kathnā.

kathnā: (v; synonymous with 'kahiṇā' and 'biān karnā') literally, to say, state, speak, utter, narrate or recount.

nā: (p; synonymous with and often written as just 'n'; pronounced as 'nāṅ') no, not or indicative of a negative implication or connotation.

jāh(i): (v, pl, present tense, third person; synonymous with 'uh jāṅde han'; 'jā sakde han'; 'jā sakdīāṅ han'; pronounced as 'jāheṅ') they go or can go. See jāṇā (d (v)).

kathīā nā jāh(i): (synonymous with 'kītīāṅ nahīṅ jā sakdīāṅ') literally, cannot be stated, narrated, or explained.

The essence of that state of spiritual enlightenment just cannot be described.

Je ko kahai pichhai pachhutāi

je: (conj; synonymous with 'yadī' and 'agar') if or in case. See je.

ko: (pron; abbrev for and synonymous with 'koī') someone, anyone, or another; many or several. See ko.

kahai: (v, s, present tense, third person; synonymous with 'ākhdā-' or 'kahiṅdā-' 'hai'; 'varṇan-' or 'vakhyān-' 'kardā hai') sets forth, utters, expounds, explicates, or sings His Glory. See kahiṇā (b).

pichhai: (pronounced as 'pichhchhai') (adv; synonymous with 'pichhchhoṅ', 'magroṅ', and 'samān bīt jāṇ bād') literally, later, thereafter, afterwards, or subsequently. See pichhai.

pachhutāi: (a) (indeclinable past participle or perfect participle - 'pūran pūrab kārdaṅtak'; synonymous with 'pachhutā ke'), and (b) (v, s, present tense, third person; synonymous with 'pachhutāuṅdā hai') see pachhutāuṇā.

pachhutāuṇā: (v; synonymous with 'paschātāv karnā') to regret, repent or feel remorse; to be penitent or contrite, especially about one's misdeeds or at not achieving one's objective/s.

One regrets thereafter, and must eat the proverbial humble pie, should one dare to expound that inner state.

Tithai gharīai surat(i) mat(i) *man*(i) budh(i)

surat(i): (n, f; one of four parts of '*Man*(u)' in Gurmat; synonymous with 'dhiān', 'tavajjo', 'birtī', 'suchet pan' and 'vīchār') focus or attention; alertness or conscious state of mind; meditation or reflection; proclivity or predisposition. This empirical world is replete with distractions and hence the reason why one's focus becomes an absolute sine qua non for the successful completion of any task in hand. The following verses from the SGGS beautifully capture this vulnerable condition:

Hordes follow the way of the 'Paṅḍits' but only Kabir engages in this uphill struggle en route to 'Nām-realisation'.[474]

One wavers between being truly ecstatic and being dejected and despondent. Inflicted with greed, one is forever searching in all directions, for more.[502]

mat(i): (n, f; synonymous with 'akal', 'giān', 'samajh' and 'siāṇap') knowledge, intellect, wisdom, and ability to reason or discern. This is one of the aspects or functions of '*man*' in Gurmat.

man(i): (locative case - 'adhikaraṇ kārak'; synonymous with '*man* vich') in one's conscious self ('Jīvātmāṅ', '*Man*' or 'Hirdā'). See '*man*'.

budh(i): (n, f; synonymous with 'bibek') one of the functions of '*Man*' in Gurmat. It is the faculty for wisdom, intellect and rationality which gives clarity and sharpness to one's thought process and judgement, and for the discernment of right and wrong.

There is no doubt that our actions (thoughts, speech, and deeds) will become subject to His scrutiny. However, that process has its roots and first steps in one's conscious self; hence, the great emphasis, in this Pauṛī, on fashioning one's conscious self. The following verses from the SGGS aptly capture this sentiment:

'Whatever is in one's conscious self takes root and bears fruit; otherwise, mere words are like castles in the air'.[503]

Explore the depths of your conscious self, for this is how you realise 'Nām(u)', the source of all treasures and inner bliss.[316]

There, one forges the 'surat(i)', 'mat(i)', and 'budh(i)' of one's Man.

Tithai ghaṛīai surā sidhā kī sudh(i)

surā: (a) (n, m, pl) human beings with divine attributes ('dayavī guṇ'), and (b) (genitive case - 'saṅbaṅdh kārak'; synonymous with 'surāṅ-' or 'devtiaṅ-' 'dī'; pronounced as 'surāṅ') literally, of demi-gods or or those with divine attributes. See sur(i) (a, f, g).

sidhā: (n, m, pl; genitive case - 'saṅbaṅdh kārak'; synonymous with 'sidhāṅ' dī') of Sidhās. See sidh.

sidh: (n, m, pl) spiritually high ranking 'yogīs' who have achieved: (a) eight unique or mythical psychic, miraculous or supernatural powers, and (b) sidh(i).

sudh(i): (a) (n, f; synonymous with 'khabar', 'sudh-budh' or 'hosh') awareness, perceptiveness, presence of mind or alertness, (b) (n, f; synonymous with 'samajh', 'sūjh', 'sojhī' or 'jāṇkārī') perception, understanding or comprehension, and (c) (n, f; synonymous with 'vivek shakat(i)') rational or discerning ability; wisdom or prudence; power of deductive reasoning.

surā sidhā kī sudh(i): alertness, perceptiveness, prudence, and discernment of demi-gods and 'Sidhās'.

There, one forges one's perceptiveness, prudence, and discernment similar to that of the sages and 'sidhās'.

Conceptual summary

Spiritual awakening and enlightenment reign supreme in the realm of knowledge and wisdom, where one enjoys the same joy and bliss as one gets from melodious music and countless wondrous events.

The forged state of one's conscious self is supremely beautiful in this realm of spiritual effort, and so wonderfully beautiful that should one dare define the essence of its beauty, one would subsequently come to regret it, as it is simply ineffable.

One forges and fashions the focus, wisdom, and discerning ability of one's '*Man*' and one's perceptiveness, prudence, and discernment similar to that of the sages and 'sidhās'.

Having surrendered to the Guru's Divine Word and Message, one now vows to follow it with absolute faith and commitment and, indeed, to implement it in one's daily life. One boldly faces the daily challenges of 'Māyā' but, with unwavering faith in one's freshly imbibed spiritual knowledge, wisdom and God's Grace, one successfully overcomes all attempts of 'Māyā' to uproot and deflect one from the path of 'Nām-consciousness'.

PAUṚĪ 37
ਪਉੜੀ ੩੭॥

Karam khaṅḍ kī bāṇī jor(u).
ਕਰਮ ਖੰਡ ਕੀ ਬਾਣੀ ਜੋਰੁ॥

Tithai, hor(u) n koī hor(u).
ਤਿਥੈ, ਹੋਰੁ ਨ ਕੋਈ ਹੋਰੁ॥

Tithai, jodh mahābal sūr.
ਤਿਥੈ, ਜੋਧ ਮਹਾਬਲ ਸੂਰ॥

Tin mah(i), Rām(u) rahiā bharpūr.
ਤਿਨ ਮਹਿ, ਰਾਮੁ ਰਹਿਆ ਭਰਪੂਰ॥

Tithai, sīto sītā mahimā māh(i).
ਤਿਥੈ, ਸੀਤੋ ਸੀਤਾ ਮਹਿਮਾ ਮਾਹਿ॥

Tā ke rūp, n kathne jāh(i).
ਤਾ ਕੇ ਰੂਪ, ਨ ਕਥਨੇ ਜਾਹਿ॥

Nā oh(i) marah(i), n ṭhāge jāh(i).
ਨਾ ਓਹਿ ਮਰਹਿ, ਨ ਠਾਗੇ ਜਾਹਿ॥

Jin kai, Rām(u) vasai *man* māh(i).
ਜਿਨ ਕੈ, ਰਾਮੁ ਵਸੈ ਮਨ ਮਾਹਿ॥

Tithai, bhagat vasah(i) ke loa.
ਤਿਥੈ, ਭਗਤ ਵਸਹਿ ਕੇ ਲੋਅ॥

Karah(i) anaṅd(u), sachā *man*(i) soi.
ਕਰਹਿ ਅਨੰਦੁ, ਸਚਾ ਮਨਿ ਸੋਇ॥

Sach(i) khaṅḍ(i), vasai niraṅkār(u).
ਸਚ ਖੰਡਿ, ਵਸੈ ਨਿਰੰਕਾਰੁ॥

Kar(i) kar(i) vekhai, nadar(i) nihāl.
ਕਰਿ ਕਰਿ ਵੇਖੈ, ਨਦਰਿ ਨਿਹਾਲ॥

Tithai, khaṅḍ, maṅḍal, varbhaṅḍ.
ਤਿਥੈ, ਖੰਡ, ਮੰਡਲ, ਵਰਭੰਡ॥

Je ko kathai, ta aṅt n aṅt.
ਜੇ ਕੋ ਕਥੈ, ਤ ਅੰਤ ਨ ਅੰਤ॥

Tithai, loa, loa, ākār.
ਤਿਥੈ, ਲੋਅ, ਲੋਅ, ਆਕਾਰ॥

Jiv jiv hukam, tivai tiv kār.
ਜਿਵ ਜਿਵ ਹੁਕਮੁ, ਤਿਵੈ ਤਿਵ ਕਾਰ॥

Vekhai, vigsai, kar(i) vīchār(u).
ਵੇਖੈ, ਵਿਗਸੈ, ਕਰਿ ਵੀਚਾਰੁ॥

Nānak, kathnā karṛā sār(u). (37)
ਨਾਨਕ, ਕਥਨਾ ਕਰੜਾ ਸਾਰੁ॥ ੩੭॥

One now experiences a state of lasting inner equanimity ('Sahaj') even in the face of extremes of worldly bliss and adversity. Having thus subdued 'Māyā', one is now able to perceive, with the Grace of God, the everlasting, unstruck sound ('anhad-' 'nād' or 'dhun(i)') and to experience a state of lasting inner bliss ('Anand'), as is endorsed by the following verses from the SGGS:

One shuts off all means of quickly turning one's focus outward (nine sensory organs) and succeeds in intensely focusing on one's conscious self and achieving lasting inner bliss ('Anand' - 'dasam duār'). There, through the Gurū's instructions, one perceives the everlasting, unstruck 'dhun(i)', day and night.[504]

Where there was flirtatiousness I can now perceive that celestial, unstruck sound. I have achieved perfect harmony and realised 'Nām(u)' through the Grace of the Gurū. Godly attributes, previously lying dormant in my 'Hirdā', now shine brightly like lightning. Now I see Him near, not far, and He pervades my entire conscious self ('Hirdā'). Where, before, there was the dim light of an oil lamp there is, now, the constant bright light of the sun. Its success is rooted in my achievement of lasting equanimity ('Sahaj') through the Grace of the Gurū.[505]

The celestial, unstruck sound resonates in that fortunate 'Hirdā' where there is the effulgent glow of 'Nām(u)'.[506]

The Creator Lord worked a miracle and enabled me to perceive the celestial, unstruck sound. The egocentrics strayed and failed but He revealed it to the God-centric. The Creator Lord, Cause of all Causes, makes it all happen.[507]

'He who reveals the presence of 'Nām(u)' within one's 'Hirdā', is a 'Sat(i)gurū'. There resonates loudly the celestial unstruck sound, heralding His imminent revelation.[508]

The perception of this everlasting, unstruck sound signifies the advent of an experiential perception of the full glow of 'Nām(u)' within one's 'Hirdā', the ultimate goal of one's life.

One's genuine love and desire, the blessings of the Divine Words and Wisdom ('Gur prasād'), absolute faith, unwavering determination and hard work, and God's Grace, were crucial in reaching thus far. In spite of enjoying a state of lasting inner equanimity and bliss, 'Jīvātmāṅ's' intense love and burning desire to be with 'Parmātmāṅ', from whom it has been separated for so long, is now unbearable. Gurmat describes this state of a 'Gursikh' as 'Birhāṅ' or 'Sik' which is beautifully captured in the following verses from the the SGGS:

His 'bhagats' always keep Him close to their hearts ('Hirdās'), both when engaged in their daily activities outside and at home. They always remember and contemplate 'Nām(u)', for they are truly imbued with His love.[509]

'I now love my sleep, for I find my beloved in my dreams', O' my friend.[510]

'When shall I see my Lord, the love of my 'Hirdā'/ '*Man*'? Being asleep is better than being awake, for I can savour some moments with Him in my dreams'.[511]

'O' [chātrik-like] Seeker! Do not wail or crave, just submit to His Will. By so doing, you will not only lose this craving but your love for Him will quadruple'.[512]

Nothing appeases my inner torment or the affliction of separation from You despite all the means at my disposal. Thus separated, I can barely survive, for life, thus, is the life of a crazy desperado.[513]

Karam khaṅḍ kī bāṇī jor(u)

karam: (a) (n, f; pers; synonymous with 'dyā', 'kripā', 'meharbānī', 'rahmat' or 'bakhshīsh') kindness, favour, grace, mercy, or compassion. It is, however, noteworthy that one is only deserving of His Grace when one lives in perfect harmony with 'Nām(u)'. It is perhaps incorrect to label this stage as the stage of 'shubh-'or 'naitik-' 'karam' as one has already successfully fashioned one's 'surat(i)', 'mat(i)', '*man*(i)' and 'budh(i)'. See karam.

khaṅḍ: (n, m) (a) (synonymous with 'avasthā') state, stage, condition, domain, or realm. See khaṅḍ (j).

kī: (a) (prep, f; synonymous with 'dī') of or belonging to. See kī.

bāṇī: (n, f; synonymous with 'rachnā', 'baṇtar' and 'banāvaṭ') creation, composition, production, any work of art, craft, or literature; structure, build or design. See bāṇī.

jor(u): (a) (n, f; pers; synonymous with 'zor(u)', 'bal', 'himmat', 'shaktī' and 'samrathā') bravery, strength, power, or ability. See jor(u).

With one's conscious self already forged and fashioned beautifully, one is in perfect harmony with 'Nām(u)' and one has the inner strength to repulse all attacks of 'Māyā'.

One now eagerly and longingly awaits His Grace and one's goal ('Sachkhaṅḍ', the 'so dar(u)', or 'mahal murār(i)') when one perceives 'Nām(u)', the eternal Reality in one's 'Hirdā' ('nij ghar(u)'). The following verses of the SGGS highlight the significance of receiving His Grace:

Past noble deeds trigger the gift of this human body but it is through His Grace that one finds release ('Moksh') from 'Haumaiṅ', 'Moh' and innate 'Vikārī' tendencies ('Māyā') in this life and 'Āvāgavan' at death. See Pauṛī 4, pp. 102-3.

One who submits to His Will, gets His approval and realises the full glow of 'Nām(u)' within their 'Hirdā'.[514]

By aligning me perfectly with 'Nām(u)', the Beneficent Lord has dispelled all my inner 'vikārī' tendencies.[515]

He whom God grants His Grace, realises the way to 'Nām-realisation'. He then aligns perfectly with and merges with the Primal Soul like water with water.[516]

Align me with Yourself, for I give in now and surrender at Your door. Save me, for, having wandered about aimlessly for long enough, I am now tired, O' compassionate Lord![517]

The main attributes of the state of one's conscious self, in the realm of grace, are power and strength.

Tithai hor(u) n koī hor(u)

tithai: (adv; synonymous with 'othe' and 'vahāṅ') there or therein.

hor(u): (adj; synonymous with 'aur' and 'is toṅ-' 'vadh' or 'chhuṭ') more, additional, or different. The reference here is to any aspect of 'Māyā' or the visible, empirical world, as one's conscious self is now perfectly and absolutely attuned to 'Nām-consciousness'. See hor(u).

n: (p; pronounced as 'nāṅ') no, not or implying a negative connotation.

koī: (pron and adj; synonymous with 'koī ik') literally, anyone, someone or rare one.

hor(u) n koī hor(u): nothing other than absolute and perfect harmony with 'Nām(u)'.

Nothing else, except perfect harmony with 'Nām(u)', exists in one's conscious self.

Tithai jodh mahābal sūr

jodh: (n, m, pl; synonymous with 'yodhā') literally, braves, knights, or warriors, especially those who fight injustice, tyranny, oppression, a holy war or engage in battle with their 'innate evil tendencies'.

mahābal: (adj, m; synonymous with 'balvān', 'balvaṅt', 'mahābalī' and 'at(i) tākatvar') a complex word comprising 'mahā' (great) + 'bal' (might or power), i.e., very strong and powerful; mighty and brave.

sūr: (adj, m; synonymous with 'bahādur', 'yodhā' and 'sūrbīr') literally, brave, valiant, courageous, or intrepid warriors. In essence, the braves who fight 'dharam yudh' ('holy war') for a noble and righteous cause in the wider world and/or the evil disposition of their inner self.

See next verse (paṅkat(i)).

Tin mah(i) Rām(u) rahiā bharpūr

tin: (pron and adj, pl, third person; synonymous with 'tinā', 'tin(h)' and 'tin(h)ā') they or their. See tin(i).

mah(i): (prep; synonymous with 'māh(i)', 'aṅdar' or 'vichkār') inside, within, or in the midst of.

Rām: (n, m) (a) Lord Rāmā, of the Hindu epic Ramāyan, son of King Dasrath, and implicit here is (b) (n and adj, m, s; synonymous with 'ramiā hoiā') 'Nām(u)', the all-pervasive and immanent form of the transcendent God.

rahiā: (a) (present participle - 'kriyā-phal kirdaṅt'; synonymous with 'us dā-' 'rahinā' or 'rahiṇā') literally, one's stay, (b) (v, present continuous of 'rahiṇā'; synonymous with 'rah rahiā hai'), and (c) (v, present tense; synonymous with 'rahiṅdā hai') literally, resides or remains. See rahiṇā (a and b).

bharpūr: (adj) (a) (synonymous with 'labā-lab- 'or 'pūran-' 'bhariā hoiā') literally, filled to the brim or brimful, and (b) (synonymous with 'paripūraṇ' and 'sarv-vyāpak') ubiquitous, all-pervasive, or omnipresent.

Those who have 'Nām(u)' permeating through their entire being, are the real mighty and brave.

Tithai sīto sītā mahimā māh(i)

sīto: (a) (past participle - 'bhūt kirdaṅt'; synonymous with 'vāhiā hoiā') ploughed; see vāhuṇā (a), and implicit here is (b) (past participle - 'bhūt kirdaṅt'; synonymous with 'proiā' and 'sītā hoiā') see siūṇā.

siūṇā: (v) to sew, stitch or make a seam interweave and interlock.

sītā: (a) (n, f) daughter of Rājā Janak and consort of Lord Rāmā of Ramāyanā, (b) (v, past tense of 'siūṇā') stitched or sewed, and implicit here is (c) (past participle - 'bhūt kirdaṅt'; synonymous with 'sītā hoiā') inextricably sewn, stitched, knitted, interwoven, and bound together.

mahimā: (n, f; synonymous with 'ustat(i)', 'vaḍiāī', 'bazurgī', 'jas', 'upmā', 'sobhā' or 'siphat sālāh') literally, praise, fame, tribute, eulogy, or glory. In essence, His Glory or 'siphat-sālāh'.

māh(i): (prep; synonymous with 'vichkār', 'bhītar' or 'aṅdar'; pronounced as 'māh(i)ṅ') literally, inside, within or in the midst of.

See next verse (paṅkat(i)').

Tā ke rūp n kathne jāh(i)

tā: (synonymous with 't'; pronounced as 'tāṅ') (pron, pl; synonymous with 'un(h)āṅ' and 'tin(h)āṅ') they or their. See tā.

ke: (a) (prep, m; synonymous with 'de') of or for. See ke.

rūp: (n, m) (a) (synonymous with 'shakal', 'sūrat', 'sarūp' and 'ākār') literally, form, shape, looks, or appearance, (b) (n, f; synonymous with 'khūbsūrtī', 'sauṅdryā' and 'suṅdartā') literally, good looks, cuteness, beauty, or elegance. The reference here is to the conscious self which, adorned with godly attributes, is now beautiful and elegant.

kathne: (conj v- 'saṅyugat kriyā'; synonymous with 'kahe' and 'ākhe') see kathnā.

kathnā: (a) (n, f; infinitive mood - 'bhāvārth kārdaṅtak'; synonymous with 'vyākhiā' and 'biān') commentary, elaboration, exegesis, or discourse, and (b) (v; synonymous with 'kahiṇā and biān karnā'; pronounced as 'kathnāṅ') literally, to say, state, speak, utter, narrate or recount.

jāh(i): (a) (v, pl, present tense, third person; synonymous with 'uh jāṅde han' or 'jā sakde han'; pronounced as 'jāheṅ') they go or can go, and (b) (conj v, m, pl), e.g., 'n kathne jāh(i)' - cannot be described. See jāh(i) and jāṇā (d).

Those whose beauty and grace are beyond words, are wholly and inextricably rapt in His Glory in that state.

nā oh(i) marah(i) n ṭhāge jāh(i)

nā: (p; synonymous with and often written as just 'n'; pronounced as 'nāṅ') no, not or indicative of a negative implication or connotation.

oh(i): (pron and adj, pl; synonymous with 'oh' and 'vahī') they or precisely they.

marah(i): (a) (v, s, present tense, second person; synonymous with 'tusīṅ marde-' or 'mar jāṅde-' 'ho'; pronounced as 'marheṅ'), (b) (v, pl, present tense, first person; synonymous with 'asīṅ mar jāṅde hāṅ'), (c) (imperative mood - 'saṅbhāv bhvikht kāl - kiās, sharat or bekparvāhī bodhak'; synonymous with 'je mar-' 'jāvāṅ' or 'jā-ī-e'), (d) (v, s, future tense, third person; synonymous with 'uh marange'; pronounced as 'marheṅ'), and (e) (v, pl, present tense, third person; synonymous with 'uh marde-' or 'mar jāṅde-' 'han'; pronounced as 'marheṅ') suffer spiritual downfall or death before their physical death. See marnā (c).

marnā: (v; synonymous with 'marṇā') (a) (synonymous with 'dehāṅt', 'sarīrak maut' or 'mrityū ho jāṇī') to pass away physically, die, expire, or decease, (b) (synonymous with 'jīvat marnā') to shed or lose completely the influence of 'Haumaiṅ', and implicit here is (c) (synonymous with 'ātmak maut ho jāṇī') to suffer spiritual downfall or death during one's lifetime.

ṭhāge: (a) (past participle - 'bhūt kirdaṅt'; synonymous with 'ṭhāge hoe manukh'), and implicit here is (b) (conj v, pl, present tense, third person; synonymous with 'chhal nāl luṭṭe-' or 'ṭhagge-' 'jāṅde han') see ṭhagṇā.

ṭhagṇā: (v; synonymous with 'dhokhe nāl dhan māl harnā') to deceive, cheat, swindle, rob or loot.

n ṭhāge jāh(i): (synonymous with 'chhal nāl luṭṭe-' or 'ṭhagge-' 'nahī jāṅde' or 'jā sakde') literally, cannot be cheated, swindled or robbed. In essence, they cannot be robbed of their precious godly attributes; 'Māyā' cannot beguile and rob them of their godly attributes; they are immune to attacks of 'Māyā'.

See next verse ('paṅkat(i)').

Jin kai rām(u) vasai *man* māh(i)

jin: (pron, pl; synonymous with 'jis', 'jin(h)' and 'jin(h)ā') literally, they, who or whosoever.

kai: (prep; synonymous with 'kā', 'ke', 'kī', 'dā', 'de' or 'dī') of. See kai.

vasai: (synonymous with 'basai') (a) (imperative mood - 'saṅbhāv bhvikht kāl - kiās, sharat or ichhā bodhak', s, third/first person; synonymous with 'je vas jāve'), and implicit here is (b) (v, s, present tense, third person; synonymous with 'vasdā hai' or 'vas jāṅdā hai'; pronounced as 'vasaiṅ') see vasanā (c).

vasanā: (v) (synonymous with 'basaṇā' and 'vasaṇā') (a) (synonymous with 'nivās karnā') literally, to live, inhabit, dwell or reside, (b) (synonymous with 'ras jāṇā') to permeate and overwhelm, and implicit here is (c) to permeate, overwhelm and manifest in one's '*Man*' or 'Hirdā'. See vasanā.

man: (n, m, s) one's conscious self, 'Hirdā' or 'Jīvātmāṅ'.

māh(i): (prep; synonymous with 'vichkār', 'bhītar' or 'aṅdar'; pronounced as 'māh(i)ṅ') literally, inside, within or in the midst of.

Those whose 'Hirdās' are attuned perfectly to and overwhelmed by 'Nām(u)', neither succumb to the attacks of 'Māyā' nor suffer spiritual death from them.

Tithai bhagat vasah(i) ke loa

bhagat: (n, m, pl; synonymous with 'shradhāvān', 'upāsak' or 'bhagtī karan vāle') devotees who worship their deity, preceptor or god, with faith and conviction.

However, implicit here is devotees, votaries or they who have perceived the celestial 'Nād' ('Nām(u)'), who live by His Will, and whose every thought ('*Man*'), utterance ('Bachan') and deed ('Karam') is in perfect harmony with 'Nām(u)'. In Gurmat such a 'bhagat' is synonymous with a 'Sańt', 'Sādh', Gurū and 'Brahm-gyānī'. See bhagat.

vasah(i): (a) (v, s, present tense, second person; synonymous with 'tusīṅ vasde ho'; pronounced as 'vas-heṅ'), (b) (v, s, future tense, second person; synonymous with 'tusīṅ vasoge'; pronounced as 'vas-heṅ'), and (c) (v, pl, present tense, third person; synonymous with 'uh vasde han'; pronounced as 'vas-heṅ') see vāsṇā.

ke: (a) (adj; synonymous with 'ka-ī' and 'anek') many. See ke.

loa: (n, pl; synonymous with 'lok', 'khańḍ' and 'bhavan') islands, countries, or continents; domains, spheres or planets in a system. See loa.

See next verse ('pańkat(i)').

Karah(i) anańd(u) sachā *man*(i) soi

karah(i): (v, pl, present tense, third person; synonymous with 'uh karde-' or 'kardīāṅ-' 'han' or 'kar sakde han'; pronounced as 'karheṅ') do, perform, or carry out. See karah(i) and karnā (g).

anańd(u): (n, m, s; synonymous with 'Sahaj') a state of lasting inner equanimity and supreme inner bliss that one achieves: (i) with perfect alignment with 'Nām(u)', (ii) when innate inner drives and repressed desires ('T'rishnā') in one's '*Man*' no longer relentlessly drive one to satisfy one's urges, and (iii) when 'Māyā' is no longer able to ensnare one into its net. See anańd(u).

sachā: ((skt) 'satya' and (gmkh) 'sat(i)') (a) (n, m, s; synonymous with 'sadīvī jyot(i)' - the Primal Soul) the eternal Reality - the transcendent Lord or 'Nām(u)', It's immanent form. See sachā.

man(i): (locative case - 'adhikaraṇ kārak'; synonymous with '*man* vich') literally, in their conscious self.

soi: (pron and adj; synonymous with 'oh' or 'ohī') he, she, it or they; the same. See soi.

With their 'Man' attuned perfectly to 'Nām(u)', His true devotees from many worlds relish this state of perfect inner equipoise and bliss.

Sach(i) khaṅḍ(i) vasai niraṅkār(u)

sach(i): (locative case - 'adhikaraṇ kārak'; synonymous with 'sach vich') literally, in the eternal Reality ('Pārbrahm' or 'Kartār'). However, implicit here is the state of being in perfect alignment with 'Nām(u)'.

khaṅḍ(i): (locative case - 'adhikaraṇ kārak'; synonymous with 'khaṅḍ vich') see khaṅḍ (j).

sach(i) khaṅḍ(i): literally, in the realm of the eternal Reality.

vasai: (v, s, present tense, third person; synonymous with 'vas jāṅdā hai') See vasanā (d).

niraṅkār(u): (adj, m; synonymous with 'Nirākār') 'Nirākār' is a complex word comprising 'nir' (without) + 'ākār' (form, shape, or the three dimensional outline of something), i.e., one without a physical shape. The reference is to the non-physical, spiritual and the immanent or transcendent form of God.

vasai niraṅkār(u): literally, the formless One ('Nām(u)') exists. In reality, though 'Nām(u)' - the immanent form of the transcendent Lord, being omnipresent, exists within the mortal body, it is still beyond the grasp of the 'Jīvātmāṅ' (conscious self, '*Man*' or 'Hirdā'). However, implicit here is the state of 'Nām(u)' pervading and manifesting its full glow in one's 'Hirdā' or when one has the experiential revelation of the Primal Soul within one's 'Hirdā' as is explicated in the following verses from the SGGS:

Whilst 'Nām(u)' pervades all, Its full glow or expression occurs only in the conscious self ('*Man*' or 'Hirdā') of those who have His Grace ('nadrī karam(i)') and Seal of Approval ('nīsāṇ(u)'). See Pauṛī 34, pages 407-8.

He who submits to His Will and gets His Seal of Approval, realises the full glow of 'Nām(u)' within his 'Hirdā'.[514]

He called me into His Court where I received His Robe of Honour ('His siphat sālāh dā kapṛā/siropāu').[518]

He who enjoys the full glow of 'Nām(u)' in his 'Hirdā', is 'Jīvan mukat'. Recognise that there is no difference between him and the Lord as true', says Nānak.[519]

The Lord is pleased with me; thus, the service of Your servant has borne fruit. By uttering and contemplating 'Nām(u)' my worldly worries and innate evil 'Vikārī' tendencies have vanished. By Your Grace, You have mercifully approved my lifetime's toil and devotion in Your Name.[520]

As water mingles imperceptibly with water, so has 'Jīvātmāṅ' now become immersed in 'Parmātmāṅ'. I am forever a sacrifice unto You, for I have now found release from 'Āvāgavan'.[521]

By His Grace, I have acceded to the status of the Lord and have realised Him. I have now become one with Him and none can find us different.[522]

See next verse ('paṅkat(i)').

Kar(i) kar(i) vekhai nadar(i) nihāl

kar(i) kar(i): (indeclinable past participle or perfect participle - 'pūran pūrab kārdaṅtak'; synonymous with 'kar kar ke') literally, having created. See karnā (f (iii)).

vekhai: (v, s, present tense, third person; synonymous with 'vekhdā hai' and 'dekh bhāl' or 'saṅbhāl kardā hai'; pronounced as 'vekhaiṅ') see vekhai and vekhṇā (g).

nadir(i): (n, f; instrumental case - 'karaṇ kārak'; synonymous with 'kripā drisṭ(i)-' or 'mehar dī nazar-' 'nāl' or 'duārā') with or through His Grace or Blessing. See nadir(i).

nihāl: (a) (v; synonymous with 'nihār', 'nihārnā', 'dekhṇā', 'takṇā' or 'nirīkhaṇ karnā') to look, observe or carefully examine, and implicit here is (b) (adj; synonymous with 'khush', 'anaṅd-chit' or 'prasaṅn') delighted, ecstatic and inspirited, and (c) (adj; synonymous with 'kāmyāb' or 'murādmaṅd') satisfied or satiated and ecstatic or delighted at (i) having a wish granted, (ii) exalted or elevated to a higher post, rank or spiritual level, and (iii) being successful in achieving one's ambition, e.g., realisation of 'Nām(u)'.

The Primal Soul, the eternal Reality, manifests its full glow within one's 'Hirdā' in this realm of eternal Truth and one really perceives Him creating, caring for, and supporting His creation with His compassionate Grace.

Tithai khaṅḍ maṅḍal varbhaṅḍ

khaṅḍ: (n, m, pl) planets ('khaṅḍ') in the universe (brahmaṅḍ). See khaṅḍ (c).

maṅḍal: (n, m, pl; synonymous with 'golākār gherā' and 'dāyrah') circular orbits; planetary systems, with planets orbiting around a sun or star. See maṅḍal.

varbhaṅḍ: (n, m, pl; synonymous with 'brahmānḍ') literally, cosmos, sum total of all galaxies or the whole universe/s.

One perceives countless planets, planetary systems, and the entire universe in action therein.

Je ko kathai t aṅt n aṅt

je: (a) (pron; pl of 'jo'; synonymous with 'jihṛe') they, who, whoever, whosoever. (conj; synonymous with 'yadī' and 'agar') if or in case. See je.

ko: (pron and adj; abbrev for and synonymous with 'koī') someone, anyone, or another; many or several. See ko.

kathai: (a) (v, s, present tense, third person; synonymous with 'kathdā or ākhdā hai'), and implicit here is (b) (v, s, imperative mood - 'saṅbhāv bhvikht kāl', third person; synonymous with 'kathnā chāhe', 'kathe', 'ākhe' and 'dasaṇ lagge') see kathnā.

je ko kathai: (imperative mood - 'saṅbhāv bhvikht kāl - kiās bodhak'; synonymous with 'je koī biān karnā chāhe') literally, should one dare speculate.

t: (synonymous with 'tā'; pronounced as 'tāṅ') (p and adv; synonymous with 'tad', 'tadoṅ', or 'udoṅ') then, thus, because of, or, therefore. See t.

aṅt: (n, m; synonymous with 'oṛak', 'sīmā' and 'had') end, boundary, finale, or extremity. See aṅt.

aṅt n aṅt: [there is] no end, boundary, or finale.

t aṅt n aṅt: literally, [one realises that] there is no end to the endless.

Daring to speculate about the extent of the universe is futile even in this state of one's spiritual development, for there is no end to the endless.

Tithai loa loa ākār

loa: (a) (n, pl; synonymous with 'lok', 'khaṅḍ' and 'bhavan') islands, countries, or continents; domains, spheres or planets in a system, and (b) (n, m, pl) worlds (inhabitable planets) or countries. See loa.

loa loa: (synonymous with 'ka-ī-' or 'beaṅt-' 'bhavan') countless habitable regions, countries, or worlds.

ākār: (n, m, pl; synonymous with 'akār', 'sarūp' and 'rachnā') three dimensional shapes, sizes, forms, figures, appearances, or outlines of the empirical world. In essence, the diverse empirical world with whatever diverse form of inanimate and sentient life forms.

See next verse ('paṅkat(i)').

Jiv jiv hukam tivai tiv kār

jiv jiv: (adv; synonymous with 'jioṅ', 'jis prakār', 'jaise' and 'jiveṅ') howsoever, as, in the manner of, as though, for instance.

hukam: (n, m; (arab); synonymous with 'phurmān', 'āgiā' and 'ādesh') order, decree, or command. See hukam(u).

tivai: (adv; synonymous with 'tiv', 'taise' and 'us prakār'; pronounced as 'tivaiṅ') similarly, or in the same manner, accordingly.

tiv: (adv; synonymous with 'tiveṅ') similarly or in the same manner.

kār: (n; synonymous with 'karanyog kaṅm') worthwhile or useful work, job, or action they act out, live or perform. See kār.

One perceives countless planets, supporting appropriate inanimate and perhaps sentient life forms therein, all evolving according to His Divine Order.

Vekhai vigsai kar(i) vīchār(u)

vigsai: (a) (v, s, present tense, third person; synonymous with 'pasār-' 'vikās-' or 'phailāu-' 'huṅdā hai'; pronounced as 'vigsaiṅ') see vigsanā, and implicit here is (b) (v, s, present tense, third person; synonymous with 'vigsadā-' or 'khiṛdā-' 'hai'; 'khush-' or 'prasaṅn-' 'huṅdā hai'; pronounced as 'vigsaiṅ') see vigsanā.

kar(i): (indeclinable past participle or perfect participle - 'pūran pūrab kārdaṅtak'; synonymous with 'kar ke') having done. See karnā (a).

vīchār(u): (a) (synonymous with 'kudrat de lekhe dī-' 'bīchār' and/or 'bibek') consultation, speculation, consideration, or deliberation, and (b) (n, m; synonymous with 'nirṇā' and 'phaislā') conclusion, judgement or decision. See vīchār(u).

See next verse ('paṅkat(i)').

Nānak kathnā karṛā sār(u)

Nānak: (n, m, s) the (u) of 'Nānak(u)' is missing because of its vocative case - 'saṅbodhan kārak'.

kathna: (a) (n, f; infinitive mood - 'bhāvārth kārdaṅtak'; synonymous with 'vyākhiā' and 'biān') commentary, elaboration, exegesis, or discourse, and (b) (v; synonymous with 'kahiṇā' and 'biān karnā') literally, to say, state, speak, utter, narrate or recount. In essence, to describe 'what is in His mind'.

karṛā: (adj) (a) (synonymous with 'kaṭhor' and 'sakhat') hard, rigid, sturdy, or stiff; callous, cruel or heartless, and implicit here is (b) (synonymous with 'aukhā', 'kaṭhin' and 'mushkil') difficult, arduous, knotty, intricate or problematic.

sār(u): (n, m; synonymous with 'lohā' and 'phaulād') iron metal. See sār(u).

karṛā sār(u): literally, hard like steel.

kathnā karṛā sār(u): (a) literally, to describe what is in His Mind [even in this realm of Sach(i) khaṅḍ(i)] is as hard as biting into steel, and (b) to describe one's inner state at the time of experiential revelation of 'Nām(u)' within one's 'Hirdā' is as hard as biting into steel. The following verse from the SGGS beautifully captures this sentiment:

Fifty-two letters of the Sanskrit alphabet can describe everything within our grasp in the whole world. However, these letters would prove inadequate and useless in expounding the state of oneness between 'Jīvātmāṅ' and 'Parmātmāṅ'.[523]

'Whilst rejoicing and watching over everything, He nurtures and cares for it all as it evolves. However, to describe one's inner state during the

experiential revelation of 'Nām(u)' within one's 'Hirdā' and to know what's in His mind is as hard as biting into steel', O' Nānak!

Conceptual summary

The main attribute of this state of one's conscious self in the realm of grace is that of power and strength, and nothing else, except that perfect harmony with 'Nām(u)', exists in therein. Many who are mighty and brave, with 'Nām(u)' permeating through their entire being, cherish it. Indeed, they, whose beauty and grace are just beyond words, are wholly and inextricably rapt in His Glory. Furthermore, they, whose 'Hirdās' are attuned perfectly to and overwhelmed by 'Nām(u)', neither succumb to the attacks of 'Māyā' nor suffer spiritual death from them.

With their '*Man*' attuned perfectly to 'Nām(u)', His true devotees from many worlds, relish this state of perfect inner equipoise and bliss. The Primal Soul, the eternal Reality, manifests its full glow within one's 'Hirdā' and one really begins to perceive Him creating, caring for and supporting His creation with His compassionate Grace. One now truly perceives countless planets, constellations, and universes; one perceives countless habitable worlds and infinite life forms therein, all evolving according to His Divine Order.

'Whilst rejoicing and watching over everything, He nurtures and cares for it all as it evolves. However, to describe one's inner state during this experiential revelation and what is in His Mind is as hard as biting into steel', O' Nānak!

Having achieved lasting inner equipoise ('Sahaj') and bliss ('Anańd') and with no lingering impeding baggage of 'Haumaiṅ', 'Moh', innate evil 'Vikārī' tendencies, one is now ready to perceive the full glow of the Primal Soul within one's 'Hirdā'. Indeed, at the right moment and with God's Grace, 'Parmātmāṅ' elects to express itself fully and 'Jīvātmāṅ' then becomes its exact functional replica.

One now realises one's true self and perceives the all-powerful, all-knowing, and all-pervasive 'Nām(u)', the Primal Soul, in real time action - creation (unity/unicity into diversity), preservation and assimilation back into itself, all happening spontaneously within the bounds of His Divine Order.

PAUṚĪ 38
ਪਉੜੀ ੩੮॥

Jat(u) pāhārā, dhīraj(u) suniār(u).
ਜਤੁ ਪਾਹਾਰਾ, ਧੀਰਜੁ ਸੁਨਿਆਰੁ॥

Ahraṇ(i) mat(i), ved(u) hathīār(u).
ਅਹਰਣਿ ਮਤਿ, ਵੇਦੁ ਹਥੀਆਰੁ॥

Bhau khalā, agn(i) taptāu.
ਭਉ ਖਲਾ, ਅਗਨਿ ਤਪ ਤਾਉ॥

Bhāṅḍā bhāu, aṅmrit(u) tit(u) ḍhāl(i).
ਭਾਂਡਾ ਭਾਉ, ਅੰਮ੍ਰਿਤੁ ਤਿਤੁ ਢਾਲਿ॥

Ghaṛīai, sabad(u) sachī ṭaksāl.
ਘੜੀਐ, ਸਬਦੁ ਸਚੀ ਟਕਸਾਲ॥

Jin kau nadar(i) karam(u), tin kār.
ਜਿਨ ਕਉ ਨਦਰਿ ਕਰਮੁ, ਤਿਨ ਕਾਰ॥

Nānak, nadrī, nadar(i) nihāl. (38)
ਨਾਨਕ, ਨਦਰੀ, ਨਦਰਿ ਨਿਹਾਲ॥ ੩੮॥

The process of forging and fashioning a 'kuṛiār *Man*' into a 'sachiār *Man*' is compared and contrasted with a nugget of gold being turned into a beautiful piece of jewellery in the forge of a goldsmith. A small nugget of gold is carefully placed in a crucible and smelted in an orderly fashion. It is then moulded into the ultimate desired shape by being poured it into a diecast, allowed to cool a little and hammered whilst still malleable. This process of controlled reheating, cooling, and hammering ('forging') is repeated until the desired ultimate shape is produced. Its rough edges are then milled and smoothed and the outer surfaces polished. It is finally stamped, which denotes and declares the mark of approval.

In contrast, one's conscious self ('*Man*' or 'Hirdā'), lacking many beautiful attributes in its default or natural state ('Kuṛiār'), expresses only its unattractive and undesirable characteristics of 'Haumaiṅ', 'Moh' and innate evil 'Vikārī' tendencies. It needs to be forged and fashioned into a 'Sachiār', the conscious self in perfect harmony with 'Nām(u)' where

'Nām(u)' pervades it absolutely and the full glow of 'Nām-consciousness' shines through in daily life.

Jat(u) pāhārā, dhīraj(u) suniār(u)

jat(u): (a) (adv; synonymous with 'jidhar' and 'jithe') where, whither, in or to which side or direction, (b) (adv; synonymous with 'jidhroṅ' and 'jithoṅ') where from or from which side or direction, (c) (adv; synonymous with 'jad', 'jadoṅ' and 'jis same') when or whenever, and implicit here is (d) (n, m) the act of absolute control over one's five sensorimotor organs, with particular emphasis on chastity and continence. In a broader sense, 'jat(u)' is righteous thoughts, speech, sight, hearing, touch, smell, deeds and direction. Its focus and emphasis on continence alone is wrong and not supported by Gurmat, as outlined in the following verses from the SGGS:

If celibacy could save one from 'Haumaiṅ', 'Moh' and innate 'Vikārī' tendencies ('Māyā'), why then no eunuchs could achieve 'Sahaj' and 'anaṅd' ('Moksh').[524]

If one strives, but fails, to control one's lust despite performing the accepted rituals, one's conscious self ('*man*(u)') wavers and errs in a state of confusion and suffers its consequence.[525]

One's innate nature, desires and drives spontaneously direct one's conscious self towards their fulfilment. Driven by 'Haumaiṅ', 'Moh', innate evil 'Vikārī' tendencies and one's unmet desires ('Trisnā'), one is easily led astray. One therefore always needs to be on one's guard.

pāhārā: (a) (n, m; synonymous with 'prasār', 'phailāu' and 'visthār') expanse, development, amplification, or growth, and implicit here is (b) (n, m; synonymous with 'luhār-' or 'suniār-' 'dī bhaṭhī') literally, a smithy, the workshop or forge of a blacksmith or goldsmith. A goldsmith keeps a constant and careful watch over all aspects of his workplace, for not only is the raw material extremely valuable but the process is also extremely delicate and precise requiring the patience of a saint. 'Rome was not built in a day' as the saying goes; one needs to be extremely patient in fashioning one's conscious self.

dhīraj: (n, f; synonymous with '*man* dī driṛtā', 'ṭikāu', 'hauṅslā', 'sabar', 'shāṅtī', 'gaṅbhīrtā') literally, patience, composure, forbearance, tranquility, reserve, morale, fortitude, and resoluteness. 'Haste makes waste' and 'patience is indeed a virtue' and we know only too well that one often comes to regret a decision taken in haste and without due consideration. That is precisely the sentiment expressed in the following verse from the SGGS:

One would not even think of committing an evil act if one were fully aware of its dire consequences in the long run.[526]

Both 'Jat(u)' and 'dhīraj' are considered as pre-eminent in the propagation of moral and ethical virtues and values. They both help in the development of one's moral and ethical conduct and are thus often considered beneficial during the stage of 'dharam khaṅḍ'.

suniār: (n, m; synonymous with 'sunār') a goldsmith.

Make restraint and self-control your forge and nurture the patience of a goldsmith.

Ahraṇ(i) mat(i), ved(u) hathīār(u)

ahraṇ(i): (n, m; synonymous with 'lohe dā piṅḍ') an anvil, a heavy block of iron, on which a smith works his metals.

mat(i): (a) (n, f; synonymous with 'akal', 'giān', 'samajh' and 'siāṇap') knowledge, intellect, wisdom, and the ability to reason. This is one of the aspects or functions of '*man*' in Gurmat. See mat(i) and '*man*'.

ved(u): (n, m, s; synonymous with 'bed(u)') literally, each one of the four vedas of the Hindus - 'Rig', 'Sām', 'Yajur' and 'Atharvan'. However, as the noun is singular, the tacit reference here is to Divine Knowledge and Wisdom from any holy 'graṅth'.

hathīār(u): (a) (n, m, s; synonymous with 'ghātak shastar') literally, a device, an implement, or a weapon, and implicit here is (b) (n, m, s; synonymous with 'saṅd' and 'auzār') literally, an implement or a tool.

Both 'Mat(i)' and 'Budh(i)' are suggestive of and relate to 'Giān khaṅḍ's' stage of one's spiritual development. 'Giān' is the initial knowledge ('mat(i)') from an external source and deductive reasoning or discernment ('budh(i)') is dependent on it. Intuition ('anubhav giān'), however, is knowledge and/or deductive reasoning based on one's gut instinct or experiential ability and not on conscious reasoning. Intution, in consonance with 'Nām-consciousness', is 'bibek budh(i)' or 'sudh(i)'. 'Mat(i)' and 'Budh(i)' need to evolve to 'uchī mat(i)' and 'bibek budh(i)' respectively through the process alluded to above in 'Pauṛī' 36.

Let your own intellect ('mat(i)') be your anvil and Divine Knowledge and Wisdom your hammer.

Bhau khalā, agan(i) taptāu

bhau: (a) (n, m; synonymous with 'bhya' (skt), 'bhai', 'ḍar' or 'khauph') fear, fright, dread, or apprehension. In essence, the reference here is to 'nirmal bhau' of God, i.e., due reverence and just fear of the Divine Order ('Hukam'). Only the very naïve forget that the evil thoughts, foul utterances, and sinful deeds that we commit cannot escape His judgment and verdict but the wise amongst us always remember that we reap what we sow. The following verses from the SGGS beautifully express this sentiment:

One neither struggles nor engenders any desire to align with 'Nām(u)' without harbouring any faith or fear in the Divine Order.[527]

Realising His Writ and Justice, and all-pervasiveness, one commits to living in harmony with 'Nām(u)'.[528]

khalā: (a) (v; past tense; synonymous with 'khaṛā' and 'khaṛotā') literally, stood upright or standing still, (b) (n, m; synonymous with 'mūrakh') a fool, simpleton, or an idiot, and implicit here is (c) (n, f; synonymous with 'dhauṅkaṇī'; pronounced as 'khalāṅ') bellows - a portable or fixed device for blowing a blast of air into the fire. The rate at which blasts of air are driven into the fire governs and controls both the final temperature and the maintenance of that steady state as well.

agan(i): (n, f; synonymous with and pronounced as 'agnī') literally, fire. In essence, energy - the very first of the five primordial aspects of creation - others being air (gases), water (liquids), Earth ('dharat(i)' - solids), and 'ākāsh' (ether or space).

tap: (n, m; synonymous with 'tapasyā') strict discipline, austerities, or penances - deliberate self-punishment, viz. tolerance of extreme cold in winter or heat in summer; prolonged fasting, silence or the adoption of strange posture, and other austere practices, in order to gain full control over one's conscious self ('*Man*'). See tap(u).

tāu: (a) (n, m; synonymous with 'tāp', 'sek' and 'āṅch') heat or warmth; hurt, harm or danger, and (b) (n, f; synonymous with 'tapan' and 'tap karan dī kriyā') the act or process of taptāuṇā.

taptāuṇā: (v) (a) to heat or warm, (b) to annoy, trouble or torment, and (c) to impose strict self-discipline, austerities, or penances in order to gain full control over one's conscious self.

taptāu: (a) (n, m; synonymous with 'tapasyā dā kashṭ') the deliberate imposition and suffering due to strict self-discipline, austerities, or penances in order to gain control over one's conscious self, and implicit here is (b) (synonymous with 'ghāl ghālaṇī'; 'tapāṅ dā-' 'tapṇā' or 'tapāuṇā'; 'kamāī karnī') the process of moving forward with conviction and steadfastness despite the hurdles, problems, distress and innate 'vikārī' tendencies en route; the act of putting in prolonged, determined and intense effort or painstaking toil.

Thus, remembering one's moral or ethical vulnerabilities, inevitable physical death, the need to live by His Will and the need to be innately and spontaneously good and altruistic, require active engagement and effort, dogged determination, and strict discipline; all point to the 'Saram khaṅḍ' stage of one's spiritual development.

Let awe, reverence, and fear of the Divine Order be your bellows, and the toil of strict self-discipline and contemplation, your blazing fire.

Bhāṅḍā bhāu, aṅmrit(u) tit(u) ḍhāl(i)

bhāṅḍā: (n, m) (a) (synonymous with 'bartan') a utensil, vessel, pot, or a container, (b) (n, f; synonymous with 'kuṭhālī') literally, a goldsmith's melting pot or crucible, and implicit here is (c) (n, m; synonymous with 'sarir') literally, the physical body. In essence, it is the melting pot or the crucible where one's '*Man*' or conscious self will be subject to smelting with extreme love and care.

bhāu: (a) (n) (n, m; synonymous with 'prem' and 'piār') love or deep affection. In essence, it implies cordial and courteous interaction and dealings with each other and/or the expression of love or deep affection for God. This sincere and undying love for God and 'Nām-consciousness' could be construed as part of the 'Karam khaṅḍ' stage of one's spiritual development. See bhāu. However, the following verses from the SGGS allude to some pre-conditions that must first be met:

Only one who has love for the Lord who has due reverence and just fear of the Divine Order in their '*man*'.[529]

Just as love for alignment with 'Nām(u)' does not flourish without ideological convergence with the truly enlightened, similarly, one does not commit to surrender to 'Nām(u)' and live by His Will without this love and reverence within.[530]

One feels little love for the Lord and fails to serve and worship Him without harbouring a just fear of the Divine Order. One develops this by ideologically converging with a Gurū, and both God's love and just fear enhance one's service and worship of Him.[531]

bhāṅḍā bhāu: (synonymous with 'prem rūp bhāṅḍā') literally, the body as the crucible of love. In essence, the reference is to soften and plasticise the '*Man*', in this body, with love and care.

aṅmrit(u): (n and adj, m; synonymous with 'Amrit') a compound word containing two parts: 'aṅ' (without) + 'mrit' (death). 'Mrit' is an abbreviation for the Hindi or Sanskrit word 'mrityū', meaning death. The word 'Aṅmrit' really means that which defies death or something that has an immortalising effect. Death here does not refer to the physical death or bodily demise of a being but to their spiritual downfall or death ('Ātmak maut') - succumbing to one's ego-consciousness ('Haumaiṅ', 'Moh', 'Māiā' and 'Vikārs'). The only authentic 'Aṅmrit' in Gurmat is 'Nām(u)':

'There is but one elixir that immortalises one, i.e., 'Nām(u) Aṅmrit' and there is none other'.[532]

The reference here is to 'Nām(u) Aṅmrit', the spiritually uplifting and enlightening words, knowledge and wisdom of the perfect Gurū, which make one immune to spiritual downfall or death. 'Aṅmrit(u)' is equated here with a diecast, as '*Man*' needs to be forged and fashioned into that exact mould.

tit(u): (a) (adv; synonymous with 'uthe' or 'vahāṅ') there or therein, (b) (pron; synonymous with 'us') that, (c) (pron; instrumental case - 'karaṇ kārak; synonymous with 'us-' 'nāl', 'rāhīṅ', 'duārā', 'sadkā' or 'anusār'), and implicit here is (d) (pron; accusative case - 'karam kārak'; synonymous with 'us nūṅ'). In essence, the tacit reference here is to one's conscious self ('*Man*').

ḍhāl(i): (a) (indeclinable past participle or perfect participle - 'pūran pūrab kārdaṅtak'; synonymous with 'ḍhāl ke') by melting and casting, and implicit here is (b) (v, imperative mood - 'hukmī bhvikht', second person; synonymous with 'pighlā ke saṅche vich pā'; 'ḍhālo' or 'ḍhāl lavo') literally, melt and cast. See 'ḍhālṇā'.

ḍhālṇā: (v) (a) (synonymous with 'ṭhos padārath nūṅ puṅghrāuṇā') to melt, plasticise, mould, or cast into a form or shape, and (b) (synonymous with 'ṭhaṅḍā-', 'shāṅt-' or 'rāzī-' 'karnā'; 'manāuṇā') to coax and cajole, mollify, persuade and bring round to one's view.

aṅmrit(u) tit(u) ḍhāl(i): (synonymous with 'aṅmrit de saṅche vich ḍhālo') literally, pour and cast it in the diecast of 'aṅmrit(u)'.

With love and care as your crucible, mould your 'Man' in the diecast of spiritual knowledge and wisdom (the revealed Word or 'Gurbānī' – manifestation of 'Nām(u)').

Ghaṛīai, sabad(u) sachī ṭaksāl

ghaṛīai: (a) (v, pl, first person, imperative mood - 'hukmī bhvikht'; synonymous with 'sānūṅ ghaṛ laiṇā chāhīdā hai'), and implicit here is (b) (v, s, present tense, third person; synonymous with 'ghaṛīdā hai' and 'ghaṛiā jāṅdā hai') literally, is forged, fashioned, or moulded. See ghaṛnā.

sabad(u): (n, m) (a) His Glory or Praise, (b) 'Anhad Sabad', the 'Primordial Nād' ('Nām(u)') through which God communicates with His Creation, (c) Gurū's Word (Gurbānī) utterances or the written word of a person who has experienced the full glow of 'Nām(u)' within his 'Hirdā', and whose every thought, utterance or deed is in perfect harmony with 'Nām(u)', and implicit here is (d) (instrumental case - 'karaṇ kārak'; synonymous with 'sabad-' 'nāl', 'rāhīṅ', 'duārā' or 'sadkā') literally, with, by, through or by virtue of.

A Gurū's word, inspired by and spoken at the behest of 'Anhad Sabad' ('Nām(u)') is its surrogate, the 'Baikharī Bānī' that mortals can hear. On the contrary, 'Anhad Sabad', its source, cannot be heard but only perceived in a state of perfect harmony with 'Nām(u)' and with the Grace of God. Notably, it embodies not only God's Glory but also Divine Wisdom for the path to 'Nām-realisation'. A Gurū's word is thus a medium which an ordinary person can use to discover and tread the path of 'Nām-consciousness', achieve perfect harmony with and eventually realise and perceive 'Nām(u)' within their 'Hirdā'.

sachī: (a) (adj, f; synonymous with 'sadīvī' and 'aṭal') eternal, (b) (adj, f; synonymous with 'asal', 'suhird' or 'nishkapṭ') real, pure, and sincere, (c) (adj, f) (synonymous with 'nirmal' and 'pavitr') perfect, flawless, or immaculate, and (d) (synonymous with 'hukam baṅdh') conforming to or in harmony with 'Nām(u)'.

ṭaksāl: (a) (n, m; synonymous with 'satsaṅg', sādhsaṅg' and 'uttam saṅgat') literally, company or association of the enlightened where deliberation or chanting of Nam(u) is pre-eminent, (b) (n, f; synonymous with 'ṭake-' or 'sikke-' 'baṇāun dā ghar') literally, a royal mint, and (c) (n, f; synonymous with 'uttam sikhyā deṇ vālī pāṭhshālā') literally, seminary for Christians and Jews; 'madrassā' for Muslims, and 'damdami ṭaksāl' or a missionary college for Sikhs.

sachī ṭaksāl: (a) (n, f; synonymous with Gurū and 'Gurū dī Saṅgat') literally, the company or association of a Gurū who has realised 'Nām(u)', and whose every thought ('*Man*'), utterance ('Bachan') and deed ('Karam') is in perfect harmony with it. In essence, 'Gurū dī Saṅgat' is not just his companionship but ideological convergence which entails surrender to a Gurū's Will, contemplating his Divine Word (Gurbānī), imbibing it in one's 'Hirdā' and implementing it in one's daily life, (b) (n, f, s; synonymous with 'Sachī ṭaksāl jithe sachā sabad baṇdā hai') literally, a mint where the 'true word' is produced; in essence, the source of the Divine Word, and (c) (genitive case - 'saṅbaṅdh kārak; synonymous with 'sachī ṭaksāl de').

sabad(u) sachī ṭaksāl: (instrumental case - 'karaṇ kārak'; synonymous with 'Gurū or Sachī ṭaksāl de Sabad-' 'nāl', 'rāhīṅ' or 'duārā') literally, with, by or through the Gurū's word (Gurbānī).

In essence, here the word 'ghaṛīai' refers to the final stages of the process of forging and diecasting, where the moulded raw product is then milled and polished to smooth off any residue of unevenness, i.e., any lingering trace of 'Haumaiṅ', 'Moh' and innate 'Vikārī' tendencies. One's conscious self is now attuned perfectly to and becomes the embodiment of, 'Nam-consciousness'.

Finally, one smooths off any residual nonuniformity of 'Man' by deliberating and imbibing the perfect Gurū's Divine Word in the company of 'sādhsaṅgat'.

Jin kau nadar(i) karam(u), tin kār

jin: (pron, pl; synonymous with 'jin(h)' and 'jin(h)ā') literally, they, who or whosoever.

kau: (prep; synonymous with 'tāṅī', 'ko', 'nūṅ', 'neṅ', 'toṅ', 'dā/kā' or 'la-ī') to, for, from, upto. See kau.

nadar(i): (n, f; synonymous with 'kripā drisṭ(i)') literally, gracious glance, look of favour or an expression of compassion. See nadar(i).

karam(u): (n; (arab); synonymous with 'kripā', 'meharbānī' and 'bakhshīsh') grace, blessing, mercy, compassion, or favour. It is, however, noteworthy that whilst God grants us all that we need for our daily survival, one only finds and begin to tread the path to 'Nam-consciousness' when one genuinely and actively seeks and becomes worthy of His Grace. See karam(u).

jin kau nadar(i) karam(u): literally, they who are blessed with His Gracious Glance. In essence, those who get to submit to the Gurū's Divine Word and Wisdom, ideologically converge with it and genuinely strive to live by God's Will.

tin: (pron, pl, third person; synonymous with 'tinā', 'tin(h)' and 'tin(h)ā') literally, they, them, or theirs.

kār: (n, m; synonymous with 'karanyog-' 'kaṅm' or 'kriyā') worthwhile work, job, or an action. The tacit reference here is to the whole process of forging and diecasting, with particular emphasis on the end product. See kār.

tin kār: literally, (a) only they engage in this process or (b) this job of turning a nugget into a beautiful piece of jewellery is for them only.

They who are blessed with His Gracious Glance, engage, and succeed in this task.

Nānak, nadrī, nadar(i) nihāl

Nānak: (n, m, s) the (u) of 'Nānak(u)' is missing because of its vocative case - 'saṅbodhan kārak'.

nadrī: (a) (adj; synonymous with 'nadar karan vālā' or 'kartār'; pronounced as 'nadrī') one with the ability to give a compassionate glance, i.e., God, and (b) (genitive case - 'saṅbaṅdh kārak'; synonymous with 'nadar karan vāle dī'). See nadrī and nadar(i) (c).

nadar(i): (instrumental case - 'karaṇ kārak'; synonymous with 'kripā drisṭ(i)-' or 'mehar dī nazar-' 'nāl' or 'duārā') with or through His Grace or Blessing. See nadar(i).

nihāl: (a) (v; synonymous with 'nihār', 'nihārnā', 'dekhṇā', 'takṇā' or 'nirīkhaṇ karnā') to look, observe or carefully examine, and implicit here is (b) (adj; synonymous with 'khush', 'anaṅd-chit' or 'prasaṅn') delighted, ecstatic and inspirited, and (c) (adj; synonymous with 'kāmyāb' or 'murādmaṅd') satisfied or satiated and ecstatic or delighted at (i) having a wish granted, (ii) exalted or elevated to a higher post, rank or spiritual level, and (iii) being successful in achieving one's ambition, e.g., realisation of 'Nām(u)'.

'The Gracious Lord, through His Gracious Glance, blesses them with inner equipoise, bliss and enlightenment', O' Nānak!

Conceptual summary

Make restraint and rigorous self-control your forge and nurture the patience of a goldsmith within you. Let worldly knowledge and wisdom be your anvil and Divine Knowledge and Wisdom your hammer.

Let awe, reverence, and fear of the Divine Order be your bellows and the toil of strict self-discipline and contemplation your blazing fire. With love and care as your crucible, mould your '*Man*' in the diecast of 'Nām(u)'.

Finally, mill and polish off any residue of difference or seamier aspect by deliberating and imbibing the perfect Gurū's Divine Word when 'Jīvātmāṅ' becomes an exact functional replica of 'Parmātmāṅ'.

Only they, who are blessed with His Gracious Glance, engage and succeed in this task. 'The Gracious Lord, through His Gracious Glance, blesses them with inner equipoise, bliss and enlightenment', O' Nānak!

The key question, right at the outset, was: 'How can a 'kūṛiār(u)' turn into a 'sachiār(u)'? Or put another way: 'How can one fashion one's 'Jīvātmāṅ' (conscious self, '*Man*' or 'Hirdā') into an exact functional replica of 'Parmātmāṅ'? A few basic questions that must immediately spring to one's mind before one can even begin to speculate about the answers to this vexed, and as yet unanswered, question are as follows: 'Who am I?', 'What am I here for?' 'Can I get there by myself?' 'Who can guide me and show me the path?'

Equally, we must recognise that these are not questions for one who is already knee-deep in the quicksand of the material world, its comforts and pleasures and who is happily allowing himself to sink still deeper.

For progression to a higher plane in the spiritual sense, one must realise that one is not this functioning body but 'Jīvātmāṅ', a dysfunctional or partially functional replica of 'Parmātmāṅ', gifted to this body with the opportunity to break through the obstructing wall or barrier that prevents 'Parmātmāṅ' from casting its exact functional image in us. Secondly, one must appreciate one's limitations in this non-physical or spiritual field and be ready to submit to another who has first-hand knowledge in this sphere. A Gurū is one such person who has perceived the full glow of this all-pervasive and creative Primal Soul in his conscious self and can guide us not only in our understanding of the Divine Order and Will but also in how to live by His Will.

The key ingredients of our correct understanding of life in general are as follows: For survival, growth and evolution, the creation of a centre of consciousness is a pre-requisite for all elemental, non-sentient, and sentient life, as no life can exist without such a centre of consciousness, with a degree of autonomy, to serve both as its guardian and guide. This centre of consciousness ('Jīvātmāṅ') comes into being when the Primal Soul ('Parmātmāṅ') interacts with and manifests itself in the physical body.

Creation of 'Jīvātmāṅ' (conscious self, '*Man*' or 'Hirdā') is God's way of creating diversity from unity. 'Jīvātmāṅ' is nothing but a partial and functional surrogate of 'Parmātmāṅ'. The degree of expression of 'Parmātmāṅ', along with a degree of autonomy (free will) and endowed attributes, virtues and values result in a functional unit with a unique conscious self, innate nature, predispositions, potential, and the ability not only to survive, grow and interact with the surrounding world, but also to evolve.

Infinite permutations in the endowed mixture of these attributes, virtues and values in different beings engender different responses to the same interaction in different beings and this in turn generates numerous scenarios and role models for us to deliberate on, to reject or from which to learn. Accumulated karmā and 'Saṅskārs' form the basis of His Judgement, and one's future destiny ('Mastak de lekh') depends on one's determined degree of alignment with His Will.

To carry out or live by His Will is the goal of all life forms.

EPILOGUE

SALOK
ਸਲੋਕੁ॥

Pavaṇ(u) gurū, pāṇī pitā, mātā dharat(i) mahat(u).
ਪਵਣੁ ਗੁਰੂ, ਪਾਣੀ ਪਿਤਾ, ਮਾਤਾ ਧਰਤਿ ਮਹਤੁ॥

Divas(u) rāt(i) dui, dāī dāiā, khelai sagal jagat(u).
ਦਿਵਸੁ ਰਾਤਿ ਦੁਇ, ਦਾਈ ਦਾਇਆ, ਖੇਲੈ ਸਗਲ ਜਗਤੁ॥

Chaṅgiāīā, buriāīā, vāchai dharam(u) hadūr(i).
ਚੰਗਿਆਈਆ ਬੁਰਿਆਈਆ, ਵਾਚੈ ਧਰਮੁ ਹਦੂਰਿ॥

Karmī āpo āpṇī, ke neṛai, ke dūr(i).
ਕਰਮੀ ਆਪੋ ਆਪਣੀ, ਕੇ ਨੇੜੈ, ਕੇ ਦੂਰਿ॥

Jinī Nām(u) dhiāiā, gae masakat(i) ghāl(i).
ਜਿਨੀ ਨਾਮੁ ਧਿਆਇਆ, ਗਏ ਮਸਕਤਿ ਘਾਲਿ॥

Nānak, te mukh ujle, ketī chhuṭī nāl(i). (1)
ਨਾਨਕ, ਤੇ ਮੁਖ ਉਜਲੇ, ਕੇਤੀ ਛੁਟੀ ਨਾਲਿ॥ ੧॥

This empirical world is God's stage or theatre where His theatrical performance/pageant ('khel'/'līlā') is being performed. For all such performances, the planets and the Earth serve as 'Space', day and night as 'Time', and air, water, fire, elements and ether as 'Substance'. In 'Pauṛī' 34, Gurū Nānak, categorically states that this Earth is here for all humankind to learn and practise righteousness - a 'Dharamsāl' ('dharam kamāuṇ dī thāṅ'). It is a place where, with the God-given golden opportunity of a human birth, we must seek to understand our rightful place in the ecosphere, to learn about our purpose and goal in life and the path we must tread in order to succeed in living by the Will of God. We must also remember that our deeds are subject to God's careful scrutiny. Those who follow their ego-consciousness ('Haumaiṅ') and remain engrossed in the empirical world, get further and further away from their goal. For them, this world remains forever a stage where all the men and women are merely players; they make their entrances, misled by 'Haumaiṅ' and driven by 'Trisnā' just act out their chosen roles and suffer the consequences. In contrast, those who submit to the Gurū's Divine Wisdom and strive to shed their 'Haumaiṅ' and align perfectly with 'Nām-consciousness', succeed, and realise their goal of 'Nām-realisation.' Moreover, they altruistically help others on this path too, and are honoured for having fully discharged their duties to the letter and spirit.

Salok

salok: (a) (n, m; synonymous with 's' ('vahī') + 'lok' ('lok' and 'desh') the same people and the same country, (b) (n, f; synonymous with 'ustat(i)-' or 'yash-' 'de gīt') tribute, eulogy, or praise; songs of praise, and (c) (n, m) synonymous with 'chhaṅd' or stanza in poetry. In essence, it refers to words of praise or 'Siphat Sālāh dī bāṇī'. This second 'Salok', an epilogue, represents the gist or the very essence of this composition ('up-saṅhār').

Pavaṇ(u) gurū, pāṇī pitā, mātā dharat(i) mahat(u)

pavaṇ(u): (n, f; synonymous with 'havā', 'vāyū', 'pavan' and 'suās') (a) literally, air or breath, and (b) the divine spark or energy ('prāṇ' or 'prāṇāma-ī shakat(i)').

gurū: (n, m) a complex word comprising 'gu' (darkness or ignorance) + 'rū' (light or knowledge) and means that which takes one out of darkness or a state of ignorance into light or a state of knowedge and wisdom.

Pavaṇ is contrasted here with Gurū: in the absence of the former, we suffer physical death and in the absence of the latter we suffer spiritual downfall or death. Spiritual life begins when we submit to the Gurū (Divine Word) and vow to imbibe the Divine Wisdom and live by His Will. Alternatively, 'Nam(u)', being the divine spark and 'anhad sabad', is also being portrayed here as our primeval gurū ('ād(i)' gurū).

pāṇī: (n, m; synonymous with 'jal') water.

pitā: (n, m; synonymous with 'bāp', 'janam deṇ vālā' and 'janak') literally, father, dad, or sire.

‘Pāṇī’ is contrasted here with ‘Pitā’: just as no life is possible without water, so no human life is possible without a father.

mātā: (n, f; synonymous with ‘māṅ’, ‘janam deṇ vālī’ and ‘janan(i)’) literally, mother.

dharat(i): (n, f; synonymous with ‘dhartī’, ‘bhūmī’, ‘zamīn’ and ‘prithvī’) literally, the soil, land, or earth. Whilst fertile soil and healthy seeds are pre-requisites for growth, no growth is possible without the other essential ingredient, water. Hence, a paternal figure is likened to water.

mahat(u): (a) (n, f; synonymous with ‘buḍhā’ and ‘bazurg’) literally, an elderly man, (b) (adj; synonymous with ‘vaḍḍā’) big, large, huge or tall, (c) (n, f; synonymous with ‘bazurgī’ and ‘vaḍiāī’) status of respect and veneration, respectability and venerability; esteem, honour, praise or eulogy, and implicit here is (d) (adj; skt; synonymous with ‘visthār vālī’, ‘vistrit’, ‘phailiā hoiā’ or ‘phailī hoī’) vast, extensive, diffuse, widespread or pervasive. In essence, this is because the Earth supports all life forms.

Mother is contrasted with Earth: both are great, generous, and large-hearted, and nurture life that grows within them.

Just as air is like a Gurū, and water like a father, a mother is like the great Earth.

Alternatively, this verse could also be construed as referring to ‘Nam(u)’ as being the key ingredient of God’s world-stage or theatre (‘khel’ or /‘līlā’) – our empirical world – where It acts as the mother, father and consciousness.

Divas(u) rāt(i) dui, dāī dāiā, khelai sagal jagat(u)

divas(u): (n, m, s; synonymous with ‘roz’ and ‘din’) (a) literally, a day of the week. In essence, the time when we actively perform our roles and engage with the empirical world, and (b) (n, m; synonymous with ‘giān’ or ‘chānaṇ’) knowledge, dispeller of the darkness of ignorance.

rāt(i): (a) (n, f; synonymous with ‘jīvan dā smāṅ’) (fig) lifetime, (b) (n, f, s; synonymous with ‘nis’) a night, and (c) (n, f; synonymous with ‘agiāntā’ or ‘aṅdherā’) literally, ignorance. In essence, the time when we rest, sleep, and recuperate or the knowledge or ignorance with which we act out on this world-stage.

dui: (a) (adj; synonymous with ‘do’) literally, two, and implicit here is (b) (adj, pl; synonymous with ‘duhū’, ‘dohāṅ’, ‘doveṅ’ and ‘donoṅ’) both.

dāī: (a) (suff that turns a word into adj, e.g., ‘sukh-dāī’) that which comforts or soothes, (b) (n, f) a midwife, and (c) (n, f; synonymous with ‘bachche dī khiḍāvī’ or ‘āyāh’) a babysitter or nanny.

dāiā: (n, m; synonymous with ‘bachche dā khiḍāvā’) a male childminder or babysitter.

dāī dāiā: the role of child-minders is the symbolic representation of a supportive and nurturing role, essential for the well-being and development of a child into a well-adapted and independent adult. Alternatively, day and night represent our ability, within the spectrum of knowledge and ignorance, and the dimension of time, within which we act out on this world-stage.

khelai: (a) (v, s, present tense, second person; synonymous with ‘tūṅ kheldā haiṅ’ or ‘tusīṅ khelde ho’), (b) (imperative mood - ‘saṅbhāv bhvikht kāl’, s, third/first person; synonymous with ‘je-’ ‘tusīṅ’ or ‘asīṅ’ ‘khelīe’), and (c) (v, s, present tense, third person: synonymous with ‘uh kheldā hai’) see khelaṇā.

khelaṇā: (v; synonymous with ‘kheḍnā’ and ‘kheḍṇā’) literally, to play, sport or role play. In essence, the tacit reference is to the diverse life forms playing out their unique roles.

sagal: (adj, synonymous with ‘sagl’, ‘sarv’, ‘sarab, ‘sabh’, ‘sabhe’, ‘sāre’ and ‘tmām’) all, entire, whole or totality of something.

jagat(u): (n, m, s; synonymous with ‘saṅsār’ or ‘srisṭ(i)’) literally, the world or universe. In essence, the whole sentient world.

The diverse life forms of this whole world act out their roles within the supportive constraints of time and ability.

Chaṅgiāīā, buriāīā, vāchai dharam(u) hadūr(i)

chaṅgiāīā: (n, f; synonymous with ‘chaṅgā-pan’, ‘bhaliāīāṅ’ and ‘nekīāṅ’; pronounced as ‘chaṅgiāīāṅ’) good deeds, altruism, goodness, virtues, righteousness, or good attributes.

buriāīā: (n, f, pl; synonymous with ‘burāīāṅ’ and ‘badīāṅ’; antonym of ‘chaṅgiāīāṅ’; pronounced as ‘buriāīāṅ’) evils, wickednesses or depravities.

chaṅgiāīā buriāīā: literally, [our] good and bad deeds, i.e., our 'lekhā'.

vāchai: (a) (synonymous with 'paṛtāl kardā hai') see paṛtāl karnī, and implicit here is (b) (v, s, present tense, third person; synonymous with 'paṛdā hai', 'kathan kardā hai', 'paṛ ke suṇāuṅdā hai' and 'paṛtāle jāṅde han') see vāchaṇā.

vāchaṇā: (v) (a) synonymous with 'paṛnā', 'kathnā' and 'paṛ ke suṇāunā') to read, recite or illustrate, and (b) (synonymous with 'paṛtālaṇā' or 'paṛtāl karnī') to check, audit, scrutinize and verify.

dharam(u): (a) (n, m, s) 'dharamrāj' a mythological character in Hindu mythology who is appointed to carry out God's justice. However, Gurmat does not give any credence to this notion of a specific agent or appointee for the role but fully endorses the view that our deeds shall be subject to His scrutiny (see 'Pauṛī' 34). Implicit here is (b) (synonymous with 'maryādā') a moral, ethical or religious code of conduct, especially that which is in line with 'Nām(u)' or 'Nām-consciousness'. However, the reference here is to the Divine Order ('Hukam(u)'), which creates, supports, and sustains, governs and guides the entire creation and way of life in complete congruence with 'Nām(u)' or 'Nām-consciouosness' ('Hukam anusārī')'. See dharam.

hadūr(i): (a) (locative case - 'adhikaraṇ kārak'; synonymous with 'lokāṅ de sā(h)maṇe' or 'khulle maidān vich') out in the open, in front of everyone, and (b) (arab; locative case - 'adhikaraṇ kārak'; synonymous with 'sanmukh', 'rūbrū' and 'hadūrī-' or 'hazūrī-' 'vich') literally, in His presence.

vāchai dharam(u) hadūr(i): literally, 'Dharamrāj' scrutinises one's 'lekhā' and makes a judgement in God's presence. Our 'karam' (thoughts, speech and deeds) will be subject to His Scrutiny and Judgement as alluded to in Pauṛī 34 but Gurmat does not give any credence to the above view as everything, including jurisprudence, is bound by His Divine Order and His judgement is delivered instantaneously and without any delay. The following verses of the SGGS vouch for this day of judgement:

'Hear the real edict', O *man*! You will be asked to submit your account at God's Court and they who have not settled their accounts, will be summoned and the Angel Israel will be ready to execute the due punishment. 'Jīvātmāṅ', trapped in that blind and narrow alley, will find no room for escape. They who lived life by His Will, will be honoured and the rest will lose out and suffer the consequences.[533]

[Gurū Nānak is addressing a believer in Islam here]

Judgement at His Court, where both a master and servant are deemed equal, is based on real facts only. The Omniscient Lord knows our innermost self without a single word being uttered.[534]

Our good and bad deeds are, and shall be, subject to His closer scrutiny at death.

Karmī āpo āpṇī, ke neṛai, ke dūr(i)

karmī: (a) (instrumental case - 'karaṇ kārak'; synonymous with 'karam-' or 'mehar-' 'sadkā'; pronounced as 'karmīṅ'), through His Grace or Mercy, and implicit here is (b) (instrumental case - 'karaṇ kārak'; synonymous with 'karmāṅ-' 'karke' or 'anusār'; pronounced as 'karmīṅ') due to or by virtue of one's past karmā. See karmī.

āpo āpṇī: (adj, f; synonymous with 'swai dī', 'khud dī' and 'āpṇe dī') literally, personal; apertaining to or belonging to self. The phrase 'āpo āpṇī' is used as opposed to 'āpo apṇā' (adj, m) because it relates to the word 'karmī' (pronounced as 'karmīṅ' which gives the false impression of it being of the female gender).

ke: (adj; synonymous with 'ka-ī' and 'anek') many. See ke.

neṛai: (adv; synonymous with 'nikaṭ', 'kol', 'pās', 'nazdīk') literally, close by, close to, near or in the vicinity of. In essence, close to 'Nām-consciousness' or 'Nām(u)'.

dūr(i): (adv; synonymous with 'vith-', 'phāsle-' or 'dūrī-' 'te' or 'kar ke') literally, far, far away, remote, or distant. In essence, far or remote from 'Nām-consciousness' or 'Nām(u)'.

ke neṛai ke dūr(i): literally, some would be nearer whilst others further away from 'Nām(u)' or 'Nām-consciousness'. In essence, this judgment reflects the degree or extent of one's perfect alignment with 'Nām(u)' or 'Nām-consciousness. They who are judged to be aligned perfectly with 'Nām-consciousness' in this life, enjoy the status of 'Jīvan Mukt', and are released from the cycle of transmigration ('Āvāgavan') in the hereafter. In contrast, they who fail to achieve perfect alignment with 'Nām(u)', are afforded appropriate attributes dependent upon His judgement and remain in the cycle of transmigration.

The degree of our alignment with 'Nām-consciousness' is determined solely on the basis of our intention and good and bad deeds.

Jinī Nām(u) dhiāiā, gae masakat(i) ghāl(i)

jinī: (pron, pl; nominative case - 'kartā kārak'; synonymous with 'jināṅ-' or 'jin(h)āṅ' 'neṅ'; pronounced as 'jinīṅ' or 'jin(h)īṅ') they, whom or whomsoever.

Nām(u): (n, m, s) the immanent form of the transcendent God. This one word alone encompasses all the known and unknown attributes of the immanent form of God.

dhiāiā: (v; present perfect tense, third person; synonymous with 'simriā-' or 'dhiāiā-' 'hai') have contemplated or reflected upon. See dhiāunā.

dhiāunā: (v; synonymous with 'dhiāvṇā', 'sumarnā' and 'arādhanā') to focus and totally immerse oneself in reflecting on the persona or the attributes of a being or an object of one's reverence with the aim of expressing the very same attributes in one's own life.

gae: (v, pl, present tense, third person; synonymous with 'jāṅde han') go or depart having done. In essence, the tacit reference here is to departing after having lived one's entire lifetime.

masakat(i): (a) (n, f; arab; synonymous with 'taklīph' and 'kashṭ'; pronounced as 'mushakat') hardship, agony, torture, or painful experience, (b) (n, f; synonymous with 'mihnat', 'ghālaṇā' or 'ghāl kamāī') hard work, labour or toil.

ghāl(i): (indeclinable past participle or perfect participle - 'pūran pūrab kārdaṅtak') (a) (synonymous with 'ghāl kar ke' or 'mihnat kar ke') having toiled or worked hard, and (b) (synonymous with 'saphlī kar ke') having succeeded or having fulfilled one's desired objective. See ghālṇā (e).

ghālṇā: (a) (v; synonymous with 'ghalṇā' and 'bhejaṇā') to send, post, dispatch or transmit, (b) (v; synonymous with 'prahār karnā' and 'vār karnā') to strike, attack or assault, (c) (v; synonymous with 'barbād karnā' and 'tbāh karnā') to ruin, destroy or annihilate, (d) (n, f; synonymous with 'kamāī') literally, wages, earnings, profit, gains, savings or achievements, and (e) (v; synonymous with 'mihnat karnī') to slog, toil or work hard.

They who contemplated upon and aligned perfectly with 'Nām(u)', depart, having successfully achieved the fruits of their hard work.

Nānak, te mukh ujle, ketī chhuṭī nāl(i)

Nānak: (n, m, s) the (u) of 'Nānak(u)' is missing because of its vocative case - 'sanbodhan kārak'.

te: (genitive case - 'sanbandh kārak'; synonymous with 'un(h)āṅ de') literally, theirs. See te.

mukh: (a) (adj; synonymous with 'mukhīā' or 'pradhān') head, chief or leader, and implicit here is (b) (n, m, pl; synonymous with 'mūṅh' and 'chehre') literally, faces.

ujle: (adj, pl; synonymous with 'sāph', 'svachh', 'nirmal' and 'chamkīle') literally, clean, immaculate, bright, and shining, or shining white; in essence, free from the bondage of 'vikārs'.

ketī: (a) (adj; synonymous with 'ka-ī' and 'anek') many, several, numerous or countless, and (b) genitive case - 'sanbandh kārak'; synonymous with 'ka-ī-āṅ-' or 'ka-ī jīvāṅ-' 'dā/dī') of many beings. See ketī.

chhuṭī: (a) (n, f; synonymous with 'rukhsat' and 'vidāigī') literally, leave, departure, parting, farewell or send off, and implicit here is (b) (n, f; synonymous with 'chhuṭkārā', 'rihāī' and 'mukat(i)') release or freedom from 'Haumaiṅ', 'Moh' and innate evil tendencies ('Māyā') in one's lifetime, and from the cycle of transmigration ('Āvāgavan') at the end of one's lifetime and (c) (v; synonymous with 'mukat(i) ho ga-ī') were liberated or found release or freedom.

nāl(i): (adv; synonymous with 'sāth' or 'saṅg') literally, with or in the company of. In the company of, or along with, 'Gurmukhs'.

'Their faces reflect and radiate their inner bliss, and many others too find liberation in their company', O' Nānak!

Conceptual summary

Just as breath is crucial to physical life, so is a Gurū vital for spiritual enlightenment and life. Similarly, while fertile, and well-prepared soil and good seeds are pre-requisite for growth, no growth occurs without the other essential element, water. A paternal figure is, therefore, likened to water. Just as a mother nurtures her unborn child, so the great mother Earth provides succour to all beings.

Both survival and growth, whether individual or corporate, are observed as functions of time; thus, day and night provide another dimension, essential for the growth and maturation of the diverse life forms and for the acting out of their worldly roles and activities.

The good and bad deeds of all beings, based on their degree of alignment with 'Nām-consciousness', are scrutinised and disclosed at His Court, and His judgement of their Karmā determines their proximity to or distance from Him. Whilst some are rewarded and become increasingly God-orientated, and finally achieve liberation, others increasingly retreat from the true path and remain lost in the cycle of birth and death.

'They who surrendered to the Guru's Divine Word and contemplated upon and aligned perfectly with 'Nām(u)' willingly and lovingly, depart having successfully achieved the fruits of their hard work. Their faces reflect and radiate inner bliss with His Seal of Approval and many others, too, who are ideologically convergent with them, find liberation in their company', O' Nānak!

GLOSSARY OF TERMS

ād: (a) (p; synonymous with 'vagairā' and 'ādik') et cetera, (b) (adj; skt; synonymous with 'ād(i)', 'pahilā' and 'muḍhlā') original, elemental, primary, primeval, or primordial, (c) (n, m; synonymous with 'āranbh' and 'muḍh') beginning, origin, inception, source or root, and (d) (n, m; synonymous with 'mūl kāraṇ') primary cause.

ād(i): (a) (n, m; synonymous with 'brahm' and 'kartar') the Primeval, Primordial or Primal Soul, and (b) (ablative case - 'apādān kārak'; synonymous with 'muḍh' (ād 'toṅ'- see ād (b and c)) literally, in the beginning or before the beginning of time, primary, original, primeval, or primordial. In essence, the reference here is to God, the Creator, who was there before the beginning of time. See ād (b, c, and d).

ādes(u): (n, f, s; pronounced as 'ādesh(u)') (a) (synonymous with 'sikhyā' and 'nasīhat') teaching, counsel, instruction, precept, admonition, or warning, (b) (synonymous with 'khabar' and 'sudh') awareness, knowledge or alertness, (c) (synonymous with 'āgyā' and 'hukam') command, directive, mandate or order, and (d) (synonymous with 'namaskār' or 'praṇām') a humble bow of and submission, deferential homage, salutation or obeisance.

agaṅm: (adj, m; synonymous with 'agam'; pronounced as 'agaṅm') (a) (synonymous with 'achall') that which is fixed or does not move, stationary, and immovable, and (b) (synonymous with 'apahuṅch') inaccessible, unreachable, unapproachable, unfathomable or beyond human reach.

ākhah(i): (a) (v, s, present tense, second person; synonymous with 'tūṅ ākhdā haiṅ' or 'tusīṅ ākhde ho'; pronounced as 'ākhaheṅ'), (b) (v, s, future tense, second person; synonymous with 'tuṅ ākheṅgā' or 'tusīṅ ākhoge'), (c) ('saṅbhāv bhvikht kāl - kiās, sharat or prernā bodhak'; synonymous with 'je tusīṅ- ' 'ākho'or 'kaho'), (d) (v, pl, future tense, third person; synonymos with 'uh ākhaṇge', and (e) (v, pl, present tense, third person; synonymous with 'ākhde han'; pronounced as 'ākhaheṅ') see ākhṇā.

ākhaṇ(i): (infinitive mood - 'bhāvārth kārdaṅtak') (a) (genitive case - 'saṅbaṅdh kārak'; synonymous with 'ākhaṇ dā') of saying, (b) (instrumental case - 'karaṇ kārak'; synonymous with 'ākhaṇ nāl') with saying, (c) (locative case - 'adhikaraṇ kārak'; synonymous with 'kahan- 'or 'ākhaṇ-' 'vich') in stating, (d) (accusative case - 'karam kārak'; synonymous with 'kahaṇ nūn') literally, to state, and (e) (v, pl, present tense; synonymous with 'ākhde han') [they] say, utter or express. See ākhṇā.

ākhṇā: (v; synonymous with 'bolaṇā', 'kahiṇā', 'kathan karnā' or 'vakhyān karnā') to say, utter, express, define or expound.

Aṅmrit Bānī: The phrase literally means immortalising (Aṅmrit) utterances (Bānī). It is synonymous with 'Gurbānī': 'Gur' (that which spiritually enlightens) + 'Bānī' (words or utterances of 'Gurūs') i.e., words or utterances ('Bachan') of those who have realised 'Nām', and whose every thought ('*Man*'), utterance ('Bachan') or action ('Karam') is entirely in perfect harmony with it.

'Recognise the words of the Gurū as eternally true as it is God Himself who has commanded the words to be thus spoken'.[182] 'I speak only when You instruct me to do so and put the words into my mouth'.[543]

anād(i): (a) (n, m; synonymous with 'aṅn ād(i)' or 'khāṇ pīṇ de padārath'; pronounced 'anād') food items fit for consumption, (b) (adj) a complex word comprising 'a' ('binā' or 'rahit' - without) + 'nād(i)' ('dhun(i)') i.e., without any sound, and implicit here is (c) (adj) a complex word comprising 'an' ('binā' or 'rahit' - without) + 'ād(i)' (āraṅbh', muḍh' - origin or beginning) i.e., that has no beginning.

anāhat(i): (a) (adj) a complex word comprising 'an' ('binā' or 'rahit'- without) + 'āhat(i)' ('choṭ', 'saṭṭ', 'ṭhokar', 'aghāt' or 'prahār'- strike, blow, whack or knock) unstruck, e.g., unstruck sound or 'dhun(i)', and implicit here is (b) (adj) a complex word comprising 'an' (without) + 'āhat' ('death' or 'destruction') i.e., literally, everlasting or eternal.

anaṅd: (a) (a) (n, m; synonymous with 'anad', 'khushī' and 'prasaṅtā') transient happiness, delight, jubilation, rejoicing and contentment, and implicit here is (b) (n, f; synonymous with 'Sahaj') It is an experiential state of lasting inner bliss in one's conscious self ('Jīvātmāṅ' '*Man*' or 'Hirdā') which dawns when one achieves lasting inner equanimity ('Sahaj') with submission to and perfect alignment with 'Nām(u)' and God's Grace. 'Nām-' or 'God-' consciousness then supersedes or overwhelms one's ego-consciousness. The key characteristics of this state are: (i) one's conscious self is no longer restless or flirtatious and is immune to the adverse effects or assaults of 'Haumaiṅ', 'Moh' or innate 'Vikārī' tendencies ('Māyā'), (ii) one's innate inner drives and repressed desires ('T'rishnā') no longer relentlessly drive one to satisfy one's urges, (iii) 'Māyā' is no longer able to ensnare one into its net, and (iv) it represents the supreme position in spiritual progress or evolution when one perceives the Divine Word ('Anhad Sabad' or 'Nām(u)'), signifying the advent of 'Nām-realisation', and perceives, with God's Grace, the full glow of 'Nām(u)' within one's 'Hirdā'.

anīl: (a) (adj) a complex word comprising 'a' (without or beyond) + 'nīl' (10^{12}; synonymous with 'nīl giṇtī rahit or 'giṇtī toṅ pare') countless or infinite, (b) (adj; a complex word comprising 'a' (without or beyond) + 'nīl' (nīlā raṅg); synonymous with 'chiṭṭā' and 'ujlā') literally, plain white or without a blue tinge; in essence, white, pure, untainted and immaculate, and (c) (adj; synonymous with 'māyā'raṅg rahit') literally, unadulterated, not contaminated or defiled with the black dye or colour of 'Māyā'.

aṅt(u): (a) (n, m; synonymous with 'phal', 'natījā' and 'priṇām') result or consequence, (b) (n, f; synonymous with 'aṅtkāl', 'samāpat(i)' and 'khātmā') death or demise, and (c) (n, m; synonymous with 'oṛak', 'sīmā' and 'hadd') end, boundary, finale, or extremity.

aṅtahkaran: (n, m) the inner sensorimotor organ that orchestrates the five external sensorimotor organs of the body and which supposedly has the following four parts according to Hindu religious texts: (a) '*Man*', the seat of the spontaneous and constant flow of ideas ('Saṅkalps') and counter-ideas ('Vikalps'), (b) 'Budh(i)', the seat of deliberation and decision making, (c) 'Chit', where the process of memory ('Sumarṇ') occurs, and (d) 'Ahaṅkār', which links one with the empirical world and leads to the development of a sense of 'Mamtā' ('merā pan', 'khudī' and 'apṇat'), a strong feeling of ownership, possessiveness and partiality.

ātmā: (n, f; synonymous with Soul, Primal Soul or 'Nām(u)'; pronounced as 'Ātmāṅ') Being the immanent form of the transcendent Lord, it pervades everything but remains distinct[64] and immune to the influence of 'Māyā' and hence the term 'Nām-niraṅjan' (See Pauṛī 12-15) which is often attached to 'Nām(u)'. 'The glory of 'Ātmāṅ' is infinite and wondrous. It has no mother or father; it is never born, nor does it ever die, and it never ages with time. It is beyond the influence of 'Moh', 'Māyā' and 'Vikārs'; it is immune to pain and suffering, and no amount of joy or pain disturbs its state of equipoise. It has no friend or foe, it is unaffected by virtue or sin, and is forever merged in the Primal Soul. It is omnipotent, the source of the entire empirical world and the ever alert and awake consciousness in every being. It is infinite and eternal; it has caused the three types of attributes: (i) complete subservience to ego-consciousness, (ii) total subservience to 'Nam-consciousness', and (iii) the numerous shades in between these two opposites - the three gunas of 'Māyā', and the great ignorance ('Avidyā' or 'Bharam') is nothing but its mere shadow. Though the Primal Soul is omniscient and undeceivable, impenetrable and mysterious, it is, nevertheless, compassionate and merciful to the meek. Its power, ability and expanse are infinite, and Nanak is forever a sacrifice unto Him'.[41]

It is, therefore, immortal and eternal. 'God abides in the Soul, and the Soul abides in God'.[41, 114] Its interaction with any constituent of the creation mysteriously causes a manifestation of its shadow or functional expression, somewhat partial or imperfect surrogate, 'Jīvātmāṅ', which enables elemental or inanimate objects, without any sentience, to assume a shape and to perform only an ascribed function. Its greater expression is seen in living forms: plants and animals, where there is a greater degree of sentience as well as autonomy of function. Its highest expression is in humans, and hence the reason that humans have the ability and the potential to align perfectly with God-consciousness and realise or perceive God. It is also termed 'Paṅch-bhū-ātmāṅ' which alludes to the fact that it pervades all parts of the creation made up of the five basic elements - air, water, fire (energy), 'prithv(i)', and space.

In Gurbanī, although 'Jīvātmāṅ' pervades the entire body, its ultimate expression or manifestation is said to occur in one's conscious self ('Hirdā' or '*Man*'). 'Haumaiṅ', 'Moh', one's accumulated 'Saṅskārs' and 'Saṅjog(u)' and 'Vijog(u)' contribute to this process and help determine the conscious self, the unique innate nature, and other attributes that a body expresses in its lifetime. 'Jīvātmāṅ' cannot become the perfect surrogate of 'Ātmāṅ' as long as even a trace of 'Haumaiṅ' exists in oneself and without it one's conscious self can never be in perfect harmony with 'Nām(u)' and one cannot achieve the status of a 'Jīvan Mukt'. Once one rids oneself of this baggage or interference of 'Haumaiṅ', 'Moh' and innate 'Vikārī' tendencies, one's 'Jīvātmāṅ' becomes 'nirmal' or immaculate 'Jīvātmāṅ'. Put another way, 'Ātmāṅ' can functionally express itself fully or 'Jīvātmāṅ' becomes just a mirror image of 'Ātmāṅ' - one's real self. One is now free from 'Āvāgavan', the cycle of transmigration.

āuṇā: (synonymous with 'āvṇā') (a) (c; synonymous with 'pahuṅch jāṇā' or 'pargaṭ hoṇā') to come, arrive or appear, (b) (v; synonymous with 'janam laiṇā') to be born and come into this world, and (c) (conj v and suff) (i) 'bisvās(u) āuṇā' - to have faith or firm belief; (ii) 'nazar āuṇā' - to become visible; (iii) 'pasaṅd āuṇā' - to suit; (iv) 'kām āuṇā' - to serve a useful purpose; (v) 'saraṇ(i)' or 'saṅgat(i) vich āuṇā' - to submit to someone and seek their sanctuary, (vi) 'toṭ(i) n āuṇā' - to experience no shortfall and (vii) 'kapṛā āuṇā' - to receive the gift of this body or to receive 'prem paṭolā' or 'siphat-salāh dā kapṛā'.

āvah(i): (a) (v, s, present tense, second person; synonymous with 'tuṅ āuṅdā haiṅ' or 'tusīṅ āuṅde ho'), (b) (v, s, future tense, first person; synonymous with 'asīṅ āvāṅge'), (c) (v, s, 'saṅbhāv bhvikht kāl sharat bodhak - kiās, sharat or ichhā bodhak', second person; synonymous with 'je tūṅ ā jāveṅ'), (d) (v, pl, future tense, third person; synonymous with 'uh-' 'ā jāṇge', 'āuṇge', 'āvaṇge' or 'āveṅge'), and (e) (v, pl, present tense, third person; synonymous with 'uh āuṅde han'; pronounced as 'āvaheṅ') see āvṇā or āuṇā.

bakhsīs: (synonymous with 'bakhsh' and 'bakhshīsh') (a) (n, f; synonymous with 'dāt' or 'dān') gift, boon, largesse, or benefaction, (b) (n, m; synonymous with 'inām') literally, reward or award, and (c) (n, f;

synonymous with 'rahmat', 'kripā', 'da-i-ā' or 'meharbānī') grace, mercy or blessing.

bāṇ(i): (a) (instrumental case - 'karaṇ kārak'; synonymous with 'vāṇ-' 'se', 'nāl', 'rāhīṅ', 'duārā' or 'sadkā') literally, with or through an arrow, (b) (n, f; synonymous with 'ādat' and 'subhāu') habit, predisposition or innate nature, (c) (n, f; skt; synonymous with 'āvāz' and 'sur') literally, sound or the act of vocalisation, (d) (n, f; synonymous with 'bol', 'vachan', 'kathan' and 'vyākhiā') speech, utterance, sermon, precept or oral exegesis, (e) (n, f; synonymous with 'bāṇī') inspired Divine Words of knowledge and wisdom or utterances of one who has realised 'Nām(u)', (f) (n, f; synonymous with 'bolī') language, dialect or mode of communication and (g) (genitive case -'saṅbaṅdh kārak'; synonymous with 'bāṇī-' or 'bolī-' 'dā') of language or spoken words.

bāṇī: (a) (n, f; synonymous with 'ghabrāhaṭ', 'utāvalī', 'shīghartā' and 'chaṭpaṭī') eagerness, agitation, fluster, uneasiness or nervousness, (b) (n, m; synonymous with 'vaṅnī', 'varṇ' or 'raṅg') colour or dye, (c) (instrumental case - 'karaṇ kārak'; synonymous with 'vāṇāṅ nāl' and 'tīrāṅ sadkā') with or through arrows, (d) (synonymous with 'baṇī- 'or 'rachī-' 'hoī') literally, made of, (e) (n, f; synonymous with 'baṇtar','rachnā and 'banāvaṭ') creation, structure or design; work of art, craft or literature, (f) (n, f; synonymous with 'vāṇī', 'kathan' and 'vyākhiā') elaboration, critique, annotation or exegesis, (g) (n, f; synonymous with 'padrachnā', 'tasnīph' and 'kāvya rachnā') poetical rendering, (h) (n, f; synonymous with 'Anhad nād or bāṇī', 'Parā-Vāk' or 'Parā- Bānī') literally, phrases that allude to sound, vibrations of the Divine Word, (i) (n, f; synonymous with Gurbāṇī or the Gurū's 'bachan', 'bol', 'hukam', 'adesh' or 'updesh') spiritually uplifting and divinely inspired words of knowledge and wisdom or utterances of one who has realised 'Nām(u)', and whose every thought, utterance and deed is in harmony with 'Nām(u)', and (j) (n, f; synonymous with 'bāṇ(i)', 'bāṇīāṅ' and 'bolīāṅ') languages, dialects or modes of communication.

baṅnaṇā: (v) (a) (synonymous with 'rokaṇā') to stop, check, resist, block, or ban, (b) (synonymous with 'rukāvaṭ pāuṇī') to deliberately obstruct, impede or hinder, and (c) (synonymous with 'bāṅdhanā' and 'baṅn laiṇā') to tie, bind, restrain or imprison; to gather and pack.

bhagat: (n, m, pl; synonymous with 'shradhāvān', 'upāsak' or 'bhagtī karan vāle') devotees who worship God with faith and conviction and yearn to be with Him like a true lover ('Jīvātmāṅ' - the bride) who eagerly awaits her beloved ('Parmātmāṅ' - God, the husband).

It is believed that Gurū Hargobiṅd Sāhib, the sixth Gurū, described the following four types of 'bhagats': (a) 'kāmnāvān bhagat' - they who worship their God for money ('dhan'), material assets ('saṅpadā') and offspring ('saṅtān'), (b) 'ārat bhagats' - they who worship their God in order to rid themselves of their ills and sorrows, (c) 'giānī bhagats' - they who worship their God as being omnipresent and all-pervasive, and (d) 'upāsak bhagats' - they who regard God as their husband and worship Him faithfully as His wives.

However, implicit here is devotees, votaries or they who have realised 'Nām(u)', who live by His Will, and whose every thought ('*Man*'), utterance ('Bachan') and deed ('Karam') is in perfect harmony with 'Nām(u)'. Such a 'bhagat' is synonymous with a 'Saṅt', 'Sādh', Gurū and 'Brahm-gyānī' in Gurmat as cited in the following verses of the SGGS:

'One who submits to His Will, is a 'bhagat' or else is just a charade', O' Nānak.[340]

'One who appears innocent despite being wise, powerless despite being blessed with power, and who shares with others even when there is little to share is a rare true bhagat'.[341]

bhāi: (a) (n, m; synonymous with 'bhāv' or 'vichār') one's view, drift of thought, instinct, or gut feeling, (b) (n, m; synonymous with 'bhāg' or 'hissā') part, portion, segment or fraction, (c) (n, m; synonymous with 'bhāv' or 'hāv bhāv') bodily expression of inner feelings, (d) (n, f; synonymous with 'āshā' or 'marzī') wish, discretion or choice, (e) (n, m; synonymous with 'raṅg' or 'varaṇ') colour, hue or complexion, (f) (n, m; synonymous with 'prakār', 'ḍhaṅg' or 'kisam') kind, sort, category, variety or manner, (g) (n, f; synonymous with 'dashā' or 'hālat') condition or state, (h) (n, m; synonymous with 'sidhāṅt' or 'tatv') underlying doctrine, principle, tenet or theory; source of everything, eternal truth, and (i) (n, f; synonymous with 'prem') literally, love, intense fondness, amity or preference, and (j) (locative case - 'adhikaraṇ kārak'; synonymous with 'prem vich') in love or to have deep affection and reverence for. In essence, those who are in love with or express deep devotion and reverence for Him.

bhakh(i): (a) (indeclinable past participle or perfect participle - 'pūran pūrab kārdaṅtak'; synonymous with 'bhakshaṇ-' or 'khā-' 'ke') literally, by eating or having eaten; see bhakshaṇā, (b) (adj; synonymous with 'khāṇ yog') worth eating or fit for eating, (c) (v, pl, present tense, third person; synonymous with 'khāṅde han'), and (d) (v, pl, present tense, third person; synonymous with 'hochhiāṅ- 'or 'hābṛiāṅ- ''vāṅg khāṅde han') eat impatiently and voraciously, and in an undignified manner.

bhakshaṇā: (v; synonymous with 'khāṇā', 'chabbṇā' and 'bhojan karnā') to dine or eat.

bhār: (a) (n, s; synonymous with 'ahsān', 'pharz' and 'jumevārī') (fig.) burden of responsibility, onus, or obligation, and (b) (n, m; synonymous with 'bojh' or 'vazan') literally, weight, load, luggage or cargo. In essence, the reference here is to the enormous amount or weight of all non-sentient and sentient life and material objects, useful or valuable for its survival, comfort and pleasure.

bharnā: (a) (v; synonymous with 'tuṅnaṇā') to stuff, plug or cram, (b) (v; synonymous with 'libaṛnā') to be soiled, stained or defiled, and (c) (conj. v and suff.) (i) (synonymous with 'phīs-', 'tax-', 'bakāiā-' or 'jurmānā-' 'deṇā') to pay or deposit fees, taxes, dues or penalties, (ii) (synonymous with 'zakham dā bhar jāṇā') [for a wound] to heal, (iii) (synonymous with 'dastāvez bharnā') to fill in and complete a form or proforma, (iv) (synonymous with 'gaḍḍī bharnī') to load a carriage, (v) (synonymous with 'baṅdūk vich golī bharnī) to load a firearm, (vi) (fig.) (synonymous with 'jo-' 'ḍoldā nahīṅ' or 'ṭikiā rahiṅdā hai') does not waver and becomes resolute - the implication being that as one gathers and fills up with the attributes of 'Nām(u)' or as one gradually aligns with 'Nām(u)', one is less likely to waver and be influenced by 'Māyā', and (vii) (synonymous with 'khālī nūṅ pūran karnā') to fill in or fill up.

bhāu: (a) (n, m; synonymous with 'nirakh' and 'mul') price, cost, value or worth, (b) (n, m; synonymous with 'prabhāv' and 'asar') effect or influence, (c) (skt, n, m; synonymous with 'bhāg' and 'hissā') a part, portion, segment or fraction, (d) (n; abbrv for 'bhavjal' or 'Saṅsār-sāgar') the empirical world or world stage, (e) (skt) 'bhav' - janam/maran, i.e., cycle of birth and death or 'Āvāgavan', (f) (n, f; synonymous with 'hoṅd') existence or presence, (g) (synonymous with 'bhramaṇā', 'bhauṇā' or 'bhaṭkaṇā') going astray and wandering about aimlessly, and being in a state of dubiety and indecision, (h) (n, m; synonymous with 'hukam(u)') Divine Order, (i) (n, f; synonymous with 'dashā' and 'hālat') state, condition, position or circumstances, (j) (n, m; synonymous with 'saṅkalp' or 'khayāl') a notion, concept or an idea, (k) (synonymous with 'vāk dā-' 'matlab' or 'sāraṅsh') gist of a sentence, (l) (n, m; synonymous with 'bhai' (skt), 'ḍar' and 'khauph') fear, dread or apprehension of 'd' and 'e', the Divine Order ('hukam(u)' as well as of losing something towards which one has 'Moh' (money, assets, health, beauty, rank, fame, and one's kith and kin) in 'Haumaiṅ', (m) (n, m; synonymous with 'shradhā' and 'vishvāsh') faith, trust, confidence or devotion and (n) (n, m; synonymous with 'sneh', 'prem' and 'piār') love or deep affection.

bhāuṇā: (v, synonymous with 'bhāvṇā' and 'piārā- 'or 'chaṅgā-' 'lagṇā') literally, to find appealing, desirable, suitable, deserving or worthy.

bhāvai: (a) (v, s, present tense, third person; synonymous with 'bhāuṅdā hai'), (b) (v, s, 'saṅbhāv bhvikht kāl - kiās or ichhā bodhak', third person; synonymous with 'bhā jāve'), and (c) (v, s, present tense, second person; synonymous with 'tainūṅ bhāuṅdā hai') see bhāuṇā.

bhavsāgar: (n, m) A compound word comprising 'bhav' (world, birth and cycle of transmigration) + 'sāgar' (a sea or an ocean), i.e., literally, the world ocean ('Saṅsār Sāgar'). The term 'bhavsāgar' is a metaphor for the world stage, which in many ways describes the salient features of rough and stormy seas, with the emphasis being on the inherent dangers involved in crossing over to the other end. One's unrestrained and insatiable desire for more and more of the empirical world and its pleasures ('Trishnā') is likened to the mountainous waves of the stormy ocean. The lure of the material world and its pleasures which not only intoxicates and captivates but also blurs one's ability to discern their transient nature and foresee the potential dangers of engrossment therein ('Moh') is likened to a whirlpool ('Ghuṅmaṇ-gherī') and quagmire or quicksand ('daldal'), which sucks one deeper and deeper, making one's escape virtually impossible without the help of another outside of it.

One's conscious self ('*Man*', 'Hirdā' or 'Jīvātmāṅ') is inherently not attuned to 'Nām' or 'Nām-consciousness' because of the filth ('Mal' or 'Mail') of 'Haumaiṅ' and 'Saṅskārs' accumulated during the present and previous lifetimes which adversely influence and modify the expression of the immaculate 'Ātmāṅ'. Hence, the expression of 'Ātmāṅ, in this imperfect or impure state, is termed 'Jīvātmāṅ'.

In this default state, one's conscious self operates purely for the fulfilment of self-interest and self-pride, regardless of any consequences to humanity, other sentient life or nature in general. One now fails to appreciate the whole world as one family, the principles of the universal Fatherhood of God and Brotherhood of Man, and of unity in diversity. Instead, one considers oneself to have an independent existence, independent of the Divine Order ('Hukam(u)'). One's conscious self, corrupted with the attributes alluded to above, is characterised as suffering from 'Haumaiṅ'.

Thus, misled by 'Haumaiṅ' and detached from 'Nām-consciousness', one easily succumbs to evil predispositions because of one's previous 'Saṅskārs', and committing evil deeds ('Vikārs') and sinful acts ('Pāp'). 'Jīvātmāṅ' thus gets bound to the cycle of transmigration and remains entrapped until it rids itself of 'Hauṅmai' and 'Saṅskārs' accumulated over previous lives and aligns perfectly with 'Nām(u)' or 'Nām-consciousness'. 'Jīvātmāṅ' is then regarded as 'nirmal Jīvātmāṅ' and 'Jīvan-mukt' during that lifetime, eventually finding release from the cycle of transmigration ('Āvāgavan') when it merges with 'Parmātmāṅ' (the Primal soul or God) at death. This journey of 'Jīvātmāṅ' is likened to swimming across the 'Bhavsāgar' successfully, its allotted task.

bhī: (a) ('bhūt kāl bodhak') indicative of past tense, (b) (conj; synonymous with 'yadī' and 'je') if, in case or provided, (c) (conj; synonymous with 'ate' and 'aur') and, (d) (synonymous with 'tad- 'or 'tau- ''bhī') even then, (e) (synonymous with 'yakīnan', 'ap(i)' or 'nischya hī') surely, certainly and without doubt, and (f) (adv, synonymous with 'bhī' and 'vī') also or too.

bh(i): (a) (synonymous with 'yakīnan', 'ap(i)', 'nischit' or 'nirsaṅdeh') surely, certainly and without doubt, (b) (adv; synonymous with 'punah' and 'pher') again, (c) (conj; synonymous with 'aur' and 'ate'), and (d) (p and adv; synonymous with 'bhī' and 'vī') also or too.

bhram(u): (n, m; synonymous with 'bharam') (a) (n, f; synonymous with 'ghuṅmaṇ-gherī') a whirlpool, (b) (n, f; synonymous with 'ghumār dā chak') a potter's wheel, (c) (n, m; synonymous with 'bharam', 'bhulekhā' or 'mithyā-gyān') fallacy, misunderstanding or misconception. Its five recognised forms are: (i) the creator is not the only Primal Soul, (ii) the empirical world is an evil, immoral, sinful and flawed act of creation of God, (iii) the empirical world is an everlasting reality, (iv) one is not the soul ('Ātmāṅ') but the mortal body whose brain and nervous system orchestrate all its sensorimotor responses and interactions with the world outside, and (v) one is not only totally independent of the creator and its creation but also independent of the Divine Order and one is in possession of the ultimate intellect, wisdom, and discriminatory ability, (d) (n, f; synonymous with dubiety or 'dubidā' in Gurmat) a state of mistrust, misgiving, apprehension, inner turmoil and confusion in one's mind between the two options of 'Haumaiṅ' and 'Nām(u)', or ego-consciousness and 'Nām-consciousness', and (e) (n, f; synonymous with 'ghumaṇā' or 'bhaṭkaṇā') a state of confusion and fruitless and aimless wandering in the empirical world because of misconception and a sense of loss of direction alluded to above.

'Haumaiṅ' is the root cause of 'bharam' which is a state of misconception and confusion about oneself, the creation, the creator, and their inter-relationship which leads to dubiety, a loss of sense of direction, and, eventually, aimless wandering in the material world.

bujhaṇā: (v) (a) (synonymous with 'jalde hoi dā shāṅt ho jāṇā') calming down or putting out of fire or a burning object, (b) (synonymous with 'jagde hoi dā bujh jāṇā') to go out or put off a light source, (c) (synonymous with 'piās dā bujh jāṇā') quenching of thirst, and (d) (synonymous with 'bodh hoṇā', 'jāṇ jāṇā' or 'samajhaṇā') to realise, comprehend, infer, deduce or solve.

bujhāuṇā: (v) (a) 'giān krāuṇā' or 'samjhāuṇā' - to make one understand, grasp, realise or perceive, (b) 'bhet kholṇā' - to reveal or divulge a secret, to spill the beans or to unravel a mystery and (c) (i) (suff.) 'ag bujhauṇā' - to put out or extinguish a fire, (ii) 'batīāṅ bujhauṇā' - to switch off the lights, and (iii) 'piās bujhauṇā'- to quench one's thirst.

chalai: (a) (v, s, present tense, second person; synonymous with 'tūṅ chaldā haiṅ' or 'tusīṅ chalde ho'; pronounced as 'chalaiṅ'), (b) (v, s, present tense, third person; synonymous with 'uh chaldā-' or 'turdā-' 'hai'; pronounced as 'chalaiṅ'), (c) ('saṅbhāv bhvikht kāl - kiās, sharat bodhak'; synonymous with ' je chalaṇ' or 'je turan') literally, [if] walk, and (d) (fig.) v; synonymous with 'kise nāl khaṛā hoṇā') to stand by someone.

chalāuṇā: (v; synonymous with 'chalāvaṇā') (a) to set in motion, to cause to move or to start or drive something, (b) to discharge or fire (a firearm), (c) to shoot an arrow, and (d) to manage, govern, conduct, or direct.

chalṇā: (v (a to f)) (a) (synonymous with 'turnā') to move, walk or proceed, (b) (synonymous with 'pāṇī dā vagṇā') [for water] to flow, (c) (synonymous with 'kise dā sāth deṇā') to accompany, (d) for a machine to work or function, (e) to fire or discharge a gun, or explode an explosive, (f) to pass as a genuine article, and (g) (infinitive mood - 'bhāvārth kārdaṅtak'; synonymous with 'turnā' or 'gaman') walking or movement.

chup: (a) (n, f; synonymous with 'khāmoshī' and 'maun') silence, muteness, quietness, or speechlessness, (b) (adj; synonymous with 'khāmosh' and 'maunī') silent or quiet, and (c) (interj) shut up, silent, hush or listen.

chup rahiṇā: (v) to hold one's tongue, to remain silent, and to endure patiently.

chupai: (pronounced as 'chupaiṅ') (a) (synonymous with 'chup hi') only silence or muteness, (b) (ablative case - 'apādān kārak'; synonymous with 'chup-' or 'khamoshī-' 'toṅ' or 'se') from keeping quiet or keeping one's mouth shut, (c) (instrumental case -'karaṇ kārak'; synonymous with 'chup rakhaṇ-' 'nāl', 'rāhīṅ', 'duārā' or 'sadkā') with, through or by virtue of keeping silence, (d) (locative case - 'adhikaraṇ kārak'; synonymous with 'chup rakhaṇ vich') in maintaining silence or remaining speechless. A certain sect of yogīs observes and maintains a ritual of prolonged silence, especially with their eyes closed, to still their flirtatious ('chaṅchal') minds ('*Man*') with this exercise.

dar: (a) (n, m, s; pers; 'dwār', 'duār', 'dahlīz', 'chaukhaṭ' and 'darvāzā') literally, the bottom part of the threshold of a door or door - a movable barrier to the entrance of a room, a building, or the outermost part of a house, and (b) (n, m, s; abbrev. for 'darbār') a Court. Remember, both the transcendent God and 'Nām(u)', His immanent form, are non-physical, all-pervasive, and omnipresent.

dāt(i): (a) (n, m; synonymous with 'dātā' and 'dānī') a giver, donor or a bestower; generous, benevolent, charitable or munificent, (b) (n, f, pl.; synonymous with dātāṅ; pronounced as 'dātīṅ) literally, many dāts, (c) (n, f; synonymous with 'ditī hoī vastū') free gift, donation or grant with no ulterior motive of expecting anything in return, (d) (n, f; synonymous with 'dān karnyog vastū') a worthwhile free gift, and (e) (n, m; synonymous with 'dān', 'khairāt'; n, f; synonymous with 'bakhshīsh') blessing, grace, boon, bestowal or largesse; in essence, His Bounty.

dātār: (n, adj, s; synonymous with 'dātā, 'dāt deṇ vāle', 'dānī' or 'dānshīl') (a) a complex word comprising 'dāt' (a free gift, donation or grant) + 'ār' (synonymous with 'hār', 'vān' or 'vāle' - they who implement the attributes of the noun), i.e., they who give, donate or bestow gifts, and implicit here is (b) a complex word comprising 'dāt' (a free gift, donation or grant) + 'ār' ('ālya' or 'ghar' - source or fount) they who bestow gifts and whose treasures are boundless. However, implicit here is the ever beneficent and benevolent God ('sarab thok kā dātā').

de: (a) (n; abbrev for 'daivī'; synonymous with 'devtiāṅ nāl saṅbaṅdhat' or 'devtiāṅ de') of or relating to Hindu demi-gods, (b) (n, f ; abbrev for 'devtā' or 'devī') literally, demi-god or demi-goddess, (c) (prep; synonymous with 'kā', 'ke', 'dā') of, (d) (Indeclinable past participle or perfect participle - 'pūran pūrab kārdaṅtak'; synonymous with 'dei' or 'ਦੇਇ' - 'de ke') literally, having granted, and (e) (v, s, present tense, third person; synonymous with 'de(i)', 'ਦੇਇ' or 'deṅdā hai') literally, offers, confers, bestows or grants.

deh(i): (a) (v, s, present tense, second person; synonymous with 'tūṅ deṅdā haiṅ' or 'tusiṅ deṅde ho') you give, provide, confer or grant, (b) (v, pl, present tense, third person; synonymous with 'uh deṅde han') they give or provide, (c) (v, pl, future tense, third person; synonymous with 'uh deṇge') they will give or provide, and (d) (v, s, imperative mood - 'hukmī bhvikht-benat(i) bodhak', first or second person; synonymous with 'mainūṅ-' 'deu' or 'davo'; 'tūṅ deh' and 'tusīṅ deo') literally, give or grant; in essence, O' Lord! Grant us.

dehlī dīpak: literally means an earthenware lamp that gives light in both directions. However, it refers to a word that joins with two or three words in a sentence in grammar.

deṇā: (a) (v) give, provide or supply, (b) (v; synonymous with 'dān karnā') to offer, present, contribute, sacrifice or donate, (c) (synonymous with 'pradān- 'or 'arpaṇ- ''karnā' and 'bakhshaṇā') to confer, grant or bestow, and (d) (conj. v and suff) e.g. 'milā deṇā'-to introduce or bring together.

dev: (n, m, pl; abbrev. for 'devtā' and 'devte') (a) (synonymous with 'pūjyā devtā dī mūrtī') an idol of a god or a demi-god, (b) Gurūs, (c) noble, virtuous or ideal persons, (d) sacred material, e.g. 'an' (foods as source of energy), 'pāṇī' (water), 'baisaṅtar' (fire or energy), 'lūṇ' (salt) and ghrit' ('ghee' or clarified butter), (e) (n, m; synonymous with 'pārbrahm' or 'kartār') creator or God, and (f) (synonymous with 'devtās' and 'sur') eternal beings with divine powers who live in heaven in Hindu mythology.

dharam: (n, m, s) (a) (synonymous with 'Dharamrāj' and 'rājā dharam(u)', (b) (synonymous with 'shubh karam') altruistic, pious or noble deeds, (c) (synonymous with 'maṅtav', 'pharz' or 'kartav') aim, purpose or duty, (d) (synonymous with 'rasam', 'rivāj' or 'rīt(i)') custom, tradition or common practice, (e) (synonymous with 'nyāy' or 'insāph') equity, reparation or justice, (f) (synonymous with 'mazhab' and 'dīn') faith, creed or religion, and (g) (synonymous with 'maryādā') a moral, ethical or religious code of conduct, especially that which is in line with

‘Nām(u)’ or ‘Nām-consciousness’. However, implicit here is the Divine Order (‘Hukam(u)’), which creates, supports, and sustains, governs and guides the entire creation and way of life in complete congruence with ‘Nām(u)’ or ‘Nām-consciousness’ (‘Hukam anusārī’).

dharam rāj: (n, m, s; synonymous with ‘rājā dharam’) Lord of moral justice - a character in Hindu mythology who is appointed to carry out God's justice; his residence, throne, and the huge register for everyone’s account of good and bad deeds, under the supervision of ‘Chitr’, are titled ‘Kalīchī’, ‘Vichārbhū’, and ‘Agrsaṅdhānī’ respectively. In contrast, ‘sachā āp(i) sachā darbār(u)’ - the eternal Lord is omnipresent, and His Court, too, is truly just (see Pauṛi 34). The Lord of Gurū Nānak is omnipotent, omnipresent and omniscient; if He can create the universe in the flicker of an eyelid, then He can deliver perfect justice for one and all too.

dībāṇ(u): (a) (n, m; synonymous with ‘māli maṅtrī’) a finance minister of a Moghul emperors, (b) (n, m; synonymous with ‘insāph karan vālā’ or ‘hākim’) a qazi, magistrate, governor or an administrator of justice, (c) (n, m; synonymous with ‘divān’or ‘darbār’) a large hall where a king/emperor holds audience, and (d) (n, f; synonymous with ‘kachahirī’) a royal court or a court of justice. His Court is priceless because His justice is based solely on evidence (one’s ‘karmā’) and no favour or bias and cannot be bought with anything.

eh(u): (a) (n, m; synonymous with ‘eh lok’) literally, this world, (b) (adj, m; synonymous with ‘aisā’) like, similar to, or resembling this, and (c) (pron and adj, m, s; synonymous with ‘yahī’ and ‘keval eh’) this or precisely this.

ek(u): (a) (adj, m; synonymous with ‘Kartār’) literally, one. However, the reference is to the one and only God or ‘Nām(u)’, its persona and attributes as captured in Gurbānī, (b) (adj, m; synonymous with ‘adutī’) unique, unrivalled, or peerless, and (c) (adv; synonymous with ‘siraph’ or ‘keval’) only, merely, just or simply.

gāh: (a) (n, f; skt; synonymous with ‘gaṅmbhīrtā’ or ‘ḍuṅghiāī’) seriousness, solemnity or gravity; depth, (b) (n, f; pers; synonymous with ‘jag(h)ā’ or ‘thāṅ’) place, location, position or situation, (c) (n, m; synonymous with ‘maslaṇ-’ or ‘kuchlaṇ-’ ‘dī kriyā’ and ‘gāhuṇā’) the act of trampling, crushing or threshing, (d) (adj; synonymous with ‘sūjh-’ or ‘samjhaṇ-’ ‘vāle’) they who have truly grasped and understood the issue or problem, (e) (n, m; synonymous with ‘gāhak’, ‘kharīdār’ and ‘vākaph’) customers, buyers or seekers; well acquainted or well aware, and (f) (n, m; synonymous with ‘grahaṇ-’ or ‘aṅgīkār-’ ‘karan dī kriyā’) real comprehension or grasp of an issue; acceptance of an offering.

gat(i): (a) (n, f; synonymous with ‘chāl’) speed or pace, (b) (n, m; synonymous with ‘vidh(i)’, ‘jugat(i)’, ‘tarīkā’ or ‘ḍhaṅg’) a technique, path or way of life towards one’s spiritual goal, (c) (adj; synonymous with ‘prāpat hoiā’ or ‘miliā’) acquired goods or status, (d) (n, f; synonymous with ‘prāpatī’ or ‘lābh’) gain, profit or achievement, (e) (n, m; synonymous with ‘mārag’ or ‘rastā’) way, path or road, (f) (n, f; synonymous with ‘līlā’ or ‘khel’) wondrous act or ploy, (g) (n, f; synonymous with ‘shudhī’ or ‘pavitartā’) purity, sanctity or holiness, (h) (n, f; synonymous with ‘moksh’ or ‘mukat(i)’) liberation from: (i) ‘Haumaiṅ’, ‘Moh’, ‘Māyā’ and ‘Vikār’ in this life ('Jīvan Mukat(i)') and (ii) ‘Āvāgavan’, the cycle of transmigration, at death (‘Param gat(i)’), and implicit here is (i) (n, f; synonymous with ‘hālat’, ‘avasthā’, ‘dashā’ or ‘darjā’) one’s inner or spiritual state, status or rank, with ‘Sahaj’ or ‘Anaṅd’ being the highest spiritual status or rank.

gāvah(i): (a) (v, s, present tense, second person; synonymous with ‘tuṅ gāuṅdā haiṅ’ or ‘tusīṅ gāuṅde ho’), (b) (v, pl, present tense, first person; synonymous with ‘asīṅ gāuṅde hāṅ’), (c) (v, s, ‘saṅbhāv bhvikht kāl - sharat bodhak’, second/first person; synonymous with ‘je tūṅ gavaheṅ’ or ‘je asīṅ gāvīe’), (d) (v, pl, future tense, third person; synonymous with ‘uh-’ ‘gāuṇge’or ’gāvaṇge’), and (e) (v, pl, present tense, third person; synonymous with ‘uh gāuṅde han’; pronounced as ‘gāvaheṅ’) see gāvṇā.

gāvai: (a) (v, s, present tense, second person; synonymous with ‘tūṅ gāuṅdā haiṅ’ or ‘tusīṅ gāuṅde ho’), (b) (‘saṅbhāv bhvikht kāl - kiās, sharat, ichhā or bevasī bodhak’, s, third/first person; synonymous with ‘je maiṅ gāvāṅ’ or ‘je tusīṅ gāvo’), and (c) (v, s, present tense, third person: synonymous with ‘uh gāuṅdā hai’; pronounced as ‘gāvaiṅ’) see gāvṇā.

gāvṇā: (v, synonymous with 'gāuṇā' and 'gāvnā') (a) literally, to sing, chant or recite, (b) to sing His Praise or Glory, and (c) to express the endowed attributes, gifted on the basis of one's past Karmāor by God's Will, in one's daily life.

ghar(u): (a) (n, m, s; synonymous with 'grih' and 'nivās') literally, home, (b) n, m, s; synonymous with 'sarīr' and 'deh') one's body, (c) (n, f; synonymous with 'sur' and 'tāl' in music) beat, rhythm and a tonic note, (d) (n, m; synonymous with 'Shāstr') a holy book that contains the credo of a belief system or dharma, (e) (n, m; synonymous with 'rutbā' and 'padvī') rank, status, position or title, (f) (n, f; synonymous with 'ghar vālī', 'zorū' and 'vahuṭī') wife, (g) (n, m; synonymous with 'kul', 'vaṅsh' and 'khāndān') pedigree, lineage, ancestry, dynasty, house; caste, tribe or race, and implicit here is (h) (n, m; synonymous with conscious self, '*Man*' and 'Hirdā') an abstract but innermost part of one's body where one's 'Jīvātmāṅ' abides, and where it eventually perceives 'Nām(u)' or 'Parmātmāṅ'.

ghaṛnā: (v) (a) (synonymous with 'rachṇā' and 'baṇāuṇā') to make, design, construct, manufacture or create, and (b) (synonymous with 'chhilṇā' and 'trāshaṇā') to chisel, carve, sculpt, fashion, or smooth. However, spiritually it implies ridding oneself of one's 'Haumaiṅ', 'Moh' and innate 'Vikārī' tendencies ('Māyā' or 'Auguṇs') and imbibing and amassing noble attributes, virtues, and values ('ruhānī guṇas') in one's 'Hirdā'.

giān: (n, m, s) (a) (synonymous with 'bodh', 'ilam' and 'samajh') knowledge, insight, comprehension, or intelligence, (b) (synonymous with 'vivek' or 'bibek') intuitive insight and knowledge of moral, ethical and spiritual correctness or godliness, (c) (synonymous with 'tat(u)-' 'ruhānī-' or 'brahm-' 'giān(u)'; 'ruhānī-' 'jāgratā' or 'sojhī') divine knowledge about the one eternal Reality, its pervasiveness, sustaining and creative power; being the fount of all attributes; an understanding of the Divine Will and the true path to a realisation or perception of the eternal Reality, and (d) (genitive case - 'saṅbaṅdh kārak'; synonymous with 'giān dī vīchār') deliberation over the Divine Wisdom and Knowledge.

grace: (n, f; synonymous with 'Karam' (arab), 'Mehar' (pers), 'Nadar' (skt), 'Kirpā', 'Ma-i-ā', 'Bakhshīsh' and 'Prasād'). The term God of Grace is only meaningful in an evolving world where His Grace can operate. Similarly, the term God of Will ('Razā') presupposes that God wants His creation to evolve freely though not chaotically but, in a direction and with an aim, according to His Will. The clue to this direction is His attributes and the aim for humankind is to evolve from being egocentric ('Manmukh') to God-centric ('Gurmukh'), with the supreme goal in life being to live by His Will.

God is the ultimate provider for all in the creation and gives freely according to what He judges to be deserved. For anything else, He must judge us to be worthy of His Grace as He is the fount of all attributes, virtues and values and we cannot get anything by our effort alone (see Pauṛī 21). 'Ik Oaṅkār' can only be realised or perceived through His Grace, as Gurū Nānak states in his Credal Statement ('Mūl Maṅtra'). This is further endorsed in the following verse of the SGGS:

'By virtue of one's good 'Karmā', 'Jīvātmāṅ', clothed in a body, is born, but its liberation ('Moksh') from 'Haumaiṅ', 'Moh' and innate 'Vikārī' tendencies ('Māyā') ('Jīvan Mukat(i)') and the cycle of birth and death ('Āvāgavan') is only through God's Grace'. See Pauṛī 4.

It is not the performance of religious rites and rituals which is valued in the end but a life lived in harmony with 'Nām(u)'. It is true that one reaps what one sows[260] but the extrapolation of this truth does not mean that there is a mechanistic or purely methodical system of liberation where God's Grace is redundant. One must submit to 'Nām(u)' unreservedly and lovingly, live in complete harmony with His Will, and patiently await His favourable glance ('Nadar' - His Grace) in order to realise Him eventually.

guṇ: (n, m, pl) (a) (synonymous with 'lābh' and 'phal') gain, profit or outcome, (b) (synonymous with 'vidyā', 'hunnar' and 'kalā') knowledge, education or skill, and (c) (synonymous with 'visheshaṇ', 'siphat', 'khūbī', 'khāsīat', 'lachhaṇ' and 'subhāu' or 'tāsīr') literally, characteristics, properties or attributes of something, and the tacit reference here is to the Glory or attributive aspects of 'Nām(u)', and (d) (genitive case - 'sanbandh kārak'; synonymous with 'guṇāṅ-' 'de' or 'dī') of guṇ.

gur(u): (n, m, s; abbrev. for Gurū; synonymous with 'āchārīā') a complex word comprising 'gu' (darkness or ignorance) + 'rū' (light or knowledge), i.e., one who takes others out of darkness or ignorance and brings them into a state of light or wisdom. It also has its roots in the word 'gri', meaning (a) to engulf and/or devour, and (b) to inform, instruct or make another understand, i.e., that which destroys ignorance and makes another understand the eternal Reality.

'Anhad-' 'Sabad' or 'Nād' ('Nām(u)') is the primordial and the perfect enlightener (Gurū). However, in Gurmat, a Gurū is (a) one who has perceived or experienced the full glow of 'Nām(u)' within one's conscious self (*'Man'* or 'Hirdā') and whose every thought ('*Man*'), utterance ('Bachan') and deed ('Karam') is in perfect harmony with It, and (b) the Divine Words of such a person ('bāṇī', 'bachan', 'bol' or 'updes', and Divine Wisdom and Knowledge ('brahm giān') which brings about this change and provides us with the path to 'Nam-realisation'. Hence, in Gurmat, a Gurū is also defined as the 'Sabad Gurū', i.e., the spiritual or Divine Wisdom packaged or loaded in the Gurū's words.

hai: (a) (n, m; skt; 'hyā'; synonymous with 'ghoṛā') a horse, (b) (interj; synonymous with 'dukh bodhak'; pronounced as 'hā-i') literally, oh!, (c) (interj; synonymous with 'shok bodhak'; pronounced as 'haiṅ') literally, what!, and (d) (aux v, present tense) literally, am, is or are: I am, he is or they are, referring to the present time.

haumai: (n, f; pronounced as 'Haumaiṅ') 'Haumaiṅ' is a compound word, comprising 'Hauṅ' (I) + 'mai' (I), i.e., that which emphasises the self or 'I'. Similarly, the word 'Ahaṅkār' also has two components: 'Ahaṅ' ('I') + 'kār' (unchanging or consistent over a long period, i.e., continuous emphasis on 'self' or 'I'). Egoism and egotism certainly come closer but do not fully express all the attributes of 'Haumai'.

It is Gurū Nānak's firm belief that God, the Creator of the universe, is both immanent in and yet remains distinct from the creation. 'Nām(u)', His immanent form, not only creates the basic ingredients that evolve into the empirical world that exists today, but it also pervades the entire creation in the form of a soul ('Ātmāṅ'). The degree of expression of this soul imparts a variable degree of ability and autonomy to interact with the world outside; the greater the degree of expression of soul and autonomy or free will, the greater is the burden of responsibility for their actions on the individual being.

According to Gurmat, the fusion of the soul ('Ātmāṅ') with the physical body not only initiates 'life' in general but it also, ultimately, gives rise to its functional and somewhat imperfect surrogate, 'Jīvātmāṅ' which, in turn, becomes one's centre of consciousness (conscious self, '*Man*' or 'Hirdā'), gives rise to one's innate nature and, and influences the development of its mental and physical attributes.

A sense of the conscious self (consciousness coupled with a degree of autonomy) is a biological necessity for one's survival and progress in life in general. It imparts a sense of distinctiveness, and not only separates one from another of the same species but also from members of other species ('ਹਉ' or 'Ha-u'). To exist in symbiosis and in harmony with the rest of the world is to live life in line with 'Nām-consciousness'. In contrast, existing purely for the fulfilment of self-interest, with a total disregard for others and of life in general, is ego-consciousness. Furthermore, operating in this default state of ego-consciousness we erroneously consider our existence to be independent not only of inanimate and other sentient life but also of God and His Divine Order ('Hukam(u)'. In Gurmat, ego-consciousness, coupled with this malady is defined as 'Haumaiṅ'.

The eternal transcendent Reality first creates its immanent form ('Nām(u)'), followed by 'Haumaiṅ', 'Moh' and 'Saṅjog(u)' and 'Vijog(u)', before it initiates the process of creation ('diversity from unity'), with every aspect of its unfolding, or evolution under the autonomous and absolute control of the Divine Order ('Hukam(u)').[49-50, 52-3] According to Gurbānī, 'Haumaiṅ' is crucial to the process of evolution and, indeed, is thus causally related to man's apex position in this hierarchical system. However, having conquered the struggle against rival species and the environment in general, because of one's exaggerated and ill-developed 'Haumaiṅ', one finds it difficult to use all one's talents and to live in harmony with one's fellow human beings and the environment. Thus, leaving aside any real threat, even an apparent threat to individual identity or interests unmasks one's profound self-centredness and becomes a trigger for acts of brazen violence, brutality and tyranny in the form of ruthless oppression and exploitation of other human beings, other species, and of nature in general. History is replete with examples of people, religious groups or nations terrorising, oppressing, and exploiting fellow human beings, other nations, flora and fauna and nature in general.

In 'Haumaiṅ', one is self-willed ('Manmukh') as opposed to being obedient to His Will ('Gurmukh'), in Gurmat; in other words, one lives in the default state of ego-consciousness as opposed to that of 'Nām-consciousness'. Misled by 'Haumaiṅ', lured by 'Moh' and driven by the 'Vikārī' tendencies of one's innate nature (due to the influence of one's accumulated 'Saṅskārs'), one succumbs to one's ignoble innate nature, and the five cardinal tendencies, and commits evil deeds. Then, one reaps what one sows, and one's karmā binds one to the cycle of transmigration ('Āvāgavan'). On the other hand, one who rids oneself of one's 'Haumaiṅ', 'Moh' and innate 'Vikārī' tendencies ('Māyā') and lives by His Will, achieves 'Moksh' ('Jīvan Mukat(i)') in this life and release from Āvāgavan' in the hereafter ('Param Mukat(i)') when it merges with the Primal Soul. (See Pauṛī 2).

According to Gurbānī, 'Haumaiṅ' is a chronic disease, and its cure lies in truly understanding it. The following few quotations from Gurbānī further illustrate the concept of 'Haumaiṅ':

'Husband (the immanent 'Nām(u)') and wife (the 'Jīvātmāṅ') live side by side but the impregnable wall of 'Haumaiṅ' separates them'.[262]

'Haumaiṅ' is a chronic malady; its remedy lies in attuning oneself to 'Nām(u)' by God's Grace'.[265]

'Nām(u)' and 'Haumaiṅ' are opposed to each other; the two cannot co-exist at the same place'.[79]

'Haumaiṅ' ceases to exist when one is imbued with 'Nām(u)'.[270]

Thus, liberation from 'Haumaiṅ' and the cycle of birth and death is achieved through alignment with 'Nām(u)' and God-consciousness.

hoi: (a) (v, s, present tense; synonymous with 'huṅdī-' or 'huṅdā-' 'hai'; 'ho jāṅdī-' or 'ho jāṅdā-' 'hai'; 'ho sakdā hai') literally, occurs, comes to be or becomes; can occur, happen or become, (b) (v, s, present continuous; synonymous with 'ho rahī-' or 'ho rahā-' 'hai') is taking place or happening, (c) (indeclinable past participle or perfect participle - 'pūran pūrab kārdaṅtak'; synonymous with 'ho ke') having become or having been, and (d) (v, s, 'saṅbhāv bhvikht kāl - kiās bodhak', third person; synonymous with 'ho jāve', 'hove' or 'ho sake') literally, were to become or were to be.

hor(u): (a) (pron; synonymous with 'anya', 'dūjā', 'dūsrā' and 'vakhrā') another, different and someone or something else, and (b) (adj; synonymous with 'aur' and 'is toṅ vadh or chhuṭ' and 'adhik') another, more or in addition.

hovai: (a) (v, s, 'saṅbhāv bhvikht kāl - kiās/ichhā bodhak', third person; synonymous with 'hove', 'ho jāve' or 'je huṅdā') were to exist, occur or become, and (b) (v, s, present tense, third person; synonymous with 'ho jāṅdī/jāṅdā hai'; 'huṅdā-' or 'huṅdī-' 'hai'; 'ho sakdā hai') exists, occurs, or becomes.

hovṇā: (a) (v; synonymous with 'hoṇā', 'ghaṭṇā' or 'vāparnā') to happen, occur, come about or befall, (b) (v; synonymous with 'astitv hoṇā' or 'paidā hoṇā') to be, to exist or to be born, and (c) (conj v and suff.) which denotes 'occurrence' of the activity associated with the noun or primary verb, e.g. (i) 'sūchā hovṇā' - to become clean and pure, to become free from pollutants or defilement, (ii) 'palīt hoṇā' - to become unclean, polluted or defiled, and (iii) 'sir(i) bhār(u) hoṇā' - literally, to carry or bear the burden of guilt, the crime or punishment of this error.

hukam(i): (a) (locative case - 'adhikaraṇ kārak'; synonymous with 'hukam vich') within the limits of His 'hukam(u)', and (b) (instrumental case - 'karaṇ kārak'; 'hukam- ' 'nāl', 'rāhīṅ', 'duārā', 'sadkā' or 'anusārī') with, through, by virtue of or according to 'hukam(u)'.

hukam(u): (n, m) (a) (synonymous with 'rāi', 'phaislā' and 'nirṇā') judgement or decision, and (b) (arab; synonymous with 'phurmān', 'āgiā', 'ādesh' and 'razā') order, decree, command or will. The reference here is to the one Divine Order, with all the other natural laws subservient to it. Whilst human beings, with the greatest expression of 'Ātmāṅ' and free will or autonomy, can elect to act anywhere within the spectrum of good or bad actions, only an action or deed which would please God would be judged to be by His Will ('Raza').

hukamī: (synonymous with 'hukmī') (a) (adj; synonymous with 'hākim' and 'hukam karan vālā'; pronounced as 'hukamī' or 'hukmī') king, sovereign, ruler, or commander, (b) (genitive case - 'saṅbaṅdh kārak'; synonymous with 'hukamī dā') of ruler or sovereign, (c) (locative case - 'adhikaraṇ kārak'; synonymous with 'hukam vich') in or by 'hukam', and (d) (instrumental case - 'karaṇ kārak'; synonymous with 'hukam' 'nāl', 'duārā', 'rāhīṅ' or 'anusār'; pronounced as 'hukamīṅ' or 'hukmīṅ') literally, legally, by lawful means or within the constraints of the law. In essence, according to the Divine Order or by His Will.

ik(u): (a) (adj) one, first of the 1-9 numerals. In essence, one and only one, unique, unparalleled or unrivalled, (b) (adj, s, m; synonymous with 'ikallā') alone, by oneself, single-handed or unaided, (c) (adj, s, m; synonymous with 'lāsāni' or 'adutī') unique, unparalleled or without a match, (d) (n, m) creator or 'Kartār' (God), and (e) (indefinite pron; synonymous with 'ik(i)' or 'koī') someone or anyone from a variable set of numbers. It refers to the One Absolute God, unique and unrivalled, who is 'Niraṅkār' (without any physical form or any perceivable attributes in this form), and transcendent (unfathomable and beyond the grasp of human senses and intellect).

jā: (a) (n, f; (pers) 'thāṅ' or 'jagā') place, (b) (prep; (siṅdhī) synonymous with 'dā') e.g. 'mahiṅjā' (mine), (c) (v, s, imperative mood - 'hukmī bhvikht', second person; synonymous with 'jāh' or 'jāo') see jāṇā, (d) (pron and adj; synonymous with 'jis' or 'jihṛā') who, whom, which or that, (e) (adv; synonymous with 'jab', 'jadoṅ' or 'jis vele') when or since, (f) (p and conj; synonymous with 'je', 'jāṅ', 'yad(i)' or 'agar') if, and (g) (pron; synonymous with 'jis') who, whom, which or that.

jāh(i): (a) (adj; synonymous with 'jaisā' or 'jehā') resembling, same as or like that, (b) (pron; synonymous with 'jis nūṅ' or 'jise') to whom, (c) (v, s, present tense, second person; synonymous with 'tūṅ jāṅdāṅ haiṅ' or 'tusīṅ jāṅde ho'; pronounced as 'jāheṅ') you go, (d) (v, pl, present tense, first person; synonymous with 'asīṅ jāṅde hāṅ') we go, (e) (v, s, 'saṅbhāv bhvikht kāl - shradhā or ichhā bodhak', second person; synonymous with 'tusīṅ-' 'jāvo' or 'gaman karo'), (f) (v, pl, future tense, third person; synonymous with 'uh jāṇge') they will go, (g) (v, pl, present tense, third person'; synonymous with 'uh-' 'jāṅde han' or 'jā sakde' 'han'; 'dūr ho- 'or 'miṭ-' 'jāṅde han'; pronounced as 'jāhen') they go or can go; will vanish or cease to exist, and (h) (conj v and suff), e.g. 'pāe jāh(i)' - 'pāe-'or 'labhe ja-' 'sakde han' - can be got or found; 'n kathne jāh(i)' - cannot be described.

jāi: (a) (n, f; synonymous with 'beṭī' and 'putrī') a daughter, (b) (n, f; synonymous with 'janam' and 'utpat(i)') birth, genesis, or growth, (c) (v; synonymous with 'jaṇī' and 'paidā kītī') gave birth to or brought forth, (d) (adj; synonymous with 'ajāīṅ' and 'vyarth') useless, futile, fruitless or meaningless, (e) (n, f; pers; synonymous with 'jag(h)ā' or 'thāṅ') place, spot or location, (f) (v, s, present tense, third person) (i) 'chale jaṅdā-' or 'jā sakdā-' 'hai' - goes or can go; see jāṇā, (ii) 'mar miṭ jaṅdā hai' - ceases to exist, (iii) 'dūr ho jaṅdā hai' - vanishes, (iv) 'agge turdā hai' - proceeds or moves forward, (v) 'jaṅmdā hai'/'paidā huṅdā hai' - takes birth or is born; see jaṅmṇā, (g) (indeclinable past participle or perfect participle - 'pūran pūrab kārdaṅtak'; synonymous with 'jā-' or 'pahuṅch-' 'ke') by going or having reached, (h) (v, s, 'saṅbhāv bhvikht kāl - kiās bodhak', second person; synonymous with 'jāve' and 'miṭe'; synonymous with 'jāvāṅ' or 'jāṅvāṅ'; pronounced as 'jāīṅ') vanish or disappear; shall I or could I go, and (i) (conj v and suff.) as part of the conjunct verb it helps to complete the meaning of the primary verb, e.g. (i) 'n jāi lakhiā' - cannot be ascertained or realised, (ii) 'ghāṭ(i) n jāi' - [His status] does not suffer or shrink, (iii) 'pāiā jāi' - prāpat kitā jā sakdā hai (can be achieved or realised), and (iv) 'ākhiā n jāi' - cannot be stated, described or elaborated, (v) 'visar(i) jāīṅ' or 'visar(i) jāṅvāṅ' - [I] might forget or overlook; (vi) 'birthī jāi' - becomes futile, worthless or fruitless, (vii) 'bhasmaṅt(u) jāi' - burns or turns to ashes, (viii) 'thāpiā n jāi' - cannot be conceived, created or appointed, and (ix) 'likhiā n jāi' - that cannot be written or recorded.

jāī: (a) (n, f; synonymous with 'beṭī' and 'putrī') a daughter, (b) (n, f; synonymous with 'janam' and 'utpat(i)') birth, genesis, or growth, (c) (v; synonymous with 'jaṇī' and 'paidā kītī') gave birth to or brought forth, (d) (adj; synonymous with 'ajāīṅ' and 'vyarth') useless, futile, fruitless or meaningless, (e) (n, f; pers; synonymous with 'jag(h)ā' or 'thāṅ') place, spot or location, (f) (v, s, present tense, third person; synonymous with 'chale jāṅdā/jāṅdī hai' or 'jā sakdā hai') departs or goes; can go or depart; see jāṇā, (g) (v, s, present tense, third person; synonymous with 'jaṅmdā-', 'jaṅmdī-', or 'paidā huṅdā/huṅdī-' 'hai') comes to be, takes birth or is born; see jaṅmṇā, (h) (indeclinable past participle or perfect participle - 'pūran pūrab kārdaṅtak'; synonymous with 'jā-' or 'pahuṅch-' 'ke') by going or having reached, (i) (v, s, 'saṅbhāv bhvikht kāl - kiās bodhak', second person; synonymous with 'jāve' and 'miṭe'; synonymous with 'jāvāṅ' or 'jāṅvāṅ'; pronounced as 'jāīṅ') vanish or disappear; shall I or could I go, and (j) (conj v and suff.) as part of the conjuct verb it helps to complete the meaning of the primary verb, e.g. (i) 'n jāī lakhiā' - cannot be ascertained or realised, (ii) 'ghāṭ(i) n jāī' - [His status] does not suffer or shrink, (iii) 'pāiā jāī' - prāpat kitā jā sakdā hai (can be achieved or realised), and (iv) 'ākhiā n jāī' - cannot be stated, described or elaborated, (v) 'visar(i) jāīṅ' or 'visar(i) jāṅvāṅ' - [I] might forget or overlook; (vi) 'birthī jāī' - becomes futile, worthless or fruitless, (vii) 'bhasmaṅt(u) jāī' - burns or turns to ashes, (viii) 'thāpiā n jāī' - cannot be conceived, created or appointed, (ix) 'sāth(i) n jāī' - does not go or accompany someone, and (x) 'kahṇā kathan(u) n jāī' - a narrative of God's Glory and 'Divine Order' cannot be expressed.

jāṇā: (a) (v; synonymous with 'chalṇā' and 'gaman karnā') to walk, go or proceed, (b) (v, s, present tense, first person; synonymous with 'jāṇ-' or 'samajh-' 'laiṅdā hāṅ') I get to know, understand or realise, (c) (v, s, 'saṅbhāv bhvikht kāl - ichhā bodhak', first person; synonymous with 'maiṅ jāṇ-' or 'samajh-' 'lavāṅ') if I could grasp or perceive, (d) (conj v) (i) 'chale-', 'tur-'or 'chhaḍ-' 'jāṇā' - literally, to go, depart or leave, (ii) 'dūr ho jāṇā' - to disappear, (iii) 'mar-' or 'miṭ-' 'jāṇā' - to die, cease to exist, or vanish, (iv) 'thak jāṇā' - to become tired, (v) 'kathan n jāṇā' - cannot be narrated, explained or explicated, (vi) 'vāriā-'or 'bal(i)hār-' 'jāṇā' - to be willing to lay down one's life for another to whom one is devoted and for whom one has an immensely high regard for, (vii) 'jor kar ke jāṇā' - to leave having coerced or inflicted oppression and cruelty upon on others, (viii) 'likh lai jāṇā' - to take a written account of one's 'saṅskārs' with oneself, and (ix) 'thāpiā jāṇā' or 'kise kaṅm-' or 'padvī' 'te niyukt ho jāṇā' - to be appointed to a job or position.

jāṇah(i): (a) (v, s, present tense, second person; synonymous with 'tuṅ jāṇdā hai' or 'tusīṅ jāṇde ho'; pronounced as 'jāṇaheṅ'), (b) (v, pl, present tense, first person; synonymous with 'asīṅ jāṇde hāṅ'), (c) (v, s, 'saṅbhāv bhvikht kāl - kiās, sharat, shradhā, ichhā bodhak', second person; synonymous with 'je asīṅ jāṇ la-ī-e' or 'je tusīṅ jāṇ lavo'), (d) (v, pl, future tense, third person; synonymous with 'jāṇange'; pronounced as 'jāṇaheṅ'), and (e) (v, pl, present tense, third person; synonymous with 'uh jāṇde han'; pronounced as jānaheṅ') see jāṇana.

jāṇai: (a) (v, s, present tense, second person; synonymous with 'tūṅ jāṇdā haiṅ' or 'tusīṅ samajde ho'), (b) ('saṅbhāv bhvikht kāl - kiās, sharat, ichhā or bevasī bodhak', s, third/first person; synonymous with 'je maiṅ/tusīṅ-' 'jāṇ lavoṅ', 'jānaṇā chāhīe' or 'jānaṇ dā yatan karīe'), and (c) (v, s, present tense, third person: synonymous with 'uh jāṇdā hai') see jāṇanā.

jāṇanā: (v; synonymous with 'jānaṇā') (a) (synonymous with 'pachhāṇanā' and 'vākphīyat pāuṇī') to become acquainted or familiar with, (b) (synonymous with 'samjhaṇā' and 'giān hāsal karnā') to know or understand, (c) (synonymous with 'savīkār karnā' and 'maṅnaṇā') to recognise, regard or unreservedly accept, and (d) (synonymous with 'anubhav karnā') to realise or perceive.

jāṇīai: (a) (v, s, present tense, second/third person; synonymous with 'tusīṅ samajh/anubhav kar laiṅde ho' or 'uh samajh/anubhav kar laiṅde han') literally, get to know or understand, (b) ('saṅbhāv bhvikht kāl - kiās, sharat, ichhā or bevasī bodhak', s, third/first person; synonymous with 'je asīṅ samajh jāīe', 'uh samajh jāṇ' or 'uh jāṇia- 'or 'pargaṭ ho-' 'jāve') literally, if one could or were to know/understand, (c) (v, pl, imperative mood - 'hukmī bhvikht', first person; synonymous with 'sānūṅ samajh laiṇā chāhīdā hai') literally, we should know or understand, and (d) (v, s, present tense, third person, 'karam vāch' (passive voice); synonymous with 'uh jāṇiā jāṅdā hai' or 'us nūṅ' 'samajh-' or 'anubhav kar-' 'laīdā hai') [he] can become evident or revealed.

jaṅmaṇā: (v; synonymous with 'paidā hoṇā' and 'utpat(i) hoṇī') to take birth, to be born or to incarnate.

jāpai: (a) (v, s, present tense, third person; synonymous with 'japdā hai') reflects, meditates or contemplates, (b) (v, s, present tense, second person; synonymous with 'tusīṅ mahsus- 'or 'partīt-' 'karde ho') [you] feel or perceive, (c) (v, s, 'saṅbhāv bhvikht kāl - ichhā, bevasī or prashan bodhak'; synonymous with 'jāṇīe'; 'samajh- 'or 'anubhav kar-' 'la-ī-e'), (d) (v, s, present tense, third person; synonymous with 'jāṇīdā-' or 'sojhī āuṅdī-' 'hai') gets to know or understand, and (e) (v, s, present tense, third person; synonymous with 'jāpdā-', 'bhāsdā-'or 'lagdā-' 'hai'; 'pratīt-', 'mālūm-' or 'mahsus-' 'huṅdā hai') appears, looks, feels, seems or perceives.

jāpṇā: (a) (v; synonymous with 'bhāsṇā', 'mālūm hoṇā', 'partīt hoṇā', and 'pragaṭ hoṇā') to look, find, seem, feel, perceive or appear, and (b) (v; synonymous with 'samajh-' or 'sojhī-' 'āuṅdī 'hai') to apprehend or recognise.

je: (a) (pron; pl of 'jo'; synonymous with 'jihṛe') they, who, whoever, whosoever, and (b) (conj; synonymous with 'je kar', 'yadī' and 'agar') if or in case.

jīa: (a) (n, m; synonymous with '*Man*', 'Chit', 'Hirdā') Conscious-self, (b) (n, f; synonymous with 'jīvan' and 'ziṅdagī') spiritual life, (c) (n, f; synonymous with 'Rūh', 'Jīvātmāṅ' and 'Jiṅd' (pers)) soul, and (d) (n, pl; synonymous with 'jīv') all sentient beings, and (e) (n; synonymous with 'prāṇī') persons or human beings.

jit(u): (a) (n, f, x; synonymous with 'jīt', 'jīt(i)', 'phate' or 'phatah(i)') victory, triumph or success, (b) (adj; especially if used as a suffix, e.g. 'Indrajit(u)') one who gains victory, triumph or success over one's sensory-motor organs; Meghnāth, Son of Rāvan, who gained victory over Indra Dev, (c) (adv; synonymous with 'jidhar' and 'jis pāse') whither, where or in which direction, (d) (adv, pron and adj; synonymous with 'jadoṅ', 'jis vele' and 'jab ke') when, (e) (instrumental case - 'karaṇ kārak'; synonymous with 'jis-' 'nāl', 'duārā' or 'sadka') with, through or by virtue of, (f) (ablative case - 'apāḍān kārak'; synonymous with 'jis toṅ') from whom or which, (g) (pron; synonymous with 'jis') who, which, that or whom, and (h) (adv; synonymous with 'jidhar', 'jithe' and 'yahāṅ') whither or in/to which direction; where.

jor(u): (pronounced as 'zor(u)' from b to e) (a) (n, m; synonymous with 'joṛ' and 'milāp') joint, bond, link or connection, (b) (n, f; pers;

synonymous with ‘zor(u)’, ‘bal’, ‘himmat’, ‘shaktī’ and ‘samrathā’) bravery, strength, power or ability, (c) (n, m; synonymous with ‘āsrā’ or ‘sahārā’) support or prop, (d) (n, m; synonymous with ‘dhakkā’, ‘zulam’ and ‘vadhīkīāṅ’) coercion, use of force, oppression, cruelty or persecution, and (e) (n, m; synonymous with ‘vas’) authority, control or controlling power.

jugat(i): (a) (n, m; synonymous with ‘iṅtzām’ and ‘parbaṅdh’) arrangement or system, (b) (n, f; synonymous with ‘yogitā’, ‘yogyatā’ and ‘samrathā’) ability, capability, authority or power, (c) (n, f; synonymous with ‘saṅsārk kāmyābī’ and ‘saphaltā’) achievement, success or triumph, (d) (n, m; synonymous with ‘tarak’ and ‘dalīl’) logic, reasoning or rationale, (e) (n, f; synonymous with ‘tadbīr’) plan, procedure or scheme, and (f) (n, m; synonymous with ‘rahiṇī bahiṇī’ and ‘jīvan-’ ‘jāch’, ‘tarīkā’ or ‘ḍhaṅg’) literally, way of life, art of living or method, technique or procedure.

kā: (a) (adj; synonymous with ‘kuchh’, ‘kujh’ or ‘kiṅchit’) some, miniscule or tiny amount, (b) (pron; synonymous with ‘kis’) which, (c) (synonymous with ‘koī’) any or someone, (d) (pron; synonymous with ‘kiā’) what, and (e) (prep, m; synonymous with ‘dā’) of.

kahai: (a) (v, s, present tense, second person; synonymous with ‘tūṅ kahiṅdā haiṅ’ or ‘tusīṅ kahiṅde ho’; pronounced as ‘kahaiṅ’), (b) (v, s, present tense, third person; synonymous with ‘ākhdā-’ or ‘kahiṅdā-’ ‘hai’; ‘varṇan-’ or ‘vakhyān-’ ‘kardā hai’) sets forth, utters, expounds, explicates or sings His Glory, and (c) (v, s, third person, ‘saṅbhāv bhvikht kāl - kiās bodhak’; synonymous with ‘biān-’ or ‘vakhyān-’ ‘ākhe/kare’ ‘bhī’) were to express, expound, explicate or elaborate.

kahaṇ(u): (infinitive mood - ‘bhāvārth kārdaṅtak’; synonymous with ‘kahaṇ(u)’) (a) (n, f; synonymous with ‘phaṛ’ or ‘phaṛ(h)’) a boast, (b) (n, m; synonymous with ‘bachan’ and ‘bol’) literally, words, (c) (n, m, s; synonymous with ‘biān’ and ‘kathan’) statement, description, or narration in words, and (d) (n, f; synonymous with ‘siphat sālāh’) praise, eulogy or glory.

kahiṇā/kahinā: (a) ('bhāvārth kārdaṅtak'; synonymous with 'ākhṇā', 'ākhaṇ(u)', 'kathan' or 'kathnā') comment, utterance or observation, and (b) (v; synonymous with 'ākhṇā', 'kathnā' or 'kahinā'; 'varṇan-' or 'vakhyān-' 'karnā') literally, to say, utter, recount, narrate or state; to set forth, explain, expound or elucidate. However, implicit here is 'siphat sālāh karnī' or to sing His Glory.

kai: (a) (conj; synonymous with 'bhāṅveṅ', 'chāhe', 'athvā' or 'jāṅ') even if, even though, although, either or, albeit, (b) (adv; synonymous with 'shāid' or 'kadāchit') may be or possibly, (c) (adj; synonymous with 'kitne' or 'ka-ī') some, a few, many, several or numerous, (d) (pron, adj; synonymous with 'kis' or 'kihṛe') who, what or which, (e) (synonymous with 'kāraṇ') because of, (f) (prep; synonymous with 'se', 'nāl' or 'toṅ') with or from, (g) (prep; synonymous with 'kā', 'ke', 'kī', 'dā', 'de' or 'dī') of, and (h) (pron: genitive case - 'saṅbaṅdh kārak'; synonymous with 'kis de') whose.

kāl(u): (a) (n, m, s; synonymous with 'velā' and 'smāṅ') time, period or era, (b) (synonymous with 'kriyā de vāparn dā samāṅ', i.e., tense) 'vartmān' (present), 'bhūt' (past) and 'bhvikh' (future), (c) (synonymous with 'kal' or 'aglā din') the next day, (d) (n, m, s; synonymous with 'ghāṭ', 'kamī', 'kaihar', 'toṭ' and 'auṛ') extreme scarcity of food or famine, (e) (synonymous with 'yam' or 'yamā') Angel of Death, and (f) (n, f; synonymous with 'mrityū' and 'maut') literally, the process and the time of both physical and spiritual demise or death. The fear of death is pre-eminent amongst all the emotions that human beings experience. The real 'I' or 'self' is 'Jīvātmāṅ', which is indestructible and 'spiritual demise or death' refers to succumbing to one's ego-consciousness ('Haumaiṅ'), 'Moh', 'Māiā' and 'Vikārs'.

kār: (a) (n, m; 'dharam dā tax') a religious tax, (b) (n, f; synonymous with 'rekhā and 'lakīr') a line or a boundary, (c) (n, m; abbrev for 'ahaṅkār') egotism, pride, conceit or arrogance, (d) (suff that turns a word to a 'kartā' or 'karan vālā' - a doer or performer of an act), e.g. 'mīnākār', one who is skilled in inset work in stone, metal or other art work, 'charam kār' - a leatherworker ('chamār'), 'loh kār' - a blacksmith ('luhār'), and 'suwarn kār' - a goldsmith ('suniār') (e) (suff that turns the word to an adj; synonymous with 'ik ras' or 'jis vich tabdīlī n āve') unchanging, uniform and continuous, e.g., 'na(ṅ)nākār' - persistent refusal and 'jhanatkār' - uniform and continuous melodious sound, (f) (n, m; synonymous with 'karanyog kaṅm and kiriyā') work, job, or an action, (g) (synonymous with 'srisṭ(i) rachnā') literally, the act of creation and its evolution with time. In essence, the reference here is to the way of the world, how the world moves or flows and evolution (both in the Darwinian and a spiritual sense).

kar(i): (a) (v, s, imperative mood - 'hukmī bhvikht', second person; synonymous with 'tūṅ kar' and 'tusīṅ karo'), (b) (locative case - 'adhikaraṇ kārak'; synonymous with 'hath-' 'vich' or 'uppar') literally, in or on one's hands, and (c) (indeclinable past participle; perfect participle - 'pūran pūrab kārdaṅtak'; synomymous with 'kar ke') having done or carried out an act.

kar(i) kar(i): (indeclinable past participle or perfect participle - 'pūran pūrab kārdaṅtak'; synonymous with 'kar kar ke', 'paidā kar ke' and 'sirj ke') literally, having created. See karnā (a).

karah(i): (a) (v, s, present tense, second person; synonymous with 'tūṅ kardā haiṅ' or 'tusīṅ karde ho'; pronounced as 'karheṅ') you do, (b) (v, s, present tense, first person; synonymous with 'asīṅ karde hāṅ') we do, (c) ('saṅbhāv bhvikht kāl - kiās, sharat or ichhā bodhak', pl, second person; synonymous with 'je tusīṅ karo') if you do, (d) (v, pl, future tense, third person; synonymous with 'uh karaṇge') they will do, and (e) (v, pl, present tense, third person; synonymous with 'uh karde-' or 'kardīāṅ-' 'han' or 'kar sakde han'; pronounced as 'karheṅ') do, perform or carry out.

karam(u): (n, m) (a) a collective noun for thoughts, utterances and deeds. Hindu sages and scholars describe three types of deeds (skt: synonymous with 'kaṅm'), (i) 'kriyamāṇ' - those that are being carried out, (ii) 'prārabd' - those that form the basis of one's present life, and (iii) 'saṅchit' or 'siṅchit' - those that one has accumulated from past lives whose debt is still owed, (b) (n, m; synonymous with 'amal' or 'karnī') conduct or character, (c) (n, f; synonymous with 'bhāg' or 'kismat') fate, fortune or destiny, (d) (n, m; synonymous with 'kartav' or 'pharz') duty, (e) (n, m; synonymous with 'karam kāṅḍ') commonly agreed rituals or ritualistic acts or duties thought to be propitious amongst followers of a faith, and (f) (n, f; pers; synonymous with 'dyā', 'kripā', 'meharbānī' and 'bakhshīsh') grace, mercy, blessing, compassion or favour. It is, however, noteworthy that one is only worthy of His Grace when one actively seeks and genuinely strives to live by His Will and in perfect harmony with 'Nām(u)'.

karam phal ('Law of Karmā'): (n, m) The reaction or result of 'Karmās' manifests either immediately, at some point in the future, in this life or in another life according to the Law of 'Karmā'. One's innate nature, drives or unmet desires can usually be gauged from recurrent thoughts in one's mind, for the latter represent the mirror image of the former. Repeatedly translating a thought into action and experiencing its outcome leaves an imprint on one's conscious self ('*man*') in the form of a habit. The influence of such persistent habits termed 'Saṅskārs', accumulated during one's current and previous lives, not only affects and modifies one's future innate nature but also one's subsequent perception and behaviour. This is also how the baggage of one's bad Karmā keeps one bound to the process of reincarnation. Whilst Gurū Nānak accepts this in principle, he does not accept its implied rigidity or inevitability. 'They, to whom He shows His Mercy, enshrine 'Nām(u)' in their '*man*' ('Hirdā'); an account of their deeds is then torn up, and all their dues considered settled at His Court'. [535]

Good karmā may procure one a human life, but liberation from the cycle of birth and death ('Moksh') is occurs only through His Grace. Mere rituals do not carry any merit; liberation is only achieved by submitting to and living by His Will ('Nām-consciousness'). See Pauṛī 1.

kare: (a) (v, s, present tense, third person; synonymous with 'kar sakdā' 'hai' or 'hove') and (b) ('saṅbhāv bhvikht kāl - kiās, sharat, ichhā bodhak'; synonymous with 'kar-' or 'bakhsh-' 'deve') see karnā.

karmī: (a) (adj, m; synonymous with 'karīm') merciful, compassionate or benevolent - implicit here is God, (b) (nominative case - 'kartā kārak'; synonymous with 'karam kartā') one who undertakes the responsibility of thoughts, speech or deeds, (c) (n, m; synonymous with 'karam kāṇḍī') one who commits to commonly agreed rituals or ritualistic acts or duties thought to be propitious amongst followers of a faith, (d) (instrumental case - ‘karaṇ kārak’; synonymous with ‘karam-’ or ‘mehar-’ ‘sadkā'; pronounced as ‘karmīṅ’), through His Grace or Mercy, and (e) (instrumental case - ‘karaṇ kārak’; synonymous with ‘karmāṅ-’ ‘karke' or ‘anusār’; pronounced as ‘karmīṅ’) due to or by virtue of one’s past karmā.

karnā: (a) (n, m, pl; synonymous with ‘kaṅn’) literally, ears, (b) (n, f; synonymous with ‘rachnā’, ‘krit’ or ‘s(i)rishṭ(i)’) creation or universe, (c) (n, m; synonymous with ‘kāraṇ’ or ‘sbabb’) cause, purpose or motive (d) (n, m, synonymous with ‘kītā-’ ‘kaṅm' or ‘kāraj’) a task, duty or a job, (e) (n, m; synonymous with ‘karanyog kanm’) a worthwhile action, function or purpose, (f) (adj, m; synonymous with ‘karan vālā’ or ‘karan de samrath’) literally, doer or one who undertakes or carries out; able to carry out or undertake, (g) (v; synonymous with ‘kise kāraj de karan dī kriyā’) to do, undertake or perform an action or a task, (h) (v; synonymous with ‘karam nūṅ amlī jāmā deṇā’) to adopt, implement or put into practice, (i) (conj v and suff), e.g., (i) ‘pradān karnā’ - to grant or bestow, (ii) ‘bakhshish karnā’ - to show grace or mercy, (iii) ‘paidā karnā’ - to produce, create, grow, bring forth or give birth, (iv) ‘vīchār(u) karnā’ - to ponder, deliberate or reflect, and (v) ‘kheh karnā’ - to destroy.

karṇā: (a) (n, m, pl; synonymous with ‘kaṅn’) literally, ears, (b) (n, f; synonymous with ‘karuṇā’, ‘kripā’ or ‘mehar’) favour, grace, mercy, compassion or benevolence, (c) (n, f; synonymous with ‘rachnā’, ‘krit’ or ‘s(i)rishṭ(i)’) creation or universe, (d) (n, m; synonymous with ‘kāraṇ’ and ‘sbabb’) cause, purpose or motive, (e) (adj, m; synonymous with ‘karan vālā’ or ‘karan de samrath’) literally, doer or one who undertakes or carries out; able to carry out or undertake, (f) (v; synonymous with ‘kise kāraj de karan dī kriyā’) to do, undertake or perform an action or a task, (g) (v; synonymous with ‘karam nūṅ amlī jāmā deṇā’) to adopt, implement or put into practice, (h) (n, m; synonymous with ‘karaṇyog-’ ‘kītā kaṅm’ or ‘kāraj’) worthwhile tasks or duties carried out, and (i) (conj v. and suff.) e.g. (i) ‘pradān karnā’ - to grant or bestow and (ii) ‘bakhshish karnā’ - to show grace or mercy, (iii) ‘paidā karnā’ - to produce, create, grow, bring forth or give birth, and, (iv) ‘vīchār(u) karnā’ - to ponder, deliberate or reflect.

kau: (a) (prep; synonymous with ‘tāṅī’, ‘ko’, ‘nūṅ’, ‘neṅ’, ‘toṅ’, ‘dā/kā’ or ‘la-ī’) to, for, from, up to, in return and of, (b) (adv; synonymous with ‘kad’ or ‘kab’) when.

ke: (a) (conj; synonymous with ‘athvā’, ‘agar’, ‘yad(i)’ and ‘jāṅ’) if, either, or, (b) (pron; synonymous with ‘koī’) someone or anybody, (c) (adj; synonymous with ‘ka-ī’ and ‘anek’) many or numerous, and (d) (prep, m; synonymous with ‘de’) of.

ketī: (a) (adj; synonymous with ‘kitnī’ and ‘kiṅnī’) how much or how many, (b) (adj; synonymous with ‘kaī’ and ‘anek’) many, several, numerous or countless, and (c) genitive case - ‘saṅbaṅdh kārak’; synonymous with ‘ka-ī-āṅ- ’or ‘ka-ī jīvāṅ-’ ‘dā/dī’) of many beings.

ketiā: (a) (adj, f; synonymous with ‘kitnīā’ and ‘kiṅnīā’; pronounced as ‘ketīāṅ’) literally, many or how many? (b) (adj, m; genitive case - ‘saṅbaṅdh kārak’; synonymous with ‘kaīāṅ’, ‘kiṅnīāṅ-’ or ‘kitniāṅ-’ ‘dī’; pronounced as ‘ketiāṅ’) many, of many, or how many? and (c) (accusative case - ‘karam kārak’ nūṅ synonymous with kaīāṅ-’ or ‘kitniāṅ-’ ‘nūṅ’; pronounced as ‘ketiāṅ’) to many.

khāh(i): (a) (v, s, present tense, second person; synonymous with ‘tūṅ khāṅdā haiṅ’ or ‘tusīṅ khāṅde ho’; pronounced as ‘khāheṅ’), (b) (v, pl, present tense, first person; synonymous with ‘asīṅ khāṅde hāṅ’), (c) (v, s, ‘saṅbhāv bhvikht kāl - kiās, sharat, ichhā bodhak’, first/second person; synonymous with ‘je asīṅ/tusīṅ khāvīe’), (d) (v, s, future tense, third person; synonymous with ‘uh khāṇge’) they will partake of food, and (e) (v, pl, present tense, third person; synonymous with ‘uh khāṅde han’; pronounced as ‘khāheṅ’) literally, they dine, eat, partake of food, consume or ingest; (fig) they suffer the consequences of their deeds.

khāṇā: (a) (n, m; synonymous with ‘bhojan’ or ‘khāṇyog padārth’) food fit for consumption, (b) (v) (synonymous with ‘bhojan karnā’, ‘sevan karnā’ and ‘chhakṇā’) to eat or dine, (c) (conj. v and suff.) (i) (synonymous with ‘hār-’ or ‘shikast-’; ‘kapṭ-’, ‘phreb-’ or ‘dhokhā-’; ‘kuṭṭ-’, ‘mār-’ or ‘piṭāī-’; ‘siṭṭā-’, ‘phal-’ or ‘priṇām-’ ‘khāṇā’) to suffer or endure defeat, deceit, beating or consequence, (ii) (synonymous with ‘prāi dhan vich’ ‘ghālā mālā’ ‘or ‘khurd burd’ ‘karnā’) to misappropriate or embezzle, iii) (synonymous with 'sauṅh-', 'shapt-' or 'kasam-' 'khāṇā') to take an oath, and (iv) (synonymous with 'haulī haulī-''khornā' or 'kaṭṇā') to erode or corrode.

khaṅḍ(u): (n, m) (a) (synonymous with 'tukṛā' and 'hissā') a part, portion, segment, section, fragment, (b) (synonymous with 'kāṅḍ' and 'adhayāy') a chapter, scene or episode, (c) a planet ('khaṅḍ') in the universe ('brahmaṅḍ'), (d) (synonymous with 'dīp', 'desh' and 'asthān' a continent, a country or region of a country, (e) (n, f; synonymous with 'maṅzal') ultimate goal or destination, (f) (n, f; synonymous with 'khaṛg') a sword, (g) (n, f; synonymous with 'chīnī') sugar, (h) (n, m; synonymous with 'khaṅḍ hoṇā') break up, disintegration or destruction, (i) (n, m; synonymous with 'darjā') grade, rank or status, and (j) (synonymous with 'avasthā') state, stage, condition, domain or realm.

ki: (a) (adj; synonymous with 'kitnā' and 'ketā') how much, (b) (p/conj) that, (c) (synonymous with 'yā' and 'athvā'), (d) (pron; synonymous with 'kis(u)' and 'kis') who or whom, and (e) (interrogative; synonymous with 'kiā' and 'kī') what?

kī: (a) (v. form; synonymous with 'karī' or 'kītī') did or carried out, (b) (pron; synonymous with 'kiā') what, (c) (adv; synonymous with 'kioṅ') why, and (d) (prep, f; synonymous with 'dī') of or belonging to.

kiā: (pron, p; synonymous with 'kā', 'kī' or 'ke') of, belonging to, (c) (adv; synonymous with 'kis trāṅ' or 'kis prakār') how, somehow, or whatever way or kind, (d) (pron; synonymous with 'kyā' or 'ki') what, and (e) (p; synonymous with 'prashan bodhak') used in the interrogative sense.

kirat: (n, f; synonymous with 'Saṅskārs') The imprint or conditioning, accumulated over many previous lives during evolution, gives us our unique conscious self, innate nature, drives and self-awareness. This, in turn, affects our perception or conscious experience, and predisposition towards a unique set of ideas and counter-ideas that spontaneously arise within the conscious self ('Man'), and eventually influence our behaviour. This is 'Kirat', 'Siṅchit karmā' or 'Saṅskārs'.

The legacy of one's 'Kirat' or 'Saṅskārs' influences or casts a shadow on 'Ātmāṅ' as it interacts with the body and creates its imperfect surrogate, 'Jīvātmāṅ' which, in turn, moulds one's innate nature, personality, behaviour, and general direction in life accordingly. Thus, governed by the Divine Law, and dancing to the tune set by 'Kirat' in this life, we go round and round the merry-go-round of transmigration.[258] 'None can erase the writ of 'Kirat'; one attains salvation by aligning with the Gurū's Word.[536] Release from this cycle of transmigration is only through submitting to and aligning with the Gurū's Word (in essence, 'Nām(u)').

kītā: (a) (n, m; synonymous with 'karanyog kaṅm') worthwhile actions or deeds to be undertaken, (b) (n, f; synonymous with 'krit') creation, (c) (v, s, past or present perfect; synonymous with 'kītā sī'; 'kītā-' or 'sirjiā' 'hai') actions taken or deeds done; actions have been taken or deeds have been done, (d) (present participle - 'kriyā-phal kirdaṅt'; synonymous with 'ih saṅsār us dā-' 'rachiā-', 'sirjiā-' or 'baṇāiā-' 'hoiā hai') [It is His] creation; see karnā, baṇāuṇā and sirjaṇā, and (e) (past participle - 'bhūt kirdaṅt'; synonymous with 'āpṇā kītā kaṅm'; 'us dā-' 'sirjiā' or 'baṇāiā' 'saṅsār') literally, deeds that one carried out; the universe created by Him.

ko: (a) (pron; synonymous with 'kauṇ') who, (b) (prep; synonymous with 'kā' or 'dā') of, (c) (prep; synonymous with 'nūṅ') to, and (d) (pron and adj; abbrev for and synonymous with 'koī') someone, anyone or another; many or several.

koi: (a) (indefinite pronoun; synonymous with 'koī virlā' or 'ik adhā') rarely or an occasional someone, (b) (pron and (adj; synonymous with 'koī') any, some or certain.

lai: (a) (indeclinable past participle or perfect participle - 'pūran pūrab kārdaṅtak'; synonymous with 'lai ke') see laiṇā, (b) (p; synonymous with 'tīk' or 'tak') up to, (c) (n, f; synonymous with 'lya-' or 'liv-' 'vich līn ho jāṇā') to merge, become rapt or absorbed, (d) (n, f; synonymous with 'lya-', 'sur-' and 'tāl-' 'vich rahiṇā') literally, to stay with the beat or rhythm, and (e) (v, s, present tense, third person; synonymous with 'laiṅdā hai') see laiṇā.

lāi: (a) (v, s, imperative mood - 'hukmī bhvikht', second person; synonymous with 'lā-' or 'lagā-' 'lai' or 'lavo') do, engage or carry out, (b) (indeclinable past participle or perfect participle - 'pūran pūrab kārdaṅtak'; synonymous with 'lā-', 'lagā-' or 'joṛ-' 'ke') having done, engaged or carried out, and (c) (v, s, present tense, third person; synonymous with 'maldā-' or 'maldī', 'lāuṅdā-', 'lāuṅdī-' 'joṛdā-' or 'joṛdī-' 'hai') rub or apply, do, engage or carry out. See lāuṇā.

laiṇā: (a) (v; synonymous with 'aṅgīkār karnā') to receive or take, (b) (v; synonymous with 'grahaṇ-', 'hāsal-' or 'prāpat-' 'karnā'; 'kharidaṇā'; 'khaṭṭṇā') to get, obtain or acquire; to buy; to earn, and (c) (conj v and suff) it helps towards completion of the task implicit in the primary verb or the attached noun/pronoun), e.g., (i) e.g. 'Nām laiṇā' (synonymous with 'Nām Japnā' or 'Siphat sālāh karnī') to recount, chant or sing His Glory, and (ii) 'jīa laiṇā' - to take back the 'Jiṅdāṅ' or 'Jīvātmāṅs'.

lāuṇā: (v, m; synonymous with 'lāvṇā' or 'lagāuṇā': 'lāuṇī' is its female counterpart) (a) (synonymous with 'malṇā') to apply - as in ointment, (b) (synonymous with 'joṛnā', 'melṇā' or 'saṅbaṅdh baṇāunā') to align, join or connect with, (c) (conj. v or suff.) (i) ('kaṅm lāuṇā'; synonymous with 'niyukt karnā' or 'thāpṇā') to appoint, engage or assign to a duty, (ii) 'tālā lāuṇā' - to lock, (iii) 'aṅdāzā lāuṇā' - to guess, (iv) 'agg lāuṇā' - to light a fire or to set fire to and (v) 'liv lāuṇī' - to focus, concentrate and contemplate.

lekh: (a) (n, m; synonymous with 'likhit', 'rachnā' or 'nibaṅdh') an essay, an article, a write-up, or a composition, (b) (n, f; synonymous with 'rekhā' and 'lakīr') literally, lines, streaks, narrow stripes, furrows or fine wrinkles. In essence, the lines or furrows on one's palms, which apparently reflect or foretell one's fate or destiny, and (c) (n, f; synonymous with 'likhat', 'tahrīr', 'bhāg', 'kismat' and 'nasīb') literally, fate or destiny. In reality, it represents an account of one's lot or destiny (the sum total of one's attributes, innate nature, circumstances and opportunities for the realisation or otherwise of one's potential in life), which is written on one's forehead according to Hindu belief.

lekhā: (a) (v, present perfect tense; synonymous with 'likhiā') literally, has been written, (b) (n, m; synonymous with 'likhiā hoiā hisāb') an account of everyone's good and bad 'Karmā', and implicit here is (c) (n, f; synonymous with 'lekh') one's fate or destiny, based on the judgement of one's Karmā ('hisāb' of one's 'sanskārs') and written on one's forehead according to popular and Hindu belief.

likh(i): a) (v; synonymous with 'likhna' or 'likhṇā') literally, to write or note down, (b) (genitive case - 'saṅbaṅdh kārak'; synonymous with 'likhaṇ dī') of noting down or writing something in black and white, (c) (indeclinable past participle or perfect participle - 'pūran pūrab kārdaṅtak'; synonymous with 'likh ke') literally, by writing or having written, (d) (accusative case - 'karam kārak'; synonymous with 'likhe hoe nūṅ') that which has been so recorded or an account thus written or recorded, and (e) (instrumental case - 'karaṇ kārak'; synonymous with 'likhe anusār') literally, according to the writ of His Divine Order; in essence, everything one is endowed with in one's destiny is judged on the basis of one's previous 'Karmā'.

likhiā: (a) (v, pl, present perfect) literally, [they] have all written, (b) (conj v) e.g., (i) 'likhiā n jāi' - literally, 'that cannot be written, noted or recorded' and (ii) 'ih likhiā ga-i-ā hai' - this has been written or recorded, (c) (adj, m; past participle - 'bhūt kirdaṅt'; synonymous with 'us dī likhit' or 'us dā likhiā lekh') literally, His written directive or writ, and (d) (n, m; present participle - 'kriyā-phal kirdaṅt'; synonymous with 'likhit', 'lekhā', 'mastak te likhe hoi lekh' or 'tahrīr') literally, a written directive or writ that has been worked out and allotted on the basis of one's deeds in the previous life/lives and which forms the basis of one's fate, fortune or destiny in this life.

likhṇā: (v; synonymous with 'likhat vich liāuṇā') literally, to write, scribe or note down.

loa: (a) (n, pl; synonymous with 'log' and 'jan') people or humanity, (b) (n, f; synonymous with 'chānaṇā', 'prakāsh' and 'nūr') light, brightness or dawn, and (c) (n, pl; synonymous with 'lok', 'desh', 'khaṅḍ' and 'bhavan') islands, countries, continents, domains, spheres or planets in a system, e.g., 'trilok' of the Hindu belief and the seven planets below and above Earth in the Islamic tradition.

mai: (a) (n; synonymous with 'ah(ṅ)'; pronounced as 'maiṅ') literally, I, (b) (n, f; synonymous with 'abhiman' and 'ahaṅkār') ego or egotism, (c) (p; synonymous with 'aṅdar' or 'vich') inside or within, (d) (n, f; synonymous with 'mad', 'madirā' and 'shrāb') alcohol, (e) (synonymous with 'mya' and if used as a suff.) huge or excessive, e.g., 'suvarṇ-mya' or 'anaṅd-mya', and (f) (pron; synonymous with 'merā', 'mere', 'mujhe' and 'mainūṅ') mine or to me.

man: (n, m; synonymous with 'Hirdā', 'Panch-bhū-ātmāṅ' and 'Jīvātmāṅ' in Gurbanī) '*Man*', in the italicised version, is pronounced 'Mun', a sound that rhymes with 'Sun'. The word 'Manas', in Rig Veda, implies Soul or 'Jīvātmāṅ'. '*Man*' is also described as one of the four parts of 'Aṅtahkaran', the ultimate sensorimotor organ within the innermost part of one's body, which, according to the Hindu religious texts, orchestrates one's external sensorimotor organs.

The presumed four parts of 'Aṅtahkaran' are as follows: (a) '*Man*', the seat of constant generation of ideas ('Saṅkalps') and counter-ideas ('Vikalps'), (b) 'Budh(i)', the seat of deliberation and decision making, (c) 'Chit', where the process of memory ('Sumarṇ') occurs, and (d) 'Ahaṅkār', which links one with the external physical world, and leads to the development of a sense of ownership ('Mamtā').

Gurbānī, however, defines '*Man*' as follows: 'O' '*Man*'! 'Thou art the very spark of the Divine Light; recognise thy essence as such'. '*Man*' tūṅ jot(i) sarūp(u) hai āpṇā mūl(u) pachhāṇ(u).[59] The following verse in Gurbānī describes different aspects of '*Man*': 'Tithai ghaṛīai surat(i), mat(i), *man*(i) budh(i)',**[537]** alludes to fashioning or refining one's keen attention, focus, and inclinations ('surat(i)'), cognition and intellect ('mat(i)'), and ability to deliberate and to make decisions ('budh(i)'). '*Man*' is the conscious self, the seat of constant and spontaneous generation of ideas ('Saṅkalps') and counter-ideas ('Vikalps'), based upon one's 'Haumaiṅ', innate nature, drives and desires ('Saṅskārs'), in order to satisfy one's self-interests.

Mat(i) is knowlege and/or wisdom ('Giān') imbibed from other sources, e.g., the spoken or written words of a teacher/Gurū. In contrast, intuitive knowlege or wisdom ('Anubhavī giān') is spontaneous and innate and comes forth or manifests without conscious reasoning. It is perceived and permanently stored in one's memory ('chit') after careful scrutiny and deliberation of one's acquired knowledge and/or wisdom.

In the spiritual world, ideological convergence with the Gurū's Divine Word and Wisdom transforms one's 'anubhavī giān' into 'uchī' or 'nirmal mat(i)'.

Budh(i) is one's deductive reasoning or ability to discern and is dependent upon and limited by the scope of one's 'Mat(i)'. 'Bibek budh(i)', on the contrary, exploits one's superior intuitive knowledge and/or wisdom ('uchī mat(i)') and aids one in arriving at decisions more closely aligned with 'Nām-consciousness'. To believe or not in what is not seen or perceived, or what exists primarily in spirit form only, poses a very difficult conundrum. Unshakeable belief in the being of the Primal Soul rests on the spiritual knowledge and wisdom which one gains on ideologically converging with the Gurū's Divine Word and Wisdom. This is what is referred to as one's 'bibek budh(i)' or one's third eye, in the more colloquial vernacular.

One whose '*Man*' is dominated and driven by 'Haumaiṅ' is a 'Manmukh', and Gurū Nānak describes such a person as follows:

'Day and night are like two seasons; wrath and lust are his two fields; he carefully waters them with greed; he sows in them the seed of falsehood; 'Moh' is his ploughman; evil thoughts are his plough and evil is the crop that he reaps, cuts and eats; when he is called to account for his deeds, he shows nothing worthwhile, and thus leaves this world having wasted this life'.[538]

'Jīvātmāṅ', without the baggage of 'Haumaiṅ', 'Moh', innate 'Vikārī' tendencies and 'Sanskārs' ('Māyā') is immaculate ('nirmal 'Jīvātmāṅ') and as such represents a perfect expression of 'Ātmāṅ'. In essence, the two are identical in this state. However, 'Jīvātmāṅ', misguided and misled by 'Haumaiṅ' and bewitched by 'Moh' and 'Māyā', becomes engrossed in the material world and in meaningless rituals, and thus remains bound to the physical body and its cycle of transmigration. [58] Equally, we must not forget that one's conscious-self or '*Man*' has the potential to assume the attributes of whatever it becomes aligned with. For instance, it acts as 'Māiā' if it aligns with ego-consciousness, displays the true attributes of 'Ātmāṅ' if it harmonises with 'Nām-consciousness', and in total ignorance, comes to regard itself as completely egoistic and just a physical body.[59]

maṅḍal: (a) (n, m, pl; synonymous with 'ka-ī-' 'dunīāṅ', 'saṅsār' and 'jagat') many worlds, (b) (n, m, pl; synonymous with 'ilāke') many regions in a country, (c) (n, pl; synonymous with 'sabhā' and 'dīwāns') societies, conventions, assemblies or religious congregations, (d) (n, m, pl; synonymous with 'groh', 'samudāya' and 'smūh') groups, congregations, multitudes, swarms or crowds, and (e) (n, m; synonymous with 'golākār gherā' and 'dāyrah') many circular orbits; many planetary systems, with planets orbiting around a sun or star.

maṅgah(i): (a) (v, s, present tense, second person; synonymous with 'tūṅ maṅgdā haiṅ or 'tusīṅ maṅgde ho'), (b) (v, s, 'saṅbhāv bhvikht kāl - kiās, sharat, ichhā, prernā bodhak', second person; synonymous with 'je maṅg la-ī-e'), (c) (v, pl, present tense, first person; synonymous with 'asīṅ maṅgde hāṅ'), (d) (v, pl, future tense, third person; synonymous with 'uh maṅgaṇge'), and (e) (v, pl, present tense, third person; synonymous with 'uh maṅgde han'; pronounced as 'maṅgaheṅ') see maṅgṇā.

maṅgṇā: (v; synonymous with 'maṅgṇā' and 'yāchnā karnī') literally, to ask, demand, borrow, request, seek or beg. However, it can also imply plead, implore, beseech, or supplicate.

maṅnaṇā: (v) (a) (synonymous with 'pūjaṇā' and 'upāsanā karnī') literally, to worship, (b) (n, s; infinitive mood - 'bhāvārth kārdaṅtak'; synonymous with 'maṅnat', 'mnaut' or 'māntā') a belief or postulate (c) (v; synonymous with 'aṅgikār karnā', 'maṅn lainā', 'manzūr karnā' and 'abhyās karnā') to accept, to confess to have absolute faith in, to comply with and follow, and to ideologically converge, and implicit here is (c) to submit to the Gurū's Divine Word and Wisdom willingly, lovingly and unreservedly, to deliberate over and then imbibe its essence in one's conscious self with absolute faith and conviction, and to strive to live life by 'Nām-consciousness' (God's Will).

mat(i): (a) (n, f; synonymous with 'shrāb') literally, alcohol, (b) (adj; synonymous with 'matvālā', 'mast', 'madmast' and 'mad-hosh') drunk, intoxicated, ecstatic or enraptured, (c) (n, f; synonymous with 'rāe') opinion, counsel, suggestion or advice, (d) (n, f; synonymous with 'sikhiā') teaching, precept or instruction, (e) (synonymous with 'matāṅ', ‘shāyad’ or ‘kadāchit’) lest, because of the possibility of or perhaps, (f) (particle; synonymous with ‘nished bodhak’) no or implying a negative meaning, (g) (n, m; synonymous with ‘ahaṅkār’ and ‘mamtā’) one of the four components of ‘Aṅtahkaran’ and that which binds one to the material world and generates a strong feeling of ownership, possessiveness and partiality, and (h) (n, f; synonymous with ‘akal’, ‘giān’, ‘samajh’ and ‘siāṇap’) literally, knowledge, intellect or wisdom. It forms the basis of the ability to reason or to discern. It is one of the functions or aspects of *'Man'* in Gurmat.

māyā: (n, f; synonymous with ‘Māiā’) Some of the popular or commonly accepted meanings of ‘Māyā’ are as follows: (a) (synonymous with ‘dhan and ‘saṅpadā’) money or assets, (b) (synonymous with ‘mātā’) mother, (c) (synonymous with ‘ma-i-ā’ or ‘maya’) grace, compassion or mercy, (d) (synonymous with ‘kapaṭ’, ‘chhal’ or ‘dhokhā’) trickery, guile, fraud, sham or duplicity, (d) (synonymous with ‘avidyā’, ‘bhram’ or ‘bhulekhā’) misconception, ignorance or illusion, which causes dubiety (‘dubidā’), (e) God's creative power with which infinite and diverse life forms appear, and (f) that which lures one to the physical world and its transitory pleasures in preference to living life in complete harmony with ‘Nām(u)’ or ‘Nām-consciousness’.

However, it is often used in the context of (a) the transitory nature of the empirical world in relation to humankind, and (b) that which lures one to the material world, its comforts, and pleasures, and leads one farther away from living life in perfect harmony with ‘Nām-consciousness’. See also ‘Bhram’.

It is also described as ‘triguṇī- ’or ‘treguṇī-’ ‘Māiā’ because it imparts a varied mixture of three different attributes or characteristics (‘guṇ’) to the sentient beings of the world. These are ‘Rajo-’ (or ‘Rajav-’), ‘Tamo’ (or ‘Tamas-’) and ‘Sato-’ (or ‘Satav-’) ‘guṇ’. 'Rajo guṇ’ is the basis for ‘Moh’ and self-conceit or egotism, ‘Tamo guṇ’ forms the basis of ignorance and wrath, and ‘Sato guṇ’ nurtures compassion, mercy, forgiveness, peace and tranquillity, and benefaction.

In many Hindu religious books, ‘Māyā’ is described as an illusion or the power of illusion. The universe is described as an illusion, and demi-gods, like Indra, used ‘Māyā’ to create this illusion. All human activity in this empirical world is considered worthless, and hence the constant drive to leave home and go to the forests, to become detached from the world of 'Māyā', and to strive to find 'Brahman'.

Gurū Nānak, however, states that 'God creates the universe, and permeates it'.[33] 'The world is as true as God Himself'.[468] There is, therefore, nothing illusory about this empirical world. God is often described in the SGGS as: (a) immanent in creation, loving, forgiving, merciful, guiding and enlightening the erring and the sinner, and (b) the Creator that allows the creation a degree of autonomy (free will), assessing the deeds of each being in the light of His Will, and helping the erring in their spiritual growth. Various other verses clearly outline the concepts of the Fatherhood of God and Brotherhood of Man, the whole universe being one big family and eco-system, and God-consciousness as the role model for humankind.

However, as the intrinsic or default state of the consciousness of human beings is egoistic, we fail to grasp this concept of unity in diversity and life in harmony and, instead, we emphasise preservation and the pursuit of self-interest as the basis of life. This conflicting assumption and aberrant way of looking at the basic reality of unity in diversity, and life in harmony with the world is 'Māyā'. In ego is 'Māyā'.[50] Whosoever is afflicted by duality is the slave of 'Māyā'.[16] Intoxicated with 'Māyā', one is vain and mean, and therefore gets farther away from God.[266] For one who is not in communion with God, 'Māyā' is just an illusion, like a dry blade of grass afire, the passing shadow of a summer cloud, the momentary flooding after tropical rain.[267] 'Māyā' can also be defined as that which causes us to forget God, and by which attachment to the empirical world and a sense of duality are produced.[268]

The problem of 'Māyā' lies not in grasping the concept but in one's moral and ethical frailty. Thus, misled by one's unrestrained drives, insatiable desires, and ego-consciousness one commits evil deeds against others, and against the world in general.

milṇā: (v; synonymous with 'milnā') (a) (synonymous with 'prāpat hoṇā') to find, get or receive, (b) (synonymous with 'saṅpark vich āuṇā') to meet, get together, come across, visit or encounter physically, (c) (synonymous with 'ral mil jāṇā') to mix, merge, dissolve, annex or be absorbed, (d) (synonymous with 'samrūp hoṇā') to match, resemble, tally, align or harmonise (e) (synonymous with 'anubhav karnā', '*man* kar ke milṇā' and 'yathārath rūp vich vekhṇā') to realise or perceive, and

(f) (conj. v; synonymous with 'japhphī pāuṇā', 'galvakṛī pāuṇā' and 'gal lāuṇā') to hug or embrace.

A casual crossing over of paths by two people does not equate with formal acquaintance. Instead, in Gurmat, a true acquaintance occurs when two minds converge.[539-40]

n(h)āuṇā: (v; synonymous with 'shoch-', 'majan-', 'gusal-' or 'ishnān-' 'karnā') to bathe.

nād: (n, f) (a) (synonymous with 'saṅkh') conch, (b) (synonymous with 'saṅgīt') the melodious vocal and enchanting musical sounds of rāgs, (c) (synonymous with 'avāz' - sounds of different pitch, amplitude and timbre from different objects, instruments and diverse life forms; 'dhuni(i)' and 'swar' with its three scales in music, e.g., maṅdr (low scale) - which resonates from one's abdomen ('hirdya'), 'madhyam' (middle scale) - which resonates from one's throat ('kaṅṭh'), and 'tār' (high scale) - which resonates from one's forehead ('mastak'), and (d) (synonymous with 'Anhad/anhat-' 'Sabad', 'Dhun(i)' or 'nād'; 'parā-vāk' or 'parā- bānī') is the unstruck, everlasting primordial sound that is perceived but not heard with the ears, and the Divine Word through which God communicates with His creation. One who perceives 'anhad nād' realises 'Nām(u)' - the Immanent form of God. Yogīs wear a conch around the neck and its sound alerts and summons all to a meal.

nadar(i): (n, f) (a) (arab; synonymous with 'drist(i)', 'nigāh' and 'nazar') sight, vision, watch or notice, (b) (locative case - 'adhikaraṇ kārak'; synonymous with 'drist(i)-', 'nigāh-' and 'nazar-' 'vich') literally, in one's sight or notice, (c) (instrumental case - 'karaṇ kārak'; synonymous with 'drist(i)-', 'nigāh-' and 'nazar-' 'nāl' or 'duārā') literally, with or through one's sight, vision, field of vision, watch or notice, (d) (instrumental case -'karaṇ kārak'; synonymous with 'kripā drisṭ(i)-' or 'mehar dī nazar-' 'nāl' or 'duārā') with or through His Grace or Blessing, and (e) (locative case - 'adhikaraṇ kārak'; synonymous with 'kripā drisṭ(i)-' or 'mehar dī nazar-' 'vich') literally, in His Gracious or Merciful Gaze.

nadrī: (a) (n; f; synonymous with 'nazar' and 'drishṭ(i)') sight or vision, (b) (locative case - 'adhikaraṇ kārak'; synonymous with 'nazar vich';

pronounced as 'nadrīṅ') in one's sight or vision, (c) (adj; synonymous with 'nadar karan vālā' or 'kartār'; pronounced as 'nadrī') one with a compassionate glance, i.e., God, (d) (instrumental case - 'karaṇ kārak'; synonymous with 'mehar dī nadar nāl' and 'kripā drisṭ(i) sadkā'; pronounced as 'nadrīṅ') through His Grace or Mercy, and (e) (genitive case - 'saṅbaṅdh kārak'; synonymous with 'nadar karan vāle'dī') literally, of God.

nāhī: (a) (v, s, present tense; synonymous with 'n(h)āuṅdā-' or 'isnān kardā' 'hai'; pronounced as 'nāhīṅ') bathes, (b) (adj, m; synonymous with 'varjaṇ vālā' or 'prat(i)baṅdhak') administrator, enforcer, or one who forbids, and (c) (p; synonymous with 'nāṅ' or 'nahīṅ'; pronounced as 'nāhīṅ') no, not or implying a negative connotation.

nāi: (a) (n, m, s; synonymous with 'nāu') 'Nām(u)'-the immanent form of God; 'nāv': (pl of nāu'), (b) (n, m; synonymous with 'niāi', 'insāph' and 'niyam'; pronounced as 'nyāi' or 'niāi') order, governance and justice, (c) (instrumental case - 'karaṇ kārak'; synonymous with 'Nām(u)-' 'nāl', 'rāhīṅ', 'duārā' or 'sadkā') with, through or by virtue of the Grace of 'Nām(u), (d) (locative case - 'adhikaraṇ kārak; synonymous with 'Nām(u) vich') in 'Nām(u)', and (e) (indeclinable past participle or perfect participle - 'pūran pūrab kārdaṅtak'; synonymous with 'shoch kar-', 'gusal kar-', 'ishnān kar-', and 'n(h)āi-' 'ke'; pronounced as 'n(h)āi') by bathing or having bathed.

Nām(u): (n, m, s) refers to the immanent form of the transcendent God. Although the transcendent God is 'agaṅm' (immutable and beyond our reach), and 'agochar' (unfathomable or beyond the grasp of human senses), 'Nām(u)', His immanent form, can be perceived. This one word alone encompasses all the known and unknown attributes of this immanent form of God. In particular, it symbolises (a) God's creative power ('Kartā', 'Kartār', the Creator), (b) the Divine Order, the sum total of all the Laws of Nature ('Hukam(u)') that sustain and govern the creation, (c) the Divine Word, with which He communicates and guides His creation ('Sabad', 'Anhad Sabad' or 'Anhad Nād'), and (d) the Divine Will, symbolising how He wishes and directs the entire universe to unfold, evolve and pan out with time in 'Nām-consciousness'. In reality, 'Nām(u)' is used as a surrogate for all the attributes of the one transcendent God, both known and unknown to us.

One who absolutely surrenders to 'Nām(u)' and aligns perfectly with 'Nām-consciousness', becomes a 'Gurmukh' and achieves lasting inner equanimity ('Sahaj') or bliss ('Anaṅd'). Once 'Nām(u)' manifests in such a person's 'Hirdā', their every thought, utterance or deed becomes aligned perfectly with 'Nām(u)', and such a person enjoys the title of a Gurū. A Gurū's utterances, in the form of sermons for spiritual guidance for humanity and/or in the form of God's Praise/Glory, is referred to as Gurbānī, which enjoys the status of the 'Sabad', 'Aṅmrit Bānī'or the Divine Word.

The immanence of God underscores the reality, as opposed to the illusory nature of the universe, the purposefulness of life, and the capacity for relationship with God. If God were purely transcendent, there would be no purpose in pursuing a moral, ethical, or spiritual life, and any feeling of love or yearning for Him would become meaningless. The immanence of God inextricably links Him with the universe. 'Nām(u)', in this immanent form, is the fount or ocean of attributes, values and virtues. Since all qualities conform to a spectrum or continuum, this aspect of God gives credence, validity, and direction to a moral, ethical, and spiritual life in this universe.

The attributes, values, and virtues that Gurū Nānak associates with God clearly allude to the way His Will works, and thus they become the gold standard or ideals for which human beings should strive. His loving, forgiving, guiding, encouraging, and benevolent nature alludes to His keen desire to nurture, sustain, and guide the creation towards its goals.

'Nām(u)', in the form of His Word ('Anhad Sabad'), is the Primordial or the 'Ād(i) Gurū'. Those who imbibe and align perfectly with the Divine Word or the Gurū's Word (Gurbanī) align with and live in harmony with God, 'Nām(u)' or 'Nām-consciousness', perceive, with God's Grace, the 'Anhad Sabad', and remain in direct communion with 'Nām(u)' forever.

'Nām Japṇā' and some other phrases that convey somewhat similar sentiments are: (a) 'Nām Simarnā', (b) 'Nām Dhiāuṇā', and (c) 'Nām Ārādhanā'.

Nām Japṇā: is the devout and repetitious uttering of the divine name, Wāhigurū (the wonderful Lord or Enlightener - also known as 'Gur Maṅtrā'), 'Mūl Maṅtrā' (the Credal Statement) or the essence of a part of Gurbānī from the SGGS, loud enough to be heard in one's immediate proximity, such that the persona and attributes it conjures up become the focus of one's devotion. The eventual aim of this exercise is to imbibe the same attributes in one's 'Hirdā' and spontaneously express them in one's daily life. This is the first step or stage in the path to 'Nām-realisation'.

Nām Simarn: (synonymous with 'Nām Simarnā' or 'Nām Sumarnā') literally, the word 'Simarnā' means: (a) to remember, (b) to keep in mind, (c) to recollect or recall, and (d) to reflect, contemplate or meditate on the attributes of the object of one's devotion. 'Nām Simarṇā' is to focus deeply and lovingly upon and to contemplate the persona and attributes of 'Nām(u)', such that they are always at the forefront of one's mind. However, one does not need to vocalise the 'Gur Maṅtrā', 'Mūl Maṅtrā' or one's feelings or emotions.

Nām Dhiāṇā: (synonymous with 'Nām Dhiāvaṇā' or 'Nām Dhiāuaṇā') is to focus upon and totally immerse oneself in reflection on the persona or attributes of 'Nām(u)'. The eventual aim of this exercise is to imbibe the same attributes in one's 'Hirdā' and spontaneously express them in one's daily life.

Nām Ārādhanā: (synonymous with 'Arādhanā') literally the word 'Arādhanā' means: (a) to serve willingly or wait upon in order to please someone, (b) to serve another unconditionally, (c) to do 'Upāsanā', which in turn, literally means to sit beside one or to come closer to one, and (d) to worship. To sit beside one is not the same as to be in close physical proximity with someone but simply to align or to converge ideologically with someone as stated in the following verses of the SGGS:

A meeting of two bodies does not represent a meeting; however, the meeting of two minds or true ideological convergence is a real meeting.[539]

A meeting of two minds or true ideological convergence is counted as a real meeting; mere deliberation without concomitant submission does not work, no matter how desperate or eager one is to concur.[540]

To worship someone is simply to meditate upon or contemplate such that one not only imbibes their attributes but also expresses them in one's daily life.

The implication of all these phrases is to focus on and contemplate or meditate on something such that one imbibes the attributes of the object of one's contemplation and then spontaneously expresses them in one's daily life. A mere mortal has no concept of any attributes of 'Nām(u)', and thus relies on the Divine Words of Wisdom of a Gurū or 'Sat(i)gurū' (Gurbānī or 'Baikhari Bāṇī' - the spoken word) as highlighted in this verse of the SGGS:

Everything is created by 'Nām(u)'. However, one cannot align with and realise 'Nām(u)' without submitting to a 'Sat(i)gur'.[541]

One thus learns about the persona and the attributes of 'Nām(u)' through Gurbanī, which then becomes the centre of one's focus and contemplation. Gurbānī (God's Word expressed through a living Gurū, who has realised 'Nām(u)' - the immanent form of the transcendent God), thus becomes one's aide-memoire and the road map on the path to 'Nām-realisation'. Gurbānī uttered or vocalised repeatedly and gently such that it is barely audible even to one's own ears is called 'Madhyamā Bānī'.

In time, the essence of the imbibed attributes, values and virtues then comes to pervade one's whole being ('Nām vas jāṇā'), and one's conscious self ('Jīvātmāṅ', '*Man*' or 'Hirdā') becomes totally imbued ('Nām nāl ratiā' or 'Nām nāl raṅgiā jāṇā') with 'Nām(u)'. One now lives in perfect harmony with 'Nām(u)' and does not require any conscious effort in the daily, regular or constant vocalisation of 'Gur-Mantrā', 'Mūl Mantrā' or Gurbānī. The 'Bānī' that pervades one's whole being at this stage is described as 'Pashyaṅtī Bānī'.

In the fullness of time and with God's Grace, one attains a lasting state of inner equanimity ('Sahaj') and bliss ('Anaṅd'), when one perceives the 'Anhad Nād' ('Parā-Vāk' and 'Parā Bānī', both synonymous with the Divine Word) which symbolises the experiential revelation of 'Nām(u)' within one's '*Man*' or 'Hirdā'.

'Nām(u)', the immanent form of God, now fully manifests in such a person, and one's every thought ('*Man*'), utterance ('Bachan') and deed ('karam') from then on is in absolute harmony with 'Nām(u)'. This is 'Nām-realisation'. Such a person is now in complete control of all aspects of their conscious self ('*Man*', 'Hirdā' or 'Jīvātmāṅ'), and their innate nature, inner drives, and desires, and is now truly an enlightened person (Gurū, 'Sant', 'Sādh' or 'Brahm-gyānī'), the ultimate stage in one's spiritual progress. One is now free from the shackles of 'Haumaiṅ', 'Moh', and 'Panj Vikārs' ('Māyā') and has achieved the stage of 'Jīvan Mukt'. The immaculate soul of such a person, now defined as 'nirmal Jīvātmāṅ', merges, through God's Grace, with the Primal Soul (the transcendent Lord) at death, and thus finds release from the cycle of transmigration.

nāth: (n, m) (a) (synonymous with 'khasam', 'bhartā' and 'pat(i)') husband, (b) (synonymous with 'swāmī' and 'mālik') Master, Protector and God, (c) (synonymous with 'nath') nose ring - a piece of jewellery usually worn by married women, (d) (synonymous with 'nakel') nose string for animals, and (e) a sect of Hindu ascetics or any member of a sect who follow their Yogīrāj Gorakhnāth or Lord Shiva and have achieved the pinnacle of success on that path.

nāu: (a) (n, s; synonymous with 'nām') literally, a name, that which relates to and characterises an object or being, (b) (n, m; synonymous with 'nyāy' or 'insāph') justice, (c) (n, f; synonymous with 'nāv' and 'kishtī') a boat, (d) (n, m; synonymous with 'snān' and 'ishnān'; pronounced as 'n(h)āu') bath or ablutions, (e) (n, f; synonymous with 'nāmaṇā', 'vaḍiāī', 'ustat(i)' and 'mahimā') praise, renown, fame, eulogy, glory or tribute, (f) (v, s, present tense, first person; synonymous with 'n(h)aunda hai'; pronounced as 'n(h)āu') undertakes ablutions or bathes, and (g) (n, s; synonymous with 'Nām(u)') 'Nām(u)', as the one word, is also the embodiment of all His attributes, both those known and unknown to us, and His being and immanent form.

nāv: (a) (a) (n, m, s) Nām(u), the immanent form of God and other ascribed names for God, (b) (n, m, pl; (pers); synonymous with 'kishtī', 'naukā' or 'jahāz') ships, (c) (n, m, pl; synonymous with 'nāṅv') literally, names, for the countless non-sentient elements and sentient beings in the universe, and (d) (n, pl; genitive case - 'saṅbaṅdh kārak'; synonymous with 'nāvāṅ de') of different names.

nīch(u): (a) (n; synonymous with 'gulām' and 'dās') a slave or a humble servant, (b) (adj); synonymous with 'karam kar ke nīvāṅ' or 'kāmā'; 'jāt(i) kar ke nīvāṅ') low in rank or status, low in terms of a feudal or social class system or a 'Shūdra' of the Hindu caste system, i.e., one who undertakes a lowly, menial job which no one else will do, and (c) (adj; synonymous with 'nimāṇā', 'nitāṇā', 'nāchīz' and 'guṇhīn') low in terms of noble attributes, virtues and values, i.e., one who is mean, miserly, callous or spiteful or one with innate evil tendencies, and (d) lowly, lacking virtues or good attributes.

niṅmaṇā: (v; synonymous with 'baṇāuṇā', 'rachṇā' and 'garabh vich pālaṇā karnī') to conceive and nurture.

niraṅkār(u): (adj, m, s; synonymous with 'nirākār' or 'ākār rahit') 'Nirākār' is a complex word comprising 'nir' (without) + 'ākār' (form, shape or the three dimensional outline of something), i.e., one without a physical shape. The reference here is to the non-physical, spiritual or the transcendent form of God.

nīsāṇ(u): (n, m, s) (a) (synonymous with 'nagārā' or 'dhauṅsā') a large kettledrum or war drum , (b) (synonymous with 'dhvajj' or 'jhaṅḍā') flag or banner, (c) (synonymous with 'lachhaṇ') literally, attributes or characteristics, (d) (synonymous with 'lekh', 'likhat' or 'tahrīr') destiny or fate - supposedly, a testimony, based on one's Karmāand supposedly written on one's forehead at birth ('mastak de lekh'), and (e) (synonymous with 'nishān' and 'chin(h)'; pronounced as 'nīshāṇ') mark, sign, brand, logo or trademark; seal or mark of His approval.

niyukt karnā: (v; synonymous with 'kise kaṅm vich-' or 'kise padvī te-' 'lāuṇā') to nominate and appoint to a post or position.

pāh(i): (a) (adv; synonymous with 'pās', 'nāl', 'kol', 'smīp' and 'nazdīk'; 'agge' or 'sanmukh') near; before or in front of respectively, (b) (v, s, present tense, second person; synonymous with 'tusīṅ 'paiṅde-', 'jāṅde' 'ho'; 'suṭṭe jāṅde ho'; 'prāpat karde ho'; 'pāuṅde ho'; 'tatpar- ' 'huṅde ho' or 'lagde ho'), (c) (v, pl, present tense, first person; synonymous with 'asīṅ pāuṅde hāṅ'), (d) (v, pl, future tense, third person; synonymous with 'uh-' 'paiṇge-', 'jāṇge-' or 'suṭṭe jāṇge'; 'prāpat karange'; 'pāuṇge'; 'tatpar hoṇge' or 'lagde hoṇge') literally, lie, go; get thrown away; attain or obtain; appear eager and ready, (e) (conj v), e.g., (i) 'pāh(i) jāi' - achieve, (ii) 'mukar(u) pāh(i)' - deny, renege or disclaim, and (f) (v, pl, present tense, third person; synonymous with 'pāuṅde han', 'jāṅde han', 'tatpar huṅde han' and 'lagde han'; pronounced as pāheṅ') achieve, go, get ready and eager to act or engage. See paiṇā and pāuṇā.

pāi: (a) (indeclinable past participle or perfect participle - 'pūran pūrab kārdaṅtak'; synonymous with 'pā ke', 'paidā kar ke' or 'prāpat kar ke') by achieving or having achieved, acquired or produced, (b) (v, s, present tense, third person; synonymous with 'pāuṅdā hai' or prāpat kardā hai'; 'paiṅdā- 'or 'paṛtā-' 'hai') finds, achieves or realises; lies down or falls; see pāuṇā, (c) (n, m; synonymous with 'charan', 'pāoṅ' and 'pair') feet, (d) (accusative case - 'karam kārak'; synonymous with 'pairāṅ nūṅ') literally, to feet, and (e) (n, m; synonymous with 'ihsās', 'shakat(i)', 'bal', 'pāiāṅ' and 'hauṅsalā'; pronounced as 'pā(i)ṅ') a feeling or realisation; courage and moral strength.

pāīā: (a) (n, m; synonymous with 'pā' or 'pāu') a quarter of any basic unit of weight, (b) (v, s, f, present perfect tense, second person; synonymous with 'hāsal or prāpat kītī hai'; 'khaṭṭī hai'; 'pahnī hai'; 'milāī or pā dittī hai'; 'anubhav kītī hai') has achieved; gained; worn; added, poured or put; realised or perceived respectively), (c) (v, s, present tense, first person; synonymous with 'maiṅ pāuṅdī-', 'hāsal-' or 'prāpat kardī' 'hāṅ') I achieve, (d) (present participle - 'kriyā-phal kirdaṅt'; synonymous with 'jo kichh(u) pāīā), and (e) (v, past tense; synonymous with 'hāsal-' or 'prāpat-' 'kītī hai') see pāuṇā (a and c).

pāiā: (a) (v, s, present perfect tense, first/third person; synonymous with 'hāsal or prāpat kītā'; 'khaṭṭiā'; 'pahniā'; 'milāiā or pā dittā hai'; 'anubhav- ''kītā hai'-has achieved; gained; worn; added, poured, put; realised or perceived respectively, (b) (v, s, past tense, first person; synonymous with 'maiṅ prāpat- 'or 'hāsal- ''kītā') achieved, (c) (v, s, present tense, first person; synonymous with 'maiṅ- ' 'pāuṅdā', 'hāsal' or 'prāpat kardā-' 'hāṅ') I achieve, and (d) (present participle - 'kriyā-phal kirdaṅt'; synonymous with 'jo kichh(u) pāiā') see pāuṇā.

paiṇā: (a) (v; synonymous with 'pravesh karnā') to enter, (b) (v; synonymous with 'leṭaṇā') to lie down or to sleep, (c) (v; synonymous with 'paṛnā' and 'ḍigṇā') to fall, kneel or lie down and touch another's feet , to humbly submit and seek another's protection, and (d) (conjunct

v) as such it denotes completion of the action implied in the primary verb, e.g., (i) 'ḍig paiṇa' - to fall, (ii) 'sarnī paiṇa' - to surrender and seek another's refuge, (iii) 'gal(i) phās paiṇī' - to have a noose put around one's neck, and (iv) 'nīsāṇ(u) paiṇa' - to be marked up and out, (v) 'thak paiṇa' - to lie down and rest having succumbed to exhaustion and fatigue, and (vi) 'mukar(u) paiṇā' - to deny, renege or go back upon.

pāp: (n, m, pl; antonym of 'puṅn'; synonymous with 'ashubh-' or 'māṛe-' 'karam'; 'dushkaram' and 'kukaram') (a) evil thoughts, sins, or misdeeds, exploitatory or detrimental in nature to oneself or other beings, and responsible for one's own 'spiritual downfall', and (b) (n, m; synonymous with 'pāpī birtī or subhāu') innate evil tendencies.

parvāṇ: (a) (n, m; synonymous with 'vaṭṭā') literally, weight or weights used in a scale, (b) (n, m; synonymous with 'pramāṇ') literally, proof, testimony or evidence, (c) (adj, m; synonymous with 'parvān(u)', 'maṅnaṇyog' or 'mān-niya') credible, plausible or trustworthy, (d) (adj, m; synonymous with 'pramān duārā sidh', 'pratakhkh' or 'zāhir') evident, tangible and explicit, and (e) (adj; synonymous with 'pramāṇit' or 'surkharū'; 'manzūr-', 'kabūl-', 'aṅgīkār-' or 'makbūl-' 'kītā hoiā') approved, authenticated, sanctioned or authorised [by the all-pervasive 'Nām(u)'].

pat(i): (a) (n, m; synonymous with 'bhartā', 'patī' and 'khāvaṅd') husband, (b) n, m; synonymous with 'swāmī' and 'mālik') Lord or Master, (c) (n, m; synonymous with 'paudā' and 'būṭā') a plant, (d) (n, m; synonymous with 'dhan' and 'saṅpadā') wealth or assets, (e) (n, m; synonymous with 'jāt(i)', 'pāt(i)', 'got' and 'kul') caste or sub-caste, and (f) (n, f; synonymous with 'mān', izzat' and 'pratishṭā') honour, good name, self-respect, prestige, renown, reputation or glory.

pāt(i)sāh: (n, m; synonymous with 'pādshah' and 'bādshah' and pronounced as 'pātshāh') a complex word comprising 'pāt' + 'sāh'.

pāt: (i) (n, m; synonymous with 'pattā') leaf, (ii) (n, m; synonymous with 'par', 'khaṅbh' or 'paṅkh') wing, (iii) (v, s; abbrev. for 'pāvat'; synonymous with 'pāuṅdā hai') gets, achievcs or receives; literally, wears but (fig.) endures, (iv) (v, s; synonymous with 'ḍigdā hai') literally, falls or sinks to a lowly position, (v) (n, m; synonymous with ‘rakshak’ and ‘rakhiak’) protector, saviour or guardian, and (vi) (n, m; synonymous with ‘takhat’ and ‘siṅghāsan’) a throne or royal seat, and (vii) (n, f; synonymous with ‘mān’, izzat’ and ‘pratishṭā’) honour, good name, self-respect, prestige, renown, reputation or glory.

sāh: (n, m; pronounced as ‘shāh(u)’) (a) (n, m; synonymous with ‘suās’, ‘svās’ and ‘dam’) breath, (b) (n, m; synonymous with ‘bādshāh’ (pers), ‘sultān’ and ‘rājā’) a king or an emperor, (c) (n, m; synonymous with ‘shāh’ and ‘shāhūkār’) rich merchant, banker or moneylender, (d) an honorific title for Muslim Saints, ‘Pīrs’ and ‘Sayīads’ and (e) (n, m; synonymous with ‘swāmī’, ‘mālik’ or ‘pat(i)’) Master, Lord and Husband.

pāt(i)sāh: (n, m; synonymous with ‘pādshāh’ and ‘bādshāh’) literally, Lord Protector and Lord Master of the imperial throne, i.e., a king. However, the term ‘sachche pāt(i)sāh’ implies eternal kings, those who have realised ‘Nām(u)’ - the source of all attributes, knowledge, wisdom, wealth and power, and the term pāt(i)sāhī pāt(i)sāh(u) denotes (a) King of Kings, and (b) the Most Reverend of all.

pāt(i)sāhib: (n, m) a complex word comprising ‘pāt’ + ‘sāhib’ (‘pat(i)’, 'swāmī' and 'mālik' - husband, master or lord. Literally, Lord Protector or Master.

pāuṇā: (v) (a) synonymous with ‘prāpat karṇā’, ‘laiṇā’; ‘labhṇā’; and ‘savīkār karnā’) to get, acquire or achieve; to find; to receive or accept, (b) (synonymous with ‘lābh hoṇā’, ‘lāhevaṅd hoṇā’ and ‘phāidā uṭhāuṇā’) to profit, (c) (synonymous with ‘anubhav karnā’) to perceive or realise, and (d) (conj. v and suff) (i) (synonymous with ‘paṇī-’ or ‘tel’ ‘pāuṇā') to add, mix or pour, (ii) (synonymous with ‘kapṛe-’ or ‘gahṇe-’ ‘pāuṇā') to put on clothes or ornaments, (iii) (synonymous with ‘shor pāuṇā’) to make a noise, (iv) (synonymous with ‘ghar pāuṇā’) to make or construct a house or dwelling, (v) (synonymous with ‘chiṭhi pāuṇā’) to post a letter, (vi) (synonymous with ‘kurāhe pāuṇā’) to lead one astray, (vii) (synonymous with ‘kīmat(i) pāuṇā’) to put a value on or determine the worth of something, (viii) (synonymous with ‘Prabh(u) pāuṇā’) to align perfectly with and then realise ‘Nām(u)’, through God's Grace, (ix) (synonymous with ‘rasnā Nām pāuṇā’) to get or receive the gift of ‘Nām Japṇā’, and (x) ‘bisrām pāuṇā’ -to achieve a state of tranquillity.

pavah(i): (a) (v, s, present tense, second person; synonymous with 'tūṅ paiṅdā haiṅ'; 'tusīṅ paiṅde ho'), (b) (v, s, 'saṅbhāv bhvikht kāl - sharat bodhak', second person; synonymous with 'je tūṅ paveṅ'), (c) (v, pl, present tense, first person; synonymous with 'asīṅ paiṅde hāṅ'), (d) (v, pl, future tense, third person; synonymous with 'uh paiṇge'; pronounced as 'pavaheṅ'), and (e) (v, pl, present tense, third person; synonymous with 'uh paiṅde-' or 'pai jāṅde-' 'han') see paiṇā.

pāvah(i): (a) (v, s, present tense, second person; synonymous with 'tūṅ pāuṅdā haiṅ' or 'tusīṅ pāuṅde ho'; pronounced as 'pāvaheṅ'), (b) (v, s, 'saṅbhāv bhvikht kāl - kiās, sharat, or ichhā bodhak', second person; synonymous with 'je tūṅ pā laveṅ'), (c) (v, pl, future tense, third person; synonymous with 'uh-' 'pāuṅge' or pā laiṅge'; pronounced as 'pāvaheṅ', (d) (v, pl, present tense, first person; synonymous with 'asīṅ pāuṅde hāṅ'), and (e) (v, pl, present tense, third person; synonymous with 'uh pāuṅde han'; pronounced as 'pāvaheṅ') see pāuṇā (a).

pichhai: (pronounced as 'pichhchhai') (a) (n and adj; synonymous with 'pichhvāṛ' or 'pichhlā pāsā') literally, rear or back, (b) (conj v) (i) (adv; synonymous with 'pichhe toṅ') from behind, (ii) (ph; 'pichhe pai jāṇā') to harass, torment or to persecute, (iii) (ph; 'pichhe rah jāṇā') to lag behind or to be left behind, (iv) (conj v; synonymous with 'pichhe lagṇā') to follow, to be led by or to imitate, (c) (adv; synonymous with 'pichhle pāse') literally, behind or in the rear, and (d) (adv; synonymous with 'pichhoṅ', 'magroṅ', and 'samān bīt jāṇ bād') literally, later, thereafter, afterwards or subsequently.

pīr: (a) (n, f; synonymous with 'pīṛā' or 'pīṛ') suffering or agony, (b) (n, f; synonymous with 'viptā' or 'biptā') adversity, calamity or serious difficulty, (c) (indeclinable past participle or perfect participle - 'pūran pūrab kārdaṅtak'; synonymous with 'pīṛ ke') having been crushed in a press - see 'pīṛnā', (d) (n, m; synonymous with 'pīlā') yellow in colour, (f) (n, m, pl; pers; synonymous with 'buḍhā', 'birdh', 'kamzor' and 'bazurg') respectable old and frail men, and (g) (n, m, pl; synonymous with 'aulīyā') religious or spiritual teachers or holy men in Islam.

pīṛnā: (v) (synonymous with 'kasṇā', 'ghuṭṇā', 'dabāuṇā') to tighten, squeeze or compress.

puṅn: (n, m;) (a) (synonymous with 'sukaram'; 'bhale-', 'uttam-', 'sukrit', 'shubh-', 'sreshṭ-', 'pavitr-' or 'nek-' 'karam') acts of virtue, merit, charity, or altruism, and (b) acts deemed good and auspicious, and of positive value in one's spiritual progress in Hindu belief.

purī: (a) (n, m, s: synonymous with 'nagar' or 'shahar') a city, (b) (n, f) one of the fourteen holy places according to Hindu mythology, e.g., dev purī, pātāl purī, jaganāth purī etc., (c) (n, f; synonymous with 'deh' or 'sarīr') the physical body, (d) (n, f; synonymous with 'nadī') a river, and (e) (adj and v; synonymous with 'pūrī') completed or fulfilled.

rachṇā: (v) (a) to make, create, form, construct, prepare or produce, (b) to pervade, permeate and saturate, and (c) to become deeply attached, absorbed, or engrossed.

rāh(u): (n, m) (a) (synonymous with 'mazhab' and 'dharam') creed, faith, religious denomination or religion, (b) (synonymous with 'tarikā' and 'ḍhaṅg') way, technique or method, (c) (synonymous with 'niyam', 'maryādā' and 'kānūn') rule, tradition, principle, precept, law or code of conduct, (d) (synonymous with 'mārag', 'rastā' and 'paṅth') literally, the way or path, and (e) (n, f; synonymous with 'saṅsār dī kār') literally, unfolding, panning out or the evolution of the world. However, implicit here is the affairs, the way and the direction of the world or the moral, ethical and spiritual path that leads to 'Nām-realisation'.

rahah(i): (a) (v, s, present tense, second person; synonymous with 'tūn rahiṅdā haiṅ' or 'tusīṅ rahiṅde ho'), (b) (v, s, present tense, first person; synonymous with 'asīṅ rahiṅde hāṅ'), (c) (imperative mood - 'saṅbhāv bhvikht kāl - kiās, sharat or ichhā bodhak', pl, second person; synonymous with 'je tusīṅ raho'), (d) (v, pl, future tense, third person; synonymous with 'uh rahiṇge'), and (e) (v, pl, present tense, third person; synonymous with 'uh rahiṅde han'; pronounced as 'raheṅ') literally, live, reside or remain. See rahiṇā.

rahiṇā: (v; synonymous with 'rahṇā') (a) (synonymous with 'nivās karnā' and 'rahāish karnī') to live or reside, (b) (synonymous with 'rukṇā' or 'ṭhaharnā') to remain, to stay on or to stop in that state, (c) (synonymous with 'chhaḍṇā' or 'tiāgṇā') to forsake, give up, sacrifice or renounce, (d) (synonymous with 'chhuṭṇā', 'bachṇā' or 'chhuṭkārā pāuṇā') to escape, to avoid being entrapped or to be spared, and (e) (synonymous with 'thakṇā' or 'thak jāṇā') literally, to get or become tired, fatigued, exhausted or weary or to give up, having become weary and exhausted.

rajāī: (a) (n, f; synonymous with 'leph') quilt, (b) (adj; synonymous with 'saṅtushṭ' and 'rajjiā hoiā') satisfied, content or satiated, (c) (locative case - 'adhikaraṇ kārak'; synonymous with 'razā-', 'hukam-' or 'bhāṇe' 'vich') by His Will, (d) (n, m, s; synonymous with 'razā vālā'; pronounced as 'razāī') literally, 'Kartār'/God, and (e) (genitive case - 'saṅbaṅdh kārak'; synonymous with 'razāī-' and 'razā vale-' 'dā'; pronounced as 'razāīṅ') of one whose 'razā' it is. In essence, the reference is to God or 'Nām(u)' - His immanent form.

rakhṇā: (v; synonymous with 'rākhanā') (a) (synonymous with 'pālṇā') to nurture and sustain, (b) (synonymous with 'kaṅm te lāuṇā' or 'kaṅm sauṅpaṇā') to assign a duty, task or function, (c) (synonymous with 'ṭikāuṇā') literally, to put, place or lay something safely and securely, (d) (synonymous with 'dhāran-' or 'grahaṇ-' 'karnā') to achieve and hold on to something, and (e) (synonymous with 'rakhyā karnā', 'bachāuṇā' or 'hiphāzat karnī') to watch, guard or protect from evil or danger; to defend someone's honour or good name.

raṅg(u): (n, m, s) (a) (synonymous with 'prem', 'prīt(i)' or 'anūrāg') love or affection, (b) (synonymous with 'Sahaj' and 'anaṅd') inner equipoise, tranquillity and bliss, (c) (synonymous with 'khushī' or 'mauj') joy, pleasure or whim, (d) (synonymous with 'tamāshā') a show or spectacle of fun and entertainment, (e) (synonymous with 'shobhā') fame or glory, (f) (synonymous with 'raṅk') poor or penniless, (g) synonymous with 'dhaṅn' or 'saṅpadā') money or assets, (h) (n, m and adv; synonymous with 'kisam' or 'prakār') sort, category, manner or modes, (i) (synonymous with 'līlā', 'khel' or 'kautak') objects or acts that inspire awe, wonder or intense delight, pleasure or joy; His awe-inspiring act of the creation of the universe and its diversity ('jagat tamāshā'), and (j) (synonymous with 'varaṇ') literally colour, hue or complexion.

ratan: (a) (n, m, pl; synonymous with 'kīmatī paththar' and 'adbhut vastū') literally, uniquely beautiful and precious objects or stones, e.g., jewels, rubies, (b) (n, pl; synonymous with fourteen priceless objects which demi-gods obtained after churning the oceans according to mythological stories in 'Purānās', (c) (n, m; synonymous with 'utam padārath') cereals or grain ('aṅn' or 'anāj'), water ('pāṇī'), fire ('baisaṅtr'), salt ('lūṇ'), and clarified butter ('ghrit' or 'ghī'), (d) (n, m, s; synonymous with 'ratan padārath') the priceless 'Nām(u)' - the persona and attributes of the transcendent God, (e) (n, m, pl; synonymous with 'ratan rūp' and 'guṇvān manukh') 'saṅts', 'sādhs', 'bhagats', gurūs, and 'brahmgyānīs', and (e) (n, m, pl; synonymous with 'ratan rūp' and 'amolak guṇ') priceless godly attributes, virtues and values.

razā: (a) (n, f; synonymous with 'maṅzūrī' and 'aṅgīkār') consent, approval or sanction, (b) (arab; n, f; synonymous with 'prasaṅtā' and 'khushnūdī') literally, happiness, delight or pleasure, and (c) (n, m; synonymous with 'bhāṇā', 'ichhā' and 'marzī') literally, wish, desire or will. 'Hukam(u)' and 'Razā' are virtually synonymous, but the latter represents that which appeals to Him, e.g., willing, loving and unreserved surrender to His Divine Order or Will, and this is how one becomes worthy of His Grace.

sach(u): (synonymous with 'satya' (skt); 'sat(i)', 'sāch(u)', 'sachā' and 'sāchā' (gmkh) in Gurbānī) (a) (adj; synonymous with 'sadīvī') eternal, (b) (n, m, s; synonymous with 'sadīvī jyot(i) sarūp-', 'Pārbrahm', 'Kartār-'or 'sat(i) chit anaṅd') the eternal Truth or Reality, pure consciousness, eternal equipoise and Bliss; 'Nām(u)' - the formless and immanent form of the transcendent God, (c) (adj; synonymous with 'sarab kalā bharpūr(i)', 'par(i)pūran' and 'sarab-vyāpak') omnipotent, omniscient, and omnipresent, (d) (adj; synonymous with 'satya' and 'hoṅd-' or 'hastī-' 'vālā') real and not imaginary, (e) (adj; synonymous with 'shuch(i)', 'nirmal' or 'pavitr'; 'pūrā', 'mukaṅmal' and 'ukāī rahit') perfect, flawless and immaculate, (f) (n; synonymous with 'sadīvī sukh' and 'ātmak aḍoltā') 'Sahaj' or 'Anaṅd', and (g) (adj; synonymous with 'satya', 'mithya de virudh' or 'jhūth dā abhāv') the eternal Truth. The word captures and highlights the key aspects of the persona and attributes of that perfect, all-powerful, immaculate, and eternal Truth and Reality that we refer to as the Creator or God.

sahaj: (a) (n and adj; synonymous with 'jauṛā') born at the same time or a twin, (b) (n, m; synonymous with 's(v)bhāv', 'ādat' and 'phitrat') innate nature, temperament or disposition, (c) (n, m; synonymous with 'bibek' or 'vichār') intellect, rationality or deductive reasoning, (d) (n, m; synonymous with 'ruhānī-' or 'brahm-' 'giān') spiritual knowledge, (e) (adv; synonymous with 'niryatan') without much effort or endeavour, (g) (adj; synonymous with 's(v)bhāvik') natural, instinctive or spontaneous, (h) (synonymous with 'āsānī') ease and effortlessness, and (i) (n, m) (synonymous with 'anaṅd') lasting inner bliss. However, in Gurmat, it usually denotes unshakeable and lasting inner peace and equipoise which one achieves through reflective contemplation of the Divine Word in the face of extremes of emotions, and it is in this state that one experiences 'anaṅd' and then the manifestation of 'Nām(u)' within one's '*Man*' *or* 'Hirdā'.

sahaj(i): (a) (instrumental case - 'karaṇ kārak'; synonymous with 'giān karke') knowingly, (b) (adv; synonymous with 's(v)bhāvik' and 'kudratī') instinctively, naturally or intuitively, (c) (synonymous with 'sadāchārī-' or 'sushīltā-' 'dā') of or due to good manners, behaviour or culture, (d) (adv; synonymous with 'haule haule') gradually, slowly or step by step, (e) (instrumental case - 'karaṇ kārak'; synonymous with 'dhīraj-' and 'shāntī-' 'nāl') patiently and peacefully, (f) (locative case - 'adhikaraṇ kārak'; synonymous with 'Sahaj-' or 'Brahm-' 'vich') in sahaj (God), and (g) (locative case - 'adhikaraṇ kārak'; synonymous with 'shudh sarūp ātmā de aḍol subhāu vich') in a state of lasting inner equanimity.

samāī: (a) (n, f; synonymous with 'shāṅt(i)' or 'sahanshīltā') peace or tranquillity; patience or tolerance, (b) (n, f; synonymous with 'līntā') state of being engrossed or rapt; merger, (c) (n, f; (pers.) synonymous with 'suṇvāī') hearing, e.g., of a petition, (d) (adj, m, s; synonymous with 'sharnāgtāṅ nuṅ sharan vich lain vālā') guardian or protector, (e) (v, s, present tense, third person; synonymous with 'samāiā hai' or 'līn huṅdī hai') becomes engrossed or absorbed, (f) (v, s, present perfect, third person; synonymous with 'pāī-' or 'rakh diṭṭī-' 'hai'; 'ral mil gaī hai') has been added and dissolved, and implicit here is (g) (adj; synonymous with 'viāpak-' or 'vyāpak-' 'hai') diffusive or pervasive.

samāuṇā: (v; synonymous with 'samāvaṇā') (a) (synonymous with 'ral mil jāṇā' or 'līn hoṇā') to dissolve or merge, (b) (synonymous with 'abhed hoṇā') to permeate or pervade something and become part of that; be absorbed or assimilated, (c) (synonymous with 'liv lāuṇī') to focus or fixate singularly on something for a long period, and (d) (conj v and suff.) 'jotī jot(i) samāuṇā' - perfect alignment of one's 'Jīvātmāṅ' with 'Parmātmāṅ' during one's lifetime ('Jīvan mukat(i)') and complete merger with the Primal Soul after death ('Paramgat(i)').

sar: (a) (n, f; synonymous with 'tāl') literally, rhythm or beat, (b) (n, m; synonymous with 'pāṇī') water, (c) (n, m; synonymous with 'bāṇ' or 'tīr') arrow, (d) (n, m; synonymous with 'kān(h)ā') a stick of any 'rush plant', usually 3.3m long used as an improvised measure of length, (e) (n, m; synonymous with 'svās' or 'suās') breath, (f) (n, m; synonymous with 'sir') head, (g) (adj; synonymous with 'tul(i)', 'brābar' and 'samān') matching, similar, comparable or equivalent, (h) (n & adj; synonymous with 'fateh' and 'jit') conquest or conquered, (i) (synonymous with 'yog samāṅ'; antonym is 'upsar') auspicious or propitious time, and (j) (n, m; synonymous with 'sarovar', 'jhīl', 'samuṅdar' or 'sāgar') large tanks, lakes or oceans.

sār: (a) (n, f; synonymous with 'kadar', 'kīmat' and 'mul') value or worth, (b) (n, f; synonymous with 'khabardārī' and 'saṅbhāl') care, maintenance or upkeep, (c) (n, f; synonymous with 'khabar' and 'samāchār') news, information or update, (d) (n, m; synonymous with 'niāuṅ' and 'iṅsāph') justice, fair play or equity, (e) (adj; synonymous with 'uttam' and 'sresht̤') best, perfect or ideal, (f) (adv; synonymous with 'mātr', 'pramāṇ' and 'bhar') amount, quantity, degree or proportionality, and (g) (n, m; synonymous with 'lohā' and 'phaulād') literally, iron metal but in essence, sword or other similar weapons of war made of iron.

sat: (a) (n; synonymous with 'sach(u)' or 'satya') see sach(u) and sat(i), (b) (adj, f; synonymous with 'pativrat') faithful wife, (c) (n, m, s; synonymous with 'Parmātmāṅ', 'Kartār' or 'Brahm') the eternal Reality, God, (d) (n, f, s; synonymous with 'Jīvātmāṅ' or '*Man*') conscious self, (e) (n; synonymous with 'satoguṇ') one of the three 'guṇās' or characteristics of 'māyā'; virtuous traits, (f) (n, m, s; synonymous with 'satyug') one of the four 'yugs' according to Hindu mythology, (g) (adj; synonymous with 'ark', 'sār' or 'nichoṛ') gist or essence, (h) (n; synonymous with 'subhāu') innate nature, (i) (n; synonymous with ‘dharam’) Divine Order, (j) (n; (sat(u)) synonymous with ‘puṅn’ or ‘punya-’ or ‘shubh-’ ‘karam’) noble deeds, (k) (n; (sat(u)) synonymous with ‘dān’) alms, charity or donation, and (l) (n; ‘sidhāṅt’ or ‘tātpariya’) doctrine, tenets, theories.

sat(i): (synonymous with ‘satya’ (skt); ‘sat(i)’, ‘sach(u)’, ‘sāch(u)’ and ‘sāchā’ (gmkh) in Gurbānī) (a) to (g) see sach(u); (h) (n; synonymous with ‘ythārath’, ‘tat(u)’ and ‘tath(u)’; antonym of ‘asat(i)’, ‘a-satya’ or ‘mithya’) the eternal Truth or Reality, (i) (n; synonymous with ‘shradhā’ or ‘vishvāsh’) absolute faith, reverence and devotion, (j) (synonymous with ‘ythārath gyān’, ‘asliyat di samajh’ or ‘braham gyān’) Divine Knowledge and Wisdom, and (k) (n; synonymous with ‘pratigya’, ‘vachan vaṅdh hoṇā’ or ‘praṇ karnā’) taking of an oath or giving one’s word. It primarily denotes the one and only eternal Truth, all-pervasive, and the unchanging eternal Reality that is God in the SGGS.

satī: (a) (adj, m; synonymous with ‘satya rūp’ or ‘abhināshī’) literally, eternal, i.e., God, (b) (n, f, s) a daughter of ‘Daksh’ and consort of Lord Mahadev who immolated herself in the holy fire of a ‘Yagya’ after witnessing the insult and dishonour of her husband, (c) (n, f, pl) they who elect or reluctantly submit, through social custom or pressure, to burn themselves alive on the funeral pyres of their husbands, (d) (n, f, pl; synonymous with ‘pat(i)vrat istrīs’) virtuous, chaste and faithful wives, (e) (adj; synonymous with ‘satya vaktā’) they who never lie and always speak the truth, (f) (adj; synonymous with ‘saṅjamī’) disciplined, restrained, dispassionate, temperate and placid, (g) (adj; ‘saṅtokhī’) content, and (h) (adj; synonymous with ‘dānī’ and ‘udār-ātmā’) generous, benevolent, charitable, righteous and noble.

sidh: (n, m, pl) spiritually high ranking ‘Yogīs’ who have achieved: (a) eight unique or mythical, psychic, miraculous or supernatural powers, and (b) sidh(i) which is (i) (synonymous with ‘pūraṇatā’ or ‘saphaltā’) success in achieving ‘Nirvānā’ or ‘Nām-realisation’, (ii) (synonymous with ‘ruhānī giān’) ethical, moral and spiritual wisdom and ‘bibek’ - the ability to judge right from wrong, and (iii) (synonymous with ‘saṅjam’or ‘saṅyam’) full control over one’s ‘*Man*’ and innate evil tendencies (or five cardinal drives) through their strict yogic discipline and the practice of ‘prāṇāyām’, ‘āsaṇās’ and meditation. Some consider them to be above human beings but below 'devtas', according to old Saṅskrit texts. The prominent eight of the eighteen miraculous or supernatural powers ('sidh(i)' or (sidhīs)) they harness through their yogic practice are as follows: (i) 'aṇimā' - the ability to become as small as one wishes, (ii) 'laghimā' - the ability to become as light as one wishes, (iii) 'prāpatī' - the ability to have anything material that one wants, (iv) 'prākāmayā' - the ability to have one's own way (dictatorial power), (v) 'mahimā' - the ability to become as big as one wants, (vi) 'īshitv' - the ability to assume sovereignty, supremacy or sway, (vii) 'vashitv' - the ability to get another under one's influence or control, and (viii) 'kāmāvāsāitā' - the ability to have absolute control over one's sensuality.

sir(i): (a) (n, f; synonymous with 'rachnā') creation, (b) (indeclinable past participle or perfect participle - 'pūran pūrab kārdaṅtak'; synonymous with 'rach ke') having created, (c) (adj; synonymous with 'shiromaṇī' and 'sreshṭ') supreme, ultimate, premier, apex or best, and (d) (locative case - 'adhikaraṇ kārak'; synonymous with 'sir-' 'te', 'utte', 'par' or 'uppar') literally, on, upon or above one's head.

so: (a) (nominative case - 'kartā kārak', s, third person; synonymous with 'uh') he, (b) (pron and adj; synonymous with 'ohī') the same or exactly this or that, and (c) (nominative case - 'kartā kārak', synonymous with 'us nūṅ') literally, the same or exactly him. The reference here is to God Himself, the 'dātār'.

soi: (a) (v; synonymous with 'sauṇa') to sleep, (b) (v, s, present tense, third person; synonymous with 'sauṅdā hai') literally, sleeps, (c) (n, f; synonymous with 'shobhā' or 'shuhrat') fame, renown or repute, (d) (n, f; synonymous with 'khushbū') fragrance or perfume, (e) (n, f; synonymous with 'khabar', 'sār' and 'sudh') news, information or knowledge about someone's wellbeing, and (f) (pron and adj; synonymous with 'oh' or 'ohī') literally, he, she, it or they; the same.

soī: (a) (adj; synonymous with 'suttī') asleep, and (b) (pron and adj; synonymous with 'ohī' or 'vahī') literally, the very same person or being; the same or exactly that.

su: (a) (pron; synonymous with 'swai-' or 'apne-' 'vāste' or 'laī') oneself or for oneself e.g., 's(u)prasaṅn', (b) (adj; synonymous with 'at(i)') to the superlative degree, excessive, large amount, (c) (adj; synonymous with 'uttam' or 'sresht') noble, supreme or par excellence, (d) (adj; synonymous with 'suṅdar') beautiful, (e) (a suffix to a verb that conveys the meaning of 'past tense', singular and third person), e.g., 'ditos(u)'; synonymous with 'us neṅ dittā' - He ('su') gave, offered or granted ('dito'), and (f) pron and adj; synonymous with 'so', 'uh' or 'ohī') that, he or she.

sur: (a) (n, f; synonymous with 'svar') a musical note that forms part of the scale of a rāg, (b) (adj, m; synonymous with 'sreshṭ' and 'uchā') supreme, (c) (n, m; synonymous with 'devtā') a demi-god in Hindu mythology, and (d) (n, m; pref) (i) 'sur(i)nar' (synonymous with 'manukh with dayavī guṇ') a man with godly or divine attributes, (ii) 'surjan' (synonymous with 'uttam-' or 'chaṅge-' 'purush') noble or virtuous man, (iii) 'surpat(i)' - literally, husband of 'devtās' ('devtiāṅ dā patī) i.e., Indra Dev, (iv) 'surnāth'; synonymous with 'devtiāṅ dā swāmī - the great or supreme nāth; Indra Dev, (v) 'sur-rid'; synonymous with 'shubhchiṅtak' or 'nek dil' - humane, kind-hearted, compassionate or a wellwisher, (vi) 'sur-ar(i)'; synonymous with 'daint', 'rākshak' or 'devtiāṅ dā vairī' - a demon or a giant ogre, and (vii) 'sur-gindu'; synonymous with 'amrāvatī' or 'swarg of Indra Dev' - heaven of Indra Dev.

sur(i): (a) (n, m, pl) 'devte' in Hindu mythology, (b) (n, m, s; synonymous with 'uttam purush') the reference is to God, (c) (genitive case - 'saṅbaṅdh kārak'; synonymous with 'devtiāṅ de') of 'devtās', (d) (instrumental case - 'karaṇ kārak'; synonymous with 'devtiāṅ toṇ-' 'sadkā' or 'kāraṇ') by virtue of being 'devtas', (e) (synonymous with 'bhale purash') a slightly derogatory term of address for someone in the wrong or who has gone astray, and implicit here is (f) (adj, m, pl; synonymous with 'vaḍḍe') literally, great, senior, elder, and (g) (n, m, pl) human beings with divine attributes ('dayavī guṇ').

sūr: (a) n, m, s; synonymous with 'sūraj') literally, the sun, (b) (n, m, pl; synonymous with 'shūkar' and 'sūar') literally, pigs, (c) (n, m; synonymous with 'giān dā prakāsh'; n, f; synonymous with 'ātmak roshnī') spiritual awakening or light/wisdom and (d) (adj, m; synonymous with 'bahādur', 'yodhā' and 'sūrbīr') literally, brave, valiant, courageous, or intrepid warriors. In essence, braves who fight a holy war ('dharam yudh') - with the evil disposition of their inner self and for a noble and righteous cause in the wider world.

surat(i): (a) (n, m; synonymous with 'kaṅn' and 'shrot(i)') literally, ears, (b) (v; synonymous with 'suṇanā') to listen attentively, (c) (n, f; synonymous with 'sravaṇ-shakat(i)') ability to hear, (d) (n, f; synonymous with 'uttam prit(i)') true love, (e) (n, f; synonymous with 'samajh' and 'sojhī') spiritual knowledge or wisdom, (f) (n, f; synonymous with 'khabargirī') guarding, looking out for or taking care of, (g) (n, m; synonymous with 'chit') one of four parts of the 'Aṅtahkaran' which deals with memory, and (h) (n, f; one of four parts of '*Man*(u)' in Gurmat; synonymous with 'dhiān', 'tavajjo', 'birtī', 'suchet pan' and 'vīchār') focus, attention; alertness, conscious state of mind; meditation or reflection; proclivity or predisposition.

surtī: (a) (n, f; synonymous with 'samaj', 'sojhī', 'giān' and 'mat(i)') spiritual knowledge or wisdom, state of inner/spiritual awakening or alertness, (b) (n; synonymous with 'surat(i)', 'dhiān', 'tavajjo' or 'liv') focus or attention, (c) (n and adj; synonymous with 'dharam gayātā') one who understands and follows a righteous path or code of conduct, (d) (n and adj; synonymous with 'ved gayātā') one who understands the Vedic knowledge, (e) (n; synonymous with 'jis vich surat joṛīe') one on which or on whom one focuses and contemplates, (f) (adj; synonymous with 'uchī surat vāle') they who are spiritually awakened or alert, (g) (instrumental case - 'karaṇ kārak'; synonymous with 'samādhī-' or 'dhiān-' 'lāuṇ nāl'; pronounced as 'surtīn') with or by focussing and contemplating upon, and (h) (locative case - 'adhikaraṇ kārak'; synonymous with 'surat vich'; pronounced as 'surtīṅ') in focussing. In essence, it is 'ātmak jāg vich', i.e., in spiritual awakening or alertness.

sūt: (a) (n, m) a unit of measurement, 1/8th of an inch, (b) (n, m; synonymous with 'tāgā', 'sūtr' and 'ḍor') yarn or spun thread, e.g., that which is passed through individual beads in order to gather and bind them in an orderly way into a chain or a rosary, (c) (n, m; synonymous with 'janeū') a sacred thread worn by upper class Hindus at initiation, (d) (adj;

synonymous with ‘ṭhīk’, ‘sahī’ and ‘drust’) proper or correct, and (e) (n, m; synonymous with ‘prabaṅdh’, ‘iṅtzām’ and ‘nizām’) literally, management, preparation or provision; (fig.) Divine Order.

t: (synonymous with ‘tā’; pronounced as ‘tāṅ’) (a) (p or adv; synonymous with ‘yakīnan’) surely, certainly, or without fail, (b) (synonymous with ‘nirā’, ‘nirol’ and ‘keval’) only, alone, merely or simply, (c) (pron; synonymous with ‘tis(u)’, ‘is(u)’, ‘us(u)’, and ‘jis(u)’) this, that, he or she; with whom or whomsoever, (d) (pron, synonymous with ‘un(h)āṅ’ and ‘tin(h)āṅ’) they or theirs, (e) (adv; synonymous with ‘uthe’, ‘othe’ and ‘tis asthān’) there or at that place, and (f) (p and adv; synonymous with ‘tad’, ‘tadoṅ’, or ‘udoṅ’) then, thus, because of, or therefore.

tā: (synonymous with ‘t’; pronounced as 'tāṅ') (a) (n; abbrev for ‘tāp’, ‘sek’ or ‘āṅch’) heat, harm or danger, (b) (pron; synonymous with ‘us’, ‘tis’ or ‘tin(h)’) he or she; his, her or theirs, (c) (pron, pl; synonymous with ‘un(h)āṅ’ and ‘tin(h)āṅ’) they or their, (d) (nominative case - ‘kartā kārak’; synonymous with ‘us neṅ’) him or her, (e) (p and adv; synonymous with ‘tab’, ‘tad’, ‘tadoṅ’, or ‘udoṅ’) then, thus, because of or therefore, (f) (prep; synonymous with ‘toṅ’) from, and (g) (suff) suffix to a noun or an adjective, e.g., ‘mitartā’ and ‘shatr(u)tā’.

tai: (a) (pron; synonymous with ‘tūṅ’) you, (b) (synonymous with ‘us-’, ‘un(h)āṅ-’, ‘tis-’ or ‘tin(h)āṅ-’ ‘de’) his, hers or their, (c) (pron; synonymous with ‘tainūṅ’, ‘tis nūṅ’, ‘tise’ and ‘tujhe’) to you, (d) (pron; synonymous with ‘terī’ and ‘tere’) you or yours, (e) (n, f; synonymous with ‘asthān’ and ‘jag(h)ā’) place, (f) (pron and conj; synonymous with ‘toṅ’) from or than, (g) (prep; synonymous with ‘kā’, ‘dā’, ‘dī’, ‘ke’ and ‘de’) of, (g) (adj; synonymous with ‘tiṅn’) three, and implicit here is (h) (conj; synonymous with ‘aur’ and ‘ate’) literally, and.

tap(u): (a) (n, m, s; synonymous with ‘tej’) glory, eminence or effulgence, (b) (n, m, s; synonymous with ‘bukhār’) high temperature or fever; (c) (fig) (n; synonymous with ‘josh’, ‘utejnā’ or ‘khalbalī’; ‘ḍar’, ‘bhau’ or ‘taukhlā’; ‘chiṅtā’, ‘phikr’, ‘preshānī’ or ‘vyākultā’) excitement, fear or anxiety, (d) (n, f; synonymous with ‘agan(i)’ or ‘garmī’) fire or heat, and implicit here is (e) (n, f; synonymous with ‘tapassiā’, ‘tap karnā’, ‘tap sādhnā’ or ‘tap tāuṇā’) strict discipline, austerities, penances or acts of deliberate self-punishment, e.g., tolerance of extreme cold in winters or heat in summers, prolonged fasting, silence or adoption of strange posture, etc., all to gain full control over one's conscious self or '*Man*'.

te: (a) (conj; abbrev for 'ate') and, (b) (p; synonymous with 'toṅ' and 'se') from, (c) (adv; synonymous with 'rāhīṅ' or 'duārā') through, (d) (pron; synonymous with 've', 'oh' and 'vah') they, (e) (genitive case - 'saṅbaṅdh kārak'; synonymous with 'un(h)āṅ de') literally, theirs, and (f) (prep and adv; synonymous with 'utte' and 'uppar') on or above.

thāpṇā: (v) (a) (synonymous with 'sthāpṇā', 'asthāpṇā', 'lāuṇā' and 'niyukt karnā') to appoint, designate, install, or instate respectfully, (b) (synonymous with 'niṅmaṇā', 'rachṇā', 'sirjaṇā', 'upjaṇā' and 'paidā karnā') to gestate, give birth, grow, produce or create, and (c) (synonymous with 'ṭikā ke rakhṇā' and 'ṭikāuṇā') to put or place carefully.

thit(i): (a) (n, m; synonymous with 'sithit(i)' and 'ṭhahrāo') pause, stillness or tranquility, and (b) (n, m, s; synonymous with 'tith(i)' and 'mit(i)') a day or date according to the movement of the moon around the Earth. The term 'sudī' is attached to each day as the moon gets bigger or fuller, and the day of the full moon is called 'Pūranmāshī' or 'Punniāṅ'; the term 'badī' is attached to each day as the moon gets smaller or darker, and the day when the moon is not visible is called 'Massiā'. Each half is ascribed fifteen days.

tin(i): (a) (n, m; synonymous with 'triṇ', 'tiṇkā', 'tīlā', 'ghāh' or 'phūs') dried up grass or a blade of grass, (b) (adj; synonymous with 'trai' and 'tīn') literally, number three, (c) (pron, m, s; locative case - 'adhikaraṇ kārak'; synonymous with 'tis pās') with him or her, and (d) (m, s; nominative case - 'kartā kārak'; synonymous with 'tis hī ne') just he or she.

tis(u): (a) (nominative case - 'kartā kārak'; synonymous with 'us ne') literally, he, (b) (accusative case - 'karam kārak'; synonymous with 'tis nūṅ') to him, (c) (genitive case - 'saṅbaṅdh kārak'; synonymous with 'us-' 'de', 'dī', 'ke' or 'kī') literally, his, and (d) (pron and adj, m, s; synonymous with 'us') literally, he, she or that person.

upāī: (a) (v, past tense; synonymous with 'paidā kītī'), and (b) (v, s, present perfect, third person; synonymous with 'rachī-', 'utpan kītī- 'or 'paidā kītī-' 'hai') has been created.

upjanā: (v; synonymous with 'upjaṇā', 'jaṅmaṇā', 'janam laiṇā', 'paidā hoṇā', 'ugṇā' or 'aṅkurit hoṇā') to grow, originate, sprout, produce, create or to be born.

utarnā: (v; synonymous with 'utarṇā') (a) (v; synonymous with 'thalle' or 'nīche utarnā') to come down, alight, dismount, descend or disembark, (b) (synonymous with 'raṅg dā phikkā paiṇā') to fade, blanch or bleach, (c) (synonymous with 'tāp-' or 'nashe-' 'dā' 'dūr hoṇā' or 'ghaṭṇā') to lessen, subside or abate, (d) (synonymous with 'pāṇī de paddar dā ghaṭṇā', 'muṛnā' or 'pichhchhe haṭṇā') to ebb, subside or recede, (e) (synonymous with 'janam laiṇā' or 'dūsrā sarir dhāran karnā') to be born, (f) (synonymous with 'ākāsh toṅ dhartī te āuṇā', 'avtarnā' or 'avtār dharnā') to incarnate, and (g) (synonymous with 'mail- 'or 'dard-'/'pīṛ-' 'dā dūr hoṇā' or 'miṭṇā') to disappear, cease to exist or vanish.

vaḍā: (adj, m) (a) (synonymous with 'at(i)' and 'bahut') very much, plenty, plentiful or abundant, (b) (synonymous with 'visthar vala') big, huge, large, or tall, (c) (synonymous with 'birdh' or 'virdh') senior or elder, and (d) (synonymous with 'mukhīā', 'shiromani' and 'sresht') principal, premier or most superior.

vār: (n, m pl) (a) (synonymous with 'jaṅg' and 'yudh') war, (b) (synonymous with 'yudh saṅbaṅdhī kāvya' and 'prabhū mahimā bharī bāṇī') a poetic style of writing, especially relating the valour and chivalry of warriors or in praise of God, (c) (n, m; synonymous with 'hamlā') attack, blow, strike or assault, (d) (synonymous with 'urlā kinārā') the near end, (e) (synonymous with 'avsar', 'velā' and 'maukā') opportunity, (f) (synonymous with 'duār' and 'darvāzā') threshold or door, (g) (synonymous with 'chir', 'der' and 'ḍhil') delay, (h) (synonymous with 'vārnā', 'kurbānī' and 'nichhāvar') sacrifice, (i) (synonymous with 'vāṛ') boundary fence or hedge, (j) (suff; synonymous with 'vān' or 'vālā') e.g., 'sazāvār', and (k) (n, f; synonymous with 'daphā', 'ber' or 'vārī') counter or 'number of times', and (l) (synonymous with 'din') days of the week based on the movement of the Earth around the sun.

varbhaṅḍā: (n, m, pl; synonymous with 'brahmāṅḍs' or 'varbhaṅḍs') literally, many universes; sum total of all galaxies and universes.

vasanā: (v) (synonymous with 'basaṇā' and 'vasaṇā') (a) (synonymous with 'var(h)ṇā', 'varsanā' or 'mīṅh paiṇā') to rain, (b) (synonymous with 'nivās karnā') literally, to live, inhabit, dwell or reside, (c) (synonymous with 'abād karnā') literally, to settle down to live or to populate or to colonise, and (d) (synonymous with 'ras jāṇā') to permeate and overwhelm, and (e) to permeate, overwhelm and manifest in one's conscious self, '*Man*' or 'Hirdā'.

vekhai: (a) (v, s, present tense, third person; synonymous with 'vekhdā hai'; pronounced as 'vekhaiṅ') literally, looks, watches or observes, and (b) (v, s, present tense, third person; synonymous with 'vekhdā hai', 'dekh bhāl' or 'saṅbhāl kardā hai'; pronounced as 'vekhaiṅ') literally, cares, maintains, guards and protects.

vekhṇā: (v) (a) (synonymous with 'dekhṇā') to see, look, gaze, behold or observe, (b) (synonymous with 'khoj/paṛtāl karnī') to search, inspect or examine, (c) (synonymous with 'vichār karnī') to view or consider, (d) (synonymous with 'sāvdhān rahiṇā') to watch or look out, (e) to notice and/or mark, (f) (synonymous with 'mahisūs karnā') to experience or perceive, and (g) (synonymous with 'dekh bhāl-' and 'sanbhāl-' 'karnī') to guard, care, support and sustain.

ves(u): (a) (n, m, s; synonymous with 'kiryā', 'karam' and 'amal') conduct, character, practice or way of life, (b) (n, m, s; synonymous with 'kukaram') misdeeds, evil deeds or wickedness, (c) (n, m, s; synonymous with 'ghar' and 'nivās asthān') literally, house or abode. In essence, '*Man*' - literally, the abode of all ideas ('saṅkalps') and counter-ideas ('vikalps'), (d) (n, f; synonymous with 'bhaiṛī vādī') a defiled, evil, vile, wicked, immoral or profligate nature, (e) (n, f; synonymous with 'vaṇaj' and 'vapār') trade, business or dealings, (f) (synonymous with 'shiṅgār') make-up, adornment, embellishment or beautification, (g) (synonymous with 'bhes', 'libās' 'poshāk' and 'pahirāvā') dress, garb or attire, and (h) (n; synonymous with 'bhekh', 'shakal' and 'rūp') form, figure, appearance, caricature or silhouette.

vīchār(u): (a) (v, s, imperative mood - 'hukmī bhvikht', second person; synonymous with 'vīchār karo') reflect, ponder or contemplate, (b) (n, m; synonymous with 'saṅkalp', 'khyāl' and 'phurnā') a thought, an idea, a notion or a concept, (c) (n, m; synonymous with 'anumān' and 'aṅdāzā') estimate, guess or conjecture, (d) (n, f; synonymous with 'rāi', 'bhāv' and 'ihsās') a feeling, a view or an opinion, (e) (n, f; synonymous with 'vivek', 'tatv dā nirṇā' or 'aslīyat jāṇan dī kriyā') study, reflection, deliberation, cogitation or speculation, (f) (synonymous with 'kudrat de lekhe dī-' 'bīchār' and/or 'bibek') consultation, speculation, consideration or deliberation, and (g) (n, m; synonymous with 'nirṇā' and 'phaislā') conclusion, judgement or decision.

vichāre: (a) (v, s, present tense, third person; synonymous with 'bīchāre' and 'vīchārdā hai'), (b) (v, s, 'saṅbhāv bhvikht kāl - prashan and bevasī bodhak', first person; synonymous with 'maiṅ kī vichār-' 'karāṅ- ' or 'kar sakdā hāṅ'), (c) (v, pl, present tense; synonymous with 'bīchārde' and 'vīchārde han'), and (d) (indeclinable past participle or perfect participle - 'pūran pūrab kārdaṅtak'; synonymous with vichār kar ke') by focusing on and contemplating noble and godly attributes.

vīchārnā: (v; synonymous with 'bīchārnā' and 'tat dā nirṇai karnā') to deliberate, ponder, reflect, or deduce.

vigsanā: (v; synonymous with 'biksanā', 'bigsanā', 'vigsanā' or 'vigsaṇā') (a) (synonymous with 'khiṛnā' or 'viksit hoṇā') to develop, flourish or blossom; for a grain to pop into popcorn; to smile or burst into laughter, and (b) (synonymous with 'khush-' or 'prasaṅn-' 'hoṇā') to rejoice or be delighted, content and satisfied.

visarnā: (v; synonymous with 'bisarnā', 'chete nā rahiṇā' and 'bhulṇā') to forget, to fail to remember or to overlook.

visārnā: (a) (synonymous with 'bhulaṇā' and 'bhul jāṇā') to forget, to fail to remember or to lose completely from memory, and (b) (synonymous with 'aṇgaihlī karnī', 'lāparvāhī karnī', 'dhiān nā deṇā' 'uk jāṇā' and 'nazar aṅdāz karnā') to overlook or neglect.

vīsrah(i): (a) (v, s, present tense, second person ; synonymous with 'tūṅ visar-' or 'bhul-' 'jāṅdāṅ haiṅ'; 'tusīṅ visar-' or 'bhul-' 'jāṅde ho', (b) (v, s, 'saṅbhāv bhvikht kāl - sharat bodhak', second person; synonymous with 'je tūṅ visar-'or 'bhul- ''jāveṅ'), (c) (v, pl, future tense, third person ; synonymous with 'uh visar-' or 'bhul-' 'jāṇge'), and (d) (v, pl, present tense, third person; synonymous with 'uh visar-' or 'bhul-' 'jāṅde han'; pronounced as 'vīsraheṅ').

vuṛna: (v) (a) (synonymous with 'cheshṭā-', 'yatan-' or 'uddam-' 'karnā') to strive or endeavour, (b) (synonymous with 'vagṇā' and 'vahiṇā') to seep, leak, flow; to blow, and (c) (synonymous with 'chalṇā' and 'turnā') to move from a fixed point.

REFERENCES

1. SGGS, 266, 13 'Sarab dharam maih sresaṭ dharam(u). Har(i) ko Nām(u) jap(i) nirmal karam(u)'.
2. Gurbani Viakaran de Sarl Nem. Sikh Missionary College, Ludhiana.
3. Gurbani Viakaran. Professor Sahib Singh. Publishers: Singh Brothers, Amritsar.
4. Gurbani Da Sarl Viakaran-both (vol. 1 and 2). Joginder Singh Talvarha. Publishers: Singh Brothers, Amritsar.
5. Naveen Gurbani Viakaran. Giani Haribans Singh. Publishers: Gurbani Prakashan, 17a, Dogra Street, Patiala.
6. Mahan Kosh. Bhai Kahn Singh Nabha.
7. Sri Guru Granth Sahib Darpan. Professor Sahib Singh.
8. Sri Guru Granth Sahib (English translation) vol. 1-4. Dr Gopal Singh.
9. Sri Guru Granth Sahib (English translatin) vol. 1-8. Manmohan Singh.
10. Teachings of the Sikh Gurus. Christopher Shackle and Arvind-pal Singh Mandair. Published by Routledge, 2 Park Square, Milton Park, Abington, Oxon OX14 4RN.
11. Ibid., p. 611, line 19 'Ek(u) pitā ekas ke ham bārik tū merā gur hāī'.
12. Dasam Granth: Akal Ustat(i). Hindū turak koū rāphzī imām sāphī Mānas kī jāt(i) sabai ekai pahichānbo. p. 19, 15. 85.
13. SGGS, 946, 3 Haumaiṅ vich(i) jag(u) upjai purakhā nām(i) visarīai dukh(u) pāī.
14. Ibid., p. 560, line 12 Haumaiṅ nāvai nāl(i) virodh(u) hai dui na vasah(i) ik ṭhāi.
15. Ibid., p. 12, line 6 Bhaī prāpat mānukh dehurīā. Gobiṅd milaṇ kī ih terī barīā.
16. Ibid., p. 12, line 15-6 Deh(u) sajaṇ asīsaṛīā jio(u) hovai sāhib sio mel(u).
17. Ibid., p. 651, line 19; p. 652, line 1 Is(u) jag mah(i) purakh(u) ek(u) hai hor saglī nār(i) sabāī. Sabh(i) ghaṭ bhogvai alipat(u) rahai alakh(u) n lakhiā jāī.
18. Ibid., p. 1298, line 14 Kīrat(i) prabh kī gāo(u) merī rasnā.
19. Guru Nanak in the Eyes of Non-Sikhs (Mohsin Fani), trans. David Shea and Anthony Troyer, ed. Sarjit Singh Bal, Publication Bureau, Panjab University, 1969, p. 5.
20. The Sikh Religion, History and Character (London, 1909): Introduction, Max Arthur Macauliffe.

21. Sikhism: A Faith for the Modern Man. G.S. Gill, 1989, p. 52. Quotation by H.L. Bradshaw.
22. The Religion of the Sikhs. London, 1914. Dorothy Field.
23. Selections from the Sacred Writings of the Sikhs (UNESCO, 1960), Foreword p. 9 by Arnold Toynbee.
24. Advanced Studies in Sikhism. Ed. Jasbir Singh Mann and Harbans Singh Saron. 1988, Chapter 1 by Noel Q. King.
25. Sri Guru Granth Sahib. Translation and annotation by Dr. Gopal Singh. 7th Edition, Vol. 1, p. XIX, 'Introduction' Pearl S. Buck.
26. Guru Granth Sahib, Light House of Humanity. Dr Kuldeep Singh. 2003, p. 18. Quotation of Dr Janet Lant.
27. "that if some lucky men survive the onslaught of the third world war of atomic and hydrogen bombs, then the Sikh religion will be the only means of guiding them." Quotation of Sir Bertrand Russell.
28. Thought For The Month (Barah Maha). Dr K.S. Ryatt. 2018 Published by S.A.V.E., Printed by Printwell, 146, Industrial Focal Point, Amritsar.
29. SGGS, p. 290, lines 16-9 and p. 291, line 1; Salok(u). Sargun nirgun Niraṅkār suṅn samādhī āp(i). Āpan kīā Nankā āpe hī phir(i) Jāp(i). Astpadī: Jab akār(u) eh(u) kachh(u) na drisṭetā... Nānak karnā'i-hār(u) na dūjā.
30. Ibid., p. 945-6, line 15; Rūp(u) na hoto rekh na kāī ta sabad(i) kahā liv lāī...Gao(u)n(u) gagan(u) jab tabah(i) na hotao(u) tribhavaṅ jot(i) āpe niraṅkār.
31. Ibid., p. 1035, lines 9-19; Arbad narbad dhuṅdhūkārā...p. 1036, lines 1-10.
32. Ibid., p. 113, lines 7-8; Ekam ekai āp(u) upāiā. Dubidhā dūjā tribidh(i) māiā. Chauthī 'Pauṛī' gurmukh(i) ūchī sacho sach(u) kamāvaṇiā.
33. Ibid., p. 463, line 4; Āpīnai āp(u) sājio āpīnai rachio nāo(u). Duyī kudrat(i) sājīai kar(i) āsaṇ(u) ḍiṭho chāo(u).
34. Ibid., p. 916, line 4; Ekaṅkār(u) niraṅjan(u) nirbhao(u) sabh jal(i) thal(i) rahiā samāī.
35. Ibid., p. 19, line 18; Sāche te pavanā bhaiā pavanai te jal(u) hoe. Jal te tribhavaṇ(u) sajiā ghat(i) ghat(i) jot(i) samoe.
36. Ibid., p. 4. line 9-10; Jetā kītā tetā nāo.
37. Ibid., p. 4. line 10; Viṇ(u) nāvai nāhī ko thāo(u).
38. Ibid., p. 131, line 14; Ikas(u) te hoio anaṅtā Nānak ekas māh(i) smāe jīo(u).

39. Dasam Granth, p. 1387, 'Kabyo bāch bentī'. Chaupaī. Jab udkarakh karā kartārā. Prajā dharat tab deh apārā. Jab ākarakh karat ho kabahūṅ. Tum mai milat deh dhar sabahūṅ.
40. SGGS, p. 787-8, line 19 Kartai kāraṇ(u) jin(i) kīā so jāṇai soī.
41. Ibid., p. 868, lines 12-9 Acharj kathā mahā anūp. Prātmā Pārbrahm kā rūp(u). ...Nānak tā kai bal(i) bal(i) jāe.
42. Ibid., p. 1030, lines 9-10 Paṅch tat(u) mil(i) kāiā kīnī...Ātam rām(u) rām(u) hai ātam Har(i) pāīai sabad(i) vichārā he.
43. Ibid., p. 374, lines 5-6 Avar jon(i) terī panihārī. Is dhartī mah(i) terī sikdārī.
44. Ibid., p. 921, lines 14-5 Eh sarīrā meriā Har(i) tum mah(i) jot(i) rakhī tā tū jag mah(i) āiā.
45. Ibid., p. 736, lines 5-6 Sabh(u) jīo(u) piṅḍ(u) dīā tudh(u) āpe tudh(u) āpe kārai lāiā. Jehā tuṅ hukam(u) karah(i) tehe ko karam kamāvai jehā tudh(u) dhur(i) likh(i) pāiā.
46. Ibid., p. 12, lines 6-9 Bhaī prāpat mānukh dehurīā. Gobiṅd milaṇ kī ih terī barīā.
47. Ibid., p. 1075, lines 14-5 Lakh chaorāsī jon(i) sabāī. Mānas kao(u) Prabh dīī vadhiāī. Is 'Pauṛī' te jo nar(u) chūkai so āi jāi dukh(u) pāidā.
48. Ibid., p. 913, lines 7-19 Is(u) pāni te jin(i) tu ghariā.... Apvitr pvitr jin(i) tū kariā. Sagal jon(i) mah(i) tū sir(i) dhariā. Ab tū sījh bhāvai nahī sījhai. Kāraj(u) savarai *man* prabh(u) dhiāījai. ...Nānak dās saṅg pāthar tariā.
49. Ibid., p. 176, lines 10-16 Kaī janam bhae kīṭ pataṅgā...Kah(u) Nānak Har(i) Har(i) guṇ gāi.
50. Ibid., p. 466, lines 14-5 Hao(u) vich(i) māiā hao(u) vich(i) chhāiā. Haumai kar(i) kar(i) jaṅt upāiā.
51. Ibid., p. 946, lines 2-3 Kit(u) kit(u) bidh(i) jag(u) upjai purakhā kit(u) kit(u) dukh(i) binas(i) jāī. Haumai vich(i) jag(u) upjai purakhā nām(i) visriai dukh(u) pāī.
52. Ibid., p. 491, line 16 Paṅch bhū ātmā vas(i) karah(i) tā tīrath karah(i) nivās(u).
53. Ibid., p. 1128, lines 18-9 Mūl(u) moh(u) kar(i) kartai jagat(u) upāiā. Mamtā lāi bharam(i) bho(u)lāiā.
54. Ibid., p. 509, lines 9-10 Saṅjog(u) vijog(u) upāion(u) srisṭ(i) kā mūl(u) rachāiā. Hukmī srisṭ(i) sājīan(u) jotī jot(i) milāiā.
55. Ibid., p. 1258, lines 12-3 Haumai vaḍā rog(u) hai sir(i) māre jamkāl(i).
56. Ibid., p. 1263, lines 4-5 Dhan pir kā ik hī saṅg(i) vāsā vich(i) haumai bhīt(i) krārī. Gur(i) pūrai haumai bhīt(i) torī jan Nānak mile banvārī.

57. Ibid., p. 466, line 14 Hao(u) vich(i) māiā hao(u) vich(i) chhāiā.
58. Ibid., p. 415, line 10 ‘Ih(u) *man*(u) ‘Karmā’ih(u) *man*(u) dharmā. Ih(u) *man*(u) paṅch tat(u) te janamā.
59. Ibid., p. 342, line 5 ‘Ih(u) *man*(u) saktī ih(u) *man*(u) sīu. Ih(u) *man*(u) paṅch tat ko jīu.
60. Ibid., p. 441, line 3 *Man* tūṅ jot(i) sarūp(u) hai āpṇā mūl(u) pachhāṇ(u).
61. Ibid., p. 43, line 3 Prāṇī tū āiā lāhā laiṇ. Lagā kit(u) kuphakṛe sabh mukdī chalī raiṇ(i).
62. Ibid., 1219, lines 15-6 Āio sunan paṛan ko bāṇī. Nām(u) visār(i) lagah(i) an lālach(i) birthā janam(u) prāṇī.
63. Ibid., p. 751, lines 18-19; p. 752, line 1-6 Mānas janam(u) dulaṅbh(u) gurmukh(i) pāiā...Mai dījai nām nivās(u) Har(i) guṇ gāvsī.
64. Ibid., p. 294, line 14 Sabh kai madh(i) alipato rahai.
65. Ibid., p. 464, line 16 Nānak nirbhao(u) nirankār(u) sach(u) ek(u).
66. Ibid., p. 1 Ik o'ankār sat(i)nām(u) kartā purakh(u) nirbhao(u) nirvair(u) akāl mūrat(i) ajūnī saibhaṅ gur prasād(i).
67. Ibid., p. 918, lines 12-5 Agam agochrā terā aṅt(u) nā pāiā...Kahai Nānak tū sadā agaṅm(u) hai terā aṅt(u) nā pāiā.
68. Ibid., p. 103, lines 12-4 Tūṅ merā pitā tūṅhai merā mātā...Tūṅ merā rākhā sabhnī thāī tā bhao(u) kehā kāṛā jīo(u).
69. Ibid., p. 660, lines 1-2 Jīo(u) ḍarat(u) hai āpṇā kai sio(u) karī pukār. Dukh visāraṇ(u) seviā sadā sadā dātār(u). Sāhib(u) merā nīt navā sadā sadā dātār(u).
70. Ibid., p. 2, line 3 Sāchā Sāhib sāch(u) nāi bhākhiā bhāo(u) apār(u).
71. Ibid., p. 263, line 19; p. 264, lines 1-4 Dīn dard dukh bhaṅjanā ghat(i) ghat(i) nāth anāth...Astpadī. Jah māt pitā sut mīt na bhāī. ...Nānak pāvah(u) sūkh ghanere.
72. Ibid., p. 828, lines 3-4 Hamro sahāo(u) sadā sad bhūlan tumro birad(u) patit udharn.
73. Ibid., p. 859, lines 1-2 Har(i) jāṇai sabh(u) kichh(u) jo jīe(i) vartai Prabh(u) ghāliā kisai kā ik(u) til(u) nā gavāī.
74. Ibid., p. 859, lines 18-9 Mere *man* āsā kar(i) Har(i) prītam kī jo terā ghāliā sabh(u) thāi pāī.
75. Ibid., p. 830, lines 1-2 Aṅdhule ṭik nirdhan dhan(u) pāio Prabh Nānak anik gunī.
76. Ibid., p. 4, lines 15-6 Sabh(i) guṇ tere mai nāhī koi. Viṇ(u) guṇ kīte bhagat(i) nā hoi.

77. Ibid., p. 850, lines 6-9 Sabh vaḍiāīā Har(i) nām vich(i) Har(i) gurmukh(i) dhiāīai.
78. Ibid., p. 284, lines 11-14 Nām ke dhāre sagle jaṅt... Nānak chao(u)the pad mah(i) so jan(u) gat(i) pāe.
79. Ibid., p. 560, line 12 Haumai nāvai nāl(i) virodh(u) hai dui nā vasah(i) ik ṭhāi.
80. Ibid., p. 940, lines 13-4 Hukam(u) bismād(u) hukam(i) pachhāṇai jīa jugat(i) sach(u) jāṇai soī.
81. Ibid., p. 466, lines 18-9 Haumai dīragh rog(u) hai dāru bhī is(u) māhe. Kirpā kare je āpṇī tā gur kā sabad(u) kamāh(i).
82. Ibid., p. 235, lines 10-1 Jab ih(u) *man* mah(i) karat gumānā. Tab ih(u) bāvar(u) phirat bigānā. Jab ih(u) hūā sagal kī rīnā. Ta te ramaīā ghat(i) ghat(i) chīnā.
83. Ibid., p. 1258, lines 4-6 Trai guṇ sabhā dhāt hai nā Har(i) bhagat(i) nā bhāi. Gat(i) mukat(i) kade nā hovaī haumai karam kamāh(i).
84. Ibid., p. 611, line 19 Ek(u) pitā ekas ke ham bārik tū merā gur hāī.
85. Ibid., p. 213, lines 11-4 Trisnā birle hī kī bujhī he. Koṭ(i) jore lākh krore *man*(u) nā hore. Parai parai hī kao(u) lujhī he.
86. Ibid., p. 510, lines 9-10 Māyā hoī nāganī jagat(i) rahī laptāi. Is kī sevā jo kare tis hī kao(u) phir(i) khāi... Nānak seī ubre ji sach(i) rahe liv lāi.
87. Ibid., p. 466, lines 9-10 Utam(u) eh(u) bichār hai jin(i) sache sio(u) chit(u) lāiā. Jagjīvan dāta pāiā.
88. Ibid., p. 1423, 12-4 Jinā ik *man*(i) ik chit(i) dhiāiā sat(i)gur sao(u) chit(u) lāi...Nānak gur pūre te pāiā sahaj(i) miliā Prabh(u) āi.
89. Dasam Graṅth, Akāl Ustat, 17. 87 Jaise ek āg te kanukā kot āg uṭhe niāre niāre hui kai pher(i) āg mai milāh(i)ṅge.
90. Ibid., p. 468, line 7 Kūṛ(i) kūṛai neh(u) lagā visriā Kartār(u).
91. Ibid., p. 302, line 16 Kūṛiār pichhāhā saṭian(i) kūṛ(u) hirdai kapaṭ(u) mahā dukh(u) pāvai.
92. Ibid., p. 3, line 14 Je ko būjhai hovai sachiār(u).
93. Ibid., p. 11, lines 14-5 Tūṅ kartā Sachiār(u) maiṅḍā sā(ṅ)ī.
94. Ibid., p. 289, lines 2-5 Gun gāvat terī utras(i) mail(u). Binas(i) jāi haumai bikh(u) phail(u)...Kahu Nānak jā kai mastak(i) lekh(u).
95. Ibid., p. 561, lines 16-8 Hao(u) jāi puchhā sohāg suhāgan(i) tusī kio(u) pāiṛā Prabh(u) merā...Āpnaṛā Prabh(u) nadar(i) kar(i) dekhai Nānak jot(i) jotī ralīai.
96. Ibid., p. 616, lines 16-7 Binsai moh(u) merā ar(u) terā binsai apnī dhārī...Jit(u) hao(u)mai garab(u) nivārī.

97. Ibid., p. 1098, lines 14-5 Mai dasih(u) mārag(u) saṅtaho kio Prabhū milāīā. *Man*(u) arpih(u) hao(u)mai tajah(u) it(u) paṅth(i) julāīā.
98. Ibid., p. 1423, lines 3-4 Hukmo seve hukam(u) arādhe hukme smai samāi. Sadā suhāgaṇ(i) ji hukmai bujhai sat(i)gur(u) sevai liv lāe.
99. Ibid., p. 22, lines 14-6 Jis(u) Satgur(u) Purakh(u) na bhetio su bhao(u)jal(i) pachai pachāi...Nānak te mukh ujle dhun(i) upjai sabad(u) nīsāṇ(u).
100. Ibid., p. 7, lines 9-11 Jor(u) na jīvaṇ(i) maraṇ(i) nah jor(u)...Jor(u) na jugatī chhutai saṅsār(u). Jis(u) hath(i) jor(u) kar(i) vekhai soi. Nānak utam(u) nīch(u) na koi.
101. Ibid., p. 736, lines 3-4 Kītā karṇā sarab rajāī kichh(u) kīchai je kar(i) sakīai. Āpṇā kitā kichhu na hovai jio(u) Har(i) bhāvai tivai rakhīai.
102. Ibid., p. 661, lines 10-2 Nadar(i) kare ta simriā jāi...Har(i) sio chit(u) lāgai phir(i) kāl(u) na khāi.
103. Ibid., p. 466, lines 7-10 Bin(u) sat(i)gur kinai na pāio bin(u) sat(i)gur kinai na pāiā...Jagjīvan dātā pāiā.
104. Ibid., p. 1242, lines 16-8 Nām(u) Niraṅjan alakh(u) hai kio lakhiā jāī...Nānak nadrī karam(u) hoi gur milīai bhāī.
105. Ibid., pp. 242-3, line 19 Kar joṛ(i) sā dhan karai bintī raiṇ din(u) ras(i) bhiṅnīā.
106. Ibid., p. 764, lines 7-8 Sāī vast(u) prāpat(i) hoī jis(u) setī *man*(u) lāiā. Andin(u) mel(u) bhaiā *man*(u) mānia ghar maṅdar sohāe.
107. Ibid., p. 921, lines 2-5 Jaisi agan(i) udar mah(i) taisī bāhar(i) māiā. Māiā agan(i) sabh iko jehī kartai khel(u) rachāiā...Kahe Nānak(u) gur parsādī jinā liv lāgī tinī viche māiā pāiā.
108. Ibid., p. 12, Line 3 Tit(u) sarvaṛai bhaīle nivāsā pāṇī pāvak(u) tinah(i) kīā. Paṅkaj(u) moh pag(u) nahī chālai ham dekhā tah dubīale.
109. Ibid., p. 20, line 15-6 Har(i) jap(i) jīare chhuṭīai gurmukh(i) chīnai āp(u).
110. Ibid., p. 224, line 10 Ātam(u) chīnai su tat(u) bīchāre.
111. Ibid., p. 230, line 14 Āp(u) n chīnai bājī hārī.
112. Ibid., p. 684, line 17-8 Jan Nānak bin(u) āpā chīnai miṭai n bhram kī kāī.
113. Ibid., p. 23, lines 15-7 Ih(u) tan(u) dhartī bīj(u) karamā karo salil āpāo(u) sāriṅgpāṇī...Pit suto sagal kālatr mātā tere hoh(i) nā aṅt(i) sakhāiā.
114. Ibid., p. 1153, line 9 Ātam mah(i) rām(u) rām mah(i) ātam(u) chīnas(i) gur bichārā.

115. Ibid., p. 1256, line 18 Kaṅchan kāiā nirmal haṅs(u). Jis(u) mah(i) nām(u) niraṅjan aṅs(u).
116. Ibid., p. 350, line 5 Sāhib merā eko hai. Eko hai bhāī eko hai.
117. Ibid., p. 45, line 11 Pārbrahm(u) Prabh(u) ek(u) hai dūjā nāhī koi. Jīo Piṅḍ sabh(u) tis kā jo tis(u) bhāvai su hoi.
118. Ibid., p. 1044, lines 18-9 Eko ek(u) vartai sabh(u) soī. Gurmukh(i) virlā būjhai koī. Eko rav(i) rahiā sabh aṅtar(i) tis(u) bin(u) avar(u) n koī he.
119. Dasam Graṅth, Tav Prasād Swai-i-ye: p. 19, 15:85 Kartā karīm soī rāzak rahīm Ohī dūsro n bhed koī Bbhūl bhram mānbo. Ek hī kī sev sabhhī ko gurdev ek ek hī sarūp sabhai ekai jot jānbo.
120. Dasam Graṅth, Tav Prasād Swai-i-ye: p. 19, 16. 86 Dehurā masīt soī pūjā aur namāz Ohī mānas sabhai ek bhae anek kau bhramāo hai. Ekai nain ekai kān ekai deh ekai bān khāk bād ātash au āb ko ralāu hai. Allah abhekh soī Purān au Kurān oī ek hī sarūp sabhai ek hī banāu hai.
121. Ibid., p. 1056, line 6. Sabhnā sir(i) tū eko Sāhib(u) sabde Nām(u) salāhā he.
122. Ibid., p. 287, line 17 Nirgun(u) āp(i) sargun(u) bhī ohī. Kalā dhār(i) jin(i) saglī mohī.
123. Niraṅkār ākār āp(i) nirgun sargun ek. Ekah(i) ek bakhānano Nānak ek anek. p. 250, lines 12-3.
124. Ibid., p. 1061, lines 16-7 O'aṅkār sabh sirisṭ(i) upāī. Sabh(u) khel(u) tamāsā terī vaḍiāī.
125. Ibid., p. 1066, line 1 Niraṅkār ākār(u) upāiā. Māiā moh(u) hukam(i) baṇāiā.
126. Ibid., p. 71, line 17 Tudh(u) saṅsār(u) upāiā. Sire sir(i) dhaṅdhe lāiā. Vekhah(i) kitā āpnā kar(i) kudrat(i) pāsā dhāl(i) jiu.
127. Ibid., p. 639, line 17 Jīa jaṅt pratipāldā bhāi nit nit kardā sār.
128. Ibid., p. 276, line 12 Kaī jugat(i) kīno bisthār. Kaī bār pasrio pāsār. Sadā sadā ik(u) ekaṅkār. Kaī koṭ(i) kīne bah(u) bhāt(i). Prabh te hoi Prabh māh(i) smāt(i). Tā kā aṅt(u) n jānai koi. Āpe āp(i) Nānak Prabh(u) soi.
129. Ibid., p. 387, lines 2-3 Opat(i) parlau khin mah(i) kartā. Āp(i) alepā nirgun(u) rahtā.
130. Ibid., p. 1354, lines 13-5 Ghaṭaṅt rūp(ṅ) ghaṭaṅt dīp(ṅ) ghaṭaṅt rav(i) sasīar nakhyatr gagan(ṅ). Ghaṭaṅt basudhā gir(i) tar sikhaṅḍ(ṅ). Ghaṭaṅt lalnā sut bhrāt hit(ṅ). Ghaṭaṅt kanik mānik māiā svrūp(ṅ). Nah ghaṭaṅt keval Gopāl achut. Asthir(ṅ) Nānak Sādh jan.
131. Ibid. p. 1310, line 8 O'aṅkār(i) eiko rav(i) rahiā sabh(u) ekas māh(i) samāvaigo.

132. Ibid., p. 929, line 18 O'aṅkār(i) Brahmā utpat(i).
133. Ibid., p. 1061, line 16 O'aṅkār(i) sabh srist(i) upāī.
134. Ibid., p. 1003, line 17 O' aṅkār(i) utpātī. Kīā dinas(u) sabh rātī.
135. Vārāṅ Bhāī Gurdās: 4-1-1 Oṅkār(i) akār(u) kar(i) pavaṇ(u) pāṇī baisṅtar dhārai.
136. Ibid., p. 464, lines 12-6 Bhai vich(i) pavan(u) vahai sadvāu. Bhai vich(i) chalah(i) lakh dariāu...Bhai vich(i) sūraj(u) bhai vich(i) chaṅd(u)...Bhai vich(i) āvah(i) jāvah(i) pūr.
137. Ibid., p. 943, line 1 Pavan araṅbh(u) sat(i)gur mat(i) velā. Sabad(u) gurū surat(i) dhun(i) chelā.
138. Ibid., p. 916, lines 13-4 *Man* bach kram(i) rām nām(u) chitārī.
139. Ibid., p. 1083, lines 10-1 Kirtam nām kathe tere jihbā. Sat(i)nam(u) terā parā pūrbalā'.
140. Ibid., p. 117, line 8 Utpat(i) parlau sabadai hovai. Sabde hi phir(i) Opat(i) hovai.
141. Ibid., p. 813, lines 7-8 Karaṇ kāraṇ samrath Prabh Har(i) agam apār.
142. Pūr(i) shete it(i) purushah. (Skt).
143. Purī purī basaṅtā sā Purkhā. (Skt).
144. Ibid., p. 907, lines 9-10 Ek mah(i) sarab sarab mah(i) ekā sat(i)gur(i) dekh(i) dikhāī.
145. Ibid., p. 684, 15-8 Kāhe re ban khojan jāī. Sarab nivāsī sadā alepā tohī saṅg(i) samāī. Rahāo. Puhap jio bās(u) basat(u) hai mukar māh(i) jaisae chhāī. Taise hī base niraṅtar(i) ghaṭ hī khojah(u) bhāī. Bāhar(i) bhītar(i) eko jānah(u) ih(u) Gur giān(u) batāī. Jan Nānak bin(u) āpā chīnai miṭai n bhram kī kāī.
146. Ibid., p. 5, lines 9-10 Vaḍā Sāhib ūchā thāu. Ūche ūpar(i) ūchā Nāu. Evaḍ ūchā hovai koi. Tis(u) ūche kau jāṇai soi.
147. Ibid., p. 464, line 16 Bhai vich(i) pavaṇ(u) vahai sadvāu. Bhai vich(i) chalah(i) lakh darīāu... Sagliā bhau likhiā sir(i) lekh(u). Nānak nirbhau niraṅkār sach(u) ek(u).
148. Ibid., p. 464, line 15. Nānak nirbhau niraṅkār(u) hor(i) kete rām ravāl.
149. Ibid., p. 999, line 2 Sagal samagrī ḍarah(i) biāpī bin(u) ḍar karṇaihārā.
150. Ibid., p. 592, line 2 Tis kā sarīk(u) ko nahī nā ko kanṭak(u) vairāī.
151. Ibid., p. 1038, lines 15-6 Tū akāl purakh(u) nāhi sir(i) kālā. Tū purakh(u) alekh agaṅm nirālā.
152. Dasam Graṅth, Akal Ustat(i). T(v) prasad(i). Chaupai. p. 11, 9. Kāl rahit an akāl sarūpā.
153. Ibid., p. 1136, line 4 So mukh(u) jal-u jit(u) kahah(i) ṭhākur(u) jonī.

154. Ibid., p. 6, line 13 Soī soī sadā sach(u) Sāhib(u) sāchā sāchī nāī. Hai bhi hosī jāi n jāsī rachnā jin(i) rachāī.
155. Ibid., p. 339, lines 1-2 Sankaṭ(i) nahī parai jon(i) nahī āvai Nām(u) Niraṅjan jā ko re. Kabīr ko suāmī aiso ṭhākur(u) jā kai māī n bāpo re.
156. Ibid., p. 2, lines 6-7 Thāpiā n jāi kītā n hoi. Āpe āp(i) niraṅjan(u) soi.
157. Ibid., p. 771, line 12 Merā Prabh(u) sāchā sad hī sāchā jin(i) āpe āp(u) upāiā.
158. Ibid., p. 59, lines 7-8 Bhāī re Gur bin(u) giān(u) n hoi. Pūchhah(u) Brahme Nārdai Bed Biāsai koi.
159. Ibid., p. 469, lines 16-7 Kuṅbhe badhā jal(u) rahai jal bin(u) kuṅbh(u) n hoi. Giān ka badhā *man*(u) rahai gur bin(u) giān(u) n hoi.
160. Ibid., p. 1066, lines 18-9 Har(i) jīu sabh mah(i) rahiā samāī. Gurparsādī pāiā jāī.
161. Ibid., p. 1078, lines 7-8 Ekaṅkār Sat(i)gur te pāīai hau bal(i) bal(i) gur darsāiṇā.
162. Ibid., p. 599, lines 5-6 Tat(u) Niraṅjan jot(i) sabāī sohaṅ bhed(u) n koī jīu. Apraṅpār Pārbrahm Parmesar(u) Nānak gur(u) miliā soī jīu.
163. Ibid., p. 759, lines 8-9 Sat(i)gur(u) merā sadā sadā nā āvai nā jāi. Oh(u) abināsī purakh(u) hai sabh mah(i) rahiā samāi.
164. Ibid., p. 802, lines 10-1 Saphal mūrat(i) gurdeu suāmī sarab kalā bharpūre. Nānak gur(u) Pārbrahm Parmesar(u) sadā sadā hajūre.
165. Ibid., p. 879, line 9 Gur(u) ād(i) purakh(u) Har(i) pāiā.
166. Ibid., p. 797, line 8 Āpe sat(i)gur(u) sabad(u) hai āpe. Nānak ākh(i) suṇāe āpe.
167. Dasam Graṅth, Kabyo bāch benati, Chaupaī: p. 1387, 385 Ad(i) aṅt(i) ekai avtāra. Soī gurū samjhīh(u) hamāra.
168. Ibid., p. 466, lines 7-8 Bin(u) Sat(i)gur kinai n pāio bin(u) Sat(i)gur kinai n pāiā. Sat(i)gur vich(i) āp(u) rakhion(u) kar(i) pargaṭ(u) ākh(i) suṇāiā.
169. Ibid., p. 286, line 12 Sat(i) Purakh(u) jin(i) jāniā sat(i)gur tis kā nāu. Tis kai saṅg(i) sikh(u) udhrai Nānak Har(i) gun gāu.
170. Ibid., p. 168, line 11 Jis(u) miliai *man*(i) hoi anaṅd(u) so sat(i)gur kahīai.
171. Ibid., p. 304, lines 4-5 So sat(i)gur(u) ji sach(u) dhia(i)da sach(u) sacha sat(i)gur(u) ike. Soī sat(i)gur(u) purakh(u) hai jin(i) paṅje dūt kītai vas(i) chhike.
172. Ibid., p. 287, line 2 So sat(i)gur(u) jis(u) ridai Har(i) nāu.
173. Ibid., p. 864, lines 12-3 Gur kī mahimā kathan(u) n jāi. Pārbrahm gur(u) rahiā samāi.

174. Ibid., 1421, line 11 Vāh(u) vāh(u) sat(i)gur(u) purakh(u) hai jin(i) sach(u) jātā soi. Jit(i) miliai tikh utrai tan(u) *man* sītal hoi.
175. Ibid., p. 722, lines 16-7 Jaisī mai āvai khasam kī bāṇī taisaṛā karī giān ve Lālo.
176. Ibid., p. 292, lines 5-6 Besumār athāh aganat atolai. Jio bulāvah(u) tiu Nānak dās bolai.
177. Ibid., p. 982, line 10-1 Bāṇī gurū gurū hai baṇī vich bāṇī aṅm(i)rat sāre.
178. Ibid., p. 628, line 2 Dhur kī bāṇī āī. Tin(i) saglī chiṅt miṭāī.
179. Ibid., p. 763, lines 6-7 Hau āpah(u) bol(i) n jāṇdā mai kahiā sabh(u) hukmāu jīu.
180. Ibid., p. 734, lines 18-9 Dāsan(i) dās kahai jan(u) Nānak jehā tūṅ krāih(i) tehā hau karī vakhiān(u).
181. Ibid., p. 508, line 1 Jio bolāvah(i) tiu bolah suāmī kudrat(i) kavan hamārī.
182. Ibid., p. 308, lines 5-6 Sat(i)gur kī bāṇī sat(i) sat(i) kar(i) jānah(u) gursikhah(u) Har(i) kartā āp(i) muhah(u) kaḍhāe.
183. Ibid., p. 935, line 12 Bāṇī birlau bichārsī je ko gurmukh(i) hoi. Ih bāṇī mahā purakh kī nij ghar(i) vāsā hoi.
184. Ibid., p. 594, line 11 Sat(i)gur no sabh(u) ko vekhdā jetā jagat(u) saṅsār(u). Ḍiṭhai mukat(i) n hovai jichar(u) sabad(i) n kare vīchār(u).
185. Ibid., p. 50, lines 14-5 Lakh chaurāsīh bhrmatiā dulabh janam(u) pāioi. Nānak Nām(u) samāl(i) tūṅ so din(u) neṛā āioi.
186. Ibid., p. 64, lines 16-7 Bhāī re bhagat(i) hīṇ kāhe jag(i) āiā. Pūre gur kī sev n kīnī birthā janam(u) gavāiā.
187. Ibid., p. 133, line 7 Kirat(i) karam ke vīchhuṛe kar(i) kirpā melah(u) rām(u).
188. Ibid., p. 631, lines 17-8 Phirat phirat bahute jug hārio mānas deh(u) lahī. Nānak kahat milan kī barīā simrat kahā nahī.
189. Ibid. p. 1414, line 3 Sat(i)gurū n sevio sabad(u) n rakhio urdhār(i). Dhrig tinā kā jīviā kit(u) āe saṅsār(i).
190. Ibid., p. 601, line 11 Tū guṇdātā sabad(i) pachhātā guṇ kah(i) guṇī samāṇe.
191. Ibid., p. 561, lines 16-7 Ha-u jāi puchhā sohāg sohāgaṇ(i) tusī kiu pir(u) pāiaṛā Prabh(u) merā. Mai upar(i) nadar(i) karī pir(i) sāchai mai chhodiaṛā merā terā.
192. Ibid., p. 722, lines 11-2 Jāi puchhah(u) sohāgaṇī vāhai kinī bātī sah(u) pāīai. Jo kichh(u) kare so bhalā kar(i) mānīai hikmat(i) hukam(u) chukāīai.

193. Ibid., p. 58, lines 6-7 Ha-u gur pūchha-u āpṇe gur puchh(i) kār kamā-u. Sabad(i) salāhī *man*(i) vasai haumai dukh(u) jal(i) jāu.
194. Ibid., p. 565, lines 10-1 Sabad(u) chīn(i) *man*(u) nirmal(u) hovai tā Har(i) kai gun(i) gāvai. Gurmatī āpai āp(u) pachhāṇai tā nij ghar(i) vāsā pāvai.
195. Ibid., p. 418, lines 13-5 Vaṇj(u) karah(u) makhsūd(u) laih(u) mat pachhotāvah(u). Augaṇ chhodah(u) guṇ karah(u) aise tat(u) parāvah(u).
196. Ibid., p. 921, lines 6-7 Aisā Sat(i)gur(u) je milai tisno sir(u) saupīai vichah(u) āp(u) jāi. Jis dā jīu tis(u) mil(i) rahai Har(i) vasai *man*(i) āi.
197. Ibid., p. 467, lines 11-2 Sat(i)gur miliai sach(u) pāiā jin(h) ke hirdai sach(u) vasāiā.
198. Ibid. 468, line 1 Sat(i)gur bheṭe so sukh(u) pāe. Har(i) kā Nām(u) *man*(i) vasāi.
199. Ibid., p. 468, lines 12-3 Sach(u) tāṅ par(u) jāṇīai jā ātam tīrath(i) kare nivās(u). Sat(i)gur no puchh(i) kai bah(i) rahai kare nivās(u).
200. Ibid., p. 286, lines 18-9 *Man*(u) bechai sat(i)gur kai pās(i). Tis(u) sevak ke kāraj rās(i).
201. Ibid., p. 918, line 5 Tan(u) *man*(u) dhan(u) sabh(u) saup(i) gur kau hukam(i) maṅniai pāīai.
202. Purātan Janam Sākhī: Sākhī No 10.
203. Punjābī Bhākhā te chhaṅdā-baṅdī. Dr Mohan Singh.
204. Vārāṅ Bhāī Gurdās Jī: Vār 1.
205. Ibid., p 717, line 7 Simar(i) suāmī aṅtarjāmī mānukh deh kā ih(u) ūtam phal(u).
206. Hārīt Sim(i)rit(i): A 4; S 40 to 44.
207. Ibid., p. 491, lines 1-2 Rām Rām sabh(u) ko kahai kahiai Rām(u) n hoi. Gur parsādī Rām(u) *man*(i) vasai tā phal(u) pāvai koi.
208. Ibid., p. 1199, lines 13-4 Hirdai kapaṭ(u) nit kapaṭ(u) kamāvah(i) mukhah(u) Har(i) Har(i) suṇāi. Aṅtar(i) lobh(u) mahā gubārā tuh kūṭai dukh khāi.
209. Ibid., p. 732, lines 6-7 Har(i) Har(i) karah(i) nit kapaṭ(u) kamāvah(i) hirdā sudh(u) n hoī.
210. Ibid., p 717, line 7 Simar(i) suāmī aṅtarjāmī mānukh deh kā ih(u) ūtam phal(u).
211. Ibid., p. 262, line 10 Simara-u simar(i) simar(i) sukh(u) pāva-u. Kal(i) kales tan mah(i) miṭāva-u.
212. Ibid., p. 262, line 13 Sukhmanī sukh aṅmrit Prabh Nām(u). Bhagat janā ke *man*(i) bisrām.

213. Ibid. p. 263, line 1 Prabh kā simran(u) sabh te ūchā.
214. Ibid., p. 667, lines 18-9 Jin(i) Har(i) japiā se Har(i) hoi Har(i) miliā kel kelālī.
215. Ibid., p. 670, lines 1-2 Jap(i) *man* sat(i)nām(u) sadā sat(i)nām(u). Halat(i) palat(i) mukh ūjal hoī hai nit dhiāīai Har(i) purakh(u) niraṅjanā.
216. Ibid., p. 265, lines 15-6 Har(i) ke Nām samsar(i) kachh(u) nāh(i). Nānak gurmukh(i) Nām(u) japat gat(i) pāh(i).
217. Ibid., p. 266, lines 14-5 Sagal udam mah(i) udam(u) bhalā. Har(i) kā Nām(u) japah(u) jīa sadā.
218. Ibid., p. 266, lines 16-7 Nirguniār iāniā so Prabh(u) sadā samāl(i). Jin(i) kīā tis(u) chīt(i) rākh(u) Nānak nib-hī nāl(i).
219. Ibid., p. 270, line 2 Prabh jī japat dargah mān(u) pāvah(i). Nānak pat(i) setī ghar(i) jāvah(i).
220. Ibid., p. 283, line 12 Jap(i) jan sadā sadā din(u) raiṇī. Sabh te ūch nirmal ih karṇī.
221. Ibid., p. 284, line 14 Kar(i) kirpā jis(u) āpnai Nām(i) lāe. Nānak chauthe pad mah(i) so jan(u) gat(i) pāe.
222. Ibid., p. 286, lines 4-5 Nām(u) dhan(u) Nāmo rup(u) rang(u). Nāmo sukh(u) Har(i) Nām kā sang(u).
223. Ibid., p. 288, line 2 Sāth(i) n chalai bin(u) bhajan bikhiā saglī chhār(u). Har(i) Har(i) Nām(u) kamāvanā Nānak ih(u) dhan(u) sār(u).
224. Ibid., p. 296, lines 6 and 9-10 Jis(u) *man*(i) basai sunai lāi prīt(i). Tis(u) jan āvai Har(i) Prabh(u) chīt(i). ...Sabh te ūch tā kī sobhā bāṇī. Nānak ih gun(i) Nām(u) sukhmanī.
225. Ibid., p. 779, line 11 Kirpā kījai sā mat(i) dījai āth pahar tudh(u) dhiāī.
226. Ibid., p. 39, lines 7-8 Mal(u) haumai dhotī kivai n utrai je sau tīrath nāi.
227. Ibid., p. 59, lines 4-5 Kathnai kahaṇ(i) n chhuṭīai nā paṛ(i) pustak bhār. Kāiā soch n pāīai bin(u) Har(i) bhagat(i) piār.
228. Ibid., p. 265, line 17 Soch karai dinas(u) ar(u) rāt(i). *Man* kī mail n tan te jāt(i).
229. Ibid., p. 484, lines 16-7 Jal kai majan(i) je gat(i) hovai nit nit meṅduk nāvah(i). Jaise meṅduk taise oi nar phir(i) phir(i) jonī āvah(i).
230. Ibid., p. 1367, lines 6-7 Kabīr Gaṅgā tīr ju ghar(u) karah(i) pīvah(i) nirmal nīr(u). Bin(u) Har(i) bhagat(i) n mukat(i) hoi iu kah(i) rame Kabīr.
231. Ibid., p. 558, line 10 *Man*(i) mailai sabh(u) kichh(u) mailā tan(i) dhotai *man* hachhā n hoi. Ih jagat(u) bharam(i) bhulāiā virlā bujhai koi.
232. Ibid., p. 905, lines 9-10 Aṅtar(i) mail(u) tīrath bharmījai. *Man*(u) nahī sūchā kiā soch karījai.

233. Ibid., p. 904, line 14, Nāvah(i) dhovah(i) pūjah(i) sailā. Bin(u) Har(i) rāte mailo mailā.
234. Ibid., p. 467, lines 17-8 Mon(i) vigūtā. Kiu jāgai Gur bin(u) sūtā.
235. Ibid., p. 642, lines 1-2 Mon(i) bha-iu karpātī rahiu nagan phiriu ban māhī. Taṭ tīrath sabh dhartī bhramio dubidhā chhuṭkai nāhī. *Man* kāmanā tīrath(i) jāi basio sir(i) karvat dharāe. *Man* kī mail(u) n utrai ih bidh(i) je lakh jatan karāī.
236. Ibid., p. 1128, lines 16-7 So mun(i) ji *man* kī dubidhā māre. Dubidhā mār(i) Brahm(u) bīchāre.
237. Ibid., p. 1348, lines 8-9 Bolai nāhī hoi baiṭhā monī. Aṅtar(i) kalap bhvāīai jonī.
238. Ibid., p. 1013, lines 5-6 Mūṅḍ(u) muḍāi jaṭā sikh bādhī mon(i) rahai abhimānā. Manūā ḍolai dah dis dhāvai bin(u) rat ātam giānā.
239. Ibid., p. 140, line 15 Paṛiā mūrakh(u) ākhīai jis(u) lab(u) lobh(u) ahaṅkārā.
240. Ibid., p. 147, lines 5-7 Akhaṇ(u) ākh(i) n rajiā sunaṇ(i) n raje kaṅn. Akhī dekh(i) n rajīā guṇ gāhak ik vaṅn. Bhukhiā bhukh n utrai galī bhukh n jāi. Nānak bhukhā tā rajai jā guṇ kah(i) guṇī samāi.
241. Ibid., p. 213, line 11 Trisnā birle hī kī bujhī he. 1. Rahāu. Koṭ(i) jore lakh krore *man*(u) n hore. Parai parai hī kau lujhī he.
242. Ibid., p. 278, line 19; p. 279, line 1 Sahas khaṭe lakh kau uṭh(i) dhāvai. Tripat(i) n āvai māiā pāchhai pāvai.
243. Ibid., p. 672, lines 3-5 Vaḍe vaḍe rājan ar(u) bhūman tā kī trisan n būjhi. Lapaṭ(i) rahe māiā raṅg māte lochan kachhū n sūjhi. Bikhiā mah(i) kin hī tripat(i) n pāī. Jiu pāvak(u) īdhan(i) nahī dhrāpai bin(u) Har(i) kahā aghāī. Rahāu.
244. Ibid., p. 1287, lines 13-4 Nānak sache Nām bin kisai n lathī bhukh. Rupī bhukh n utrai jāṅ dekhāṅ tāṅ bhukh. Jete ras srir ke tete lagah(i) dukh.
245. Ibid., p. 332, lines 4-5 Har(i) jas(u) sunah(i) n Har(i) gun gāvah(i). Bātan hī asmān(u) girāvah(i). Aise logan siu kiā kahīai. Jo Prabh kīe bhagat(i) te bāhaj tin te sadā ḍarāne rahīe. Rahāo.
246. Ibid., p. 356, lines 14-5 Vidiā vichārī tā parupkārī.
247. Ibid., p. 541, lines 17-8 Sahas siāṇap nah milai merī jiṅduṛīe jan Nānak gurmukh(i) jātā rām.
248. Ibid., p. 641, line 8 Saṅjam sahas siāṇapā piāre ik n chalī nāl(i).
249. Ibid., p. 655, lines 17-9 Kiā paṛīai kiā gunīai. Kiā bed purānā sunīai. Paṛe sune kiā hoī. Jau sahaj n milio soī. Har(i) ka Nām(u) n japas(i) gavārā. Kiā sochah(i) baṅ-bārā.

250. Ibid., p. 918, lines 6-8 E *man* chaṅchalā chat(u)rāī kinai n pāiā. Chat(u)rāī n pāiā kinai tu suṇ(i) maṅn meriā. Eh māiā mohaṇī jin(i) et(u) bharam(i) bhulāiā.

251. Ibid., p. 973, line 19; p. 974, line 1 Paṛīai gunīai Nām(u) sabh(u) sunīai anbha-u bhāu n darsai. Lohā kaṅchan(u) hiran hoi kaise ja-u pārsah(i) n parsai.

252. Ibid., p. 1238, line 6 Mūl(u) mat(i) parvāṇā eho Nānak(u) ākh(i) suṇāe. Karnī upar(i) hoi tapāvas(u) je ko kahai kahā-e.

253. Ibid., p. 1383, lines 4-5 Faridā darīāvai kaṅn(h)ai bagulā baiṭhā kel kare. Kel karede haṅjh no achiṅte bāj pa-e. Bāj pa-e tis(u) rab de kelāṅ visriāṅ. Jo *man*(i) chit(i) n chete san(i) galī rab kīāṅ.

254. Ibid., p. 72, line 2 Satsaṅgat(i) kaisī jāṇīai. Jithe eko Nām(u) vakhāṇīai. Eko Nām(u) hukam(u) hai sat(i)gur(i) dīā bujhāi jīu.

255. Ibid., p. 433, lines 13-4 Dadai dos(u) n deū kisai dos(u) karaṅmā āpṇiā. Jo mai kīā so mai pāiā dos(u) n dījai avar janā.

256. Ibid., p. 464, lines 12-6 Bhai vich(i) pavan(u) vahai sadvāu. Bhai vich(i) chalah(i) lakh dariāu...Bhai vich(i) sūraj(u) bhai vich(i) chaṅd(u)...Bhai vich(i) āvah(i) jāvah(i) pūr.

257. Ibid., p. 510, lines 1-2 Prabh(i) saṅsār(u) upāi kai vas(i) āpṇai kītā.

258. Ibid., p. 465, line 13 Baṅdhan baṅdh(i) bhavāe soi. Pa-i-ai kirat(i) nachai sabh(u) koi.

259. Ibid., p. 510, lines 11-2 Jo dhur(i) likhiā lekh(u) so karam kamāisī.

260. Ibid., p. 662, lines 7-8 Jaisā kare su taisā pāvai. Ap(i) bīj(i) āpe hī khāvai.

261. Ibid., p. 756, line 2 Haumai mailā jag(u) phirai mar(i) jamai vāro vār(u). Pa-i-ai kirat(i) kamāvaṇā koi n meṭaṇhār(u).

262. Ibid., p. 1263, line 4 Dhan pir kā ik hī saṅg(i) vāsā vich(i) haumai bhīt(i) karārī.

263. Ibid., p. 275, lines 10-1 Ustat(i) karah(i) anek jan aṅt(u) n pārāvār. Nānak rachnā Prabh(i) rachi bah(u) bidh(i) anik prakār.

264. Ibid., p. 1172, lines 7-8 Bikh aṅmrit kartār(i) upāe. Saṅsār birakh ka-u dui phal lāe. Āpe kartā kare karāe. Jo tis(u) bhāvai tisai khavāe.

265. Ibid., p. 466, lines 16-9 Haumai ehā jāt(i) hai haumai karam kamāh(i). Haumai eī baṅdhanā phir(i) phir(i) jonī pāh(i). Haumai kithah(u) ūpjai kit(u) saṅjam(i) ih jāi. Haumai eho hukam(u) hai paiai kirat(i) phirāh(i). Haumai dīragh rog(u) hai dārū bhī is(u) māh(i). Kirpā kare je āpṇī tā gur kā sabad(u) kamāh(i). Nānak kahai suṇah(u) janah(u) it(u) saṅjam(i) dukh jāh(i).

266. Ibid., p. 924, lines 9-10 Māiā mad(i) mātā hochhī bātā milaṇ(u) na jāī bharam dhaṛā. Kah(u) Nānak gur bin(u) nāhī sūjhai Har(i) sājan(u) sabh kai nikaṭ(i) khaṛā.
267. Ibid., p. 717, lines 5-6 Māī māiā chhal(u). Triṇ kī agan(i) megh kī chhāiā gobid bhajan bin(u) haṛ ka jal(u).
268. Ibid., p. 921, line 4 Eh māiā jit(u) Har(i) visrai moh(u) upjai bhāu dūjā lāiā.
269. Ibid., p. 1153, line 18 Dubidhā rog(u) su adhik vaḍerā māiā kā muhtāj(u) bhaiā.
270. Ibid., p. 941, lines 14-5 Nāme rāte haumai jāi. Nām(i) rate sach(i) rahe samāi...Nām(i) rate pāvah(i) mokh duār(u).
271. Ibid., p. 1327, line 11 Nāi terai tarṇā nāi pat(i) pūj.
272. Ibid., p. 654, line 5 But pūj(i) pūj(i) Hindū mūe tūrk mūe sir(u) ‘nāī.
273. Ibid., p. 958, lines 1-2 Viṇ(u) tudh(u) hor(u) ji maṅgaṇā sir(i) dukhā kai dukh. Deh(i) Nām(u) saṅtokhīā utrai *man* kī bhukh.
274. Ibid., p. 1018, lines 11-2 Māgnā māgan(u) nīkā Har(i) jas(u) gur te māgnā.
275. Ibid., p. 135, lines 2-3 Jin(h)hī chākhiā prem ras(u) se tripat(i) rahe aghāi.
276. Dasam Graṅth, T(v) Prasād(i) Svaye, p. 14, 9:29 Sāch(u) kahoṅ sun leh(u) sabhai jin prem kīu tin hī Prabh pāiu.
277. Ibid., p. 298, line 10 Jāchak jan(u) jāchai Prabh dān(u). Kar(i) kirpā devah(u) Har(i) Nām(u).
278. Ibid., p. 1428, line 12 Jagat(u) bhikhārī phirat(u) hai sabh ko dātā Rām(u). Kah(u) Nānak *man* simar(u) tih pūran hovah(i) kām.
279. Ibid., p. 676, lines 10-1 Dāt(i) piārī visriā dātārā. Jāṇai nāhi maraṇ(u) vichārā.
280. Ibid., p. 952, line 5 Har(i) kā maṅdar(u) ākhīai kāiā koṭ(u) gaṛ(u).
281. Ibid., p. 754, lines 9-10 Kāiā aṅdar(i) āpe vasai alakh(u) n lakhiā jāī. Manmukh(u) mugadh(u) būjhai nāhī bāhar(i) bhālaṇ(i) jāī.
282. Ibid. p. 827, line 6 Mai nāhī Prabh sabh(u) kichh(u) terā. Īghai nirgun ūghai sargun kel karat bich(i) suāmī merā.
283. Ibid., p. 694, line 18 Tero kīā tujhah(i) kiā arpau Nām(u) terā tuhī chavar ḍholāre.
284. Ibid., p. 1375, lines 9-10 Kabīr merā mujh mah(i) kichh(u) nahī jo kichh(u) hai so terā. Terā tujh ka-u sa-u-pate kia lāgai merā.
285. Ibid., p. 143, lines 10-3 Gorī setī tuṭai bhatār(u). Putī ganḍh(u) pavai sansār(i). Nānak(u) ākhai eh(u) bichār(u). Siphtī ganḍh(u) pavai darbār(i).

286. Ibid., p. 150, lines 13-4 Dīkhiā ākh(i) bujhāiā siphtī sach(i) same-u. Tin ka-u kiā updesīai jin gur(u) Nānak de-u.
287. Ibid., p. 255, lines 6-7 Jhālāghe uṭh(i) Nām(u) jap(i) nis(i) bāsur ārādh(i). Kāṛ(h)ā tujhai n biāpa-ī Nānak miṭai upādh(i).
288. Ibid., p. 305, lines 16-7 Gur sat(i)gur kā jo sikh(u) akhāe su bhalke uṭh(i) Har(i) Nām(u) dhiāvai.
289. Ibid., p. 743, lines 5-6 Prātāhkal(i) Har(i) Nām(u) uchārī. Īt ūt kī oṭ savārī.
290. Ibid., p. 1383, lines 15-6 Farīdā pichhal rāt(i) n jāg(i)oh(i) jīvadṛo mu(i)oh(i). Je tai rab(u) visāriā t rab(i) n visar(i)oh(i).
291. Ibid., p. 1384, lines 1-2 Pahilai paharai phulṛā phal(u) bhī pachhā rāt(i). Jo jāgaṅn(i) lāhaṅn(i) se sāī kaṅno dāt(i).
292. Ibid., p. 734, lines 5-6 Har(i) dhan(u) aṅmrit velai vatai kā bījiā bhagat khāi kharach(i) rahe nikhuṭai nāhī. Halat(i) palat(i) Har(i) dhanai kī bhagtā ka-u milī vaḍiāī.
293. Ibid., p. 1329, lines 9-10 Siphat(i) saram kā kapṛā māṅgau Har(i) guṇ Nānak ravat(u) rahai.
294. Ibid., p. 631, lines 17-8 Phirat phirat bahute jug hārio mānas deh lahī. Nānak kahat milan kī barīā simrat kahā nahī.
295. Dasam Graṅth, Akāl Purakh bāch. Chaupaī: p. 57, 32 Jo ham ko Parmesar uchrah(i). Te sabh narak kuṅḍ mah(i) parah(i).
296. Ibid., p. 1160, lines 5-6 Jo pāthar ka-u kahte dev. Tā kī birthā hovai sev. Jo pāthar kī pāṅ-ī pāi. Tis kī ghāl ajāṅ-ī jāi.
297. Ibid., p. 525, lines 7-8 Ekai pāthar kījai bhāu. Dūjai pāthar dharīai pāu. Je oh(u) deu t oh(u) bhī devā. Kah(i) Nāmdeu ham Har(i) kī sevā.
298. Ibid., p. 479, lines 7-8 Pātī torai mālinī pātī pātī jīu. Jis pāhan ka-u pātī torai so pāhan nirjīu. Pākhān gaḍh(i) kai mūrat(i) kin(h)ī de kai chhātī pāu. Je eh mūrat(i) sāchī hai ta-u gaṛ(h)aṇhāre khāu.
299. Ibid., p. 223, line 19 Jaisā sevai taiso hoi.
300. Ibid., p. 755, line 8 E *man* jaisā sevah(i) taisā hovah(i) tehe karam kamāi.
301. Ibid., p. 592, line 2 Purakhai sevah(i) se Purakh hovah(i) jinni haumai sabad(i) jalāi.
302. Ibid., p. 879, lines 6-8 So sevak(i) Rām piārī. Jo gur sabadī bichārī. So Har(i) jan(u) Har(i) Prabh bhāvai. Ah(i)nis bhagat(i) kare din(u) rātī lāj chhod(i) Har(i) ke gun gāvai.
303. Ibid., p. 300, lines 3-4 Har(i) kī ṭahal kamāvaṇī japīai Prabh kā Nām(u). Gur pūre te pāiā Nānak sukh(u) bisrām(u).

304. Ibid., p. 1298, line 14 Kīrtat(i) Prabh kī gāu merī rasnā. Anik bār kar(i) baṅdan saṅtan ūhāṅ charan Gobiṅd jī ke basnā.
305. Ibid., p. 11, lines 6-7 Jin seviā jin seviā merā Har(i) jī te Har(i) Har(i) rup(i) samāsī.
306. Ibid., p. 135, lines 2-3 Jin(h)ī chākhiā prem ras(u) se tripat(i) rahe aghā(i). Āp(u) tiag(i) bintī karah(i) leh(u) Prabhu lar(i) lāi.
307. Ibid., p. 142, lines 10-2 So jīviā jis(u) *man*(i) vasiā soi. Nānak avar(u) n jīvai koi. Je jīvai pat(i) lathī jāi. Sabh(u) harām(u) jetā kichh(u) khāi. Rāj(i) raṅg(u) māl(i) raṅg(u). Raṅg(i) ratā nachai naṅg(u). Nānak ṭhagiā muṭhā jāi. Viṇ(u) nāvai pat(i) gaiā gavāi.
308. Ibid., p. 142, lines 12-4 Kiā khādhai kiā paidhai hoi. Jā *man*(i) nāhī sachā soi. Kiā mevā kiā ghiu guṛ(u) miṭha kiā maidā kiā mās(u). Kiā kapaṛ kiā sej sukhālī kījah(i) bhog bilās. Kiā laskar kiā neb khavāsī āvai mahalī vās(u). Nānak sache Nām(u) viṇ(u) sabhe tol viṇās(u).
309. Ibid., p. 890, line 7 Tīrath nāi n utras(i) mail(u). Karam dharam sabh(i) haumai phail(u).
310. Ibid., p. 473, lines 15-6 Aṅdrah(u) jhūṭhe paij bāhar(i) dunīā aṅdar(i) phail(u). Aṭhsaṭh(i) tīrath je nāvah(i) utrai nāhī mail(u).
311. Ibid., p. 1428, line 18 Tīrath barat ar(u) dān kar(i) *man* mai dharai gumān(u). Nānak nihphal jāt tih jiu kuṅchar isnān.
312. Ibid., p. 687, line 14 Tīrath(i) nāvaṇ jāu tīrath(u) Nām(u) hai. Tīrath(u) sabad bīchār(u) aṅtar(i) giān hai.
313. Ibid., p. 961, lines 15-6 Jisno terī nadar(i) n lekhā puchhīai.
314. Ibid., p. 590, lines 2-3 Jāla-u aisī rīt(i) jit(u) mai piārā vīsarai. Nānak sāī bhalī prīt(i) jit(u) sāhib setī pat(i) rahai.
315. Ibid., p. 722, line 9 Karaṇ palāh kare bahutere sā dhan mahal(u) n pāvai. Viṇ(u) karmā kichh(u) pāīai nāhī je bahuterā dhāvai.
316. Ibid., p. 1128, lines 17-8 Is(u) *man* ka-u koī khojah(u) bhāī. *Man* khojat Nām(u) na-u nidh(i) pāī.
317. Ibid., p. 695, lines 15-6 Jo brahmaṅḍe soī piṅḍe jo khojai so pāvai. Pīpā praṇvai param tat(u) hai sat(i)gur(u) hoi lakhāvai.
318. Ibid., p. 1324, lines 10-1 Aṅtar(i) rattan javehar māṇak gur kirpā te līјai.
319. Ibid., p. 880, lines 16-7 Ratan(u) javehar(u) lāl(u) Har(i) nāmā gur(i) kāḍh(i) talī dikhlāiā. Bhāghīṇ manmukh(i) nahī līā triṇ olai lākh(u) chhupāiā.

320. Ibid., p. 1027, lines 16-7 Gur(u) sarvar(u) ham haṅs piāre. Sāgar mah(i) rattan lāl bah(u) sāre. Motī māṇak hīrā Har(i) jas(u) gāvat *man*(u) tan(u) bhīnā re.
321. Ibid., p. 360, line 16 Je ko nāu̱ dhrāe vaḍā sād kare *man*(i) bhāṇe. Khasmai nadrī kīṛā `āvai jete chugai dāṇe.
322. Ibid., p. 6, line 19 Ap(i) nāth(u) nāthī sabh jā kī ridh(i) sidh(i) avrā sād.
323. Ibid., p. 83, lines 10-1 Dātī sāhib saṅdīā kiā chalai tis(u) nāl(i). Ik jagaṅde nā lahaṅn(i) iknā sutiā de(i) uthāl(i).
324. Ibid., p. 158, line 11 Karam(u) hovai satsaṅg(i) milāi. Har(i) guṇ gāvai bais(i) su thāe.
325. Ibid., p. 231, lines 7-8 Pūrai sat(i)gur(i) sabad(u) suṇāiā. Trai guṇ meṭe chauthai chit(u) lāiā. Nānak haumai mār(i) Brahm milāiā.
326. Ibid., p. 232, line 12 Trai guṇ meṭe nirmal(u) hoi. Sahaje sāch(i) milai Prabh(u) soi.
327. Ibid., p. 414, lines 3-4 Ūtam saṅgat(i) ūtam(u) hovai. Guṇ kau dhāvai avguṇ dhovai.
328. Ibid., p. 474, line 19 Nānak hukam(u) n chalaī nāl(i) khasam chalai ardās(i).
329. Ibid., p. 593, line 18 Ridh(i) sidh(i) sabh(u) moh(u) hai 'Nām(u)' n vasai *man*(i) ā(i).
330. Ibid., p. 908, lines 3-4 Āpe mel(i) la-e guṇdātā haumai trisnā mārī. Trai guṇ meṭe chauthai vartai ehā bhagat(i) nirārī.
331. Ibid., p. 1365, lines 12-3 Kabīr jis(u) marne te jag(u) ḍarai merai *man*(i) ānaṅd(u). Marne hī te pāīai puran(u) parmānaṅd(u).
332. Ibid., p. 465, lines 2-3 Nadar(i) karah(i) je āpṇī tā nadrī sat(i)gur(u) pāiā. Eh(u) jīu bahute janam bhraṅmiā tā sat(i)gur(i) sabad(u) suṇāiā. Sat(i)gur jevaḍ(u) dātā ko nahī sabh(i) suṇ(i)ah(u) lok sabāiā. Sat(i)gur(i) miliai sach(u) pāiā jin(h)i vichah(u) āp(u) gavāiā. Jin(i) sacho sach(u) bujhāiā.
333. Ik(i) dāte ik(i) maṅgate Nām(u) terā parvāṇ(u). Nānak jin(h)ī suṇ(i) kai maṅniā ha-u tinā viṭah(u) kurbāṇ(u). p. 790, lines 4-5.
334. Ibid., p. 1239, line 12 Nām(u) niraṅjan nirmalā suṇīai sukh(u) hoī. Suṇ(i) suṇ(i) *maṅn*(i) vasāīai būjhai jan(u) koī.
335. Ibid., p. 1240, lines 1-3 Nāi suṇiai *man*(u) rahsīai Nāme sāṅt(i) āī. Nāi suṇiai *man*(u) triptīai sabh dukh gavāī. Nāi suṇiai Nāu ūpjai Nāme vadiāī.
336. Ibid., p. 329, lines 3-6 Oi ju dīsah(i) aṅbar(i) tāre. Kin(i) oi chīte chītanhāre. Kah(u) re paṅdit aṅbar(u) kā siu lāgā. Būjhai būjhanhār sabhāgā.

Sūraj chaṅd(u) karah(i) ujiārā. Sabh mah(i) pasriā brahm pasārā. Kah(u) Kabīr jānaigā soi. Hirdai Rām(u) mukh(i) Rāmai hoi.

337. Ibid., p. 466, lines 4-5 Nānak bhagtā bhukh sālāhaṇ(u) sach(u) Nām(u) ādhar(u). Sadā anaṅd(i) rahah(i) din(u) rātī guṇvaṅtiā pā chhār(u).

338. Ibid., p. 918, lines 18-9; p. 919., line 1 Bhagtā kī chāl nirālī. Chālā nirālī bhagtāh kerī bikham mārag(i) chalṇā. Lab(u) lobh(u) ahaṅkār(u) taj(i) trisnā bahut(u) nāhī bolṇā. Khaṅn(i)ah(u) tikhī vālah(u) nikī et(u) mārag(i) jāṇā. Gur parsādī jinī āp(u) tajjiā Har(i) vāsnā samāṇī. Kahai Nānak(u) chāl bhagtā jugah(u) jug(u) nirālī.

339. Ibid., p. 816, line 16 Bhagat arādhah(i) ek raṅg(i) Gobiṅd Gupāl.

340. Ibid., p. 950, lines 15-6 Nānak Har(i) kā bhāna maṅne so bhagat hoi vin(u) maṅne kach(u) nikach(u).

341. Ibid., p. 1384, lines 16-7 Mat(i) hodī hoi iāṇā. Tāṇ hode hoi nitāṇā. Aṇhode āp(u) vaṅḍāe. Ko aisā bhagat(u) sadā-e.

342. Ibid., p. 574, lines 11-2 Soī bhagat(u) dukh(u) sukh(u) samat(u) kar(i) jāṇai Har(i) Har(i) Nām(i) Har(i) rātā.

343. Ibid., p. 473, line 16 Aṭhsaṭh(i) tīraths je nāvah(i) utrai nāhī mail(u).

344. Ibid., p. 1008, lines 18-9 Bed purān kathe suṇe hāre munī anekā. Aṭhsaṭh(i) tīrath bahu ghaṇā bhram(i) thākke bhekhā. Sācho Sāhib(u) nirmalo *man*(i) mānai ekā.

345. Ibid., p. 1013, line 2 Aṭhsaṭh(i) tīrath bharam(i) vigūchah(i) kiu mal(u) dhopai pāpai.

346. Ibid., p. 1167, line 9 Bin(u) dekhe upjai nāhī āsā. Jo dīsai so hoi bināsā.

347. Ibid., p. 524, lines 3-4 Koṭ(i) bighan tis(u) lāgte jis no visrai nāu. Nānak andin(u) bilpate jiu suṅnai ghar(i) kāu.

348. Ibid., p. Jinī suṇ(i) ke maṅniā tinā nij ghar(i) vās(u).

349. Ibid., p. 645, line 18 Jinī suṇ(i) ke maṅniā Har(i) Nāu tinā hau vārīā.

350. Ibid., p. 669, line 15 Gāviā suṇiā tin kā Har(i) thāi pāvai jin sat(i)gur kī āgiā sat(i) sat(i) kar mānī.

351. Ibid., p. 285, line 10 Jā kai ridai bis(v)ās Prabh āiā. Tat(u) giān(u) tis(u) *man*(i) pragṭāiā.

352. Ibid., 1241, lines 6-7 Nāi maṅn(i)ai sukh(u) upjai nāme gat(i) hoī.

353. Ibid., 1242, lines 3-4 Nāi maṅn(i)ai durmat(i) gaī mat(i) pargaṭī āiā. Nāu maṅn(i)ai haumai gaī sabh(i) rog gavāiā.

354. Ibid., 1242, lines 4-5 Nāi maṅn(i)ai Nām(u) ūpjai sahje sukh(u) pāiā. Nāi maṅn(i)ai sāṅt(i) upjai Har(i) maṅn(i) vasāiā.

355. Ibid., 1242, line 10 Nāi maṅn(i)ai surat(i) upjai nāme mat(i) hoī.

356. Ibid., p. 441, line 3 *Man* tūṅ jot(i) sarūp(u) hai āpṇā mul(u) pachhāṇ(u).

357. Ibid., p. 1020, lines 4-5 Jam(i) jam(i) marai marai phir(i) jaṅmai. Bahut(u) sajāi pa-i-ā des(i) laṅmai. Jin(i) kītā tisai n jāṇī aṅdhā tā dukh(u) sahai prāṇīā.
358. Ibid., p. 325, line 19; p. 326, line 1-3 Asthāvar jaṅgam kīt pataṅgā. Anik janam kīe bahu raṅgā. Aise ghar ham bahut(u) basāe. Jab ham Rām garabh hoi āe. Jogi jatī tapī brahmchārī. Kab-hū rājā chhatrpat(i) kab-hū bhekhārī. Sākat marah(i) saṅt sabh(i) jīvah(i). Rām rasāin(u) rasnā pīvah(i). Kah(u) Kabīr Prabh kirpā kījai. Hār(i) pare ab purā dījai.
359. Ibid., p. 666, lines 11-2 Bahute pher pae kirpan ka-u ab kichh(u) kirpā kījai. Hoh(u) da-i-āl darsan(u) deh(u) apunā aisī bakhas karījai.
360. Ibid., p. 1104, lines 11-2 Kahai Kabīr(u) sunah(u) re saṅtah(u) khet hī karah(u) niberā. Ab kī bār bakhas(i) baṅde ka-u bahur(i) n bha-u-jal pherā.
361. Ibid., p. 622, line 3-4 Bighan bināsan sabh(i) dukh nāsan sat(i)gur(i) Nām(u) driṛāiā. Khoe pāp bhae sabh(i) pāvan jan Nānak sukh(i) ghar(i) āiā.
362. Ibid., p. 1426, lines 3-4 Paṅthā prem n jāṇ-ī bhūlī phirai gavār(i). Nānak Har(i) bisrāi kai pa-u-de narak(i) aṅdh(y)ār.
363. Ibid., p. 496, lines 3-4 Jis(u) simrat sabh(i) kilvikh nāsah(i) pitrī hoi udhāro. So Har(i) Har(i) tum(h) sad hī jāpah(u) jā kā aṅt(u) n pāro.
364. Ibid., p. Bikār pāthar galah(i) bādhe niṅd poṭ sirāi. Mahā sāgar(u) samud(u) laṅghanā pār(i) n parnā jāi.
365. Ibid., p. 9, lines 10-1 Vaḍe mere sāhibā gahir gaṅbhīrā guṇī gahīrā. Koi n jāṇai terā ketā kevaḍ(u) chīrā.
366. Ibid., p. 9, lines 10-1 Vaḍe mere sāhibā gahir gaṅbhīrā guṇī gahīrā. Koi n jāṇai terā ketā kevaḍ(u) chīrā.
367. Ibid., p. 797, lines 3-4 Atul(u) kiu toliā jai. Dūjā hoi t sojhī pāi. Tis te dūjā nāhī koi. Tis dī kīmat(i) kikū hoi.
368. Ibid., p. 1279, lines 5-6 Aṅbar(u) dharat(i) vichhoṛ(i) chaṅdoā tāṇiā. Viṇ(u) thaṅm(h)ā gagan(u) rahāi sabad(u) nisāṇiā.
369. Ibid., p. 1361, line 13 Hāth(i) klaṅm agaṅm mastak(i) lekhāvatī.
370. Ibid., p. 470, line 15 Aprādhī dūṇā nivai jo haṅtā mirgāh(i). Sīs nivāiai kiā thīai jā ridai kusudhe jāh(i).
371. Ibid., p. 642, lines 3-4 Pūjā archā baṅdan ḍaṅḍa-ut khaṭ(u) karmā rat(u) rahtā. Ha-u ha-u karat baṅdhan mah(i) pariā nah milīai ih jugtā.
372. Ibid., p. 614, lines 11-2 Ghāl n bhānai aṅtar bidh(i) jānai tā kī kar(i) *man* sevā. Kar(i) pūjā hom(i) ih(u) manūā akāl mūrat(i) gurdevā.
373. Ibid., p. 1304, lines 8-9 Anik pūjā mai bah(u) bidh(i) khojī sā pūjā ji Har(i) bhāvās(i). Maṭī kī ih putrī jorī kiā eh karam kamās(i).

374. Ibid., p. 1070, line 19 Viche grih sadā rahai udāsī jiu kamal(u) rahai vich(i) pāṇī he.
375. Ibid., p. 522, lines 10-1 Nānak Sat(i)gur(i) bheṭiai pūrī hovai jugat(i). Hasaṅdiā khelaṅdiā painaṅdiā khavaṅdiā viche hovai mukat(i).
376. Ibid., p. 74, lines 8-13 Ha-u gosāī dā pahilvānṛā. Mai gur mil(i) uch dumālaṛā. Sabh hoī chhiṅjh ikaṭhīā dy(u) baiṭhā vekhai āp(i) jīu. Vāṭ vajan(i) ṭaṅmak bherīā. Mal lathe laide pherīā. Nihate paṅj(i) juān mai gur thāpī ditī kaṅḍ(i) jīu. Sabh ikathe hoi āiā. Ghar(i) jāsan(i) vāṭ vaṭāiā. Gurmukh(i) lāhā lai ga-e manmukh chale mūl(u) gavāi jīu. P. 74, lines 8-13.
377. Ibid., p. 16, lines 13-4 Bābā hor(u) khāṇā khusī khuār(u). Jit(u) khādhai tan(u) pīṛīai *man* mah(i) chalah(i) vikār.
378. Ibid., p. 1375, lines 5-6 Kabīr jīa jo mārah(i) jor(u) kar(i) kahte hah(i) ju halāl(u). Daphtar(u) da-ī jab kāḍh(i) hai hoigā ka-un(u) havāl(u).
379. Ibid., p. 1375, lines 6-7 Kabīr jor(u) kīā so julam(u) hai le-i jabāb(u) khudāi.[2] Daphtar(i) lekhā nīksai mār muhai muh(i) khāi.
380. Ibid., p. 1103, lines 2-3 Jīa badhah(u) su dharam(u) kar(i) thāpah(u) adharam(u) kahah(u) kat bhāī. Āpas ka-u munivar kar(i) thāpah(u) kā ka-u kahah(u) kasāī.
381. Ibid., p. 483, line 5 Rojā dhare manāvai Alah(u) suādat(i) jīa saṅghārai. Āpā dekh(i) avar nahī dekhai kāhe ka-u jakh mārai.
382. Ibid., p. 1350, lines 5-6 Bed kateb kahah(u) mat jhūṭhe jhūṭhā jo n bichārai. Ja-u sabh mah(i) ek(u) khudāi kahat ha-u ta-u kiu murgī mārai.
383. Ibid., p. 745, lines 2-3 Prem bichhohā karat kasāī. Nirdai jaṅt(u) tis(u) da-i-ā n pāī.
384. Ibid., p. 322, line 10 Dūkh(u) n de-i kisai jīa pat(i) siu ghar(i) jāva-u.
385. Ibid., p. 50, line 6 Jiu kūkar(u) harkāiā dhāvai dah dis jāi. Lobhī jaṅt(u) n jāṇa-ī bhakh(u) abhakh(u) sabh khāi.
386. Ibid., p. 755, lines 8-9 Niṅdā bhalī kisai kī nāhī manmukh mugadh karaṅn(i). Muh kāle tin niṅdakā narke ghor(i) pavaṅn(i).
387. Ibid., p. 380, lines 17-8 Janam janam kī mal(u) dhovai parāī āpnā kītā pāvai. Ihā sukh(u) nahī dargah ḍhoī jam pur(i) jāi pachāvai.
388. Ibid., 261, line 14 Drisṭmān akhar hai jetā. Nānak Pārbrahm nirlepā.
389. Ibid. p. 922, line 6 Eh(u) vis(u) saṅsār(u) tum dekhde eh(u) Har(i) kā rūp(u) hai, Har(i) rūp(u) nadri āiā.
390. Ibid., p. 293, lines 18-9 So aṅtar(i) so bāhar(i) anaṅt. Ghaṭ(i) ghaṭ(i) biāp(i) rahiā bhagvaṅt.

391. Ibid., p. 267, line 19; p. 268, line 1 Bair birodh kām krodh moh. Jhūṭh bikār mahā lobh dhroh. Iāhū jugat(i) bihāne kaī janam. Nānak rākh(i) leh(u) āpan kar(i) karam.
392. Ibid., p. 651, lines 1-3 Janam janam kī is *man* ka-u mal lāgī kālā hoā siāh(u). Khaṅnlī dhotī ujlī n hovaī je sa-u dhovan(i) pāh(u). Gur parsādī jīvat(u) marai ulṭī hovai mat(i) badlāh(u). Nānak mail n laga-ī nā phir(i) jonī pāh(u).
393. Ibid., p. 1004, lines 1-2 Ha-u ha-u karam kamāṇe. Tete baṅdh galāṇe. Merī merī dhārī. Ohā pair(i) lohārī.
394. Ibid., p. 595, lines 12-3 Nānak a-u-guṇ jetṛe tete galī jaṅjīr. Je guṇ hon(i) t kaṭīan(i) se bhāī se vīr. Agai gae n maṅnīan(i) mār(i) kaḍhah(u) vepīr.
395. Ibid., p. 110, line 13 Gurmukh(i) hovai soī būjhai guṇ kah(i) guṇī samāvaṇiā.
396. Ibid., p. 592, line 2 Purakhai sevah(i) se purakh hovah(i) jinī haumai sabad(i) jalāī.
397. Ibid., p. 220, lines 13-4 Nar achet pāp te ḍar re. Dīn da-i-āl sagal bhai bhaṅjan saran(i) tāh(i) tum par(u) re.
398. Ibid., p. 135, lines 5-6 Katik(i) karam kamāvaṇe dos(u) n kāhū jog(u). Parmesar te bhuliāṅ viāpan(i) sabhe rog(u). Vemukh hoe Rām te lagan(i) janam vijog.
399. Ibid., p. 473, line 12 Kitā āpo āpṇā āpe hī lekhā saṅḍhīai. P. 473, line 12.
400. Ibid., p. 470, line 19 Maṅdā chaṅgā āpṇā āpe hī kītā pāvṇā.
401. Ibid., p. 468, line 15 Phal(u) tevaho pāīai jevehī kār kamāīai.
402. Ibid., p. 1245, lines 5-6 Aklī sāhib(u) sevīai aklī pāīai mān(u). Aklī paṛ(i) kai bujhīai aklī kīchai dān(u). Nānak ākhai rāh(u) eh(u) hor(i) galāṅ saitān.
403. Ibid., p. 466, lines 1-2 Satīā *man*(i) saṅtokh(u) upjai deṇai kai vīchār(i). De de maṅgah(i) sahsā guṇā sobh kare saṅsār.
404. Ibid., p. 1245, line 19 Ghāl(i) khāi kichh(u) hathah(u) de-i. Nānak rāh(u) pachhāṇah(i) sei.
405. Ibid., p. 117, line 8 utpat(i) parla-u sabde hovai. Sabdai hi phir(i) upat(i) hovai.
406. Ibid., p. 509, lines 2-4 Āpnā āp(u) upāion(u) tadah(u) hor(u) n koī. Matā masurat(i) āp(i) kare jo kare su hoī. Tadah(u) ākās n pātāl hai nā trai loī. Tadah(u) āpe āp(i) niraṅkār(u) hai n opat(i) hoī. Jiu tis bhāvai tivai kare tis(u) bin(u) avar(u) n koī.

407. Ibid., p. 442, lines 1-2 Sache mere sāhibā sachī terī vaḍiāī. Tūṅ pārbrahm beaṅt(u) suāmī terī kudrat(i) kahaṇ(u) n jāī.
408. Ibid., p. 789, lines 13-4 Dui dīve cha-u-dah haṭnāle. Jete jīa tete vaṇjāre.
409. Ibid., p. 9, lines 10-1Vaḍe mere sāhibā gah(i)r gaṅbhīrā guṇī gahīrā. Koi n jāṇai terā ketā kevaḍ(u) chīrā.
410. Ibid., p. 284, lines 5-6 Jā kī līlā kī mit(i) nāh(i). Sagal dev hāre avgāh(i). Pitā kā janam(u) ki jānai pūt(u). Sagal paroī apunai sūt(i).
411. Ibid., p. 284, line 4 Dhiāi dhiāi bhagtah sukh(u) pāiā. Nānak tis(u) purakh kā kinai aṅt(u) n pāiā.
412. Ibid., p. 262, line 12 Kinkā ek(u) jis(u) jīa basāvai. Tā kī mahimā ganī n āvai.
413. Ibid. p. 1368, lines 15-6 Kabīr sāt samuṅdah(i) mas(u) kar-u kalam kar-u banrāi. Basudā kāgad j-u kar-u Har(i) jas(u) likhan(u) n jāi.
414. Ibid., p. 797, lines 3-4 Atul(u) kiu toliā jāi. Dūjā hoi t sojhi pāi. Tis te dūjā nāhī koi. Tis dī kīmat(i) kīkū hoi.
415. Ibid., p. 294, line 17 Tā kī gat(i) mit(i) kahī n jāi. Dūsar hoi t sojhī pāi.
416. Ibid., p. 25, line 6 Tū darīāu dānā binā mai machhalī kaise aṅt lahā.
417. Ibid., p. 894, lines 4-5 Mahimā n jānah(i) bed. Brahme nahī jānah(i) bhed. Avtār n jānah(i) aṅt(u). Parmesar(u) parbrahm beaṅt. Apnī gat(i) āp(i) jānai. Sun(i) sun(i) avar vakhānī.
418. Ibid., p. 1218, line 17 Anbolat merī birthā jānī apnā Nām(u) japāiā.
419. Ibid., p. 624, lines 18-9 Har(i) aṅtarjānī sabh bidh(i) jāṇai tā kis(u) pah(i) ākh(i) suṇāīai.
420. Ibid., p. 863, lines 11-2 Bīo pūchh(i) n maslat(i) dharai. Jo kichh(u) karai su apah(i) karai.
421. Ibid., p. 9, line 9 Suṇ(i) vaḍā ākhai sabh(u) koi. Kevaḍ vaḍā ḍīthā hoi.
422. Ibid., p. 724, lines 6-7 Tū kāhe ḍolah(i) prāṇīā tudh(u) rākhaigā Sirjaṇhār(u). Jin(i) paidāis(i) tu kīā soī de-i ādhār(u).
423. Vārāṅ, Bhāī Gurdās Jī, p. 606, 35-08-06 Nā tis(u) bhāre parbatāṅ asmān khahāṅde. Nā tis(u) bhāre koṭ gaṛ(h) ghar bār disāṅde. Nā tis(u) bhāre sāirāṅ nad vāh vahaṅde. Nā tis(u) bhāre taruvaraṅ phal suphal phalaṅde. Nā tis(u) bhāre jīa jaṅt aṇgaṇat phiraṅde. Bhāre bhuīṅ akirtghaṇ maṅdī hū maṅde. Ed. 2010.
424. Vārāṅ, Bhāī Gurdās Jī, p. 606, 35-09-06 Mad vich(i) ridhā pāi kai kute dā mās(u). Dhariā māṇas khoprī tis(u) maṅdī vās(u). Ratū bhariā kapṛā kar(i) kajaṇ(u) tās(u). Dhak(i) lai chalī chūhṛī kar(i) bhog bilās(u). Ākh(i)

suṇāe puchhiā lāhe visvās(u). Nadrī pavai akirtghaṇ(u) mat(u) hoi viṇās(u). Ed. 2010.

425. SGGS, p. 469, lines 9-10 Dukh(u) dārū sukh(u) rog(u) bha-i-ā jā sukh(u) tām(i) n hoī. Tūṅ kartā karṇā mai nāhī jā ha-u karī n hoī.

426. Ibid., p. 958, lines 12-3 Siphat(i) salāhaṇ(u) bhagat(i) virle ditīan(u). Sa-u-pe jis(u) bhaṅḍār phir(i) puchh n lītīan(u).

427. Ibid., p. 604, lines 2-3 Dātai dāt(i) rakhī hath(i) apṇai jis(u) bhāvai tis(u) de-ī. Nānak Nām(i) rate sukh(u) pāiā dargah jāpah(i) se-ī.

428. Ibid., p. 9, lines 9-10 Kīmat(i) pāi n kahiā jāi. Kahaṇai vāle tere rahe samāi.

429. Ibid., p. 294, line 4 Mol(i) nā pāīai guṇah amol.

430. Ibid., p. 921, lines 5-6 Har(i) āp(i) amulak(u) hai mul(i) n pāiā jāi. Mul(i) n pāiā jāi kisai viṭah(u) rahe lok vil-lāi.

431. Ibid., p. 293, lines 6-7 Sach(u) vāpār(u) karah(u) vāpārī. Dargah nib-hai khep tumārī.

432. Ibid., p. 749, line 3 Janam maraṇ duhahū mah(i) nāhī jan parupkārī āe. Jīa dān(u) de bhagtī lāin(i) Har(i) siu lain(i) milāe.

433. Ibid., p. 186, lines 2-3 Khāvah(i) kharchah(i) ral(i) mil(i) bhāi. Toṭ(i) n āvai vadhado jāī.

434. Ibid., p. 13, lines 17-8 Jā ka-u āe soī bihājhah(u) Har(i) gur te manah(i) baserā.

435. Ibid., p. 289, line 1 Āp(i) japah(u) avrā Nām(u) japāvah(u).

436. Ibid., p. 110, lines 12-3 Merā Prabh(u) nirmal(u) agam apārā. Bin(u) takṛī tolai saṅsārā.

437. Ibid., p. 629, line 16 Jis no bakhas(i) laih(i) mere piāre so jas(u) terā gāvai.

438. Ibid., p. 9, lines 13-4 Tudh(u) viṇ(u) sidhī kinai n pāīā. Karam(i) milai nāhī ṭhāk(i) rahāīā.

439. Ibid., p. 877, lines 3-4 Jit(u) dar(i) vasah(i) kavan(u) dar(u) kahīai darā bhītar(i) dar(u) kavan lahai. Jis(u) dar kāraṇ(i) phirā udāsī so dar(u) koī āi kahai.

440. Ibid., p. 296, line 11 Jal(i) thal(i) mahial(i) pūriā Suāmī Sirjanhār(u). Anik bhāṅt(i) hoi pasriā Nānak ekaṅkār(u).

441. Ibid., p. 83, line 19 Kudrat(i) kar(i) kai vasiā soi.

442. Ibid., p. 570, lines 6-7 Khoṭe khare sabh(i) parkhīan(i) tit(u) sache kai darbārā Rām. Khoṭe dargah suṭīan(i) ūbhe karan(i) pukārā Rām.

443. Ibid., p. 474, line 19 Nānak hukam(u) n chala-ī nāl(i) khasam chalai ardās(i).

444. Ibid., p. 642, lines 4-5 Jog Sidh āsaṇ chaurāsih ey bhī kar(i) kar(i) rahiā. Vaḍī ārjā phir(i) phir(i) janamai Har(i) siu saṅg(u) n gahiā.
445. Ibid., p. 558, lines 11-5 Sidhā ke āsaṇ je sikhai indrī vas(i) kar(i) kamāi. *Man* kī mail n utrai haumai mail(u) n jāi.
446. Ibid, p. 650, lines 6-8 Bin(u) nāvai painaṇ(u) khāṇ(u) sabh(u) bād(i) hai dhig(u) sidhī dhig(u) karmāt(i). Sā sidh(i) sā karmāt(i) hai achiṅt(u) kare jis(u) dāt(i). Nānak gurmukh(i) Har(i) Nām(u) *man*(i) vasai ehā sidh(i) ehā karmāt(i).
447. Ibid., p. 14, lines 11-3 Sidh(u) hovā sidh(i) lāī ridh(i) ākhā āu. Gupat(u) pargaṭ(u) hoi baisā lok(u) rākhai bhāu. Mat(u) dekh(i) bhūlā visrai terā chit(i) n āvai nāu.
448. Ibid., p. 522, lines 10-1 Nānak Sat(i)gur(i) bheṭ(i)ai pūrī hovai jugat(i). Hasaṅdiā khelaṅdiā painaṅdiā khavaṅdiā vichai hovai mukat(i).
449. Ibid., p. 522, line 15 Udam(u) karediā jīu tūṅ kamāvadiā sukh bhuṅch(u). Dhiā(i)d(i)a tūṅ Prabh(u) mil(u) Nānak utri chiṅt.
450. Ibid., p. 465, lines 14-5 Nachaṇ(u) kudaṇ(u) *man* kā chāu. Nānak jin(h) *man*(i) bhau tin(h)ā *man*(i) bhāu.
451. Ibid., p. 1245, line 19 Ghāl(i) khāi kichh(u) hathah(u) de-i. Nānak rāh(u) pachhāṇah(i) sei.
452. Ibid., p. 283, lines 13-4 Jā kai *man*(i) Gur kī partit(i). Tis(u) jan āvai Har(i) Prabh(u) chīt(i).
453. Ibid., p. 1105, lines 16-7 Āpas ka-u diragh(u) kar(i) jānai auran ka-u lag māt. Mansā bāchā karmanā mai dekhe dojak jāt.
454. Ibid., p. 946, lines 13-4 Nāme hī te sabh(u) pargaṭ(u) hovai Nāme sojhī pāī.
455. Ibid., p. 273, line 2 Brahm giānī kā bhojan giān.
456. Ibid., p. 917, line 10 Sāch(u) nām(u) ādhār(u) merā jin(i) bhukhā sabh(i) gavāīā.
457. Ibid., p. 684, line 4 Tripat(i) bhaī sach(u) bhojan(u) khāiā. *Man*(i) tan(i) rasnā Nām(u) dhiāiā.
458. Ibid., p. 653, lines 12-3 Nak(i) nath khasam hath kirat(u) dhake de. Jahā dāṇe tahāṅ khāṇe Nānakā sach(u) he.
459. Ibid., p. 11, line 18 Jiā jaṅt sabh(i) terā khel(u). Vijog(i) mil(i) vichhuṛiā saṅjogi mel(u).
460. Ibid., p. 509, lines 9-10 Saṅjog(u) vijog(u) upā(i)on(u) s(i)risṭ(i) kā mūl(u) rachāiā. Hukmī s(i)risṭ(i) sājīan(u) jotī jot(i) milāiā.
461. Ibid., p. 700, lines 2-3 Māt pitā banitā sut baṅdhap isṭ mīt ar(u) bhāī. Pūrab janam ke mile saṅjogī aṅtah ko n sahāī.

462. Ibid., p. 294, lines 13-4 Āvan jān(u) ik(u) khel(u) banāiā. Āgiākārī kīnī māiā.
463. Ibid., p. 1066, lines 1-2 Niraṅkār(i) ākār(u) upāiā. Māiā moh(u) hukam(i) baṇāiā. Āpe khel kare sabh(i) kartā suṇ(i) sāchā *man*(i) vasāidā.
464. Ibid., p. 10, lines 9-10 Kāhe re *man* chitvah(i) udam jā āhar(i) Har(i) jīu pariā. Sail pathar mah(i) jaṅt upāe tā kā rijak āgai kar(i) dhariā.
465. Ibid., p. 130, lines 18-9 Pahilo de taiṅ rijak(u) samāhā. Pichho de taiṅ jaṅt(u) upāhā. Tudh(u) jevaḍ(u) dātā avar(u) n suāmī lavai n koī lāvaṇiā.
466. Ibid., p. 893, line 16 toṭ(i) n āvai akhuṭ bhaṅḍār.
467. Ibid., p. 284, line 16 Sat(i) karam(u) jā kī rachnā sat(i). Mūl(u) sat(i) sat(i) utpat(i).
468. Ibid., p. 284, line 19 Āp(i) sat(i) kīā sabh(u) sat(i).
469. Ibid., p. 85, lines 1-2 Galī asī chaṅgīā āchārī burīāh(u). Manah(u) kasudhā kālīā bāhar(i) chiṭvīāh.
470. Ibid., p. 263, line 3 Prabh kai simran(i) *man* kī mal jāi.
471. Ibid., p. 941, lines 5-6 Gurmukh(i) rom(i) rom(i) Har(i) dhiāvai. Nānak gurmukh(i) sach(i) samāvai.
472. Ibid., p. 1375-6, lines 18-9 and 1 Nāmā māiā mohiā kahai Trilochan mīt. Kāhe chhīpah(u) chhāīlai Rām n lāvah(u) chīt. Nāmā kahe Tilochanā mukh te Rām sanmāl(i). Hāth pāu kar(i) kām sabh chīt Niraṅjan nāl(i).
473. Ibid., p. 972, lines 14-5 Ānīle kāgad(u) kāṭīle gūḍī ākās madhe bharmīale. Paṅch janā siu bāt bata-ūā chīt su ḍorī rakhīale. *Man*(u) Rām Nāmā bedhīale. Jaise kanik kalā chit(u) mānḍīale.
474. Ibid., p. 1373, lines 7-8 Kabīr jih mārag(i) Paṅḍit gae pāchhai parī bahīr. Ik avghaṭ ghāṭī Rām kī tih chaṛ(i) rahio Kabīr.
475. Ibid., p. 276, line 19 Karan karāvan karnai jog(u). Jo tis(u) bhāvai soī hog(u).
476. Ibid., p. 277, lines 6-7 Kah(u) mānukh te kiā hoi āvai. Jo tis(u) bhāvai so karāvai. Is kai hāth(i) hoi tā sabh(u) kichh(u) le-i. Jo tis(u) bhāvai soī kare-i.
477. Ibid., p. 206, lines 8-9 Kāṭh kī putrī kahā karai bapurī khilāvanhāro jānai. Jaisā bhekh(u) karāvai bājīgar(u) oh(u) taiso hī sāj(u) ānai.
478. Ibid., p. 11, lines 1-3 Tūṅ ghaṭ ghaṭ aṅtar(i) sarab niraṅtar(i) jī Har(i) eko purakh samāṇā. Ik(i) dāte ik(i) bhekhārī jī sabh(i) tere choj viḍāṇā. Tūṅ āpe dātā āpe bhugtā jī ha-u tudh(u) bin(u) avar n jāṇā.
479. Ibid., p. 471, lines 18-9 Jaṅmaṇ(u) marṇā hukam(u) hai bhāṇai āvai jāi'.
480. Ibid., p. 685, line 19; p. 1022, line 18 Maraṇ likhāi maṅḍal mah(i) āe'.

481. Ibid., p. 254, lines 10-1 Ghaṇ ghāle sabh divas sās nah baḍhan ghaṭan til(u) sār. Jīvan lorah(i) bharam moh Nānak teū gavār.
482. Ibid., p. 9, lines 12-3 Sabh(i) sat sabh(i) tap sabh(i) chaṅgiāīā. Sidhā purkhā kīā vaḍiāīā. Tudh(u) vin sidhi kinai n paia.
483. Ibid., p. 604, line 2 Dātai dāt(i) rakhī hath(i) apnai jis(u) bhāvai tis(u) de-ī.
484. Ibid., p. 917, line 8 Ghar(i) t terai sabh(u) kichh(u) hai jis(u) deh(i) su pāva-e.
485. Ibid., p. 485, line 4 Sabh(u) gobiṅd(u) hai sabh(u) gobiṅd(u) hai gobiṅd(u) bin(u) nahī koī.
486. Ibid., p. 988, lines 16-7 Sabhai ghaṭ Rām(u) bolai Rāmā bolai. Rām binā ko bolai re.
487. Ibid., p. 1381, lines 17-8 Farīdā khālak khalak mah(i) khalak vasai rab māh(i). Maṅdā kis no ākhīai jā tis bin(u) koī nāh(i).
488. Ibid., p. 1219, lines 15-6 Āio sunan paran ka-u bāṇī. Nām(u) visār(i) lagah(i) an lālach(i) birthā janam(u) prānī.
489. Ibid., 43, line 3 p. Prāṇī tūṅ āiā lāhā laiṇ(i). Lagā kit(u) kuphakaṛe sabh mukdī chalī raiṇ(i).
490. Ibid. p. 463, lines 16-7 Nānak jīa upāi kai likh(i) nāvai dharam(u) bahāliā. Othai sache hī sach(i) nibṛai chuṇ(i) vakh(i) kaḍhe jajmāliā.
491. Ibid., p. 705, lines 9-10 Bīj(u) bovas(i) bhog bhogah(i) kīā apṇā pāva-e.
492. Ibid., p. 488, line 8 Dilah(u) muhabat(i) jin(h) se-ī sachiā. Jin(h) *man*(i) hor(u) mukh(i) hor(u) si kāṅḍhe kachiā.
493. Ibid., p. 62, lines 11-2 Sachah(u) orai sabh(u) ko upar(i) sach(u) āchār(u).
494. Ibid., p. 789, lines 8-9 Nānak badrā māl kā bhītar(i) dhariā āṇ(i). Khoṭe khare parkhīan(i) sāhib kai dībāṇ(i).
495. Ibid., p. 1241, lines 5-6 Hukam(i) chalāe āpṇai karmī vahai kalām.
496. Ibid., p. 720, line 1 Har(i) āpe paṅch tat(u) bisthārā vich(i) dhātū paṅch āp(i) pāvai.
497. Ibid., p. 736, lines 6-7 Paṅch tat(u) kar(i) tudh(u) srisṭ(i) sabh sājī koī chhevā kario je kichh kītā hovai.
498. Ibid., p. 1167, lines 12-3 Phal kāran phūli banrāi. Phal(u) lāgā tab phūl(u) bilāi. Giānai kāran karam abhiās(u). Giān(u) bhaiā tah karamah nās(u).
499. Ibid., p. 331, line 18 Dekho bhāī gyān kī āī āṅdhī. Sabhai uḍānī bhram kī ṭāṭī rahai n māiā bāṅdhī.

500. Ibid., p. 469, line 10 Bal(i)hārī kudrat(i) vasiā. Terā aṅt(u) n jāī lakhiā.
501. Ibid., p. 26, lines 1-2 Vich(i) dunīā sev kamāī-ai. Tā dargah baisaṇ(u) pāī-ai.
502. Ibid., p. 876, lines 12-3 Kab-hū jīaṛā ūbh(i) chaṛat(u) hai kab-hū jāi pa-i-āle. Lobhī jīaṛā thir(u) n rahat(u) hai chāre kuṅḍā bhāle.
503. Ibid., p. 474, line 11 Jo jī(i) hoi so ugvai muh kā kahiā vāu.
504. Ibid., p. 124, lines 13-4 Na-u dar thāke dhāvat(u) rahā-e. Dasvai nij ghar(i) vāsā pā-e. Othai anhad sabad vājah(i) din(u) rātī gurmatī sabad(i) suṇāvaṇiā.
505. Ibid., p. 657, lines 1-4 Jotī jot(i) samānī. Mai gur parsādī jānī. Ratan kamal kothārī. Chamkār bījul tahī. Nerai nāhī dūr(i). Nij ātmai rahiā bharpūr(i). Jah anhat sūr ujyārā. Tah dīpak jalai chhaṅchhārā. Gur parsādī jāniā. Jan(u) Nāmā sahaj samāniā.
506. Ibid., p. 917, line 13 Vāje paṅch sabad tit(u) ghar(i) sabhāgai. Ghar(i) sabhāgai sabad vāje kalā jit(u) ghar(i) dhārīā.
507. Ibid., p. 1154, lines 3-4 Tin(i) kartai ik(u) chalat(u) upāiā. Anhad bāṇī sabad(i) suṇāiā. Manmukh(i) bhūle gurmukh(i) bujhāiā. Kāraṇ(u) kartā kardā āiā.
508. Ibid., p. 1291, lines 1-2 Ghar mah(i) ghar(u) dekhāi de-i so Sat(i)gur(u) purakh(u) sujāṇ(u). Paṅch sabad dhun(i)kār dhun(i) tah bājai sabad(u) nīsāṇ(u).
509. Ibid., p. 197, lines 10-2 Bāhar(i) rākhio ridai samāl(i). Ghar(i) āe Goviṅd(u) lai nāl(i). Har(i) Har(i) Nām(u) saṅtan kai saṅg(i). *Man*(u) tan(u) rātā Rām kai raṅg(i).
510. Ibid., p. 249, lines 17-8 Sun(i) sakhīe merī nīd bhalī mai āpnarā pir(u) miliā.
511. Ibid., p. 816, lines 9-10 Kab dekha-u Prabh(u) āpnā ātam kai rang(i). Jāgan te supnā bhalā basīai Prabh saṅg(i).
512. Ibid., p. 1282, lines 5-6 Bābīhā nā bil-lāi nā tarsāi eh(u) *man*(u) khasam kā hukam(u) maṅn(i). Nānak hukam(i) maṅniai tikh utrai chaṛai chavgal(i) vaṅn(u).
513. Ibid., p. 1368, lines 9-10 Kabīr birah(u) bhuyaṅgam(u) *man*(i) basai *man*(u) n mānai koi. Rām biogī nā jīai jīai t ba-urā hoi.
514. Ibid., p. 471, line 13 Hukam(i) maṅn(i)ai hovai parvāṇ(u) tā khasmai kā mahal pāisī.
515. Ibid., p. 681, line 18 Kaṅṭh(i) lāi avguṇ sabh(i) meṭe da-i-āl purakh bakhsaṅd.

516. Ibid., p. 633-4, lines 19 and 1 Gur kirpā jih nar ka-u kīnī tih ih jugat(i) pachhānī. Nānak līn bha-i-o gobiṅd siu jiu pānī saṅg pānī.

517. Ibid., p. 709, lines 12-3 Mel(i) laih(u) da-i-āl ḍhah(i) pa-e duāriā. Rakh(i) levah(u) dīn da-i-āl bhramat bah(u) hāriā.

518. Ibid., p. 150, lines 17-9 Ḍhāḍhī sachai mahal(i) khasam(i) bulāiā. Sachī siphat(i) sālāh kapṛā pāiā.

519. Ibid., p. 1428, lines 14-5 Jih ghaṭ(i) simran(u) Rām ko so nar(u) muktā jān(u). Tih(i) nar Har(i) aṅtar(u) nahī Nānak sāchī mān(u).

520. Ibid., p. 295, lines 14-5 Suprasaṅn bha-e gurdev. Pūran hoi sevak kī sev. Āl jaṅjāl bikār te rahte. Rām nām sun(i) rasnā kahte. Kar(i) prasād(u) da-iā Prabh(i) dhārī. Nānak nib-hī khep hamārī.

521. Ibid., p. 278, lines 4-5 Jio jal mah(i) jal(u) ai khaṭānā. Tio jotī saṅg(i) jot(i) samānā. Miṭ(i) ga-e gavan pā-e bisrām. Nānak Prabh kai sad kurbān.

522. Ibid., p. 969, lines 17-8 Ab ta-u jai chaḍhe siṅghāsan(i) mile hai sāriṅgpānī. Rām Kabīrā ek bha-e hai koi n sakai pachhānī.

523. Ibid., p. 340, line 4 Bāvan achhar lok trai sabh(u) kachh(u) in hī māh(i). Ey akhar khir(i) jāhige oi akhar in mah(i) nāh(i).

524. Ibid., p. 324, lines 7-8 Biṅd(u) rākh(i) jo tarīai bhāī. Khusrai kiu n param gat(i) pāī.

525. Ibid., p. 906, lines 1-2 Jatan karai biṅd(u) kivai n rahāi. Manuā ḍolai narke pāī.

526. Ibid., p. 474, lines 7-8 Maṅdā mūl(i) n kīcha-ī de laṅmī nadar(i) nihālīai.

527. Ibid., p. 788, line 13 Bhai bin bhagat(i) n hovai Nām(i) n lagai piār(u).

528. Ibid., p. 774, line 3 Nirmal(u) bhau pāiā Har(i) guṇ gāiā Har(i) vekhai Rām(u) hadūre.

529. Ibid., p. 465, lines 14-5 Nānak jin(h) *man*(i) bha-u tin(h) *man*(i) bhāu.

530. Ibid., p. 694, line 12-3 Sādhsaṅgat(i) binā bhāu nahīṅ upjai bhāv bin(u) bhagat(i) nahī hoi terī.

531. Ibid., p. 788, line 13 Bhai bin bhagat(i) n hovai Nām(i) n lagai piār(u). Sat(i)gur(i) miliai bha-u ūpjai bhai bhāi raṅg(u) savār(i).

532. Ibid., p. 1238, lines 18-9 Nānak aṅmrit(u) ek(u) hai dujā aṅmrit(u) nāh(i).

533. Ibid., p. 953, lines 13-5 Nānak ākhai re manā suṇīai sikh sahī. Lekhā rab(u) maṅgnesīā baiṭhā kaḍh(i) vahī. Talbā pa-u-san(i) ākīā bākī jinā rahī. Ajrāīl phrestā hosī āi ta-ī. Āvaṇ(u) jāṇ(u) n sujha-ī bhīṛī galī phahī. Kūṛ nikhuṭe Nānakā oṛak(i) sach(i) rahī.

534. Ibid., p. 621, lines 9-10 Tah sāch niā(i) niberā. Ūhā sam thākur(u) sam cherā. Aṅtarjāmī jānai. Bin(u) bolat āp(i) pachhānai.
535. Ibid., p. 698, lines 1-2 Jin kau kripā karī jagjīvan Har(i) ur(i) dhārio *man* mājhā. Dharam rāi dar(i) kāgad phāre jan Nānak lekhā samjhā.
536. Ibid., p. 1052, lines 14-5 Kirat(u) na koī meṭaṇhārā. Gur kai sabdai mokh duārā. Pūrab(i) likhiā so phal pāiā jin(i) āp(u) mār(i) pachhāta he.
537. Ibid., p. 8, line 2 Tithai ghaṛīai surat(i) mat(i) *man*(i) budh(i). Tithai ghaṛīai surā sidhā kī sudh(i).
538. Ibid., p. 955, lines 3-5 Sāvaṇ(u) rāt(i) ahāṛ(u) dih(u) kām(u) krodh(u) dui khet. Lab vatr darog(u) bīu hālī rāhak(u) het...Nānak lekhai maṅgiai aut(u) jaṇedā jāi.
539. Ibid., p. 791, lines 16-7 Miliai miliā nā milai milai miliā je hoi. Aṅtar ātmai jo milai miliā kahīai soi.
540. Ibid., p. 725, lines 6-7 Jo dil(i) miliā su mil(i) rahiā miliā kahīai re soī. Je bahu terā lochīai bātī mel(u) n hoī.
541. Ibid., p. 753, lines 6-7 Nāmai hī te sabh(u) kichh(u) hoā bin(u) sat(i)gur nām(u) na jāpai.
542. The Name of My Beloved - Verses of the Sikh Gurus. Nikky-Guninder Kaur Singh. HarperCollins Publishers, 77-85 Fulham Palace Road, London W6 8JB.
543. Ibid., p. 566, lines 2-5 Tā mai kahiā kahaṇ(u) jā tujhai kahāiā.

ABOUT THE AUTHOR

Kamaljit S. Ryatt, M.D. (Manc.), F.R.C.P. (Lond.) is a retired Consultant Dermatologist & Hon. Senior Lecturer, Walsall Hospitals NHS Trust, West Birmingham & Sandwell NHS Trust, and University of Birmingham. He studied at Roundhay Grammar School, Leeds, for four years before joining the Medical School at Manchester in 1968. After his initial training posts, he joined Prof. N.R. Rowell, Prof. W.J. Cunliffe, and Dr J.A. Cotterill at the Department of Dermatology, Leeds General Infirmary, as a Lecturer/Hon. Senior Registrar for five years. Thereafter, he joined Professor H.I. Maibach, UCSF, as a Smith & Nephew Foundation Fellow in 1984 for a year before returning to Birmingham, UK, as a Consultant Dermatologist and Hon. Senior Lecturer. He worked as an Accredited Specialist in dermatology from 1985 and retired from the NHS in 2011.

Despite his medical background, he has always had a great interest in metaphysics and comparative religion. The late Piara Singh Sambhi and the numerous visiting scholars to his house, both from India and the UK, the late Dr. W. Owen Cole and Prof. Bakhshish Singh (Leeds), in particular, guided his initial studies in the Sikh faith. Thereafter, both Dr Rajinder Singh Gill (Hayes, London) and Mr Avtar Singh 'Missionary' (Birmingham, UK) played a significant role in his studies and in his deeper understanding of the Srī Gurū Granth Sāhib, the Sikh Holy Scriptures.

SPIRITUAL EVOLUTION

The focus of this book is the following fundamental article of the Sikh faith: In order to create diversity from unity, God created an altered and imperfect expression of a centre of consciousness in all aspects of creation which Gurū Nānak defines as 'Haumai'. Thus, with 'Haumai' as our default and active state, our world view is incongruous with that of universal consciousness or God. Gurū Nānak, the first of the ten Sikh gurūs and founder of Sikhism, posits that, having evolved over countless millennia and enjoying supreme status in the entire creation of sentient life, human beings have a rare and golden opportunity to realign and harmonise with God or universal-consciousness.

Being inextricably linked with creation through His immanent form, God is also the fount of all attributes, values and virtues which allude to the purpose and direction of His Will or God-consciousness. The gap that exists between our imperfect consciousness ('Haumai') and universal or God-consciousness manifests in us as being 'Manmukh' or 'Kuṛiār' (self-centred being). However, Gurū Nānak emphatically states that unprompted and innate expression of God-consciousness is congrous with being a 'Sachiār' or 'Gurmukh' (God-centred being) and for this to be our goal in this life.

In *Spiritual Evolution* the author attempts to elucidate this central tenet at the heart of the Sikh Holy Scriptures: How do we become godlike and shatter this wall of ignorance that stands between us and the all-pervasive eternal Reality within us? ('Kiv sachiārā hoīai kiv kūṛai tuṭai pāl(i)?') and the answer that Gurū Nānak offers is that 'We must learn to live by His Will as His writ' ('Hukam(i) rajāī chalṇā Nānak likhiā nāl(i)'). Our path for this goal is thus perfect realignment and harmony with God-consciousness or God.

Each chapter offers an in depth analysis and explanation, in chronological order, of the 38 segments ('Pauṛīs') which make up the writings of Gurū Nānak's 'Jap(u)' in the Srī Gurū Granth Sāhib (SGGS). Carefully and methodically translating into English the original script written in 'Gurmukhī' and other regional languages and dialects, the author facilitates an understanding and appreciation of the sublime truths of the SGGS for both the reader exploring the Sikh Holy Scriptures for the first time and for the already committed reader seeking to deepen their faith.

REVIEWS

Dr Kamaljit Singh Ryatt is to be thanked for so painstakingly sharing his interpretation of Guru Nanak's significant composition, Jap(u). It is a foundational Sikh text that is basic both to Sikhs' theology and to their devotional lives.

Realising that his readers (as Sikhs and non-Sikhs, scholars, and lay people) will have very different levels of prior linguistic and religious knowledge, Dr Ryatt systematically addresses their various needs, whether for linguistic analysis or for conceptual summaries.

Congratulations to Dr Ryatt for his fine attunement with the Guru's insights and for his meticulous attention to detail throughout. His work is itself an example of Sikhs' principle of *seva* (selfless service) as he demonstrates his tireless commitment to providing greater access to the Guru's timeless teaching and thus to the spiritual evolution of humanity.

Eleanor Nesbitt
Professor Emeritus
Centre for Education Studies
University of Warwick
Coventry CV4 7AL

Dr Ryatt's second book *Spiritual Evolution* is a welcome addition to the body of literature which focusses on the hermeneutics of the Guru Granth Sahib. Ryatt's years of research are clearly demonstrated in the logical and coherent structure of the book which takes the reader from the basics to the more in-depth analysis of Sikh teachings from the Guru Granth Sahib. Thus, *Spiritual Evolution* is suitable for both those beginning an exploration of the Sikh teachings, as well as those readers who wish to explore further perspectives into the relevance and meaning of the key tenets contained within the Guru Granth Sahib. The universality of the Guru Granth Sahib is clearly expressed through practical means by its inclusion of not only the teachings of the Sikh Gurus, but also the teachings of Hindu and Muslim devotees too. Sikh teachings address the balance between human efforts and free will through the concept of the five realms of existence, referred to as the *Panj Khand*, which, as Ryatt highlights, further accentuates the human birth as the golden opportunity through which to reach the goal of Sikhi.

This is for the consciousness to be elevated from the level of that of the *manmukh* (self-orientated) to that of the *gurmukh* (egoless and orientated towards selfless service to others). From an exploration of the human predicament to the goal of the human birth, Ryatt undertakes in-depth analysis by engaging the reader with a well nuanced perspective on the core messages of the Guru Granth Sahib. He explores the Sikh perspective on theories such as cosmology and teleology in a sophisticated manner which allows for critical analysis of Sikh teachings.

I congratulate Dr K S Ryatt on this endeavour which will give rise to scholarly discussions on the depth of meaning one finds in the Guru Granth Sahib.

Dr Opinderjit Kaur Takhar MBE,
Associate Professor of Sikh Studies and Director of the Centre for Sikh and Panjabi Studies, University of Wolverhampton UK.

Dr Kamaljit Ryatt's *Spiritual Evolution* is an invitation to the reader to travel on a journey of scholarship and spirituality through an exploration of Guru Nanak's *Jap-jī*, the thirty-eight stanzas ('*pauṛī*', literally 'steps on a staircase') of which provide the heart of this capacious book. In each case, Dr Ryatt helpfully furnishes the text in Gurmukhi script with a transliteration into Roman characters, then provides copious and illuminating line-by-line notes on the etymology and range of meaning of each item of the vocabulary deployed. With comments often added in from other parts of the Sikh scriptures, we are then offered an English translation of every line of the stanza, which leads for each '*pauṛī*' into, first, a conceptual summary and, second, a general comment which locates the message of each stanza within the overall doctrinal and ethical system of Sikhī.

This is therefore a book which operates at several different levels, each leading on to another. Beginning with a mass of semantic, grammatical, and syntactical analysis, it pays very close attention to the contents of this text, so well-known to and beloved of practising Sikhs but so little-known to those outside the community. However, this analysis is no mere academic exercise: the teaching of the *Jap-jī*, which sets out a vision of God, of the possibility of our relationship to God, and of the creative divine Word which communicates the possibility of that relationship through divine grace, is an invitation to spiritual growth and transformation. I am conscious that in describing Guru Nanak's text in this way I have used language shaped by my own Christian faith, and doubtless in so doing I run the risk of distorting or misrepresenting authentic Sikh teaching; indeed, one of the salutary aspects of a volume as careful in its scholarly examination of textual detail as this, is precisely that it can provide a corrective to sweeping generalisations. Nevertheless, it has been remarked that one of the notable characteristics of the '*Mul Mantra*' which prefixes the *Jap-ji* is that, while emphatically credal in character, it is in no sense exclusive or partisan in its formulation, but rather open to all. It has also been said of the '*Mul Mantra*' that, while almost defying translation in its resonant concision, it positively invites exposition; Dr Ryatt's book can perhaps be seen as an encouragement and an aid to all, of whatever faith, to embark on the unfolding of its rich and dense theological core.

Building on textual analysis and spiritual exposition, the journey continues to point to changes to the way in which the reader sees and lives his or her life. Indeed, this expectation of a practical outcome is embedded in the very concept of *jap*. This literally means the act of repetitive utterance of a sacred word or collection of words, and hence word-based meditation or contemplation, but in one of his lapidary lexical comments, Dr Ryatt explains: '*Nām japnā*' is mandatory in *Gurmat* and its sole purpose is to cleanse, uplift and evolve spirit, and to transform oneself by imbibing the attributes of *Nām* in one's conscious self ... and then to be able to express them spontaneously in one's daily life'.

For me, this has irresistible parallels with some of the ways in which Christians have traditionally practised memorisation, recitation, and reflection on passages of scriptures. In Western monastic life, for example, monks and nuns would devote time to *lectio divina*, 'divine reading', savouring the life-giving words of the Bible over and over again, in a pattern so reminiscent of deep digestion that it was given the name *ruminatio*, the prolonged process by which cattle assimilate their food. The purpose of such monastic *lectio* or *ruminatio* was always, as in Dr Ryatt's account, for the conversion of life, the living out in this existence of a life oriented towards union with God and closer alignment with divine values. Of course, the scriptural starting points for Sikhs and for Christians are very dissimilar, as they are for people of other faiths (though it should be remembered that the Sikh scriptures include writings which could also be described as 'Hindu' and 'Muslim'). So also, the doctrinal, spiritual and ethical teachings of the faiths are widely divergent, and at many points are not susceptible of agreement. With full recognition of those differences, though, for one Christian at least, Dr Ryatt's journey through textual study and spiritual exploration to practical action is a path which can be recognised as resonant, sympathetic, and admirable.

Most Reverend Michael Ipgrave
Bishop of Lichfield

The transmission of a religious faith both geographically and from generation to generation brings with it both difficulties and wonderful benefits. In terms of the latter the Sikh diaspora has enabled those of us of other faith communities to explore the richness of Sikh spirituality, not as something which is 'other', but which contributes to humanity's attempt to understand something of the nature of that Being at the basis of our own being. The other side of the coin is that whereas in the Panjab one is simply immersed in Sikhi, in the UK one has to actively learn about the faith. Those Sikhs of a generation born here face the challenge of learning a language and script that is not always part of their everyday lives. It is at this point that Dr Ryatt's new book becomes his gift to his fellow Sikhs and beyond, to those of us of other faith communities for whom mutual interfaith exploration can lead to a deepening of spirituality.

Spiritual Evolution is a labour of love and faithfulness, introducing us to Guru Nanak's thought and his experience of life lived in harmony with eternal Reality. Yet it was an insight from Kabir that struck me forcefully. In a passage (pp. 412-3) dealing with the way in which we humans are so often caught up in a preoccupation with our own self-centredness, we sometimes experience a moment of sheer insight. The author reminds us of Kabir's words: 'Look, O friends! The storm of new ideas and insight ('eureka moment') has struck. It has blown away the thatched roof of misconception and dubiety propped up by 'māiā'.' That translation itself is indicative of the nature of the book. It uses inclusive, modern language, yet has the capacity to take one's mind back to the vulnerability, both of the meagre huts of the poor and also of the inadequacy of the human mind, to fathom the depths of the Divine One.

It is important to draw the reader's attention to the Preface. Here the concise introduction to the essence of the theology of Sikhi is of immense value. It is not written in the language of saccharined piety, but nonetheless emphasises the need to set self aside to find the guidance of God's gracious Word. To those for whom Sikh theological terminology requires to be unpacked we are also provided with a very comprehensive glossary the likes of which is often found in books only published in India.

At the end of the summary of Paurī 3 (pp. 88-89), like the Sikh Gurus, Dr Ryatt indicates that we human beings fail in our own strength and perceptions to gauge the full extent of the Divine One. The search for better understanding is an ongoing struggle throughout life. This translation and commentary is, in this day and age, an important contribution to that striving for spiritual comprehension.

However, this is never enough. I recall one of the Guru's sayings, translated in a way which defies English grammar but beautifully illustrates the full meaning of the saying: 'Truth is highest, but higher still is truthful living.' That concept of service and honest hard work together with a rejection of empty ritual, whilst aligning oneself with the will of the One, is at the heart of this significant and valuable book.

Rev'd Dr John Parry
London.